Earth-honoring Faith

EARTH-HONORING FAITH

FAITH

Religious Ethics in a New Key

LARRY L. RASMUSSEN

OXFORD
UNIVERSITY PRESS

OXFORD
UNIVERSITY PRESS

Oxford University Press is a department of the University of Oxford.
It furthers the University's objective of excellence in research,
scholarship, and education by publishing worldwide.

Oxford   New York
Auckland   Cape Town   Dar es Salaam   Hong Kong   Karachi
Kuala Lumpur   Madrid   Melbourne   Mexico City   Nairobi
New Delhi   Shanghai   Taipei   Toronto

With offices in
Argentina   Austria   Brazil   Chile   Czech Republic   France   Greece
Guatemala   Hungary   Italy   Japan   Poland   Portugal   Singapore
South Korea   Switzerland   Thailand   Turkey   Ukraine   Vietnam

Oxford is a registered trade mark of Oxford University Press in the UK and certain other countries.

Published in the United States of America by Oxford University Press
198 Madison Avenue, New York, NY 10016

© Oxford University Press 2013

Library of Congress Cataloging-in-Publication Data
Rasmussen, Larry L.
Earth-honoring faith : religious ethics in a new key / Larry L. Rasmussen.
p. cm.
Includes bibliographical references (p.) and index.
ISBN 978-0-19-991700-6 (hardcover : alk. paper) 1. Human ecology—Religious aspects—Christianity.
2. Ecotheology. 3. Christian ethics. I. Title.
BT695.5.R375   2013
241'.691—dc23   2012004162

3 5 7 9 8 6 4 2
Printed in the United States of America
on acid-free paper

To St. Olaf College
The United Church of Santa Fe
and
GreenFaith

Our whole life is startlingly moral.
—HENRY DAVID THOREAU, *Walden*

*Using the same old materials of earth, air, fire, and water,
every twenty-four hours, God creates something new out of
them. . . . Every morning you wake up to something that in
all eternity never was before and never will be again. And
the you that wakes up was never the same before and will
never be the same again either.*
—FREDERICK BUECHNER, *Wishful Thinking: A Theological ABC*

Contents

Acknowledgments

ST. OLAF COLLEGE, the United Church of Santa Fe, and GreenFaith: Interfaith Partners in Action for the Earth have all drawn, critically, upon cherished traditions in order to be the best Earth citizens they can. Each has nurtured its Earth-honoring mission for the sake of present and future generations. And each has shown exemplary leadership in creation awareness and care. I am grateful and pleased to dedicate this volume to them.

I have others to thank. Ghost Ranch, Abiquiu, New Mexico, has hosted an annual June seminar on Earth-honoring Faith. Beit Tikva Congregation, Santa Fe, New Mexico, has graciously invited me into the choir for "The Days of Awe" (the High Holy Days) and introduced me to materials I have used in this volume. Friends have read portions of this manuscript and responded with good advice: Andrew Black, Rita Nakashima Brock, Thomas Christensen, James Cone, Jacquelyn Helin, Dieter Hessel, Karen Marrolli, Kevin O'Brian, Aana Vigen, Steven Rockefeller, Cynthia Moe-Lobeda, Brandon Johnson, Glen Stassen, Chester Topple, and Andrew Rasmussen. Charlotte Steinhardt and Cynthia Read at Oxford University Press responded promptly to every query about manuscript preparation. Andrew Attaway of Making Words Behave (www.makingwordsbehave.com) supplied valuable editorial comment. Nicole Dunn, fiber artist, Los Alamos, New Mexico (www.dunnquilting.com), created the quilt that is this book's cover image; and Wendy McEahern of Wendy McEahern Photography, Santa Fe (wmphotosantafe.com), photographed it. Nyla Rasmussen has been part of creating and revising this volume at every point.

I am also thankful for invitations to share ideas for this volume as they developed. Materials include the Robert McAfee Brown Lectures, First Presbyterian Church, Palo Alto, California; the Batalden Lectures, Augsburg

College, Minneapolis, Minnesota; the Grounds for Hope Conferences, Drew University, Madison, New Jersey; the Picard Lectures, United Theological Seminary, New Brighton, Minnesota; the Kellogg Lectures, Episcopal Divinity School, Cambridge, Massachusetts; the Geering Lectures, St. Andrews on the Terrace, Wellington, New Zealand; the William Weber Lectures on Governance and Society, Kalamazoo College, Kalamazoo, Michigan; the McAllister Inaugural Lecture, Carroll College, Waukesha, Wisconsin; a conference plenary address, Gadjah Mada University, Yogjakarta, Indonesia; the Zerby Lecture, Bates College, Lewiston, Maine; the Zabriskie Lecture for Peace and Justice, All Souls Cathedral, Asheville, North Carolina; the University Lecture, Great Theologians Series, Seattle University, Seattle, Washington; the Killeen Chair Convocation Address, St. Norbert College, Du Pere, Wisconsin; the Heritage Lecture, St. Olaf College, Northfield, Minnesota; the Heritage Lecture, Lutheran School of Theology at Chicago, Chicago, Illinois; the Brennen Guth Lecture in Environmental Philosophy, University of Montana, Missoula, Montana; the Donohoe Lectures, Arizona Council of Churches, Phoenix, Arizona; a plenary address, the Nobel Science Conference on Water, Gustavus Adolphus College, St. Peter, Minnesota; commencement addresses at Trinity Lutheran Seminary, Columbus, Ohio, and the Lutheran School of Theology at Chicago, Chicago, Illinois; and the Prayer Breakfast Address of the Festival of Faiths, Louisville, Kentucky. In addition I have drawn on numerous published articles, essays, and book chapters. All are cited in the chapter notes.

Permission has been granted for use of the following: Denise Levertov, "Beginners," *Candles in Babylon* (New York: New Directions Publishing Corporation; Tarset, Northumberland: Bloodaxe Books); Dietrich Bonhoeffer, *Letters and Papers from Prison* (New York: Simon & Schuster; London: SCM Press); *The Animals' Lawsuit Against Humanity* (Louisville, Ky.: Fons Vitae); Simone Weil, *Two Moral Essays* (Wallingford, Penn.: Pendle Hill Publications); Hayim Bialik, "After My Death," *Songs from Bialik: Selected Poems of Hayim Nahman Bialik* (Syracuse: Syracuse University Press); W. Steffen et al., *Global Change and the Earth System: A Planet Under Pressure* (Heidelberg: Springer Verlag); Thich Nhat Hanh, *The World We Have* (Berkeley, Calif.: Parallax Press); Mary Oliver, "The Summer Day," *House of Light* (Boston: Beacon Press); Fyodor Dostoyevsky, *The Brothers Karamazov* (New York: Alfred A. Knopf); Larry Rasmussen, "Asceticism and Consumption," *Crosscurrents* 57, no. 4 (2009): 498–513; Martin Luther King Jr., "The World

House," *Where Do We Go From Here: Chaos or Community?* (Boston: Beacon Press). Where required, permissions have been acknowledged in the notes and copyright page as well.

Larry Rasmussen
Reinhold Niebuhr Professor Emeritus of Social Ethics, Union
Theological Seminary, New York City
Santa Fe, New Mexico

Earth-honoring Faith

Prelude

VOYAGER I HAD completed its 1990 mission. It was on its way out of the solar system when Ground Control instructed it to make a U-turn and photograph each planet it had passed. In some of the photos a pale blue dot appeared.

In 1994 Carl Sagan featured that distant dot in a now-famous address at Cornell University: "That's here," he said. "That's home. That's us. On it, everyone you ever heard of, every human being who ever lived, lived out their lives. That aggregate of all our joys and sufferings, thousands of confident religions, ideologies and economic doctrines, every hunter and forager, every hero and coward, every creator and destroyer of civilizations, every king and peasant, every young couple in love, every hopeful child, every mother and father, every inventor and explorer, every teacher of morals, every corrupt politician, every superstar, every supreme leader, every saint and sinner in the history of our species, lived there on a mote of dust, suspended in a sunbeam."[1]

Homo sapiens sapiens—the wise hominids, the brainy species, the "us" Sagan speaks of—may once have been as few as six hundred individuals. That tribe of six hundred was the only surviving hominid line. There had been others; quite a few, in fact—*Sahelanthropos tchadensis, Australopithecus afarensis, Kenyanthropus platyops, Australopithecus africanus, Australopitehecus garhi, Australopithecus sediba, Australopithecus aethiopicus, Australopithecus robustus, Australopithecus boisei, Homo habilis, Homo georgicus, Homo erectus, Homo ergaster, Homo antecessor, Homo heidelbergensis, Homo neanderthalensis, Homo floresiensis.* Their home was also the pale blue dot. But their death is eternal now. In contrast, the mighty six hundred have become well over seven billion, all living on the same "mote of dust, suspended in a sunbeam."

From the Voyager's window the planet appears featureless. Every arc and corner looks like every other. Did we not know better, we might confuse it with many another desolate speck in the "great enveloping cosmic dark."[2] From this distance nothing betrays its singular privilege—life.

Up close and personal, however, this chance planet is exuberant in the way only what St. Augustine called "standing miracles" can be. Were it the size of a large birthday balloon and on exhibit at the American Museum of Natural History in New York City, with all of its features doing what they do in their own colors—jet streams and banks of white and gray cloud; ice caps and porcelain-blue seas; rivers running muddy or clear; continents of multiple shapes and hues crisscrossed with croplands and cities; furious volcanoes and tornadoes, earthquakes and typhoons; lights outlining every shoreline; plants thick enough to paint almost everything, even seawater, some hue of green; and creatures by the trillions, some of them unimaginably strange, others deep in places too dark to be seen by any but God's eye—were all this on display the line of ticket holders would be out the door, down the block, across Central Park West and into the park as far as the Sheep Meadow. "Why, there's nothing like this in all the world!" people would exclaim, half-forgetting the little ball hanging in the museum was a pitiful version of the marvel that gave them birth, the same marvel that made possible everything else in their lives, the marvel that enabled all life, before, with, and after the line around the block, and the marvel that sustains, with every breath taken and every morsel chewed, all curious onlookers to this very hour.

A tough, new place

Now Planet Home is undergoing a transformational moment, akin to those "ages" that come to pass as episodes in geologic time. But this one is different, at least for us, since it is happening not only in geologic time but in human time as well. Moreover, the brainy species is not only around for this episode but is among its causes, its reason for geophysical change. That "sweet spot"[3] of sufficient planetary stability to host all the human civilizations ever known, the late Holocene, is moving so far out of phase that the planet we were all born on and have grown accustomed to is suddenly a "tough, new" place[4] that asks in rude ways for a different way of life than the one industrialized nature delivered but cannot sustain. We awake to a surprise, then: We are far too many and many of us are far too rich, with far too much stuff and the wrong kind of economy, for the planet to bear, on our terms.

A new song

So we find ourselves awkwardly astride a turning time when we must learn to sing a new song in a strange land (Psalm 137:4). Only this time the strange land is not Babylon but the planet, and we are not Israel but all humankind. The third rock from the sun can no longer be counted on for steady seasons of seedtime and harvest; for glacial waters feeding great rivers; for sea levels trustworthy enough to permit the building of great cities; for sufficient time for flora and fauna to adjust to new insect predators and diseases, or drought and deluge; for governments capable of marshaling resources to handle disasters of greater number and intensity or to allay the conflicts that arise when desperate people are rendered helpless and homeless en masse; for rainfall and snowpack and enough resources to assure that future generations will survive and thrive on their diminished planet; and for ocean biochemistry stable enough to maintain the eons-old underwater rainforests.

How, then, do we hymn the Earth differently? How do we write and sing a new song for a strange land, even though it be our own? How do we do it with our neighbors, all our neighbors—human and other-than-human—when Earth is "hot, flat and crowded"[5] and borders and walls no longer protect? Where do we turn when we discover that the religion we have lived by since the industrial-technological era emerged—eternal and exponential economic growth—is an illusion, dogma masquerading as common sense and kept alive by willpower and little else?[6]

Wicked problems like climate change, the death of nature in key locales (coral reefs, rainforests, permafrost belts), and the need for a different socio-economic-political order are problems that cannot be solved with the same means and ways of life that created them. The old wineskins do not hold, the old cloth tears (Luke 5:33–39). A new era of responsibility asks for new capacities to devise different ways of living.

That requires courage—the courage to "lift the veil"[7] and be relentlessly honest about the human causes of Earth's degradation; the courage to undertake a compassionate retreat from the world of those causes; the courage to live with the anguish of a diminished planet; the courage to embark on "ventures of which we cannot see the ending, by paths as yet untrodden, through perils unknown";[8] the courage, in short, to compose, sing, and enter a new song.

Gimme some new-time religion

We do not start from scratch. There is no scratch to start from in a world long underway. This is not about beginning, but re-beginning. And traditions of transformation are at hand for working at the foundations of human character and conduct, with the moral authority to shape lives both inwardly and outwardly; traditions rooted in patterns of death and renewal, birth and rebirth, and able to sustain ways of life marked by rites of passage and close community.

The world's religions are among such traditions. Science is indispensable because it can tell us what is happening to our changing planet. It provides both sound data and big ideas about what makes the universe tick. Religion is certainly no substitute for science. It is less exacting and trustworthy about things empirical, and less rigorous about testing its claims.

Yet few people will die for a pie chart. Data, even the good data of sound science, do not of themselves upend habitual and cherished ways, including dysfunctional ones. Nor do big ideas about how things work. Something with more tenacity, commitment, and loyalty; something with a reach deep enough to summon sacrifice; something that lays claim to cosmic meaning and locates us in communities that transcend our egos and surpass our modest moment in time; something that speaks to our longings and the mystery of our lives; something that offers renewable moral-spiritual energy for hard transitions; and something that keeps open the door of hope—some such power as this needs to join all that good science and good technology bring.

That something is not only religion, of course. There are other transforming agents, not least education, the arts, and healthy families. But religion bears remarkable powers that are ignored or dismissed to the peril of those riding the same small ark on the same rising seas. It is foolish not to tap millennia of fluency in the arts of life instruction and renewal, just as it is foolish to overlook the religious loyalties of some ten thousand religions and 85 percent of the planet's peoples. The dismissal of religion by its cultured despisers is, in any event, an exercise in futility. It runs against the grain of a species that is incorrigibly religious.

It is also foolish to dismiss those who know what moves people. We are moved by fear and terror and by love and beauty. Religions know these powers. They also know the pain and ruin that follow *Homo sapiens* who sense terror and act in fear but have no experience of a beautiful world or love for it.

That said, the powers of the world's faiths are not up to the present task in most of their present forms. In part this is because their prescientific worldviews were formulated well before the onset of modernity. But there is another reason: Like the rest of the family they, too, lack tried and tested experience with geophysical change and planetary tipping points. Most have not had their own ecological phase, at least not this side of industrialized nature. While they have known death and rebirth as Phoenix rising, they were always greeted by nature's reliability. Not so now. Moreover, they have peopled the ranks of those standing by to witness to "the withering of the earth."[9] In a word, they are as needful of conversion to the realities of the tough new planet as other agents of change. Religious communities, too, must generate new capacities for new responsibilities on an altered planet.

Singing the Lord's song in a strange land, singing our own song on a changing planet, means religious ethics in a new key—some new-time religion. Yes, the vast repertoire of living traditions is at hand, awaiting creative spirits. Thankfully, there is far more in that repertoire than the orthodoxy of economic growth and getting-and-spending has let us see and hear, far more than modernity has considered or cared about. Still, none of the traditions this book draws upon are adequate in their present form. They, too, belong to the God-wrestle that happens when the past can no longer be the future but the future is not clear, when destiny is uncertain rather than manifest. Then a whole era experiences Jacob's struggle up close, the grapple with God down by the riverside that gave him a new identity and a new name—Israel, the one who "strove with God." The present match may leave us, too, as it did Jacob/Israel, with a limp, a blessing, and unexpected reconciliation with an estranged brother (Gen. 32–33).

Song

Ours are hard times for many. They are not for the faint of heart. They will get worse. But they are also times of exhilarating song on the part of a species that was born singing and has never ceased. Human language itself may have evolved from song sounds as early hominids responded with elation or pain to their environment and circumstances.[10] In any event, whether it's spirituals or the blues, gospel or country and western, chant or aria, choral or symphonic, classic or modern, rock or lullaby, lament or alleluia, life goes on as endless song. We can't keep from singing;[11] it's the kind of creature we are. Moreover, it's our very best attribute and the reason Song of Songs is a motif throughout this work, from the Prelude through the Interlude to the Postlude.

Song is more than lament and consolation; it is inspiration. Song bears the human spirit at its most expressive and expansive. This time, however, the song we sing must learn humbly and deeply from the changing Earth we inhabit. Its melodies and harmonies must be Earth-oriented in ways matched to our sober responsibility for a contracting planet in jeopardy at human hands.

We are not onlookers or audience this time, guilty or innocent bystanders. We are, like jazz singers and instrumentalists, both composers and performers, invited to execute our greatest work.

That greatest work is effecting the hard transition from a time of, on balance, a destructive human presence on the planet to a time of mutual enhancement in the community of life.[12]

Living well

This is a work in religious ethics. Its burning questions are the questions of all ethics: How are we to live, and for what? What makes lives, any lives and all lives, go 'round well? What is good, right, and fitting? And while this book, as any book, can do precious little by itself, it belongs to those questions. Its spirit is that of the Navajo/Diné Song of the Earth—

> Indeed I am its child,
> > Absolutely I am a child of the earth.

—and a Denise Levertov poem, "Beginners," from *Candles in Babylon*:

> But we have only begun to love the earth. We have only begun to
> > imagine the fullness of life.
> > *How could we tire of hope!—so much is in the bud.*
> How can desire fail?—we have only begun to imagine justice and
> > mercy,
> > *Only begun to envision how it might be to live as siblings*
> > *with beast and flower, not as oppressors.*
> Surely our river cannot already be hastening into the sea of nonbeing?
> > *Surely it cannot drag, in the silt, all that is innocent!*
> Not yet, not yet—there is too much broken that must be mended,
> > *Too much hurt that we have done to each other*
> > *that cannot yet be forgiven.*
> We have only begun to know the power that is in us if we would join
> > our solitudes in the communion of struggle.
> > *So much is unfolding that must complete its gesture, so much*
> > *is in the bud.*[13]

PART ONE

I

The Creature We Are

There is no animal on earth, nor yet a bird on the wing, but forms communities like you.
—QUR'AN, Sura 6:38

Of all the things in the world, the Holy One did not create a single one that is useless.
—THE BABYLONIAN TALMUD, Shabbat 77b

Dear God. Dear stars, dear trees, dear sky, dear people. Dear everything. Dear God.
—ALICE WALKER, *The Color Purple,* last letter

Born to belonging

Let us now sing the praises of famous men and women, and our ancestors in their generations. The Lord apportioned to them great glory.

There were those who made a name for themselves by their valor;
those who gave counsel by their understanding and
those who spoke prophetic truth;

those who led the people in their deliberations, and in their knowledge of the people were wise in their instruction;

those who composed musical tunes, and set verses to song;
and rich men and women who endowed with resources.
All these were honored in their generations, and were the pride of
their times.
Some of them have left behind a name, so that all declare their praise.

But of others there is no memory; they have perished as though they had never been born. So have their children after them.

Yet they also were people of mercy whose righteous deeds have not
been forgotten; their prosperity will remain with their descendents, . . .
and their glory will not be blotted out.

Their bodies returned to earth, but their name lives.
The assembly declares their wisdom, the congregation proclaims
their praise.

—Sirach 44:1–15

We are all "born to belonging."[1] When others heard our borning cry, we could
not walk, feed ourselves, don clothing, or protect ourselves from the heat, the
cold, or those who might do us harm. Only the care of others kept us alive,
just as the mentoring of others taught us our first life skills. Even as adults we
cannot make a simple No. 2 pencil on our own. We stand tall because we are
planted on the shoulders of ancestors, most unknown to us, their journeys
anchored in the legacy of the famous and the forgotten. When our dying day
comes and the fever of life has passed, we will return to the topsoil that
brought us forth, joining in yet another way the great community that birthed
us and sustains us. We are born to belonging, and we die into it; our lives are
braided into all that is. "Biosocial" is the kind of creature we are: Apart from
human community implanted in an Earth community embedded in a cosmic
community, we cannot, and do not, exist.

What is true for us as individuals is equally so for us as members of a ram-
bunctious species. If anything, our communion with all else is deepened by
the story of evolution and the hymn of the universe.[2]

When David Hillis and his colleagues in Texas wanted to display the relationship of a measly three thousand species of animals, plants, fungi, and
microbes, out of ten million or more, they decided the best image was the
Tree of Life—an ancient religious symbol, the same one Charles Darwin
chose to close his momentous work *On the Origin of Species* (1869). "The affinities of all the beings of the same class have sometimes been represented as
a great tree," Darwin wrote. "I believe this simile largely speaks the truth. . . .
As buds give rise by growth to fresh buds, and these, if vigorous, branch out
and overtop on all sides many a feebler branch, so by generation I believe it
has been with the great Tree of Life, which fills with its dead and broken
branches the crust of the earth, and covers the surface with its ever branching
and beautiful ramifications."[3] And here is Darwin's very last sentence: "There
is grandeur in this view of life, with its several powers, having been originally
breathed into a few forms or into one; and that, whilst this planet has gone

cycling on according to the fixed law of gravity, from so simple a beginning endless forms most beautiful and most wonderful have been, and are being, evolved."[4]

Hillis and his colleagues' Tree of Life is shaped a bit oddly, more like a bicycle wheel than a tree. The "endless forms most beautiful and most wonderful," all evolved from "powers . . . breathed into [only] a few forms or into one," nest on spoke-like branches ending along a rim. This revised graphic still leaves the tree so dense that it requires a visual aid, a "You are here" arrow that points to the single dot on the rim where *Homo sapiens sapiens* have perched for some two hundred thousand years.[5] From that dot on that twig, the eye travels back down the branch that joins us to chimpanzees, onto the larger branch of our common mammal ancestors, then to all vertebrates, then to all animals, and finally into the largest and deepest branches anchored in the massive trunk. Here, in the heartwood, is the ancestral home of all living things, home to what biologists have named "LUCA," the Last Universal Common Ancestor. Single-celled organisms, LUCAs were the only life the Earth's first few billion years knew anything about; multicelled organisms appeared some 600 million years ago. While a single-celled organism, such as an amoeba, is "a one-man band," a multicelled organism is already "a very large orchestra."[6] Both mediate "cellular awareness." They have receptors that detect their environment and convey the relevant meaning to the organism (an amoeba's receptor detects decaying food molecules).[7] Yet the salient point is that these humblest of all creatures began the life adventure that has evolved and branched for 3.5 or so billion years. And here is where we, too, belong, as "members and plain citizens" (Aldo Leopold) of the community of life. Though only a twig on the great Tree, humans are joined to a fierce communion.[8]

Psalm 139 has it right, then: We emerged not from one womb, but two, our mother's and Mother Earth's. As this singer says in praise of God,

> For it was you who formed my inward parts;
> > you knit me together in my mother's womb.
> I praise you, for I am fearfully and wonderfully made.
> > Wonderful are your works; that I know very well.
> My frame was not hidden from you,
> > when I was being made in secret,
> > intricately woven in the depths of the earth.
> Your eyes beheld my unformed substance.
> In your book were written all the days that were formed for me,
> > when none of them as yet existed.[9]

To be "fearfully and wonderfully made," to belong to life's drama and grandeur, is our glory.

But where does Earth belong? Where is its slow womb? And what about that passing remark, that we cannot make a No. 2 yellow lead pencil on our own?

Try making one from scratch. Where will you get the tin for the crinkled band? How will you know which ore to search for, if it's ore at all? How will you mine and process it until it's pliant enough for the thin little circle around eraser and barrel? Where will you get the rubber for the eraser? Who will suggest a certain tree's milky innards? When you do find the right tree, how will you extract an eraser from the sticky, whitish fluid? And what makes your pencil write? If it doesn't write by itself, how do you get it to do so? Who invented alphabets anyway? And speech—how did that come about?

Then there is the barrel. What's best for that, plastic, wood, or some post-consumer composite? But there is no such thing as plastic ore, composite ore, or smooth pentagonal wood 23/100ths of an inch in diameter. And don't forget to paint it. With what? What is paint, anyway? For that matter, what is color? Who invented that? How do you get the liquid just the right shade so that the No. 2 pencil is yellow and not dirty chartreuse? This pencil is obviously not a task for you by yourself. It's the work of tens of thousands of both the famous and the forgotten who, over centuries, organized and utilized vast systems of local and global knowledge, invention, mechanics, trade, and five-and-dime stores.

Still, if No. 2 yellow lead pencils were the product of *human* genius and cooperation alone, we would still have nothing, nada. How was tin ore formed, where and when, over how many eons, and by what Earthly powers? What about the tree for wood or petroleum for plastics? If your chem and bio professors assigned you to create a tree, what chemicals would you gather and how would you fix the mix to arrive at life in that specific botanical form? The same holds for the rubber, the graphite, the paint, and the color. By what nigh-eternal forces and processes did these come to be? For your humble pencil, then, you can thank the standing miracle of land, air, water, sunlight, and endless minute and enormous transactions ages in and ages out, over millions, even billions, of years. In fact, you can literally thank your lucky stars, some of which were exploding supernovas (more on that in a moment). In sum, you and your unloved No. 2 pencil were both born to belonging long, long ago. Indeed, the only real difference between you and your pencil is that you get to *experience this great adventure in your heart, mind, body, and soul* as you take your place in the chain of the famous and the forgotten. You are a brainy creature of self-consciousness and self-reflection; your pencil is not.[10]

Still, this doesn't answer the question of where Earth itself belongs and how it came to be. Was Planet Home also born to belonging? Recall those first photographs downloaded from the Hubble telescope. One, displaying haunting columns of gaseous gold and tangerine, is titled *Pillars of Creation*. Another offers a galaxy of lights, scattered as a spiral across the rich blackness of space. If we think of this galaxy as our Milky Way, we can imagine it with our familiar arrow, "You are here." This time it doesn't point to a twig in the Tree of Life but to a small smudge—Earth. Each species is not only a twig on the Tree of Life; each is far older, a late galactic version of stardust originating in the Big Bang 13 to 14 billion years ago. Our origins are stellar; we are, in Walt Whitman's words, "the journey-work of the stars."[11]

The journey-work goes like this: We are starseed, as is all else on the third rock from the sun. *Everything* is stardust. The gases necessary to make organic compounds, and therefore life, are common elements across the universe—hydrogen, oxygen, nitrogen, and carbon. They are not from our solar system alone. In fact, our sun is too cool and too young to manufacture some ninety heavy elements found on Earth. The heavy-hitters came from farther afield. Some, like uranium and plutonium, can only be created in giant exploding stars (supernovae). This means the planet's beginnings rest in nebulae—star nurseries, powerhouses of star formation. Life eventually evolved from elements blown off by supernovae formed in such nurseries.[12] Your evolution was thus billions of years in the making, by way of a particular galaxy and, eventually, the solar system of one of its billion or more stars. Milky Way citizenship, then, is membership in a cosmic community that began long before our species and our planet arrived and will be here long after our planet is a cinder. (Eco-philosopher Joanna Macy quips, "I just try to act my age. My atoms are 14 billion years old.")[13]

There are surprises all along the way, the surprises of a restless evolution where most anything is possible but no one thing is probable. Thirteen billion years ago the universe was nothing remotely similar to the universe now. Nor was the planet a billion years ago recognizable as the one we know: Oxygen was rare, nothing grew on its surface, any seas there might have been would have been shallow. Nor did life on this planet even a mere million years ago bear a notable resemblance to the life around us now. For one thing, more than 90 percent of the species that lived episodically over that stretch no longer exist. This includes mammals so wild, huge, and improbable they hardly fit human imagination. It also includes distant cousins, hominid lines that met a dead end. We have only "the dried tokens / Of their sojourn here / On the planet floor" (Maya Angelou).[14] Or, in Annie Dillard's memorable line, "Evolution loves death more than it loves you and me."[15]

Nevertheless, ordering has been hard at work. Patterning has taken shape and given shape, sometimes with unlikely mutations. "In nature improbabilities are the one stock in trade. The whole creation is one lunatic fringe" (Dillard again).[16] Yet creativity and chance are complemented by enduring universal principles.

One principle is differentiation. In the cosmos and on Planet Home, *to be* is to *be different*. The "several powers" of which Darwin spoke may have been "originally breathed into [only] a few forms or into one," but their flourishing yielded "endless forms" markedly different from one another in "ever branching and beautiful ramifications."[17] This breeds uniqueness: All creatures, including humans, are distinct in ways essential to their existence. This is nature's "outrageous bias for the novel,"[18] which it uses for survival, branching, and development. Diversity, complexity, variation, disparity, wild and endless articulation—these, so long as they continue, guarantee a constant flowering of the unique.

It has been ever thus. Dillard once more: "[T]he extravagant gesture is the very stuff of creation. After the one extravagant gesture of creation in the first place, the universe has continued to deal exclusively in extravagances, flinging intricacies and colossi down aeons of emptiness, heaping profusions on profligacies with ever-fresh vigor. The whole show has been on fire from the word go."[19]

Autopoiesis, nature's capacity to self-organize, is a second universal principle. Awesome powers of self-articulation or self-manifestation run from atom and cell to ecosystem and biome to star and galaxy. Were we to offer a friend a physicist's diagram of an atom together with an astronomer's diagram of a solar system, both the same size and color and neither labeled, she or he would be hard put to tell one from the other.

Or consider the building blocks of life, that wholly unexpected gift and wonder. Well before the discovery of DNA, physicist Erwin Schrodinger had concluded that the riot of life as we know it would need the qualities of an "aperiodic crystal," an ordered, repeating pattern with various possibilities of expression. That proved accurate not only for DNA but for the molecular structure of soils like clay.[20] Creative pattern reigns, whether intercellular or interstellar.

Life itself appears to be a self-organizing and self-perpetuating nonlinear system. Complex networks of evolved feedback loops between organisms maintain conditions for the continuation of life. At the same time that these networks create continuity and stability, they allow new organisms to emerge.[21]

Communion is the third principle. It is a synonym for creation's internal relatedness and active interdependence, what Buddhist monk Thich Nhat Hanh calls "interbeing."[22] An aboriginal material kinship can be documented everywhere in the form-producing powers manifest in planetary and cosmic evolution.[23] Dynamic relationships are the substance of existence; "nothing is itself without everything else." This "togetherness of things" is a systemic feature of evolution.[24] Mathematical biologist Martin Nowak even argues that the "master architect" of evolution, joining random mutation and natural selection, is cooperation and that this bonding of different elements already begins at the molecular level.[25] Ours is truly a *uni*verse. *E pluribus unum* could be its motto, although "out of one, many" would be more accurate than "from many, one."

Differently said, creation is bonded and braided at every turn, yet open to what has not yet been. While this is now conventional science, the Hebrew Bible has a twist on it that is important for later discussion: Creation is, from the perspective of human agency, *morally* seamless once *Homo sapiens* enters evolution's tale; the flourishing and degradation of human life is of a piece with the flourishing and degradation of land, sea, and sky. Human perversity and injustice bear consequences for the whole community of life, as do human rectitude and justice. This is so from the beginning, with Cain's killing of Abel and the subsequent cry of earth itself in agony and protest (Genesis 4:8–12). And in Christian scripture it continues to the end, with the near destruction of Earth at the hands of human empire (Revelation). Contrariwise, righteous living yields abundance for the land and its peoples.

The reason for both degradation and plenty is the same: All that is, is kin and born to belonging. All is relational. Humankind and otherkind live into one another's lives and die into one another's deaths in relationships that either sustain or subvert creatures and the land. Nothing is, without the other. Such is the way of "covenant" (the biblical term for relational living). Covenantal bonds—between God and Earth, between God and humankind, between humans and one another and the rest of life—establish, order, and sustain creation as we know it. The way of covenant, for better and worse, is the way things *are*. There is no life apart from the geological, biological, ecological, and cosmic processes that gave life birth and sustain it.

So also is the way of justice. Biblically, justice is right relation with all that is.[26] Encompassing more than intrahuman relationships, it might be called "creation justice."

Yet only modern science provides the stunning detail of creation's "integrity" as the integral, relational functioning of planetary and cosmic systems.

Consider *Homo sapiens* in light of this integral functioning. We are an infant species, arriving in the last 0.001% of the time Earth has hosted life.[27] Even then we didn't suddenly appear as a discrete species, springing full-grown from the head of Zeus. There are surprises here, too. It's mess and wonder and leftovers all the way down.

The zoo in you

We are, for example, fish, albeit fish out of water. In his book *Your Inner Fish*, biologist Neil Shubin demolishes the notion of discrete species with fixed natures by showing that our bodies took a 3.5-billion-year journey to become the kind of creature we presently are. Using fossils and modern genetic studies—bones and genes, essentially—he demonstrates that our inner ear is modified fish-head architecture. In our aquatic cousins, the bones that became our inner ear connect the upper jaw to the braincase. And our limbs are modified fins. In both cases—ears and limbs—the new bones that form in the human embryo and develop in the child are really old bones from nonhuman creatures, retooled for other purposes. Especially striking is this: Very similar genetic recipes were at work both for the modifications that make us who we are and the modifications that changed some fish to other creatures or just different fish. Similar recipes tweaked a little yielded different outcomes: "From a Few Genes, Life's Myriad Shapes."[28] *To be* is *to be different*, yes, but from the same recycled stuff. The same genes, the same parts, turn up again and again from species to species. Moreover, the basic functions of cells are the same in all life-forms, with the DNA molecule specifying the characteristics of all living organisms, from bacteria through human beings. (Not all this is good news. Knee problems plague us because fish were not designed to walk.[29])

But why the different outcomes from the same small pool of genes? How do (and did) we and our nonhuman kin evolve? Take our eyes, for example. Insects, clams, scallops, humans, and scads of other animals have photoreceptor organs. All of them use the same kind of light-gathering molecules, molecules we can trace to ancient bacteria. In our case, modified bits of ancient bacteria set up shop inside our retinas, helping us see.[30] Yet unlike most other creatures, humans developed rich color vision. Why? Probably because of changes in Earth's flora in the places our ancestors lived. As best we can tell, our kind of color vision, with three color receptors and not two like most other mammals, arose about 55 million years ago among our primate predecessors. If we correlate these genetic modifications with the fossil record, we discover a period of major changes in the forests. Before this time, the forests of our distant kin were rich in palms and figs—tasty and adequate but all roughly the same color. Life was beige. Then the plant world diversified in such a way that a more varied palette of colors emerged, which is to say, a more varied palette of foods. Natural selection favored those vision mutations that aligned with the more colorful food of the changing food supply.[31] Changing ecosystems set the parameters and posed the challenges; natural selection and social learning responded.

Our eye is only one example. Our noses and sense of smell is another fascinating chapter in the evolutionary interplay of environment and tweaked genes. So are skin and touch, teeth and diet, along with numerous other adventures in bodybuilding such as walking upright and having our head on top instead of out in front. Yet the storyline is the same: a common set of genetic tools and rules among and across species reveals that our body is a throwback to all sorts of prehistoric critters.[32] There is a "zoo in you"[33] and we're all a wondrous mess, the late, twisted offspring of weird and exotic forebears who had no idea whom they might become. To cite Shubin, "We are simply a mosaic of bits and pieces found in virtually everything else on the planet."[34] And to top it off, the scaffolding for our entire body was already present in those most ancient of creatures, single-celled animals, the ones from which all life evolved,[35] the ones deep in the heartwood of the great Tree of Life. You and I are the eventual and unlikely outcome of the humblest creatures ever to inhabit Planet Earth.[36] It's a miracle, the miracle called "life."

Which is only to say that it literally takes a universe to raise a child. Every human story, yours included, is written in the deep history of the planet and the cosmos. There we were "fearfully and wonderfully made."

Two things should grab our attention for later discussion.

First, there is no separation between what our surroundings do to us and what we do to our surroundings. Today especially, cumulative human presence and power means that what we throw at the rest of nature is as crucial as what the rest of nature throws at us. Or, rather, throws *back*, since it is all interactive, all part of the same mess and wonder. Species, and individuals within species, always have a responsive relationship to their environment.

Second, the modern world's sense of the human is a shrunken one, given what we know about our evolutionary journey. While there is a deep human longing to belong to the same order that threw the galaxies across a universe and the planets into orbit, most of the cosmological and biological processes that gave us birth do not register in our sense of ourselves. The Tree of Life as part of us and we as part of it lives somewhere outside our modern self-awareness. Modernity's prized bubble—the built environment as our true habitat—leads to "apartheid" consciousness at the species level. Like whites in apartheid South Africa, we think "our kind" can develop separately. Human beings collectively become the center and focus, drawing upon all the rest as needed. We do not regard ourselves *internally* related as kin to the rest of a shared and indispensable community that also lives embedded in the Earth and cosmos. This constricted and alienated sense of ourselves is the species counterpart of the self-absorption we will discuss later as the heart-turned-in-upon-itself (*cor curvatum in se*). And while, as biosocial creatures by nature, we might acknowledge that our deepest human need is for social bonds in committed relationships—the opposite of self-absorption—we for some reason do not extend these bonds and commitments to other-than-human life. The outcome is the kind of anthropocentrism that smothers the cosmophilia (love of the cosmos) and biophilia (love of life) native to the kind of creature we are. Biophilia, the yearning for contact with other-than-human life, and cosmophilia, the yearning to belong to the same order as the stars, then languish, and we forget we are human beings tethered marrow and bone to evolutionary and cosmic processes.

This is underscored when we add Lynn Margulis's work to Shubin's. Margulis shows, first, that each of us is a community of different species together in one body via symbiotic relationships. Our stomachs and intestines, for example, are a commune of life forms that allows us to live and develop by turning plant and animal products into energy and body parts. Second, and even more startling, something Margulis calls "serial endosymbiosis" occurs now and again on evolution's odd trek. Why do both plant chloroplasts as well as mammals share DNA, for example? And why do three of the four kingdoms of the living world—plants, animals, and protists—share eukaryotic cells (cells with a nucleus), while the fourth—bacteria—are prokaryotic only, a far simpler, more primitive type, likely akin to the first cells from which all life evolved? Margulis suspected that the chloroplasts in plant cells were once bacteria, likewise the mitochondria in all mammal eukaryotic cells. What had happened? The parts of more complex eukaryotic cells arose through a symbiosis in which one kind of cell engulfed another, and then the two cells, one inside and the other surrounding it, used each other's skills and traits to produce differentiated life components through the merger of two (or more) different species (endosymbiosis). Margulis, like Shubin, utterly demolishes the notion of discrete species with fixed natures leading separate lives.[37]

Peter Bork reports yet another dynamic. Genes need not wait until two species come together to venture off and create something new. Genes can simply leap, so to speak, from one branch of the Tree of Life to another. "Each gene has its own evolution," Bork says. "It's not inherited [only] from mother to daughter; it's inherited from a neighbor."[38] So, for example, a virus can bring genes from a previous host into the new species the virus has invaded. Genes then sometimes set up shop there, whether the virus stays or moves on.

Not that this busy past is prologue only. It is also present. The "zoo in you" occupies every waking and sleeping moment. Direct descendents of cells that came into being approximately 45 million years ago remain active in our bloodstreams just as the ions in our blood still betray their salty brine origins. And a full 10 percent of our dry body weight is other-than-human creatures, mostly microbes feeding in, on, and with us. Microbe cells outnumber the distinctively human cells 10:1. So of the quadrillion cells of our bodies, almost 90 percent are not human but tiny self-propagating organisms that have their own lives as they live in us as part of who we are. We have an inner ecosystem in which each of us is home to something like 100 trillion microbes.[39] No fewer than 400 different species of microbes, for example, live in your mouth alone (not 400 microbes, 400 *species* of microbes).[40] And you should see your gut! Every digestive system is really a host kitchen with an adjoining dining nook.[41]

Without such microorganisms we would perish within hours. The body's processes would shut down and we would die, essentially from microbe laziness or, more precisely, a successful strike, since each human body has roughly 400 billion molecules that conduct "millions of processes between trillions of atoms" unceasingly. "The total cellular activity in one human body is staggering. . . . One septillion[42] actions [take place] at any one moment. . . . In a millisecond, our body has undergone ten times more processes than there are stars in the universe, which is exactly what Charles Darwin foretold when he said science would discover that each living creation was a 'little universe, formed of a host of self-propagating organisms, inconceivably minute and as numerous as the stars of heaven.'"[43] In a word, we are alive only because of the kindness of countless strangers within us.

Not that our bodies are isolated and insulated communes. They depend utterly upon Earth's abiotic envelope. The air we breathe, its oxygen the free gift of plants, is the same air breathed by Moses, Jesus, the Buddha, Muhammad, Dorothy Day, and Derek Jeter. The planet's water is recycled as well, its sum fixed even as it changes forms constantly—liquid, solid, vapor.

Both—the atmosphere and the water—are life-essential elements our bodies share with the rest of the planet.

We would strike parallel wonder if, beyond air and water, we dug into Earth's other primal elements, soil and fire (energy). The countless strangers by whose grace we live are above, below, and around us, as well as within.

So the Tree of Life lives within us, as well as we within it, and the old fourth-century Cappadocian theologians[44] got it right: Each human being is a little universe, a microcosm of the macrocosm. We're at home in the cosmos; the cosmos is at home in us. We're creatures of a planet on which the planet's creatures inhabit and sustain us, inside and out.

The theologians, however, like the psalmists, lacked the science to know that *all else* is microcosm of the macrocosm as well, first seeded by stars on their own pilgrimage and, more proximately, by the elements of earth, air, fire, and water on their trek into the present.[45] Microcosm of macrocosm was right, yet neither theologian nor psalmist had the scientific capacity to trace the relationships of deep time—billions of years deep—that integrally bind us to all that has gone before and all that surrounds us, infinite in all directions. Call it what the World Council of Churches does: "the integrity of creation." Or simply call it "aboriginal belonging" and call us "biocommunal and geocommunal creatures *by nature*." Call it miraculous, too. St. Augustine does. The "standing miracle" of earth and sky is "a greater miracle than the rarest and most unheard-of marvels."[46]

Or share Rabbi Abraham Heschel's response: "We can never sneer at the stars, mock the dawn or scoff at the totality of being." "Sublime grandeur evokes unhesitating, unflinching awe. Away from the immense, [and] cloistered in our own concepts, we may scorn and revile everything. But standing between earth and sky, we are silenced by the sight."[47]

Yet even St. Augustine could not have imagined how miraculous—or how strange. Take *Triops*, for instance. *Triops* are bizarre aquatic-desert organisms, wee desert shrimp (yes, desert shrimp). As Craig Childs reports, these leftovers from the age of dinosaurs challenge most of our notions of life itself. They cope with extremely long periods of desert drought that "would kill every jackrabbit and human out there" by shriveling up "until they are dry as cotton balls, releasing all of their water." This is the rare state of "*anhydrobiosis. Life without water*. Basically, they die, but with the loophole of being able to come back to life."[48] Their life span from egg to death might not exceed three weeks total but, if need be, they can wait a hundred years in their self-sealed containers for the biological clock to start ticking again when conditions are right—pooled desert water and the proper temperature and light. So what defines life? As Childs notes, *Triops* metabolism is so near zero that if this creature were a human, the heart would beat three times a year. One *Triops* scientist let the words "cosmic metabolism" slip out, only to realize that could have little meaning for a creature with a lifespan of less than a month. He meant only that this metabolism is so marginal to all we know of life that it slips the categories of biological understanding.[49] It seems more akin to the slow womb of the cosmos.

Were *Triops* and life without water not bizarre enough, consider "hyperthermophiles" living without the sun's energy, without light, and without photosynthesis. Scientists have discovered a riot of life in and around deep-sea volcanic vents, some of it tolerating fluid temperatures of 575 degrees Fahrenheit, more than double water's boiling point. These "hyperthermophiles" render "hyper" a vast understatement.

Beyond these deep ocean hotspots, "the dark biosphere" of the Earth's crust itself contains great colonies of microbes living without light. Scientists wonder whether there might not be life miles into the Earth's crust that rivals, in mass, all surface life.[50]

So what can we say? Diane Ackerman puts it well: "Variety is the pledge that matter makes to living things. Think of a niche and life will fill it, think of a shape and life will explore it, think of a drama and life will stage it." Wonder, drama, and mess, all the way down.

"I personally find cactus an unlikely predicament for matter to get itself into," she goes on, "but no stranger than we humans, the lonely bipeds with the giant dreams."[51]

Big-dreaming bipeds

But who are these big-dreaming bipeds? For the moment the answer, whether from comparative anatomy (including embryology), genetics, the fossil record, biogeography, or paleoanthropology, is this: We are biosocial creatures born to belonging in a community that is cosmically deep; biosocial creatures born of Earth itself, humans from *humus* worthy of both humor and humility; and biosocial creatures whose existence is cast between the infinitely large (cosmic space) and the infinitely small (subatomic particles and microorganisms), as well as the infinitely slow (cosmic evolution over billions of years) and the infinitely fast (atoms colliding a billion times a second, bodily processes a millisecond long).[52]

What counts most for subsequent discussions is Wes Jackson's startling conclusion that the living ecosphere—the biotic and abiotic worlds together as planetary nature—"is the only truly creative force at work in the world."[53] "The scientist at the bench or the artist at the easel is only creative in the context of a civilization," and every civilization is possible only because of "the capital stock of the ecosphere"[54] and the ever-renewing way in which it works.

Jackson draws upon Stan Rowe's basic insight: Organisms do not possess "life" so much as "life" possesses organisms. We belong to that which is far more than us and we owe our existence to it. "By this hypothesis," says Rowe, "the secret of 'life' is to be sought outwardly and ecologically rather than (or as well as) inwardly and physiologically."[55]

To look outwardly and ecologically is to recognize that the ecosphere "is larger *in time* (it was here before we were), larger in *inclusiveness* (we are embedded within it), *more complexly* organized, and superior in *evolutionary creativity* (it gives rise to species, whereas we mostly only modify, through selective breeding, a few of the species the ecosphere has provided) and has greater *diversity* (a product of evolutionary creativity)."[56]

With this, Jackson and Rowe set the stage for a revolutionary shift in our thinking. It will be thinking in a new key about ourselves, how we live, and our place in the world. It will be the shift from the human subject to nature comprehensively as the starting point and measure. Yes, we remain creatures of lively symbolic consciousness. But the content of that consciousness will not be the same as the preoccupations, perspectives, and morality of the contemporary era, the industrial-technological. This will be a new song and new wineskins for new wine.

Born to meaning

"New cells are born every day and old cells die, but they have neither funerals nor birthdays."[57] We are born to belonging. We are also born to meaning. Ackerman's "lonely bipeds with the giant dreams" possess a certain kind of consciousness and a certain kind of mind, one outfitted with sophisticated cognition and insistent about making and marking meaning ("funerals and birthdays").

This kind of mind asks big questions. They may be the child's: Where did I come from? Where did Daddy come from? Where did the world come from? What happens when we die? Where do we go? Will my goldfish be there, too? Why did Grandma lose her voice when she died? Why do people get sick? Why do people hurt so much even if they are good and not naughty?

Will everything die? Why don't people tell the truth? Are they hiding something bad? Isn't everything kinda weird? Why are we here and not somewhere else? Should we live like Grandpa and Grandma, or like the people on our street? Isn't everything just wonderful!

These questions have long been ratcheted up to adult levels and turned into the journey-work of philosophers, poets, parents, theologians, and scientists. Does God exist? Why do mortals hate, pray, and sing? Why do they make both love and war, sometimes on the same day? Is there an answer to inner emptiness, genuine tragedy, or the vicissitudes of fortune? Why do the righteous suffer and the wicked prosper? Why do good things happen to bad people and bad things to good? Is peace possible? What is justice? Are irony, absurdity, and comedy the last word? What is real, anyway, and how do we know it? Do our senses tell us of the real world, or deceive us? Does our mind make things up? What truly fulfils? Can we attain genuine happiness? If so, how? How do we make good decisions? What form of government, society, and economy are best? What way of life? How will the world end? What becomes of the universe? Is it, or anything else, eternal? What is the *ultimate* origin of life and matter?

These are all questions of meaning, even cosmic meaning. We apparently can't help asking them, whether or not we answer them to anyone's lasting satisfaction. A relentless search for meaning has marked all things human since dark arms first lifted the first baby to the full moon in the awesome presence of waiting gods. Nor is it just us. We find glimmers in extinct hominid lines. Humans of one species or another have been making meaning for a very long time, long before written texts, theologians, and the country schoolhouse.

Differently said, it seems that hominids need a story to live by—or several stories, with lots of answers—and it has to add up. We are born to meaning, and we cannot help but wonder. Nor can we help but explain and instruct. We insist on explanations even for behavior with origins in deep, unconscious impulses and snap judgments. Reasoning animals that we are, we insist on plausible explanations even for the irrational.

The questions and answers are not idle or trivial. Religions and moralities emerge from them, and whole ways of life turn on them. Timeless, classic achievements embody them. So do mountains of inflicted injury.

True, many of the answers die when their stories and ways of life no longer compel and their meanings no longer convince. But questioning and answering never expire. What, after all, would human culture be apart from life's certain questions and transient answers? There would be no storytellers, musicians, artists, architects, or writers; no rituals or rites of passage; no heirlooms, legacies, or monuments; and very little nurture, few memories, and nothing to talk about.

But we began with a statement that ours is a certain kind of consciousness and a certain kind of mind, one that cultivates the art of wonder and insists on making and marking meaning. One way to describe this rather unique trait is this: We are "symbolizing" creatures, creatures of self-reflective symbolic consciousness.

The evidence is early, at the dawn of *Homo sapiens* or likely even before. Caves at Pinnacle Point, South Africa, contain ground red ochre among tools and shellfish remains that are 164,000 years old. The red ochre was probably for body painting and coloring of artifacts. Adding it to other things known about very early humans, paleoanthropologist Curtis Marean and his team concluded that already at this time humans "inhabited a cognitive world enriched by symbols."[58]

Symbols are images, representations, and gestures that let us make imaginative, "mindful" associations. Who first looked at a stone and saw an axe? Or looked at a stone, a vine, and a broken branch and saw a hammer or hunting tool? Who saw shells for trade and devised numerals—numbers as symbols—to say how many for how much of some other, and unrelated, object? Who looked at a tree and imagined all life branching and joined like a great oak, or imagined her ancestors, siblings, and children as a family "tree"? Who looked at a mountain and saw an ascent to the gods or the place where the ancestors must first have emerged into this world? Who stood at the Nile, the Amazon, the Congo, or the Mississippi and could only sing or speak poetry or tell tales or build shrines and temples, all in response to the life, power, and mystery of the mighty river? And who invented language, that vast symbol system in which sounds in the air stand in for actions, feelings, relationships, and instruction? Who made of sound a sacrament, the sacrament of song?

The etymology is telling. *Syn* means "together," *bolē* means a "throw." Symbols "throw together" some object or action and some image for it, in order to create a meaning the symbol then conveys in shorthand. It may be utterly utilitarian—a red octagon for a stop sign, a white "H" on a blue shield for a hospital, 6 or 12 for the number of apples to buy. Or it may be evocative—a wedding ring, a family heirloom, a treasured photograph, a remembered sunset, a war memorial. It may also be horrific—a swastika, a noose, the lynching tree. It may signal authority—a crown, a constitution, a gavel; or invitation and permission—an open door, a welcome mat, a handshake. It might even gather up the whole story of a people and centuries of pilgrimage—a menorah, a minaret, a Buddha, a cross, a font, a flame, a feather. The list is as long and alive as the unending trails of human imagination. Yet the purpose is always the same: to "throw things together"—images and representations, gestures and objects or actions—in order to create, convey, mark, sustain, or change meaning.

All this is so "natural" to us that we slight its significance. Symbolizing creatures can effectively detach images from their objects and relate these images to one another so as to create whole worlds of meaning via mindful imagination. We can, and do, create virtual worlds a step or more removed from the real material world. The stimulus might be the lure of enchantment and the story might have no other purpose than good, plain fun. Who didn't enjoy *Lord of the Rings, The Arabian Nights, The Chronicles of Narnia*, Harry Potter's adventures, *Avatar*, and *Star Trek*?

Symbolizing, throwing things together, might take the form of more serious story-telling. Stories of origin and destiny, the birth of a nation and a people, the epic narrative and the definitive history are almost always conveyed with symbols: a city set on a hill, a people and their Promised Land, a battle of gods bestowing favor to contending kings, George Washington crossing the Delaware as shorthand for the founding Revolution.

Or symbols might be used for serious plotting and planning, with symbolic consciousness allowing us a kind of dress rehearsal of what we might pursue and achieve. We can test possible and probable consequences of contemplated actions and alliances; we can layer meaning upon meaning for purposes of nuanced expression and communication; we can live into other times and places, walk in others' shoes, and, at least to some degree, travel their world through their eyes. We can recall our past and project our future. We can conjure up worlds, create ideals, formulate goals, and plot ways to achieve them, all for better or for worse.

Symbolic consciousness also allows us to learn lessons that stick without hard, direct experience. The child who hears the fictional account of the boy who cried wolf and remembers what happened to him in the story may file that lesson away. She doesn't need to cry wolf to see what might happen.

But the symbolizing mind is a dangerous mind, too. Symbols can be detached from the realities they initially expressed and be reinvested with meaning. Then they take on a life of their own, and a half-imagined world loses touch with reality. Map replaces territory, and we live inside our pictures of what is real and what matters.

Then we create on the basis of the map and prefer the human rendition of nature to the original. Martin Nowak's *Supercooperators: Altruism, Evolution, and Why We Need Each Other to Succeed* includes an exchange between Gustav Mahler and conductor Bruno Walter. Mahler's Third Symphony was his effort, he said, to let "nature in its totality . . . ring and resound. . . . In my own way, I would like to think I have helped to give nature her voice too." With that magnificent work, he had. In 1896 he invited Walter to glimpse the score. As they walked in the mountains, Walter admonished Mahler to take in the grand vistas, to which Mahler replied, "No use staring up there—I've already composed it all anyway into my symphony!"[59]

In Mahler's case, good results followed and a great composition was added to the high culture repertoire. But often wrong actions follow, with nature redone on the basis of human maps and the mapmakers preferring the results, the built environment, to the original.

Many maps created by the modern mind have so construed the natural world, so divested it of subjectivity and meaning, that nature is no longer imbued with the sacred, and we no longer have communal feelings toward it. From a *relational* point of view, nature is effectively dead. Modern minds imagine only an instrumental connection to nature, and we act accordingly.

We are, then, symbol-making, symbol-using, and symbol-misusing animals. Not a day goes by in which we don't marshal symbols to think what we think and say what we say. Yes, we also learn by rote imitation. But we can and do go far beyond, drawing upon the lives and experience of others over long stretches of time as these have been encoded in symbol systems, not the least of which is language.

Other animals may be symbolizing creatures as well. The chimpanzee that sees a branch, strips it bare, and creates a digging tool, for example, or gorillas that learn sign language and then teach it to their young. Whales and birds use song, that sacrament of sound, in order to communicate. Perhaps the otter has such a mind as well, hefting a stone to smash mollusks for food. But most animals, including these, live in abrupt immediacy with their environment, an immediacy that doesn't betray a capacity to detach from it in order to envision and create other worlds, or imagine different pasts and altered futures, with different ways to achieve them. For better or worse, other creatures' minds and imaginations don't seem as wild and ranging, or as fraught with consequence. They don't deal in truth so large, so important, and so mysterious that it cannot be contained by mere fact or the exigencies of the immediate world.[60]

Other animals live passionately, to be sure. But do they dream passionately? They respond to their environment in sophisticated ways, some with far keener senses than ours. But they don't picture their environment altogether differently and then upend it in keeping with utopian notions of New Harmony, the New Jerusalem, or a Thousand Year Reich. They are not "the lonely bipeds with the giant dreams" (Ackerman) who, because they are sophisticated symbolizing creatures, become the ultimate "creatures of possibility."[61] Spiritual quests, for example, don't seem part of other animals' repertoire. Few, if any, go to temple. Nor do they take up astrology as a way to read personality.

It is not our bodies, then, that truly mark us off from our relatives; it's our ability to use vast webs of symbolic communication to mediate our experience of the world and engage others across time and space. Self-reflection and symbolic consciousness mean a certain transcendence and freedom for us, compared with our other-than-human kin.

We do none of this as lone individuals. We always create meaning together; we symbolize together. We use what has been passed on to us, the product of other generations and civilizations, the yield of both the famous and the forgotten, just as we tap the vast and rich world of nature around and within us. The symbolizing mind is a *biosocial, biocommunal* mind, with symbols no more created from nothing by isolated individuals than No. 2 yellow lead pencils. Symbols are not symbols at all until they throw things together in ways humans understand together and pass along together. Symbols carry no meaning if they are not shared. Even the symbols of high creativity—Einstein's famous equations—are unintelligible apart from goods already shared in the community of knowing to which Einstein belonged.

There is a necessary caution: While our minds range freely and creatively, our kind of consciousness is inherently finite and selective. Symbols by nature capture and filter only some of the reality we inhabit. No symbols capture the whole or even tell the whole truth about the part they capture. Their power, in fact, is in a capacity to focus and limit, pushing all else aside for the sake of precision, insight, or emphasis. A lotus blossom can bear a profound message, as can a crescent, a cross, and a menorah. Each can be a vessel of life-shaping meaning. But one cannot substitute for the other. The lotus cannot substitute for the menorah or the cross for the crescent, nor can they occupy the same emotive region in the devotee's heart. Each bears its own cargo of meaning.

The limiting that is native to symbols has another implication. Not only is there no true universality for any single symbol or symbol set, just as there is no universal language and culture that can substitute for each and every language and culture, so also do inherently finite symbols frame our perception and skew our view. We are creatures of ordinary bias, and there is always an ideological taint in the way we read the world and reason about it. Our point of view is just that, a *point* of view. We see the horizon clearly enough. But the horizon is never all there is. Something always exists beyond the horizon, something that we do not see and something that, while standing here, we cannot comprehend. We can move and take in another horizon. But symbolic consciousness cannot stand in all places at the same time or, even standing in one place, take in all the reality there in some comprehensive and unfiltered way. Symbols are finite, and symbolic consciousness is bounded and contextual. Bias and partial, skewed perspective come with our kind of mind.

Differently said, "our mode of vision" is tied up with "our mode of being."[62] If our mode of being changes, if circumstances change and the life we live is altered, our way of seeing will likely change as well. We are historical creatures whose life-worlds and institutions shape our mental maps. While symbolic consciousness always organizes our perception, and limits it, it is mutable. While it always strives for meaningful totalities, they are partial, inherently biased, and temporal. Nonetheless we crave absolute categories and love to canonize our perception and judgments.[63] The bumper sticker advice is sound: Don't Believe Everything You Think.

Religion merits special mention. We said earlier that life's big questions and the symbolizing mind give rise to religion and morality. All we might conclude at this point is that every religion and morality, too, will be partial, inherently biased, temporal, and mutable as it strives for meaningful totality and truth.

Born to religion

James Miller begins an essay on "Connecting Religion and Ecology" with the story of Pharkru Pitak, the Thai Buddhist monk who in 1990 hit upon the idea of "ordaining" trees. He and his neighbors despaired of deforestation that was creating soil erosion and impoverishing the land, in turn breaking up families by sending the able-bodied off to the cities in desperate search of livelihood. What Pitak did was wrap the big old trees—the ones most desired by the timber companies—in saffron robes, ritually investing them with the status of Buddhist monks. He also hung a sign on the trees: "To destroy the forest is to destroy life." A local village authority, Suay Sisom, explained that cutting down an ordained tree produced the same karmic demerit as killing a monk. In the face of such a choice, involving the deep symbols of their culture and their understanding of karma as a moral order, the people chose not to cut down the trees themselves and not to allow others to do so.[64] The sacred values conveyed by the saffron robe had trumped the monetary value of timber for the market.[65] The choice was not easy—jobs, already in short supply, were at stake—but it was real.

I might have chosen any number of examples of the ties of religion and symbol. Here's another one.

"Earth is the icon that hangs around God's neck," said Daniel Ogan, an iconographer in Kodiak, Alaska. He was explaining the creation-rich cosmology of land, sea, and sky of "Orthodox Alaska,"[66] where the majority of clergy and laity in the Orthodox churches are native Alaskan or Creole (mixed blood, native and Russian). In St. Herman's Chapel, at the seminary in Kodiak, the "royal doors" through which the priests pass with the bread and wine of the Eucharist include not only the traditional Orthodox saints but also the totems of four native peoples—an otter, a salmon, a rose, and a raven. The salmon conveys in the speckles of its skin the stars and planets. The salmon is at home in the universe and the universe is at home in it. Add the reverence of the people for their "iconic" salmon, and their identification with its spirit, and you have a symbol so rich in meaning that it evokes prayer and devotion.

Another example: On a July afternoon in 1990, an hour or so after the school children had been dismissed for the day, an earthquake of 7+ on the Richter scale rocked Baguio, the Philippine City of Pines, and laid it low. Devastation was massive and the loss of life staggering, not least because a second strong tremor arrived forty minutes after the first—just long enough to lure people back into their weakened homes to survey the ruin and take shelter from the torrential rains that continued to fall.

The sixty-two-year-old convent of the Maryknoll Sisters was among the ruins. After emergency care, the question quickly became, What now? Rebuild somehow and take up where they had left off—primarily elementary education and advocacy work with the urban poor and the tribal communities of the surrounding mountains—or find another ministry?

Over the course of the next seven years, the answer took form: The Maryknoll Ecological Sanctuary, with its Center for the Integrity of Creation, its Fourteen Stations of the Cosmic Journey, its Environmental Theater, and its Bio-Shelter. The Ecological Sanctuary protects the remaining old-growth pines and, with diverted rainwater and recycled graywater, restores the wetlands. The Center for the Integrity of Creation hosts many meetings focused on jobs, housing, and poverty alleviation. The outdoor Environmental Theater is where most meetings begin, with prayers danced by students from the school for the deaf. The Stations of the Cosmic Journey, connected by paths across the mountain that is the sanctuary, express artistically the evolution of the universe from the Big Bang to the present. And the Bio-Shelter, itself constructed from the recycled ruins and felled trees of the earthquake, is home to the Sisters. It is simple, sleek, and high-tech in the way of "green" building, with an airiness that captures the feel and smell of the sanctuary's sunshine and pine.

All this is cast in the sacramental traditions of Roman Catholicism as that has taken shape in recent decades under the influence of thinkers such as Thomas Berry and Brian Swimme.[67] What Berry calls "the Great Work" of our time, to move from "the human devastation of Earth" to a time "when humans [are] present to the planet in a mutually beneficial manner,"[68] is what the Sisters and their Ecological Sanctuary embody in ritual and practice.

One more example: Sunday afternoon worship at the Zionist congregation in Mucheke Township, Masvingo, Zimbabwe, was vivid. Strong, solid colors; robed figures circling to the beat of drums and the jangle of tin rattles; time for instruction, hosted by a reader of scripture and an expositor of the same, verse by verse; more song and more dance and more bright sunlight whitening the canopy. Not too far into the praise, Bishop Marinda welcomes Bishop Moses, whose own green robe carries the logo of the African Association of Earthkeeping Churches across the back: an African farmer kneeling, planting a tree. Beneath the tree are the words of Colossians 1:17: "In Christ all things hold together."

"Bishop Moses" is a conferred title. It recognizes (and symbolizes) extraordinary leadership on the part of Inus Daneel, bringing the Shona people up from destitution through a grassroots movement of earth-healers. The ties to the soil of these subsistence farmers are strong. Fighters for independence from Rhodesia called themselves "Sons of the Soil." These ties found Christian voice in a cosmology of the whole community of life as framed liturgically. So tree-planting happens in the context of a Eucharist; seed dedication does as well. The first fruits of the harvest are gathered in a Feast of Booths celebration, itself borrowed from the Hebrew Bible. No cutting of trees alongside streams is allowed, in recognition of the living waters of life common to scripture, baptism, and the sacred groves of the ancestors. The young are trained in local horticulture and land preservation as their training in stewardship. All the earth of these granite hills has become the religious focus of a comprehensive guardianship, so much so that the people felt their work together needed a name—The African Association of Earthkeeping Churches (AAEC)—and a slogan: "Regaining the Lost Lands, Reclothing the Earth."[69]

These examples—the ordained trees, the icons of Orthodox Alaska, the Maryknoll Stations of the Universe Story in their Ecological Sanctuary, the AAEC—show people operating in the register of symbol and spirit.[70] They do what Miller says religion does. Through symbols and the work of symbolic consciousness, religion imaginatively construes human experience of the world so as to invest it with meaning and provide motivation, energy, and direction. Much of this is sense-making on a grand scale—"rearranging the nonreligious furniture of our mind into a coherent whole."[71] This is religious meaning cosmic in its reach (those questions of origin, destiny, and purpose), sacred in its value (those questions of morality and ultimate standing), and unifying in its drive (the coherent whole, the story that adds up).

The human experience of nature is gathered up in the process. Lasting, cross-cultural symbols are often lifted directly from nature: the sacred mountain, the rivers of crystalline waters, the Tree of Life, the caves of the gods, the deserts of our lives, the rock from which we are hewn, springs of living water, Mother Earth and Father Sky.

Note, for example, the evening Rosh Hashanah service in the Reformed tradition, commencing the Jewish High Holy Days, "The Days of Awe." In the prayer, "We Will Not Forget You," the congregation recollects, thousands of years later, its ancient beginnings as a rather irascible people gathered at the foot of a mountain.

> God of our people, hear our prayer:
> We who speak are Jews.
> Remember
> The bush You kindled once in the desert air,
> Years ago, on Horeb's lonely sand,
> That fire You lit to set the centuries aflame
> And say to us Your endless, perfect Name,
> 'I am what I will be'—
> It burns eternally now, that light
> Upon our altars now, against the night.
> And there are deserts still. We are the Jews;
> We do not forget.
> Remember
> The words You spoke in stone
> And thunder.
> The mountain smoked
> And the dismayed multitude

Stood off, hearing the first time
The words they could not refuse,
Fearing the burden and the God that set
Them into history.
And there are mountains still. We are the Jews.
We cannot forget.
We come here then. But something far more deep
Compels: the ancient desert dream we keep,
A people touched by God, a certain grace
That tells of you. We are
Locked with You in old identity,
Remembering the lightning of that place;
Something in us of Your awesome will,
Something of that mountain's thunder, still.
Love us, as much as we will let You.
We are your Jews,
We will not forget You.[72]

    This is the language of religion and nature together. That link is not only the oldest in religious discourse, but primordial; most religious symbols originate in nature—here the mountain, the burning bush, the desert dreams, the words spoken in stone and thunder, the fire, sand, and lightning of that place.

    The Rosh Hashanah language is also the language of identity: "We are your Jews," "[l]ocked with You in old identity," the congregation prays. Religious language is invariably so. It says we are born to belonging and hold citizenship in a cosmic community far surpassing our abbreviated moment in time. The imagination of symbolic consciousness has offered, via religion, an identity "that is archaically and symbolically rooted in the human experience of nature."[73]

    Religious symbols also include symbols of nature as transformed by human hands, nature recast as a built environment bearing multivalent and lasting meaning—the New Jerusalem, the Temple Mount, the Pyramids, Angkor Wat, Golgotha, a city set on a hill. But in all cases religion, a universal aspect of human culture as far back as we have records and certainly since the Neolithic revolutions of 10,000–8,000 B.C.E., addresses the big questions of life through elaborate symbol systems—rites and rituals, sacraments and stories, teaching and training, art, architecture, dress, liturgy, festival, food and drink prepared and shared. Religion distills the worlds that are native to creatures born to meaning. It does so with the presence and power of the natural world. And it does so everywhere, without pause, for good and ill. *Homo sapiens* is incorrigibly religious.

Born to morality

The Days of Awe continue with the morning Rosh Hashanah service. "We worship the power that unites all the universe into one great harmony," the congregation testifies, only to go on and say: "That oneness, however, is not yet. We see imperfection, disorder, and evil all about us. But before our eyes is a vision of perfection, order, and goodness: these too we have known in some measure. There is evil enough to break the heart, enough good to exalt the soul. Our people has experienced untold suffering and wondrous redemptions; we await a redemption more lasting and more splendid than any of the past."[74]

"[E]vil enough to break the heart, enough good to exalt the soul" is the language of morality as well as religion. So is "untold suffering" and "wondrous redemptions." Such extremes led Jeffrey Kluger to begin his essay, "What Makes Us Moral," by saying that "[if] the entire human species were a single individual, that person would long ago have been declared mad."[75] Mad, not simply because the human mind is an untamable cauldron capable of willing wholesale destruction, the kind that can create fantasy movies of cosmic wars and video games of Apocalypse, the kind that can also create real holocausts. And mad, not because of the counter extreme, a "transcendent goodness . . . so sublime we fold it into a larger 'soul.'"[76]

Disasters around the world—tsunamis in Asia, earthquakes in Haiti and Chile, a hurricane in the United States, a brutal attack on the World Trade Center or in Gaza—elicit a global outpouring of compassion, pity, and material wealth from total strangers. The same Amish community that witnesses in horror the murder of its schoolchildren embraces in forgiveness the family of the assailant. And what about the prayer left beside the body of a dead child by a prisoner in the concentration camp at Ravensbruck, Germany? "O Lord, remember not only the men and women of good will, but also those of ill will. But do not remember all the suffering they have inflicted on us: remember the fruits we have brought, thanks to this suffering—our comradeship, our loyalty, our humility, our courage, our generosity, the greatness of heart which has grown out of all this, and when they come to judgment, let all the fruits which we have borne be their forgiveness."[77] How does magnanimity steal this far into the camp of the enemy? Or yet a different example. We donate our very organs to one another, some, such as a kidney, while we are still alive. Living organisms sacrifice for one another.

No, neither the savage nor the splendid is cause on its own to diagnose madness; rather, the fact that these extremes reside in the same creature at the same time.[78] There is something of the killer in us, just as there is an angel of goodness and delight. The divine contends with the demonic, within and without. The Apollonian, with its instinct for form, beauty, and moderation, faces off against the Dionysian, with its instinct for the exuberant, irrational, and violent. We are mad with morality. Mad with morality is the kind of creature we are.

Why? The question demands an answer. But the answer begins elsewhere, with another question: What gives rise to moral experience in the first place? What creature, *because* it is moral by nature, is capable of such extremes? Or, backing away from extremes only, what creature, because it is moral, is capable of ordinary, everyday, routine acts of moral value?

The Rosh Hashanah passage provides the clue. "We see imperfection, disorder, and evil all about us. But before our eyes is a vision of perfection, order, and goodness." This is the work of reflective and imaginative symbolic consciousness. We experience one kind of world, the world that is. But we imagine another, the world that might and ought to be. This is where human life is lived, suspended in the tension and across the gaps between is, ought, and how (getting from is to ought). That tension and those gaps give rise to human moral experience, which is to say, choice and agency. Moral agency is the capacity to act in ways large and small on the difference between the world we face and the world we desire. Desires and dreams, even more than DNA, drive our actions. We are incorrigibly moral. Or, in the words of the epigraph to this book, "our lives are startlingly moral" (Thoreau).

Choices and possibilities are constrained, of course, sometimes severely. Often we cannot begin to do what we desire, and we can never do all we desire. We lack opportunity, means, and talent, though not motive. In *German Boy*, Wolfgang Samuel recalls his years as a child in war. It was an account of his life in the early to mid-1940s, much of it with his mother, sister, grandparents, and mostly absent father, all fleeing the eastward advance of the Russians. A preteen, then a teenager, he was a refugee with shorter and longer stays in different villages of his homeland as it lost the war. The boy takes on more and more responsibility for their survival but feels powerless. One passage begins, as many do, with nature mirroring the child's mood.

> Autumn days turned the leaves to gold; soon the sunshine faded, and rain and overcast skies were the rule again rather than the exception. The leaves remaining on the trees shriveled and the townspeople

turned bleak and somber again, as we stared another threatening winter in the face. . . . After the brutal beating episode in school, I never quite recovered my spirit. It depressed me to think I had absolutely no rights whatsoever as a human being. Anyone in authority could do to me whatever they wanted. If they wanted to take my grandfather and kill him, they could do that. If they wanted to imprison and abuse some hungry kids whose only offense was to steal raw sugar to moderate their hunger, then they could do it. . . . If they wanted to rape my mother and blow up my house, or nearly so, they could do it. They could do anything. I could do nothing but stoically accept my fate. And if I didn't? I knew the consequences.[79]

He didn't "stoically accept" his fate, however. Though feeling powerless for very good reason, he never stopped dreaming of surviving the war and living free somewhere where his dreams could be realized. Nor did he ever stop doing what he could to save his family and himself. Wolfgang's was yet another instance of those dreams of "perfection, order and goodness" (Rosh Hashanah) that never expire, even when we have experienced "evil enough to break the heart." Humans stubbornly seek to create a way where, at the moment, none appears.

Consciousness of a difference between good and evil, and a felt obligation to pursue the former and avoid the latter, describes us as moral creatures. Were we nonmoral creatures like plants, we would lack a sense of the morally good as distinct from the morally evil. The world would simply "be," and we would be at home in a simple state of "is," without visions of a world that is not but could be.

We would experience belonging in such a world, to be sure—the plain, real belonging of a beehive or a termite mound, an ape colony or a weaver's nest. But our belonging would not be driven by a comparable longing, the longing for a peaceable kingdom, a just world, and rest at the last. Deep and restless longing accompanies belonging as the kind of creature we are.

The is/ought/how tension in our lives, stamped with longing, invents the future. So far as we know, other animals do not imagine futures radically different from the present. Nor do they use unlimited imagination to generate foresight and scan a projected horizon for opportunities and dangers. They do not invent different futures and chase them down in the hope for something other and better. We do.

Of course, not all talk of good and evil, perfection and order, present and future, is moral talk, just as not all symbols are religious and/or moral. If we recognize Joshua Bell as a "good" or "superb" musician, always in the "right" key and playing the "right" rather than "wrong" note, we are not making moral judgments. We are using "good," "right," and "wrong" in nonmoral senses.

If I say "Rembrandt is a good painter," my judgment is aesthetic, not moral. If, however, I say, "Rembrandt was of dubious character," my judgment is moral, not aesthetic. And if you respond, "You're wrong, Rembrandt was of upstanding character," we're engaged in a moral debate, no matter whose judgment is correct.

All this is important because we are by nature irreducibly "moral" creatures. We may argue endlessly about whether an action, a course, or a whole way of life is moral or immoral. But both of those—moral and immoral—belong to the moral universe of distinctively moral creatures.[80] While we are certainly more than our moral selves, we are never less. "Moral" is the kind of creature we are.

Many other creatures are moral as well. They, too, are prosocial creatures whose lives exhibit clear moral qualities. For example, empathy—a key moral trait, perhaps *the* key moral trait—is shared by many primates. Russian primatologist Nadia Kohts raised a chimp in her home. When the chimp would find his way onto the roof and not come down in response to calling, scolding, or offers of food, Kohts would sit down and pretend to cry. The chimp would come immediately. "He tenderly takes my chin in his palm . . . as if trying to understand what is happening."[81] Or there is Binta Jua, the gorilla who rescued a three-year-old boy who fell into her zoo enclosure. She rocked the frightened child in her arms, then carried him to a door where zoo trainers could enter and collect him.[82]

Iain Douglas-Hamilton reports from Kenya's Samburu Reserve that the elephants in the herd with Babyl, a cripple who could only walk slowly, always waited. They would stop, look around to see where she was, then proceed when she caught up. Babyl belonged; and they cared enough not to abandon her. Instead they adjusted their own behavior. Marc Bekoff watched a female red fox bury her mate.[83] Maybe "funerals and birthdays,"[84] and longing, aren't exclusively human after all.

Empathy only begins the list of moral traits we observe among animals other than ourselves. Protection of the vulnerable, defense of one's group, help for the injured or trapped, loyalty to a partner, sympathy for the suffering, tenderness toward the young, pleasure at a meeting, concern for the missing, intimations of friendship, displays of affection, discipline of the wayward, clear signs of reciprocity—these and more on the part of different animals testify to salient moral qualities we share.

Animals also know pain and certainly have a point of view about how they are treated. Many show what we identify as moral emotions—anger, jealously, joy, grief, resentment, sympathy.[85] Sometimes the eyes convey an inner state. Jane Goodall writes of the sunken eyes of a young chimpanzee grieving its mother. Konrad Lorenz says the eyes of a grieving goose sink back in its head. Jody McConnery says of traumatized orphan gorillas that "[t]he light in their eyes simply goes out, and they die."[86] And it is highly doubtful, Marc Bekoff writes, that animals like "being chained, stunned, crammed into tiny cages, tied up, torn from family and friends, or isolated."[87]

This should not surprise any hominid. For if other animals are also prosocial and biosocial, like us, and if they, too, are limited in providing for themselves as individuals all that they need, then community must be created, sustained, and protected. And for that to happen, social rules and traits must be learned and nurtured, training must happen, and rewards and punishments must be meted out.

Differently said, the interests of my community must be taken into account for the sake of our survival and well-being. And taking into account community interests is the stuff of morality, pure and simple, whether as a jungle clan or on Chicago streets.

Darwin thought this moral capacity on the part of animals redounded to the collective good. "Those communities which included the greatest number of the most sympathetic members would flourish best and rear the greatest number of offspring."[88]

That said, other animals are not moral in exactly the same way. Or, more precisely, they are not moral to the same extreme. They are not mad with morality.

Other animals do exhibit culture. Primatologists have identified forty different behavioral patterns that show cultural variation among chimpanzees, for example. Tool use, grooming, and courtship rituals are among them. Different ape clans adopt different patterns for different locales and teach these to their children.[89] Too, there appear to be genuine individuals in a clan, with different personalities. Some are extroverts, some introverts, some agreeable, some neurotic. "Apes," "chimps," or "whales," as wholesale categories, much less a notion of *the* quintessential ape, chimp, or whale, is a human abstraction, in the same camp with other difference-denying abstractions—whites, blacks, Indians, Jews, Muslims, Christians, women, men—"those people." Darwin's insistence on evolutionary continuity, marked by nuanced but real difference, is borne out by animal studies. To be is to be different; it is also to belong to the same community of life.

Yet few other animals run off the rails by trying to render extinct all traces of "the other" in order to safeguard the purity and sanctity of their own tribe and culture. The group next to us—chimpanzees—come close. From time to time they do wreak havoc on one another. But they don't build large-scale institutions of forced labor and repression in order to garner economic benefits for the empire or leisure for its elite. They don't build intercontinental ballistic missiles and call them "Peacemakers" or manufacture deadly gases to protect their turf and eradicate the innocent along with the guilty. Few practice sadism or engage in utterly gratuitous violence although, again, chimpanzees may approximate this.

At the other extreme, other animals do not organize great institutions of philanthropy or adopt unknown but needy children of different cultures and races halfway around the world. They don't organize massive relief efforts for persons they don't know and will never meet. They are not mad with morality in the same way and degree humans are, for ill or good. Which is another way of saying they are not "the lonely bipeds with the great dreams." They are not symbol-making, symbol-using, and symbol-misusing creatures in the way we are, living the big questions across a projected is/ought/how gap they yearn to close with all the powers at their disposal, for weal as well as for woe.

Questions easily multiply about the kind of moral creature we are. Are we born with a moral "grammar," a parallel to what the child brings into the world as his or her complex capacity for speech? Nurture, culture, and community spell out the particulars of vocabulary, language, and morality, but do we bring something like a "starter" program into life so that, say, both selfishness ("Mine comes first") and selflessness ("Do unto others as you would have them do unto you") are seemingly written into our genes? Why do we experience what seem to be primal gut reactions about what is deeply desirable or utterly disgusting? Is it because our ancestors had to make split-second decisions in order to protect what they cherished, or simply to survive in a dangerous world?[90] Do these moral emotions of first response set the terms for the deliberations and decisions that follow, so that reason is the servant of interests?

A related question: Is there a common set of reference points, a kind of moral daypack we carry, whatever the cultural variations? Jonathan Haidt says there is and parses the moral realm with five evolved and shared factors: purity and sanctity, loyalty to the in-group, respect for authority, do as you would have done to you, and do no physical harm.[91] So, for example, four-year-olds everywhere have a sense of fairness and their "right" to equal treatment with other four-year-olds. Different communities weigh and institutionalize moral factors differently and develop different moral maps and cultures. Those differences matter. But Haidt's five factors do seem to occur and recur wherever humans take up life together— namely, everywhere.

Why does the essence spoil? Why does morality go rancid? Why are some of the moral stanzas we sing so off-key? Why is moral judgment a universal trait, as well as moral energy and zeal for a better world, but moral behavior is all over the chart, sometimes unspeakably far off the chart? Why does our kind of mind apparently have a negativity bias and register bad news more strongly than good, or remember cutting remarks longer than complimentary ones? Why do we react to a nonvenomous snake or a loud bang as real threats, while ignoring far more momentous ones, such as climate change or endemic corruption? Why are we so strongly tribal and suspicious of the other, even though the boundaries and membership of "in" groups and "out" groups change with regularity? Why walls instead of doors or open spaces? Why the tendency to demonize "the other" and justify ourselves, even when the behavior on all sides is much the same? And why does the difference of insiders and outsiders descend to such brutality at times, so that many find war exhilarating and atrocity gleeful? Why the moral extremes at the same time in the same circumstances—altruism and sacrifice in war matched to atrocity and deception?

The questions could continue. The mystery of iniquity certainly does, the mystery of why good moral substance rots. But this is an introductory chapter, the bare essentials of what we are born to and no more. And we have only walked the edges of that. We have not talked of moral tragedy, irony, or pathos. Nor have we examined the basic elements of the moral life—human character and conduct, vice and virtue, duty and responsibility, vision and value, communities and their practices, institutions and their policies.

So there is much more. Separate chapters will be given to the kind of faith and ethic we need for the kind of world we have, given the kind of creatures we are—creatures born to belonging, born to meaning, and born to morality; creatures who are, *by nature*, "moral, believing animals"[92] and "creatures of possibility," lonely bipeds with big dreams.

Next . . .

Pages about Evolutionary Adam and Eve tell us much, but they do not tell us how our interdependencies, powers, and relationships presently pattern the relationship with the rest of nature. They do not detail the kind of world that is presently ours. They tell us of human nature, but they don't tell us of the change in nature itself at human hands. Nor do they tell us how the drama of our time may alter future time, even future deep time. More must be said or we will not know what, in the face of vastly enhanced human powers and altered nature on a tough, new planet, we ought now to do and how we ought now to live.

2

The World We Have

It's a mutual, joint-stock world, in all meridians. We cannibals must help these Christians.
—HERMAN MELVILLE, *Moby-Dick*

There is no such thing as a Jewish ocean and a Lutheran sun and a Buddhist river and a Taoist forest and a Roman Catholic cornfield.
—MATTHEW FOX

IN *MOBY-DICK*, QUEEQUEG, the imposing harpooner whose faithful idol Tojo is always nearby, is taunted by a zealous young sailor who calls him "the devil."[1] When a sudden storm washes the young man overboard, Queequeg hops the rail and, several surface dives later, has the youngster in tow. Both are lifted aboard the battered schooner, the youth is revived, and Queequeg is praised. But Queequeg appears oblivious; he asks only for fresh water, gathers some dry clothes, and lights his pipe. He "seemed to be saying to himself," Melville writes: "It's a mutual, joint-stock world, in all meridians. We cannibals must help these Christians."[2]

"A mutual, joint-stock world, in all meridians" can stand as a recap of the previous chapter. Whether in deep time or shallow, we all live downhill, downwind, and downstream from everybody and everything to date; and uphill, upwind, and upstream from everyone and everything to follow.

Were the "betweenness" of life—that "relationships are the music life makes" and that words like "ecology, family, community, religion . . . all grope toward . . . connection, belonging, purpose"[3]—fully to register, different habits of mind and consciousness would settle in. Though the words initially seem awkward, "nature" and "culture" would merge as "nature-culture," "nature" and "society" as "nature-society," "biological" and "social" as "biosocial," "ecological" and "social" as "eco-social," and "economics" and "ecology" as "eco-nomics." "More-than-human" and "other-than-human" would stand in for that sweeping negative, "nonhuman." "Community" would break from its narrow human reference to gather in the rest of life, even the cosmos, and "neighbor" would include "*all that participates in being*," organic and inorganic, past, present, and future.[4] Since the planet itself is undergoing change under the impact of human presence, the geological and the social become the merged term "geosocial." Awkward as these constructions are, the remainder of this book will use them from time to time, simply to release one kind of consciousness from captivity and send it in search of a better home.

Were such revised understanding to take hold, a different symbolic consciousness would form. What we categorically label as simply "nonhuman" would disaggregate and soon bloom and dart and crow and turn golden in autumn. The "nonhuman" would breathe, suckle, climb, feast, play, and die. Lives other than ours might then appear unique and precious, even if they came eons before—or come eons after.[5] In a truly "mutual, joint-stock world" a different religious ethic, in a new key, would be heard. Planetary creation itself would become the subject of a comprehensive love, with comprehensive human responsibility its corollary. Queequeg would have understood.

First works over

What is the state of our "mutual, joint-stock world, in all meridians"? What conditions mount up around us? While answering the question entails a lengthy introduction, its conclusion is brief: Our present way of life has no durable future. Change will not come easily, however, because every way of life defends entrenched biases and protected privilege. This mandates that we be savvy about the play of human perception and the way we lean into the world. Analysis of how we take in the world and organize power is required; so is attention to how change happens.

In *The Price of the Ticket* James Baldwin writes of "do[ing] our first works over":

> In the church I come from—which is not at all the same church to which white Americans belong—we were counseled, from time to time, to do our first works over. Go back to where you started, or as far back as you can, examine all of it, travel your road again and tell the truth about it. Sing or shout or testify or keep it to yourself but *know whence you came.*[6]

To do first works over means to reexamine everything from its onset and to speak the truth as best one can.

First works, those by which we expect to work out our geo-social salvation, are layered deeply in psyche and society. They generate the "normative gaze" that frames and guides feeling and thought alike.[7] They fund our personal habits and the habits of our institutions. They show up in our modes of production and reproduction; our cultural sensibilities; and our basic aesthetic, intellectual, and moral values. They furnish the content of our symbols and consciousness. They comprise, at day's end, nothing less than our way of life.

As the incarnation of first works long underway, a way of life seems "natural"; at least it seems so, because culture is really "second nature" to us. It is what we do with nature to organize it for our own purposes and bend it to the way we live. It is nature-culture, culture as our rendition of nature. This renders a way of life so obvious to its adherents, and so firmly in place, that those who benefit barely notice its painstaking, costly, arbitrary construction. Its wisdom seems conventional, its good common. Only the stranger, some other wanderer from the borderlands, or those habituated to the "two-ness"[8] required of persons who must know two worlds in order to survive in one, are routinely aware of its quirky logic and capricious composition. Those native to their own first works treat their culture as fish do water, or plants topsoil. They grow, adjust, work with what they have, and go about their business, doing what comes naturally.

This makes any objective truth-telling difficult, since our first works construct the mindsets and sensibilities with which we attend to the world in the first place. If we benefit from that world, our first works also flatter us with biases that favor us and turn our good luck and advantages into achievements we're certain we've earned. Our motherboard is hardwired to favor the results we desire.

All this has been well known to students of human nature since the Hebrew prophets. "The heart is devious above all else," cries Jeremiah. "It is perverse—who can understand it?" (17:9). Apes may playfully deceive one another now and again, but when trickster time is over, they all giggle over their wiliness. They don't believe their own lies, nor do they think "more highly of [themselves] than [they] ought" (Rom. 12:3). Humans by contrast practice self-deception as a fine art. Mark Twain wanted to write a truthful autobiography and tried many times but gave it up. "I'm not going to write autobiography. . . . The man has yet to be born who could write the truth about himself. Autobiography is always interesting, but howsoever true its facts may be, its interpretation of them must be taken with a great deal of allowance."[9]

Few have laid out the consequences of reigning bias as succinctly as Baldwin. In an *Ebony* article written well after he had left the life of a storefront preacher, he says that "[p]eople who imagine that history flatters them (as it does, since they wrote it) are impaled on their history like a butterfly on a pin and incapable of seeing or changing themselves, or the world."[10]

Seeing afresh

How, then, do we see our way of life and its first works differently, perhaps for the first time? How do we avoid pinning ourselves down, rendering ourselves incapable of constructive change? How do we find another place to stand, with other possibilities for seeing, understanding, and responding? How do we address the "wicked problems"[11] that challenge present first works on a tough, new planet?

Learning to live in more than one world at a time is one way. Walking in others' shoes, exploring their terrain, seeing what they see and how they see it, is a human capacity that delivers empathetic insight to those willing to venture it. We can learn "two-ness" and garner the insight and wisdom won through the rigors of dual belonging.

Letting the past speak anew is a second way. This is Baldwin's "go back as far as you can, examine all of it, travel your road again and tell the truth about it."

Walter Rauschenbusch published *Christianity and the Social Crisis* in 1907, soon after the nineteenth century had closed. To draw his readers back through those tumultuous years, Rauschenbusch's imagination convenes a meeting of the Spirits of the Dead Centuries. The Spirits gather on their granite thrones in the vaulted chamber of the past to receive the latest centennial report. The Spirit of the Eighteenth Century requested the Spirit of the Nineteenth Century to "Tell thy tale, brother. Give us word of the humankind we left to thee."

> "I am the Spirit of the Wonderful Century," the Nineteenth Century begins.
>
> "I gave men mastery over nature. Discoveries and inventions, which lighted the black space of the past like lovely stars, have clustered in the Milky Way of radiance under my rule. One man does by the touch of his hand what the toil of a thousand slaves never did. Knowledge has unlocked the mines of wealth, and the hoarded wealth of to-day

creates the vaster wealth of tomorrow. Man has escaped the slavery of Necessity and is free. I freed the thoughts of men. They face the facts and know their knowledge is common to all. The deeds of the East at even are known in the West at morn. They send their whispers under the seas and across the clouds.

I broke the chains of bigotry and despotism. I made men free and equal. Every man feels the worth of his manhood.

I have touched the summit of history. I did for mankind what none of you did before. They are rich. They are wise. They are free."[12]

The Spirits sit in silence, "with troubled eyes." Eventually the Spirit of the First Century speaks. The First Century poses questions to the Nineteenth Century about its claims: "You have made men rich . . . You have made men wise . . . You have set them free . . . You have made them one."[13] The Nineteenth Century listens long, its head sinks to its breast, then it responds:

"Your shame is upon me. My great cities are as yours were. My millions live from hand to mouth. Those who toil longest have the least. My thousands sink exhausted before their days are half spent. My human wreckage multiplies. Class faces class in sullen distrust. Their freedom and knowledge has only made men keener to suffer."[14]

Now with troubled eyes of its own, the Nineteenth Century Spirit can only issue a request: "Give me a seat among you, and let me think why it has been so."[15]

If learning from the past is a second means, discerning the signs of the times is a third. Look up, down, and around to puzzle out where you are and what you see. What is happening? What are its causes, manifestations, and consequences? Check with the scientists and historians; the elders and the poets; the artists, farmers, doctors, nutritionists, engineers, and children. Check with those who benefit from present arrangements. Consult especially those who do not. What do they report as salient for the way life is presently lived? In light of the collective testimony, which first works should be retained, which modified, which abandoned?

If we combine knowing whence we've come with discernment of the present and the experience of those living in two worlds at once, the account might go like this.

It starts again with Rauschenbusch and what he and others in the nineteenth century identified as "the social question," "the social problem," or "the modern social problem." Those phrases are Ernst Troeltsch's, a contemporary of Rauschenbusch. His 1911 rendition trails Rauschenbusch's by only a few years.

> This social problem is vast and complicated. It includes the problem of the capitalist economic period and of the industrial proletariat created by it; and of the growth of militaristic and bureaucratic giant states; of the enormous increase in population, which affects colonial and world policy, of the mechanical technique, which produces enormous masses of materials and links up and mobilizes the whole world for purposes of trade, but which also treats men and labour like machines.[16]

By whatever name, "the social question" or "the modern social problem" was the effort to name the exploitative character and dislocating effects of rapidly developing industrial society. Its driving force was the economy made famous in Adam Smith's work. "Capitalism" was not yet its name when Smith penned *An Inquiry into the Nature and Causes of the Wealth of Nations* in 1776. That christening came three-quarters of a century later, courtesy of European philosophers who used it to describe an economic system in which the productive assets and the profits they produce are monopolized by a relative few, the capitalists, to the exclusion of the many. But Smith had identified its engine—the robust ways of the emerging bourgeoisie—and it was already a world-shaping power. Not that many years later, Karl Marx himself was shocked and awed by capitalism:

> The bourgeoisie, during its rule of scarce one hundred years, has created more massive and more colossal productive forces than have all preceding generations together. Subjection of Nature's forces to man, machinery, application of chemistry to industry and agriculture, steam-navigation, railways, electric telegraph, clearing of whole continents for cultivation, canalization of rivers, whole populations conjured out of the ground—what earlier century had even a presentiment that such productive forces slumbered in the lap of social labor?[17]

That was 1848, barely on the cusp of the "application of chemistry to industry and agriculture, . . . clearing of whole continents for cultivation, canalization of rivers, whole populations conjured out of the ground." And while Marx was spectacularly wrong in his prophecy that the proletariat would become the gravediggers of the bourgeoisie and that the coming socialist revolution would upend capitalism, he was, like Troeltsch and Rauschenbusch, dead on about the atomization of society and the exploitative, alienating nature of industrial orders that nonetheless captivated people with the lure of enormous productivity and mounting material prosperity. Had all three, Rauschenbusch, Troeltsch, and Marx, been present in 2000 to receive the report of the Spirit of the Twentieth Century, they would likely not have been surprised at the staying power of "the social question" or the fact it had gone global. The assault on settled community still defines our world. The gap between the rich and the rest widens while institutions of family, community, and nation-state still struggle to stave off the atomization of society amid shifting identities and unsure sovereignty. This might have saddened or angered these students of early capitalism but it probably would not have startled them.[18]

Does the Spirit of the Twentieth Century report anything else? Yes, and it went largely unnoticed by Rauschenbusch and Troeltsch, somewhat less so by Marx. In the final third of the twentieth century, "the ecological question" joined "the social question." The degradation of Earth's life forms and ecosystems threatens the community of life wherever it is found—in the air, on land, on and under the surface of the sea.[19] While the causes are multiple and complex, the ecological question, like the social question, is primarily the downside of the organization, habits, and exacting requirements of modern industrial-technological society. It manifests itself as the unending transformation of nature, a parallel to the unending transformation of society, both of them, nature-culture and nature-society, in pursuit of mammon. Its warning signs include shrinking habitat and disappearing species, eroding soils, altered gene pools, mono-cropping and industrialized agriculture, collapsing fisheries, fouled air, environment-related disease, receding forests, environmental refugees and internally displaced populations, greater urbanization, and climate volatility. Like the social question, the ecological question has gone global as well. Overlaid atop ongoing social transformation, it marks the twenty-first century world like a full-body tattoo.[20]

The fourth avenue for breakthrough understanding is the shock of recognition. It is the path we take for the remainder of this chapter. Think, for example, of Robert Oppenheimer, civilian head of the Manhattan Project. As he witnessed the opening of the Nuclear Age at the Trinity site[21] in the New Mexico desert on July 17, 1945, the words of Vishnu in Hindu scripture came to him: "I am become Death, the destroyer of worlds." "I suppose we all thought that, one way or another," Oppenheimer goes on.[22] Yes, but they also stood in stunned silence as they witnessed the mushroom cloud rise into the porcelain-blue skies over the skullcap mounds of a stretch of desert the Spanish had named Jornada del Muerto (the Journey of Death or Dead Man's March).[23] Oppenheimer and team had inaugurated a new epoch. While they knew it, and considered their work an extraordinary success, the fiery cloud left them groping for the meaning of what they had wrought.

Or consider the fall of the Berlin Wall on November 9, 1989. That year saw governments in Eastern Europe tumble nonviolently one after the next: the USSR, Poland, Czechoslovakia, the German Democratic Republic. The breached Wall meant more than the unification of different Germanys. It was the dramatic symbol for a related epochal development: State-sponsored socialism as the century's alternative to capitalism had failed, and failed miserably. The Wall's demise heralded the triumph of capitalism and the arrival of an era British Prime Minister Margaret Thatcher hailed as "TINA"—"There Is No Alternative."

Then there is that picture telecast worldwide in February 1990 of Nelson Mandela stepping out of the Victor Verster Prison and wading into masses of jubilant South Africans, on his way, after twenty-seven years in prison, to the first election and first presidency of the soon-to-be post-apartheid nation. Apartheid, the ugliest feature of an otherwise beautiful country, had tumbled, too, and, like the Berlin Wall and Eastern Europe, surprisingly nonviolently.

Life after these events—the advent of weapons of mass destruction, the fall of the Wall and state-sponsored socialism, the legal end of apartheid—would not be the same as life before. They were epoch-making, captured in symbols that have become the currency of shared meaning and the reference points for subsequent thought and action.

The shock of recognition and its revelations continue in our case, albeit in another vein. The essential backdrop is a brief history of human/Earth relations that highlights moments of great transformation.

Thresholds

The initial stage of human/Earth relations is the long period of hunter-forager, or hunter-gatherer, humanity. It's a full 95 percent of the record. But in terms of impact on the planet, that 95 percent is only prelude to the first genuine transformation, the series of changes beginning around 10,000 B.C.E. labeled the Neolithic Revolution. The Neolithic transformation, occurring simultaneously in Southwest Asia, China, and Mesoamerica, was a revolution vast and deep, with lasting effects. Initially an agricultural revolution, it resulted in the growth of settled societies. From 3000 B.C.E. to 1000 C.E. it saw the emergence of cities and craft specializations; the rise of powerful religions and philosophies and equally powerful social elites; the development of writing, horticulture, pottery, weaving, and many of the arts; the domestication of animals and plants; and the onset of population growth. Indeed, by about 2000 B.C.E. all the major crops and animals that belong to present agricultural systems around the world had been domesticated, even though agricultural systems themselves would later alter dramatically.[24]

This revolution self-consciously reconfigured nature for the sake of society and reorganized nature-society in order to produce more effectively. From now on, and in great contrast to hunter-forager society, nature-society became a humanly designed, humanly ordered, humanly set-apart rendition of nature. Among other changes, humans reduced the diversity of regional biota by planting only a few crops. That reduction of diversity and simplification of natural landscapes continued with subsequent agricultures. Compared with hunter-foragers, humans started becoming a species out of context.[25]

Hunter-foragers were not passive members of their surroundings, to be sure. Like every species, these humans responded to their environment and changed it, though not dramatically. We know they had basketry and some weaving, apparently some small-scale irrigation, and even dogs and pigs as domesticated animals. They also worshipped and nurtured a sense of the sacred. But nothing like the worlds of art, science, culture, and agriculture we have come to know developed until human society found a way whereby a growing number of people were no longer engaged in the direct production of food. Then not only farmers but builders, architects, artists, priests, philosophers, accountants, and scientists could be invented, together with their creations.

The contrasting ways of life were dramatic. Hunter-gatherers lived off the land in an "extensive" fashion. That is, they utilized resources over a large area, moving around, following the rest of nature's ways. Neolithic and subsequent farmers, by contrast, utilized the land "intensively." They created settled society and organized the landscape and its resources to suit the needs of settled humans. When cities emerged, their citizens lived more intensively still. The built environment, itself largely shorn of agriculture, was their primary habitat.

Today, with the majority of the human population now urban for the first time in human history, the rub with the rest of nature is fundamental: Nature's way is extensive, but the way of present humans has become highly intensive, over more and more territory. We are extensively intensive, effectively "mining" most everything, from soil to water to energy. Nature's "extensive" ways, however, haven't evolved in a manner attuned to mass mining and intensive extractive economies.

Wes Jackson's way of explaining the required human/Earth relationship is helpful. "The challenge for *Homo sapiens* is to learn to live within the means, not exceed the natural recharge rate of the forces at work on the earth's crust."[26] The resources of the ecosphere were produced in geologic time but humans use them in agricultural and urban time. The fundamental mismatch here might not matter so long as human populations are low and supply (fertile topsoil, good oil, clean air, and fresh water) is seemingly infinite relative to demand. But when soil loss exceeds soil regeneration and oceans acidify and energy resources are on the downside of the bell curve, then nature's natural recharge rate is history—at least until humans change their ways or dramatically decrease their numbers.

The shock of recognition here is that our present way of life exceeds the recharge rate of Earth. Edward Barbier's conclusion is that, for the very first time, we may be entering a global Age of Ecological Scarcity.[27] If that is so, the beginning of wisdom is to ask questions like Wendell Berry's: "What was here?" meaning, What was the ecosystem like before extensive human disruption? And, "What will nature require of us here?" rather than, as Jackson puts it, the childish question that seems to have been the one we've lived by, "What can we get away with?"[28]

The mention above of "priests" and the rise of "powerful religions and philosophies" needs a word for later purposes. Christianity and Islam, together with their elder, Judaism, assume in virtually every line of their sacred texts and across their practices the Earth/human relationships wrought by the Neolithic Revolution. The accounts of creation innocently ignore 95 percent of the human story, and we find God creating domesticated animals and plants, as well as wild, at the very dawn of time, just as we find human beings already cultivating and herding (Gen. 1:24, 2:15). How massive that deficit is, with its concomitant loss of human intimacy with Earth and human rapport with nature as the numinous, we will never know. The primordial ethos of the cosmos present to hunter-gatherers is largely absent now. Some cosmophilia and biophilia may still course in our veins—the Tree of Life is still within us, after all, and we within it—but the difference between praying "thy kingdom come" and "thy garden continue" is not small. Nor is the difference between an identity as Peoples of the Book and an identity as Nature Peoples; nor the difference between being local, tribal animals, living in the confines of a small company of compatriots[29] (this is true for both hunter-foragers and Neolithic settlements) and being tribal and global at once.

But the second great transformation[30] of Earth/human relations is not present in the *formation* of Jewish, Christian, and Muslim sacred texts and traditions either. That omission, too, is a significant datum, since it underscores the strangeness and newness of an ecological awareness for religions of the Book at a time when almost every faith is scattered about as part of Melville's "mutual, joint-stock world, in all meridians."

That second great transformation was the Industrial Revolution and all that followed in its wake. The benefits have been huge. No one wants to backpedal to an era when lifetimes were half as long; no one wants to live at a time before modernity had lifted millions and millions from the misery of poverty; no one wants to return to "the Great Mortality"[31] of the Plague and the scourge of pandemic disease. And no one wants to give up creature comforts even the rich of other times did not know.

Illusions

That great transformation in Earth/human relations was made possible by compact, stored energy in the form of fossil fuels—oil, coal, natural gas— joined to technologies that used them lavishly. Yet these technologies coupled to vast quantities of accessible stored energy encouraged several illusions we still live by.

First, fossil fuels let humans bypass the rhythms and requirements of nature that preindustrial populations had of necessity to observe season after season. The industrial era let peoples create their own built environment as their preferred habitat, a world created in their image apparently on their terms. Soon few bothered even to ask about the rest of nature's demands for regeneration and renewal on its own complex and nonnegotiable terms. That every human economy is always and everywhere utterly a dependent part of nature's economy seemed to pass from memory, despite the fact that Earth's economy is always the substructure for every human economy.

Bypassing nature's rhythms and requirements for its own regeneration on its own terms linked arms with a second illusion: the conviction that humans could bring the ecosphere under their control and liberate humankind from futility and toil. Assuming nature's unlimited abundance and obedience, humans could design their world with Promethean purpose. Or so we thought; we now know differently. Planetary processes are not only more complex and unpredictable than we think; they are probably more complex than we can ever think.[32] They are certainly more complex than any one species can master and control.

The third illusion is that scale somehow doesn't matter. Anyone twenty-five or younger in 2010 lived through the era when half of all the fossil fuels in human history were burned and more than half the greenhouse gases emitted at human hands sailed skyward.[33] Anyone born in 1936 and still alive in 2003 was around for 97.5 percent of all the oil ever pumped and burned.[34] In the prodigious half-century from 1950 to 2000, the global consumer economy produced, transported, and consumed as many goods and services as *throughout the entirety of prior history*.[35]

And the beat goes on. We still imagine that infinite growth on a finite planet can be arranged and that scale, whatever it be, can be managed. Even the *notion* of limits offends our way of life. The biblical judgment (Proverbs 30:8–9) that just enough *is* enough, rather than riches on the one hand, or poverty on the other, doesn't register.[36]

These illusions, when coupled with massive supplies of stored energy and the powers of science and technology tied to the industrial paradigm of extraction, production, and consumption for human ends, means that no part of other-than-human nature, from genes to grasslands to glaciers, is exempt from human-induced change. The primary human relationship to the rest of nature has become "use" alone, just as other-than-human nature's primary status has become "object" alone, rather than fellow subject. Nature symbolized as "it" has displaced nature as "thou," ending a long and deep relationship in which nature bore the spirit of life and mediated the sacred.

Nature as "it" in our consciousness has also displaced nature as "thou" in our morality. Nature is no longer a salient source, much less *the* source, of moral direction and guidance. Job's counsel goes unbidden: "But ask the animals, and they will teach you; the birds of the air, and they will tell you; ask the plants of the earth, and they will teach you; and the fish of the sea will declare to you" (Job 12:7–8). God's creatures no longer instruct us; no creatures beyond our own species instruct us. As "resources" and "capital" only, for use only, they have nothing to say. Kinship and voice are gone.

The uninvited blow to all three illusions—that we can wholly know and control the ecosphere, that its own rhythms and requirements can be bypassed or bent to our design, and that scale is little reason to fret—is every major life system in decline and the rude appearance of that wildest of wild cards, accelerated and extreme climate change. What that means for all life systems reaching for a future we only perceive through a smoky glass.

Technozoic or ecozoic?

The tumultuous activity of the industrial age, what some simply call "modernity," has thus brought us to the threshold of yet another transformation of Earth/human relations. Thomas Friedman calls it the "Energy-Climate Era"; it is Thomas Berry's "Great Work" of moving from a "technozoic" to an "ecozoic" era.

Every civilization and people has its historical project. In Berry's account, "[T]he Great Work of the classical Greek world [was] its understanding of the human mind and the creation of the Western humanist tradition; the Great Work of Israel [was] articulating a new experience of the divine in human affairs; the Great Work of Rome [was] in gathering the peoples of the Mediterranean world and of Western Europe into an ordered relation with one another.... The Great Work [of India was] to lead human thought into spiritual experiences of time and eternity and their mutual presence to each other with a unique subtlety of expression.... In America the Great Work of the First Peoples was to occupy this continent and establish an intimate rapport with the powers that brought this continent into existence in all its magnificence." And our Great Work, the task of this and the next several generations, is to effect "the transition from a period of human devastation of the Earth to a period when humans [are] present to the planet in a mutually beneficial manner."[37] For Friedman this means moving from global flattening, global warming, and global crowding in a "bright-line" historical moment—ours—to "new tools, new infrastructure, new ways of thinking, and new ways of collaborating with others."[38]

But this is to assume that this transformation is underway. A closer look at what is happening to the planet, to see whether or not we find ourselves amid a new "Great Work," or in the year 1 E.C.E.,[39] is in order. Graphs assembled by scientists tracking global trends provide the data. It's "hockey sticks" everywhere.

The International Geosphere-Biosphere Programme undertook to assemble major trends in the areas graphed below. When these scientists compared these to knowledge of earlier planetary conditions, they came to this conclusion: "Evidence from several millennia shows that the magnitude and rates of human-driving changes to the global environment are in many cases unprecedented. There is no previous analogue for the current operation of the Earth system."[40] They go so far as to announce a new era in the geological history of Earth, "the Anthropocene." "The planet is now dominated by human activities."[41]

These graphs chart the great transformation effected by the triumph of the industrial-technological paradigm (see figs. 2.1 and 2.2). They all begin with the conventional date for the onset of the Industrial Revolution, 1750, and they all reflect modernity as industrialized nature-culture. Two features surprise.

First, the "screeching acceleration"[42] on all graphs is the same, despite widely disparate subjects. What can foreign investment, the damming of rivers, fertilizer and paper consumption, ozone depletion, population growth,

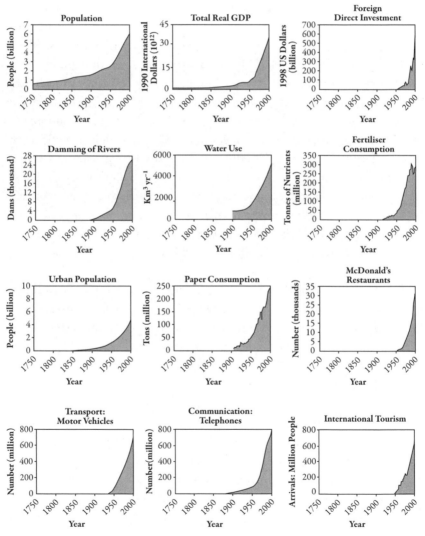

FIGURE 2.1

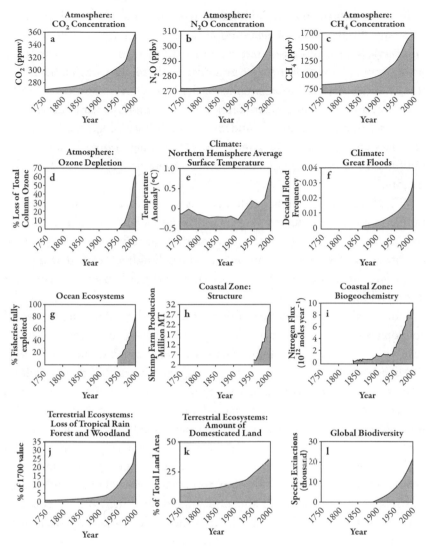

FIGURE 2.2

McDonald's restaurants, collapsed fisheries, and species extinction possibly have in common? Yet lay one graph atop the next, and you get the same abrupt curve for the same five decades. Hidden lines seem to connect dots drawn by a common hand.

Second, from 1750 until 1950 the change is gradual wherever records are available. Then, from 1950 onward, humans truly leave behind the moorings of the past and shatter the constraints and stabilities of earlier economic, demographic, and energy regimes.[43] Across much of the industrial world, the year 1950 marks the post–World War II explosion into the global consumer economy of industrial capitalism and socialism. As noted earlier, more goods and services were produced and consumed from 1950 to 2000 than in all prior history.[44] Not that the wartime militarized economy was left behind; it joined the escalation. The economics of the Korean War, the Cold War, the Vietnam War, and subsequent conflicts such as Iraq, Afghanistan, and the war on terror are no minuscule undertakings. Military budgets and the use of resources are still huge. The largest, the U.S. Pentagon budget, was $696.3 billion for 2008,[45] exceeding the Gross Domestic Product of forty-five nations.[46]

The drivers sit in the upper-left graphs of the first set—unprecedented human population matched to unprecedented global economic activity. It took all of *Homo sapiens* history—roughly 200,000 years—to arrive at 1.6 billion people by 1900. But in only the next hundred years, that number flipped—to 6.1 billion. In October 2010 it passed 7 billion and is heading for 9 to 10 billion.

Total real economic activity follows the same line, doubling the world economy since 1960 with a projected quadrupling again by 2050. Contrast that with earlier increases: John Maynard Keynes says that from a couple of thousand years before Christ until the eighteenth century, there was little change in the standard of living for most peoples, at most a 100 percent increase over those four millennia.[47] One hundred is not an impressive number over four thousand years. But when Thomas Newcomen scooped coal into a new kind of engine—a practical steam engine—in 1712 and replaced the equivalent of five hundred horses, a new age was underway. While in the early years of the industrial era, 94 percent of the world's energy was supplied by human labor and animals, and fossil fuels and water only 6 percent, by the time of the dramatic upswing of the 1950s, 93 percent of all energy was supplied by oil, coal, and natural gas. An automobile uses the energy equivalent of the labor of 2,000 human beings, a jet plane that of 700,000.[48] Yet we are the end users of this dirty fuels revolution so that now each one of us, in the words of scientist Geoffrey West, "is effectively acting as a blue whale, and it's screwing up the whole system."[49]

James Gustave Speth, who uses these graphs in *The Bridge at the Edge of the World*,[50] titles them "the Great Collision," the collision of the global human economy with the ecosphere's. The human economy has rolled along with "pathological indifference to the ecological costs."[51] Generating enormous human benefits, it also wedded economic brutality to ecological brutality by never asking what nature's economy requires for its own renewal on its own hard terms. "The great transformation" was possible only *because of* certain natural elements (compact, stored energy in the form of fossil fuels), yet nature's needs are nowhere registered. The requirements of the generative elements essential to Earth's existence and ours—earth, air, fire, water, light—are simply missing from this account. Instead, the graphs line out the degradation of these generative elements and the destabilizing of nature's economy as the collateral damage of both industrial capitalism and industrial socialism. We asked, What will nature help us do? Rarely asked was, What does nature require of us? The result, from Earth's point of view, is that "a gigantic uncontrolled experiment"[52] has been launched in which living systems decline at an accelerating rate.

Yet even Speth's collision account can understate the change in Earth/ human relations. For the hunter-forager period and throughout the Neolithic Revolution, the human story was an expression of Earth's story. Humans had to adapt to powers far in excess of their own and live by the rhythms of nature. But with the convulsive impact of the Industrial Revolution and global capitalism and consumerism, Earth's story became an expression of the human story. Earth itself changed markedly at human hands. Bill McKibben even changes the spelling to underscore that it's a "tough, new planet" called Eaarth.[53] "New planets require new habits," he adds.[54]

The most far-reaching description of radical change for *Homo sapiens* vis-à-vis the rest of the ecosphere is Wes Jackson's in "The 3.45-Billion-Year-Old Imperative and the Five Pools." The "3.45 billion" is the time life has been present; the "five pools" are the carbon pools of soil and agriculture, forest, coal, oil, and natural gas. Humans have been burning through all of them, of late at a quicker pace.

Jackson's conclusion is that we are living in the most important and challenging moment in the history of *Homo sapiens*, more important than any of our wars, more important than our walk out of Africa, more important than any of our conceptual revolutions. We have to consciously practice restraint to end our "use it till it's gone" way of life. We have to stop our deficit spending of the ecosphere and reduce our numbers if we hope to prevent widespread sociopolitical upheaval.[55]

Thomas Friedman's version complements Jackson's. No peace and security, no sustainable economic growth, no enjoyment of human rights, and no righting of remaining wrongs is possible apart from new attention to the generative elements of the planet itself. A just peace cannot be achieved apart from developing clean energy, mitigating the effects of accelerated and extreme climate change as best we can while adapting to what we cannot change, addressing conflicting claims to indispensable water, bringing to a halt the loss of indispensable biodiversity, and creating political, economic, and social structures that treat Earth as the standing miracle that births and sustains us together with the rest of life.[56]

Rendering these parenting elements of all life their due has not by and large been considered essential in the peace-and-justice traditions of the Western past, with the notable exception of native peoples. In John Rawls's renowned theory of justice as fairness, the designated "primary goods" are income, wealth, and opportunity.[57] But these are in fact secondary, all dependent on the health and well-being of the true primary goods, earth, air, fire, water. These goods have been assumed and fought over, but not nurtured in the way they require. Nor has religious ethics centered the primal elements and their health theologically and morally. They are central now. This means doing some first works over. If "world" is changed to "planet" in President Obama's 2008 Inaugural Address, we have it exactly: "For the planet has changed, and we must change with it."[58] Given our impact on the planet and new relationship to it, the changes in turn mean what the president went on to say: "What is required of us now is a new era of responsibility . . . God calls on us to shape an uncertain destiny."[59]

United States presidents never name our destiny "uncertain." It has always been "manifest," the opposite of uncertain. Yet "uncertain" is correct for a world no longer possible on its present terms but not yet accomplished in new first works. It is both "a new era of responsibility" and an era of new responsibility.

No small part of the reason for the imperative of restraint is bad design. If you wanted to create a system vulnerable to, say, terrorism, sabotage, and the dicey ways of destabilized nature, you would design one that is global in extent, technologically complex, and economically and demographically centered in a network of dense metropolitan areas located chiefly along coastlines. To create this comprehensive vulnerability, you would also use an industrial paradigm of production and consumption that pretty much runs against the grain of self-renewing nature through its use of stored energy in the form of fossil fuels that foul air, water, and soils and that generate accelerated and extreme climate change. You would design a system that achieved the following:

* put billions of pounds of toxic material into the air, water, and soil
   every year;
* measured prosperity by activity rather than legacy;

* required thousands of complex regulations to keep people and nature systems from being poisoned too quickly;
* resulted in gigantic amounts of waste;
* put valuable materials in holes all over the planet, where they can never be retrieved;
* used agricultural methods that resulted in topsoil loss rather than regeneration;
* pursued economic practices that eroded the diversity of biological species, cultural practices, and ways of life intricately fine-tuned to place.[60]

Lastly, you would organize a global economy that works best for the richest fifth of the world's peoples and poorly for the bottom two-fifths and their environments.

Epic history

Alfred Crosby offers still more documentation of a changed planet. Using a different timeline and sources, Crosby combines a new reading with old history for a picture that, at least for some, yields bracing insight.

Crosby writes of the "self-replicating and world-altering avalanche" that slid outward from Europe and upended culture and nature together on all continents except Antarctica. In effect it stitched shut the seams of Pangaea, that great landmass of Earth huddled together before continents and subcontinents rode tectonic plates to new places. Since nature itself had evolved differently on the now-parted continents, even at the same latitudes and with similar climates, the establishment of neo-European societies on every continent except Antarctica was epic for the whole community of life. In Crosby's vivid picture:

> The seams of Pangaea were closing, drawn together by the sailmaker's needle. Chickens met kiwis, cattle met kangaroos, Irish met potatoes, Comanches met horses, Incas met smallpox—all for the first time. The countdown to the extinction of the passenger pigeon and the native peoples of the Greater Antilles and of Tasmania had begun. A vast expansion in the numbers of certain other species on this planet began, led off by pigs and cattle, by certain pathogens, and by the Old World peoples who first benefited from contact with lands on the other side of the seams of Pangaea.[61]

None of this went unnoticed. Crosby himself draws on four famous authors, all writing within seventy-five years of one another.

The first is Adam Smith in *The Wealth of Nations* (1776). Reflecting on the Age of Discovery, symbolized by 1492 and the voyages of Columbus, and moving from there into the busy work of the emerging bourgeoisie, Smith wrote with remarkable confidence that "[t]he discovery of America, and that of a passage to the East Indies by the Cape of Good Hope, are the two greatest and most important events recorded in the history of mankind."[62]

But a price was paid, and Smith was aware of it.

> By uniting, in some measure, the most distant parts of the world, by enabling them to relieve one another's wants, to increase one another's enjoyments, and to encourage one another's industry, their general tendency would seem to be beneficial. To the natives, however, both of the East and West Indies, all the commercial benefits which can have resulted from these events have been sunk and lost in the dreadful misfortunes which they have occasioned. . . . [The Europeans] were enabled to commit with impunity every sort of injustice in those remote countries.[63]

Some pages earlier Smith had noted the moral and religious elements that often accompany great ventures. Reaching back to the Catholic Monarchs of Spain and their funding of Columbus for conquest, colonization, and commerce, Smith wrote: "The pious purpose of converting [native inhabitants] to Christianity sanctified the injustice of the project. But the hope of finding treasures of gold there, was the sole motive which prompted to undertake it."[64]

Little more than a half-century later, Charles Darwin, in *The Voyage of the Beagle* (1839), noted that "[w]herever the European had trod, death seems to pursue the aboriginal. We may look to the wide extent of the Americas, Polynesia, the Cape of Good Hope, and Australia, and we find the same result."[65]

And only nine years after Darwin, Karl Marx included this in the manifesto we met earlier:

> The discovery of America, the rounding of the Cape opened up fresh ground for the rising bourgeoisie. The East Indian and Chinese markets, the colonization of America, trade with the colonies, the increase in the means of exchange and in commodities, generally, gave to commerce, to navigation, to industry, an impulse never before known, and

thereby, to the revolutionary element in the tottering feudal society, a rapid development.[66]

Yet Marx, too, was cognizant of the cost to people and planet. Long before factory farming and monocropping agriculture, though not before what he called "the union of agriculture and industry," Marx observed that progress here is progress "in the art, not only of robbing the labourer, but of robbing the soil; all progress in increasing the fertility of the soil for a given time, is a progress towards ruining the lasting sources of that fertility." It saps "the original sources of all wealth—the soil and the labourer. The more a country starts its development on the foundation of modern industry, like the United States, for example, the more rapid is this process of destruction," Marx wrote in 1867.[67]

His colleague Frederick Engels drove home the point as a moral one. Engels was convinced that human alienation and land exploitation followed from a mode of interacting with nature that rendered all things commodities to be peddled for profit on the market. "Huckstering" ruled. "To make the earth an object of huckstering—the earth which is our one and all, the first condition of our existence," Engels averred, "was the last step toward making oneself an object of huckstering." "It was and is to this day," he went on, "an immorality surpassed only by the immorality of self-alienation. And the original appropriation—the monopolization of the earth by a few, the exclusion of the rest from that which is the condition of their life—yields nothing in immorality to the subsequent huckstering of the earth."[68]

Crosby's fourth citation is from Charles Lyell, a contemporary of Darwin and Marx. In his 1832 *Principles of Geology* Lyell, assessing the European-led transformation of nature and culture together, says: "Yet if we wield the sword of extermination as we advance, we have no reason to repine the havoc created."[69] Later Theodore Roosevelt would say much the same in his multi-volume bestseller, *The Winning of the West*: "The settler and the pioneer have at bottom had justice on their side. That great continent could not have been kept as nothing but a game preserve for squalid savages."[70]

It is intriguing that a moral philosopher tracking the new economy, a biologist developing evolution as a theory, a social historian and student of industrial capitalism, and a geologist, none of whom is reading the other, should all mention the discovery of the Americas and the rounding of the Cape of Good Hope as epoch-making transformations of culture and nature together. Even more intriguing are the tight historical connections of the "most important events recorded in the history of mankind" (Smith) to the revolutionary change and development of European society (Marx) and then both of these to the death of aboriginal peoples and their biosocieties and nature-cultures (Darwin), complete with testimony to the justice of this rapaciousness (Lyell). And all these recorded independently of one another, not with 1992 hindsight on the five hundred years after Columbus set sail from Cádiz, but within three-quarters of a century, beginning in 1776, a date aligned with the beginnings of the industrial era.

Crosby might have included a fifth source, the naturalist Charles Marsh. Marsh published *Man and Nature* in 1864 then changed the title in 1874 to make his point more precisely: *The Earth as Modified by Human Action*. Marsh, a bit of an oddball for his time because he focused on complex and dynamic *relationships* in nature, rather than on organisms "in and of themselves," posted a warning of what we now label the "law of unintended consequences."

> Man is dealing with dangerous weapons whenever he interferes with arrangements pre-established by a power higher than his own. The equation of animal and vegetable life is too complicated a problem for human intelligence to solve, and we can never know how wide a circle of disturbance we produce in the harmonies of nature when we throw the smallest pebble into the ocean of organic being.[71]

Crosby's sources and story, with Marsh added, suggest what Sallie McFague calls "the arrogant eye."[72] The arrogant eye is a sweeping perspective on human and other-than-human worlds that assumes nobility and superiority on the part of the viewer and sees the other in relation to the controlling center the viewer occupies.[73] One's own confreres—here the European tribes—are affirmed as the center of value, but not the others, and from this center judgments are made about worth and value elsewhere. A self-referential "we" views the world from inside its own bubble and takes the measure of "them" on the terms of "us." Here the biases and power of privilege mentioned at the outset are at work. This is Baldwin's point: History flatters those who write it in a way that renders them very unlikely to make radical corrections, however needed they may be.

The morality of such coherent arrogance, with consequences for both humankind and the rest of nature, is captured by Crosby in a passage that startles in the way bare truth does. "Again and again, during the centuries of European imperialism, the Christian view that all men are brothers was to lead to persecution of non-Europeans—he who is my brother sins to the extent that he is unlike me."[74] First affirm the intimate connection with sincere theological conviction (he is my brother, we are all children of God), then punish them for deviating from the norm (the tribal us).

Such is the fashioning of the modern world by the forces of conquest and colonization, commerce, Christianity, and (white) civilization. The modern world built upon the Age of Discovery and effected a global upending of humanity and the rest of nature via the powers of modern science and technology in league with industry and "the sailmaker's needle" (Crosby). Granted, this is well before the screeching escalation of global mass consumerism after 1950. But the hubris of dominant human powers is the same, and it becomes so routinized in economic and governing practices that its adherents regard their ways as natural rather than arrogant. It is not only considered the way we *do* live but the way to which we are entitled.

A last witness brings the account into the twentieth century: Dietrich Bonhoeffer, the young theologian and pastor caught in the maelstrom of German fascism in the early 1930s. The sudden and unexpected takeover by the Nazis forced Bonhoeffer into a critical appraisal of a German way of life he deeply loved and had largely taken for granted. In due course he would pay with his life for resisting the Hitler regime. His analysis, however, pushed beyond German culture, even though it was initiated by the turbulence of 1932 and 1933 in Berlin. It begins with a little-known address, "The Right to Self-Assertion," given at the College of Technology in 1932. Thanks in part to his grandmother, young Bonhoeffer is fascinated with Gandhi. He is also unsettled by the aggressive right-wing populism stirring among the growing ranks of National Socialists. So in order to address the subject of collective self-assertion, he contrasts two cosmological frameworks that entail different political orientations. The first framework is rooted in the Upanishads and the Sanskrit phrase *tat tvam asi*, translated as "that is you, you yourself." The sage Uddalaka uses the phrase in teaching his son, Shvetaketu, that his true essence is identical with that of all existence; the human is at home in the universe as a microcosm of the macrocosm.[75] Gandhi takes this basic orientation and develops an ethic of cosmic community in which minimal harm is done to all creatures and selective suffering is accepted in deference to the well-being of the whole. The latter—selective suffering—is chosen as a way to break the spiraling cycle of violence/counterviolence that again and again issues in escalating harm. Collective self-assertion is thus expressed as *active nonviolence*. This is communal self-assertion in the form of resistance that is anything but passive. Bonhoeffer will soon hope to appropriate Gandhian lessons for the church struggle in Germany.

The fascism marching on German streets in 1932 had a different notion of collective self-assertion. Bonhoeffer doesn't isolate fascism, however, but speaks more broadly of "European-American civilization." In contrast to India's "history of suffering," European-American civilization's is "a history of wars" in which "wars and factories" are the chief means of self-identity, self-assertion, and problem-solving.[76]

Next comes the vital point for us: This war-and-industry identity is rooted in the struggle by peoples of the West "to master nature, fight against it, to force it to [their] service. . . . This position of human mastery over nature is the fundamental theme of European-American history."[77] Later, in prison, Bonhoeffer will say that the West's aim is to be independent of nature and substitute "organization" as the immediate and controlled human environment. "Nature used to be conquered by the soul; with us it is conquered through technological organization of all kinds. What is unmediated for us, what is given, is no longer nature but organization." He will also say that while everything now, in a world coming-of-age, depends upon humankind—"[i]n the end, it all comes down to the human being"—the "power of the soul" is lacking for responsibly handling the technological and organizational power now in human hands.[78] Thus how to "claim Christ for a world coming of age" and how to forge a viable ethic of responsibility for this new epoch of human presence and power became preoccupations in Bonhoeffer's prison years.[79]

In the 1932 address, the battle is not only against nature, but "against other human beings" as well. "In the most essential sense his life means 'killing,'" Bonhoeffer says bluntly of the European.[80] Western civilization, fragmented from the rest of nature in its very consciousness, destroys natural and human communities together in an exercise of collective power with few spiritual and moral constraints (no "power of the soul"). Needless to say, Bonhoeffer rejects this kind of collective assertion, collective identity, and aggressive problem-solving. His fascination with Gandhi will continue as he grows convinced that Western, or European-American, spirituality, ethics, and politics are exhausted.[81] For a different world, spiritual-moral formation will have to begin anew.

Bonhoeffer's conviction that an aggressive war-and-industry identity expresses a fundamental alienation from nature and his contention that the essence of European-American civilization is simply to kill may initially seem overwrought. But seventy years later we can look back on by far the deadliest century in human history. Moreover, it belongs to our consciousness to declare and wage war on almost everything, even to do a great good: thus a war on poverty or on homelessness, a war on cancer or HIV/AIDS, an end to suffering, and so on.

In Daniel Maguire's words: For this mindset "problems are *assaulted*, not solved; diseases are *defeated*, not cured. We *wage war* on illness and social problems. A *killing* is made in the stock market. The Christian cross becomes a *triumph* and God *a mighty fortress*. The system is to be *beaten* and the frontiers of knowledge *pushed back*. Even poetry is *a raid on the inarticulate*. Business language smacks of the terror of the hunt; you must *corner the market, wipe out* the competition, and see that the bull displaces the bear."[82]

And industry is certainly the lead paradigm in every domain, the center and soul of a collective way of life. Not only has an industrial/postindustrial global economy outstripped all previous centuries in extraction, production, consumption, and destructive impact on both the biosphere and atmosphere, industry is omnipresent as the way we understand and organize our lives. Everything is industry, from the defense industry to the hospitality industry, the food industry to the health care industry, the entertainment industry to the mining industry, the advertising industry to the cancer industry and bio-technology.[83] Speaking of "war and industry" or "war and the machine," then, may not be overwrought; it may be the correct measure of the degree to which modernity is no longer rooted in the earth but in technology and organization, both of which let us construct a meaningful life without reference to the natural world, much less active care for it.

The shock of recognition here is that even the moral ideals and crusades of the modern era—eliminating poverty, toil, suffering, and disease and bringing civilization to the needy—witness to an aggressive identity that, whether in colonialist, capitalist, or communist mode, is an "assault on nature that is presently unearthing the earth and unworlding the world. . . . We let loose Orlando[84] in the guise of Christ, and with a look of grave concern for human suffering he devastates the land."[85]

One last example of the shock of recognition as stimulus for changing direction is climate change. It, too, prompts a fresh look at "big history," an account of planetary history in which the human story is never lifted from nature's journey and is read as part of it.

The unlimited economic growth of the "hockey stick" graphs has been possible because an energy-intensive world has largely replaced a labor-intensive world. A barrel of oil substitutes for "twenty-five thousand hours of human manual labor—more than a decade of human labor per barrel."[86] Accelerated and extreme climate change is the direct consequence of fossil-fueled energy use and policy. "Each gallon of gasoline," for example, "represents a hundred tons of ancient plants"[87] that, as gasoline, cannot be burned without emitting CO_2.

The graphs provide initial evidence of climate change. They register CO_2 concentration, average surface temperature, great floods, ocean ecosystems, coastal zone biochemistry, and global biodiversity. All share the same acceleration as the other graphs. Yet 2000, the last date on these graphs, only foreshadowed present impacts.

The decade from 2001 to 2010 was the hottest decade since recordkeeping began. 2010 was the wettest year in the historical record, and it tied 2005 for the hottest. These are related; warm air holds more water than cold air. The moister air of the atmosphere and the warmer oceans is driving weather to extremes: epic blizzards, unprecedented droughts alongside disastrous floods, bleached coral reefs (important fish nurseries), melting icecaps and glaciers. Flood damage is currently increasing by 5 percent a year across the planet.[88] In the United States, Vermont, hardly the epicenter of climate change impact, saw "three flood emergencies in the 1960s, two in the 1970s, three in the 1980s—and ten in the 1990s"[89] with ten more in the first eight years of the twentieth century and the worst in 2011. Iowa had both a one-hundred-year flood and a five-hundred-year flood within the space of fifteen years, and Nashville, Tennessee, had no place in its record books for the rains and flooding of 2009. In the summer of 2010, Russia had its highest temperatures and worst drought, with hundreds of wildfires and the failure of the wheat crop, while Pakistan suffered record monsoons, with thousands of deaths and millions of homeless, together with crop loss and the destruction of much infrastructure. At one point, one-fifth of Pakistan was under water. In 2011 one-fifth of Thailand's population was directly affected by flooding. Australia suffered unprecedented drought, then unprecedented flooding, both followed in Queensland by a monster cyclone that even brought flooding to the Outback, hundreds of miles from the coastline.

Nor are drought and more intense precipitation the sole effects of climate change. So is melting. The polar icecaps, the Greenland ice sheet, and glaciers almost everywhere are disappearing faster than earlier scenarios forecast.

Consider the Himalayan glaciers. There are three reasons for their record melting: overall warming due to increased CO_2 emissions; changing rain and snow patterns such that less new snow is replacing what melts; and pollution from vehicles and smoke covering the glaciers with carbon soot that turns their surfaces darker and less reflective, resulting in faster melting.[90] Exactly what the ripple effects will be is not clear. But these glaciers are the feeders of

Asia's great rivers. The agricultural and population centers of Asia depend upon them.

Then there is timing. Seasons are now changing and many farmers, in Sub-Saharan Africa, for instance, don't know when to plant and expect the rains—or not expect the rains because of extended drought. New pests are appearing that don't bring their natural predators with them. What about the choice of crops? Should farmers plant their traditional food crops, or switch to something else? It's become a crapshoot for subsistence farmers and a dress rehearsal for living on an altered planet.

If we turn to ocean warming, we find simplification of a worrisome sort taking place, with attendant loss of biodiversity. In some places this is also an increase in undesirables. Jellyfish is one example. They grow faster and produce more offspring in warmer waters, and nomurai jellyfish are now the scourge of Japanese fishermen, clogging their nets. A section of the Bering Sea is so full of jellyfish that it's been renamed "Slime Bank." And speaking of slime, enormous sheets of a mucus-like material have begun to appear, some 140 miles long.[91] The complex, biodiverse water-world that gave us Earth's life, including our own, is changing qualitatively. These are not the same oceans we have known for centuries and centuries.

Probably the most portentous change is ocean acidification, a consequence of saltwater absorbing more of the CO_2 pumped into the atmosphere. Oceans are now more acidic than anytime in the last 800,000 years. If the 1950 rates continue (remember the graphs), the acid will be more corrosive than at any time in the past 20 million years, according to paleo-oceanographers. The Pacific oyster industry reported in 2009 that oyster larvae mortality had increased 80 percent, likely from the acid levels. Many shellfish can't make thick enough shells, and coral reefs may be gone by the end of the century. This level and kind of change overwhelms systems that have been in place for ages.

Lastly, ocean waters absorb heat slowly and expend it slowly. This means that warming ocean waters have climate change in the pipeline for a very long time to come and that human slowing, even stopping, of CO_2 emissions will not change the near future, even though continued emissions can make the far future worse. Climate change is baked in for a while.

The point is threefold. First, the experience of the planet from 1750, and especially from 1950 on through 2010, is the result of one thing: the kind of energy that has powered the world with dirty fuels for 250 years. Second, the planet we presently inhabit is not the one that has been in place for the entire period of the human species to date. In Bill McKibben's phrase, "The Holocene is staggering."[92] Third, because of feedback loops, the epic changes can no longer be turned off. Released methane leads to warmer skies, which releases more methane. The darker ice-free Arctic waters absorb more of the sun's rays, rather than, as snow and ice, reflecting them; so melt begets melt.[93]

We can, of course, make things worse. The Arctic may hold 20 percent of the world's undiscovered oil, and the oil and gas industry is lined up to drill. BP, Conoco-Phillips, and Shell have bought leases to four million acres of the Arctic region. BP even built an artificial island close to shore to skirt rules that do not permit offshore drilling. From the rig on its island it will drill a long horizontal line to the offshore oil. At the same time new technologies for natural gas, shale gas, and tar sands oil are spurring huge extraction projects in Canada and the United States. All this means further pulses of carbon to melt more of Greenland, the Arctic, and the Himalayan glaciers.

Bottom line? The planet has changed and now we must change with it. Our destiny is uncertain because the new planet doesn't work the same way the old one did. We have new wine and new cloth, and it's too late for the old wineskins and old cloth. Or, to use McKibben's image, it's too late to "keep stacking boulders against the change that's coming on every front."[94] We'll need "to figure out what parts of our lives and our ideologies we must abandon so that we can protect the core of our societies and civilizations. There's nothing airy or speculative about this conversation: it's got to be uncomfortable, staccato, direct."[95]

The difficulty of change should not be underestimated. Corporate power intrudes. In 1989, the same year the Bush administration edited the testimony of climate science to water down its conclusions, oil and coal companies formed the Global Climate Coalition to combat efforts to shift economies away from fossil fuels. Research by the Royal Society of Britain discovered that the world's largest corporation, Exxon, had channeled millions of dollars to think tanks and supposed experts to sow doubt about the climate-change consensus of science.[96]

The difficulty is reinforced by the kind of mind we have. The initial reaction to large-scale threats to a way of life is to doubt the evidence. In fact, "the desire to disbelieve deepens as the scale of the threat grows," say economist-ethicist Clive Hamilton, in explanation of climate change denial.[97] We will try everything plausible to offer explanations for the global "weirding"—focus on minor mistakes in peer-reviewed reports; play up the power of factors other than emissions, such as sunspots, jet contrails, cosmic rays, natural cycles; ignore long-term trends and focus on short-term vacillations; consult only sources of information that align with our ideological commitments.[98]

Nonetheless, under the impact of facts that kick, denial will eventually erode. As of 2011 there is only one major political party in one industrial nation in the world, the Republican Party in the United States, that is made up of a majority of climate deniers. The ranks of those who understand that altered climates mandate doing some works over grow.

The alternative is watching them being done over, probably in catastrophic fashion. Even what *can* be done is limited by the failure to have acted in a more timely fashion in the period from 1990 to 2010. "There are degrees of screwed," says Peter Gleick, head of the Pacific Institute for Studies in Development, Environment, and Security. "And no matter how bad it is, it could be worse or less worse. There is a huge difference between a two-foot sea level rise and a ten-foot. There is a big difference between a two-degree temperature rise and a five-degree temperature rise—and that is why thinking about manageable and unmanageable comes into play, because one scenario might kill ten million and one might kill a hundred million."[99]

"Degrees of screwed" acknowledged, here is where we are now, per Thomas Friedman: We are not "post-anything" anymore, not postcolonial, postwar, post–Cold War, or post–post–Cold War, so much as we are "pre-something totally new"—the "Energy-Climate Era." Fossil fuels "are exhaustible, increasingly expensive, and politically, ecologically, and climatically toxic."[100] Moreover, the "Climate" portion of the new era crosses another line—potentially unmanageable and irreversible effects. Friedman concludes that we should seek to manage what is already "unavoidable" and avoid what will truly be "unmanageable."[101]

Response

Given all this, what should we expect as response?

The initial effort, to remember Jesus, is to patch an old garment with a piece from a new one and to pour the new wine into trusty old wineskins. The text is familiar:

> He also told them a parable: No one tears a piece from a new garment and sews it on an old garment; otherwise the new will be torn, and the piece from the new will not match the old. And no one puts new wine into old wineskins; otherwise the new wine will burst the skins and will be spilled, and the skins will be destroyed. But new wine must be put into new wineskins. And no one after drinking old wine desires new wine, but says, "The old is good." (Luke 5:36–39)

While Jesus says "no one" does this, in fact this ill-fated patching and pouring happens frequently. Indeed, Jesus' comments about the unintended consequences would seem to say that at least "someone" rather than "no one" has tried it. Were it not a regular habit, there would have been little reason to teach his disciples about it.

Key historical moments usually require outside-the-paradigm thinking. But the first try is always to try and fit new experience and knowledge inside known boxes and molds. "The old is good"(5:39). Einstein's wisdom, that we cannot solve basic problems with the same frame of mind that produced them, is ignored.[102]

To see this at work, consider a full-page advertisement in the June 2, 1998 *New York Times*, the day the American Museum of Natural History inaugurated its Hall of Biodiversity. The ad displays an eye-catching selection of flora and fauna from around the world and across the top in large letters is the sentence: "We believe in equal opportunity regardless of race, creed, gender, kingdom, phylum, class, order, family, genus, or species." The creatures then tumble down the page, followed by smaller-lettered text:

> All life is interconnected. So without a supporting cast of millions of species, human survival is far from guaranteed. This variety and interdependence of species is what's called biodiversity. And it matters to Monsanto in particular. Our business depends on making discoveries in the world of genetic information. Information that is lost forever when a species becomes extinct. Information that offers solutions in agriculture, nutrition, and medicine never before thought possible. For a population that's growing. On a planet that's not.

The logo—a growing plant—then appears next to the name and trademark— "Monsanto: Food Health Hope." The last line is: "Monsanto is honored to be a sponsor of the Hall of Biodiversity at the American Museum of Natural History. www.monsanto.com."

This ad is unthinkable apart from contemporary sciences and their impact: genetics, molecular biology, ecology, and computer science especially. Its thought-world appears to be holistic thinking based in good science. The awareness of complex, living interdependence seems central. At the outset the ad even strikes a note of egalitarian bio-democracy worthy of St. Francis. But as the text trails off we are keeping company with the soft utopianism and secular promise-and-fulfillment theology of so much industrial science and technology, and not least the new biotechnologies: "Monsanto: Food Health

Hope" and "solutions in agriculture, nutrition, and medicine never before thought possible." We are also keeping company with human subjectivism in ethics. This moral universe not only assumes that human beings are *the* sole moral arbiters, it assumes that in the end the only actions that truly matter are those affecting human beings. No court of appeal beyond the human subject exists. And by the very bottom, right-hand corner of the page, we have placed good science and a viable way of life ("Food, Health, Hope") firmly in the hands of global agribusiness.

This sounds like new wine and new cloth but in fact it is "eco-modernity."[103] Modernity worked with a set of famous dualisms, those longstanding boundaries of mind and matter, human culture and resistant nature, and the sharp distinction of humans from other creatures. These have now been erased in favor of "equal opportunity regardless of race . . . phylum . . . class . . . genus, or species" in a world where "[a]ll life is interconnected." Modernity also mirrored a largely mechanistic understanding of how things worked. Now ecological language has replaced the mechanistic. In short, this is new knowledge, new perception, and new vocabulary—apparently new cloth and new wine.

Yet eco-modernity's fundamental biases remain modernity's. The day-to-day practice of science, technology, and industry features human mind and culture as the creators, controllers, and high-tech bio-cowboys who work ecosystems and genomes as they would their ranchlands. Furthermore, the creatures on the page are generic, not particular. They are not even truly creatures, as biological individuals. They don't dart, bloom, suckle, or turn golden in autumn.[104] They are, categorically and simply, "information" and "resources." Humans are thereby recentered as masters without qualification, despite the web of interdependence, and ecology, molecular biology, genetics, and evolution itself find themselves in the employ of a morality that views "all things bright and beautiful, all creatures great and small," even "all things wise and wonderful,"[105] as information, resources, and property—in short, as pure capital. So in only one striking page, what begins as a confession of bio-democracy ends as user-friendly exploitation that promises, yet one more time, to do good by doing well, for profit and without (human) sacrifice.

Genetics as a science may render us kin to roundworms, to say nothing of giraffes and bonobos, all mirroring the "zoo in you."[106] Ecology may map in gratifying detail the awesome webbing of life. And Evolution with a capital "E" may present a dynamic universe still on its pilgrim way, with us a stupendous expression of it, even if only a wink in its regime of time. Such is indeed the new cloth and new wine of recent discovery. Yet these sciences are captured by the present political economy for an ethic that retains modernity's hubris married to entrepreneurial courage and engineering confidence. Life is chiefly a production, management, and security problem, subject to techno-logical remedies based in rigorous science and the wizardry of the market. Life is not a species problem, or a problem of the human soul or spirit, or a misshapen identity, or a matter of evil and injustice and things going wildly awry on a regular basis. The perceiving eye is still the arrogant eye.

The clincher is an irony we may miss, precisely because the inside of the box and the shape of the mold are so familiar. Monsanto's advertisement is a public endorsement of biodiversity, which is worthy of its own hall and every museumgoer's attention. Yet Monsanto's purpose is to capture as much of the market as possible for a very small number of crops whose seeds they control. The purpose is to simplify, not diversify, the stock for the sake of profit.[107] A stable of lawyers is on hand to chase down farmers who try and save seed and live independently in Monsanto Territory. So rather than, as the company says, proudly supporting the new hall that is making the case for preserving local biodiversity, Monsanto's practices undercut it. The eco-modern vocabu-lary of the advertisement speaks ecology's language while the company's prac-tices fail to learn from and support evolution's way of adapting successfully to changing conditions.

This frame of mind was already present in 1963 when the classic that launched the environmental movement, Rachel Carson's *Silent Spring*, was published. Monsanto issued a parody of Carson, entitled "Desolate Spring." It pictured America, laid waste not by pesticides, as Carson suggested, but by insects "on and under every square foot of land . . . and yes, inside man."[108]

Monsanto is only one illustration. Scolding this version of "Food Health Hope" avails little if we go no deeper.

If we ask, what is the culture of modernity, eco-modernity, and indus-try as a way of life—"the power industry, the defense industry, the commu-nications industry, the transportation industry, the agriculture industry, the food industry, the health industry, the entertainment industry, the mining industry, the education industry, the law industry, the government industry, and the religion industry," to use Wendell Berry's list[109]—the answer goes something like this: It is certainly a dream and a promise to supplant poverty, disease, and toil with an abundance that permits the good life as enriching, expanded choice. That dream, promise, and partial success has been irresistible. And while it remains the lure, it is rooted in assumptions about the ecosphere that the planet's present condition forces us to scrutinize:

Nature is a virtually limitless storehouse of resources for human use.

Humanity has the commission to use and control nature.

Nature is malleable and can be reconfigured for human ends.

Humanity has the right, perhaps even the calling, to use culture-nature's resources for an improvement in its material standard of living.

The most effective means to raise material standards of living is ongoing economic growth.

The quality of life is furthered by an economic system directed to ever-expanding material abundance.

The future is open, systematic material progress for the whole human race is possible, and through the careful use of human powers humanity can make history turn out right.

Human failures can be overcome through effective problem-solving.

Problem-solving will be effective if reason and goodwill are present, and science and technology are developed and applied in a free environment.

Science and technology are neutral means for serving chosen ends.

Modern science and technology, coupled with democracy, have helped achieve a superior civilization, first in the West, then for the rest.

What can be scientifically known and technologically done should be known and done.

The things we create are under our control.

The good life is one of productive labor and material well-being.

The successful person is one who achieves and is on his or her own.

Both social progress and individual interests are best served by achievement-oriented behavior in a competitive and entrepreneurial environment.

A work ethic is essential to human satisfaction and eco-social progress.

The diligent, hardworking, risk-taking, and educated will attain their goals.

There is freedom in material abundance.

When people have more, their freedom of choice is expanded and they can and will *be* more.[110]

All this is first cousin to Frederic Morton's *Crosstown Sabbath*. Morton, narrating the experience of riding the Forty-second Street crosstown bus in

New York City, describes the fatigue on the faces of the passengers as "classi-cally Judeo-Christian." We are imitating the God of our civilization, Morton says, the "Workaholic Supernal" who "assembled the world in Factory terms." "Before the Hebrews, no other people had a Sabbath," he writes. "No other people needed one."[111]

There is more to attend to if we are to understand the world we have: the massive role of global corporations in what has become corporate capi-talism overstepping all local, regional, and national boundaries; the Infor-mation Revolution and its transformation of the industrial paradigm; the decoding and recoding of nature itself in biotechnologies that amount to the industrialization of biological systems; the emergence of nanotechnol-ogies; the lure of planetary geo-engineering—all this and more. The past 250 to 300 years display the same frame of mind and the same anthropocen-tric universe we met in the Monsanto analysis: the arrogant eye and cultural chauvinism of one-way domination ethics, human subject to useful object, conceiving all things, living things included, as capital, information, and resources.[112]

As we've seen above, we have effective ways to recognize our collective plight and learn from it so as to make the changes needed—living in more than one world at a time; crawling back through history and letting it speak anew; discerning the signs of the times; and undergoing the shock of recogni-tion. Here are some conclusions summing up what we've learned so far; they anticipate the chapters to come:

- We don't see the world as *it is*; we see the world as *we are*. Creatures of symbolic consciousness have no unmediated apprehension of nature, their own nature included. Our *notions* of nature, not raw nature, shape our response. This holds for our apprehension of other humans as well. How do we gauge the other? Do we join, ignore, or dismiss him? Is she friend, foe, or immaterial? Is she means or end, sometimes one, sometimes the other, or both together? We can't understand the world we have and our way of life until we interrogate our perception at its deepest levels—our underlying assumptions, common biases, and reigning desires about the human and the more-than-human.
- The planet is not aging gracefully. New first works are mandatory. To cite Gustave Speth, "all that we have to do to destroy the planet's climate and biota and leave a ruined world to future generations is to keep doing ex-actly what is being done today, with no growth in the human population or the world economy."[113] Apocalypse requires no more than leveling out

the trends of 2000 C.E. and pushing on from there. But they are not leveling out. The curves still climb. It took all of human history to attain the economy of $7 trillion reached in 1950. Now $7 trillion is added each decade. In the short run, but only the short run, the ecosphere's economy is no match for global capitalism's.

- The planet is small and natural systems do not grow. There aren't more rivers to discover and dam, more oceans to fish and drill, more land masses to settle and till, more atmospheres to breathe and pollute. Yet human impacts grow larger relative to the planet's natural systems. We already use so much water that too little is left for the rest of the life we depend upon. We already capture 40 percent of nature's photosynthetic output. Deforestation and topsoil loss exceed reforestation and soil formation. Nature begs for new first works.

- The god of the world's secular religion since the Industrial Revolution has been material economic growth, sponsored by industrial socialism and industrial capitalism. It has been a blockbuster Broadway show with an unlimited run. Yet unless triumphant capitalism can be wholly "ecologized," and nature's economy made its foundation, capitalism will destroy that upon which it depends. Unfortunately, Mother Nature doesn't do bailouts.

- New technologies in energy, transportation, construction, and agriculture are vital and possible. So is wringing large efficiencies from what we already have, together with preemptory conservation of resources. But how far and how fast revolutionary technologies can come online for widespread use, in the face of entrenched resistance on the part of people and companies who are threatened by competition and obsolescence, means that it is foolish to blindly trust in technology and plead in desperation at its altar. Multiple strategies, including significant changes in human desires and habits, are required.[114]

- Doing first works over entails several long-haul transitions.

A *perspectival transition* in which we understand ourselves as a species among species no longer inhabiting the same planet *Homo sapiens* have known for a very long while. Altered perception includes a certain reenchantment that counters what Max Weber called the "disenchantment" of the world, by which nature was rendered little more than a repository of resources for human use. Reenchantment restores nature to human consciousness and feeling, nature as a community of subjects, the bearer of mystery and spirit, the ethos of the cosmos, and the womb of all the life we will ever know.

An *economic transition* in which economics and ecology merge to become "eco-nomics." Eco-nomics embeds all economic activity within the ecological limits of nature's economy and pursues the three-part agenda of production, relatively equitable distribution, and ecological regenerativity. Growth as a good is not precluded, provided it is ecologically sustainable and regenerative for the long term, reduces rather than increases the eco-social instability that large wealth and income gaps generate, and bolsters rather than undermines the capacity of local and regional communities and cultures to nurture and draw wisely upon their cultural and biological diversity. In all events, "the first law of economics must be the preservation of the Earth economy."[115]

A *demographic* transition in which human population levels off or slowly declines and the negative per person impact on the rest of nature gives way to mutual enhancement with other life.

A *polity transition* in which the basic conception of democratic capitalism shifts, if indeed democratic capitalism is retained. It shifts from (a) a society that fosters virtually unrestricted liberty to acquire and enjoy wealth, in which the right to property and its uses is more basic than the role of government as an equalizing force, to (b) a society that fosters the common good through the process of democratizing social, political, and economic power in such a way that the primary goods of the commons—earth, air, fire, water, light—are cared-for requisites of a shared good, a good for both present and future generations of humankind and otherkind.

A *policy transition* in which policies are as integrated as nature itself. Climate change, poverty, energy, food, water are all interlaced in the planetary economy. They, and the "wicked problems" they represent, cannot be siloed and targeted separately for either analysis or solution. Integrated policies need to mirror the systemic character of nature's own integral functioning, just as human technologies must cohere with the technologies of the natural world.[116]

And a *religious and moral transition* in which, because planetary health is primary and human well-being derivative, the center of ethics shifts from the self to the ecosphere as the relational matrix of our lives and responsibility. Human creatures, embedded *as* nature *in* nature, are inseparable from the rest of nature from which we have evolved, upon which we depend, and whose fate we share. Nature and its economy are the bottom line, with us and our welfare and power responsible to it. This makes planet-keeping the common calling of all religions in the same moment that the moral framework stretches beyond a fixation on the human species so as to include responsibility for the eco-societal, the biophysical, and the geo-planetary.

Next . . .

As we've seen, the Great Work before us asks for an Earth-honoring faith and a moral universe of more generous proportions than those we presently live. What kind of faith is truly Earth-honoring? What kind of ethic is its partner? What kind of faith and ethic yields zest for life through hard transitions? What kind creates renewable moral-spiritual energy to take on tasks that require generations of good work? The next chapters take each in turn—the faith we seek and the ethic we need.

3

The Faith We Seek

*There are more things in heaven and earth than are thought
of in your philosophy.*

—HAMLET TO HORATIO IN WILLIAM SHAKESPEARE'S HAMLET

AS NATURE ABHORS a vacuum, so history resists a dead end. Many of the
great religions and philosophies—biblical monotheism, Hinduism and Buddhism, Confucianism and Taoism, Greek humanist rationalism—emerged
from a long season of suffering and turbulence, roughly 900 B.C.E. to 200
B.C.E. The creativity of this era was so momentous and lasting that it earned
its own name (given to it by the philosopher Karl Jaspers), the "Axial Age."
Centuries later the Middle Ages gave way to the Renaissance in Europe, and
the Reformation and the ensuing religious wars to the Enlightenment. More
recently, slavery, then the disenfranchisement of women, and finally legal-
ized racism gave way to the ballot box and equality before the law. In the late
1980s the Cold War ended, state socialism collapsed, and new states arose in
transition toward democracy and capitalist market economies. A-bombs,
H-bombs, and intercontinental ballistic missiles (ICBMs) became massively irrelevant just as we found ourselves too broke to address human
needs and relieve Earth's distress. Not least, the shift from the energy regime
historians will call the "fossil-fuel interlude" coincides with a communications revolution—information technologies—that makes possible widespread changes in collective consciousness in short periods of time. Always
tribal, we can now be global as well. In a contracting world with shrinking
margins of error, we need to be.

In a word, the heft of history offers more than a little evidence of the Phoenix shaking off its own ashes. Death and renewal, birth and rebirth, are real.
They happen.

Now we are astride another hinge time. The industrial era stares at its ter-
minus. In its wake, the social and ecological coalesce, and the world must
enter an ecological age for which it is not prepared. The planet is no longer

the one the ancestors knew, or even the one our living elders grew accustomed to and loved. If the death-renewal-rebirth transition happens this time, it will of necessity find its way from industrial civilization to ecological civilization or, in Thomas Berry's phrase, from a "technozoic age" to an "ecozoic" one.[1]

Faith, like nature and history, abhors both a vacuum and a dead end. It does not rest. Nor will it give up. Particular faiths may fade, some even die. Still others will mimic Israel's experience and awaken to new life from roots of a tree cut down and left for dead. "A shoot shall come out from the stump of Jesse, and a branch shall grow out of his roots" (Isaiah 11:1). Someone, you can be sure, will set about making new wineskins and weaving new cloth (Luke 5:36–39).[2]

But what is the faith we seek now, for the transitions at hand and for the Great Work of this epoch? The answer begins with questions, questions that take us to more things in heaven and on earth than have inhabited our philosophy to date.

What kind of faith is life-centered, justice-committed, and Earth-honoring, with a moral universe encompassing the whole community of life, the biosphere and atmosphere together as the ecosphere? What kind imports the primal elements—earth (soil), air, fire (energy), and water—into the moral universe and centers them there? What kind interrogates past traditions of spirituality to ask for their contributions to new first works? What kind alerts us to past pitfalls? What kind uses a single stringent criterion—contributions to an Earth ethic and robust Earth community—as the plumb line that measures all impulses and aspirations? What kind illumines our responsibility, offers wellsprings of hope, and generates renewable moral/spiritual energy for hard seasons ahead? What kind is savvy about the play of power and privilege in light of the creature we are and the world we have? What kind offers the security to permit risk when we are absent the firm plateau and sure confidence we had when Earth seemed endless and nature free for the taking? What kind dares to welcome the end of the dirty fuels interlude and despoiling consumerism?

The Songs of Songs motif of *Earth-honoring Faith* speaks to the faith we seek. Song of Songs[3] is a double reference with a double meaning. It refers, of course, to the little book of love poetry[4] in the Hebrew Bible. The most "commentaried" book in the Tanach (the Hebrew Bible), as well as the one most set to music, the Psalms excepted, it is two love stories told as one. At its center is sensuous love between a young woman ("I am black and beautiful,"1:5a) and a young man ("With great delight I sat in his shadow, and his fruit was sweet to my taste," 2:3b), with a chorus of women, the Daughters of Jerusalem, offstage, their commentary a foil for the young woman's amorous declarations. The other love is every bit as real even when it is not the love declared. It is the love of these lovers for the land and its life. ("The flowers appear on the earth; the time of singing has come, and the voice of the turtledove is heard in our land," 2:12). The lovers in fact draw from the land their images for one another's charms: "O my dove, in the clefts of the rock, in the covert of the cliff, let me see your face, let me hear your voice; for your voice is sweet, and your face is lovely" (2:14). And to extol their love for one another: "I am my beloved's, and his desire is for me. Come, my beloved, let us go forth into the fields, and lodge in the villages; let us go out early to the vineyards, and see whether the vines have budded, whether the grape blossoms have opened and the pomegranates are in bloom. There I will give you my love" (7:10–12).

These loves are one. Life and creation are seamless here, as they are throughout the Hebrew Bible. Animals and birds, fruit and fauna, dew and sunshine are the vessels and vocabulary for the lovers' adoration, the holy mysteries of their world. Life is intensely present. And all of it is quietly Earth-oriented, Earth-honoring, Earth-affirming. Though theirs is only a small patch of the planet, it is a song of many songs.

The second allusion is less obvious, a line in passing in a little-remembered talk by Dietrich Bonhoeffer. A vicar in a German expatriate parish in Barcelona, he addressed the congregation in February 1929 on "Basic Questions of a Christian Ethic." Included is this:

> It is only through the depths of earth that the window of eternity opens itself up to us. . . . An ancient and profound old legend tells us about the giant Antaeus, who was stronger than all the men of the world. No one could defeat him until during one battle his adversary lifted him up off the ground; whereupon the giant lost the power that had flowed into him only from his contact with the earth. Those who would abandon the earth, who would flee the crisis of the present, will lose all the power still sustaining them by means of eternal, mysterious powers. The earth remains our mother just as God remains our father, and only those who remain true to the mother are placed by her into the father's arms. Earth and its distress—that is the Christian's Song of Songs.[5]

Bonhoeffer's allusion is an odd one. It is not odd in its affirmation of Earth as the only place where we are who we are created to be, the only place we experience sustaining powers, the only place faith can be alive and genuine. Nor is it odd for Bonhoeffer personally; he loved life and was continually thankful for Earth's gracious pleasures and powers. His prison letters, penned some fourteen years later, find him dreaming of the woods and his fiancée Maria; longing for colors, flowers, and the song of birds; happily remembering family; enjoying music and a good cigar. He writes Maria about their meeting when he is released from prison:[6] "When I picture our first reunion I don't see us talking together in a room; I instinctively see us walking in the woods, seeing and experiencing things together, in contact with the earth and reality."[7] Another letter says: "Our marriage must be a 'yes' to God's earth. It must strengthen our resolve to do and accomplish something on earth. I fear that Christians who venture to stand on earth on only one leg will stand in heaven on only one leg too."[8]

The Barcelona address is not Bonhoeffer's only mention of the Song of Songs. In the prison letters he cautions Christians about moving to the New Testament too soon and points out the Hebrew Bible's sturdy theme of God's blessing, "which itself encompasses all earthly good." "This blessing is the addressing and claiming of earthly life for God," he writes to his soul mate, Eberhard Bethge, "and it contains all [God's] promises."[9] Earlier, in another letter to Bethge, he is explicit about the Song of Songs: "God, the Eternal, wants to be loved with our whole heart, not to the detriment of earthly love or to diminish it, but as a sort of cantus firmus to which other voices of life resound in counterpoint. One of these contrapuntal themes, which keep their *full independence* but are still related to the cantus firmus, is earthly love. Even in the Bible there is the Song of Solomon, and you really can't imagine a hotter, more sensual, and glowing love than the one spoken of here (cf. 7:6!).[10] It's really good that this is in the Bible, contradicting all those who think being Christian is about tempering one's passions (where is there any such tempering in the Old Testament?). Where the cantus firmus is clear and distinct, a counterpoint can develop as mightily as it wants."[11] Two weeks later he writes: "I'll write to you in Italy about the Song of Solomon. I would in fact read it as a song about earthly love, and that is probably the best 'christological' interpretation."[12]

In this discussion of the Song of Songs Bonhoeffer has found a new image for God's love bound to earthly loves. Cantus firmus means "fixed song" or "fixed melody." As a musical style its roots are in medieval and Renaissance music where preexistent melodies, often the simple, plainsong melodies of the church, were used as a basis for new polyphonic compositions that greatly elaborated the musical texture. Popular during the Reformation, cantus firmus was solidified as a technique by Bach in his cantatas and fugues. Here it was the given melody against which counterpoint was improvised. The result was a new composition that, no matter how ornate, could always return to its core melody line, the cantus firmus. In Bonhoeffer's rendition, "the other voices of life resound" in counterpoint to this cantus firmus love of God. One of these is "earthly love,"[13] the example for which is the lovers' erotic passion in the Song of Songs. The love of God is the fixed point, the fixed melody, to which all earthly loves are related in their own rich variety, each a counterpoint that "can develop as mightily as it wants."[14] The result, says Bonhoeffer with a related musical image, is the Christian life as "polyphonic." Polyphony means "many tones" or "many voices," each important and independent while at the same time integrally related to the others. Cantus firmus–based composition is itself "the clearest illustration of polyphony: every theme developed is distinct and independent in its own right; yet, each theme is intricately related to its foundational, organizing element—the cantus firmus."[15] Polyphony is thus an integral interrelatedness that, at the same time, honors a wealth of diverse harmonic themes. In this case, love of Earth and earthly loves intermingle with their ground in the love of God, a love that will carry them through.[16] "Only this polyphony gives your life wholeness, and you know that no disaster can befall you as long as the cantus firmus continues,"[17] Bonhoeffer writes Bethge.

This-worldly prayer

The opening paragraph of Bonhoeffer's 1932 address on "Thy Kingdom Come: The Prayer of the Church for God's Kingdom on Earth" stipulates who rightly prays this first petition of the Lord's Prayer. "Only wanderers . . . who love the Earth and God as one, can believe in God's Kingdom."[18] Bonhoeffer repudiates an otherworldly Christianity: "We have been otherworldly ever since we hit upon the devious trick of being religious, even 'Christian,' at the expense of the Earth. . . . When life begins to become difficult and oppressive, one leaps boldly into the air and soars, relieved and worry-free, into the so-called eternal realm. One leapfrogs over the present, scorns the Earth; one is better than it; indeed, next to the temporal defeats, one has eternal victories that are so easily achieved."[19] This is Nietzsche's critique of Christianity; Bonhoeffer has made it his own.

Later, in prison on the day after the failed attempt on Hitler's life, when he has to reckon with his own death, Bonhoeffer will put it this way: "In the last few years I have come to know and understand more and more the profound this-worldliness of Christianity. . . . I remember a conversation that I had thirteen years ago in America with a young French pastor. We had simply asked ourselves what we really wanted to do with our lives. And he said, I want to become a saint. . . . This impressed me very much at the time. Nevertheless, I disagreed with him, saying something like: I want to learn to have faith. For a long time I did not understand the depth of this antithesis. . . . Later on I discovered, and I'm still discovering to this day, that one only learns to have faith by living in the full this-worldliness of life."[20]

Bonhoeffer is famous for this prison theme of Christian this-worldliness and for the life of faith as drinking the earthly cup to the dregs. Overlooked, however, is that Christian this-worldliness is his theme at the very beginning, not just the end; and that this Christian this-worldliness belongs to a consistent affirmation of Earth. Throughout his life and in all his theology, fidelity to God is lived as fidelity to Earth.

He doesn't romanticize Earth, however, in the manner of the day's chant of "blood and soil." Bonhoeffer knows Earth's distress and degradation, what he calls its "curse."[21] Yet he says in his comment on "Thy kingdom come," "[o]nly where Earth is fully affirmed can its curse be seriously broken through and destroyed."[22] In short, love the Earth fiercely in its distress, if you would join God's love for its renewal and redemption. We do not save what we do not love and respect.

This, then, is the odd element in Bonhoeffer's assertion about "Earth and its distress" as the Christian's Song of Songs. The Song of Songs is a biblical paean of sensuous love celebrating Earth and flesh as uninhibited, redeemed Eden.[23] No distress whatsoever mars the sheer erotic blessing the lovers know. Earth is pure desire and pleasure; the planet is paradise found. Yet Earth for Bonhoeffer is Earth with its afflictions, miseries, and degradation as well as its beauty, blessings, and joys. Earth loved encompasses its suffering and agony, the cruciform passion it knows all too well.[24]

Earth is not a planet we live "on" in some *temporary* role acted on some *temporary* stage. This is the otherworldliness unworthy of those who pray "Thy kingdom come." Earth rather is bone of our bone and flesh of our flesh and the only place in all the universe attuned to the kind of creature we are. Yet this one true abode is degraded and diminished, a shell of its possibilities and beauty. And—here is Bonhoeffer's persistent point in *Ethics* and *Letters and Papers from Prison*—those true to her will not shrink from their responsibility for her welfare, whatever hard sacrifice that responsibility brings. "Unlike believers in the redemption myths, Christians do not have an ultimate escape route out of their earthly tasks and difficulties into eternity. Like Christ ('My God . . . why have you forsaken me?'), they have to drink the cup of earthly life to the dregs."[25]

There is no living of life as life is meant to be apart from a full embrace of Earth: "Only when one loves life and the earth so much that with it everything seems to be lost and at its end may one believe in the resurrection of the dead and a new world."[26] Bonhoeffer wrote that from a prison cell. Earth, including its distress, is the Christian's Song of Songs.

Power and privilege

But what does it mean to embrace Earth now as the world we have? What does it mean to undergo a "spatial" conversion, creating an ethic of place for life on a changed planet?

Certainly it is to savor life. The rabbis teach that God will hold us accountable for all the pleasures of creation we fail to enjoy! They ought not be squandered, or left unnoticed. Nor ought the powers of good go unthanked. The pedal tone of Earth-honoring faith is gratitude for the gift of life and its goodness. Few images are more apt than Annie Dillard's: "I think the dying pray at the last not 'please,' but 'thank you,' as a guest thanks his host at the door."[27]

Yet embracing Earth and its distress is not only to savor life; it is also to save life. That requires relentless honesty about the causes of Earth's distress. Call it the path that human power and privilege have now taken. Or call it an aggressive identity that doesn't include love and respect for the planet's material elements. We have already noted Bonhoeffer's analysis, in "The Right to Self-Assertion," that a Western "war and industry" identity expressing a fundamental alienation from nature has been destructive of nature and peoples together.[28]

To this scientist E. O. Wilson adds the termination of species. "The trail of *Homo sapiens*, serial killer of the biosphere, reaches to the farthest corners of the world."[29] If the damage is this horrific and this widespread, we would do well to see if the causes reach back behind Bonhoeffer and Wilson, even behind the Enlightenment and the voyages of Columbus.

Consider the insights of two fourth-century bishop-theologians, Ambrose and Augustine. Ambrose raised the question of Earth's distress in Milan, the temporary capital of the empire because Rome was under siege. Thus he found himself both bishop of Milan and the emperor's bishop. (He had also served as governor of the province.) Here is Ambrose's question—and complaint.

Why do the injuries of nature delight you?
The world has been created for all, while you rich are trying to keep it for yourselves. Not merely the possession of the earth, but the very

sky, air and the sea are claimed for the use of the rich few. . . . Not from your own do you bestow on the poor man, but you make return from what is his. For what has been given as common for the use of all, you appropriate for yourself alone. The earth belongs to all, not to the rich.[30]

Ambrose was the teacher of Augustine, a Berber from Roman North Africa who, crossing the Mediterranean for work, taught rhetoric in Rome and then in the imperial court in Milan. Moved by the preaching of Ambrose, he was baptized by him in 387 C.E. and soon left behind the Manichaean cosmology he had carried to the capital. For Augustine the universe was no longer carved into opposing spheres of good and evil in which Earth and the world are hostile to the God of the good. Augustine, like Ambrose, now understood redeemed creation to be the *alternative* to a cosmic dualism of spiritual good and material evil. In one of his commentaries on Genesis, his third, he writes that paradise has been hidden *within* the Earth since creation, like "seeds waiting for the light of justice and mercy."[31] The world, when justice and mercy shine, is "a smiling place."[32]

But Augustine also shared his teacher's suspicions of the imperial rich and their treatment of Earth. In *The City of God*, written upon his return home to Africa as Bishop of Hippo, he reflects on the bitter experience of empires without justice and asks rhetorically, "Remove justice, and what are kingdoms but gangs of criminals on a large scale?" He goes on to say that the "ranks of the demoralized" themselves are a source of "many recruits" who in turn acquire territory, capture cities, and subdue peoples and the land for the rewards parceled out by their leaders. The grand title of "kingdom" is then conferred, clothing all this in majesty. He adds the caveat that the title is conferred "not by the renouncing of aggression but by the attainment of impunity,"[33] and he clinches his point with an exchange borrowed from Cicero:

For it was a witty and a truthful rejoinder which was given by a captured pirate to Alexander the Great. The king asked the fellow, "What is your idea, in infesting the sea?" And the pirate answered, with uninhibited insolence, "The same as yours, in infesting the earth. But because I do it with a tiny craft, I'm called a pirate; because you have a mighty army, you're called an emperor."[34]

Though both are cozy with empire, neither Ambrose nor Augustine shrinks from inveighing against imperial injustice. Ambrose in fact excommunicated

Emperor Theodosius after Theodosius ordered a massacre in Thessalonica in retaliation for the murder there of one of his guards. The bishop withheld the Eucharist from the emperor, telling him to either publicly repent or renounce his baptism and leave the community. Only after Theodosius underwent the rigors of repentance for eight months—fasting, almsgiving, and worshipping in plain clothes alongside other penitents—could he rejoin the community for the Eucharist.

For his part, Augustine rejected Eusebius's fawning account of Constantine and the empire as a Christianized earthly paradise in which Christ, with the help of Constantine's sword, triumphed over his enemies. For Augustine as for Ambrose, redeemed Earth as paradise was the *alternative* to empire. Paradise was not, contra Rome's claims, an embodiment *of* the empire. "The city of God," imperfectly expressed through the church, was the critic and judge of imperial power, "the city of man."[35]

What moves Ambrose and Augustine to denounce the injustice of courtly privilege? What fuels their courage to stand as they do against imperial power, despite their own presence in its corridors? On one level, we might surmise that it was simply the moral divide between what is and what ought to be, and their felt responsibility to address moral gaps candidly rather than complacently. "Hope has two lovely daughters, anger and courage. Anger that what is ought not to be; courage that what ought to be, might be" (attributed to Augustine).

But there is a deeper reason, a reason that renders the is/ought gap itself unacceptable and that generates hope, together with anger and courage. Neither bishop can give up on the biblical dream for the Earth: justice, community, and the common good, with "righteousness" as a good life lived in good institutions. Neither can imagine the common Earthly good as anything less than "the minimal livability necessary so that [the] individual good" of every creature can be pursued.[36] Thus neither can stifle the prophet's anger at creation violated and Earth desecrated at human hands, some—here those of the rich and imperious—more than others. Neither can imagine that Earth has not been given "as common for the use of all" (Ambrose) or that Eden might not be reborn (Augustine). The biblical dream drives their actions.

Yet the truly haunting question is Ambrose's: "Why do the injuries of nature delight you?" Or, in Augustine's words, Why do you "infest the earth"? Why the killing and harming—of human animals, other animals, trees and plants, bodies of water, and mountain valleys? Such destruction is the outcome of human choice and agency, and thus a matter of moral responsibility.

In Daniel Quinn's fanciful *Ishmael*, a gorilla (Ishmael) becomes teacher to a disillusioned young man whose hopes for a transformed world have all but expired, his idealism pummeled by too much reality. He is as demoralized by injustice and unhappiness as the citizens of empires without justice in Augustine's account. Ishmael initiates an exchange with the young man.

Ishmael thought for a moment. "Among the people of your culture, which want to destroy the world?"

"Which want to destroy it? As far as I know, no one specifically wants to destroy the world."

"And yet you do destroy it, each of you. Each of you contributes daily to the destruction of the world."

"Yes, that's so."

"Why don't you just stop?"

"Why do the injuries of nature delight you?" "Why do you infest the earth?" "Why don't you just stop?"

Why, indeed. Perhaps the reason is that we moderns have few genuine feelings for nature beyond an attachment to pets, houseplants, a favorite recreation spot, or perhaps a garden and some screensavers of pristine nature in exotic places we've never been. We seem not to notice where the meat on the plate comes from and the factory farms and slaughterhouses that produce it. (In 2010, 97 percent of the poultry eggs in the United States were laid in battery cages that gave each hen a life space of 7 inches by 7 inches.)[37] Are we so encapsulated in the built environment, and do we so prefer it as our habitat, that we live inside a bubble of nature as art on the wall, a cat in the corner, and Internet ether? Has our innate love of biological life (biophilia) and the starry skies above (cosmophilia) been so degraded that we know only processed nature, which we then confuse with the real thing? Have we grown moral calluses that protect us from the pain other creatures undergo on our behalf?

After all, the science is in: we are wreaking havoc on innumerable lives and their home habitats. We have become imperial uncreators, or decreators, in the community of life, terminators who deal death to birth itself by way of extinction; the sixth great wave of extinction, to be exact, and the first at human hands. We're running time backward, from Apocalypse to Genesis, as de-creation.

The immediate reason for extinctions and species holocaust is not shrouded in mystery. No great meteor has struck recently. No ultradramatic, deadly cycle of nature-induced climate change has yet run its full course. No

Krakatoa[38] explosion from middle earth has blotted out both sun and life. Species disappear because encroaching human habitat and the toxic downstream of human industry wipe them from the face of the Earth.

So why don't we stop?

A simpler world

Maybe the reason is another altogether, unrelated to compassion's absence and the deadening of empathy for the other-than-human. Alphonse the Wise, King of Castile and Lyon (1221–1284), had an explanation of sorts. "If the Lord Almighty had consulted me before embarking on the creation, I've have recommended something simpler." "Simpler" we did not get. Instead, we got creation as the riot of life infinite in all directions, a drama intent upon filling every niche. "The whole creation is one lunatic fringe," writes Annie Dillard, who then goes on to echo Alphonse. "If creation had been left up to me, I'm sure I wouldn't have had the imagination or courage to do more than shape a single, reasonably sized atom, smooth as a snowball, and let it go at that."[39]

Instead of creating a single, reasonably sized atom and letting it go at that, we split one and ushered in an age of WMDs—weapons of mass destruction. We also simplified, mightily. For ten millennia or so, *Homo sapiens* have been cutting and pasting biodiverse and geodiverse nature to fit the purposes of human society; or, more precisely, to fit the purposes of the more powerful forces in stratified societies. Less, as nature simplified, can be humanly more, for the rich but often for the poor as well.

A quip making the rounds among environmentalists has it about right: As complexity, human society is to the rainforest what the squeak of a mouse is to the history of music. Or, in the soil scientist's words we noted earlier, "Ecosystems are not only more complex than we think; they are more complex than we can *ever* think."[40]

So maybe our tenacious habit of dumbing-down infinitely complex nature to serve human ends more efficiently identifies the major cause of taking delight in nature's injuries. Yet even when this issues in the stark reality James Martin-Schramm and Robert Stivers open with in *Christian Environmental Ethics*, we don't call it sin or lobby lawmakers to render it a crime. "Until recently the great ecological systems of the earth were a problem for human beings," they write. "Now the reverse is true."[41] Nor do we stop, even though this "problem" now translates as a vast unplanned and uncontrolled planetary experiment.

Sole membership

Still, hell-bent simplifying may not wholly suffice as the explanation for our "delight." It works better for "infestation." In any event, neither the injuries nor the invasions took place for Ambrose and Augustine on a scale that approaches ours. And the complaints are theirs, not ours. So maybe there are further reasons and other causes, known to them but not yet to us.

A plausible one surfaces in Western moral philosophy. There the attention of recent decades and centuries is to human subjectivity and agency as they bear on moral standing. Who or what has moral standing, and on what terms? Who or what is morally included and excluded? Who counts and who does not? The answer, distilled in a single sentence, is that under present arrangements, all God's creatures other than humans are bereft of moral citizenship. This is, to be sure, no longer argued in the crass terms of the starkly human-centered, mechanistic cosmology of an earlier day when Bacon, Newton, Kant, Locke, and Descartes took no prisoners and offered no apologies for treating all nature as means only, for human ends only. Our version, as noted in the previous chapter, is eco-modernity.[42] We are keenly aware that humanity belongs to a common, interdependent creation marked by waves of biological evolution and vast cosmic processes eons in the making. Yet despite the shift from the mechanistic world of the Enlightenment and Industrial Revolution to the metabolic one of the ecologist and cosmologist, the moral universe remains strangely untouched. Despite a deep dependence that we readily acknowledge, human beings remain the decisive agents who are the sole judges of their action, without reference to any court of appeals beyond them— not nature, not God—and in keeping with ends they desire and choose. The decisive action still turns on modernity's axis: human mind and agency, powered by sophisticated science and technology, is laid out on one end, with complex, living nature construed as information and resources at the other. This, for all practical purposes, is the moral death of nature. Other-than-human nature has no life of its own, morally speaking, and no binding claims upon ours. It carries value only as a means to human purposes. Worse, its moral death seems not to matter. At least we do not name such exhilarating human agency "sin" or lower our imperial standing a notch or two. Instead, the moral language we use for this sovereign managerial stance is "stewardship," with its attendant "responsibility." That is something akin to calling the worst human-caused environmental disaster in U.S. history a "spill." The best we can do as good stewards, we conclude, is to clean up the mess and try to rule our vast empire more wisely. TINA—There Is No Alternative.

This absence of moral citizenship for other-than-human nature may explain our abuse of it even though it is less "delight" in injury than it is a lack of any feeling. Nature's injuries move us not. We are not stirred. Empathy has no reach.

Brains too small

Or maybe the reason is the kind of brains we have. As we saw in the first chapter, we respond quickly to immediate and obvious threats—the loud bang, the snake in the grass, airliners crashing into towers. But a billion pistons a day doing equal or greater damage to the air we breathe and the global temperature that is best for life doesn't register. Even graphed and put in front of us, the threat doesn't alarm. It's possible that our minds cannot take in the known consequences of our own actions when their scale quietly exceeds the worlds we know up close and when those consequences don't make any more noise than melting ice. Maybe we injure nature not so much because we're hell-bent on protecting privilege but simply because our big brains aren't that good after all. Maybe *Not-so-sapiens* better describes us.

A more pointedly theological discussion may aid our understanding. Since both Ambrose and Augustine were theologians, that kind of analysis might help us move closer to what they had in mind. While the formulations that follow are those of Protestant theologians, they make use of the analyses of Paul, Augustine, and Ambrose. First- and fourth-century explanatory power surfaces in the later theological reflection.

Crimped hearts

Take Luther and his depiction of sin as *cor curvatum in se*—the human condition as the heart turned in upon itself. This is the *human* heart, not just some individual's, or the pope's. So this is Luther's *species* analysis. Calvin says much the same about how we "tick": The center of our life in God and creation is twisted back on us in such a way that our hearts carry on a thriving business in self-serving idol-making. Sin, then, is to affirm oneself and one's confreres as of equal value, but not "the other," and to acknowledge others only in relation to oneself. "We" are ranged over against "them," with norm-making firmly in the hands of the collective "we." In recent centuries this has meant normative whiteness as the basis for judging other races, European and neo-European societies as the basis for judging other peoples and civilizations (invariably as lesser or inferior, even savage), Christianity as the measure of true religion, male status as decisive for female, heterosexual for homosexual, the able-bodied for the disabled, and so forth. The self-referential "we," viewing the world from inside its own bubble, takes the measure of "they" on the terms of "us" and not "them."

Protestants have elaborated this exclusion and arrogance as "pride" in a dazzling display of subtle forms, including the temptations of humility and false modesty. Reinhold Niebuhr's acute analysis of sin as overweening individual, social, moral, and religious pride remains a classic.[43] Niebuhr, too, meant *pan-human* nature, not simply the eccentricities of the particular neighbors we don't like. Yet Protestants, Niebuhr included, joined Catholics, the Orthodox, and others in failing to reach the logical conclusion: *the elaboration of pan-human sin as species pride and arrogance*. The species "we" that sins is set over against the "they" of the rest of nature that is sinned against, but the sinned against goes unrecognized as having comparably significant moral claims. Indeed, the pan-human "we" doesn't even conceive itself in species terms, as one species bound together in living and dying with other species in a common community.

With one notable exception: we see ourselves as a segregated species, distinctive, set apart and over. We thus end up in a very odd place, from a moral and theological point of view: a contracting Earth is jeopardized by its acclaimed stewards who don't even wince at the reality that they have become de-creators. The traditional theological analysis of sin as pan-human waywardness simply falls silent about our species being and cumulative *Homo sapiens* threats to life. Some theo-ethical black hole evidently swallowed this sensibility. After all, many human societies have known the profound interconnectedness of all life processes and creatures, and they also have felt moral claims upon them for reverence and respect that leads to the humane treatment of other biological individuals. So why not moderns? (Incidentally, this varying moral attunement to the more-than-human world carries good news: Species pride is not pan-human in a way that brooks no exceptions. Species arrogance can be jettisoned and, in some quarters, it has been.)

Privilege revisited

Yet Ambrose and Augustine were not talking about species pride on a contracting Earth, with nature in the modern world as an alienated "other." Their complaint was not about injury and infestation of some smooth pan-human sort. Their point is elsewhere, captured by C. S. Lewis in his comment that what we call human power over nature is usually the power exercised by some people over others (rich over poor for Ambrose, emperor over pirate for Augustine). Species pride is real, and the human heart is, as Jeremiah lamented, deceitful above all things.[44] But the consequences of species pride always play out in ways that are coupled with economic, social, and cultural privilege on the part of some peoples over others. All arrogance is not equal, nor are its consequences.

In a word, the crisis of nature is a crisis of justice for these bishops, and it represents a failure of the community to achieve a common good that includes Earth. To take some liberty in paraphrasing Ambrose: If you want to know why the injuries of nature continue to delight, follow the money. Track the powers of entrenched privilege and you will understand why we don't just say no and stop.

Still, even this explanation is only partial. It doesn't account for the participation of the "demoralized recruits" whom Augustine identifies as complicit in the imperious injury of nature even though they do not belong to the elite. Nor does the complaint of Ambrose, that "the earth belongs to all, not the rich," tell us all we need to know about how privilege functions. Tempting though it may be, denouncing the affluent offers little in the way of good analysis or proper response to injured nature, since overtly malevolent intent has relatively little to do with, say, accelerated climate change or the death of coral reefs and their nurseries. Ishmael is right: Most people, including most rich people, don't want to destroy the world. It isn't malice aforethought that has brought some ocean fisheries to the point of collapse. Virtue and vice as the explicit character traits of individuals can provide some explanation (Wall Street greed reflected in executive pay and bonuses, even in the face of poor performance, is a viable candidate). But it won't illumine Augustine's observation that the ranks of the demoralized themselves supply the troops for taking territory and imperious living. The play of privilege encompasses far more than the moralistic "we's" and "they's" we use to locate our enemies and negotiate our way. We will need to do better than a blame game if we wish to know why the injuries of nature delight us. Very large systemic factors attending a whole way of life are at work.

Reinhold Niebuhr can assist us here. Seven theses, largely but not exclusively from *Moral Man and Immoral Society* (1932), supply a stripped-down version of his theory of power:

"There is no ethical force strong enough to place inner checks upon the use of power if its quantity is inordinate."[45] Wherever power—political-economic

power, social power, cultural and religious power, our power over the rest of nature—is excessively concentrated, neither moral appeal nor sweet reason are significant checks, much less the means of transformation. Self-regulation by those enjoying systemic gain from their own concentrated power never suffices. Frederick Douglass made this point in classic fashion eighty-five years earlier, in 1857. "Let me give you a word of the philosophy of reforms," he said. "The whole history of the progress of human history shows that all concessions yet made to her august claims have been born of struggle. . . . If there is no struggle there is no progress." "The struggle may be a moral one," he continued, "or it may be a physical one; or it may be both moral and physical, but it must be a struggle. Power conceded nothing without a demand. It never did and it never will."[46] Like Douglass, Niebuhr knew that "when collective power . . . exploits weakness, it can never be dislodged unless [countervailing] power is raised against it."[47] In our era, the shift in capitalism to large global corporations exemplifies the concentration of power unable to reform itself of its own accord. Instead of reform these corporations seek allies to protect and extend their power—lobbyists influencing if not actually writing legislation, regulatory agencies staffed by people from the industry, scientists and lawyers hired to serve the industry's cause.

Evil and injustice flow from imbalances of power. Abuse of power follows from its concentration, whether in the family, the state, finance, or industry. True, power is necessary for the organization and maintenance of society and for social and environmental justice; powerlessness is certainly no virtue! It is the key factor in exploitation; the powerless are the most vulnerable of all, and exploited because of it. But our attention, like that of Niebuhr, Ambrose, and Augustine, is to power in the hands of those who hold it and benefit from it. That power, when unchecked, generates injustice in the process of consciously or unconsciously protecting privilege. This includes the power of privilege humans exercise when they can control nature.

This propensity to injustice on the part of reigning power often put Niebuhr on the side of the underdog and led him to an important distinction: *The disinherited have more of a right to fight for their (violated) rights than the powerful have to extend their (protected) rights.* It is thus possible to distinguish between morally justified and morally unjustified collective self-interest and self-seeking. British Petroleum or ExxonMobil singing "We Shall Overcome" means something very different from the same song on the streets of Selma or in church and temple basements. This point was never lost on Niebuhr as he measured disproportions of power and frequently took the side of countervailing power. It was axiomatic for him that

"power minus accountability equals domination."[48] Like most of his generation he did not, however, extend this insight to suffering in the ranks of
biosocial creatures other than humans. That essential point was lost, or
never made.

*The institutionalized power of privilege is often more covert than overt,
giving it the appearance of nonviolence. This nurtures self-delusion on the part
of those who wield such systemic power.* They see overt opposition to their privilege as "a power move" on the part of dissidents, while their own daily institutional habits are perceived as a force for stability and tranquility. The
systemic power of institutionalized privilege begins to appear "natural" while
the way of dissidents appears devious, disruptive, and abnormal. Niebuhr
knew this was self-serving, even if genuine, on the part of the powerful. "The
moral attitudes of dominant and privileged groups are characterized by universal self-deception and hypocrisy." There is an "unconscious and conscious
identification of their special interests with general interests and universal
values."[49]

*All this makes democracy and democratic power precious to Niebuhr, both as
a check on the ever-present imperial impulses in human nature and as the
matrix for achieving a common good.* But democracy is not the franchise
alone. Votes mean little if influence can be bought or subtly coerced. Rather,
democracy is genuine when two conditions exist. (1) When it is a form of
government in which criticism of government, even resistance to government, is built into the principle of government itself: that is, when space is
systematically created to organize countervailing power. (2) When democracy is the means of sharing political, economic, and social power in the
interests of social justice and the common good. Democracy is not, for
Niebuhr, maximal liberty married to corporate-regulated markets in the
interests of an ownership society represented by concentrated wealth. The
existence of the franchise in the context of a system "in which the fortunate
few dominate the rest"[50] is not democracy but plutocracy. Democracy
requires a balance of all three of democracy's classic values—freedom,
equality, community. More precisely, for Niebuhr, freedom and equality in
roughly equal measure are the regulative principles of a justice that pursues a
more communitarian democracy.

Given his attention to power and human nature, we can understand why
Niebuhr emphasizes both clauses in his famous defense of democracy: "Man's
capacity for justice makes democracy possible; man's inclination to injustice
makes democracy necessary."[51] A Niebuhrian brings to our discussion of why
injuries delight a suspicion of inordinate concentrations of economic, political,

and social power, even under the banner of democracy and freedom (the inclination to injustice). Likewise, a Niebuhrian always seeks to make space for countering inordinate power in the interests of a more widely shared common good, a common good that is not only desirable but also attainable (the capacity for justice).

Powerful democratic nations frequently suffer from a certain naïveté and self-delusion. They fail to recognize the sure imperialism which flows from disproportions of power between more powerful nations and less powerful, whether domestic polities are democratic or not. Indeed, the very moral idealism that bolsters the case for democracies often serves not only to justify their imperialism but also to intensify it. Power operating behind a screen of ideal ends is frequently more self-deluded and sometimes more evil in practice than when it acts in open and cynical defiance of moral ends. President George W. Bush exemplified this naïveté and self-delusion when he said straightforwardly that the United States' global mission on behalf of freedom is not imperial and ought not be viewed by others in that way. One could easily add the naïveté and self-delusion (or intended deception) reflected in the mission statements of many global corporations or other large human entities, including religious bodies.

Lastly, *religion normally intensifies power dynamics.* Religious *humility* tends to check the headstrong exercise of power and hold it accountable to norms beyond itself. It recognizes that we are judged by transcendent standards not of our own making and that we are accountable to a community, a cosmic community no less, which doesn't begin and end with our own ego and will, even our own collective ego and will. On the other hand, religious *pride* tends to foster extremism, fanaticism, intolerance, and absolutism. "Religion is humility before the absolute and self-assertion in terms of the absolute."[52]

All this is a digression, however, until we take Niebuhr on power and privilege back to the discussion of species sin and other-than-human nature as the objects of the imperial ethic of privileged humans and their demoralized recruits. While Niebuhr himself rarely made that extension, one passage comes close. Discussing "the pride of power" as "prompted by the sense of insecurity" that nature brings to life, Niebuhr says that "sometimes this lust for power expresses itself in terms of man's conquest of nature, in which the legitimate freedom and mastery of man in the world of nature is corrupted into a mere exploitation of nature. Man's sense of dependence upon nature and his reverent gratitude toward the miracle of nature's perennial abundance is destroyed by his arrogant sense of independence and his greedy effort to overcome the insecurity of nature's rhythms and seasons by garnering her store with excessive zeal and beyond natural requirements."[53] Niebuhr goes on to name greed as the form this will-to-power takes in the modern era—"greed has become . . . the besetting sin of a bourgeois culture"—and to say that modern technology "has tempted contemporary man to overestimate the possibility and the value of eliminating his insecurity in nature."[54]

Whatever their shortcomings, Niebuhr's theses on power are still largely pertinent. That includes his contention that the unconscious arrogance of established ways (the daily habits of those living the industrial paradigm, in our case) is often the most prominent exercise of power even though it is covert, not overt, and seems "natural" in the consciousness of those who wield it. We don't have to will or intend empire in order to act imperiously. The systems and culture and habits we create do it for us, a step or two removed from conscious willing and deliberated action.

Bias

There is yet another factor—the aforementioned biases of the human mind. We want to live lives in keeping with our best intentions. But we seem to possess an inordinate capacity for ideological spin and biases that reinforce our stance ("confirmation biases," in the language of psychology). The public case we make for our actions is then better than the underlying motives and judgments. Even more unsettling, we often believe the reasons we give so that we end up deceiving ourselves about what motivates us at the deepest levels. We succumb to our own ideological constructs, even when these turn reality on its head. Perhaps Luther's *cor curvatum in se*—the heart turned in upon itself—should be supplemented with *mens curvata in se*—symbolic consciousness and the mind turned in upon itself. When we're in our own heads, we're usually behind enemy lines. We trap ourselves in the "self-deception and hypocrisy" of which Niebuhr wrote.

Samuel Purchas was a seventeenth-century English man of the cloth who admired the English sailors of the Age of Discovery. In praise of them he asked, "Who ever tooke possession of the huge Ocean, and made procession about the vast Earth? Who ever discovered new Constellations, saluted the Frozen Poles, subjected the Burning Zones? And who else by the Art of Navigation have seemed to imitate Him, which laies the beames of his chambers in the Waters, and walketh on the wings of the Wind?"[55] The important matter to note is not his answer; his questions were rhetorical and his answer a foregone conclusion. Rather, the noteworthy item is that in his eyes, these sailors imitate God. But whose God is it? It is the God of the Book of Job and the great creation psalm, Psalm 104. "Him, which laies the beames of his chambers in the Waters, and walketh on the wings of the Wind." There are few chapters in all of literature that so majestically describe the Creator of the Cosmos as the transcendent ground of all being. The authors of Job and the psalm in fact designed their texts so as to set an infinite qualitative distance between the majesty and power of the Creator and the creation, on the one hand, and the puniness, transience, and vulnerability of humble humanity on the other. But in Purchas's nimble mind, it is precisely this God of surpassing transcendence whose work compares favorably with that of English sailors in small boats on high seas. They imitate this God and that sanctions their part in creating global empire.

Did we not recognize such "innocent" arrogance as this and its ability to turn argument and symbol on their heads, it would be hard to imagine how such comparisons and conceits could be honestly and easily held. The biases of mind and heart intrude upon, even form, our perception. They give reason its direction. This holds across the board for our perception and our "rational" treatment of both human and more-than-human worlds.

Joseph Sittler got it right. In an open letter in response to his faith community's statement on peace and politics, he wrote that "[e]vil is never more quietly powerful than in the assumption that it resides elsewhere. The term 'evil empire' is a description of all empires. The internal empire of every person's egocentricity is the template of historical evil."[56]

Augustine is frequently identified with the doctrine of original sin and roundly criticized for it. The criticism certainly holds for his view that sin is transmitted from one generation to the next through the act of sexual intercourse. And it's also true that the phrase "original sin" obscures more than it reveals. Yet Augustine's doctrine makes an important point: We are born with refined skills for canonizing bias, and we develop accordingly, nurturing exclusive rather than inclusive interests that we justify to ourselves in convincing fashion. It is as though we possess an unconscious mind that uses social preferences around factors such as race, gender, culture, nationality, class, and religion to set the "in" group over against the "out" group, "we" against "them." Differently said, it is as though we are all born on invisible tracks that put us in the company of others of similar mind. Yes, we can get off and board another train, and sometimes do—biases are malleable and movable. But on the new way the mind will again narrow, simplify, prejudge, and rationalize, never taking in the full complexity and meaning of the world around it and never seeing beyond its own. The persistence of these biases across the human record and in every generation would seem to merit an adjective at least akin to "original" ("pervasive and lasting," perhaps), while their consequences might well be called something akin to "sin." This sin—call it pervasive perversity—is always, like Cain's, "lurking at the door," never quite "mastered" (Genesis 4:7).

If we follow Augustine and Niebuhr on power, add to power the biases of mind and heart and the delight we take in the injuries of nature, and then recall the world graphed as "The Great Collision," we can hardly avoid coming to a harsh conclusion: Morally speaking, our present Earth/human relationship is the modern/eco-modern version of perhaps the longest-lived and most oppressive ethic of all: the ethic of masters and slaves. Applied now to other-than-human nature, it goes like this: Humanity's essence is consciousness and mind. *Homo sapiens* is the "wise" species, the brainy one. This essence distinguishes us from the rest of nature. (Our brains, not our bodies, mark us off.) The rest of nature, in the modern era, is object to us, not fellow subject. Thus is our relationship one of subject-over-object and mind-over-matter in a paradigm of domination that renders nature essentially a slave to humanity, its steward and master.

This relationship—"stewardship"—has a checkered history. Recall that the white Christian slave-owner considered himself the good steward of his slaves. Responsible for their welfare, he determined where they ought to live, how they ought to work, what family life they were allowed, and whether they remained in his domain or were sold to able stewards elsewhere. We've gotten rid of that notion for humans, more or less.[57] What remains as our slave is the rest of nature. Nature fits the classic understanding of the slave: living property to be bought, sold, and used in keeping with what is deemed necessary, desirable, and responsible on the part of the slaveholder—in this case, us. And like human slaves, nature slaves can always be replaced by other nature slaves when they are no longer desirable, are too few or too many, wear out, get sick, or die. Slaves are certainly not dispensable. But they are replaceable; one can substitute for another. This is the master/slave ethic in pure form. There is something unnerving about a stewardship that renders us keepers of creation in ways that mimic the relationship of master to slave. And there is something unsettling about how "natural" this relationship seems to millions, maybe billions, of us now.

But of course the "we" is not everyone. Some humans accrue more benefits, others accrue more burdens. Climate change visits the poor and vulnerable first and worst, yet they contribute least to its causes. *In*equality of guilt and responsibility must be kept in view even if we are all, as card-carrying members of the same species, equally capable of both justice and injustice.

Let's put this differently. There is an identifiable human nature restless enough to be endlessly creative, for better or worse. Creatures of symbolic consciousness are marked by nothing so much as active imagination, imagination of both what might be and the means to render it real. What Niebuhr called the "indeterminate possibilities of history" are the result, along with equally indeterminate ways of life. All of them will, however, be partial and skewed, suffused with self-serving ideology. In our time, such bias and ideology have issued in the orthodoxy of unlimited economic growth in a moral universe where nature is object and slave. And given our power, it means a way of life that has injured nature in such degree that we no longer live on the same planet that made this swashbuckling growth possible and affordable. Do we share a common human nature with all its potential, including its capacity for real justice? Yes. The challenge, however, is to choose our way of life well; its cosmology, its prevailing institutions, its human-to-human relationships, and its scale make all the difference.

"The earth belongs to all," Ambrose's basic contention, is actually a corollary of quite another claim he held with equal conviction—"The earth is the Lord's and all the fullness therein" (Psalm 24:1). Earth as the gift of the Creator is not "ours" as any specific and separate group. Benefits are to be shared with all, as are burdens. And "all" in our world is necessarily more than the "all" of any single species, including *Homo sapiens*. Yet Ambrose is curiously right about our crowded world, too; perhaps even more so than for his, despite the differences. His world was more generous to nature than ours, not because people were finer but because his world was less "flat, hot and crowded,"[58] with more margin for error than we have. In the fourth century, society was small and the rest of nature large. Moreover, his world and Augustine's lacked technological powers remotely comparable to ours. They could not have impacted the biosphere and atmosphere as profoundly as we do. Perhaps we ought to turn their stand on the common good around, and say that "all belongs to the Earth"; it is our singular home, fit for the kind of creatures we are. The same holds for the rest of the ecosphere, something that we understand in ways Ambrose and Augustine could not. Perhaps when our moral emotions and religious convictions grasp this core belonging—the Earth belongs to all and all belongs to Earth, which belongs to God—we will rightly name the injuries of nature at our hands "sin" and the abuse of power. This truth-telling includes unmasking the master-slave ethic we live even when we don't will or admit slavery.

New revelation

What else shall we say about Earth-honoring faith? It is a faith open to new revelation, to "more things in heaven and earth" (Hamlet) than may reside in our current philosophy. Sometimes that revelation is about the biggest picture of all, cosmology.

Fr. Georges Lemaître was the cosmologist and priest who proposed the Big Bang theory of the universe's origins. This earned the ridicule of some scientists, who suspected his theory was just a theologian's way of sneaking a Creator into science. Albert Einstein did not happen to be among those who questioned his motivation or theology; he simply thought Lemaître's physics "abominable." And since Einstein was Einstein, his judgment was enough to banish the Big Bang theory from scientific cosmology for years, until, in 1929, Edwin Hubble showed that all the distant galaxies were racing away from one another, as though powered by some aboriginal explosion. Einstein visited Hubble at the Mount Wilson Observatory in Southern California and came away saying that his earlier judgment was the biggest blunder of his career. "This is the most beautiful and satisfactory explanation of creation to which I have ever listened," he said of Fr. Lemaître's work as refined by Hubble. Einstein had had a revelation, via good science. To his credit, he accepted it.[59]

At other times revelation comes, not on the level of grand theory, but among the daily practices of our way of life—the work we do, the transportation we use, the food we eat, the water and soil we treat, the company we keep, and the ways we dispose of our wastes. ("Trash is a testimony to our beliefs," as a church's blessing of its new composter put it.)[60]

At this level—the workings of a way of life—climate change is a chapter in the history of revelation. It is the biggest thing to happen to the planet in tens of thousands of years and a rude interruption of the first works that future historians will identify as "the fossil-fuel interlude." William Rosen says the story of "Steam, Industry, and Invention," the story that gave us mechanical power, transportation power, industrial processes, cooking heat, building heat and cooling, to say nothing of a thousand uses of electricity for power and light and the worlds of plastics and artificial fertilizers for industrialized agriculture, is "The Most Powerful Idea in the World."[61] Yet try as we might to get our petrochemical groove back, or keep it going, climate change takes daily revenge, disrupting the daily habits and practices of the most conventional of lives with heat waves, wildfires, crop loss, flooding, disappearing ice sheets, drought, monster storms, and ocean acidification. The totality of these signs and results of climate change seems a revelation demanding conversion, a demand to do some first works over. Routines can no longer be routine.

But whether the questions are about cosmology, daily habit, or something else, Earth-honoring faith is an open architecture poised to receive revelation—more truth, different truth, and deeper truth than our present philosophy and conventional wisdom allow. In the words of a Hindu prayer from the Rigveda, "Let noble thoughts come from all directions."[62]

Experience of God

In 1954 Joseph Sittler vowed "as a son of earth [to] know no rest" until Earth's voices were gathered up "into a deeper and fuller understanding of faith." Earth's voices have about them "the shine of the holy," Sittler said. "A certain 'theological guilt' pursues the mind that impatiently rejects" them.[63]

The theological guilt rests with God-talk that fails to gather in all of Earth's voices to sing the hymn of creation or to reflect creation's "shine of the holy." Any God-talk that does not encompass all 13 to 15 billion years of the universe's pilgrimage to date and the immense wheeling of 50 to 100 billion galaxies, each swimming with billions of stars and who knows how many planets; any God-talk that does not gather in all species come and gone, as well as those leaving as we speak; and any God-talk that does not embrace the whole drama of life in all its misery and grandeur, is simply quaint. Shorn of the universe, the worship of God is worship of a human species idol. It is God rendered in our own smudged and diminished image. It is Luther's self-strangled heart (*cor curvatum in se*) at the species level, pridefully excluding all life and all worlds except our own. And it is the mind and consciousness so turned in upon itself (*mens curvata in se*) that it cannot enter with empathy and understanding the more-than-human world of its ancestors and kin. In "The Mass on the World," paleontologist-priest Teilhard de Chardin finds himself praying: "Shatter, my God, through the daring of your revelation the childishly timid outlook that can conceive of nothing greater or more vital in the world than the pitiable perfection of our human organism."[64]

Earth-honoring God-talk is about the mystery of matter and its drama—all of it, past, present, and future. It is an invitation to "sing with all the people of God and join in the hymn of all creation"[65] so as to give voice, however partially and inadequately, to the carnal presence of the "uncontained God."[66]

Earth-honoring faith is awe and trust in "a transcendent Presence that defies containment, definition or even comprehension."[67] Augustine's wisdom is: *Si comprehendes, non et Deus*. ("If you think you understand, it is not God you're talking about.") This means a rejection of religious certitude, any "grasping" after God in doctrinal and moral certainties that close the universe and see it only in finite, and thus limited, human terms.[68]

The language of Earth-honoring faith is invariably symbolic and mythic. It is language about how we fit into the world as the mysterious and stumbling creatures we are. We have a deep desire for a secure place that makes sense of our lives. That carries its own temptation, however. As finite creatures, any but temporary security and certitude elude us, just as they elude all life. Contingency marks all nature.

The response to this security deficit is often a religious one, commonly but not only as fundamentalisms. Human yearning often turns destructive when religion renders its creeds and way of life as once-and-for-all and nonnegotiable. Human longing is better served by a faith that rejects religion as domesticating the Infinite and corralling the Transcendent, a faith that is open to new truth and the revision of old truth.

The presence of the divine or the holy is the experience of the Intimate One who is also the Wholly Other, a Spirit so close as to be within, yet far more than we can comprehend or possess. This nongrasping awe and trust includes living with ambiguity and the inherent insecurity and vulnerability of being creatures.

While no one description of the experience of the divine in Earth-honoring faith fits all (Buddhism, for example, eschews a notion of God), many "songs" of this song will identify with panentheism and an understanding of God as Spirit. The sense of both intimacy and transcendence, the closeness of the Spirit and its wholly other dimensions, is conveyed by all in God and God in all (pan-en-theism). In words from *The Gates of Repentance*, a Jewish prayer book: "We experience our belonging to an infinity. It presses upon us, whether we go into ourselves or go beyond ourselves."[69] An "eerie proximity"[70] of the divine *in* matter joins an awesome, sometimes even terrifying, presence that surpasses everything within our reach.

Nature and the world are not of themselves divine and are not worshiped in panentheistic faiths. The Earthly may indeed be said to be sacred and holy and bear a "shine" and value not of human making. But these are *of* God rather than *being* God. The Earthly and cosmic live and move and have their being *in* God. The Spirit is present in their presence. Such is the kernel of a panentheism widely shared across religious traditions. It belongs to the song of Earth-honoring faith.

Finally, the experience of God in Earth-honoring faith understands that we live more deeply than we can think. Faith apprehends ultimacy and a primordial goodness that extends well beyond the contours and reasoned formulations of our cosmologies and moral principles. The nexus of relationships that constitute our existence is only a fragmentary, albeit precious, part of the full context of life gathered in God that we feel most deeply. Mystery envelops both what we know with some confidence and what we might sense but do not know. God is uncontained and so is much of life. The task of religions has always been to mediate the numinous and to foster ways of life that live in rapport with it.

By grace

Earth-honoring faith lives by grace. Life is a gift and a sacred trust. We did not create it, not a single blade of grass, nor do we earn it. It bears its own power, an energy that courses through the cosmos and nature as we know it. It is a power by which life creates the conditions conducive to its own continuation, a rooted confidence that life has what it takes to press on in the face of assault and uncertainty. Robert Pogue Harrison writes that life "is an excess, call it the self-ecstasy of matter." It engages in a kind of "self-exceeding" that creates new life, or more life, or different life. Some "mysterious law of surplus" makes of animate matter "the overflow of its elemental constituency." Life exists "where giving exceeds taking."[71] Organisms sacrifice themselves for others.

Such irrepressible power includes the capacity to begin anew, a power that brings wounds back to health from within battered flesh itself. Assaulted life may never be quite the same, it may in fact change dramatically, and all individual lives come to an end. But life itself does not cease.

Most religions not only affirm this power but identify it with the presence and power of the Spirit and claim it as God's own. In one way or another religions hold the conviction that the finite bears the infinite, the material bears the divine, and the transcendent is as close at hand as the neighbor, soil, air, and sunshine. So, too, they identify the Spirit with new or renewed life and the power to bring creatures to their fulfillment. A zest for life, an energy for life, is tapped in life itself, amid Earth and its distress. Nature's resilience, the generativity of Earth and the biblical "teeming" of the waters, all point to this triumph of life over death again and again, a parallel to the narrow edge that matters seems to have over antimatter in the universe. Yes, life is tragic. It is also graced.

The philosophers have long contended this. "There is a power in the universe forever on the side of those brave enough to trust it," is Montaigne's formulation in the mid-sixteenth century.[72]

Religious songwriters have found tune and text for the same trust and confidence:

> The hills are bare at Bethlehem,
> No future for the world they show:
> Yet here new life begins to grow,
> From earth's old dust a greenwood stem.
> The stars are cold at Bethlehem,
> No warmth beneath the sky'
> Yet here the radiant angels fly,
> Joy burns a fi'ry gem.
> The heart is tired at Bethlehem,
> No human dream unbroken stands;
> Yet here God comes to mortal hands,
> And hope renewed cries out: "Amen!"[73]

Preachers and theologians have preached and taught much the same, often with a justice message and as a source of inspiration. At a low point in the civil rights struggle Martin Luther King said: "When our days become dreary with low-hovering clouds of despair, and when our nights become darker than a thousand midnights, let us remember that there is a creative force in this universe, working to pull down the gigantic mountains of evil, a power that is able to make a way out of no way and transform dark yesterdays into bright tomorrows. Let us realize the arc of the moral universe is long but it bends toward justice."[74]

Nature is the theater of grace here ("from earth's old dust a greenwood stem"). "The spiritual dimensions of living on [E]arth and the ecological dimensions of living in the Spirit"[75] are the same. But cheap grace it is not. In the manner of all genuine liberation, it goes to the places where community is most ruptured and ruined. It knows "the sickened heart,"[76] defiled beauty, wasted habitat, and stunted lives. It faces "the slow terror of ecological degradation" and remembers tragedy and loss.[77] It embraces rather than bypasses Earth's distress.

There is no denying that this distress can be horrific and inexplicable. It can be the death of the innocent en masse and an affront to every sense of justice. Here the reality of Earth's pain and loss becomes the harshest of tests, even for King's "[long] arc of the moral universe." Ivan in *The Brothers Karamazov* tells Alyosha, "It's not that I don't accept God, Alyosha, I just most respectfully return him the ticket." When Alyosha asks for an explanation, Ivan's reply is the presence of suffering, the suffering of the innocent above all.

If that suffering is somehow justified, accounted for as belonging to some greater harmony, Ivan will have none of it. "[T]he entire truth is not worth such a price. . . . [T]oo high a price has been placed on harmony. We cannot afford to pay so much for admission. And therefore I hasten to return my ticket of admission. And indeed, if I am an honest man, I'm bound to hand it back as soon as possible. This I am doing. It is not God that I do not accept, Alyosha, I merely most respectfully return him the ticket."[78]

This is a fictional account in a chapter titled "Rebellion." The nonfictional is worse, seared into the modern psyche by the Holocaust. The test here could not be clearer or more demanding. Irving Greenberg, a post-Holocaust theologian, is a good and compassionate but hard mentor. For Greenberg, to fathom the Holocaust theologically with common notions of classical theism does not avail. The Holocaust as punishment for sins, for example, or as an event somehow to be understood in terms of the redemptive power of innocent suffering—these are not only offensive, they are simply ludicrous. Nor does modern atheism fare better, since none of the tenets of the Enlightenment and modernity—dogma-free reason, human autonomy, the liberal confidence in justice—failed to stop, or even explain, this massive evil. Germany itself was the leader in science and the arts, teacher to the world, and home to more Nobel laureates than any other country in the first decades of the twentieth century. The Holocaust is a grotesque instance of human evil crashing through common moral limits and shattering past categories of understanding. Greenberg not only rejects each and every rationalization, including every theological and philosophical one, but weighs all truth claims by whether or not they can be made in the presence of burning children. If there is any redemption at all in the face of such distress and destruction as this—and Greenberg believes and acts as though there can be—it will be a redemption that knows bottomless evil as a genuine reality in an unredeemed world.[79]

There is other loss, the loss of unfinished lives, whether human or other-than-human. Hayim Bialik's poem "After My Death," like this book, uses song as metaphor. But now the song is never sung.

> After my death, mourn me this way:
> "There was a man—and see, he is no more;
> before his time this man died
> and his life's song in mid-bar stopped;
> and oh, it is sad! One more song he had
> and now the song is gone for good,
> gone for good!"[80]

Like Bialik's, Dietrich Bonhoeffer's meditation on loss and unfinished lives is also cast as a musical metaphor. For him life itself is inherently fragmentary. Longing accompanies belonging, our reach always exceeds our grasp. Yet what kind of fragment makes all the difference. Some fragments "are only fit for the garbage heap (even a decent 'hell' is too good for them)," he writes from prison, while others "remain meaningful for hundreds of years." Bach's *The Art of the Fugue*, itself unfinished, is the latter kind of fragment. A Bach fugue, even an unfinished one, states its themes robustly, embellishes them, inverts some of them, and sets them in a larger framework of meaning.[81] If our life, Bonhoeffer writes, "is only the most remote reflection of such a fragment, in which, even for a short time, the various themes gradually accumulate and harmonize with one another and in which the great counterpoint is sustained from beginning to end—so that finally, when they cease, all one can do is sing the chorale 'Vor Deinem Thron tret' ich allhier'—then it is not for us, either, to complain about this fragmentary life of ours, but rather even to be glad of it." The question, he says in the same letter, is whether one can see in the fragment of life we have "what the whole was intended and designed to be, and of what material it is made."[82] Lives will be unfinished, they will be fragments. That is reality. But what do those fragments reveal about how our lives are lived, and to what end?

Life's fragmentary character carries other meanings. It marks the limits of human comprehension and accomplishment. We see only in part, through a glass darkly, from a rooted, not universal, standpoint. We are tribal. We cannot see the whole, much less "manage" it all.

A famous paragraph in Reinhold Niebuhr's *The Irony of American History* lays out the qualities of faith that might attend our creaturely ways. While only a paragraph in passing in a chapter on American illusions about "Happiness, Prosperity, and Virtue," it is also a meditation on the classic theological virtues of faith, hope, and love:

> Nothing that is worth doing can be achieved in our lifetime; therefore we must be saved by hope. Nothing which is true or beautiful or good makes complete sense in any immediate context of history; therefore we must be saved by faith. Nothing we do, however virtuous, can be accomplished alone; therefore we are saved by love. No virtuous act is quite as virtuous from the standpoint of our friend or foe as it is from our standpoint. Therefore we must be saved by the final form of love which is forgiveness.[83]

Earth-honoring faith is this kind of faith, with these virtues. The drama of life takes place within a penumbra of mystery we do not fully fathom. Faith, love, hope—and humility—in the face of the awesome power we exercise is the proper response, since the kind of creature we are has shown itself fully capable of massive, tragic destruction.

If we gaze beyond ourselves, we must also say that the rest of nature as the theater of grace cannot be romanticized any more than human nature. Nature's psalms are psalms of both beauty and terror, psalms of exuberant life, bitter suffering, utter waste, broken fragments, and mass tragedy. ("Evolution loves death more than it loves you and me," to recall Dillard.)[84] Yet the end-work of grace in nature and through it is the transformed heart, restored beauty, a life lived in gratitude and forgiveness, and even new life itself where it seemed death had cast the final ballot. "We mustn't lose our past," Bonhoeffer wrote to Maria von Wedemeyer. "It belongs to us and must remain a part of us. . . . We must continually bathe all that is past in a solution of gratitude and penitence; then we shall gain and preserve it."[85]

The twenty-first century is that moment when the same human powers that shape life on the planet can destroy much of it. While these powers cannot make *Helianthus maximus*, a simple sunflower, and human creativity doesn't extend to fashioning natural systems themselves, we can nevertheless damage and destroy, sometimes forever. With knowledge that is finite and understandings that are provisional, coupled to powers that are awesome, bathing all "in a solution of both gratitude and penitence" is more imperative than option. It is also the journeywork of grace. Not the cheap grace that asks nothing more of us than better engineering for the same way of life; but the costly grace that confesses our sins against the rest of nature and sets us to cultivating and restoring. Not the cheap grace of "indifferent silence"[86] before nature's injuries; but the costly grace that disturbs and summons, the grace of those practices of death and renewal that seek creation's repair—in Hebrew, *tikkun olam*—and its fullest possible flourishing under the conditions of brokenness. Then Earth-honoring faith, by grace, becomes the capacity to affirm life in the face of death, be reconciled to its limits and our own, and accept the whole without despair.[87] It savors life and lives it to the fullest possible extent even "in those melancholy places where the cry of the people and the cry of the earth are intermingled."[88] Indeed, to be fully alive is to face the despair and live with, rather than apart from, the anguish of those intermingled cries.

Rita Nakashima Brock and Rebecca Parker name this "ethical grace." It returns us to the idea of Earth as paradise in Ambrose and Augustine and attaches the unmerited grace "of the core goodness of life on earth" to "humanity's responsibility for sustaining it."[89] "Renovating grace" is Willis Jenkins's term.[90] The sheer availability of unending streams of grace is a surprise on a planet reeling in the throes of change.

The faith we seek, then, is one in which fidelity to God is lived as fidelity to the Earth.[91] Intimacy with Earth is intimacy with God. Such faith embraces Earth's distress and understands the dangerous downside of human privilege and power on a planet whose life-systems are in deep trouble on every front—in the water, on land, in the air. Yet it never gives up on the biblical dream, the dream of most religions, that the world can be "a smiling place" (Augustine) whenever and wherever justice and mercy meet. But a "smiling place" requires singing communities whose poets and composers know the rhythm of death and renewal, birth and rebirth; poets and composers who, through the Spirit, tap the renewable moral-spiritual energy *in* life itself for the hard transitions of hard times on a tough, new planet.

Next. . . .

No faith is without its ethic, implicit and explicit. To that we turn.

4

The Ethic We Need

CHANGE AND IMAGINATION

It is not the strongest of the species that survives, nor the most intelligent that survives, but the one that is most adaptable to change.

—CHARLES DARWIN

THE FOLLOWING FOUR chapters argue for "religious ethics in a new key." Science can provide much but it cannot provide this since, unaided, science "does not teach us what we most need to know about nature"; namely, "*how to value it.*"[1] Religion and culture do that. The new key, specifically, is religion that "ritually and symbolically" invests nature, ourselves included, "with the value and meaning that it has lost in the process of modernization."[2] This means ethics with a different moral universe and way of life, beyond industrial-technological civilization. It means ethics that undertakes a grand shift, a shift from the human self and human society as the gated moral community to a moral universe embracing all life and its generative elements. A shift, if you will, from the ego to the ecosphere as the starting point and boundary of moral reflection. Modernity's famous turn to the denatured and abstracted human subject as the site of all significant moral knowledge and consideration was a huge error; and now, because of cumulative human presence and power, it is a destructive one.

For such sweeping changes as these, the place to begin is with the nature of change itself.

The anatomy of change

In 1994 Vaclav Havel, leader of the nonviolent Velvet Revolution and president of first Czechoslovakia and then the Czech Republic, gave a Fourth of July address in Philadelphia, the cradle of American independence. He looked back on the Velvet Revolution as his own nation's turning time. The distinguishing features of such times, he said, "are a mixing and blending of cultures, and a plurality or parallelism of intellectual and spiritual worlds. . . . [t]hese are periods when all consistent value systems collapse, when cultures distant in time and space are discovered or rediscovered. . . . New meaning is gradually born from the encounter, or the intersection, of many different elements."[3]

As his speech progressed, Havel turned to modernity as an age that is ending. He faults modern science for failing "to connect with the most intrinsic nature of reality, and with natural human experience."[4] We know immeasurably more about the universe than our ancestors yet "it increasingly seems they knew something more essential about it than we do, something that escapes us."[5] He concludes that the world we experience seems disconnected, confusing, and chaotic. There are few viable integrating forces, common meanings, or inner understandings of the phenomena we experience. Experts can explain anything in the objective world, yet our lives are rudderless.

He goes on to say that while new organizational, political, and diplomatic instruments will necessarily play a role in negotiating a transition time, "such efforts are doomed to failure if they do not grow out of something deeper."[6] Then, in what surely surprised the Fourth of July crowd, Havel tactfully rejects "the fundamental ideas of modern democracy" as the "something deeper." The solution modern democratic ideas offer is still, as it were, modern, "derived from the climate of the Enlightenment and from a view of man and his relation to the world . . . characteristic of the Euro-American sphere for the last two centuries,"[7] centuries we have identified with the industrial paradigm, colonization, and commerce. While the Enlightenment idea of human rights and freedoms will be an integral part of any meaningful world order, even moral treasures such as these must "be anchored in a different place, and in a different way, than has been the case thus far."[8] In the end, Havel says, the problem of modernity is a "lost integrity," and it simply will not suffice to ground "inalienable human rights" or other moral obligations in the notion of *Homo sapiens* "as a being capable of knowing nature and the world" who regards itself as "the pinnacle of creation and lord of the world."[9] "Modern anthropocentrism" is deeply, fatally flawed, and we must reject the institutions and lifeways that issue from its ethos and spirituality.

When Havel describes the "lost integrity," he gathers in the theme with which we began: We are born to belonging. The lost integrity is the integrity of creation:

[W]e are not at all just an accidental anomaly, the microscopic caprice of a tiny particle whirling in the endless depths of the universe. Instead, we are mysteriously connected to the entire universe, we are mirrored in it, just as the entire evolution of the universe is mirrored in us. Until recently it might have seemed that we were an unhappy bit of mildew on a heavenly body whirling in space among many that have no mildew on them at all. This was something that classical science could explain. Yet the moment it begins to appear that we are deeply connected to the entire universe, science reaches the outer limits of its powers [and finds itself] between formula and story, science and myth. In that, however, science has paradoxically returned, in a roundabout way, to man, and offers him—in new clothing—his lost integrity. It does so by anchoring him once more in the cosmos.[10]

Havel continues with the acknowledgment that such knowledge may express a forgotten awareness that is encoded in all religions and in most philosophies and cultures, an awareness perhaps inscribed as primordial archetypes in all of us. This is the awareness of our being "anchored in the Earth and the universe, the awareness that we are not here alone nor for ourselves alone" but "are an integral part of higher, mysterious entities against whom it is not advisable to blaspheme."[11] Rather than blaspheming or, alternatively, resigning ourselves to the insignificance of being "an unhappy bit of mildew on a heavenly body whirling in space among many that have no mildew . . . at all,"[12] we reach for a different world order. It will come by way of honoring imperatives derived from respect for the miracle of Being, the miracle of the universe, the miracle of nature, the miracle of our own existence. "Only someone who submits to the authority of the universal order of creation, who values the right to be part of it and a participant in it, can genuinely value himself and his neighbors, and thus honor their rights as well."[13] Honoring creation properly honors the human as a unique citizen of the whole. Modern anthropocentrism severely diminishes the human and violates creation's integral patterns.

Havel finishes with the theme of international coexistence and cooperation. The theme per se is not the surprise. After all, Havel is the visiting leader of a new nation eager for aid and friends. The surprise is that coexistence and cooperation are grounded in "transcendence." This is transcendence

as a hand reached out to foreigners, to the human community, to all living creatures, to nature, to the universe; transcendence as a deeply and joyously experienced need to be in harmony even with what we ourselves are not, what we do not understand, what seems distant from us in time and space, but with which we are nevertheless mysteriously linked because, together with us, all this constitutes a single world. Transcendence as the only real alternative to extinction.[14]

Transcendence of this kind belongs to Earth-honoring faith.[15]

Take note: This is not transcendence as the distant contrast to that which is close at hand. There is not a whiff of otherworldliness or remoteness in Havel's transcendence. It is "the beyond in the midst of life" (Bonhoeffer)[16] and it comes, not by leaving behind the cultures we know, but by expanding their capacity to be inclusive and creative. Nor is the presence of this transcendence an exalted view of nature. Rather, it shows itself when the current degraded notion of nature as object and capital is set aside to make room for the normal human experience of nature as the bearer of mystery and the sacred.

With his Fourth of July address Havel has set the stage for an Earth-honoring ethic in a time of transition. But he has only set the stage; we need to say more, much more. What is the subject of ethics? What are its essential concepts and traditions? If we are born *to* morality, predisposed as social creatures for life together, are we also born *with* morality? Are there recurring moral patterns across cultures? How are they sustained and changed as need arises?

These are broad questions with generic answers, human species answers. While meaningful and important, they fade to irrelevance if they are not also concrete and contextual: What are the stipulations for a viable ethic *now*, in view of the world we have and the creature we are? How do we take responsibility for the human power we presently possess? What does religious ethics contribute? What moral issues and substance belong to the process of doing first works over at a hinge time in history? What ethic understands our reality—not as an "environmental crisis," an "economic crisis," a "climate crisis," or a crisis of world order—but all of them braided as a civilizational challenge in a time of multiple transitions to a different way of life?

These are questions for this chapter and the following three. All four are framed with attention to the kinds and levels of change required of us, as sketched by Havel and alluded to by Darwin. The task is to become a viable species, not as the most intelligent or strongest, but the most capable of the right kind of change. The Ethic We Need stands in the service of that change.

Levels of change

The kinds and levels of change are threefold. The first is the initial one that occurs to us and the easiest to pursue: Do better what we already know so as to continue, on familiar terms, the life we've achieved. No one wants to erase the benefits modernity has delivered—longer life, better health, abundance, and a greater range of choice and experience. Furthermore, we know what to do to keep these: Wring greater efficiencies from our present sources of energy and use of water. Reward technological innovation and economies of scale in the marketplace so as to replace combustion engines with electric motors and heavy gas users with hybrids. Flip the switch on sources of electricity so that roof panels directly overhead on thousands of homes, businesses, schools, churches, and temples idle the coal-fired generator a hundred miles away. Replace the produce hauled a thousand miles at high energy and clean air cost with locally grown food that gives small farmers a chance and circulates cash in the community, to the benefit of all. And treat material goods in ways that routinely reuse, recycle, and renew. All this is genuine change, accomplished for the sake of holding on to what we cherish.

Such change as this can turn counterproductive, however; at some point it usually does. When the institutions, systems, and basic perspectives are firmly in place as the commonsense way of daily life, interests often narrow to "improved means for unimproved ends"[17] and little more. An ultimately unsustainable way of life is "improved" for a few more years. This delays a necessary reckoning for its unimproved ends. Still, such reckoning does happen—at the next level of change.

That next level is the shock of recognition discussed earlier. It dawns on us, perhaps gradually, perhaps in a sudden epiphany, that this crisis demands a paradigm shift. Conventional means turn dysfunctional; doing the accustomed only makes matters worse as it is done more "efficiently." We may slow the rate of CO_2 emissions with green technologies. Yet greenhouse gas accumulation grows; the global mean temperature climbs another degree or two; and as climate change accelerates its extremes affect growing seasons and crops, pest infestation and disease, human health and coastal infrastructure, species and their habitats. Water usage per person drops significantly and so does agricultural use per acre as conservation wends its way from sea to shining sea. Yet total water use for a steadily growing global population and the shift to more meat diets among growing middle classes in Asia and South America not only cancels all gains but also leaves too little freshwater for both human beings and the rest of life. In short, even extending the trends at 2000 spells apocalypse (see the graphs in chapter 2).[18]

A famous paradox surfaces here. In 1865 William Stanley Jevons published *The Coal Question*. He said England's turn to coal couldn't last despite then-abundant sources, even with increased efficiency. He argued (italics in original) that *"[i]t is wholly a confusion of ideas to suppose that the economical use of fuel is equivalent to a diminished consumption. The very contrary is the truth."*[19] Sure enough, the years since 1865 have borne out Jevons's argument with a vengeance. Increased efficiencies have accompanied and contributed to economic growth that has outstripped the "economical use of fuel." That economic growth exceeded the per-unit saved energy so dramatically that total energy use scaled up markedly. Recall our discussion of the half-century following 1950, a time of much innovation and marked efficiencies in production, distribution, and consumption, including recycling.

Jevons's paradox might not have held had the industrial paradigm been abandoned for another. But it was not. So Jevons assumed, rightly, that continuing economic growth was the framework and the goal, and that efficiencies would play out within this framework and with this goal. Now, however, efficiencies within that same framework exacerbate its dysfunctions. They are "improved means to unimproved ends." Marked efficiencies accompanying greatly expanded energy use generates climate change.

In short, the realization dawns that some new first works are required. Revising the old ones is not sufficient. Greening unlimited consumption does not suffice. New wineskins and new cloth are needed. "Nothing succeeds like success" morphs to "nothing fails like success" as success breeds excess. Because climate change, for example, is the byproduct of everyday activities, continued habits land us in a flooded ditch.

Roger Shinn, adapting William James, calls this second-level change a "forced option." Some options are avoidable. You can take them or leave them, change your way of life or carry on as before; it's up to you. Other options are forced because decisions for something different cannot be avoided or evaded. This doesn't dictate only a single course of action; the choices are still many. But extending the status quo is not among them.[20]

This is difficult, this transition from doing better what we already do well to doing something quite other because "well" is no longer viable and options are forced. It is a blow to tried, tested, and improved ways. After all, we know how to build big dams; irrigate millions of acres of industrial farmland; keep crop production high with massive amounts of fertilizers, pesticides, and herbicides; and launch fleets of eighteen-wheelers to stock supermarkets the size of football fields with more edibles and drinkables than the world has ever seen.

The transition is also difficult because it entails, per Havel, the collapse of "consistent value systems." Our value systems are "consistent" because they belong to the tight logic of the industrial-technological paradigm. They seem the only "reasonable" course. Why not use abundant, cheap coal, for example, instead of leaving it at home in the mountain? Why not substitute natural gas for soil (ammonia as fertilizer) and oil and heavy machinery for farmers? Why not maintain continued economic growth and "a rising tide that lifts all boats" (John F. Kennedy)? We value a high-energy, fossil-fueled lifestyle, so why not find ways to continue it?

Or take a different example of extending the conventional wisdom: the marriage of democracy to capitalism. Its entrepreneurial drive and short-haul, restricted time horizons (this election cycle, these quarterly profits) has been wildly successful for millions, as has the ensuing economic growth. Yet "growing the economy" with no end in sight and democratic capitalist values fail to serve either present or future populations of nature on a contracting planet in desperate need of long time horizons and generational staying power. And what about the externalities that let democratic capitalist systems generate unprecedented wealth at the expense of huge ecological debt? Capitalism cannot be a free-rider system any more than state socialism, with nature bearing the costs of both. Yet getting the price right so as to includes all costs, including those of nature's regeneration, requires other values, other interests, other policies, and other market mechanisms. If ever-increasing economic growth is the mantra and the goal, it can only be growth congruent with nature's renewal, demands, and limits. Economic time dare not outstrip biological time.

But the collapse of consistent value systems in the times between times does not render us bereft. Not only are there creative technological solutions to some of our problems, there are also the treasures of cultures present and past, "distant in time and space." "A mixing and blending of cultures," to recall Havel, "and a plurality or parallelism of intellectual and spiritual worlds" take up the work of negotiating hard transitions. The key, we noted, is change that expands their capacity to be more inclusive and creative in searching for a new integrity "anchored in the Earth and the universe" and "honoring imperatives derived from respect for the miracle of Being, the miracle of the universe, the miracle of nature, the miracle of our own existence" (Havel).

All this said, the kind of change that follows from now-dysfunctional ways of life is what Havel experienced, a world that "seems disconnected, confusing, chaotic, with few integrating forces, common meanings, or inner understanding of the phenomena we experience."[21] It is a world in decline, even collapse. Or at least it seems so until jarring recognition moves to a third level and kind of change. Here the need for new first works is accompanied by a change of consciousness and cosmology that lets systemic change happen and guides it. This is "new meaning . . . gradually born from the encounter, or the intersection, of many different elements" (Havel). It is a different place to stand, with different optics and a different view of what does and does not make sense. It is transformed values and cultures, a new wisdom; new songs in a strange land, if you will, and different wineskins—or different cornerstones and new architecture. "Jesus said to them, 'Have you never read in the scriptures: The stone that the builders rejected has become the cornerstone?'" (Matthew 21:42a, Jesus citing Psalm 118:22).

The rejected stone or the new wine might, for example, be as simple and powerful as the realization, noted earlier, that planetary health is primary and human well-being derivative. That could in turn mean an expanded moral universe in which the present anthropocentric master-slave ethic governing our use of nature is abandoned, and policies of production, distribution, and consumption of food, energy, and water are as integrally related to one another as the systems of nature that provide them; in which the regenerative needs of soil, air, energy, and water are accounted for and factored into every use of these, including the price of consumer goods. Human "technologies would then be coherent with the technologies of the natural world"[22] and in accord with the proper first law of economics, "the preservation of the Earth economy."[23]

Or perhaps changes of consciousness and cosmology would lead to deconstructing structures that, like present food and energy systems, are "too big to fail," in favor of smaller systems, closer to home, with more transparency, more face-to-face accountability, and more flexibility, with wider margins of error during a season of climate-driven experimentation and adaptation. In a chaotic world decentralized systems are much less dangerous than centralized ones. When they fail, as some no doubt will, they yield less damage overall and are far easier to correct. (Is it wise to have only five basic food crops, each gene-engineered for the same results everywhere, in a climate-changing world, when there are no heat-resistant genes?)

Changes at the level of consciousness and cosmology might also extend rights so as to include, in some meaningful way, the lives of other animals, with implications for factory farming, diets, and the preservation of species. The vision and values of the Earth Charter, adopted by millions around the world, might inform constitutions and legislation. The ordering of those values is not accidental. Of the Charter's four major sections, the first two—Respect and Care for the Community of Life, and Ecological Integrity—lead into the next two—Social and Economic Justice, and Democracy, Nonviolence, and Peace.[24]

In short, examples are almost unlimited when fossil-fuel fundamentalism is rejected as a way of life and change happens at the level of worldviews that generate a different angle of perception. Basic ideas and values are deeply altered by such changes to consciousness and cosmology. "Do not be conformed to this world," Paul writes, "but be transformed by the renewing of your minds, so that you may discern what is the will of God—what is good and acceptable and perfect" (Romans. 12: 2). This perspectival revolution is in keeping with the kind of creature we are. For creatures of symbolic consciousness, it is mind, ideas, and values that matter most profoundly. Our creative powers of imagination, meaning, and choice are engaged when the forced options challenge our reigning life-narrative.

The dialectic of change

In addition to levels and kinds of change, there is a *dialectic* of change that commands moral attention. Two axioms make this easy to remember. The first is, *What people define as real is real in its consequences.* People act in accordance with their perception of what is happening. How they respond is in keeping with how they interpret what they see. This highlights the importance of hearts and minds for effective change. "Hearts and minds" describes the roll that personal character and cosmology play in determining people's conduct. Internalized values, virtues, and ways of "reading" the world select, as it were, among the actions we might take. They favor those most in accord with who we are and what we see. The first axiom is thus a clue to which prospective change will take hold. It will be change that either already accords with hearts and minds or changes them.

An important countertruth is captured in the second axiom: *Behavioral changes frequently precede attitudinal ones.* We act our way into new ways of seeing and thinking through changed practices. Some of these practices may be mandated or even coerced—the law of the land, the stipulations of the job, the requirements of a contract or covenant, the begrudging compromise that keeps all parties at the table, the terms of a treaty, the expectations of someone we dare not disappoint. Structure, systems, institutions, and policies all stipulate actions we might not undertake if they were left to the musings of the soul or the spontaneities of the heart. Yet, by shaping our behavior from the out-side, they change the way we live and in due course, our values. When President Truman integrated the armed forces in 1948, and black and white soldiers trained, lived, ate, and fought together, the race-related attitudes of both groups changed. Those attitudes were different from the attitudes of the very same soldiers when those soldiers trained, lived, and fought in race-segregated units. Different practices, themselves compelled, effected a different relation-ship and altered values.

When Martin Luther King broke the law and risked jail in the civil rights struggle and pleaded for others to do so, he wasn't only a moral witness for noncompliance with evil; he was putting pressure on the nation to enact and enforce new laws so that a racist nation wouldn't have to wait until racism was eradicated from each heart, mind, and soul before justice could be done for the disenfranchised. New laws would diminish the public impact of racism and eventually affect attitudes themselves.

Derrick Jensen's article, "Forget Shorter Showers: Why Personal Change Does Not Equal Political Change," may overstate the point.[25] But he is right in saying that, short of changing the fundamentals of the corporate economy and how it uses water, short of changing laws, institutions, and our collec-tive mindset, the individualist, voluntary focus on what-you-can-do-to-save-the-planet is an exercise in futility. As Bill McKibben puts it, "addition"—thousands of individual showers with an egg timer—will not save the day; only "multiplication" will. "Screw in a new light bulb? Sure," says McKibben. "Screw in a new global treaty? Now we're talking."[26] Treaties mean multiplication, multiplication that works whether we are among the conscientious or the complacent.

Yet Jensen's polemic against individual hearts-and-minds change has for-gotten our first axiom. So we must loop back to say that change undertaken by individuals who simply find it the right thing to do—those shorter showers, with or without egg timers—does matter. In the larger scheme of things, that undertaking may be no more than so-called symbolic action, but that action sends an important signal even if, of itself, it doesn't produce widespread change. Jensen fails to see that prophetic symbols and practices, even modest ones, move people in a direction that lets them embrace bigger changes when the moment is ripe and options are forced. Small changes are often the leaven of a better order. They are like water softening-up compacted soil, allowing new seeds to grow.

Consider climate change. Hoisting solar panels to rooftops here and there, starting community gardens, and reforesting floodplains, one community at a time, will not do what only bioregional, national, and international legislation and law enforcement can. Beijing, Canberra, Washington, Brasilia, Brussels, Delhi, Moscow, and the UN count more for this than my neighborhood. Yet, "there's no such thing as a useless community garden,"[27] a useless photovoltaic system, or a useless forest as preparation for systemic change.

Systemic changes usually don't materialize if they are not already present in anticipatory communities, even if those communities are modest in size and number. Anticipatory communities initially come about voluntarily; hearts, minds, and the perception of what is "real" are vital elements. Outward change springs from motivation, desire, and a driving dream. In words attributed to Gandhi, we must *become* the change we seek if we expect change to happen. Or, to cite "A Buddhist-Christian Common Word on Structural Greed," "We must be peace in order to make peace."[28]

Effective change is the result of the dialectical play of both elements: attitude and behavior. A strategy that relies on only one will be ineffective. Voluntary hearts-and-minds change will not suffice when the change needed is fundamental, extensive, and goes against the grain of entrenched ways and institutions. But coerced behavioral change fails as well if there is no preparation for it and assent to it in people's inner being.

The necessity of preparation and assent elicits four further notes on change:

1. For deep change to happen, the drag of normalcy must be resisted and conventional wisdom doubted.

This is difficult but not impossible. While W. H. Auden speaks the truth when he writes that often "[w]e would rather be ruined than changed,"[29] abiding by conventional wisdom has not compiled a good record.

Millions over the centuries lived comfortably in the Ptolemaic world. The sun rose in the east and set in the west; clearly, it circled Earth, the center of the universe. Then in 1633 Galileo propounded a heresy: Earth is a rather small rock rounding the sun. Against all the conventional wisdom—and science as well—Galileo was right, but only because he first doubted, then defied, the reigning consensus. "And yet it moves," he said of Earth to his accusers as they extracted his recantation.[30]

Another example of wrong-headed conventional wisdom: As recently as fifty years ago, geologists did not have a framework for understanding earthquakes, volcanoes, and other processes shaping the Earth. The theory Alfred Wegener proposed in 1912, that all the continents were once joined, then drifted apart, was dismissed despite the fact that a sixth grader could see the east coast of South America fitting nicely into the west coast of Africa. An unstable Earth simply didn't jibe with conventional wisdom, even among most scientists. Yet now continental drift is standard science and a part of sixth-grade texts.

Even more recently, a developing consensus saw free global markets as the most efficient allocators of resources, democracy as the most stable form of government, and liberal individualism as the foundation of a just political order. Growing prosperity and personal freedom would benefit all.[31] A short decade or two later, the rationality and impartiality of markets looks suspect, while the blindness of the global capitalist economy to the planet's health appears fatal to sustainability. The Age of Optimism and the Washington Consensus have given way to global anxiety.

In short, if widespread, deep change is to happen, conventional wisdom and institutional inertia must lose their grip. The way must be opened for the essential role of imagination.

Making change happen

2. Leadership and the first initiatives for major change, including perspectival change, usually come from minority communities at the edges or bottom of society.

Good leaders normally know two worlds well: the neglected or oppressed world and the privileged, reigning one. Good leaders are driven by the dream of a better world—and some rage. When Joseph's brothers complained, "Here comes the dreamer again" (Genesis 37:19), they were right, but they didn't imagine that the dreamy brother they sold into slavery would save them as an astute secretary of agriculture in Pharaoh's court. And Martin Luther King, the dreamer who knew two worlds, did not electrify the world by proclaiming, in Lincoln's shadow, "I Have a Nightmare," even though he had many. One of them—the assassin's bullet—killed him. The dream drives the action, and when the time is right and the soil prepared, the dream takes hold.

The numbers need not be impressive. The civil rights movement at its height found only 5 to 7 percent of the American public directly engaged. Many decisive events, like the sit-ins, involved less than a quarter of one percent! Small is often powerful. Think of the Buddha, Lao-tzu, Jesus, Gandhi, Sojourner Truth, and Harriet Tubman. Their first followers were few. Two important climate change campaigns, the worldwide 350.org movement and its 10/10/10 Global Work Day, started with Bill McKibben and seven students at Middlebury College in Vermont. All this is evidence for an observation widely attributed to Margaret Mead: "Never doubt that a small group of thoughtful, committed citizens can change the world. Indeed, it is the only thing that ever has."[32]

3. While almost every change movement is begun by the dreamers, it fails if influential allies in privileged circles are not forthcoming.

The task is to alter systems so that required *behavioral* changes lead to better policies, new habits, and a different way of life; that requires the powers of multiplication. A movement's prophetic symbols and practices matter only if they help move from voluntary addition to mandatory multiplication. The abolitionist's cause could stir many a heart but it could not end slavery until those with sufficient power to outlaw it took up the cause. The Occupy Wall Street movement can protest Wall Street's occupation of America but until the Occupy movement forces others with more leverage to legislate different corporate banking and finance practices, Wall Street will continue to occupy America.

In sum, effective change means altering perception and habits one story at a time; one shower and song at a time; one child, parent, and boss at a time. In this sense, every revolution starts small and gets smaller. It's one-by-one-by-one-by-one. But deep change is finally effective only when it is also behavior changed via mutual enforcement mutually agreed upon, whether hearts and minds are wholly ready or not. This is systemic change, structural change, and, when far-reaching enough, paradigm change.

4. Change that addresses today's wicked problems for the sake of new first works requires that we understand complex adaptive systems.

The industrial paradigm is skilled in linear thinking and linear change. Linear solutions—one problem, one remedy, linked by tight causation—assume change that happens evenly in proportion to some single controlling factor. But the industrial paradigm is not skilled in thinking about the nonlinear change it now produces on a mass scale. In a contracting and crowded world on an unsustainable path, that paradigm generates huge interlocking problems: rapid urbanization, climate change, hunger and poverty, ecosystemic degradation, population growth, disease, joblessness, market turmoil, and so forth. These interact in such a way that seemingly small change in one sector—global mean temperature, new investment instruments in global financial markets, the introduction of an invasive plant or toxic substance, an uptick in ocean acidification—can effect system-wide consequences.[33] When this nonlinear change takes over, the effects are out of proportion to the initiating cause. Thresholds are crossed and tipping points reached. (Extreme weather events and new climate patterns in the wake of small temperature changes in ocean waters and the atmosphere is one example.)[34]

Understanding this nonlinear change means understanding how complex adaptive systems work; that is, how systems of many interacting elements mutually condition behavior in ways that are not readily foreseeable, much less predictable or controllable. High uncertainty may reign as well as fluid boundaries of both space and time. This means learning from complex interactions in the very process of adapting to them, a posture that is far more ecological than mechanical. It means a deep respect for the integrity of a changing creation in which members of *Homo sapiens* are among the witting and unwitting change agents. It means finding human technologies that are congruent with nature's own changing technologies in a season of multiple transitions. The key is sustainable adaptation: What kind of change takes into account the integral functioning of dynamic, complex systems and is in accord with them? Effective systemic, structural, and paradigm change depends on understanding nonlinear change and how complex adaptive systems work.

Shakers and movers

What forces lead to change? Some students of change emphasize *social movements*—people acting together to bring about change in keeping with a cause. The change itself varies wildly. Some movements aim for regressive change, change that stops change and returns life to some desired, and often imagined, state. An example here is the Ku Klux Klan's effort to "take America back" to an imagined white Protestant purity. Some movements, such as the transformation of laissez-faire capitalism to social welfare capitalism, are reformist about the institutions of society. Some, like the breakup of the Soviet Union, are secessionist. All are social movements as the means of change.

Other observers highlight *the forces of nature*. The death of the dinosaurs allowed mammals, until then very small (mouse-size to small dog–size), to become the megafauna of a different environment. The human population that populated the Americas depended on a land bridge from Asia. That land bridge later disappeared. In our own time climate change is creating pervasive change through rising sea levels, extreme drought and deluge, and altered seasons affecting flora and fauna, pests, diseases, and predators. The current rendezvous with extinction and the loss of biodiversity through the gene pool reduction of industrialized agriculture and the destruction of habitat and species is also a force of nature, albeit this time with heavy human influence. Future generations are inheriting a gene-poor world that will constrain their opportunities. This is a marked sea change from their ancestors' world.

Still other students focus on *the power of technology*. Think of an invention— the ship, the plow, the printing press, the internal combustion engine, gunpowder, weapons of mass destruction, immunizations, birth control pills, automobiles, cameras, and computers—and it's clear that world-altering change has followed in the wake of new or improved technologies. (An aside: the industrial-technological age invests remarkable faith in technology. The industrial paradigm's general rule of thumb has always been to ask more of technology and less of one another.)[35]

Cultural diffusion is still another source of change. One society or culture adopts the ways and means of another—steel from Damascus, paper from China, Arabic numerals via India, philosophy and critical thinking from Greece, symphonic music from Europe, "pop" culture from the United States, art and architecture from innumerable locales, staple foods from many sources (wheat from the Fertile Crescent, potatoes from Peru, corn from Mexico, rice from Asia), imperial law and engineering from Rome, democracy's first steps from Greece, market capitalism from Europe. Cultures and their habits are created and altered, sometimes to a surprising degree, through processes of exchange and adaptation.

It goes without saying that these sources of change—social movements, forces of nature, technology, and cultural diffusion—are not independent of one another. They weave together, often creating outcomes that could never have been predicted or foreseen. When Thomas Newcomen scooped coal into the belly of the first "Atmospheric Steam Engine" in 1712 and substituted fossil fuel power for horses, he had no inkling whatsoever of the consequences of his invention—vast technological change, changes in culture and society, changes in nature itself.

Ethics and morality

All of the levels, sources, and species of change, as well as its dialectic, engage moral choice and agency whenever and wherever humans are a part of them. Because ours is an era of planetary geophysical change interlaced with social, political, economic, cultural, and technological change, very little falls out-side The Ethic We Need. Change of this kind and range is about how we live and for what, the very heart of morality and ethics. Religious communities trade in ways of life, the home page of ethics. They do so at every level, from cosmology to causes; from institutions and polities to rites, practices, and pol-icies; from communal food and drink and song to quiet contemplation about the ultimate meaning and purpose of life. Religious communities thus join others to engage the forced options we face.

Next . . .

If the extensive change we have described is about how we live and for what, then "our whole life is startlingly moral"[36] and it seems wise to introduce for-mal ethical categories. Shared notions about how we understand and speak of ourselves as moral creatures can aid our deliberation of The Ethic We Need.

5

The Ethic We Need

GOOD THEORY

Due to the precedent that has been set, the South African community is laying claim to all 200 pairs of the boots donated by their Red Cross. We shall wear each pair for three days to signal our right to what is our own property, and then shall be glad to lend some out when not in use to any non-South Africans who request our generous help.

—The two South Africans detained by the Japanese
in Shantung Compound, Weihsien, China, During World War II.

Categories and concepts

There is no "app" for good moral judgment. This means that the tools of ethics do not of themselves grant wisdom. But good theory does enable us to think more clearly, thereby enhancing moral deliberation and aiding thoughtful character formation and conduct. All stand in the service of better-informed choices when the options are forced.[1]

A hiking image may be helpful. When the hike is in open country with few distinctive landmarks and where the trail is easily lost because the same cobbles are underfoot everywhere, good hikers build cairns. Cairns are modest rock towers easily visible against a treeless horizon. They let hikers map the next section of the trail. They are not the trail itself; they are orientation points that let hikers forge a trail across unknown territory.

What are the cairns that let us hike the moral life? What "think withs" help us understand where we are going? What markers guide and orient when a different way of life must be forged but much of the territory is treeless? Some "think-with" markers follow.

1. Language

"Ethics" has a Greek root. Its noun form is *tō ēthos*. The parallel in Latin is *mos*, from which derive the words "mores," "morality," and "morale." *Tō ēthos* originally referred to a sheltering place for animals, a stall. The animal's safe habitat, it offered security and sustenance—nourishment and sufficient comfort and familiarity to provide a sense of home. The "stable" meant "stability," a secure place to be.

The verb form is *eiōtha*. "To be accustomed to" is the meaning, a parallel to *mos* ("mores" are customs). Here is one of the oldest meanings of morality—behavior according to custom. Customary behavior, routine conduct, does for human society what the stall does for domesticated animals; it provides stability and security, a comfort zone. These sustain a "stable" society.[2]

To shift images, but not meanings, morality is a kind of social glue. It enables people to get on with their lives in ways that assume stability, familiarity, and trust. It is not surprising, then, that when society comes "unglued," there is a move to moral repair and order, even if some of it comes by way of force—the police or army called on to restore order and keep the peace. Life together requires minimal moral stipulations; it cannot be lived in a moral void. When morality breaks down, so does society. Amorality and immorality run amok breed chaos.

Shared morality as essential social glue means that the most important ethic is rarely written.[3] Layered in culture and largely assumed, it often goes unacknowledged even by those who practice it day in and day out as their way of life. Ordinary behavior guided by a shared ethic is considered "natural," simply the way things are. For many, probably most, life is quite inconceivable and unmanageable apart from such underlying and unspoken morality.

But, of course, ways of life and their moralities *are* challenged from within and without, not least in a time when technology, culture, society, and even nature change at an accelerating pace. The formerly unspoken is contested and renegotiated. Ways of life themselves may die; some do. This takes us to a second cairn.

2. Ethics versus morality

With the rise of early humanistic rationalism, a gift of the Axial Age,[4] Greeks came to distinguish "morality" from "ethics." Morality continued to refer to behavior according to custom, in keeping with one's place in society and its way of life. But with the rise of philosophy as a critical, reflective enterprise, ethics came to mean behavior according to reason. Ethics subjected common morality to analytical reflection and, after extended give-and-take, recommended behavior on the basis of reasoned argument. Ethics might indeed confirm customary behavior, thereby ratifying the standing morality. But it might also recommend a break with custom, a "better" morality that should give rise to new and different habits and customs.

Ethics, in other words, required that morality be "justified," that it be subjected to chains of evidence and publicly reasoned arguments in order to make its case persuasively in the town square. Custom alone, even custom long practiced, such as patriarchy's status for women or the institution of slavery, was not of itself sufficient reason for sustaining a given moral course. The most common standards required a reason beyond "we've always done it that way." Morality, all morality, any morality, needed to make its case in the court of public reason.

In short, "ethics" came to mean critical reflection on the moral dimensions of human experience while "morality" referred to the standards of character and conduct people customarily use to guide their choices and actions.

While that distinction is the chief difference between "ethics" and "morality," it's also necessary to attend carefully to these words in their context. People use "morality" and "ethics" in many different ways, often interchangeably and beyond the distinction we have drawn. Sometimes "ethics" means a stipulated code of acceptable or unacceptable behavior—legal ethics, medical ethics, classroom and examination ethics, journalism ethics, officeholder ethics. Sometimes it's the character and conduct entailed in a whole way of life—Stoic ethics, Buddhist ethics, Jewish ethics. Ethics may also name the particular interests and schools of the critical reflective enterprise we mentioned above. Then it's "philosophical ethics" in the tradition of Aristotle or Kant, or it's "utilitarian," "deontological," or "virtue" ethics. "Theological ethics" is also an enterprise, the moral life among Christians as the Orthodox, Roman Catholics, Calvinists, Lutherans, or Anabaptists express it and reflect upon it, or as a theologian in one of these traditions elaborates and recommends it—Augustine's ethics, Aquinas's, Thomas Merton's, or Dorothy Day's. Muslims, Hindus, and Buddhists all have comparable schools and figures. The orientation and ethics of Theravada, Mahayana, and Vajrayana Buddhism, for example, are not identical. Nor are those of Shiite, Suni, and Sufi Muslims, despite commonalities.

Meanings, then, are multiple, and listening well is a standing requirement. The languages of morality and ethics range far beyond critical reason; they engage all that forges and sustains a way of life. But for our purposes, morality refers to the sources and standards of character and conduct that people use on a daily basis, while ethics denotes the critical, rational exchange they undertake in search of a sounder and more viable morality, a search that can extend to a different way of life altogether.

3. Moral theory

Ethical analysis has identified different understandings of what counts as the heart of moral experience. Commonly called "moral theory," these understandings take the form of an integrated body of basic approaches to the moral life. Key dimensions of morality as well as recurring patterns are illumined. While the following formulations of moral theory developed in Western philosophical traditions, readers standing in other traditions will readily compare them to their own, since moral experience is universally shared.

An episode from World War II provides a good case study. When the Japanese invaded China, they rounded up all the non-Chinese and put them in camps, one of which was the Weihsien Compound in Shandong province. Initially about fifteen hundred people were interred in the camp, mostly from Europe and the United States, but also Eurasians, South Americans, and South Africans. Japanese soldiers were assigned to control all goods entering and leaving the camp, but the internal administrative tasks were assigned to the detainees. People little known to one another were thus given the daunting task of creating a working community essentially from scratch. As Langdon Gilkey, a detainee who narrated life in the compound notes,[5] this was society reduced to a microcosm in which fundamental social dynamics were visible for all to see.

On a cold January day in 1945, an unexpected delivery arrived at the camp. One donkey cart after another passed through the gates to offload 1,500 parcels, each packed with food or clothing.

The source of this manna was the American Red Cross. Not surprisingly, then, many of the 200 Americans (of the then 1,450 detainees) laid claim to the parcels. With a nod to the country of origin, the Japanese commandant ruled that each U.S. citizen would receive one-and-a-half parcels, all other prisoners one each. The math worked perfectly. But a number of Americans protested vigorously. Americans, they said, should decide the distribution of American goods. The commandant temporarily retracted his ruling and postponed the distribution until the community had discussed the matter and reported back to him.

That discussion included an exchange between two of the Americans, an elderly missionary named Grant and the young schoolteacher Gilkey. Grant, according to Gilkey, wanted to argue the "moral" side of the affair: "'I always look at things, Gilkey, from the moral point of view.' 'Fascinated,' Gilkey comments, 'I heard him out.'"[6]

> "I want to make sure that there be a moral quality to the use we make of these fine American goods. Now as you are well aware, Gilkey, there is no virtue whatever in being *forced* to share. We Americans should be given the parcels, all right. Then each of us should be left to exercise his own moral judgment in deciding what to do with them. We will share, but not on order from the enemy, for then it would not be moral."[7]

Gilkey, pursuing the meaning of "moral," asked how many parcels the Americans would likely share. Each would likely give away a couple, Grant replied. That meant less than one-fourth parcel for each non-American, Gilkey responded, rather than the parcel apiece the commandant initially ordered. "Would that be moral sharing when all of us are equally hungry and in need?" Gilkey put to Grant. "Grant looked at me in bafflement," Gilkey reports, "that was not at all what he meant by 'moral.'" "I don't understand you," he said. "If the Japanese share it *for* us, no one is doing a good act, and so there's no morality in it anywhere."[8]

Gilkey next contrasts Grant's understanding of "moral" with his own. Grant contended that human actions that are not the free acts of individuals cannot be genuinely "moral." If we do not act from choice and do not express who we are in our choices, or who we strive to be, then genuine morality is absent. We may well *act*, under compulsion, but the wellspring of such action is not authentic morality, even if beneficial consequences are elicited. The wellsprings of true morality are in character, free will, and free choice. Acts that mirror freely undertaken responsibility are "moral." Others are not.

Gilkey counters Grant by arguing that Grant's theory of morality ignores a basic moral fact: Moral action has to do primarily with relations between persons in a community. Thus moral actions are those in which the neighbor's needs are measured together with one's own as part of the same relational framework; immoral acts are those in which the neighbor is forgotten or ignored in deference to the self. Gilkey's conclusion is that moral action, certainly if it is to be called "Christian" (Grant is a Christian missionary), expresses "in the outward form of an act a concern for the neighbor's welfare, which concern is, if anything is, the substance of inner virtue."[9]

Gilkey's moral theory differs sharply from Grant's because for Gilkey the heart of morality is not in character and individual free choice but in values that are realized in tangible social consequences and ends, values that are in fact tested *by* those consequences and ends. (As if to agree, David Brooks, writing on "The Responsibility Deficit" in the *New York Times*, says straightforwardly, "The heart of any moral system is the connection between action and consequences."[10]) In Gilkey's case, the roughly equal sharing of critical goods on the basis of common need is the salient value, a value rooted in an even more fundamental tenet; namely, the equality of persons in inescapable relationship to one another. Each one's welfare is placed in the same frame of moral reference, and on the same terms, as my own. The result for Gilkey is to find that action "moral" that expresses genuine care for neighbors in its consequences, whatever the source and even if compelled. Indeed, for Gilkey, genuine "inner virtue" is to cultivate this consequences orientation for all our actions. Our actions are judged by outcomes rather than by dispositions, motives, or unconstrained individual choice. To live the good life means to create and share in the general welfare by way of moral goods, such as liberty, equality, and community, that are realized in society.

If we step back from Grant and Gilkey,[11] we observe different moral theories at work: character ethics and consequences ethics. Each identifies genuine morality differently, just as each underscores a different dimension of moral experience (character for one, conduct for the other).

Character ethics is also known as "virtue" ethics. Its answer to the question, How is the good life achieved? is this: Choose the qualities that mark the good person and the good society and internalize these as the habits of heart, soul, and mind. When habitual, these qualities express who we are at the core; they exhibit our moral identity and drive our actions. They create the good society from the inside out, as the outcome of the kind of persons we are. The focus of attention is on the moral agents, from whom actions flow as water from a spring.

Communities and societies, cultures and subcultures, as well as individuals, bear moral traits. They are self-conscious about some while utterly unaware of others belonging to the unwritten moral substratum of society. Either way, groups achieve "character" and express character traits. Empathy and compassion, a disposition to treat persons as equals, and an insistence on justice as fair play may be so widely shared that they are part of a whole society's character; so is honoring the elders, respecting those in authority, and making the welfare of future generations part of present policies and decisions. Dignity, self-determination, love as equal regard, and a willingness to sacrifice might be present as well, whether in the same group or another. On the other hand, social character might also include tolerance for cheating on taxes or corruption in high places. Taking advantage of the power of public office might be expected. People's notions of justice might sanction honor killings and the death penalty in one society and find them abhorrent in another. Likewise, large inequalities of income and wealth might be accepted in some societies and deeply opposed in others. Whatever the particular constellation of virtues and vices, the morality that flows from cultivated personal and communal character is, for character ethics, morality at its most authentic. Authentic moral actions are conceived in reference to those who perform them, as matters of identity and integrity. These moral subjects, whether individual persons or groups large and small, are the center of attention and assessment.

Virtue ethics has numerous schools and exemplars. The one articulated by Grant is far from the best. There are ongoing debates in virtue ethics about which virtues have priority, who and what best embodies them, and what kind of moral formation and discernment cultivates the desired individual and collective character. Alfred Borgmann's *Real American Ethics*, for example, proposes that a good virtue ethic now must account for "economy and design." He thereby gives prominence to a matter that falls outside Grant's purview altogether. Why economy and design? Borgmann argues that greater attention must be given to "Churchill's principle": "We shape our buildings, and afterward our buildings shape us."[12] Just as we construct our habitat, our "stable," so our habitat "constructs" us. In the modern world, the global corporate capitalist economy is so overwhelming a force that it promotes its own strong culture, one that instills and rewards certain virtues and values while discouraging or dismissing others. It effectively creates its own morality and brings about attitudinal change through the market habits it rewards. As a system it generates moral consequences that shape hearts and minds and affect how we, as moral agents, view the world and act in it. It's the phantom cosmology of our era. Borgmann concludes that we should self-consciously make economy and design the subject of virtue and character formation, rather than let individual and collective character be formed by external forces that are not truly external at all. For Borgmann, character formation, the very heart of virtue ethics, includes a long hard look at the way the economy is organized and public space is designed since daily behavior, whether consciously willed or simply assumed as the way things are, affects motives, dispositions, attitudes, intentions, desires, even perception itself.[13] We shape the buildings that shape us. Good virtue ethics thus works for better systemic alternatives. Such attention to institutions and their behavior may not have occurred to Grant even though Grant and Borgmann are both exponents of virtue ethics.

Aristotle's *Ethics* is a classic statement of virtue ethics. Like Borgmann, Aristotle is keenly aware that while character shapes decisions and actions, practices and actions mold character. In the words of the *Nicomachean Ethics*: "We become just by doing just acts, temperate by doing temperate acts, brave by doing brave acts."[14]

The experience of the African Association of Earthkeeping Churches we visited in chapter 1 nicely illustrates the point of Aristotle and Borgmann: being shapes doing, doing shapes being. Since the African seminarians are farmers, they and their families cannot pack up their households to move to a campus a considerable distance from field, forest, and livelihood. Instead they gather in appointed villages where the faculty comes to them for weekly classes. The program is called Theological Education by Extension (TEI).

On a visit to Zimbabwe I went along for a round of classes. The professor posed a question: "What did we formerly believe?" Hands shot up, a student was called on, and the answer came: "We believed that Jesus Christ died for our sins." Not an answer I expected as a "former" belief, I awaited the follow-up. "What do we now believe?" came next. Hands high again, and a reply: "We now believe Jesus Christ died for all creation." The practices of Earth-keeping—soil amendment, reforestation, water catchment, erosion control, tree nurseries and botany lessons, animal husbandry, all of it accompanied by education, training, and religious expression in liturgy and song—had altered the perception, theology, even the identity of this Pentecostal alliance. Creation and its redemption had replaced the earlier focus on personal sin and salvation in these farmers' understanding of Jesus Christ. Earth-keeping practices worked on the heart and mind and, cast as Earth-honoring faith, were internalized as part of a transformed collective identity in what was literally a changed environment. As the farmers reconstructed their habitat, their habitat reconstructed them, their faith and ethic included.

Were we to ask about virtue ethics for the Great Work, we might land on what Mary Evelyn Tucker identifies as the common values most religions hold in relation to the natural world. She summarizes them as "reverence, respect, restraint, redistribution, responsibility and renewal." If we were advocates of a virtue ethic in the manner of Aristotle or Borgmann, but simultaneously advocates of this ethic as Earth-honoring faith, the outcome would approach Tucker's. "[R]eligions can advocate reverence for the Earth and its profound cosmological processes, respect for the Earth's myriad species, an extension of ethics to include all life forms, restraint in the use of natural resources combined with support for effective alternative technologies and equitable redistribution of wealth. They can establish a broader acknowledgment of human responsibility for the continuity of life on our planet and help renew the energies of hope for the transformative work to be done."[15] These are Great Work virtues.

Gilkey's ethics, by contrast, are straightforward "teleological" ethics, with a different location for the heart of morality. *Telos* is Greek for end, goal, or purpose; teleological ethics are outcome-oriented and tested. Gilkey's morality is so solidly teleological that even the use of force is justified by the praiseworthy end it achieves: needy neighbors obtain needed supplies.

But just as Grant, Borgmann, and Aristotle present varieties of virtue ethics, so Gilkey's is not the only kind of teleological, or consequences, ethics. We have already cited a prominent version that belongs to an entire epoch: utilitarian ethics, the working ethic of the industrial paradigm. Here non-human and other-than-human natures are the means for realizing human ends, purposes, and goals. "Use," or utility, defines the human/rest of nature relationship in such a consistent and thoroughgoing manner that we named it a continuation of the supreme "use" ethic—master/slave.

There is little reflection in this consistent-use ethic on duties or obligations to the rest of nature, or on any rights that other-than-human nature may or ought to hold. Nor is there much reflection on virtues incumbent upon the users as users. (The virtues of the good steward as manager are the exception.)

To his credit, Gilkey's own teleological ethic, unlike the utilitarian version of industrialism, is keenly aware of human responsibility for the natural world. His *Maker of Heaven and Earth* and *Nature, Reality, and the Sacred* published in 1959 and 1993, respectively, were significant steps toward an ecological theology.[16] Moreover, like Borgmann and Aristotle, he is aware of the interplay of actions and character, just as he is aware of our axioms of change. Sharing the parcels at the hands of the enemy expresses in outward form "a concern for the neighbor's welfare, which concern is, if anything is, the substance of inner virtue." Still, the decisive moral test is not with the doer ("inner virtue") but with the deed (shared parcels). Gilkey concludes his account: "In such a view all actions which help to feed the hungry neighbor are moral, even if the final instrument is an impersonal arm of government. Thus, as I argued to Grant, efforts designed to bring about a universal sharing were moral, efforts to block such a sharing, immoral."[17] So while virtue is no doubt present and important for Gilkey, even for it the test resides in the quality of actions as judged by their outcome. For Gilkey and all purveyors of consequences ethics, authentic morality is known by its fruits.

The parcel distribution had an amusing sequel. As the mountain of goods from the American Red Cross was sorted, two hundred pairs of boots sent by the South African Red Cross appeared. A grand total of two South Africans were in the camp at the time. The next day they posted a notice: "Due to the precedent that has been set, the South African community is laying claim to all 200 pairs of the boots donated by their Red Cross. We shall wear each pair for three days to signal our right to what is our own property, and then shall be glad to lend some out when not in use to any non–South Africans who request our generous help."[18] The morality play continued!

A third moral theory, neither Grant's nor Gilkey's, centers on obligation, or duty. In philosophical ethics it is called "deontological ethics," from the Greek *de + ontos*—"from being itself," "out of being," or "rooted in being." That is, life itself—"being"—imposes requirements incumbent upon all. Living together as prosocial creatures mandates ground rules, and inescapable relationships entail shared responsibilities. (We noted in chapter 1 that this holds for other social animals as well, a strong indication that morality as obligation belongs to mammalian evolution.) Or, to recall Havel, there are imperatives that derive "from respect for the miracle of Being, the miracle of the universe, the miracle of nature, the miracle of our own existence." They are to be honored rather than blasphemed.[19]

A widely used text in biomedical ethics by Beauchamp and Childress offers a hypothetical case for duty and obligation as an element of universal moral experience. Imagine you and a friend are mountain climbing. Your friend falls. When you reach him, it is obvious he is severely injured. In his dying moments he begs you to keep a promise. You readily agree. He reveals he has a tidy sum of money, nearly a million dollars, that he acquired by dint of hard work and good investments. He tells you where the money is and asks that you deliver it to an uncle who helped him at a crucial moment in the past. Your friend dies.[20]

You know three things. You made a promise; only you know about the million dollars; and your friend's uncle, whom you know as well, is both rich and likely to squander your friend's earnings. Furthermore, you can easily identify needier causes. Would the money in their hands not be a more fitting memorial to your friend? Should you or should you not break your promise to your friend, sworn at his deathbed, if the outcome is better consequences? He will never know, of course. Neither will the uncle.

Promise-keeping and truth-telling are examples of fundamental duties. In answer to the moral question, What is the good life and how are we to live it?, the chief concern here is not consequences determined, or virtue determined, but obligation determined. What are we duty-bound to do? What bottom-line morality do we owe one another, maybe even Being itself (if Havel and most religions are correct)? To whom are we obliged, and what are we obliged to do, given the investment of life itself in our hands? In this particular case, the judgment at issue is whether you should break your promise to your friend in order to use his money for worthier ends. Whatever your actual decision, the very existence of a strong sense that you should not break a solemn promise is testimony to obligation as a core reality of the moral life. (It is also testimony that the truths of duty ethics and consequences ethic might conflict, just as the truths of virtue might conflict with those of duty and consequences.)

Promise-keeping and truth-telling are hardly the only examples of ground rules. Extending respect and trust are others. Life cannot be lived well, if at all, out of basic distrust or mistrust. If everyone and everything is untrustworthy all of the time, nothing can be done to anyone's lasting satisfaction. Elemental trust is an indispensable eco-social requirement.

Respect and equal regard, too, are necessary for the good life. How we treat one another counts for most everything. Equal regard as basic respect means we treat others in the manner we ourselves wish to be treated. Some formulation of the Golden Rule thereby emerges in every culture, not only as good advice to squabbling kids but as a universal principle applicable to all. Negatively stated, lack of basic respect results in corrosive double standards. Some humans are regarded as less than human or human in ways that are inferior to the ways of my tribe. "Mine" and "ours" trump "you" and "yours." Absent respect and equal regard, "my" and "our" actions lose all sense of fair play and easily turn arbitrary, indifferent, or oppressive. Injustice, with its corrosive effects for life together, follows.

Immanuel Kant is regarded as the premier expositor of a consistent-duty ethic. His key notion is the "categorical imperative." It designates an unconditional requirement, an obligation that is binding in all circumstances. The kind of principles we should use to set the framework, possibilities, and limits of the moral life are principles that meet the test of the categorical imperative.

The first formulation of the categorical imperative goes like this: "Act only according to that maxim whereby you can at the same time will that it should become a universal law." No double standards. Not one law for me and my tribe but another for you and your ilk. The test of genuine morality is whether you can will for others what you will for yourself.

The second formulation of the categorical imperative is, "So act in every case as to treat humanity, whether in your own person or in that of another, as an end, and never a means only." Women as only a means to fulfill male desires, or any relationship governed by use alone, with no respect or inherent value accorded persons as worthy in their own right—these, like slavery, are "out." They don't pass the test of "ends, not means only."

The third formulation works from Kant's notion of a "kingdom of ends" to which humans belong and for which they are the legislators. "Every human being must so act as if he were through his maxim always a legislating member in the universal kingdom of ends." If you, like Moses or Hammurabi, were the lawgiver, what laws would be binding upon all? What moral framework and substantive duties would govern your little kingdom (your family, your town, your neighborhood, your bioregion)? The stipulated guideline is, Always act as though you were the giver of such laws as the laws for all.

Think of duty ethics this way. If, as in John Rawls's neo-Kantian theory of justice, you were placed behind a veil of ignorance so that you could not know in advance your position or status in the future society of which you will be a member, what rules would you legislate as binding? If you cannot know how your interests and your life will play out in the future, what terms do you recommend as the initial terms for everyone? What institutions abiding by what rules and practices would you create?[21]

Kant wants morality that is not susceptible to self-serving distortions. We consistently engage in ideological twists and turns that serve our limited interests. We construe our vices as virtues; we confirm our biases; we even believe our lies. Imperatives that are "categorical," or right for any and every person in similar circumstances (i.e., "universal"), minimize the influence of our distorting interests. Kant's moral universalism thus yields public guidelines that are independent of the interests of the persons posing and deciding moral issues.

Contrasted with the other theories, this means that, for duty ethics, neither the virtue of the person nor the consequences of her actions is the decisive test of moral value; the fundamental requirements of life together and universal applicability are. Stealing, lying, breaking promises, rape, and torture cannot be moral yardsticks and recommended norms and behaviors. If they were universally practiced and approved, nature-society would be impossible. Or if somehow nature-society were remotely possible on such terms, then it would be a place we'd do everything possible to escape in favor of a habitat that valued respect and fair play. We would seek the shelter of a better stable.

Here are two examples that, on the face of it, are different. The first recalls the thesis of duty ethics that our lives as eco-social creatures impose moral requirements on us; the second illustrates the universal reach of these duties.

The Hebrews had lived far too long as the bottom tier in a great civilization run on slave labor by a priestly caste—Pharaoh's Egypt. Liberation came with the first recorded slave revolt in history and the exodus into the wilderness. But now what? Shorn of their familiar habitat and livelihood in the fleshpots of Egypt and without its imposed order, how will the ragtag band of former slaves govern themselves so as to make a life together? They complain vehemently to Moses: "Why did you bring us out of Egypt, to kill us and our children and livestock with thirst?" (Exodus 17:3b). So what will they do with their new freedom? In their own version of Shantung Compound, but without the Japanese (i.e., the Egyptians), they need to establish the requisites for living together. What will the rules be? What does life together as a functioning community require? The answer is the Ten Commandments and chapter after chapter of legislation. The Ten Commandments and the Covenant Code are ground rules articulated as fundamental moral duties in the presence of the God who, unlike Egypt's gods, knows their suffering (Exodus 20:12–16; Exodus 21–23). And Moses, though also remembered as prophet and leader, is venerated above all as Lawgiver. Israel and its leaders discover the forces in human experience that give rise to an ethic of basic obligations. If a people, any people, never lives easily with moral bottom-lines, without them it does not live at all. Even the libertarian has to legislate the conditions for hands-off freedom.

It should be added that these stipulations—commandments and covenants—belong to a moral order that, in Israel's experience, is authored by none other than the God of the universe, who sided with slaves against the empire's gods. Commandments and covenants manifest, in this case as in the case of many religions, an existence that is rooted in God, the same God who flung stars across the sky and moved upon the primordial waters to order all creation. (In Havel's secular rendition, life imperatives derive from respect for interconnected miracles: Being, the universe, nature, and our own existence.)

Israel's wilderness experience is more typical than exceptional. Any people whose circumstances require them to create a life together need to settle on moral baselines that bind individual and institutional behavior. Not by coincidence, these are frequently inscribed as founding "constitutions," a subject of great interest to Kant. Such provisions "constitute" that which is incumbent upon all citizens. They comprise the basic bodywork for a nation as it grows and changes. If basic change is needed, it will come as amendments to the founding documents or, in more drastic cases, as a new constitution. But whether newly drafted or amended, constitutions attest to how essential the rule of law is. Obligation is not optional for creatures who by nature are born—and fated—to longing and belonging. A biosocial nature—we only live by the kindness of strangers, even if it is compelled—requires some minimum shared terms for getting along.

The great transition of the Hebrews from an oppressive and static order to freedom and uncertainty was taxing. At times the devil they knew seemed preferable to the one they didn't: "If only we had died by the hand of the Lord in the land of Egypt, when we sat by the fleshpots and ate our fill of bread; for you have brought us out into this wilderness to kill this whole assembly with hunger" (Exodus 16:3). Jewish teaching, insightful about the colonization of the mind and the need to get along, especially under duress, says it was *necessary* to spend forty years in the wilderness. Only then would a generation arise that had not internalized Egypt's oppression.

Which is only to say that drafting a constitution, ratifying it, living with it, and interpreting it rarely proceeds smoothly. People in transition bring truths and counter-truths, with moral argument a part of both. Experience, even the same experience, rarely yields consensus, even on something as fundamental as ground rules for living together. Constitutions require deliberation as well as, at some point, an end to deliberation by agreeing to accept the results of voting or the authority of designated leaders.

Many a constitution has a bill of rights, our second example of deontological ethics at work. Human rights as a strong moral presence with a global reach inscribed in law and protected by it are chiefly a modern phenomenon. The Enlightenment's quest for a universal morality as legislated by autonomous human reason, set against the moral horror of World War I, World War II, and the Holocaust, gave rise in the immediate post–World War II years to the Universal Declaration of Human Rights, adopted by the United Nations General Assembly in 1948. The drafters posited human dignity as the bedrock of these rights. In Kantian terms, no human being can be regarded as an instrument only; all persons bear inherent value as ends in themselves. The parallel in religious communities is that all are, without exception, children of God and precious in God's sight.

But what is a "right"? To have "rights" or a "right" is to hold a legitimate claim or entitlement to something, the recognition of which is required of others. Or, in keeping with our focus on morality, a right is a universal moral claim made a binding legal one. We are duty-bound to honor these rights, no exceptions allowed. If, because of egregious behavior, a right *is* suspended— say in the case of known felons or persons under arrest as terrorists—it must meet a heavy burden of proof and pertain to all similar cases in the same way (be "universal"). Even such exceptional suspension of rights testifies, precisely *as* exception, to their status as strong moral claims.

Israel in the wilderness and the Universal Declaration of Human Rights illustrate deontological ethics as morality marked by universal obligation, whether the forms are moral principles, commandments, laws, codes, covenants, rights, or constitutions. Life together pushes for morality that is binding on all parties in similar circumstances.

But we have not yet raised a crucial issue. Do we have a root obligation to other-than-human nature, to community and society in their comprehensive sense? (Every community and society belongs to nature. The built environment is a part of nature no less than the unbuilt one.) Why do there seem to be no binding claims upon us on the part of the generative elements of all life—earth (soil), air, fire (energy), water? Why are the requirements of their condition not duties incumbent upon us as those who depend upon them utterly for our life? Is it because other-than-human nature lacks dignity in our moral universe, gets no basic respect, and is relegated to the status of means only, never ends? Is it not morally irresponsible, even reprehensible, to ignore that which provides and sustains life? If so, ethics as the reasoned critique of reigning morality wants to know whether that is sufficient cause and good argument, or only bad cosmology and a fateful human mistake.

The Earth Charter thinks this lack of respect for nature and its moral claims is bad cosmology and a fateful mistake. While eschewing the language of rights per se, the Charter joins our examples of duty ethics by including universal human responsibilities toward the rest of nature. The very first section, Respect and Care for the Community of Life, lays out four basic principles:

1. Respect Earth and life in all its diversity.
2. Care for the community of life with understanding, compassion, and love.
3. Build democratic societies that are just, participatory, sustainable, and peaceful.
4. Secure Earth's bounty and beauty for present and future generations.

Each principle has two subordinate principles that provide more content. The pattern repeats itself when the Charter then moves on to Ecological Integrity, Social and Economic Justice, and Democracy, Nonviolence and Peace.[22] The outcome of a global process of achieving consensus across all sectors of society, with special attention to the views of historically underrepresented peoples as well as the world's religions, the Charter is a remarkable example of the possibilities of a common ethic of obligation to nature in a comprehensive sense.

To summarize moral theory: We have identified notably different ways to underline what is most important in the moral life and how it is tested. They cluster around three moral realities continually present in human experience:

the quality of human character, individually and collectively; the goals and consequences of human action and human responsibility for them; and the binding rules that living together requires as incumbent upon all. Given various names, we have used the idiom of character ethics (virtue), consequence ethics (teleological), and duty ethics (deontological). Whatever the names, these realities cross all cultures and all recorded human time. The morality we are born to takes varied, recurring, enduring forms.

Two notes finish the discussion.

Moral theory is the effort to reflect systematically upon the dimensions and forms of human moral experience. It highlights the different and sometimes conflicting "logics" in the moralities we live: Which is most vital and the heart of the matter at any given moment—character, consequences, or obligation? Which do we most live by, and how does it matter?

Yet lived moral experience will always be richer and more dynamic than our theories. Theories by nature abstract from experience in ways that simplify it for the sake of an illuminating focus and explanatory power. But however elegant and powerful the theories, we still feel the tug and tensions of all three—character, consequences/goals, and duty—often without settled resolution. That should tell us that no one of these approaches of itself, in either religious or secular articulation, captures the whole. No single theory, even when sound and consistent, encompasses the length, breadth, depth, and complexity of human morality, nor does any one resolve competing claims to lasting satisfaction.

That said, good theory offers good maps, and maps are useful, sometimes indispensable. They aid the moral trek. Or, to shift images, good theory illumines different dimensions of our moral experience to help us see the kind of creature we are and what is at stake in the world we inhabit as creatures who are mad with morality and in need of morally formed judgment.

But map is not territory, and we live in the territory. Good ethics facilitates moral understanding. Understanding morality, however, does not substitute for living it any more than a good recipe or pictures of food satisfy hunger or watching a dance takes the place of dancing. Good theory serves the moral life; it never substitutes for it.

Finally, the reader may have noticed that the examples in this discussion have moved freely between those we associate with society (Shantung Compound, the mountain-climbing friends, Israel) and the nature-focused discussions of previous chapters. That free flow is intentional.

The reason is twofold: First, human society and nature are inseparable. Nothing is gained, and much goes awry, if we bifurcate society and nature or nature and humanity. It's always nature-society, it's eco-social humanity together with the rest of nature, whether we name it so or not. The varied examples thus share the same space even when different points are highlighted. Second, the moral theory outlined here pertains to our experience as a whole. We do not have, and do not seek, a fourth theory, one reserved for other-than-human nature in our experience. The Ethic We Need is not some segregated, autonomous "environmental ethic" with fundamentally different moral categories. The Ethic We Need is an inclusive ethic tailored to the world we have in light of the kind of creatures we are and the changes we face. Human character, ends, and obligation all pertain, as do the other categories and concerns we will explore. None drop out as the moral universe moves its boundary from the ego to the ecosphere. But neither are other categories added, not even when present working moralities need to be reframed and rewritten. Other virtues and different character may well be necessary, or other consequences as the outcome of different policies and habits, or a restatement of our obligations to present and future generations of both human and more-than-human life—a major theme of this book is that these content changes are vital. But changes of substance expand the formal categories rather than replace them. The baselines of moral theory—character, consequences, obligation—remain. An adequate account of human responsibility for nature-society incorporates them all.

4. Moral vision

A conference on organ transplants was considering health care policy. Various issues of moral import had surfaced in the plenary sessions—equal access to services, the role of regulation (who decides, using what criteria), and the economic ramifications of organ demand. When the next speaker took the podium, it was apparent that he suffered from a severe deformity. He required special support for his congenitally misshapen back to address the assemblage of physicians, lawyers, health care administrators, and biomedical ethicists.

The young man spoke matter-of-factly about his condition and went on to say that in many ancient civilizations the disabled were put to death. This had happened in the United States as well and, even now, in certain cases the disabled were not allowed to live.

The audience was skeptical about the latter claim. Several people challenged him from the floor. His reply was a question: If two persons could avoid death, and could anticipate significantly prolonged life from an organ transplant, and if the only difference between them was that one was notably disabled and the other not, who would receive the transplant?

At first the surgeons on hand defended their practice of excluding significantly disabled persons, all other things being equal. They did so with arguments the majority deemed reasonable. Yet before long they began to realize the consequences of their train of thought: The young man who had quietly put the question to them would not, in their considered judgment, be given the transplant that would allow him to live. Quiet moral shock set in as it came clear to them that they had not considered the disabled to be fully persons.

Roy Branson, a conference participant who reported on the event, commented: "In the silences between their sentences the participants sensed that they had passed beyond the discussion of ethical, economic, medical, and legal terms to glimpse new horizons of responsibility. Their sense of humanity had expanded."[23]

What, from a moral point of view, happened here? What occurred as their "sense of humanity . . . expanded"?

For discussion's sake, let us presume the transplant surgeons were persons of acceptable character. They genuinely cared for their patients, they were dedicated to the relief of suffering, and they were skillful in the treatment of those in their care. Most, if not all, demonstrated the moral and technical virtues expected of good physicians. They had taken the Hippocratic Oath and were conscientious about their profession's duties. They were vigilant above all when facing the hard decisions, those life and death choices made unavoidable by limited supplies of life-saving organs.

We have, then, persons of character who attend to their professional obligations with a keen sense of responsibility and a desire to provide the best outcome that resources permit. Still, the young man's challenge nagged at them: Had their compassion been restricted to certain classes of patients? Had their understanding of the social good been prejudicial? Did congenitally deformed persons lack the status of full persons?

When the answer to those questions turned to "yes" as "[t]heir sense of humanity . . . expanded," it signaled the intrusion of a modified moral vision. They saw things somewhat differently, the consequence of altered lenses and vision. If we tracked them after the conference, we would likely find that all the elements of the moral life we called moral theory were affected in due course: some of the virtues important to the profession, some of its policies and their consequences, some of the basic obligations themselves. Moral vision has that kind of sweep and impact for a simple reason: Though often subtle and unnoticed, our moral vision is our integrated grasp of the moral realm overall. A synonym of moral imagination, it casts the moral world and it can recast it.

Differently said, moral vision provides the basic storyline for the morality we live by, or seek to live by. We could call it the narrative line rather than the vision. It's not the full story, so it doesn't provide every detail. The storyline for a television series doesn't include every twist and turn of character or lay out every conversation and action for every installment. The characters and the plot change. Yet they do so within a narrative that aligns with who they are and what they do. They are "in character;" they fit the tale and the tale fits them.

Moral vision and moral narrative may change, and do. But then the story changes, as do the optics, and a different life is lived. In the first centuries of the Common Era, the philosophical schools of Greece and Rome each claimed their own distinctive way of life. Each taught "the Way," whether Stoic, Epicurean, or Cynic, or, within the Judaism and Christianity of the first centuries, Essene, Gnostic, Ebionite, or proto-Orthodox. Competition was keen, and to change membership from one school to another was called "conversion." Conversion meant resocialization in accord with a different narrative of the good life. It entailed an altered moral vision that affected outlook, character, action, relationships, and responsibilities.

Moral vision may change at glacial speed. But like glaciers, it can move mountains. Take the example of slavery: Throughout all of recorded human history, including the present, some humans have made slaves of others. The arrangements and conditions have varied; some systems, like chattel slavery, were extraordinarily brutal. Others were less so, sometimes stamped with the paternalism of familial care, even family membership. In all cases, slavery was "moral" in that the full range of moral experience and justification was brought to bear on it. Virtue was taught: The master should show care for the slave; the slave should respect and obey the master. Rules were laid down and enforced by law or custom. And while the rules were rules of inequality, both masters and slaves were to abide by them. The social good was an important consideration, with slavery defended as a matter of social necessity integral to a cherished way of life. Finally, on yet another level, slavery was defended as rooted in the order of the universe itself and presented, from Aristotle until abolition, as nature's own mandate. The arguments made for slavery always included moral ones that were deemed important, whether those rested in natural law, scripture, or the practical imperatives of civilization and the economy.

To cite an example. When secession was the agenda of Southern states in the United States in 1860, most said the reason was the Northern threat to do away with slavery. Revisionists underscore states' rights as the precipitating cause of the War Between the States/Civil War, but state declarations at the time argued the *im*morality of abolishing the institution of slavery. South Carolina declared: "The non-slaveholding states . . . have denounced as sinful the institution of slavery" and "have encouraged and assisted thousands of our slaves to leave their homes." Mississippi said: "Our position is thoroughly identified with the institution of slavery—the greatest material interest of the world." Georgia: "A brief history of the rise, progress, and policy of anti-slavery and the political organization into whose hands the administration of the Federal Government has been committed will fully justify the pronounced verdict of the people of Georgia [to secede]." Abraham Lincoln was dismissed as "an obscure and illiterate man" whose "opinions and purposes are hostile to slavery."[24] Theirs was a states' rights issue: but the chief states' right issue was the right of slaveholders to protect a way of life that required slaves. It accorded with a sincerely held moral vision aligned with material economic interests.

Yet the day came, first here, then there, and never without conflict, including secession and war, when slavery was condemned as inherently immoral. Slaves had long yearned to breathe free. Many, at the risk of their lives, rebelled in the name of that freedom and their dignity as children of God. But now non-slaves, too, caught a vision of the fundamental equality of all persons and the right of all persons to live as free citizens. (Words in the Jefferson Memorial Rotunda, Washington, D.C., include the following, from Jefferson, the slave-holder. They are excerpted from his "Commerce between Master and Slave," written in 1782. "I tremble for my country when I reflect that God is just, that his justice can not sleep for ever.")[25] Those once scorned as utopian dreamers— they had imagined a society without slaves—were vindicated as the day came, not when each and every trace was banished forever from the Earth, but when slavery was no longer the reigning vision or reality, the day when the morality upholding it no longer held.

If an eco-centric ethic displaced the anthropocentrism of the industrial paradigm or if there were an Earth-friendly successor to democratic capitalism, the shift would be as dramatic and far-reaching as abolition. At present, many can no more imagine such departures from our received moral vision than earlier generations could imagine society without slavery or the "natural" sub-ordination of women, or than Romans could imagine the end of the empire. Yet such shifts of moral vision occur. They usually occur as a process of death and renewal, or birth and rebirth, often with strong religious overtones. They happen as an altered moral vision moves multitudes, however slowly, into a different moral environment. They occur in conjunction with the kinds and levels of change we cited in the previous chapter.

Consider the direct appeal of Arundhati Roy that so many in the Southern Hemisphere, together with indigenous and minority peoples of the Northern, find compelling. While she pleads for a certain "philosophical space," it is a moral space as well. "The first step towards reimagining a world gone terribly wrong," she writes, "would be to stop the annihilation of those who have a different imagination—an imagination that is outside capitalism as well as communism. An imagination which has an altogether different understanding of what constitutes happiness and fulfillment."[26]

Such imagination brings with it its own requirements: "To gain this philosophical space, it is necessary to concede some physical space for the survival of those who may look like the keepers of our past, but who may really be the guides to our future. To do this, we have to ask our rulers: Can you leave the water in the rivers? The trees in the forest? Can you leave the bauxite in the mountain? . . . If they say they cannot, then perhaps they should stop preaching morality to the victims of their wars."[27]

Moral vision is powerful. When the spirit of the age aligns with a different moral vision, it may even leave the coal in the mountain and create another livelihood for the miner.

Religious communities are among the sources of moral visions. We finish this discussion with an extended example from the Christian tradition. Like other moral visions or narratives, it sets the basic terms; it does not map every policy or supply every detail.

We might call this a vision of "ecological civilization" as the alternative to industrial civilization. Its nucleus is *oikos*, Greek for "house" and "household." *Oikos* is the root of "ecumenics," "ecology," and "economy," with house and household referring to the households of faith of early Christians, even to Earth itself as the "world house."[28] The *oikoumenē*, whence come "ecumenics" and "ecumenical," is the whole inhabited earth or imperial claims to it. (The Roman Empire referred to itself as the *oikoumenē*.) The emphasis of *oikoumenē* falls on the unity of the household—all belong to the same family—and nurturing this unity across the expanse of inhabited terrain. Thus the Christian households of faith (*oikoi*) made a conscious effort to stand for the whole church in each place, scattered as it was on three continents around the Mediterranean basin. This identity and mission required instruction, called *oikeiosis*. The word was borrowed from the Stoics, for whom it meant "appropriation" in the sense of making something one's own, whether as a member of the family, society, the human race collectively, or the world (*cosmos*) as a whole. Instruction included basic teaching, core practices, and rites of passage. If an alternative way of life to that of the empire was to take shape, community formation, including moral formation of both character and conduct, was required.

The Christian householder himself or herself was the *oikonomos*, literally "the economist," the one who knows the house rules (*oikos* + *nomos*, law) and cares for the material well-being of its members. (*Oikonomos* is often translated as "steward" or "trustee," even though "economist" is the more exact rendering.)

Household dwellers are *oikeioi*. Their task, too, is to build the community and share the gifts of the Spirit for the common good. First Corinthians 12:4–7 puts it like this: "Now there are varieties of gifts, but the same Spirit; and there are varieties of services, but the same Lord; and there are varieties of activities, but it is the same God who activates all of them in everyone. To each is given the manifestation of the Spirit for the common good." This common good includes meeting one another's material needs (Acts 2:44). This is designated *oikodomé*, the continual up-building of the household, the *oikos*. Such care requires intimate knowledge of community structures and dynamics. It requires knowing the household's logic and laws, which is exactly what "ecology" means (*oikos* + *logos*), knowledge of relationships that build up and sustain.

Oikos is, then, a knowledge and vision of economics, ecology, and ecumenics as interrelated dimensions of the same world. Economics means knowing how things work and managing "home systems" (ecosystems) in such a way that the material requirements of the whole household of life (*oikoumenê*) are met and sustained. Economics is the orderly manner by which the goods of the world household are shared for the common good.

This ancient unitary vision accords with the seamlessness, or integrity, of creation in the Hebrew Bible, mentioned earlier. Creation is the abode, the dwelling place, of God's creating, redeeming, and sustaining Spirit; the transcendent God is "home" here, as are humans and all life. Early theologians even referred to the way by which creation is upheld and redeemed as the "economy of God" (*oikonomia tou Theou*). Some theological traditions still do.[29]

The same seamlessness, or integrity, continues with the conviction that this vast cosmos is a *shared* home. All are born to belonging, and all—human beings and otherkind—are co-inhabitants who live into one another's lives and die into one another's deaths in a complex set of relationships that sustain (or degrade) the life of creatures and the land.

And where are we now? What does this antique vision teach us? Daniel Bell ended *The Cultural Contradictions of Capitalism* in search of a unifying vision. *The Cultural Contradictions* was Bell's study of a world coming apart by virtue of living out its own logic. He sought alternative scaffolding and reached back to the Greeks and *oikos* for a coherent culture and a moral vision for life together amid present fragmentation.[30] Curiously, however, his cultural and economic critique largely omitted the ecological. His *oikos* quest for a durable present and future thus needs its own amendment. His question might now go like this: In keeping with the world-house vision of *oikos*, can Earth's human economy be rendered compatible with Ecumenical and Ecological Earth?

To achieve such compatibility, major shifts in economics and economic ethics are needed. They would embody and express the changed moral vision.

The aim of economic life would need to shift from maximizing the production of goods and services to a three-part agenda of production, relatively equitable distribution, and ecological regenerativity. All economic activity would need to operate within the ecological limits of the planet and in the face of its hot and crowded condition. "Eco-nomics" replaces economics and ecology by joining both.

The new eco-nomic paradigm would reject growth and high consumption as *the* mark of mature economies. This does not preclude growth as *a* good; it only says that growth must be ecologically sustainable as well as regenerative, for the long term. It must reduce rather than increase the wealth and income gaps within and between nations and regions, a formidable challenge in that climate change will exacerbate these inequalities. Those contributing least to climate change will likely suffer the most. And it should bolster rather than undermine local communities and cultures in order to draw wisely from their cultural and biological diversity.

The new economic paradigm would also reject freedom as unrestrained political and market individualism and cultivate freedom as thriving in community in ways that contribute to personal well-being and the common good, including the goods of the commons (soil, air, water, energy).

The chief obstacles to an effective transition from the fossil-fuel era will not likely be technological. Sustainable and regenerative technologies already exist in part and can be elicited with imagination and the proper political-economic incentives. The chief obstacles will be the political-economic and sociocultural dimensions of ways of life that remain addicted to fossil fuels, that have not yet come to terms with the limits of planetary systems, that assume happiness and fulfillment are based on unending material consumption of goods and services, and that think and invest for short-term rather than long-term ends in a political economy that operates with a different metabolism from that of the rest of nature. All of these, too, belong to a moral vision, that of the industrial-technological era.

An effective transition would also take into account the well-being of future generations, the future generations of both human and other life. "*All* the children*,*" to cite Thomas Berry's dedication.[31]

In the end the most basic issue for "eco-nomics" and ethics is *how* we live, and *for what;* and it is at this crucial juncture that moral and religious convictions and commitments are vital to a successful transformation and transition. The answer does not lie in trying to retrieve and replicate the economy and economic ethics of the biblical communities. Theirs was a Neolithic pastoral world that became urbanized. The planet was large and richly endowed with a small human population at home in places they knew well generation in and generation out. Ours is an industrial and postindustrial planet that is human-dominated, resource-stressed, environmentally degraded, and on the move. That said, the *oikos* conception of Earth, with creation's integrity at its core, is perhaps more timely than ever. Certainly a spirituality and ethic for the long haul is needed, one that receives life as a gift and knows our place in creation. It knows the significance of our striving as well, even in the face of inevitable corruptions and losses. Not least, the very purpose of eco-nomics in the biblical world carries new force on this side of modern economics; namely, to cultivate the material conditions for the continuation of life. To renew the face of the Earth (Psalm 104) as the work of the divine economy is the shared human calling.

The extended example of *oikos* should not overwhelm the main points: the inevitability of a moral vision for human living, and the power of moral vision as a means of far-reaching change for The Ethic We Need.

Just as inevitable is some notion of justice, yet another cairn on the moral horizon.

5. Justice theory

In *The Republic*, Plato gives Glaucon a classic ethics assignment. Glaucon is to say how he would recognize a just person. What, Plato asks, would demonstrate the sure presence of justice? The truly just person, Glaucon replies, would be one "of true simplicity of character who . . . wants to be and not to seem good. We must not allow him to seem good, for if he does he will have all the rewards and honours paid to the one who has a reputation for justice, and we should not be able to tell whether his motive is love of justice or love of the rewards and honours. We must strip him of everything except his justice."[32] Glaucon continues:

He must have the worst of reputations for wrongdoing even though he has done no wrong, so we can test his justice and see if he weakens in the face of unpopularity and all that goes with it. We shall give him an undeserved and lifelong reputation for wickedness and make him stick to his chosen course until his death. . . . They will say that the just man, as we have pictured him, will be scourged, tortured, and imprisoned, his eyes will be put out and after enduring every humiliation he will be crucified.[33]

For sheer brutality this description is numbing, as is the startling parallel to Isaiah's Suffering Servant and the crucifixion of Jesus. But Plato pursues his question: In what does justice reside?[34]

Together with "love" and "compassion," "justice" is the most common and enduring of norms in religious ethics. Even beyond religious ethics, every moral environment holds some conception of justice and a demand for it.

Concepts of what justice is and where it resides differ, however. All of them belong to moral theory and reflect moral vision, though no one theory commands universal assent. What comprises justice is, like the substance of each and every moral base point, a contested notion.

Michael Sandel's bestseller, *Justice: What's the Right Thing to Do?* organizes varied approaches to justice, from antiquity to the present. It includes Glaucon's answer that justice is above all a strong imprint of character. Justice as virtue is only one conception, however.

"To ask whether a society is just," Sandel says, "is to ask how it distributes the things we prize—income and wealth, duties and rights, powers and opportunities, offices and honors."[35] What are people due, and why? How do they get what they are due? These questions, the questions of justice, endure. The answers are never singular. Notions vary about what counts as the heart and measure of justice.

People have thought about justice as the distribution of social goods in three ways that cross time and cultures. One centers on human welfare: That society is just that maximizes human welfare. A second conception says human freedom is the heart and soul of justice: That society is just that respects, protects, and expands freedom. The third we met in Glaucon's reply that justice is a deeply held element of character: That society is just that cultivates justice as the very core of people's being.

Not surprisingly, these understandings roughly parallel standard moral theory. One school uses teleological ethics. It says, in effect: Be goal-oriented in your choices and actions so as to increase justice as the common good. Reduce suffering, improve the standard of living, enhance well-being. In other words, maximize human welfare.

Utilitarianism, an example of justice as maximizing welfare, is a version of teleological ethics. Jeremy Bentham is Sandel's choice for a classic account of utilitarian justice. Here the lead principle is to increase happiness, calculated as the balance of pleasure over pain. The right thing to do, the just thing, is to act in a manner that maximizes pleasure or happiness and prevents or alleviates pain and suffering. As in consequences ethics generally, good actions count above all; here the worthiest actions are those yielding pleasure and avoiding or alleviating pain.[36] Utilitarianism isn't the only example of justice as the maximizing of human welfare, but it will suffice for the moment. We should add that Bentham's utilitarianism, the balance of pleasure over pain as the measure and outcome of our actions, is not identical to the brand of utilitarianism in our earlier discussion of "use" or "utility" as the sole guideline for our relationship to all nature beyond human nature. This only underscores for justice what we also found with moral theory: Each camp includes differing versions. Indeed, the fiercest arguments are often family feuds.

Another school focuses on human freedom to choose and act. Do that which maximizes human freedom, with the caveat that you will the same freedom for all others that you claim for yourself. Or, act in such a way that the good you seek for yourself you seek for others as well. No double standards. The regulative principle is equal treatment of similar cases. We met this as deontological ethics. Here the assumption for justice is that the right thing to do—our duty—is to enhance human freedom and take responsibility for our actions. Not surprisingly, this notion of justice prizes fairness and embraces universal rights. Rights and fair play respect, frame, and protect human freedom.

To this camp of justice-as-fairness, Sandel adds another, the free-market libertarians. For them justice consists in upholding the choices made by consenting adults. Respecting voluntary choice is the way justice as maximum human freedom is upheld. A laser-like focus is on the human subject, the doer of the deeds, and his or her capacity to make unconstrained or minimally constrained choices, then take personal responsibility for them.

Sandel's examples of the fairness camp and the free-market camp nicely illustrate what we noted for justice as maximizing human welfare. Arguments flourish within each school about what best embodies its broad notion of justice. The fairness and free-market camps don't mean the same thing even when both begin and end with human freedom and understand justice as the exercise and enhancement of that freedom. Different moral narratives divide them.

The third school focuses on personal and collective virtue. What kinds of people do we strive to be in what kind of society? What qualities should be internalized as the body politic's identity and bearing? What "excellences" of character mark the good society and citizen? The cultivation of heart, mind, and soul matters most. Integrity is a prime mark of the good life as it was for Glaucon. Our choices and actions accord with the kinds of people we are and seek to be. A just citizenry is the key to the good society and the good life.

Sandel sorts through these orientations and notions of justice, from antiquity to the twentieth century. He shows their pertinence for the issues every society faces, and he highlights the important differences within schools that otherwise share the same focus—human welfare, freedom, or virtue. Finally, following his ethical critique of the contending schools, he offers his own preferred theory in a chapter titled "Justice and the Common Good." It underscores the human community as the matrix of justice and identifies the essential topics of common-good justice: citizenship, sacrifice, and service; equality, solidarity, and civic virtue; and a politics of moral engagement. He is explicit about his preference for a "civic" or "republican" notion of freedom over the "liberal" or "free market" one. The latter protects an individual's rights to choose and pursue his or her own values and ends, while respecting a similar liberty for other persons. Civic freedom, by contrast, is more demanding: "To be free is to share in self-government and shape the forces that govern collective life. This requires citizens to possess certain habits, dispositions, and qualities that orient them to the common good rather than to self-interested concerns." Differently said, citizens must have "a tie to the community whose fate is at stake."[37] Free-market justice ignores the constitutive importance of the communal matrix of life, while common-good justice recognizes the degree to which our lives are inevitably a shared undertaking in a shared world. While Sandel's is a mixed theory that draws from all three basic notions, it is also a coherent one attuned to his analysis of present needs. By his lights, it's The Justice We Need for The Ethic We Need.

Were we to continue the kind of analysis of justice theory that Sandel undertakes, but include his proposed theory, we might say the following. Both the classic notions and his own proposal suffer a grave omission. Like the justice theories he finds wanting, Sandel's alternative also fails to account for the primal goods that make possible any and every common human good. While his theory focuses on the common human good, the goods of the planetary commons upon which every human good depends seem morally to count very little. Why, just as in the three classic notions, are the goods of nature evidently assumed by Sandel, then apparently ignored as needing no justice-attention and no justice of their own? Why does the ecosphere disappear while the collective human ego remains front and center? In an era when the goods of the planetary commons are in jeopardy at human hands, that omission undercuts everything any justice must have as its own material base. Given the cumulative

impact of planetary human power, it also omits a massive arena of human responsibility. Thus Sandel, too, is trapped in the profound Western dualism of
humanity and nature even when that dualism seems disallowed by all the
empirical evidence that both the story of evolution and the present "hot, flat,
and crowded" planet affords. Were that dualism not so destructive of the very
commons shared by the whole community of life, disengaging the human so as
to concentrate on abstracted human justice might not matter. But because
such abstraction and bifurcation is globally destructive, justice theory needs to
be reframed in ways that grant all life and its generative elements their due,
which is the very heart of justice. Sandel's own proper focus for justice—the
common good—is severely compromised by a constricted notion of the community (of life) for whom justice is due.

Justice theory as it now stands, in all but most indigenous communities,
generates a relationship of alienation. It renders external to the self that which
is inextricably a part of one's very existence and it makes a fellow subject an
object, relating to her, him, or it as an external entity only. Whether the cause
is indifference, ignorance, exploitation, dismissal, or rejection, the other is
distanced and objectified despite that fact that self and other are bound to
one another in a shared existence. Where intersubjectivity and mutuality are
called for, alienation defines the relationship.[38]

Sandel's book cover accurately images the volume. Disembodied human
heads are arranged to spell out "JUSTICE." The absence of the primal elements
in Sandel, together with the absence of an understanding that the community
of life is more than the disembodied species on the book's cover, is morally
justified only if the material reality upon which we wholly depend is itself morally irrelevant, only if other life and what gives rise to and sustains it do not
matter for moral theory and justice theory. But since we are at the top of the
food chain, ought not our present moral universe be upended so that what first
counts are life's essential elements? Does not the very possibility of justice
between humans, and between humans and other creation kin, start with the
health—quantitative and qualitative—of earth, air, fire, water, and light? What
life is there apart from the health of the biotic and abiotic together as the ecosphere? And why should the ecosphere, of which we are part and parcel from
well before birth until long after death, be object to us rather than subject?

Our justice theory, then, critiques the representation of justice in the dominant Western traditions as well as Sandel's personal proposal for justice adequate to our present circumstances. But it cannot stop there. Ethics has a
constructive task and not only an analytical one, so it is incumbent on us to
offer an alternative.

Let's call it "creation justice." It could also be called "restoration justice," provided that includes ecological restoration. The land, an ecosystem, a watershed, a crippled forest and its life, a mined-out mountain range and those who live with the scars—all these receive their due, are restored at the hands of those who have done egregious harm. It might be ecological restoration, such as the restoration of healthy habitat downstream from mining or factory farming, where water and ground have become toxic. It might be the restoration of bodies of water and their life, together with their dependent human communities, when these have been damaged by oil "spills" or the dead zones created by pesticide and herbicide runoff. Or it might be slowing, then reversing, further ocean acidification.

Restoration isn't enough, however. Creation justice is also the nurture of practices that prevent harm in the first place. An agriculture that builds topsoil rather than sending it downstream and that integrates animals into the biodynamic upbuilding of the land; manufacturing processes that avoid toxicity; energy generation from renewable and nonpolluting sources; food that does not sacrifice nutrition to profit.

Creation justice of this kind would be justice theory with a moral vision that reaches across the community of life and includes its primal elements. The question of what soil, air, water, and energy require for their own regeneration and renewal on their own terms would be a justice question, not only a scientific one. The question whether there are biotic rights and animal rights, that is, whether more than humans hold a legal claim to a healthy environment, would be a justice question. The question whether future generations of both human and other life—*all* the children—have claims upon present generations would be a justice question. The question whether there are certain "ecological" virtues crucial to human character formation itself would be a justice question.

Or, if we shift from justice and virtue and justice and rights to justice and duty, the outcome might be another categorical imperative in the manner of Kant. Douglas Sturm's version is this: "So act within the circumstances at hand that the life of the entire community and each of its participants might, so far as possible, flourish."[39]

More examples of changes could be given, but enough has been said to establish that this is an altered and expanded notion of justice. Here a moral vision different from the ones framing both the classic notions of justice and Sandel's shapes justice theory—the moral universe encompasses more citizens than we hominids. While the range of moral theory and vision is the same— virtue, obligation, ends and consequences—the substance is different.

Creation justice is not bereft of antecedents. Indigenous peoples across the globe have tried their best since the onset of colonization, conquest, and the Industrial Revolution to say that the community of life's own integral functioning was being violated by foreign notions of justice and human organization that did not recognize that peoples and their lands were inextricably linked together. Mother Earth and Father Sky were under assault by forces alien to their ways, but in the end Mother Earth and Father Sky would prevail. They would "bat last," so to speak. Yet had the creation justice of these communities been acknowledged, and had their own Earth-honoring faiths been given their due, damage of apocalyptic proportion to both peoples and their lands might have been avoided.

Communities embracing creation justice did not all end in apocalypse. Even when they did, not all their treasures were lost. Riches survived, some of them whimsical, even comical, though painfully poignant. *The Animals' Lawsuit against Humanity* is a thousand-year-old "animal rights" tale penned in Arabic by members of a Sufi order in the region of Basra, Iraq. The Islamic "Order of the Pure Brethren" sponsored the *Animals' Lawsuit* as treatise twenty-five in an encyclopedic set of fifty-one essays on the mysteries and meaning of life. Later, in 1316 C.E., the *Lawsuit* was translated into Hebrew by Rabbi Kalonymus ben Kalonymus at the behest of a Christian king, Charles of Anjou, who also had it translated into Latin. The story became popular in the nineteenth and early twentieth centuries, especially in European Jewish communities, where the Hebrew version was translated into Yiddish, German, and Spanish. The recent English version was adapted by two Jews and a Christian and illustrated by a Muslim woman from Pakistan in the employ of a Saudi princess.[40]

No summary can do justice to the witty exchanges of puzzled horses, snorting oxen, rumbling elephants, spitting camels, oddly agreeable mules, flighty birds, patient frogs, and the others as they bring their pointed lawsuit before Bersaf, King of the Spirits on the Isle of Tsagone.

Tsagone, in the middle of the Green Sea and part of the Kingdom of the Spirits (or, in some versions, the Kingdom of the Birds), was an island on which the animals lived "long, long ago . . . free from the persecution by human beings." No human had ever visited Tsagone until a great storm upended a passing ship whose sailors were tossed into the sea close enough for a swim to Tsagone's beaches. They lifted their eyes to heaven in gratitude to God for their salvation, then looked around to discover they were stranded in a lush "land of innocence" where none of the animals were afraid. "A golden opportunity if I ever saw one," says the sailor Tama. "We can be kings here! We can rule this place, and make our own way. God blesses us!"[41]

The sailors do rule, substituting animal slave labor for human toil until "the beasts were filled with awe and dread" and beg for mercy, not least because some had also become savory meat. In due course the animals rally together and take their complaints to King Bersaf the Wise, "pure and honest, God-fearing and shunning evil, hospitable to guests, a defender of the poor, merciful toward the unfortunate, a dispenser of gifts and charity, far removed from oppression, despising iniquity, opposing villainy with great conviction and with great anger—there isn't another like him in all creation!" The virtuous King "grew green with inner rage as he heard [the animals'] sad tale." His sense of justice severely offended, he sent his messengers to gather the animals and the humans to the king's court for a trial. "No life should undergo such abuse. These humans have lost sight of the life within you," he tells the animals.[42]

The animals themselves are clear about their due. "'Justice!' exclaimed Ox. He shouted again and again, 'Justice! Justice! We deserve Justice!' And the beasts began to chant together. A slow rumble turned into a towering thunder of voices, 'Justice! Justice! Justice!' Their hearts began to rise as they felt the solidarity of their purpose; hope began to ascend in their eyes, and they ventured off to the King's Court together."[43]

From there the tale proceeds as a winsome study of human and other animal nature carried out in court exchanges, with running commentary or questions by the king and his sages. Each animal notes the odd features of the others: Why a long neck and big body, small ears and a short tail for the camel, but a long beard and no fat tail to cover its bony nakedness for the goat? Why big ears attached to a little body for the rabbit? "You don't even understand the basics!" interrupts Mule, who goes on to argue, in effect, for the ways of natural selection long before Darwin: "God . . . made each of us in a particular shape to give each species a specific advantage."[44]

The long exposition of each species' genius, punctuated by differences of opinions among the animals, doesn't deter them from making a common case in the presence of the Spirits in the king's court. Curiously, the animals don't regard humans as inherently evil, despite the animals' considerable suffering and sacrifice (as dead meat) at their captors' hands. Like other species, humans, too, have a particular and appropriate bodily form in accord with their habitat. Nothing more should be made of it than that, however. Mule explains: "The Creator did not create humanity in an upright form as proof that they are lords. Nor did the Creator make our bodies bent over as a sign that we are slaves. Rather, the Creator did this in wonderful wisdom, making each body in a form most suitable to its environment."[45]

How Bersaf the Wise rules in the end I leave the reader to discover. I include only the beginning of the long song composed to honor the outcome, the joint offering of the Nightingale and Hochmah the Wise Woman:

> Let the seas sing out in thunderous voice
> While the sky and the earth together rejoice
> Let the mountain peaks chant a joyous song
> And the rivers clap hands, a happy throng.
> When the great forest trees dance and sway,
> Hear what the wild winds have to say.[46]

The ensuing pages retell the whole tale in song form as "what the wild winds say," ending with credits ("music by Nightingale; lyrics by Hochmah[47] Human") and King Bersaf's closing speech and blessing.[48]

In his introduction to the *Lawsuit*, Muslim eco-theologian Seyyed Hossein Nasr asks his own creation justice questions, aimed at a present-day audience: "What are our rights over other creatures and what are the limits of their rights? What about the rights of animals? What is the goal of human life and what is our role vis-à-vis the rest of God's creation while we seek to attain that goal?"[49] Answers to such questions are, for him, both urgent and practical: "These are questions of momentous import at a time when human beings have adopted modes of living totally out of harmony with the natural environment and a way of life based on complete disregard for the life of other creatures, a way of life which has made modern human beings an endangering and at the same time an endangered species."[50]

The *Animals' Lawsuit* is remarkable in its own right, as well as delightful, eye-catching, and wise in the way good children's books are. It is not idiosyncratic, however. With other such treasures, it belongs to one of the broadest and deepest of all religious themes: a vision of paradise as creation's flourishing. In religious lore, music, and scripture, life is always a crowded, satisfying affair that exudes abundance. Moreover, images of creation's flourishing and the planet as paradise are coupled to an understanding of justice that issues in creation's redemption. Justice is due creation, and its doing yields shared abundance. This is the common storyline and the moral narrative. But the retrieval of forgotten treasures and the rereading of sacred scriptures and traditions for the present ecological moment has only begun. The "endangering species" (Nasr) has good work to do.

As we return to justice theory per se, a point made about moral theory bears repeating. Like moral theories, justice theories abstract from the richness of human moral experience in order to achieve clarity about that experience and to point to what is at stake in different perspectives. Such theory-work may help us decide what counts most—human welfare, freedom, the kinds of persons we are, or the requirements of and for life itself. Yet, to say it again, while maps are vital aids for showing us the way, they are not the territory, and we live in the territory. Justice theories, then, are not discrete, fixed-menu choices. We err badly, with the character and well-being of society at stake, if we organize all eco-social goods and their institutions around a single abstracted concept (like market freedom, for example). Sandel is right to draw from several traditions in order to create a richer version appropriate for our time. We suggest the same but with a critical addition—that which is due the ecosphere itself.

Such work as this—laying out notions of justice and assessing them—illustrates critical and constructive ethical reflection on human morality. That belongs to the broader discussions of moral theory, moral vision, and justice theory that have developed in varied traditions with different notions of what most counts as the good life. These discussions are, in effect, extended arguments about ways of life and how they are to be lived. They illumine our agreements and disagreements with one another even when theory and vision cannot, of themselves, banish the kind of conflict that arises from differing life orientations.

We can add that the best learning medium for moral theory and justice theory is rarely theory itself. We said earlier that the most important ethic is rarely written. It is layered in a culture and its institutions, woven into its habits and rites, and learned via multiple media: a good constitution, the catechesis of a good upbringing, the presence of persons who are worthy of imitation, iconic experiences, well-run institutions, and preserved, conserved, and cared-for landscapes. It might also be a good story, like *The Animals' Lawsuit against Humanity*, or a good song ("If I had a hammer . . .").

Next . . .

The decades ahead will engage deep change. Vaclav Havel has guided our initial efforts to think about the change entailed in the profound transition from modernity to its successor. In the background was Darwin's wisdom: "It is not the strongest of the species that survives, nor the most intelligent that survives, but the one that is most adaptable to change."

The same backdrop of change and forced options continues as we turn from moral theory, moral vision, and justice theory to community as the matrix of morality.

6

The Ethic We Need

COMMUNITY MATRIX

You should come home, Amir jan. There is a way to be
good again.
—*The Kite Runner*, Screenplay by Daniel Benioff

Community

While birth already finds us fitted out with rudimentary moral instincts, most morality is ensemble work, a community enterprise and achievement, in keeping with the prosocial creatures we are. Anomie, normlessness, chaos, and drift leave us restless because we are by nature relational beings who know that the only life we have, and can have, is life together. Our natural condition is not, per Hobbes, the war of each against the other and all against all. Our natural condition is a shared instinct to create coteries and communities held together in no small part by moral rules, some of them laws backed by force. Conservatives and others are wrong in saying that religion is indispensable for social and moral order. But internalized norms and public rules of behavior—shared mores and morality—*are* necessary for society, with or without religious sanction. Community virtues, values, and obligations are not arbitrary constraints on individual choice and impingements of freedom—that's the quintessentially adolescent "take" on morality. They are—morality is—"the precondition for any kind of cooperative enterprise"[1] at all. There is no community life apart from morality, and there is no moral life apart from communities.

The need and desire for ecosocial relatedness is inborn. By nature we insist on community, even if that community is a trench-coated gang or a teen clique. We're community beings. Symbolic consciousness allows all manner of influential communities to inhabit the "is/ought/how" world: real communities, imagined ones, or, most often, combinations of the two. Moreover, in the modern world, daily life is typically intersected by several communities. We're multiply situated selves for whom home, work, education, recreation, our circles of friendship, and the sources of material provision such as food and clothing are rarely the same cluster of people at the same address. We live in overlapping communities that we carry with us.

Yes, individuals often rise above the moral level of their communities— they are not simple community clones. Recall the life principle that "to be is to be different." But their self-identified morality will be their particular twist on materials provided by their own or other communities.

The word "conscience" makes the point nicely. Often defined as the still, small, individual voice within, its etymology strikes another chord. Both "conscious" and "conscience" ("con" and "scientia," *con + sciere*) mean "knowing together," "knowing with," "knowing in relation to," or simply "joint awareness." Conscience is the expression of personal moral character, and character is formed in community. In conscience the emotional and the mindful are linked to the ethical as the expression of a community's way of life. Even the moral daypack we may be born with is the evolutionary outcome of antecedent communities of belonging. This is community in multiple dimensions, from parent-to-child and friend-to-friend to community as broad as the horizon and as expansive as a backyard enveloped in stars.

Religious traditions have long assumed that communities are essential to the life of faith and morality. They have also assumed that community's scope is as close as the neighbor at hand and as boundless as creation. For Hindus the whole world is a single family—*vasudhaiva kutumbakam*. For Buddhists the *sangha* (community, assembly) expands to encompass the four directions and all beings. Muslims interpret the *umma* (Muslim community) so as to include all who have oriented their lives toward God (Allah). Jews honor the covenant with Noah as a covenant with all peoples together with "every living creature of all flesh" and Earth itself "for all future generations" (Genesis 9). Christians, as noted, appropriated the image and language of *oikos* to envision the whole inhabited Earth as an ecumenical, ecological community.[2] And community for indigenous peoples normally includes the whole environment, both biotic and abiotic, in the places they have lived in for a long time and held sacred.

But what are the communities we need for new first works? What kind serve the Great Work? What does ecological civilization ask of us?

Some things are elementary. We know what most people want: a faith to live by and a grounded moral life in a world that adds up and fosters their survival and interests. Basic needs must be met—food, shelter, clothing, meaningful work, security, festivity, and song. Such needs cannot be met apart from communities, human and more-than-human. Helplessness, loneliness, and poverty are all inimical to well-being and meeting basic needs.

Coupled to such needs is the most fundamental need of all, beyond sheer survival—biosocial and ecosocial bonds in committed relationships. That need creates communities and sustains them. It does so by way of a dynamic intrinsic to our nature as moral creatures: Our lives are only realized and fulfilled by caring for that which is more than us but of which we are inextricably part. When glimpses of human wholeness arrive, they do so in the openness of our lives to others and their lives to ours. Meeting their needs as they meet ours, giving and receiving with some measure of reciprocity—this is the core of what fulfillment we experience. Included is sacrifice for the communities that sustain and nurture us, whether family, neighborhood, and nation, or soil, air, water, and fire. Fostering biosocial and ecosocial bonds in committed relationships, in order to survive and thrive, is the way genuine living happens.

The same holds for communities themselves. They only live well by reaching beyond their immediate and seemingly defined borders, whether family, clan, ethnic group, city, or country. Howard Thurman's observation is wise: "Community cannot feed on itself; it can only flourish with the coming of others from beyond, their unknown and undiscovered brothers."[3]

For an individualistic culture of material excess, casual waste, and casual relationships, the necessity of this kind of strong and open belonging is not intuitive or assumed. Self-absorption fed by nonstop advertising and so-called "social networking" has a stronger hold than collective commitment. The "happiness literature" of recent years is a corrective. Here is a summary.

Since 1950 or so, the story line for the industrial-technological era has grounded human fulfillment in material abundance. Whether the system was capitalism or socialism, pursuing happiness via consumerism was the strategy. In the famous 1959 "kitchen debate," then U.S. vice president Richard Nixon and Soviet premier Nikita Khrushchev argued over who would "bury" whom with abundant consumer goods, providing a cameo moment. In due course capitalism won hands down, thanks in part to one of history's finer ironies—Communist China's embrace of turbo-capitalism. On a smaller scale, Vietnamese Communists bled the great "container" of Communism, the United States, of blood and treasure, then took on capitalist ways as well.

Up to a certain point, there is a positive correlation of material well-being and happiness. If you are abjectly poor, you need to *have* more to *be* more. Basic needs of food, shelter, clothing, meaningful labor, security, festivity, and song must be met if people are to experience well-being.

Yet for affluent nations and affluent strata within poorer nations, a fat bank account and high levels of material possessions prove a weak substitute for genuine well-being. Out of hope and habit, goods as *the* good are turned to over and over again in one shopping spree or another; but the yield is not contentment. A sense of fulfillment is expected, but not realized. At some point economic growth tops out in its capacity to meet the spirit's relentless needs, and levels of happiness do not improve with improved standards of living. Consumer remorse may even set in as a new house or car, moving to a nicer climate, and collecting labor-saving devices in every room have about as much pay-off as a golf cart has on the golfer's score or a new pair of running shoes has on lung capacity. With telling insight Tibor Scitovsky calls this "mature" consumerist economy "the joyless economy."[4]

While sages have long said that money cannot buy happiness, the additional surprise for affluent societies is that some have actually experienced a decline in social well-being even as consumerism continues to rise. Why? Robert Lane, in *The Loss of Happiness in Market Democracies*, hypothesizes that there "is a kind of famine of warm interpersonal relations, of easy-to-reach neighbors, of encircling, inclusive memberships, and of solid family life. There is much evidence that for people lacking in social support of this kind, unemployment has more serious effects, illnesses are more deadly, disappointment with one's children is harder to bear, bouts of depression last longer, and frustration and failed expectations of all kinds are more traumatic." Lane comments: "Something has gone wrong. The economism that made Americans both rich and happy at one point in history is misleading them, is offering more money, which does not make them happy, instead of more companionship, which probably would."[5, 6]

Companionship, that telltale sign of committed relationships, is external to market economics and accumulated goods. It cannot be priced, bought, or sold. To continue, then, to look for happiness and fulfillment in getting, spending, and having is delusional, once poverty has been addressed and an ample cupboard has banished fear about the next meal. Ed Diener and Martin Seligman sum it up this way: "The quality of people's social relationships is crucial to their well-being. People need supportive, positive relationships and social belonging to sustain well-being. . . . [T]he need to belong, to have close and long-term social relationships, is a fundamental human need."[7] "The primary good that we distribute to one another is membership in some human community,"[8] Michael Walzer says in his discussion of justice. Martin Buber uses still grander terms: "The primary aspiration of all history is a genuine community of human beings."[9]

Wisdom about what truly counts is never wholly lost on us, however misdirected we may be. What most counts comes home to us with some regularity, frequently in those circumstances when our lives or the lives of loved ones are threatened—a fire, a flood, a disease, the death of a friend. It comes clearest as we grow old. Ask any gray-hair how she or he would like to be remembered. The answer is never "I became far richer than my friends" or "I fooled a lot of people at their own game" or "I left many good people behind as I crawled over them to the top" or "I had the highest IQ in the class and outsmarted them all." The retrospection of old age, like most eulogies, appeals instead to moral character, yet one more sign of how engraved with morality our biosocial nature is. People want to be remembered as good friends, fathers or mothers, generous spirits who did well by the community and blessed it with their presence. They want to be remembered among those who gave of themselves for a good that will outlast them. They want their lives to continue in the lives of those who follow after.

What else do we know about community and morality? We know community is indispensable to moral formation. This is nicely mirrored in some key terms. "Conscience" has already been mentioned. Our sense of obligation is weak without conscience. So the question for ecological civilization is whether conscience registers loyalties, affections, and responsibilities that include other animals, land, sea, and sky.[10]

Now add to conscience another quintessential moral word, "character." Like "ethics," "character" has a Greek root. *Charaktēr* literally means "engraving tool" and by extension the mark made by the engraving tool. Metaphorically *charaktēr* came to mean the distinctive marks of a person. Character bore his or her qualities as these were "engraved" as habits of the heart and personality.

Later, a second meaning evolved: If a person is a person "with character," she or he displays moral integrity and good judgment. He is judged a "good" person, with courage to do the right and the good. Or she has moral stamina and exhibits moral consistency and coherence over time. Here "character" means not only the moral personality of a person, whatever that might be, for good or ill; it refers to laudable moral qualities as the mark or stamp of a person. He or she "possesses" character.

While to untrained ears character can sound individualistic, it is not, though it is deeply personal. The moral being of a person or group (groups have character, too), however distinctive it may be, comes via life in community: relationships form character. Although all of us are disposed to morality by birth, the specific contours and qualities that develop as our own are nurtured and shaped through the dynamics, substance, and influence of community relationships. For the young, it is especially communities of first belonging, communities of intimacy, those communities that heard our borning cry and first words. These "engrave" character and set it on its way. Specific, continuing, and changing relationships, including our relationships with other-than-human creation, are the soil of character formation. No "I" springs fully formed from the brow of Zeus. The self, as Buddhists emphasize, is temporal, contingent, and relational.

In sum, conscience is the ethical compass of character and character is formed in community, as our convictions and commitments are. There is no conscience-gene. We may be disposed to be moral creatures by virtue of a biosocial and ecosocial nature that dreams of a better world, but none of us is morally finished at birth. "Community and commitments, and the trials thereof, grow people up," says Richard Rohr,[11] pointing to culture, community, and the way our life is organized as the matrix of moral development and maturation.

The community or communities may, as noted above, include imaginary ones. We dream of worlds that are not yet but might be, and we usually have some plans to see them happen. This "is/ought/how" gap fuels the moral life, supplies its drive. Yet even the furnishings of imagined communities are elaborations on furnishings we already know or entertain; and that, like the No. 2 yellow lead pencil, is the gift of others, humans and other-than-human. A moral tabula rasa doesn't exist. The moral life is never created ex nihilo.

Moral development can go awry, of course, from a normative point of view. "I wrestled all night with my conscience," Jacob Burckhardt is said to have announced to his friends one morning, "but I won." Who doesn't win? Unshakable belief is not, by reason of its strength, truth. Communities of longing and belonging have frequently fed hungry spirits with a militant idealism that turned destructive. *Religio*, a "uniting bond," may rally the masses and intensify their fervor with the conviction that a whole cargo of cosmic meaning supports their imperious resolve. The ensuing crusade may be horrific, complete with inquisitions and beheadings. Often such religious passion is matched only by secular moral conviction held with religious intensity, like Communism and fascism. Which is only to say that nothing, not conscience, collective character, ideology, or worldview, is exempt from the measure of a moral plumb line. Nothing gets a free pass, even the noblest endeavors. For all communities, "ethics" judges "morality."

If we know what people want deep down—to survive, belong, and flourish— and if we know that community is the matrix of human character and conduct, what, to return to our earlier question, are the communities we most need now? What conscience, character, and conduct are most fitting? An answer requires a closer look at recent communities of moral formation, how they have fared amid what kind of biosocial ecology, and how they might now respond in healthy and helpful ways for the sake of a renewed order.

Civil society

In the modern era, most communities of moral formation have been associated with "civil society," that "set of relational networks" that fill a "space of unco-erced human association."[12] Families, schools, synagogues, churches, mosques, temples, and all manner of voluntary societies and nongovernmental organiza-tions, together with communications media and social networks, belong to civil society. Cultural production, family life, the work of voluntary organizations, and much public discourse are all at home in civil society.

The civil society communities that perhaps shape human character and conduct most thoroughly are those that influence us during the years from birth to early adulthood. For most people the basic lines of character are nor-mally in place by age twenty-five or so. If their day-to-day conduct changes much thereafter, it is usually because of changed circumstances, habitat, and roles, rather than markedly altered character.

Civil society communities most formative of character typically share history, memory, and a common story. They assume some continuity of rela-tionships and place, with a more or less stable (that word again!) environ-ment for "growing people up" (Rohr). Relational chaos and high mobility, if absent carefully crafted moral havens, militate against moral development and maturation.

Civil society also offers a place of high participation to community mem-bers from all ranks and with diverse gifts. (Many communities assign strict roles and "place," however, creating a static and oppressive order with its own morals sheriff and posse. High participation isn't a guarantee of justice.)

Civil society has a history that affects the communities traditionally asso-ciated with it. The fate of modern moral formation belongs to that history. Makers of the modern world, like Adam Smith, assumed that the reliable institutions of civil society would effectively form character and prepare the citizenry for the rough-and-tumble of public life. Smith, a moral philosopher, opens *The Theory of Moral Sentiments* with his view of the social nature of the moral universe itself. "How selfish soever man may be supposed, there are evidently some principles in his nature which interest him in the fortunes of others, and render their happiness necessary to him, though he derives nothing from it except the pleasure of seeing it."[13] We are so constituted that the welfare of others is necessary to our own. The health and joys of our own spirit, as well as our moral duty, reside in community.

Mutual well-being isn't a given for Smith, however. Even though "some principles in [human] nature" press for it, virtues, values, and obligation must be learned and supported. Since Smith is especially concerned that other-regarding responsibility be nurtured, his advice is that each person "endeavor, as much as he can, to put himself in the situation of the other, and to bring home to himself every little circumstance of distress which can possibly occur to the sufferer."[14] This anticipates what scientists discovered later among many mammals: We learn sympathy through empathy, with empathy arguably the most basic moral sentiment of all for social animals.

Smith always considered *The Theory of Moral Sentiments* (1759) the necessary complement to *The Wealth of Nations* (1776). He never trusted market morality as a morality for society at large. Nor did he think civil society's communities should be organized on the terms of the economy. "Economic man" was not the whole "man" but only the individual when trundling off to "truck, barter, and exchange."[15] Moreover, "economic man" was driven by a deception, the deception that happiness and fulfillment came with success in the marketplace. It was nonetheless a fruitful deception, Smith argued, because it "rouses and keeps in continual motion the industry of mankind."[16] Old age would reveal the emptiness of possessions, he went on, even if society as a whole was well served by ambition and reward.

Smith was also aware that the emerging economy's habilitation of material desire could father moral corruption. As Alan Wolfe notes, it is the "great founder of capitalist economics" who says that a "disposition to admire, and almost to worship, the rich and the powerful, and to despise, or, at least, to neglect persons of poor and mean condition, though necessary both to establish and to maintain the distinction of ranks and order in society, is, at the same time, the great and most universal cause of the corruption of our moral sentiments."[17]

But not only did Smith not trust market morality as a morality for society as a whole, he did not conceive of capitalist *society*. He never spoke of "the market" but only of "markets." The market is a notion of things to come, with market behavior largely determining culture and the tenor of civil society itself. Smith by contrast envisioned and applauded a capitalist *economy* within society held together by noncapitalist moral sentiments nurtured by the robust communities of civil society. He certainly considered self-interested actions a virtue for generating wealth, and he viewed self-interested calculations as the proper way to make economic decisions. But economic morality was not to determine society and culture as a whole, nor was it to be the primary shaper of collective character and conduct. "The economy" was not to colonize noneconomic lifeworlds. Rather, familial and other face-to-face relationships associated with companionship and the ways of small towns had their own crucial task of domesticating ambition and desire and holding in check the urges to self-indulgence and gratification. In a complicated social ecology, these communitarian relationships would foster nonmarket virtues that would cultivate empathy and extend social responsibility. Social responsibility would in turn keep the potentially corrupting ways of commerce and self-directed economic choice from substituting for and poisoning the common good. Responsibility, directed to mutual well-being, would in fact channel market energies so as to serve the common good.

In yet another twist, Smith even contended that moral sentiments in the form of nonmarket values were essential for good market activity, though market activity did not supply them. Honesty, discipline, thrift, cooperation, keeping one's word, hard work, and deferred gratification are not initially learned on the job. While good work might value and nurture them, they are first learned elsewhere. Yet they are as crucial to business as new technologies are. For Smith, civil society funded corporate moral culture rather than the reverse.

The moral bottom line for Smith, then, was that religion and the family, together with other institutions of civil society, had the task not only of reigning in the appetites and providing a counterweight to acquisitive individualism but also of nursing a whole set of virtues necessary for an orderly moral life amid modernity's restless change. He assumed several things: the existence of civil society distinct from the sector organized by economic principles and "industry"; the existence of face-to-face communities of moral formation as a vital part of civil society; and the moral work of these communities as indispensable to society as a whole, including the emerging economy that was so effective in generating "the wealth of nations."[18]

Smith was hardly alone. Many other Enlightenment thinkers pondered human control of desire and the passions. Deadly religious wars in Europe brought the resolve to find less destructive ways to channel human drives. Economic activity in the form of the emerging economy of capitalism offered promise. Since all people desire to improve their condition, might not the pursuit of individual private interest, if properly regulated, be the psychological force that nonviolently aligns human interests and fervor? Might not "capturing a market" be more attractive and beneficial "than looting a village"?[19] Might not the strong human drive of self-interest, if channeled to the increase of material well-being, be blessed and seen as legitimate rather than sinful?

Alan Wolfe's *Whose Keeper?: Social Science and Moral Obligation* tracks the fate of Smith's, and the Enlightenment's, social ecology. "Capitalism lived its first hundred years off the precapitalist morality it inherited from traditional religion and social structure,"[20] Wolfe writes, referring to medieval and Reformation Christendom. Capitalism then proceeded to live its second hundred years "off the moral capital of social democracy,"[21] a reference to the economic reform movements of the nineteenth and twentieth centuries. Precapitalist communities taught self-restraint, charity, and an organic sense of society. These were a brake on the acquisitiveness gaining ground everywhere among the rising bourgeoisie and a check on the justification of limitless accumulated wealth. Then about the time the traditional religious, family, and community bonds were weakening under the impact of industrialization, social democracy supplied moral energy and substance. Social democracy's sense of solidarity, its concern to protect the weak and neglected together with the unemployed, and its vision of the common good—these joined efforts to discipline private power with public power (the state). Thus did movements of social democracy, such as government programs to address social dislocation and unemployment, together with union organizing and immigrant self-help organizations, take the hard edge off the inequalities and neglect generated by the market. (The memorial to Franklin Delano Roosevelt in Washington, D.C., nicely captures the ethos and moral substance of social democracy.)

Two notes supplement Wolfe. First, social democracy, too, drew from the legacy of the traditional communities of moral formation that Smith and the Enlightenment assumed would continue. The very rhetoric of these movements—unions, immigrant self-help organizations, and reform coalitions such as the suffragettes and abolitionists—was communitarian and even familial. Members greeted one another as "brother" and "sister" and invoked the spirit of family struggle and celebration. They echoed the tone and Pentecostal enthusiasm of religious communities and often functioned as a substitute church for many. A strong faith and ardent hope were at home here, as was quasi-religious enthusiasm. This was a throwback to the intimate relationships of intact communities. Second, important to both social democracy and the traditional moral communities Wolfe associates with medieval and Reformation Christendom were Jewish communities in Europe and the "New World." Jews, both observant and secular, were influential in social democratic movements in ways disproportionate to their numbers. They had a keen sense of social justice, forged strong alliances with other minorities, and fostered bonds of solidarity across class lines.

Thomas Bender's *Community and Social Change* describes what happened next. He cites Edward Ross's prescient report from the late 1800s. "Powerful forces are more and more transforming *community* into *society*, replacing living tissue with structures held together by rivets and screws."[22] The industrial world—"rivets and screws"—was on the move, and communities associated with place were being transformed into ones heavily influenced by the worlds of business, government, mass transportation, mass media, and metropolitan living. Society was becoming a gathering of interdependent strangers who shared a common but largely anonymous and disconnected life. And—this is key for communities of moral formation—markets and the state were far more able than local communities to coordinate the existence formed and impacted by fast-moving interdependence.

Traditional communities that had shared history, memory, and a common story were being upended by what Karl Polanyi called "the Great Transformation" that left feudalism in ruins and created modernity via industrialization and the creative power of the new capitalist economy. The Great Transformation broke apart settled communities and triggered mass migration.[23] Its rationalization, mobility, and transformation of all things into commodities for market exchange destroyed the kind of long-haul communities that created identity and story on the basis of generational solidarity and a shared sense of place. Communities glued together by tradition could not withstand the mobility of labor and capital required by the new economy. Nor could they withstand the fascination of the new worlds this economy opened to those who would climb aboard. If members of these settled communities were to get with the program, they would have to move, both literally and figuratively. To be free came to mean being "on one's own."

In a word, traditional communities of moral formation were rooted, precapitalist communities, and the new economy undercut their stability together with their values, their dreams, and their longstanding organization; in short, their way of life.[24] What was happening was a further transformation, "the second bourgeois revolution." Essentially, this post-Smith capitalism meant that industrial-technological modernity as calculating market logic within democracy as interest-driven association triumphed as a culture and as society itself. Smith's assumption that communities of moral formation could be safely tucked within society as formed from *both* market *and* nonmarket moralities no longer held. The second bourgeois revolution denied what the first deemed necessary—noneconomic ties of trust and solidarity as a related but separate sector. Rather, the second revolution said that all society and its decisions can be fashioned and executed in the manner expressed by good economic actors—with the calculation of self- and group interest in relationships that are fundamentally instrumental in character. It doesn't matter whether the domain is family, politics, or temple, rational self-interest is the one language everyone not only understands but can apply to all decisions and actions.

Gary Becker, a Nobel laureate from the Chicago School of economics, is clear he is departing from Smith when he argues that individuals are all "utility maximizers" who operate from a relatively consistent set of personal preferences. Maximizing utility provides "a valuable unified framework for understanding *all* human behavior," as well as a framework for our moral decisions.[25] Quite apart from direct market exchange, market behavior and logic supplies all the guidance needed for the thousands of decisions we make. "The market" as a way of life replaces "markets" as only a sector of society. Market morality is a consistent "use" morality that, together with its doctrine of human nature, contrasts with Smith's refusal to extend the logic of self-interest into noneconomic territory. Becker straightforwardly says that market principles and logic comprise a mental process "applicable to all human behavior."[26]

Becker's view has won the day, although he mirrors rather than invents the notion that the world is at the disposal of self-interested individuals and groups who make and unmake relationships in accord with utility. Value resides in the subjective choices of sovereign groups and individuals and nowhere else.

In different language, all goods, including social goods, are commodities in a picture of the good life as one of "choice" and "opportunity." Human fulfillment comes about through the autonomous choices by which individuals and groups fashion their own worlds. Citizens are entrepreneurs, producers, and consumers in the first instance, and the market is both the means of assuring a fullness of choices and the source of the logic of choice itself. Indeed, once market morality includes civil society, all that society truly requires is market-like savvy and governments that protect space for it. Then what Ronald Reagan called "the magic of the market" can work its wonders for society as a whole. This is capitalism as a way of being and not as an economic form only. Society is built up from the economy, in keeping with the economy's ethos and morality, an ethos and morality of utilitarian expediency. Or, to repeat what we said earlier, this is modern culture as calculating market logic within democracy as interest-group formation and interaction. This is also the form the industrial paradigm and its moral world took after the collapse of the socialist alternative. The drift was from having a capitalist market economy to becoming a capitalist market society.[27] Not least, this remained in place for "eco-modernity" (see above) despite the shift from the mechanical to the ecological as "new wine" language. The colonization of lifeworlds by the economy was complete. Whereas for Smith the economy was embedded in social relations and nonmarket morality, for present modernity and eco-modernity social relations and morality are embedded in the economy.

If we bring ethical analysis to this triumphant morality, we tally a triple loss. First, interest-group associations substitute poorly for communities of basic moral formation. Consequently, society suffers too few first-level moral resources for life together as interdependent strangers on a crowded and diminished planet. Lacking healthy, home-grown base communities of moral formation, such as stable, intact families, schools, and neighborhoods, modernity does not reproduce the moral character it needs for its own existence. "Utility maximizers" do not readily cultivate sufficient empathy, nor does self-interested calculation generate sufficient fellow feeling. Neither do utility maximizers learn the kind of social responsibility that affirms sacrifice for the common good, once self-interest is blessed to justify the unlimited accumulation of wealth. (To think "the magic of the market" will create the common good from the self-interested utilitarianism of sovereign choice really *does* require belief in magic.)

Stunted democracy is the second loss. Two of the classic democratic values—equality and community (fraternity)—are neglected, if not forgotten, by the second bourgeois revolution. Liberty as freedom in and for an "ownership society" is the single value needed and promoted. President George W. Bush's second inaugural address can be taken as emblematic. The synonyms "liberty," "free," and "freedom" are used forty times in a text of three-and-a-half pages. "Equal" is used once, "community" not at all, though there is an assumption that individual freedom creates community and a unified and morally exemplary nation. The moral investment is all in freedom as "the only force of history" that can "break the reign of hatred and resentment and . . . reward the hopes of the decent and tolerant. . . . There is no justice without freedom, and there can be no human rights without human liberty." To his credit, President Bush, like Adam Smith, includes attention to private moral character as crucial to this freedom. "In America's ideal of freedom, the public interest depends on private character—on integrity, and tolerance toward others, and the rule of conscience in our lives. That edifice of character is built in families, supported by communities with standards, and sustained in our national life by the truths of Sinai, the Sermon on the Mount, the words of the Koran, and the varied faiths of our people."

The goal of private (and public) character is "the ownership society," a goal in keeping with the second bourgeois revolution. "To give every American a stake in the promise and future of our country, we will bring the highest standards to our schools, and build an ownership society. We will widen the ownership of homes and businesses, retirement savings and health insurance— preparing our people for the challenges of life in a free society."

The president is also aware that humans need to belong to a community that surpasses their present moment and present wants. Yet that membership, too, rests in the free choice of sovereign individuals. "You have seen that life is fragile, and evil is real, and courage triumphs. Make the choice to serve in a cause larger than your wants, larger than yourself—and in your days you will add not just to the wealth of our country, but to its character."[28] All in all, it is clear that democracy is wholly invested, from a moral point of view, in free-dom/liberty as *the* truly determinative value—and sometimes the only one. Democracy as the democratizing of economic, social, and political power for the sake of equality and community is all but abandoned. Not least, the classic democratic understanding of freedom, namely, freedom from oppression and rule by others, is largely abandoned as well in favor of freedom as market free-dom. The American Dream is ownership. The determination of society by the economy is complete.

A look at the fate of economic equality confirms this. In the United States in 1987, the top 1 percent of taxpayers received 12.3 percent of all pretax income; but by 2007, only twenty years later, the share of the top 1 percent had nearly doubled to 23.5 percent. The share of the bottom half fell, in the same period, from 15.6 percent to 12.2 percent.[29] Wealth, as contrasted with income, is even more dramatically unequal. The top 1 percent in 2007 con-trolled 40 percent; twenty-five years earlier it was 33 percent.[30] In practical terms this means, writes Joseph Stiglitz, that "the more divided a society becomes in terms of wealth, the more reluctant the wealthy become to spend money on common needs. The rich don't need to rely on government for parks or education or medical care or personal security—they can buy all these things for themselves. In the process, they become more distant from ordinary people, losing whatever empathy they may once have had. They also worry about strong government—one that could use its powers to adjust the balance, take some of their wealth, and invest it for the common good."[31] Yet to lose empathy and the common good, albeit in the name of freedom, is to forfeit democracy itself.

This concentration of wealth has gone global. The richest 1 percent con-trol 43 percent of the world's assets; the wealthiest 10 percent have 83 percent, and the bottom 50 percent control hardly any capital at all.[32] It's a case of the global rich and the rest. Given the enormous influence of capital in funding business, charities, and other not-for-profits, as well as influencing the political process, this means that economic inequality rules, even in many democracies. Richard Wilkinson and Kate Pickett may well argue, in *The Spirit Level: Why Greater Equality Makes Society Stronger*, that more equal societies fare better on most every count—less crime, less infant mortality, less discrimination, less social conflict, better health, and longer lives—but given the distribution of economic power, their argument cannot prevail.[33]

The third loss is nature itself. A devastating neglect of nature and its requirements, matched to unprecedented wealth, are the "strongest" marks of modernity as the triumph of free-market magic. Here an irony surfaces: "Free riders" are scorned by capitalist industrial orders, yet these same orders are saddled with a free-rider problem they barely recognize. "Free riders" are those who consume more than their share of a public resource, or who shoulder less than their fair share of its costs. Because market logic treats nature as essentially worthless apart from human interest, human labor, human demand, and human use, citizens living the industrial-technological paradigm all freeload off the ecosphere. They do not pay the full costs of either its goods or its services.

In different words, much of nature is treated as economic "externalities." Economic externalities are the indirect negative (or positive) side effects of economic acts that are not included in the price. So, for example, a valuable good such as coal-generated electricity is produced, but the smog, acid rain, and global warming also produced are not factored into the cost. While public health, along with the air, land, and water, may suffer, utility rates don't include the cost of that suffering or its amelioration. In short, the same kind of capitalism that undercuts stable communities of moral formation fails to internalize all the real costs of production and to replenish resources and habitat for present and future generations of human and other life. Left to itself, capitalism is a freeloader on welfare (nature's) and nature is the loser, big time.

Market and state

But what has taken the place of civil society's traditional communities of human moral formation? We noted that these communities were simply not up to the task of morally coordinating the existence and impact of millions, now billions, of interdependent strangers who share a "globalized" life on a dynamic, but contracting, planet.

Two great institutions have stepped in—the market and the state. As models of society itself, market and state—or Big Economics and Big Politics—have, in effect, become proxies for the moral work that traditionally fell to civil society.

They suffice, many argue. Society on the model of the market can muster most of what is needed, and society on the model of the state can do the rest, if one includes governmental action at local, regional, national, and international levels.

It is easy to see why so much moral hope has been dumped into the ample laps of market and state. Positioning the moral life in local communities of face-to-face relationships cannot serve mass society very well, however personally fulfilling such intimate communities would be for most people. Other agents will have to do what society must: regulate behavior and address our obligations to one another as gathered strangers who occupy planetary space together and share limited resources under constrained but interlocking conditions. Since our daily habits touch lives far removed from us—persons and lands we never see and do not know—and since their habits reciprocate, we need frameworks and mechanisms civil society does not readily provide. How, other than by way of the global economy and the state, will we act and decide in ways that achieve a global good and hold us accountable for it?

Nothing can match markets, for example, in creating a spontaneous and dynamic order from millions of independent, decentralized decisions. Neither a network of communities nor the state can by conscious decision begin to match the market's ability to allocate resources. It utterly charms its worshippers and critics alike with a degree of order and efficiency independent of human goodness, government coercion, or even extensive knowledge.[34] Markets have astounding self-organizing capacities. Yes, there are critical shortcomings in the present arrangements (the freerider problem is one). But these can be addressed and, in any event, good order and efficiency are themselves desirable moral goods.

Moreover, the vigor of capitalist markets coordinated with a democratic polity has already proven itself morally. It has released millions from the grip of command economies and societies, from feudalism and aristocracy to communism. In the process it has fostered creativity and extended freedom. This is as much a moral achievement as a political and economic one.

Nor, many would claim, should unprecedented wealth be disparaged as a moral achievement. Granted, its benefits could be done in by destabilizing inequalities, plundered nature, and the spiritual vacuity of consumerism as a way of life. The future may see heightened conflict as too many people compete for too few essential resources. But since what is not produced cannot be distributed, to have gained the capacity to solve the classic economic problem of sufficient production of needed goods and services is without doubt a substantial moral achievement. The task is to address the downside of wealth creation without destroying the means.

Markets, then, do important moral work, and the state has corrected many of their shortcomings. Government has been a counterforce to the injustices put in place or left in place by the economy—poverty, unemployment, homelessness, extremes of wealth and income, the disruption of close communities. It has also used regulation and relief to temper the negative fallout of market "externalities."

In a word, modernity and eco-modernity, having lamed many traditional communities of moral formation, turned with considerable effect to market and state as moral proxies. Some of this was sheer necessity: No other instruments seemed able to address the mass conditions of transformational change in a restless world on the move. Thus government at various levels provided the means to subject citizens to the rule of law and subordinate individual loyalties to a larger good and a more inclusive framework of responsibility. In parallel fashion, the market took the infinite number of disparate choices people made and created a coherent order. Market and state together delivered needed goods and services and they did so in a way that avoided the oppressions of command economies.

But unfortunately the marriage of market and state, Big Politics and Big Economics, like many modern marriages, hasn't worked out—unless one is enamored with the kind of ripsaw capitalism available to an authoritarian command economy under the direction of the Communist Party—the China model. But assuming a preference for more freedom and some combination of genuine democracy and capitalism, we have to confess that as moral proxies, market and state have come up short.

For all their benefits, capitalist markets not only lived off the moral capital and natural capital of earlier centuries, they failed to effectively replace the depleted capital of both the ecosphere and moral community. This has meant the development, quite against the official ideology, of elaborately bureaucratized and expensive societies. Why? Because society could not handle in the more informal ways of face-to-face intact communities the array of problems every society faces when the bonds of belonging are atomized and society's moral base is thinned to a veneer of what it is needed. The supposedly freest society then becomes one of the most litigious; and regions known for their no-holds-barred, deregulated individualism, such as the Los Angeles basin, turn out to be regions strapped with innumerable regulations and regulators. Fully against its own intentions, the political form of the second bourgeois revolution is professionalized interest-group bureaucracy assailed (and funded) by professionalized interest-group lobbies. Capitalist society becomes oddly bureaucratic and armed with lawyers because the market fails to provide a widespread, grassroots moral guidance system powered by trust and confidence.

The sheer cost of this is staggering. If it is mildly true that crime does not pay, it is true with a vengeance that societies suffering the breakdowns that stem from moral anorexia face a long list of expensive socio-environmental problems. Adequate protection and security; the price of enacting and enforcing laws and regulations aimed to check abuse and corruption; the reality of substantial subsidies for privileged sectors in business, government, and industry; the social-welfare check for family breakdown (domestic violence, unwanted children and spouses); the cleanup costs for willfully violating the environment; the environmental costs to nature and health of externalizing many production and consumption costs; the costs of first failing to develop alternatives to dirty fuels and then the cost of putting alternatives in place; the loss of public revenues through cheating on taxes; the homeland security and military costs of fearing the global neighbors—these only begin to tally the cost of neglecting conscious attention to robust moral community.

Curiously, the state as model for society and moral proxy suffered much the same outcome as the maximally deregulated market. If we take the decades of state-sponsored socialism as an example, we note bold efforts to provide comprehensive moral formation. These states dictated the substance of education, including moral education. They learned that they needed to supply what all human societies require, that is, rites and rituals for human passage: for birth, puberty, marriage, retirement, and death, together with a string of socialist "holy" days, heroes, saints, and martyrs, all complete with special observances. They designated the forms and recipients of charity and tried on all fronts to face the full range of human needs. They reached farther into family life and the monitoring of voluntary organizations than any previous governments. They told farmers how to farm, teachers how to teach, doctors how to doctor, and writers how to write. It was perhaps the most comprehensive effort ever made to institutionalize moral obligation under governmental auspices. It also failed on a scale commensurate with its own bulk and reach. Most ironic of all, this kind of socialism did few things as badly as socialization itself. "Growing people up" (Rohr) via biosocial and ecosocial bonds in committed relationships that had a real purchase on heart, mind, and soul— this it failed to do. Evidently that takes a different kind of moral community than the state provides, necessary though government and governance are for life together.

Cold War conservatives knew where the fault lines in socialism's moral experiment lay. Their bible, Friedrich Hayek's *The Road to Serfdom*, said it well. Hayek held in disdain any state that peered into the nooks and crannies of citizens' lives and led them by the hand (Hayek's colleague and admirer, Milton Friedman, famously called this the "nanny state"). But the gravest loss is not the one Nixon and Khrushchev argued over—who would lose the consumer wars. Rather, Hayek says, "The most important change which extensive government control produces is a psychological change, an alteration in the character of the people."[35] Wills are softened and peoples' energies are enervated and stupefied "till each nation is reduced to be nothing better than a flock of timid and industrial animals, of which government is the shepherd."[36]

What Hayek and conservatives overlooked, however, is that the market, too, if extended as the model of society itself, "produces . . . a psychological change, an alteration in the character of the people." It does so in quite a different way, by reifying markets so that they seem to belong to some natural state, as though God created them. Markets and "the" market are human constructs at each and every turn. They are subject to moral assessment and choice at every level and are the outcome of those choices. This is obscured, however, and social relations are mystified by "the magic of the market" and the options "markets" present! Human choices embodying human values are then defended as economic "necessity" and the outcome of some supposed unchanging human nature. (Aren't we all utility maximizers?) Here the sense of personal moral responsibility and agency is also dulled and deflected. This might be considered a different version of the "flock of timid and industrial animals" Hayek feared, since reified free markets numb people's sense of their own moral agency, responsibility, and accountability. Then, when things go badly, the regulations, instruments, and institutions that were so carefully constructed and taken advantage of by those with the power of privilege (for obscene salaries and "windfall" bonuses) are considered "too big too fail" and must be rescued—by government no less!

That capitalist conservatives, by subjecting all life to the morality of the corporate bazaar and then treating it as a force of nature, join central-command socialists in dumbing down personal moral agency, responsibility, and accountability is another fine irony.

In sum, market society, with its impersonal efficiency and reliance on imperious egoism, and state society, with its impersonal social policy and reliance on imperious bureaucratic responsibility, have both failed to reproduce the moral base they needed in the citizenry, just as they both failed to deliver what they both promised—the common good. Neither mustered the very morality it depended upon—social solidarity, loyalty, trust in authority, civility, and consideration in human relations, to say nothing of empathy, compassion, faith, hope, and love. While the history books rightly record that democratic capitalism won and central-command socialism lost as economic and political systems, from the point of view of morality, the socialist experiment was a worse-case scenario of moral deficiencies that capitalist societies shared. Cold War competitors depleted the souls and soil of both nature and community.

There is another moral angle on this. The Big Economics and Big Politics of modernity and eco-modernity consists of thinking without thanking. Martin Heidegger's reflections on technology and modernity led him to search for some other kind of thinking than the utilitarian, calculating thinking of the industrial age. Devoid of empathy, sympathy, affectation, communion, wonder, praise, and any heartfelt love of place, modernity's thought would only bend the world to an alien end and leave the soul an arid place. Heidegger reached back to some common ecological roots. The German *denken* (thinking) is kin to *danken* (thanking), just as, in Old English, the noun for "thought" is *thanc*, which is a grateful connection to others. The language of nurturing and communion, with a sense for life as a gift, should shape our thinking (Part II of this book pursues this).

Faced with the double depletion of souls and soil, and in pursuit of another kind of thinking, Nobel laureate Octavio Paz wrote an essay on "Poetry and the Free Market" in 1991 that prefigures the Fourth of July address of Havel we cited earlier. We reach for a "re-beginning," Paz writes, "the resurgence of buried realities, the reappearance of what was forgotten and repressed," a return to origins. "Now that the cruel utopias that bloodied our century have vanished" the time has come "to begin a radical . . . reform of liberal capitalist society" and of the impoverished nations on the periphery.[37]

In sum, the twenty-first century will need to develop other ways of enacting moral formation and obligation than those represented by society-as-market and society-as-state. Big Economics and Big Politics are worthies that have not cultivated sufficient moral substance either by way of the market's rational quest of individual and collective self-interest or the state's coercive external authority. Both have exaggerated the role of artifact over organism and engineering over the kind of slow growth across generations that moral formation requires. Both have been captured by the morality of expedient utility and a master-slave treatment of nature. The question is not whether there will be markets and governments and whether they will have important moral roles; they will. But they cannot do what only more intimate, personal congeries of committed, organic relationships can. What they have done, in a negative vein, is diminish people's sense of moral agency and responsibility for the planet's elemental health. They have substituted either the rules of market transactions or the rules of policy and law for the moral capacities and struggles that have to be learned as moral freedom in the company of others, including strangers. So modernity's question, including eco-modernity's, is still left largely unanswered, despite the valiant efforts of market and state as moral proxies: How do we muster the perspectives and practices by which we come to know and live the far-reaching moral consequences we ourselves create through unprecedented, cumulative human power?

Communitarian and associational ties

The question doesn't land in the same place it arose. Another transformation has occurred, one that complicates, if not displaces, national efforts to meet moral requisites via the work of efficient markets and the state as a conscientious moral force. In the United States, for example, there was, in Michael Sandel's words, the attempt "to expand the scope of democratic institutions to catch up with the scale of economic life."[38] The effort was to shift political community and citizenship from small, local forms to national political association in tandem with a vibrant national economy, and it was in part successful— the New Deal of Franklin Roosevelt and the Great Society of Lyndon Johnson, for example.

But now the economy has gone global and once again outgrown the forms of political community. Economic supply lines and structures of power, technology, finance, and information all spill over national boundaries, and populations find themselves without democratic authority to regulate this global economy. Some hope that global philanthro-capitalism will address the continuing social problems. Bill Gates, Warren Buffett, and the international billionaires' club of generous givers are looked to for leadership. Policymaking billionaires and philanthro-capitalism, however, cannot of themselves supply what Sandel thinks necessary: a sense of global community with grass-roots moral substance. And without that, how "will governments and institutions of civil society be able to generate support for human rights initiatives, for international relief operations, for global environmental accords, and for attempts to regulate the effects of unfettered global capital markets?" Sandel asks. Not "by a kind of commercial, popular American culture," he adds. That falls short of the cosmopolitan global ethic needed and does not form the character and conduct it requires.[39]

So how do we collectively effect a global ethic? Sandel places his hope in the remnants of civil society. A cosmopolitan ethic with global reach will not succeed "unless it recognizes that most the time we live our lives by smaller solidarities. It would be a mistake to think that we can restore self-government simply by pushing sovereignty and citizenship upward."[40] In an important sense, then, an ethic of smaller-scale neighborly space matters *more* in a globalized world, not less. "The global media and markets that shape our lives beckon us to a world beyond boundaries and belonging, but the civic resources we need to master those forces, or at least to contend with them, are still to be found in the places and stories, the memories and meanings, that situate us in the world, that give our lives their moral particularity. . . . The task for politics now is to cultivate these civic resources, to repair the civic life on which democracy depends."[41]

Sandel's is a good start. Civil society does continue to exist and its communities are indispensable. We continue to experience communitarian connections of affection, friendship, voluntary action, family, faith, and education. We are also "joiners" with associational ties to all manner of formal and informal organizations offline and online. While the settled, intact, traditional communities of precapitalist days are still under assault or largely gone, the combination of communitarian and associational ties in their present form holds promise. What needs to be done can be done in small-scale communities of committed relationships tied, with the help of digital connections, into larger networks—communities of communities. We can learn trust; temper both individualism and deflected responsibility as moral styles; agree to freely serve; hone leadership skills for work together; have and raise children; learn to give to charities; volunteer for dirty, difficult, and unpleasant jobs; clean up after ourselves; restrain appetites; take out the garbage; help friends; care for siblings, parents, children, relatives, and friends; learn to return books to the library; observe meaning-giving traditions; receive and internalize all manner of moral direction, including basic moral rules and social etiquette; find out by increments what moral responsibility means from childhood up; develop qualities of character; practice decision-making; acquire a moral language; nurture moral sentiments and sensibilities; take responsibility for a pet, plant, or sibling; recover from serious mistakes; find our first models of behavior in the world around us; treat the rest of nature as kith and kin; recycle, reuse, and renew; craft organizations for transitional and transformational change at various levels; and learn to forgive and start anew. In short, we can discover in microcosm how the bewildering world works and how to find our way in it.

While such examples only begin a very long list, the tally shows what communities of communitarian and associational ties can do that national states, international treaties, and markets, including global markets, do less well. Again, this is not to set one over against the others, but to complement. Modernity's grand moral experiments—market and state as moral proxies, now tied to planetary culture—have extended moral obligation to millions of people in ways local communities could not and of themselves cannot. They rescued significant populations from the whims and crude injustices of entrenched local ways of life, in the process transforming traditional behavioral patterns and setting them on a new level of dignity and respect. They advanced human rights and extended the franchise. Of late, millennia of patriarchy and homophobia have also been significantly chipped away by modern currents running counter to the instincts of traditional communities and their social conservatives. The gains of the civil rights movement as written into new law was mentioned earlier. It, too, was the battle of the state against entrenched racist elements of tight local communities defending their traditional way of life.

No one, then, denies that modernity and eco-modernity have earned worthy moral capital we wish to keep—individual freedom, human rights, critical thought, tolerance, a large role for voluntary associations, and an awareness of planetary damage that has elicited ecological thinking and practice as a massive planetary movement. These have become part of the moral endowment we draw upon. But of themselves they do not "do" sufficient moral formation. Nor do they, of themselves, create the communities that do. Tolerance doesn't forge strong commitments to the other's well-being, human rights aren't the means of falling in love, and individual freedom isn't of itself a tie that binds. Ecological thinking is no doubt recognized as indispensable now but it, like the others, can be adjusted to fit the industrial paradigm and the master-slave ethic; indeed, it has been.

Communities that live by communitarian and associational ties and do the kind of growing people up we cited above are, then, the necessary complement of market, state, and globalized culture. Alan Wolfe says these communities provide "a kind of trial heat" for the more difficult business "of taking the perspective of future generations, responding to the needs of strangers, or learning to live within diverse cultures."[42] They certainly are a trial heat, but they are much more. They are a decades-long training program as well.[43]

An important word of caution is in order: "Community" as the matrix of the moral life is no more a model for society as a whole, and no more likely to succeed, than market and state are. Local and intimate communities can be as unjust and tyrannical as any others, and have been. "Family" and "home," indispensable as they are, are frequently the first mentors of injustice, even violence. Moreover, such community as this can make exactly the same mistake as market and state: It can acculturate to modernity/eco-modernity at too high a price. Then it, too, fails to exit the industrial-technological world we have and make the mandatory transitions to an ecological age. If moral formation for the Great Work is to happen, it will need transformed, not traditional, communities of moral formation. A return to either Adam Smith or Karl Marx will not avail us, giants of insight though they were.

The discontinuities we face are too severe, and the driving systems of modernity/eco-modernity too inept, for market, state, and civil society to successfully meet the challenges of our collective historical turning point. All major sectors will be part of the efforts at new first works but none, as it stands, is viable as the way forward. Cherished old wineskins will not do.

All this adds up to two assignments. We must meet certain "adaptive challenges," and we must create "anticipatory communities" as part of the successful negotiation out of the fossil-fuel interlude. These anticipatory communities will necessarily include communities practiced in death and renewal as life's deep rhythms, communities that wash all things in gratitude and contrition, in forgiveness and re-beginnings. Doing what we do presently, only more efficiently, will not suffice because the self-organizing capacities of global markets are in fundamental conflict with the self-organizing capacities of ecosystems New wineskins are needed. These are classic religious themes, and in later chapters we will turn to the contributions religious communities bring to these tasks. For now we finish with the recognition that civil society, market, and state in a globalizing world will face what Ronald Heifetz, in *Leadership without Easy Answers*, calls the "adaptive challenge."

Adaptive challenges

For Heifitz, meeting adaptive challenges in hard transitions entails "creative deviance on the front line."[44] Because much conventional wisdom now proves dysfunctional and doesn't move to the second and third levels of change we discussed earlier, creative deviance on the front lines of a way of life, amid the major institutions and systems people live in and by, is more promising.

This undertaking is made possible through a unifying vision worked out by diverse parties willing to suspend the conventional wisdom for collective imagination and creativity. To recall our levels of change, such cooperation happens with changes of vision at the level of cosmology/worldview.

The leadership to meet adaptive challenges often comes from the foot of the table. It arises with dissenters and entrepreneurs who have known for a long while that the prevailing arrangements have not served well. Market leaders represented by large, entrenched corporations generally have too much to lose to take the risks needed for creative innovations that might put them out of business. Some do show creative direction, however, through innovative pilot projects that can happen at their company's edge without risking its center.

But whether the leadership comes from the foot, sides, or head of the table, those who initiate change frequently do so in the form of the "anticipatory communities" we will meet in later chapters.

Multiple experiments are encouraged for successful adaptation, with innovation arising from a number of constituencies, not just the professional experts. Professionals may also be innovators, however, as might those presently at the head of the table. Recall Havel's insight that creativity arises from diverse constituencies addressing the experience of discontinuity.

Finally, a new unity issues from the joint action of many parties. This draws upon the capacity of civil society to elicit high levels of participation among different bodies making common cause together (again Havel: the "mixing and blending of cultures, and a plurality or parallelism of intellectual and spiritual worlds").[45, 46]

One of Heifetz's examples of a local community meeting an adaptive challenge nicely combines civil society, market, and state. While the example doesn't create communities of basic moral formation, it does show how existing elements of civil society, market, and state can begin to reshape morality in incrementally helpful ways. That, too, belongs to The Ethic We Need.

William Ruckelshaus, head of the U.S. Environmental Protection Agency (EPA) in 1993, had to resolve a conflict. A copper plant near Tacoma, Washington, was a major polluter. It was also a major employer, with an annual payroll of $23 million. Jobs, the local economy, and public health were all at issue, as was treatment of the land and atmosphere. Under the Clean Air Act of 1970, Ruckelshaus and the EPA had the authority to decide the plant's fate. But Ruckelshaus declined to use this authority and instead insisted on a decision process involving the community at large. He explained with a quotation from Thomas Jefferson: "If we think [the people] not enlightened enough to exercise their control with a wholesome discretion, the remedy is not to take it from them, but to inform their discretion."

Going beyond the law's requirements for hearings, the EPA organized a series of public workshops that included plant workers, union representatives, local citizen organizations, and environmental groups. The format provided participants with education about plant emissions, incidence of disease, and the local economic implications of various possible courses of action, as well as time for prepared testimony and open deliberation. What the community eventually decided together was not in the minds of Ruckelshaus, local EPA officials, or the citizens themselves in their various organizations when the process began. The collective decision was that Tacoma's economy needed to diversify and that this process must include retraining for present plant workers so as to wean the community from dependence on the offending smelter. The community had decided for itself what it wanted collectively for the future.

Heifetz identifies several principles at work here. First, Ruckelshaus identified the gap between the reality people faced and their aspirations. It was their "is/ought/how" gap. This confronted them with their "adaptive challenge." Second, in facing this adaptive challenge, Ruckelshaus helped regulate the level of distress that emerged as difficult issues were confronted by parties with differing stakes and biases. He did this by providing a structure that let people educate the EPA and one another ("inform their discretion") in the course of a well-paced deliberative process. Third, he devised a strategy that shifted responsibility for describing the problem and offering solutions from the EPA to the primary stakeholders themselves—community members collectively. Within the boundaries of the law, yet somewhat outside the box, Ruckelshaus had relocated authority and trust to the community, along with responsibility for creative actions. It was a nice example of recruiting the better angels of human nature in a setting ready-made for armies of lawyers, costly legal battles, and alienated constituencies.[47] It was also an example of strengthening those local communities where the moral substance of a successful cosmopolitan ethic must have its roots.

This example may appear small-scale, even trivial, given the large-scale character of the Great Work. But the Great Work will also need thousands of small-scale examples, fashioned from the inside. Indeed, most contributions will be small in this way, yet large in their accumulation. Small changes, multiplied enough times, accumulate to tipping points.

A second and more far-reaching example touches upon first works. The adaptive challenge in this case was severe: It was to reconstruct life amid the destruction of war and the ashes of a defeated nation—Italy in 1945. But the default options—reforming and rebuilding either prefascist or fascist institutions—seemed neither possible nor desirable.

As a local effort at reconstruction, the Focolare Movement had started in 1943 as a group of women in Trent, Italy, around the leadership of twenty-three-year-old Chiara Lubich. The word *Focolare* is Italian for hearth or family fireplace and was chosen as a symbol pointing to the reconstruction of life by a small group around an intimate center and energy point—the experience of the love of God. Roman Catholic in origin but now an interfaith outreach and committed to living all of life in the light of the Gospel, the movement has several million followers in more than 180 countries. Of particular interest for our economy/ecology concerns is a global economic project begun by Focolare members in Brazil: the "Economy of Communion in Freedom." The heart of this now dispersed, worldwide economy is business and finance dedicated to radical Gospel values in the workplace with a view to building a socially just and environmentally sustainable economic order. While the original inspiration is Roman Catholic sacramentalism with a strong sense of the mystical body of Christ, many Focolare members are not Catholic, and some are not Christian. Nonetheless, common principles and a shared sacramental spirituality permeate the Economy of Communion.

In the Economy of Communion enterprises operate within the free market, use numerous common business practices, and abide by business regulations. But they divide all their profits three ways: one-third to the poor, one-third for business reinvestment, and one-third for the moral formation of people in Focolare spirituality. As of 2003 there were 769 small- and medium-size businesses in the Economy of Communion network, in Europe, Latin America, North America, Asia, Australia, and Africa. Of the total, 194 were engaged in production, 156 in commerce, and 343 in services. Only ten have more than a hundred employees.

The Economy of Communion is reformist in that it lives by communitarian values within an economic order dominated by instrumental values. The effort is to bring religious-moral substance into the workplace as a community place, within a capitalist framework. Distinctive emphases toward this end follow, all of them a conscious outgrowth of Focolare spirituality. *Work* is viewed as co-creating with God. It offers both personal fulfillment and a means of community service. *Trade, finance, and industry* are oriented to communitarian ends, such as alleviating poverty and spreading the wealth. Debt is strongly discouraged, although low-interest microfinancing and other alternative financing structures have been developed in recent years. Trade, finance, and industry are not meant, in any event, to promote or bolster a consumer lifestyle. They are means to help create communities of material sufficiency and equality. *Wealth and possessions* are put at the disposal of the common good. Focolare members are encouraged to live simply, voluntarily offering any surplus resources to the communion of goods. Tithing is expected. A strong trust in providence ("God will provide!") has been a theme since the movement's. *Economic exchange* is viewed as a meeting of moral agents or "ethical actors." The market is appreciated and used for its efficiency but the social function of every economic encounter is communion: The rationale for economic exchange is building up human community in face-to-face exchanges among persons who take responsibility for themselves and others, much like the rationale for local farmers' markets in many locales around the world. *Protection of the environment* is part of economic activity itself, and is the object of both personal responsibility and corporate policy. Economy and environment are not conceptualized separately; together they belong to the eco-nomics of the commons. *Technological progress* is viewed positively when it expresses creativity directed to community well-being. The health of the community assumes a healthy economy and environment; both can be enhanced with scientific knowledge and appropriate technology.[48]

Focolare captures one community's efforts to undertake the challenges of new first works. It understands the critical role of moral formation on spiritual grounds and never separates this from conscious attention to the concrete practices of institutions that add up to a way of life. And all of it is measured by a comprehensive notion of justice.

Focolare's reconstruction was in response to the devastation of war and the unacceptable character of Italian prewar systems. Despite its relevance for present conditions it was not elicited by ecospheric crises. Transition Towns were.

The Transition Towns network emerged in the United Kingdom under the tutelage of permaculture designer Rob Hopkins. His hometown, Totnes, Northumberland, adapted his university-based work in 2005 and expanded it in 2006. It has caught on quickly. As of 2010 there are 300 communities recognized as Transition Towns in the United Kingdom and over 400 more in 34 countries, among them Chile, Australia, New Zealand, the United States, and Italy. Begun as local initiatives in response to climate change, peak oil, and (lack of) sustainability, the essence of the Transition Town concept is building resilience at the community level. Issues and concerns range widely, including sustainable local food production ("food feet, not food miles"), fostering a local economy with more equality, seeking an alternative to economic growth, creating high-energy efficiency from renewable sources, and aiming at the satisfactions of working together in community to tap sources of hope and address fears of local, regional, and planetary loss. Since these initiatives are local, they vary widely. Different communities work on different fronts. All are oriented to practical solutions, however, and all are shared via social networking and Transition Towns websites or ezines: for example, "10 First Steps for a Transition Town Initiative," published January 1, 2007, by *Transition Cultures*; and "Starting Out, Deepening, Connecting, Building, Daring to Dream" as free-of-charge resources for new efforts, available on www.transitionnetwork.org. "Bringing a New World to Life" is the 2011 theme for http://transitionus.org, the U.S. website.

In short, the Transition Towns movement is an example of socio-environmental and economic localization consciously exiting the industrial-technological paradigm in search of a viable grassroots alternative.

Joel Salatin's Polyface Farm is the final example of recreating grassroots moral community in light of the adaptive challenge of moving into an ecological age. Salatin, who calls himself an "alternative farmer" and a "Christian libertarian environmentalist" and who manages a truly "postindustrial" farm,[49] watches—and opposes—the takeover of farming as the industrialization of biological systems, including the "industrial organic" system of fossil-fueled corporate farms that mass-produce organic crops. One corporate enterprise, Earthbound Farm, grows 80 percent of the organic lettuce in the United States.[50] (Michael Pollan calls this "Supermarket Pastoral"[51] as chains like Wal-Mart and Whole Foods colorfully arrange fruits and vegetables to paint still-lifes worthy of a Dutch canvas.) Yet petroleum fruits and vegetables Salatin cannot accept, anymore that he can FedEx meat from "organic feedlots" across the county. Nor can he bring himself to raise "free-range" chickens that, after five or six weeks of confinement, are offered a little door leading to a small enclosed yard where they enjoy with gay abandon the last two weeks of their lives.[52] All these industrial organic meals are part of an industry, "the food industry," that fails to exit a paradigm which has morphed from "nothing succeeds like success" to "nothing fails like success." Ecological values like diversity, complexity, symbiosis, and interdependent relationships are crowded out by their opposites, the industrial values of specialization, economies of scale, mechanization, and biological simplification. Nature's logic proves no match for capitalism's and the old wineskins prevail. Unchecked, "every paradigm exceeds its point of efficiency," Salatin offers as a general rule, as though he knew the Chinese proverb that 400 years of efficiency will bring down any civilization. "The industrial paradigm in agriculture has come to the end of its workability," he continues, and there is less topsoil, less fertility, fewer species, and less life at the same time that new lexicon entries appear—campylobacter,

E-coli, mad cow, listeria, salmonella.[53] For Salatin, then, "the Fall" is the human hubris that reckons it can, and does, treat nature like a profit machine, grinding everything under its wheels for the sake of the bottom line.

But if such is the Fall, redemption is the kind of Darwinian pragmatism Salatin practices—that which symbiotically adapts to survive indefinitely on the sometimes changing terms of its own habitat. Peasant agricultural systems that managed to bring forth food from the same ground year after year after year without depleting the soil is one example. Salatin's "Polyface Farm" is another, a science-informed postindustrial way to read local nature and mimic it. It is also an effort at creating a moral community in his rural Virginia neighborhood, a community that is an alternative to the industrial paradigm and that of Big Economics and Big Politics.

Next . . .

The Ethic We Need requires not only reworking our conceptions of justice for a comprehensive creation justice, or reworking moral theory for different constellations of Earth-honoring virtue, obligation, and consequences. It means revamping communities of moral formation for renewed civil society as well as for new systems of economy and governance. The adaptive challenges will no doubt be very difficult, since we begin with substantial community deficits as well as the biophysical and geophysical constraints of a diminished planet. The list of challenges is long: the unsustainable nature of present agricultural practice as industry; capitalist economies out of sync with nature's economy; the destruction of indigenous cultures and peoples who lived "too close" to local nature and its rhythms; the breakdown of intact community and organic traditions; the disintegrative effects for society, psyche, and nature of living out the image of mastery and control as the primary image for human refashioning of the world; the mountains of debt incurred by maintaining civilization and paying for its infrastructure and debris, costs far exceeding those needed to build it in the first place; the immiseration of the growing urban poor and the evacuation of many rural areas in the manner of Appalachia; the movement of "environmental refugees" and "climagration" because the land, seasons, deluge, and drought no longer sustain populations where they have lived for decades, sometimes centuries; forms of oppression of women, many minorities, and Third World and indigenous peoples that arise from forces which extract local resources for export and oppress land, people, and the rest of nature together; and the onset, amid abundance itself, of frazzled nerves, anxiety, addiction, stress, rootlessness, fatigue, and depression as common diseases of the spirit.[54]

Not least, the adaptive challenges will entail a different notion of ourselves as humans, a "reinvention of the human at the species level" (Berry). The epigraph we chose for this chapter says it nicely: "You should come home, Amir jan. There is a way to be good again." Part IV of The Ethic We Need supplies more of the resources we need for this adventure of finding a way to be good again.

7

The Ethic We Need

TILLING AND KEEPING

History is replete with ecological disasters; the most
flourishing lands of antiquity seem to have been under a
malediction.

—RENÉ DUBOS, *A God Within*

IN THE EARLY 1970s famed microbiologist René Dubos joined other
prominent scientists to prepare a report for the United Nations titled *Only One*
Earth: The Care and Maintenance of a Small Planet. While this report pre-
dated the attention given to accelerated and extreme climate change, it did not
predate many of the trends graphed in chapter 2. The post–World War II
assault on nature was underway, "hockey stick" trends were everywhere, unsustainability was on track, and an eco-crisis was in place. Yet Dubos's point in
another work, "Franciscan Conservation versus Benedictine Stewardship,"[1] is
that regional ecological disasters belong to an even longer stretch of human
history; not all degradation is a product of industry. So Dubos begins "Franciscan
Conservation" with the Fertile Crescent, home to the great civilizations of
Mesopotamia, Persia, and Egypt as well as lesser kingdoms such as Israel.
Wealthy, powerful, and fertile for long periods of time, this was the cradle of
civilization and the site of epoch-making accomplishments—the domestication of plants and animals, writing, accounting, and great art and architecture.
Now, however, Fertile Crescent lands are among the planet's poorest, and their
most ancient cities are mounds of unforgiving desert. A time traveler might
well conclude that they had fallen under some spell of malediction.

Civilization and barbarism are not incompatible; the Fertile Crescent
found itself both the world's mentor and its cockpit. The "Five Horsemen of
the Apocalypse" that periodically ravage humanity—"climate change, migration, famine, epidemics and state failure"[2]—all had their day in the region, as
did warfare and civil strife.

Such causes do not suffice as explanation, however, apart from two specific factors—the depletion of fertile soils and the exhaustion of water sources. Both resulted from prolonged occupation of the same territory by relatively large numbers of people pursuing a particular way of life. Wars might cease and civil strife and epidemic disease might wane, but famished soils and water do not recover on the same timescale as the peoples who exploit them.[3] Bodies of water that have become salt and sand flats through human overuse do not miraculously revive as freshwater lakes, even in the wake of good rains. Nor does topsoil regenerate at the speed of human propagation. When large numbers of human beings live life at a metabolic rate outstripping the rest of nature's—when, in other words, humans fail to fit in on nature's terms—first other-than-human nature suffers and then, sure as death and taxes, people do.

We can draw several conclusions from the UN report and Dubos's chapter on Franciscan and Benedictine values in *A God Within*. They pertain to more than the post-1950 world; they brand settled human history as a whole.

First, all civilizations are mortal, with their well-being and/or decline linked to their stewardship of land, sea, and air. Circumstances may alter massively, as in the economic takeoff after World War II (see above). As a result, the whole planet is now impacted. Even forbidding places with no significant local human presence, like Antarctica, much of Greenland, and the northernmost areas of the Arctic, today feel the long reach of industrial carbon and its sea-changing effects. We share in the same mortality that marks all civilizations. And our longevity ultimately turns on the same factor: the relationship of civilizations to the very habitats that allowed and sustained their existence.

This implies that little-noticed continuities in the human/Earth relationship, whether local, regional, or global, may be as important and destructive as the harsh unveilings of apocalypse. Slow, subtle changes may be as momentous over the long haul as sudden dramatic ones. After all, the tipping point of a cataclysm almost always arrives as a small number—an additional degree or two of median temperature, one more day's rain on steep and saturated land, the silting or drying up of water sources for irrigation systems, a little more fertilizer runoff from each field bordering the river, the shift of the jet stream seventy-five miles north.

A second conclusion accompanies the first: We do well to scour the past again for lessons we ignore at our peril. (Think of works such as Jared Diamond's *Guns, Germs, and Steel* and *Collapse*. Both will be considered later.)

The third conclusion turns on human nature: We are identifiably the same kind of creature that has had a dicey relationship with the rest of nature in every locale. Human character has changed little since Homer. As we scour the past and trace continuity and discontinuity in our treatment of nature, do we garner wisdom about how we ought to live? Do the discoveries we make yield moral guidance for the present and future? Do we learn something sufficiently revelatory that at "the end of all our exploring" we return home only to "know the place for the first time"?[4]

It is certainly clear that human/Earth relationships have varied widely and the differences have mattered immensely. An "Infertile Arc" does not describe the fate of every Fertile Crescent. Some ways of living have been bright-line moments in history, hospitable to life and memorable for "man and beast" alike across long stretches of time.

Granted, such moral progress may compare poorly to the leaps in human knowledge and technological powers that now threaten the planet. There is truth in Daniel Maguire's comment that we moderns may be "morally prenatal" at the same time that we live "armed to the teeth" with weapons not only against our enemies but against the Earth. Our technology may have advanced beyond the capabilities of our morality to serve as its guide and taskmaster. So species drop around us "like canaries in a doomed mine" in the same moment that we split atoms and genes.[5] In any case, even hospitable ways of life fall short of Eden Reborn and Paradise Regained. Golden Ages long ago and far away never really existed, at least never as aspirin-free and delightful as their portrayals in literature and history. Such pictures of history owe more to the longings of the human heart and imagination than the data of experience. Rather, death and renewal have patterned life since time immemorial: never life without death, or renewal without struggle and pain.

From ego to ecosphere

We have been arguing for a seismic shift in the moral universe and in our industrial/postindustrial way of life. It is a shift from the encapsulated human self and human society to the ecosphere as center, boundary, and subject; from human justice to creation justice; and from my bounded human community to the unbounded community of all life. The first member of each pair—human self and society, human justice, my community—belongs warp and woof to the second—ecosphere, creation justice, the community of life. They can exist nowhere else. The reverse, however, does not hold in most modern mentalities and moralities. The state of the ecosphere, creation justice, and the comprehensive community of life is not lived as inextricably bound to the daily workings of human self and society, human justice, and my community. This failure of reciprocity is modernity's critical flaw. We have also argued for explicit attention to the primal elements—earth, air, fire, water—as morally significant. The materials of life have claims upon us for their well-being—and ours.

What we have not done, however, is treat the primal elements as the subject of explicit ethical analysis. While a full treatment would require another book, *The Ethic We Need* should at least show the makings of a sound approach.

We will consider earth as soil, the dust from which we came and to which we return. The aim is to demonstrate how integrally our lives, and all lives, are bound up with this primal element, and how a shift in moral theory and community might treat it as an indispensable subject of ethics.

Following these discussions we will finish our ethics primer with the most important "cairn" not yet visited—method in ethics. Method largely determines the shape of content. *How* we think, and with *what*, has the same definitive outcome for our morality as the sculptor working her clay.

The Fertile Crescent revisited

In 1942 the U.S. Soil Conservation Service distributed a report prepared by Walter Lowdermilk, the chief of its research division. Titled "Conquest of the Land through Seven Thousand Years," the report takes the reader to the Fertile Crescent and the beginnings of agriculture on the alluvial plains of Mesopotamia. To recall the biblical image, it was a land of "milk and honey." Or, if one consults the earliest recorded work of all literature, *The Epic of Gilgamesh*, a land of plains and cedar forests with abundant fauna. As Gilgamesh, a king who reigned sometime between 2700 and 2500 B.C.E., laments the death of his friend Enkidu, he sorrowfully sings of the land:

> May the bear, the hyena, the panther, the tiger, the leopard, the lion, the oxen, the deer, the ibex, and all the wild creatures of the plain weep for you. May your tracks in the Cedar Forest weep for you unceasingly, both night and day. May the Ula River, along whose banks we used to walk, weep for you. May the pure Euphrates, where we used to draw water for our waterskins, weep for you.[6]

The presence of megafauna, a large forest, the Euphrates running clear, is reminiscent of reports by European tribes arriving in the "New" World. The Passaic River, flowing through what is now Newark, New Jersey, is described as so thick with silvery Atlantic salmon they could be scooped up by people on the banks. Now the Passaic hosts some of the largest toxic waste sites in the United States. They are fenced in and under lock and key because health dangers await any trespassers.

But Lowdermilk's concern was the soils of the Middle East. His team studied the terrain of Lebanon, the Sinai Peninsula, and the famous ruins of Petra, Jordan, Syria, Cyprus, and North Africa. He didn't search out Greece in the same period, but if he had, he might have recalled one of the most famous passages of ecological history. Plato's account of archaic Greece in the *Critias* parallels what Lowdermilk found in the Fertile Crescent.

> What now remains of the formerly rich land is like the skeleton of a sick man, with all the fat and soft earth having wasted away and only the bare framework remaining. Formerly, many of the mountains were arable. The plains that were full of rich soil are now marshes. Hills that were once covered with forests and produced abundant pasture now produce only food for bees. Once the land was enriched by yearly rains, which were not lost, as they are now, by flowing the bare land into the sea. The soil was deep, it absorbed and kept the water in the loamy soil, and the water that soaked into the hills fed springs and running streams everywhere. Now the abandoned shrines at spots where formerly there were springs attest that our description of the land is true.[7]

Everywhere Lowdermilk went, he found similar results: washed-off soils, silted canals, meager flora and fauna, the ruins of dead cities. "Now that the soils are gone, all is gone,"[8] he concluded. A later Gilgamesh might have lamented the passing of his land as well as his friend.

Wes Jackson adds two matters to Lowdermilk's report. First, the Phoenicians, Greeks, Carthaginians, and Romans all established distant colonies when their homelands gave out. They consciously and sometimes brutally imported carrying capacity from elsewhere to substitute for what their own stewardship had destroyed. Second, these traders and colonizers were confident that human technological solutions would carry the day. Their elite would figure something out. Jackson quotes Cicero in what might easily have been modernity's bottom line two millennia later: "By means of our hands we endeavor to create as it were a second world within the world of nature."[9]

Lowdermilk returned to the United States to make what must have been a shocking announcement: The United States was on the same path as the ancients. He had gathered erosion data from across the country, only to find that soil was eroding faster than it was being generated. He warned the U.S.

government that ours was a "self-destructive agriculture," adding that, unlike the earlier solutions of European and other empires, no new continents were now available.[10]

An update of Lowdermilk's survey confirms the self-destructive course, except that now it holds for the planet as a whole. "Nearly 40% of the soils of the world are now seriously degraded," reports Jackson. "Globally, nearly one-third of the land devoted to farming has been lost to erosion since 1960 [recall our graphs in chapter 2], and continues to be lost at a rate of some twenty-five million acres a year."[11]

If Jackson is right about the ecosphere as the only truly creative force, if Aldo Leopold is right that "[h]ealth is the capacity of the land for self-renewal,"[12] and if Dubos is correct about malediction falling with certainty upon those who rob the soil of its fertility, we had best look anew at humans and humus. Change more profound than a better fertilizer or genetic modification or another large find of potash is needed. We turn to another angle on soil, this one religious.

The sacred 'neath our soles

A prayer of Henry David Thoreau goes like this.[13]

> Lord of skies, you walk among us
> in the plain brown soil of earth.
> How you've chosen to be present
> often seems of little worth.
> You have chosen common bushes,
> kindled them with heaven's fire,
> spoken through unlikely prophets
> heralding your love's desire . . .
> Heaven is under our feet as well as over our heads.
>   [Amen]

Ask a religious community this question: "What's the most important thing about being human?" Frequently the answer is, "We harbor a soul." For the follow-up question, ask, "Why is the soul the vital element?" The reply is: "The soul is our medium of contact with the sacred, and it animates life itself (*animus* is Latin for soul). We've got soul."

Both answers are correct—the soul is the animating element of our humanity and the way we touch the divine. But "soul" can also be spelled s-o-l-e. Where is our soul/sole? On the bottom side of bare feet, in touch with the sacred beneath our sole, the soil.

Soil and sole have always been in touch. So have soil and soul. Socrates knew about the latter. Here he is making the case for philosophy—he calls it "the art of dialectic"—to Phaedrus, who thinks philosophy a pastime at best. No, says Socrates, philosophy (the word means love of wisdom) is about sowing seeds:

> [A] man employs the art of dialectic, and, fastening upon a suitable soul, plants and sows in it truths accompanied by knowledge. Such truths can defend themselves as well as the man who planted them; they are not sterile, but contain a seed from which fresh truths spring up on other minds; in this way they secure immortality for it, and confer upon the man who possesses it the highest happiness which it is possible for a human being to enjoy.[14]

Socrates' analogy is correct: Soil and soul share a natural affinity. Both are living substances and to the degree that life "animates" them both, both lend themselves to cultivation, whether of immortal truth or new life.[15]

Among religions Jainism might understand soul best of all. Soul is *jiva*, derived from the Sanskrit root (*jiv*) for "live." "Soul" expresses an omnipresent life force. All life has soul, wherever that life is found. *Jiva* is effectively a synonym for "living being." Passages from the *Acaranga Sutra*, a fourth-century B.C.E. text, are striking. "There are living beings living in the earth, living in grass, living on leaves, or living in wood, living in cow dung, living in dustheaps" (I:1:4). The recesses of the soil, the waters, even the air, bears life that, having soul, seeks to persist.

> All things are fond of life.
> They like pleasure, they hate pain,
> They shun destruction.
> They like life and long to live,
> To all, life is dear. (I:2:3)[16]

But back to the soul's cultivation. Religious leaders know about soul cultivation, as do good parents, teachers, artists, and friends. But do we understand it's also about soils? "Cultivation" is the gardener's and the farmer's caretaking activity. Fast-forward from Socrates to Luther. Luther read Hebrew and noticed the soil/soul connection. *Ha 'ādām*—Adam, earth creature,

earthling, groundling—is created from *ādāmâ*—living soil in some transla-
tions, "red clay," "topsoil," or "humus" in others. As we will see, *ādāmâ* is an
active, generative agent in the Hebrew Bible and Jewish traditions. Because of
our very origins—Adam from *ādāmâ*—our vocation is to be *shomrei ādāmâ*,
soil guardians, earth custodians, cultivators who till and keep and care. "To till
and keep" (Genesis 2:15) is literally "to serve and preserve" (*l'ovdah ul' shom-
rah*), a Hebrew synonym for cultivate.

And who, in due course, is Adam's companion? *Hava*, in Hebrew, Eve in
English. *Hava* literally means "living"; Eve, the bearer of life, its progenitor.
Stay close to the mythic character of the language here: Adam and Eve, "Soil"
and "Life." Such is the identity from which the human vocation of *shomrei
ādāmâ*, soil guardians and cultivators, arises. The sacred is beneath our soles.
We arise from it, live a little while upon it to cultivate it, and return to it.

The Koran (*Qur'an*), after spelling out the wonders of creation at the
hands of Allah, asks a question: "If anything could make you marvel, then you
should surely marvel at those who say: 'When we are dust, shall we be restored
to a new creation?'" (13:5).[17] This is meant as a question of doubt on the part
of those who, the Koran says, "deny their Lord." That is, if Allah created us
from dust (soil), and rolled out the heavens and the Earth and all therein, why
would you doubt that another new creation is possible?

Incidentally, the *Qur'an* offers a lovely image for the offspring of Adam
and Eve—"companions of the gardens." Such companionship carries conditions: "Those who believe and work righteousness, and humble themselves
before their Lord, they will be companions of the garden, to dwell there for
aye!" (*Qur'an*, The Prophet Hud, Sutra 11:23).[18]

But let us return to "cultivation" and Luther. God's sublunary habitation
in the sacred soil beneath our soles is somewhere near the center of Luther's
theology. For him, "the finite bears the infinite"; nature's creatures are God's
"masks" or, in another image, the "wrappings" and trappings of God. God's
presence fills "all things, even the tiniest leaf"[19] and "every little seed."[20] Not
only is the divine wholly present "in a grain, on a grain, over a grain," Luther
even finds the very "footprints" of God in those of a mouse. They have "such
pretty feet and delicate hair," he says.[21] Nice soles.

All of this is cause for astonishment: "If you were to search out everything
about a kernel of wheat in the field, you would be so amazed that you would
die."[22]

Luther's Hebrew tells him that *ha 'ādām*, the farmer, is the creature of
ādāmâh assigned to till and keep this arable topsoil. All of Adam's descendents—Cain, Abel, Noah, Abraham, Isaac, Jacob—are farmers and landholders,

tilling the soil and tending the flocks. Shouldn't it be striking for Jews, Christians, and Muslims that, unlike the heroes of the neighbors in Sumeria and Mesopotamia, the archetypal ancestral figures of prehistory are farmers and shepherds and not kings and warriors? Of course we may prefer to be a king or warrior when we learn from Luther's commentary that "the cultivator came from a clod."

Where do good clods go from here? Switch to Latin. It is no coincidence that the "cultivator" gives rise to "culture" and to "cultus" (worship). All share the same root, and "root" is the right image for what lives here, in the soil. Culture, agriculture, and the ritual response of marvel and wonder to the miracle beneath our feet and all around us—this is the matrix (mother or womb) of our life together. Do not be surprised, then, that the breath (*ruah*) that gives humans life is the same *ruah* that animates other animals and the plants. They've got soul, too. Do not be surprised that virtually all the Jewish holy days had their origins in agricultural festivals. In the Yahwist's account in the Pentateuch, for example, the liturgical year is carried out at agricultural centers like Shechem, Hebron, Bethel, and Beersheba, at altars built by farmers near sacred oak trees, where the ritual celebrations are based on the three primary harvests of the Canaanite highlands: barley and wheat in the spring and first fruits in the fall. Do not be surprised, either, that the word for oak (*elon*) is related to the word for God (*el*) and that the ancestral theophanies are invariably associated with an oak tree or a grove, a mountaintop, or a spring of living water. And do not be surprised that this Yahwistic account in which the human is servant of the land is in tension with the Priestly account. In the Priestly account, humankind is in the position of controlling ruler over the rest of nature, accorded such status by God.

The tension between the Pentateuch's Yahwistic and Priestly accounts, which reflects a tension within the human soul, shows in their descriptions of Israel's altars. In the Priestly account Moses receives instructions from God on Sinai (Exodus 27:1–8, 38:1–7). The altar is an elaborate human achievement—large (ten feet on a side), built with acacia wood overlaid with bronze, and home to designated instruments and vessels for the priestly offerings. This altar reflects the highest human technology of metal and woodwork of the time. By contrast, the Yahwist's altar is built of unadorned earth and no more. More precisely it is built of arable topsoil, *'ādāmâh*, home to the farmer's life and the source of it. Fieldstones are permitted, but they are not to be cut. Nor are the local stonecutters to make any inscriptions. These are pristine natural forms, without human profanation. The Yahwist's altar symbolizes the dependence of the people on the land God has given them, the land that roots them.

The Priestly altar symbolizes the achievement of the people who rule the land, as mediated by priests.[23] Humility, service, and limit contrast with stewardly power and control, with both understood as commands of God.

Yet the main point is the nexus of cultus (worship), culture, and agriculture—we belong to these as the miraculous clods who are cultivators by calling. Humans are here to maintain the fertility of the soil for ongoing life, to "renew the face of the earth," in the phrase of Psalm 104, and to give glory to God. The ancients would have understood Wendell Berry: "In talking about topsoil, it is hard to avoid the language of religion."[24] So put aside the superstition of some religions that soul and soil are separate categories. Decent land use is less about economics than about cultivation and the state of our souls, together with the state of soil. How a people treats soil tells you much about their way of life and its soul. (That so much agricultural work is regarded as demeaning, fit only for underpaid menial labor on the part of workers accorded little respect, is a direct commentary on the state of society.)

Islam knows the linkage of soil and soul intimately in its central ritual, the call to prayer five times a day. *Flh* is the root of *felah* (farmer) and *felaheen* (farmers). That root means "cultivate," and the call to prayer is *Haya al felah, hoya al salah*, said twice: "Come to (self-)cultivation." Islam's most marked daily ritual is a call to cultivate soil and soul together.

A turn from Hebrew and Arabic to English loses nothing in translation. "Hum" is the root for "human," "humus," "humble," and "humility," also *homo* in *Homo sapiens*. That we are good dirt is worthy of a little "humor" on our part.[25] In any event, the next time someone asks, "Where are you from?" consider replying, "From six inches of topsoil and a little rain. How about you?"

But let's talk dirt. What do we know about dirt? Not much. What Leonardo da Vinci said centuries ago still holds: we know more about the stars in the skies than about the soil underfoot. Microbe scientist Susan Lachine says it is likely that we have identified fewer than 1/10th of 1 percent of the microbes in the soil! And it's clear that dirt, "the ecstatic skin of the Earth,"[26] is home to more life *in* the ground than all the life proudly striding about on the surface. Annie Dillard's census of one square foot of Virginia topsoil one piddling inch deep turned up "an average of 1,356 living creatures . . . including 865 mites, 265 springtails, 22 millipedes, 19 adult beetles, and various numbers of 12 other forms."[27] And those were only the critters visible to the naked eye. Two billion or so bacteria and millions of fungi, protozoans, algae, and innumerable other creatures aren't tallied in Dillard's *ʾădāmâh* census.

Here is William Logan on "Clay and Life."

At Christmas, I was out on the prairie again. Third time in a year. It seems like I can't stay away [he lives in New York City]. This time, I came up out of Council Grove, Kansas, at seven a.m., just around sunrise. For about a minute and a half, I saw the sun and the full moon balanced evenly at the opposite ends of the sky. And here was I, riding along the bald and slightly arched surface of the earth, halfway between the two.

What are we doing on this planet, and how did we get here? It took only a glance to tell that there would not be anything like us found on the yellow sun or the fast-paling moon. The Earth has one thing that neither sun nor moon has ever had.

And that one thing is clay.[28]

Logan the soil scientist, who had his office in one of the towers of the Cathedral of St. John the Divine in New York, writes elaborately of the microscopic structure of clay. Then he says this, just as if he's writing in church:

Isaiah, describing how God would cause righteousness and praise to arise, compared the act to a garden which "causes what is sown in it to spring up." The ground itself is as active as the seed. The seeds of organic life, attracted to the patterns of a clay matrix [matrix, the old word for "womb"], might well have found there the structure that makes all of us possible, and the means to maintain and reproduce it.[29]

" The ground itself is as active as the seed." Rainer Maria Rilke's version is this:

> Though he works and worries, the farmer
> never reaches down to where the seed turns
> into summer. The earth *grants*.[30]

First Nations, probably most indigenous peoples, have been clear that the earth, the soil, "grants." The wisdom of Chief Luther Standing Bear is shared:

There is a road in the hearts of all of us, hidden and seldom traveled, which leads to an unknown, secret place.

The old people came literally to love the soil, and they sat or reclined on the ground, with the feeling of being close to a mothering power.

Their teepees were built upon the earth and their altars were made of earth.

The soil was soothing, strengthening, cleansing and healing, that is why the old Indian still sits upon the earth instead of propping himself up and away from its life-giving forces.

For him, to sit or lie upon the ground is to be able to think more deeply and to feel more keenly. He can see more clearly into the mysteries of life and come closer in kinship to other lives around him.[31]

The "mothering power" of which Chief Luther Standing Bear speaks is echoed among the Navajo (Diné). "Mother" for the Diné applies to all things that bring forth, nurture, and sustain life, and not solely to one's biological mother or other motherly caregivers, such as a child's aunts. The cornfields are called "mother"; so, too, sheep herds—and, of course, Mother Earth.[32]

Nelson Mandela, imprisoned for twenty-seven years on Robben Island, also learned that the earth "grants." He persuaded his warders to allow him a foot of reclaimed soil for tomatoes and flowers tight against the wall of the otherwise solid concrete exercise yard. He also persuaded them to allow use of thirty-two empty oil drums for growing vegetables and fruits. These were earth's signs of life where few existed. His hands in the fertile soil, joining the wonders of gardening, that ur-human vocation, saved him, he said.[33]

For the Hebrew Bible, too, the earth "grants." "And God said, 'Let the earth [soil] bring forth living creatures of every kind. . . . And it was so" (Genesis 1:24). "The earth" is the agent of creation, at God's command. "Bring forth" is a maternal verb. The ground mothers forth life; earth delivers. Incidentally God also says, in exactly parallel fashion, "Let the waters bring forth swarms of living creatures" (Genesis 1:20). Water is creation's agent as well. Water and soil "grant."

As if to combine these agents, Logan quotes biologist Hayman Hartman: "There are only two things in the universe that require liquid water for their existence: organic life and clay."[34]

So in the beginning was clay. Water and the labor of living organisms made humus of it. Life itself, at God's behest, created conditions that favor its continuation. The ecosphere is a creative force, *the* creative force. One might even be moved to give thanks to relentless bacteria and other microorganisms that, over millions of years as the primitive gardeners par excellence, have more soul than we knew. They, created and abetted from an abiotic world, worked the terrain and made it fit for growth in a riot of shapes and colors. A late manifestation of this "ecstatic skin of Earth" is the person reading this.

Put it as Robert Pogue Harrison does: "Life is an excess, call it the self-ecstasy of matter."[35] An overload of vitality, a surge of surplus, gives rise to life, then more life, then different life. We humans do not create; we cannot create a single blade of grass. Soil and seed do that as their dance of self-ecstasy. Earth grants. We, when we're most human, cultivate. But that is when we are at our truest and best. At our worst, we destroy soils so that grass does not grow and species die an eternal death.

Harrison draws ethical conclusions from the soil's "overgiving," this continuous "self-exceeding" or "self-transcendence" of natural forms bent on creating and re-creating, death and renewal. The soil must give a little more than it takes away if it is to replenish itself. It must run Genesis forward, not backward, or it dies. The same holds for biospiritual and ecospiritual human cultivators and for human culture as a whole, for nations, marriages, friendships, institutions. Like clay itself, they must be open enclosures who give of themselves in a responsive environment that lives by reciprocity. Nothing continues to live apart from "self-imparting generosity," the active tilling-and-keeping of Adam and Eve—Soil and Life.[36]

The error from which the world suffers

Our failure to be in touch with soil arises from a certain habit of abstraction and reduction. We focus on plants, animals, and peoples as *the* important life entities. Even in science the attention is to the species, populations, and communities of ecosystems. When we abstract these as *the* subjects of singular attention, "rather than the globe's miraculous life-filled skin," in Stan Rowe's phrase, and the life of the generative, parental elements—soil, air, fire, water, light—then we have it profoundly wrong. "It is from this error," says Stan Rowe, "that the whole world suffers."[37] Organisms do not, cannot, stand on their own. Only unified ecological systems as a whole, with their "miraculous life-filled skin," confer life.[38]

We could end here with a homiletical flourish on the wonder of sacred soil and the species wonder that moves Maya Angelou to poetry. She tells of "a brave and startling truth," a truth about us.

> We are the miraculous,
> the true wonder of this world
> That is when, and only when
> We come to it.[39]

Angelou is almost right. The species *Homo sapiens* truly is a wonder. But not *the* wonder. *The* wonder is overgiving life itself, the issue of sacred soil. So we must finish elsewhere, with the kind of warning McKibben issues: We moderns are running Genesis backwards,[40] despite, and in the face of, life's insistence upon Genesis going forward. Topsoil, for example, is being lost faster than it is being created. Most places take about five hundred years to create an inch of topsoil, the same amount we are losing in a matter of decades.

Ancient texts hold the clue to why we are wayward. Cultivators and their technologies have become alienated from their origins in 'ădāmăh; and when these alienated humans muster enough power to try and control their nature and destiny, the cultivators violate creation's integrity. Choosing the Tree of Knowledge *over* the Tree of Life,[41] instead of taking the measure from the Tree of Life and placing knowledge in service to it, boomerangs. The result is a rude and crude justice that disciplines human ignorance and hubris by foiling efforts to control life on our terms. To eat from the Tree of Knowledge as *the* source of power, rather than feasting in gratitude on the Tree of Life, itself the *axis mundi*, the center of the Garden, is to fall from grace.

The first recorded violation of creation's integrity is the killing of Abel by Cain. The death is "in the field" (Genesis 4:8) at the hands of "a tiller of the ground" (Genesis 4:2). Strikingly, it is not Adam and Eve who cry out at the slaying, but 'ădāmăh, the ground (Genesis 4:10). 'Ădāmăh, the source of ongoing life that is to be nurtured by the waters of life, is violated by receiving human blood instead, the result of human violence. The consequence of this primal bloodletting is that the ground "will no longer yield to you its strength" (God to Cain, Genesis 4:12). The ground itself is cursed ("because of you" says Genesis 3:17). Fratricide is also ecocide. Apparently everything is of a piece.

Cain's response testifies further to creation's integrity and belonging: To be alienated from 'ădāmăh is more punishment than Cain can bear. "Today you have driven me from the soil," he says to God in agony, "and I shall be hidden from your face; I shall be a fugitive and a wanderer on Earth" (Genesis 4:14). Cain, alienated from his own origins in fertile soil and his vocation as its tiller, is homeless on Earth and estranged from God. Banished from the Garden of Delight (*gan-eden*), he settles in the land of Nod (Genesis 4:16). But it is a strange settlement, since *nod* is Hebrew for "wandering."

And with this primordial divorce from the soil, even God's face is hidden. If and when nature is lost to the senses, God is as well.

God, however, does not abandon Cain. Cain cries, "I shall be a fugitive and a wanderer on the earth, and anyone who meets me may kill me" (Genesis 4:14). The All-Compassionate and Merciful One then marks Cain so that he does not suffer the same death he inflicted upon Abel. Mercy exceeds justice. Renewed life, albeit in diminished terms, is offered.

This alienation from God and soil, and the resultant curse whereby the ground does not yield its strength, is accompanied by one last dimension, the ethical. Cain, that "tiller of the ground" (Genesis 4:2), answers God's question of Abel's whereabouts with his own question: "I do not know; am I my brother's keeper?" (Genesis 4:9b). Cain's is a denial posed as a question. It means: I am not my brother's keeper. What is my brother to me? Cain actually never calls Abel his brother until God's question puts it that way, and then he only turns it back so as to deny or refuse the tie. Is this the reason Abel in Hebrew (*Hevel*) means a vapor, nothingness, meaninglessness?[42]

But the tiller is to be the keeper as well. Tilling and keeping belong together as the vocation (Genesis 2:15) of those whose life is of the soil and whose task is to renew the planet's ecstatic skin. Cultivation is about earth care. When these miracle clods are genuine cultivators, they join the soil's overgiving, they nourish its self-imparting generosity, they keep as they till, and the ground yields its strength. When cultivators till without keeping, when they become takers only and not givers, when they are no longer brother or sister or neighbor, but only fugitives alienated from the God of life, when they fail to subordinate the Tree of Knowledge to the Tree of Life, then soul/sole and soil are no longer joined and the sacred is leached from both the ground and its tillers.

Wes Jackson says it differently, as a scientist and in ways reminiscent of chapter 1, "The Creature We Are": "Our very being was shaped by a seamless series of changing ecosystems embedded within an ever-changing ecosphere over hundreds of millions of years. Its ability to support humans into a distant future was not on the line."[43] But now it is. Why? Because since our Neolithic settlements we've been burning through the five pools of relatively nonrenewable energy, the first of which is soil. (Forests, coal, oil, and natural gas are the others.) We've become a species out of context, wandering fugitives defined by consumption more than cultivation and a way of life that defies mutual enhancement. Yet there can be no future in incurring endless ecological debt and then asking Mother Nature for a bailout. Colonizers and consumers must be reborn as keepers. Mother Nature doesn't do bailouts. The onetime Fertile Crescent, home to the Garden of Delights (*gan-eden*), is testimony.

Tilling and keeping: The moral bottom line

If we weave religious perspectives together with scientific ones and ask, for example, Why is mountaintop removal and an economy of pure extraction wrong? the answer might go as follows: because, to cite Harrison, it "has nothing to do with the humility, devotion, and curatorial vocation of the gardener." That striking reply—that it's wrong because, as gardeners by nature we're the "companions of the gardens" (an image from Islam)[44]— comes from somewhere outside the industrial paradigm and its logic. "Gardener" has no status for industry, including industrial agriculture. The gardener's way of relating to the rest of nature is alien even to agribusiness. But consider it in view of mountaintop removal as modern industrial technology par excellence (vis-à-vis soil). For when "it comes to the soil—that is, the entirety of the natural resources locked away in the earth—the drive of modern technology is to extract, remove, and deplete rather than to cultivate, enhance, and foster."[45] To "cultivate, enhance, and foster" is exactly the gardener's calling. By contrast, scalping the mountains removes more than it gives back; it tills, violently, but it does not keep. It visits like a malediction and leaves the ground cursed, without true repair, much less enhancement. The Fertile Crescent—anywhere—is rendered infertile.

The primitive religious question returns: Where is our soul? And the primitive religious answer replies: Soul is where sole is, under our feet, in touch with soil.

Thoreau was right:

> Lord of skies, you walk among us
> in the plain brown soil of earth.
> How you've chosen to be present
> often seems of little worth.
> You have chosen common bushes,
> kindled them with heaven's fire,
> spoken through unlikely prophets
> heralding your love's desire . . .
> Heaven is under our feet as well as over our heads.

To "read" soil—and ourselves—from inside ancient religious cosmologies and texts is one thing, necessary and powerful. By thinking in the presence of a primal element, religious inquiry takes us to dimensions of an Earth-honoring ethic that even the focus on community in the foregoing chapter did not interrogate. To read soil and recent history is another powerful approach. We continue with that.

Environmental justice and the land

The rise of the environmental justice (EJ) movement is a mustard-seed story. The movement began with the United Church of Christ's landmark study, *Toxic Wastes and Race in the United States*.[46] The authors were not Environmental Protection Agency (EPA) employees, members of the business community, or representatives of large environmental organizations; they were a small staff in a little office of the United Church of Christ (UCC) Commission for Racial Justice at the Interchurch Center in New York City. Simply by overlaying government data on the location of hazardous waste sites atop U.S. census data, the report documented environmental racism and sparked what would become the environmental justice movement. Later studies, including those of the EPA, confirmed what *Toxic Wastes and Race in the United States* showed: Three in five African Americans lived in communities with abandoned toxic-waste sites. Three of the five largest commercial hazardous-waste landfills were in predominantly African American or Latino American communities. These accounted for approximately 40 percent of the nation's estimated landfill capacity. Overall, poorer communities fared far worse than affluent ones as sites of commercial toxic waste, and poorer people of color fared worse than poor whites. Since poor women and children, especially poor women and children of color, fared worse than men in most communities, negative gender and generational factors correlated as well. Yet these populations and their communities did not generate the poisons.

In a word, race, class, age, and gender were all correlated to systemically biased environmental practices. Different communities suffered different consequences. Human beings did not all breathe the same air, drink the same water, or sail in the same boat. As if to conjure up Milan and St. Ambrose ("Why do the injuries of nature delight you?"), injustice was authorized. It was authorized by privilege and the many ways privilege organizes power and practice.

In 2007 the United Church of Christ revisited these findings and issued *Toxic Wastes and Race in the United States, 1987–2007*. The update documents real victories that followed the national and worldwide attention generated by the original report, together with the resistance it spawned in countless communities tired of being dumped on. Yet the racial and socioeconomic disparities persisted, and the conclusions in the 2007 report parallel those of

1987—race matters, place matters, class matters, and gender matters. Unequal protection still places communities of color at special risk; the most polluting industries still go to the places where land, labor, and lives are cheap as they chase profits and the bottom line around the globe; and current environmental protection still fails to provide equal protection to low-income communities of people of color.

Not long after the 1987 report, and in response to it, the First National People of Color Environmental Leadership Summit was convened in Washington, D.C., in October 1991. It adopted seventeen principles of environmental justice, introduced by a preamble that makes clear their provenance:

> We, the people of color, gathered together at this multinational People of Color Environmental Leadership Summit, to begin to build a national and international movement of all peoples of color to fight the destruction and taking of our lands and communities, do hereby reestablish our spiritual interdependence to the sacredness of Mother Earth; to respect and celebrate each of our cultures, languages and beliefs about the natural world and our roles in healing ourselves; to insure environmental justice; to promote economic alternatives which would contribute to the development of environmentally safe livelihoods; and, to secure our political, economic and cultural liberation that has been denied for over 500 years of colonization and oppression, resulting in the poisoning of our communities and land and the genocide of our peoples, do affirm and adopt these Principles of Environmental Justice.[47]

Waste—poisoning—was not the half of it, as the EJ movement knew full well. It is only one item among consequences that flow from global industry, trade, and finance. The truly generative forces of eco-injustice are historically unprecedented extraction of renewable and nonrenewable resources; the processing, distribution, and consumption of these for global markets (waste is a spinoff of this); and the competitive scramble to find cheaper resources and take advantage of low wages and less stringent environmental conditions along with other ways to externalize or "socialize" costs to the public (e.g., tax breaks) in the interests of private gain. When these factors interact, they generate cumulative socio-environmental consequences for people and the rest of nature. This impact often includes the fraying of community bonds, with psychic and cultural consequences, as well as the depleting of community resources.[48]

Our specific subject, however, is the EJ movement and the land, the soil. "[T]o secure our political, economic and cultural liberation that has been denied for over 500 years of colonization and oppression, resulting in the poisoning of our communities and land and the genocide of our peoples" (the preamble) is the necessary lead-in for what is a complex tale. To tell it from inside the biases of power and privilege, including the power and privilege of established environmental groups and their assent to the institutions and laws of the governing paradigm, is to tell it only partially and poorly.

A different story line

A perennial topic in eco-literature is the nature of the eco-crisis. How is the ecological crisis understood? How is it presented? Never far from this is a discussion of human alienation from the rest of nature in the modern era.

The point initially made over and again by prominent analyses, including those in this book, is the threat all of us face together, a threat that issues from our collective and cumulative assault on nature. We all live in the same biosphere, breathe the same air, share the same ozone layer, alter the same climate, eat food from the same soils and seas, and harvest the same acid rain whether we're just or unjust, rich or poor. Likewise we all share a common good on the basis of common planetary citizenship, perhaps best captured in the picture of Earth as the blue, white, green, and tan jewel making its appointed rounds. An earlier generation followed Adlai Stevenson in speaking of "Spaceship Earth." The clear implication was that we are all on board, all members of the same crew, and all headed for the same rendezvous with destiny. Some, like Margaret Mead, thought that the experience of "Earthrise," vividly photographed from the moon in a Kodak moment, might be the harbinger of a new age with a new sense of responsibility. "Only in the last quarter of my life," she said in 1977, "have we come to know what it means to be custodians of the future of the Earth. . . . We did not know this before, except in little pieces. . . . It was not until we saw the picture of the Earth from the moon that we realized how small and how helpless this planet is—something that we must hold in our arms and care for."[49]

Without for a minute denying a collective crisis or a shared planetary home, the EJ movement found it necessary to make noise, a lot of noise, to show that not all are being poisoned equally, or even breathing the same air. As we mentioned in passing above, not all drink the same water, nor do all share the same access to land use and environmental decision-making. Not all benefit equally from environmental redress and progress, either.

The chief reason is the way privilege rigs the game. Sometimes this is unbeknownst even to the environmentalists who most benefit—the core constituency of environmental professionals who are at home in the strata of

U.S. society that are least likely to experience environmental injustice in their neighborhoods, livelihoods, or bodies. At the same time they are most likely to see the "green" progress they help generate. They have a part in planning their own neighborhoods as well as distant ones. ("People get Ph.D.s to plan for our neighborhood," comments Alexei Torres-Fleming, founder of the interfaith Youth Ministries for Peace and Justice in New York City's South Bronx. "When do we get to plan for our neighborhood?"[50])

It is not only socially created hazards and disasters that are unequally distributed. Even natural disasters—earthquakes, hurricanes, landslides—wreak more death and injury on the least protected, who are disproportionately poor and colored, and who are offered less in the way of resources for amelioration and recovery.

These outcomes of markedly different socio-economic locations and destinies can be deeply ironic. Consider soils. The peoples who have the deepest cultural-spiritual ties to the land on this continent, the very peoples whose Great Work together was to achieve intimate rapport with the powers of the continents themselves[51]—the First Nations of the Americas—occupy the most devastated lands. They share its worst soils. And a people enslaved to work the land and learn its ways as its toilers, tillers, and keepers—African Americans— are more landless after their emancipation than any other segment of the U.S. population. They have lost their meager soils and, in search of livelihood, pound city sidewalks instead.

In short, neither the causes of environmental degradation, nor the costs and the benefits, have ever been distributed equally. Whole peoples have been fed "with the bread of tears" and given "bowls of tears" to drink.[52] Given present orderings of power, it will not be different for climate change or the applications of genetic science.

Another subject rife in eco-literature, including this book—human alienation from nature—also falls out differently for the EJ movement. For veterans of environmental racism, any proper account of this alienation includes the role of plain coercion in the transformations that have befallen lands, cultures, and peoples. Moreover, any proper account understands that these brute transformations befell the soils, cultures, and peoples together,[53] a recognition noted in the observations we cited earlier from Darwin, Marx, Smith, and Lyell via Crosby. Rather than such accounts as these, human alienation in most eco-literature is described as subtle and long-term, a millennial weave of processes with powerful origins in the triumph of Greek, Gnostic, and Docetic dualisms that eventually merged with Cartesian mechanistic cosmologies and forged a tacit partnership with modern science and technology. In due course these aided and abetted the new economy (capitalism), the Industrial Revolution, and the growth of great urban centers. A chapter or two on major transitions in agriculture is usually included in this extended narrative as well, starting with the Neolithic domestication of plants and animals.

If the reader rests well among the privileged, she might surmise that all this was evolutionary social change of a rather banal sort, smoothed out by time and the normal bias of canonical histories. Little, if anything, is included about slavery, for example, as the forced relationship to the land of a significant population. Nor does environmental history point out that, in contrast to serfdom, slavery is a consequence of the transition to monocropping of cash crops that require cheap, mass labor—tobacco, cotton, sugarcane. Forcing blacks to work the land as chattel doesn't register as an ecological issue, even an eco-justice one, in the dominant accounts, even though the process of human domination and the exploitation of nature occurred at exactly the same time by way of integrally related dynamics centering on the land.[54] Sethe, in Toni Morrison's *Beloved*, wakes from plantation nightmares wondering if hell might not also be such a pretty place.[55]

Nor, as mentioned, is the disproportionate loss of the lands of African American farmers and their resettlement in large cities in neighborhoods with a minimal direct functional relationship to the rest of nature a part of the environmentalist's story. The lot of uprooted Mexicans simply set adrift through the acquisition of two-fifths of Mexico's territory by the United States in the war of 1846–48 is not a chapter in U.S. environmental history, either. Land grant squabbles, alive to this day in the Southwestern United States and dating back to Spanish and Mexican governance, don't appear in environmental histories. Little Latino/Latina and Hispanic history does.

The trail of broken treaties and violence done to Native Americans may get a little more play than the Great Migration north of African Americans or the lot of dispossessed Spanish- and Mexican-Americans. But it merits sparse attention in standard environmental histories as well, even when the subject is human alienation from the great lands stretching from sea to shining sea. When such ravages are noted, it is usually in the form of regrets for lost indigenous wisdom and/or the appropriation of the remaining remnants of First Nations' Earth-honoring spiritualities. So the plundering continues, albeit much more politely, with an affirmation of diversity and multiculturalism.

In a word, the moral world of the dominant environmental consciousness rarely considers forced residence and working of the land or forced removal from it. The history of coercion, brutality, cultural genocide, and worse does not have much significance in the moral memory or presentation of such organizations and their supporters. In stark contrast, they are always part of the deep memory of the EJ movement. The moral worlds of EJ and other environmentalists differ markedly from one another in their attention to the relationship of the land and its keepers.

How this plays out is fruitfully pursued in an interview with environmental justice pioneer Carl Anthony. Anthony gently points out the suspicion that arises when participants in healing-the-Earth ceremonies are admonished to hear the voice of Earth in all that surrounds them and especially nonhuman nature crying out in pain. Yet they are not admonished to hear the cry of other peoples, though these, like themselves, are also songs of Earth and nature. Or, participants are admonished to "think like a mountain" and take their place as humans in the Council of All Beings. But they are not, if they are white, admonished to think like peoples of color or take their place among those who belong to other strata of class, race, gender, or culture. The environmentally sensitive are admonished to attend to the impending collapse of ecosystems, vanishing wetlands, melting glaciers, disappearing polar bears, and bleaching coral reefs. But Depression-era employment levels, degraded city neighborhoods, or the health of the rural poor and their habitat are somehow not environmental issues. Anthony's own conclusion is that unnamed whiteness is at work here, and it resists any genuinely multicultural self. That is, whites do not listen to these omitted stories, own them, and learn from them, despite the fact that a large percentage of Native Americans and African Americans carry Euro-American genes as well. White privilege and purity taboos seem to fend off more inclusive, complex, or complete narratives. By way of contrast, the EJ movement argues that a genuinely multicultural self reflecting an inclusive history would deconstruct whiteness and include as mainstream environmental analysis the long and bloody history of the transformation of peoples—all peoples—and the land, all of it, together. Anthony goes on to say that until this kind of ethical and social-psychological analysis is forthcoming, alarmist discourse about environmental dangers that do not include those who live prosaic lives with uncertain futures and uncertain resources in already alarmingly degraded environments will be suspect. Isn't such talk one more diversion on the part of those who intend to retain political and economic control and to exclude peoples of color even from environmental policy affecting their own communities? [56]

To discuss human alienation from the land without this history and perspective is an intellectual crime. But it is also a moral one, since it reveals the cover-up, denial, and amnesia of (white) privilege still hard at work.

What would happen if we started from another place, and asked not about environmental history and the land in EJ perspective, but about the moral community it assumes and the place of land and soils in it?

Marx and Muir

Earlier we cited the preamble to the "Principles of Environmental Justice" adopted in Washington, D.C., in 1991. The first of the seventeen principles then follows: "Environmental justice affirms the sacredness of Mother Earth, ecological unity and the interdependence of all species, and the right to be free from ecological destruction." The whole community of life, including soils and the land, is embraced here as the relevant moral community. A key element of any theory of justice, namely, membership in the moral community— who has standing and who does not, who is due what and who is not—is thus answered in ways far more generous than most justice theories in either Western jurisprudence or philosophy. Western theories of justice, crafted on Roman, Kantian, Cartesian, and Lockean assumptions, assume that morality is an artifact of human culture devised to aid the negotiation of human-to-human relations, and human-to-human relations only. Sentience beyond human sentience counts for little, sometimes nothing. And ecosystems and the land, much less the ecosphere as a whole, do not have separate standing of any kind in this moral world.

Mary Midgeley's list of those missing in action in most social contract ethics, for example, borders on the ludicrous. Missing are our ancestors, posterity, the senile, the insane, "the foetus" (ranging down to "human vegetables"), embryos, sentient animals, nonsentient animals, plants of all kinds, artifacts including works of art, inanimate but structured objects (rivers, rocks), unchosen groups of all kinds (including families and species, ecosystems, landscapes, villages, warrens, cities), countries, the biosphere, and God.[57] "As far as the numbers go," Midgeley says with British understatement, "this is no minority of the beings with whom we have to deal."[58] The present human interests of social contract advocates trump the interests of all other lives and habitats. As a consequence, our most commonly utilized moral discourse simply leaves out the greater part of our actual obligations. In contrast, with its preamble and first principle, the EJ movement moves closer to The Earth Charter, which arose separately from the EJ movement but has included its voice. The Earth Charter's own preamble includes this: "Earth, our home, is alive with a unique community of life." Earth's "vitality, diversity, and beauty" is itself "a sacred trust." Far-reaching moral imperatives then follow:

We must join together to bring forth a sustainable global society founded on respect for nature, universal human rights, economic jus-tice, and a culture of peace. Towards this end, it is imperative that we, the peoples of Earth, declare our responsibility to one another, to the greater community of life, and to future generations.[59]

With this vital issue of moral membership and standing for the whole com-munity of life stated at the outset, the EJ movement's focus on social justice moves in quickly, already in the second principle: "Environmental justice demands that public policy be based on mutual respect and justice for all peo-ples, free from any form of discrimination and bias." The remaining principles largely intersect public policy and the democratic creation of healthy environ-ments, beginning with the land: protection from nuclear testing and waste; issues around the production and disposal of toxic/hazardous wastes and poisons; the rights of workers to a safe and healthy environment; a fundamental right to the political, economic, cultural, and environmental self-determination of all peoples; participation as equal partners on every level of decision-making; opposition to the destructive operations of multinational corporations and compensation to the victims of environmental injustice; the need for urban and rural ecological policies to clean up and rebuild cities and rural areas in balance with nature; and the honoring of the cultural integrity of all communities, pro-viding fair access for all to the full range of resources.[60]

Behind all these, and truly a matter of first works and re-formation, the larger issue is the viability of the industrial/postindustrial paradigm and the kind of corporate global capitalism that fuels it. Here is the working grammar of the modern world, the force of a distinct age at serious odds with both social justice and environmental sustainability, including the sustainability of soils. There is, for example, a school of technocentric, eco-efficient environ-mentalism that argues for a managerial approach to environmental prob-lems and assumes that they can be addressed without fundamental changes in present patterns of production and consumption or in present values and perspectives. The ranks of business-oriented sustainable development are at home here. Justice matters to many in these ranks, and its strategy is transparent: include peoples presently excluded from the benefits of global capitalism and its dynamic markets. Generate the wealth through which local environmental degradation can be addressed. But another school, growing with each melting glacial range in the Andes and Alaska and every disappear-ing forest, presupposes radical changes in our relationship with one another (as humans) and with the other-than-human world. These social, political, and economic changes are of such a basic nature that sustainability can only be achieved on grounds qualitatively different from present ways.[61] Justice here questions the boundaries of present moral community itself together with its timeframe. Moral consideration is due not only to *Homo sapiens*, present and future, but other-than-human members of the community of life, present and future. These are basic qualifications that neither present Kantian ethics nor social-contract utilitarianism meet, much less the dominant practices of capitalism. For the moment I only note that, by and large, peoples experiencing environmental racism join the ranks of the backlash against economic globalization and the backlash against tempered environmentalism played by the rules of corporate capitalism and free-trade agreements. They instead push a critique that means doing first works over. At the same time, their strategies are generally community- and network-based. The focus is to decentralize power through achievable incremental change in keeping with subsidiarity. This push for "local democracy in a global era,"[62] or "grassroots democracy,"[63] may eventually be radical and far-reaching in its consequences. That, at least, is the hope of the EJ movement.

It may be too flip to call this position "Karl Marx meets John Muir." The EJ ethic of outrage, resistance, and patient plodding is rooted in the raw experience of injustice long done to peoples and the land together. Its critical substance issues from that experience, whether Marx or Muir are noted or not (usually they are not). Still, the EJ position can be articulated with the insights of Engels, Marx, and Muir. Marx joins Muir in asserting, now in Marx's words, that "nature is [man's] body, with which he must remain in continuous interchange if he is not to die. That man's physical and spiritual life is linked to nature means simply that nature is linked to itself, for man is part of nature."[64] In a word, we are inextricably of Earth and soil—body, soul, mind, and spirit—whether in the wilderness or the urban core. With this basic insight, Marx and his colleague Friedrich Engels go on to reiterate their critical, characteristic point that humans are always transforming nature with means that are socially organized, above all by the different modes of production (capitalism is their chief, though not exclusive, subject here). In the modern era, technology has rendered capital, and to some extent labor, increasingly mobile. Land by contrast is not mobile, although increasingly it is radically transformed—in the twentieth century human beings moved more rocks and soil than did volcanoes, glaciers, and the tectonic plates that build mountains.[65] A global economy that impacts all, local soils and landscapes included, is the world-shaping result.[66]

For Marx and Engels, a downside of the social transformation of nature-society by modern modes of production is that large-scale agriculture and large-scale industry enervate both land and laborer. Capitalist agriculture, Marx observed long before mass use of monocropping and factory farms, is progress in "the art, not only of robbing the laborer, but of robbing the soil; all progress in increasing the fertility of the soil for a given time, is a progress towards ruining the lasting sources of that fertility." It saps "the original sources of all wealth—the soil and the laborer."[67] Engels was convinced that both human alienation and land exploitation followed from a mode of interacting with nature that rendered all things commodities to be peddled for profit. "To make the earth an object of huckstering—the earth which is our one and all, the first condition of our existence—was the last step toward making oneself an object of huckstering."[68]

This digression into the work of Marx and Engels is made because the EJ movement shares their perspective, albeit from EJ experience, not the study of Marx and Engels. The movement also concludes that there are common patterns of exploitation of land and peoples in the modern era, and systems of social organization and privilege are the key to this exploitation. Thus it is not a surprise that the EJ movement has, for example, now taken on biotechnology and genetics. While this is a world neither Marx nor Muir dreamt of, the orienting analysis still holds. Discussing the controversies whirling around genetically modified foods and the transformation of agriculture, Richard Lewontin says that the creation and adoption of genetically modified organisms are "but the latest steps in this long historical development [of capital-intensive industrial agriculture]." Here, in the production and sale of the staples of life, modernity's characteristic engineering and entrepreneurial mode is seeking to effect "its last consolidation in spheres of life that seemed set apart." Lewontin is referring to the secret life of the cell and the radical ways heredity in all life-forms is subject to manipulation by genetic science. His conclusion is that "for the farmer there is no escape from engineering, whether it be mechanical, chemical, electrical, or genetic."[69]

One must add that in the eyes of the EJ movement, the comprehensive social organization of nature is also the key to a more just order, for human nature as well as for the rest. Systemic issues of power and the modes of its organization and use are thus the focus for EJ work. To point out that ours is increasingly a humanly dominated ecosphere only underscores the point. If the Anthropocene is an engineered world, then it all turns on human power and morality. In E. O. Wilson's words near the end of *Consilience: The Unity of Knowledge*:

> We are learning that ethics is everything. . . . Freedom means restraint. . . .
> The free market is a wondrous device, but to suppose that it or any other

value-neutral process—the balance of power in international politics, for example, or the development of genetic research—will yield of themselves optimal outcomes is to have the kind of naïve faith that belongs to an older, simpler world. Fundamentalism can be economic or scientific as well as religious. Without a moral vision, we will fail. And that vision, to be shared, only emerges from conversation—from talking and listening to one another across boundaries of class, income, race and faith.[70]

Tensions

Before we leave the EJ movement, we register an unresolved tension. Major environmental organizations have been stung by criticisms issuing from the EJ movement. In response they have come to place issues of urban ecology and environmental racism on their own agendas and added "equity" to "economy" and "ecology" as the three essentials of "sustainable development." "Equity" refers to social justice as a measure of whether people and communities are enriched or degraded by a given policy and its implementation. That concern, underwritten at the federal level in the United States by an executive order of President Bill Clinton that requires measuring the equity consequences of proposed federal policies, exists because of the noise generated by the EJ movement, together with responsiveness on the part of the established environmental organizations.

Does this recent sensitivity to social injustice and equity as a norm of sustainability truly address the EJ critique and take on its moral world? The literature of eco-design and the programs of the big environmental organizations by and large show the same relationship of "equity" to "economy" that pervades neoclassical economics; social and environmental goods are essentially parceled out as issues of *distribution*. The political economy produces wealth that can then be directed to ameliorate poverty or improve the environment. In a word, global and domestic capitalism as "the economy" is thereby assumed as a given for purposes of production and consumption, and equity is about a fairer distribution of its goods and bads.

Members of the EJ movement are, by contrast, more critical of the basic systemic arrangements themselves. They want to know about the initial justice of the economy's ground rules and policies and not simply about the distribution of its outcomes. Production itself needs interrogation and change. While social justice *is* still distributive justice, the chief element for the EJ movement is not the final product, the distribution of goods and ser-vices as endpoint commodities. It is the distribution of policymaking power. Specifically, it is a community's capacity for optimal self-organizing, self-provisioning, and self-sufficiency. "When do we get to plan for our commu-nity?" (Alexei Torres-Fleming's question). The three "e's" of sustainable development—equity, economy, ecology—could be benchmarks for the cre-ation and distribution of presently unshared power. But they are not so on current terms, because they continue to invest in the basic institutions and practices of the industrial paradigm in corporate capitalist hands, and they do so in ways that favor presently privileged institutions and social strata. The normative gaze of human supremacy is coupled, in this case, to rich-world supremacy.[71]

This clarification of equity and power in the social ecology of the EJ move-ment vis-à-vis other environmentalists doesn't resolve the real Marx/Muir tension within EJ ranks, however. That tension rests with unresolved anthro-pocentrism. This, too, has consequences for soils and the land.

As noted, in most sustainable development discussion "environmental jus-tice" as equity refers to the distribution of environmental goods and bads among human populations. It doesn't normally include justice to the (other-than-human) environment. Equity doesn't, for example, commonly require us to ask about the interests of other creatures and seek to determine what they require to realize their potential. No biotic rights are drawn from the principles of equity in most discussions of sustainable development. And many in the EJ movement are content to sit well with this. M. Dowie's survey of EJ agendas found that "the central concern . . . is human health"[72] and that wilderness, natural-resource conservation, and public lands policies are peripheral. Robert Bullard's discussion of equity in the EJ movement itself lists three types: proce-dural, geographic, and social. The first is about fairness in policy formulation and enforcement, the second is about the burden of environmental hazards that different communities carry, and the third is about the role that social fac-tors such as race, ethnicity, class, culture, lifestyles, and political power play in environmental decision-making.[73] Despite the founding document of the EJ movement, "The Principles of Environmental Justice," none of these notions of equity has the whole community of life in view. Nor does Bullard's own out-lined "framework for environmental justice" and its five principles of "the right to protection, prevention of harm, shifting the burden of proof, obviating proof of intent to discriminate, and targeting resources to redress inequities."[74]

Differently said, Muir has disappeared from this horizon, together with the need to render soils and the land and its more-than-human populations their due as a justice need with a seamless connection to human well-being. This leaves some basic questions unanswered. Using Andrew Dobson's distinctions, exactly what is it that is to be sustained? Is it "critical natural capital," that nature which is the precondition for human surviving and thriving? Is it "irreversible nature" that, once lost, cannot be renewed (like the Fertile Crescent's fertility)? Or is it "natural value," a goodness about nature as a whole that carries with it an ascription of value to the whole ecosphere in its own right, quite apart from human uses or even presence? And why is nature in any of these notions to be sustained? For reasons of human welfare? Because of duties to nature that transcend human welfare? Some combination of utility and transcendent obligation? Does environmental justice mean justice *to* the environment or the just distribution among humans of environmental goods and bads?[75] Does peace *on* Earth include peace *with* the Earth?

Were these questions not enough, there are the old, gnawing ones present to every ethics discussion since Socrates fruitfully intimidated his students. Is justice based in need, desert, or inherent rights? For the moment, we draw a distinction between environmental justice and ecojustice. Environmental justice attends chiefly to a set of procedural and political tasks in light of society's power arrangements and how they play out. Ecojustice, by way of contrast, focuses on the cosmic connections that envelop human life and the rest of nature. These differing standards are nicely captured by Willis Jenkins: "While the ethics of ecojustice evaluated right relations directly in reference to creation's own dignity, advocates of environmental justice critiqued environmental degradations with respect to human dignity."[76] For our discussion this means that while these notions are not inherently contradictory, how *ʾādāmâ* fares may rest on the weight given one or the other. (In this book the tilt is toward the former, with ecojustice encompassed by creation justice.)

Method

The distinction just drawn by Jenkins—environmental justice or ecojustice— rests in differences of method. It exemplifies a "think with" and how we use it as we "think about" moral matters. The way our "think withs" affect how we "think about" morality is the subject of method in ethics. This is so whether the issue is soils and souls or any other.

Everyone has an ethical method. It's a standing cairn on the moral landscape. Method may not be explicit or even conscious; most people don't ask what their method is or subject it to reflection and analysis. But it is always at work as people make choices and live their morality.

Dissecting the word introduces it. "*Meta*" means "inclusive of," "gathering in the whole," "taking the full range of." "*Hodos*" means "the way." "Method" is a way of taking in the whole of an inquiry. What is the overall design of our ethical thinking? What is its infrastructure, its components and processes? What are the salient sources we use, governed by what overriding framework and values and directed to what ends? How do these elements interact so as to yield the morality and ethic that is ours?

Since we have proposed "Religious Ethics in a New Key," and tried in these last pages to scratch the surface using one of the primal elements, we might profitably step back and set out the chief methodological moves made thus far in this book. It is a fitting way to bring this Ethics 101 primer to a close.

The aim is not to introduce new subject matter. Rather, it is to be self-conscious about the ethical method we've already used to this point. While that entails further commentary, it is commentary on what has gone before.

As religious ethics "in a new key," we have proposed a moral universe different from that of modernity. It is a universe with a different infrastructure and additional sources of moral knowledge and wisdom. We laid out much of this earlier, naming it "a seismic shift from the encapsulated human self and human society to the ecosphere as center, boundary and subject; from human justice to creation justice; and from my bounded human community to the unbounded community of all life."[77] We also proposed a stringent criterion by which to measure all our moral and religious impulses. Are they Earth-honoring? Do they contribute to Earth's preservation and restoration? Is life and what it requires the better because of them? Are the parental elements of life accorded their place? Has the shift from ego to ecosphere as the center of moral work been made? Does it re-form itself around the human vocation of tilling and keeping in such a way as to move into new first works for the age of the Anthropocene?

Further, we have used a variety of sources for insight and reflection—science, religion and religious traditions, empirical and historical studies, literature and song, philosophy and theology, the gleanings of everyday wisdom, and a variety of real-life examples. Of the sciences, those focused on the ecosphere and its health hold high place, as does the experience of individuals and persons whose livelihood and thought are tied directly to the ecosphere and local conditions. Not least, we have assumed that nature in its many forms is always a teacher, though not always a teacher of morality in any simple, straightforward sense. Not all sources need be named at this point to recognize that *which* sources are used, and their relative influence, always counts for the moral and ethical outcome. To be conscious of method is to be aware of sources and how they are used.

We tied all this to a structural analysis of human privilege and power. Power analysis is a methodological tool in its own right, the absence of which omits critically important factors. In this case we have proposed the interacting factors of race, class, gender, culture, and species power. How does human power interact with both the vulnerabilities and the constructive possibilities within human society and the rest of nature? Some further commentary on these factors is in order.

Take the ethic implicit in Earth-honoring faith. To say, for example, that "planetary health is primary, and human well-being derivative," is, as a matter of method, to seek a nonanthropocentric moral theory that gives primacy to the ecosphere. Because we are born into a great web of belonging, the health of that web is the initial and basic frame of moral reference. The ethical method of Earth-honoring faith thus first asks how the health of the primal elements is secured and then, from there, how the well-being of human life and other life is secured in relation to it. It asks questions of our working moral theory such as these: What individual and collective virtues, what consequences of our decisions and actions, and what fundamental obligations does this web of belonging, this communion, require of us?

Differently said, an Earth-honoring ethic, with a method in keeping with its expanded moral universe, answers the religious question, Who is the neighbor I am to love as I love myself? in the way of H. Richard Niebuhr. The neighbor is "the near one and the far one; the one removed from me by distances in time and space, in convictions and loyalties. [The neighbor] is man and he is angel and he is animal and inorganic being, all that participates in being."[78]

The legal definition of the term "neighbor" was handed down in a 1932 decision of the British House of Lords on bottling contaminated ginger beer: Our neighbor is anyone or anything that we think may reasonably be affected by our actions.[79] The meaning of neighbor, then, is not only its literal meaning, "the nearby farmer," or, more loosely, "the nigh one." The neighbor in a webbed world is the far one as well, both in time and space. It's the "zoo in you" extended,[80] the neighbor in a million guises as the articulated form of creation to whom justice, as the fullest possible flourishing of creation, is due. So the House of Lords got it right in ruling that the neighbor is "anyone or anything... affected by our actions." The water of life is the neighbor, as is the soil-womb from which we come. The air we breathe is neighbor, as is the energy we burn. ("My skin is happy on the black dirt, which speaks a language my bones understand," is Barbara Brown Taylor's sense of neighborly belonging.)[81] The enemy is the neighbor, too, as well as those for whom we willingly sacrifice. Those affected by my actions are thus almost infinite in extent and with no preordained boundaries, given the complex supracommunity of the ecosphere. My actions certainly cross the boundaries Jesus gathered up in the Who-is-my-neighbor parable of the Good Samaritan—boundaries of religion, class, social standing, function in society, address, and purity codes. Responsibility of this kind *does* pertain to "all that participates in being"(Niebuhr).

The complex ethical infrastructure we propose admittedly creates moral conundrums and uncertainties. Earth-honoring ethic is a path we will have to make by walking it, without cairns at every point we need them. Morality, too, is contested in a period of hard transitions. Consider the questions that follow if, as a matter of working method, we view the ecosphere as the all-encompassing neighbor: How do we conceptualize moral claims in this broader community of life and its generative elements? How do we negotiate conflicts? Are "rights," whether human, animal, or biotic, the best path? If "respect" for other-than-human nature is preferred to "rights," how is such respect given moral and legal substance? What standing do "inanimate but structured objects (rivers, rock)" (Mary Midgely) have? In what ways do moral norms for human interactions—compassion, mercy, empathy, sacrifice, justice—pertain to human/more-than-human relationships? In the same way they pertain to human/human interaction, or differently? Is sentience and sensation of pleasure and pain the primary measure?

Or, from another methodological reference point, that of the sources of our morality, how do we "read" these sources from the experience of Earth? If in religious traditions, for example, desert spirituality mirrors the desert, mountain spirituality the mountains, and coastal spirituality the oceans, do these deserts, mountains, and oceans pose claims of moral responsibility because they are among the agents of our moral-spiritual formation and expression? Or, if culture is invariably made possible and affected by landscape, and is understood as invariably nature-culture, does the accompanying landscape require a conscious ethic of place on the part of the cultures present there? Does it shape a culture's responsibilities for beauty and restoration? Does it offer an angle for assessing a culture's way of life that is not otherwise provided? If, for example, I live in Santa Fe, New Mexico, I know that Santa Fe would not be what it is ethnically, linguistically, aesthetically, apart from the interplay of three strong cultures and their ties to the land—Puebloan Indian, Hispanic, and Anglo. The valley of the Rio Grande, bounded by the Sangre de Christo and Jemez ranges of the Rocky Mountains and the red-rock mesa country of the southern reaches of the Colorado Plateau, forge both the condition and ethos of northern New Mexico. The cultures and charms of Santa Fe are inextricable from the high mountain desert of which it is part. All this repeats but does not yet answer our questions: How does an Earth-honoring ethic "read" cultures and spiritualities from the perspective and experience of Earth in a given locale? And how do these cultures and spiritualities reckon their place as affected now by other locales as well, nestled as they are in a global community of communities?[82] What responsibilities, both local and global, follow from the ties to place?

In short, the method of Earth-honoring ethic we propose broadens, deepens, and renders more complex the factors that human beings consider as they raise and answer moral queries. The kind of people we strive to be, the kind of life we seek to live, and the kind of path we wish to take in getting there are all made conceptually more difficult by shifting from the ego to the ecosphere as the center of moral attention and method.

Is the task impossible? Is the world much too much "with us" (Wordsworth)? If the task is not impossible, how might the new responsibilities of a new era on a tough, new planet be put in place? We mention two means, as a start.

One is constitutions and the law. The postapartheid South African constitution, for example, mandates that South Africans' use of water not exceed what native ecosystems require. Water use must be regulated in ways that meet human and ecosystemic needs together. This is recognition that, from the point of view of the planet's integral functioning, human and ecosystemic needs *are* bound together in a hydrological system that is ultimately one. And it is recognition that the rule of law is a way to carry out basic moral responsibility whether South African hearts and minds would voluntarily undertake their water responsibility or not.

To those who say, "You can't legislate morality," the reply is that often little else is legislated. Constitutions and the law stipulate the baselines of obligation for citizens, what can and cannot be done. Most of this carries moral content.

Still, the you-can't-legislate-morality advocates have an important point: We will not secure the support, or even the imagination, for effective legislation if the expanded moral universe is not first created by the practices of anticipatory communities functioning as communities of moral formation. If the seeds of an Earth ethic are not planted and watered in our initial communities of moral formation, they will not germinate and grow. To recall our earlier discussion, market and state as proxies cannot of themselves replace intimate communities of moral nurture and do not effectively substitute for them. Furthermore, to do what markets and states can do for life together requires moral resources and support they do not of themselves provide. They, too, draw from the communities of civil society. "You can't legislate morality" is recognition that bottom-line responsibility for an expanded moral universe must have a place in the hearts, souls, and minds of the people if deep change is to be sustained.[83] Newly learned responsibility is initially achieved through citizenship in core communities beyond the communities of law and market exchange.

It bears remembering what these communities do. Our overall horizon of moral expectation, the very sense of reality that so deeply affects moral development, is inculcated early on in family dynamics and the patterns of other first communities of intimacy. As feminists point out so effectively, gender and sexual patterns as basic biosocial patterns are learned here, to the point of rendering the cultural "natural"—second nature treated as simply "the way things are." So, too, are a whole range of ways we conceive body and spirit, reason and senses, ourselves, our neighbors, and the rest of nature. Likewise, the language through which reality is mediated and ordered is learned in this school, with indelible moral effects. If, for example, our God-talk teaches that human relationships along stipulated lines of above-and-below authority are the theologically and morally proper relations both to God and one another, then a way of life has been learned as we learn to talk. And if our nature-talk always puts the other-than-human world outside us and as an object of use to a species that arrogates all mind to itself, then children learn with language itself that the natural world is theirs to exploit. In short, the life-fashioning threads that run between these close-in schools of morality and peoples' wider expectations are strong fiber. Home and neighborhood, school, temple, and the company we keep are the first schools of justice and injustice. Creation justice begins at home.

In sum, it is clear that the moral difficulty posed by expanding the moral universe is genuine. It is not impossible, however. After all, many peoples and cultures have lived with a community-of-life ethic that accorded high standing to the parental elements of earth, air, fire, and water. Many of these peoples and cultures have even done so in the tough, new context of imposing forces that originated far from the reach of their local practices, like colonization or regional climate change. Yet who wants those negative imposing forces to continue to reign?

In any event, the moral difficulty of a different moral universe pales beside the mound of real-world troubles we face if the conventional ways of industrial-technological ethics remain in place and the ecosphere and creation justice are not given their due. Of course, simply conceptualizing our responsibility anew and facing its hard questions will not of itself achieve the needed moral universe anymore than moral theory and justice theory, as theory, achieve what they seek. Nonetheless, getting the "think withs" and the symbols right is a necessary and powerful tool (see fig. 7.1).

Perhaps we have said enough to make clear how significant method is as a standing element of any morality and ethic. Method matters; it shapes the whole and structures the outcome. Awareness of it aids moral clarity and deliberation.

Next . . .

As we bring Part I—The Creature We Are, The World We Have, The Faith We Seek, and The Ethic We Need—to a close, we turn to the communities required for the long, hard transition to ecological civilization, and to the shared religious resources they can draw upon for Earth-honoring living.

Justice : The surviving and thriving of planetary creation
Love : Belonging and equal regard
Responsibility : Care for planetary health

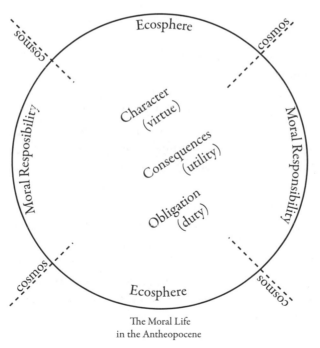

The Moral Life
in the Antheopocene

FIGURE 7.1

Interlude

As I went down to the river to pray,
studyin' about that good ol' way
and who shall wear the starry crown
good Lord, show me the way.
O sisters, let's go down,
let's go down, come on down.
O sisters, let's go down,
down to the river to pray.
O brothers, let's go down,
let's go down, come on down.
O brothers, let's go down,
down to the river to pray.

Earth can industrialize but once in the manner and on the scale it has. The throbbing modern world cannot be replicated and extended indefinitely.[1] Costs cannot be met; natural resources are not as abundant and available as they were for previous epochs; climate change and the needs of a human population of seven, then eight, then nine or ten billion, to say nothing of the needs of the rest of nature, will multiply the wicked problems already crowding the horizon; and psychic energy to continue on the same road will wane as the agricultural, industrial, and information revolutions slow down and lose their allure. The adaptive challenges pile up.[2]

To meet them a different Earth faith bearing other moral-spiritual energy and issuing in an Earth ethic appropriate to the altered world is in order. Part I cleared a conceptual path for this better way. While conceptual clarity is necessary, it cannot suffice. What suffice are not good ideas, critical though they be, but good communities; in our case, anticipatory communities meeting adaptive challenges.

"Anticipatory communities" are home places where it is possible to reimagine worlds and reorder possibilities, places where new or renewed practices give focus to an ecological and postindustrial way of life. Such communities have the qualities of a haven, a set-apart and safe place yet a place open to creative risk. Here basic moral formation happens by conscious choice and not by default (simply conforming to the ethos and unwritten ethic of the surrounding culture). Here eco-social virtues are consciously cultivated and embodied in community practices.[3] Here the fault lines of modernity are exposed.

Robert Pogue Harrison ends a late chapter of *Gardens* by quoting these words of Marco Polo in Italo Calvino's *Invisible Cities*: "There are two ways to escape suffering from the inferno where we live every day, that we form by being together." The first is "to accept the inferno and become such a part of it that you can no longer see it." The second "is risky and demands constant vigilance and apprehension: seek and learn to recognize who and what, in the midst of the inferno, are not inferno, then make them endure, give them space."[4] That space and apprehension is the space and apprehension of anticipatory communities.

Fortunately, communities with a flair for this kind of creativity are springing up everywhere. *Orion* magazine has a starter list: "[L]ocal economics and local currency, community transition, permaculture, corporate responsibility, alternative health, alternative energy and clean technology, local energy, social and economic justice, sustainable cities, alternative housing, efficient building practices and ecological design, climate action, regional agriculture and food systems, and holistic education. All of these are moving forward."[5]

The editors go on to say that "the movement in favor of truth and beauty has always been a hard, slow road. We know it always will be. But it has never been simpler for the people who want to express their values to take steps that contribute to positive, meaningful change."[6]

In Part II, we present the strong strands, the deep traditions that religious ethics brings to the work of anticipatory communities. But those millennial traditions do not stand on their own; they serve religious discipleship. Discipleship is the classic religious name for learning a way of life. It is "studyin' about that good ol' way" (or new way). Discipleship—as the Way, as a Call, and as Practices—is thus the bridge from Part I to Part II.

The Way

New religions are rarely the offspring of bejeweled emperors and royal decrees. They are usually born of a few undaunted, poorly dressed disciples. Religions are not, however, on that account modest. They provide nothing less than a cosmic story of which we and all else are parts, offering a grand narrative about the origin, destiny, meaning, and end of life. And they propose a manner of life in keeping with that meaning. They provide the practices, rituals, and disciplines appropriate to the cosmic story. They stipulate a "way."

The stories religious traditions tell, as part of the Way, are as diverse as the peoples who tell them.[7] The ways of life embodying the varied stories are similarly diverse, a note struck by the deep traditions of subsequent chapters. Nonetheless there always *is* a story, a grand narrative threaded with familiar tales told innumerable times, now and again with new twists and turns and chapters.

Secondly, there is tradition, woven of numerous paths tried and taken and argued about without end, sometimes ferociously. If the tradition belongs to a living faith it is rich, varied, and changing. The deep traditions discussed here are, if open to Earth-honoring reform, the living traditions of the dead rather than the dead traditions of the living.

Thirdly, there is a key leader, a sage, a messiah, a guru who teaches a way of life that incarnates the grand story and its meaning. Moreover—and this is not a marginal point—the revered leader teaches a way and walks a path that is in tension with, if not in outright conflict with, conventional wisdom and ways. Death can come early for such charismatic leaders, and often it does not come gently. But whether death comes prematurely by violence or arrives as the quiet end to fourscore years and ten, the life of the sage or messiah somehow triumphs even in the precincts of the tomb. Whether the leader's way is weal, woe, or both together, his or her path is sufficiently idiosyncratic to appear as something new on the Earth. This is Prince Siddhartha become the Buddha in fifth-century B.C.E. India; it's Lao-tzu in sixth-century B.C.E. China; it's Moses from Egypt to the wilderness; it's Jesus and his messianic renewal movement in the Roman Empire; it's the Prophet Muhammad ("Muhammad" is Arabic for "The Praised") in sixth-century C.E. Mecca.

In sum, new religions are almost always born in discipleship; they spring, mustard seed fashion, from small beginnings; and they are marked by a sage or charismatic healer who embodies an alternative way, a way taken up by the "disciplined" ones who think they wield a power against which the gates of hell will not prevail.

Moral impulse

Such chutzpah invariably gives discipleship a strong moral sense and vigorous moral impulse. Discipleship does not *create* moral consciousness; that belongs to the kind of creature we are. But it strengthens and channels it. Its disciplined dedication to a better way works at the "ought" and "how" sides of the "is/ought/how" gap and focuses the human impulse to create a better world. It generates energy to be, in our own persons, the kind of change we seek and to create the kind of world we ought in the form of anticipatory communities. This is a dreamed-of future burrowing into the recalcitrant present. This is life in pursuit of "the beloved community" (Martin Luther King Jr.), the Kingdom come on Earth as in heaven. This is discipleship "as transformation through an alternative community and the reversal of conventional wisdom."[8] These are children of hope on a road that does *not* lead to Rome.[9]

Discipleship's strong moral impulse can be frustrated, of course. Some people live complacent lives all of the time and, thanks to the drag of normalcy, all people do so some of the time. The strong world of "is" and its powers are always at hand, including its power over human imaginations. Many Christians of Augustine's time couldn't conceive a world other than the Roman Empire, even when they had experienced it as their enemy, and even as Goths, Visigoths, and Vandals ransacked it. In the same way, there are Christians in the United States who cannot conceive their own Christian life apart from "America." This capture of the imagination by what is, and its attendant complacency, enfeebles discipleship. Civil religion substitutes for discipleship, as culturally captive faith excludes a more radical way.

Paradoxically, discipleship can also be enfeebled by mislocating "ought." There are lives lived so completely in other worlds that the only real thing, morally speaking, is their "disconnect" with this world. Here religious imagination leads away from this world rather than deeper into it. Otherworldliness more accurately describes this faith than does the fire of renewal and first things done over. "In heaven" replaces "on Earth." Deeper communion with God translates as diminished communion with Earth. Rather than the Kingdom coming, we leave. And while such faith freely uses the rhetoric of discipleship, this discipleship is often privatized, strangely aloof, and small-minded. Its obsession is "my salvation." As measured by the righteousness of Israel and Jesus, Gandhi or the Dalai Lama, such discipleship is muted. It is not about "the whole of earthly life."

Yet this is an aside. The point is that discipleship generates moral energies and channels the moral impulses that arise from our human nature as creatures that live their lives across a yawning is/ought/how gap. It generates a Way that, while it knows the deep joy of a life centered in God and the hymn of the cosmos, also is life on the edge, life lived in tension with the principalities and powers of the age.

All this is discipleship described in generic terms, pan-religious and pan-human. That has its virtues. But the disciple's life is not lived there. So we turn to living historical traditions and begin with the children of Abraham, Sarah, and Hagar.

Public discipleship

Discipleship as "the Way" is common to Judaism, Islam, and Christianity. In Judaism it's *halakah* (sometimes called "the walk") and *imitatio Dei*. In Islam it's *shari'a* (the pathway to water) and submission to Allah. In Christianity it's the way of Jesus and *imitatio Christi*. All are notions of a life lived as a "People of God"; and all assume that this life not only *ought*, but *can*, by grace, be lived as a matter of daily habit and daily bread, even though the Way may be as demanding as the Sermon on the Mount, the Torah instruction in the wilderness, or the seven pillars of Islam.

What about the public face of discipleship? Discipleship is "public" in three ways in the Abrahamic traditions. Discipleship is about a "*people of the Way*" and a *community* pattern of life. This people is a "public" in its own right. To use early Christians as an example, Tertullian calls the second-century church a *secta dei* or a *societas dei* (a society of God); Paul calls the first-century churches a "body" that constitutes a new humanity; Peter calls this people "a holy nation," "a chosen race," "a peculiar people." These images are quintessentially public. That is, they are images of a structured social body, like the polis itself, where decisions are made, roles are assigned, and powers are exercised for life together in keeping with the commitments and values of the discipleship community. The word "church" is quintessentially public as well. *Ekklesia* in Greek means a called meeting or an assembly, like a town meeting. The *ekklesia* gathers to deliberate and discern, on behalf of the wider society, how the common life of its members is to be ordered.[10]

This public, as the community of disciples, displays a recurring pattern. The pattern is usually present when a new religion is born and breaks out again when it renews itself. Its elements are these:

- A sense of divine power as the power for peoplehood.
- A basic equality that dignifies the varied gifts of varied members.
- Forms of address that tend more toward "brother" and "sister" than titles.
- A sharing of resources with a view to need.
- An effort to cross natural-social boundaries for a more inclusive community.

- An uneasy relationship with every dominant order, every "Caesar."
- An empowerment of all members, either as laity or within a new religious order.
- A conviction that somehow all this is good news and a vanguard example for the wider world.[11]

Secondly, the Abrahamic Way is "public" in that it is lived across the whole of earthly life. The Way is a comprehensively righteous, or just, life. It is a manner of living that suffuses the whole and marks the meaning of the whole in its practices. This whole includes what is unsatisfactorily named "spirituality": a world within to match the world without, including the world aspired to—moral, religious, and natural-cultural dimensions aligned with technical and institutional ones. Earth-honoring spirituality would make certain this whole is truly so, by including, even centering on, planetary health as the responsibility of this public.

Thirdly, the Way is publicly visible. It is marked by practices that are strong enough to form the next generation and assure that the faith has children and the children have faith; practices that are strange enough to arouse the curious and gather them in for initiation; and practices that are intelligible enough to provide sound reasons for a faith that moves mountains and peoples. If the Way cannot be seen and fathomed, it is un-believable.

For Jews, Muslims, and Christians, then, discipleship is a righteous life in a community faithful to God. Posting markers on this journey is a collective undertaking that is, at the same time, deeply personal, a matter of heart, soul, and mind. There are hidden dimensions and quiet, even empty, spaces the disciple hardly dares enter, except in prayer or contemplation. They are no better known than Dag Hammarskjold's Who, Someone, or Something to which he answered with his very being. But even these worlds within worlds, wheels within wheels, and mysteries within mysteries are the internal recesses of a public faith intended to be no less than a witness to the nations.

The call

Discipleship as the Way of a People is invariably associated with a call to follow and a long obedience. The call is usually presented by a guru, messianic figure, or revered leader as an address asking for an unequivocal commitment. Jesus' call, for example, is direct, personal, and public, a call to ordinary people in their workaday world to fold up the nets, or close out the tax accounts, and pack up for a different future.

But the call may not be so stark, even in the same religious tradition. Consider the call experience of a consummately public figure, a secretary-general of the United Nations. It doesn't conform to the classic call to discipleship, yet it has all the marks of integrity as such a call. The secretary-general writes:

> I don't know Who—or what—put the question. I don't know when it was put. I don't even remember answering. But at some moment, I did answer *Yes* to Someone—or Something—and from that hour I was certain that existence is meaningful and that, therefore my life, in self-surrender had a goal.
>
> From that moment I have known what it means "not to look back," and to "take no thought for the morrow."
>
> Led by the Ariadne's thread of my answer through the labyrinth of life, I realized that the Way leads to a triumph which is a catastrophe, and to a catastrophe which is a triumph, that the price for committing one's life would be reproach, and that the only elevation possible to a person lies in the depths of humiliation. After that, the word "courage" lost its meaning, since nothing could be taken from me.
>
> As I continued along the Way, I learned, step by step, word by word, that behind every saying in the Gospels stands one person and one person's experience. Also behind the prayer that the cup might pass from him and his promise to drink it. Also behind each of the words from the Cross.[12]

As noted above, the classic discourse for discipleship in many religious traditions is that of "the Way" and resolute assent to it, a life-committing "Yes" rendered at a particular moment. Similarly, to answer "Yes" to that Someone—or Something, as Hammarskjold's text has it—inscribes life as meaningful, despite all: a joyous life and an abundant life, a life that savors living, yet a life that entails drinking the earthly cup to the dregs and even taking up the cross. "When Christ calls, he bids one come and die."[13]

The cited passage above is from Hammarskjold's book, published in English as *Markings*. The original Swedish is *Vagmarken*, "Markers of the Way" or "Road Markers"; "cairns," if you wish. Hammarskjold's account could not be more deeply personal. Yet this is a consummately public figure and exemplary world citizen on an exacting and uncertain journey.

Though the secretary-general's allusion to discipleship and the Way as "Road Markers" is peppered with allusions to Jesus and his Way, the title "Road Markers" or "Markers of the Way" is not a recollection of Jesus but

Jeremiah: "Set up road markers for yourself, make yourself guideposts; consider well the highway, the road by which you went" (Jeremiah 31:21).

And who are those instructed by Jeremiah? Not individual travelers, though Hammarskjold is certain he is being addressed at the core of his being. The instructed are the wayward People of God, "wayward" in both senses—a People on the Way and a People gone astray. Jeremiah continues: "Return, O virgin Israel, return to these your cities. How long will you waver, O faithless daughter? For the Lord has created a new thing on the earth; a woman encompasses a man" (31: 21b–22).

"A new thing on the earth; a woman encompasses a man." For a faith and way of life that was, at that time, deeply, unrelentingly patriarchal, Jeremiah's word, "a woman encompasses a man," is startling. It is sufficiently outside the paradigm to have had sober biblical scholars arguing over its interpretation for centuries. Though they have not reached a consensus, their varied readings have this in common: Here is a sharp reversal of expected roles and a new departure; and this "new thing on the earth" is, for Jeremiah, the Lord's doing. This is discipleship as dying to the old and being reborn to the new. In the words of one congregation's Whole Earth Covenant, this faith "may call us to even more radical action than we presently envision."[14]

What might be learned about the Way from the consummately public and consummately private Hammarskjold? What might be said about religious discipleship if Hammarskjold uncovers important dimensions of it?

At least this: The Way is often unexpected and only partially known and tracked. Perhaps it is precisely because the disciples' Way cannot be known that the instruction is to set up road markers, make guideposts, and consider well the road taken as well as the road forsaken.

Secondly, discipleship is a pilgrimage, a pilgrimage sometimes in the venturesome, uncertain, and dangerous manner of Abraham and Sarah and Hagar, where fortune is matched to misfortune, and where desert and bare survival are matched to grace, faith, and "a new thing upon the earth." In this case, the new thing upon the earth is no less than the birth of two peoples and their Ways, Judaism and Islam. Other religions will have their counterpart tales of heroic beginnings (or modest ones) and continued pilgrimage.

Finally, the Spirit may take disciples where they did not expect or wish to go, like Jonah and Jeremiah. The disciples' expectations may even be reversed, and God may, for a good that disciples cannot even imagine, do a new thing upon the earth. "The woman encompasses the man"; "The stone that is rejected becomes the cornerstone" (Acts 12:11b).

Hammarskjold, as secretary-general of the United Nations, came to know such vicissitudes well, and long before one of them took his life in a plane crash. He had prepared for history's complexities through his own habits of moral-spiritual discernment, though one must read more of "Markers of the Way" in order to tease this out. The immediate point is not about Hammarskjold, however. It is rather that irony and uncertainty, pathos and tragedy, as well as "a new thing upon the earth," all belong to discipleship. The deep traditions we will be examining assume this. They lived it, and it shaped them.

"Do[ing] a new thing upon the earth" adds another element of Earth-honoring discipleship across interfaith and ecumenical borders. The Way is made by treading it. It is forged, from time to time, on new ground. Discipleship is not only "studyin' the good ol' way," but stark innovation. *Improvisation: The Drama of Christian Ethics* may be the title of Samuel Wells's book on Christian discipleship, but "improvisation" pertains to other faiths as well. As times and history change and ages come and go, discipleship is necessarily a drama of improvisation.

Such is now our drama. Religious discipleship has never before lived with a globally threatened ecosphere, or genome knowledge for unimagined germ-line transformations, or weapons of mass destruction available to desperate states and rogue actors, or the unprecedented organizational possibilities that instant, worldwide electronic communication offers to grassroots organizations as well as corporate powerhouses. Improvisation is of necessity the shape of discipleship for Earth-honoring faith. Hard transitions are not negotiated without it.

Yet improvisation as the experience of discipleship is exactly what marked its borning cry as new religion. Discipleship was the groundbreaking way of life that set out on a new path cut by a leader who didn't expect to live the life or found the movement that ensued. The language was often that of obedience and submission and staying a set course, but a close look finds unscripted drama and making the path by walking it.

In any event, there *is* a Way. However uncertain and improvised the venture is, discipleship is not oblivion or chaos. Nor is it the prison of aimlessness or depression. In Hammarskjold's image, the thread of Ariadne is the slender but certain guide through the labyrinth of life. There is a Way, and it has markers.

Practices

The steady markers of the Way, the reason the Way is not waywardness, and even the raw materials of improvisation, all turn on the same thing, the *practices* of discipleship. Beliefs, creeds, theology, and cosmology are all empty apart from the practices of discipleship. These practices, or disciplines, provide a spiritual-moral guidance system even when the practices themselves are not overtly moral or ethical in tone or formulation. The practices first create, then continue, the alternative path of the Way; like a fine potter shaping a bowl, they craft the disciples' life.

We can call the recurring core practices of discipleship its "focal" practices. There are also ancillary practices, many of which are the stuff of necessary improvisation when the standard ways of doing things fail. (That starter list from *Orion*, cited above, is a list of improvised ancillary practices.)

Sometimes core practices and ancillary practices are merged to display unusual power. The examples of the nature and power of symbols in chapter 1 do that—the Buddhist ordination of trees in order to save them, or the Maryknoll adaptation of Catholic "stations" to tell the story of the universe "flaming forth from the heart of God." But we will treat focal practices separately, at least initially.

Focal practices embody dramatic distillations of the grand story, the foundation narrative, of a faith. These distillations take the form of repeated individual and communal actions. They speak to something deep in human nature, and they bear moral substance whether it is named or not. They take place in the present, but they bespeak a world longed for, a world in the making; the world of "might be," Nirvana, Eden, Paradise, the "beloved community."

While each religious tradition has its own set of markers and focal practices, there are some that surface over and over again across time and in almost every locale. Hospitality, taking in the stranger and gathering for a sacred meal, may be universal as a community practice of discipleship. Learning to say Yes or No, the hard work of discerning the personal path that "chooses life," is an ongoing discipline. So is keeping Sabbath, or a counterpart observance of sacred time and space, with appropriate ritual and festivity; and honoring the body, whether at birth, through the course of life, or in the hour of death and passage. Illness and healing, too, are often surrounded with community practices of a known pattern, as are feasting and fasting and ablutions. And there is "singing our lives," testimony and witness, those gatherings where the discipleship community shares its story and offers it up in spoken or sung praise, anguish, or doubt. Peacemaking and nonviolent conflict resolution has, in some form or another, always been a prime discipline as well. Not least, forgiveness is a core pan-religious practice, the means by which the heart is unburdened and grace sufficient to embark anew is offered. While only a bare sampling, and without the specific form or name given by each religious community, these at least illustrate focal practices that characterize discipleship. The deep traditions that follow in Part II will exemplify further how substantive focal practices are.[15]

Next . . .

Exploring discipleship as Earth-honoring Way, Call, and Practices suffices as the transition between our meditations on the creature we are, the world we have, the faith we seek, and the ethic we need, and a constructive response that takes the form of renewed deep religious traditions speaking to Earth-destructive forces. Discipleship captures well the heart of a religious ethic and life, and discipleship communities are the kind needed—those anticipatory communities facing adaptive challenges—to do the basic moral-spiritual formation necessary for making a way in tough, challenging times when our destiny is uncertain rather than manifest.

PART TWO

8

Asceticism and Consumerism

Confirm thy soul in self-control, thy liberty in law.
—STANZA, *America the Beautiful*

THOUSANDS KNOW THE opening line of Wordsworth's sonnet, "The World Is Too Much with Us." Most have forgotten what follows.[1]

> The world is too much with us; late and soon,
> Getting and spending, we lay waste our powers:
> Little we see in Nature that is ours;
> We have given our hearts away, a sordid boon!
> This sea that bares her bosom to the moon:
> The winds that will be howling at all hours,
> And are up gathered now like sleeping flowers;
> For this, for everything, we are out of tune;
> It moves us not.[2]

Has "getting and spending"—consumerism—so laid waste our powers, sent our hearts packing, and alienated our souls that we no longer belong to nature and see ourselves in it? Has commoditization so deadened the living world, so leached away the sacred, that even plaintive winds and open seas don't wash our spirits and move them to mystery and wonder? Are we this bereft, this "out of tune," this unmoved?

Wordsworth himself thought so, and chose a conspicuous departure from Christianity as the way back, or ahead.

> Great God! I'd rather be
> A Pagan suckled in a creed outworn;
> So might I, standing on this pleasant lea,
> Have glimpses that would make me less forlorn:
> Have sight of Proteus rising from the sea;
> Or hear old Triton blow his wreathed horn.[3]

His preference for a pagan "creed outworn" notwithstanding, might there be for us, if not for him, other religious traditions that would render us "less forlorn"?

To answer that question, this chapter makes some assumptions. It assumes that Wordsworth speaks poetic truth about a consumerist world so "much with us" that nature "moves us not." It also assumes that the political economy is more than production and exchange; it is the phantom cosmology of our time, with consumerism its daily demand and dead nature its measure of success ("The more quickly the living world is converted into dead products, the higher the GNP").[4]

At the same time, this chapter assumes that thousands (it is likelier millions) seek a spiritual home and habitat beyond global consumerism. Some may choose Wordsworth's path: an ancient (or recent) nature-honoring creed. Others may choose retrieval, continuation, or reformation of some ancient or newborn religious asceticism. This time, however, it will be a conversion to God and the Earth in the same moment, with Earth-honoring disciplines, virtues, and habits.[5]

Such is the path chosen here. It carries its own assumption: Asceticism speaks to something deep in the human spirit and is a requirement of authentic humanity. Self-mastery, self-control, restraint, pleasure, and wonder are home to us on our better days. "Confirm thy soul in self-control, thy liberty in law" is not alien, even when it battles other impulses.

This path has its own questions as well. Are there religious asceticisms that address the spiritual vacuity of consumerism and its irresponsible use of the Earth? Are there ascetic traditions that indict modern religious expressions for their loss of nature and their alliances with industrialism and consumerism as their preferred habitat and home? Are there other ways to link asceticism and modernity than the one unwittingly forged in the partnership of inner-worldly asceticism and early capitalism? Are there reborn asceticisms that love the Earth fiercely in a spiritually rich but materially simple way of life?

In short, is there in asceticism, old and new, a hope-borne answer for a world still "too much with us"?

Consumerism: The mature economy

How did we come to this place? Whence the global phenomenon of mass affluence? We know the outcome well (The World We Have) and some of the history (conquest, colonization, commerce, and Christianity together as "civilization" and the Great Transformation). But more needs be said about the phantom cosmology that undergirds its pulsing social-psychological drive.

Wordsworth's contemporary Alexis de Tocqueville is famous for capturing the lasting character of U.S. society in his *Democracy in America* (1835). For our purposes, however, the more relevant diagnosis appears in an equally remarkable but lesser-known work, *The American Commonwealth* (1888) by James Bryce. "All that need be here said," Bryce writes, "is that a people with comparatively little around it in the way of historic memories and associations to touch its emotion, a people whose energy is chiefly absorbed in commerce and the development of the material resources of its territory, a people consumed by a feverish activity that gives little opportunity for reflection or for the contemplation of nature, seems most of all to need to have its horizon widened, its sense of awe and mystery touched, by whatever calls it away from the busy world of sight and sound into the stillness of faith and meditation."[6]

Bryce doesn't quite say that what this people, "consumed by a feverish activity" and little given to reflection and contemplation of nature, need in order to be human is asceticism and a sense for the sacred and the mystical. But he comes close. In any event, what this people, joining others, eventually wrought is mass affluence as not only the base but the systemic demand of what became the global economy. The conditions for abundance on this scale were set in motion by those "whose energy is chiefly absorbed in commerce and the development of the material resources of its territory" and who were far too preoccupied with the "busy world of sight and sound" to fall quietly and willingly into mystery and meditation.

The roots of mass consumption go deep—Bryce is already looking back in 1888. But the single most decisive turn, as we have noted, came in the wide wake of World War II, first in the United States, then in Europe, followed closely by Japan and East and South Asia, and now in privileged social strata across the globe.

The stage was set by the privations of the Depression, the sacrifices of the war years, the return home of tens of thousands of troops, all in their working years, and the need to rebuild Europe and East Asia after history's most destructive war. These compelled a response that was anticipated by the Roosevelt and Truman administrations. New Dealer Robert Nathan's *Mobilizing for Abundance* appeared in 1944. In 1946 former head of the wartime Office of Price Administration Chester Bowles offered *Tomorrow without Fear*. Both were programmatic works and both argued for consumerism as the successor to wartime mobilization of the economy. Roosevelt himself put a key element in place only months before his death. Aboard a warship in the Red Sea out-fitted like a desert oasis, complete with a small herd of sheep, Roosevelt cut a deal with the House of Saud. United States support for Ibn Saud and his family as the rulers of Saudi Arabia was exchanged for a guarantee of an unlimited flow of oil and oil profits.[7]

Yet energy agreements and programmatic ideas go nowhere without enabling legislation. Truman's signature to the Employment Act of 1946 put the programs into play. "The propensity to consume"[8]—that is the explicit language of the act—became federal policy.

Still, even federal policy of itself did not suffice. A world economy was in view and it needed new institutions for the postwar world. In July 1944 world leaders gathered for just that purpose in Bretton Woods, New Hampshire. United States Secretary of the Treasury Henry Morgenthau presided and, in his opening speech, laid out the infinite-growth assumption of global con-sumerism. All peoples of Earth were to enjoy "the fruits of material progress on an earth infinitely blessed with natural resources." They need only embrace the "elementary economic axiom . . . that prosperity has no fixed limits. It is not a finite substance to be diminished by division."[9]

It was an assumption and mainstay of economic theory and policy that would last. Larry Summers, a later head economist of a Bretton Woods institu-tion, the World Bank (also Secretary of the Treasury under President Clinton, president of Harvard University, and economic adviser to President Obama), argued against any limits to growth, even on a changing planet: "There are no . . . limits to the carrying capacity of the earth that are likely to bind any time in the foreseeable future. There isn't a risk of an apocalypse due to global warming or anything else. *The idea that we should put limits on growth because of some natural limit is a profound error.*"[10]

All postwar economic sectors soon found their bible in W. W. Rostow's *The Stages of Economic Growth: A Non-Communist Manifesto*, published to great acclaim in 1953 and reissued periodically thereafter. Rostow's vision was genuinely global. All societies everywhere are included in one or another of his five stages of economic growth: the traditional society, the preconditions for takeoff, the takeoff, the drive to maturity, and the age of high mass con-sumption.[11] Progression from one stage to the next borrowed a key term from biology and nature's unfolding and applied it, with a new meaning, to the political economy: "development." Of crucial note is that the *telos*, the final stage, of this "natural" development is an economy of "high mass consump-tion." Defined as "the mature economy," this is the proper goal of "the feverish activity" of a people "whose energy is chiefly absorbed in commerce" (Bryce).

The world had seen nothing like the long post–World War II boom. For the twentieth century as a whole, the economy expanded 14-fold, energy use 16-fold, industrial output 40-fold, carbon dioxide emissions 13-fold, and water use 8-fold.[12] Ten times more energy was used in that century than during the previous millennium, more tons of topsoil were lost than were formed over the previous millennium, and more rocks and soil were moved by humans in the twentieth century than by volcanoes, glaciers, and tectonic plates![13] Yet the bulk of this fundamental change came after 1950 (recall the graphs in chapter 2), and, if Alan Durning's calculations are correct, global consumer classes produced and consumed as many goods and services in the half century from 1950 to 2000 as throughout *the entire period of history prior to that date*.[14]

The moral argument was straightforward: All this "getting and spending" clearly redounded to the common good. The popular press shared this conviction with planners, corporate officers, and consumers. A *Life* photo essay, titled "Family Status Must Improve—It Should Buy More for Itself to Better the Living of Others," appeared in the pages of the nation's most popular magazine in 1947. In before-and-after pictures, working-class families in modest surroundings became middle-class suburbanites with ranch-style houses, big yards, and appliance-rich kitchens. *Life* was only illustrating what a study by the prestigious Twentieth Century Fund had recommended: "To achieve a health and decency standard for everyone by 1960, each U.S. family should acquire, in addition to a pleasant roof over its head, a vacuum cleaner, washing machine, stove, electric refrigerator, telephone, electric toaster, and such miscellaneous household supplies as matching dishes, silverware, cooking utensils, tools, cleaning materials, stationery, and postage stamps."[15]

Bride magazine (less prestigious than the Twentieth Century Fund but far more popular) was equally avid. Its widely consulted *Handbook for Newlyweds* carried a clear message: "When you buy the dozens of things you never bought or even thought of before, you are helping to build greater security for the industries of this country. What you buy and how you buy it is very vital to your new life and to our whole American way of living."[16] After the 9/11 terrorist attacks in New York and Washington, D.C., President Bush commended shopping as a concrete, responsible way that Americans could respond. It, too, was somehow linked to "greater security."

Focus on the United States is almost beside the point, however. The 1950 to 2000 explosion Durning describes as without precedent, and still accelerating, is only in part "Made in America." A *New York Times* feature article opens with this: "After construction workers finish plastering a replica of the Arc de Triomphe and buffing the imitation streets of Hollywood, Paris and

Amsterdam, a giant new shopping theme park here will proclaim itself the world's largest shopping mall."[17] Las Vegas? Good guess. Phoenix? Certainly plausible. But no, it's Dongguan, of course. And Dongguan is only one of the many "great malls of China" in process.[18] Four are larger than the United States' largest, the Mall of America in Minneapolis/St. Paul. Two are larger than the West Edmonton Mall in Alberta, heretofore the world's largest. By 2010, seven of the world's ten largest malls were in China. Beijing's Golden Resources Mall covers six million feet (the world's largest office building, the Pentagon, is a trifling 3.7 million).[19] Guangzhou's mall already attracts 600,000 shoppers a day, arriving by bus, train, plane, car, and bicycle. And China is only the avant-garde of the Asian century in the global economy. The Neo-European tribes have fearsome competitors.

Consumerism as soulcraft

Further examples of life, liberty, and the pursuit of shopping as the actual or aspired way of life for billions would be redundant. Besides, further documentation of this kind evades the true question: Is consumerism as a way of life tolerable for Earth and in keeping with our well-being? "Putting scarcity behind us has been pleasant," writes conservative pundit George Will, "but has it been good for us—meaning good for our souls?"[20]

Well before Will, others answered with an emphatic "No." When G. K. Chesterton paid Times Square a visit in 1922, he observed not only serious hedonism, but something else. All the "colours and fires" of that place were being attached to an endless flow of commodities. Light and fire—previously linked to powerful sacred meanings—were now part of the "new illumination" of mass advertising. And this "illumination," Chesterton concluded, "has made people weary of proclaiming great things, by perpetually using it to proclaim small things."[21] H. L. Mencken's version, typical of his populist cynicism, was similar: "Beneath all that false tinsel there's real tinsel." That a life of taking, built upon the carefully cultivated desire for small things, distracts and thwarts the true self is the perennial protest of religious asceticism. When gratification replaces gratitude, and "gluttony becomes a destiny," then a "paltry and degenerate hedonism"[22] subverts the genuinely human; self-absorption traps the true self.

Chesterton would not live to see Times Square illuminated on a scale that would make 1922's "colours and fire" dark and drab by comparison. Nor would he see how successful the political economy's formation of character and cosmology would be. And he certainly could not have imagined the role 24/7/365 advertising would play. (In the United States, monies spent on advertising now exceed those spent on public education from preschool through high school. Since budgets are moral documents, these sums register our lived values.) Desires were created, fed, and nurtured; habits were generated; and the life of goods defined the good life. In short, "the economy" successfully engaged in soulcraft and worldview. It is the phantom cosmology, the shaper of values and the maker of morals. It not only says this is the way we live; it says this is the way we ought to.

There is more, and it is vital. Materialism and acquisitiveness were not simply the choices some citizens might make; materialism and acquisitiveness became systemic requirements of life together, entrenched requisites of the good life. This is institutionalized spirituality and morality, with economic globalization the most universal of faiths. Avarice and greed are not, then, left to the insensitive few; they are structural needs of the political economy. As the day-to-day institutional practice of the "mature" economy of "high mass consumption" (Rostow), they are no longer even required as motive and disposition. Thus persons who are not greedy by disposition share a way of life with those who are. They fly the same planes, drive the same cars, need the same infrastructure, share the same diet, attain the same degrees, work the same jobs, live in the same housing developments, send the kids to the same schools, try their best to get the same economy "back on track," overuse the same soil and water, and lift the same emissions into the atmosphere.

Max Weber, a contemporary of Chesterton, saw this captivity coming. A "disenchanted," or utterly secular, world fired by "economic compulsion" detaches life from "the highest spiritual and cultural values," he wrote in 1904. This compulsion in turn creates "specialists without spirit" as well as "sensualists without heart" who imagine "this nullity" to be "a level of civilization never before achieved." "In the field of its highest development, in the United States," he adds, "the pursuit of wealth, stripped of its religious and ethical meaning, tends to become associated with purely mundane passions, which often give it the character of sport."[23] (One "plays" the stock market, for example, and "bets" on this or that investment.) Then, as we've noticed, democracy becomes the liberty to acquire wealth and use it as one wishes in the ownership society, rather than a system of government used as an equalizing force for the common good and the democratizing of economic, political, and social power.

Yet Weber's own question is, What happens when a capitalist order truly takes hold and daily striving is severed from religious and ethical meaning and from a sense of religious calling and moral duty? Specifically, what happens when "victorious capitalism, since it [now] rests *on mechanical foundations,*"[24] no longer needs the religious asceticism that helped establish it? That is, what happens when people who, with religious zeal and vocation worked hard and saved but led frugal lives, no longer live a simple life? Wealth for inner-worldly ascetics such as the Puritans, Weber wrote, was to lie on the shoulders of the saints "like a light cloak, which can be thrown aside at any moment." But "fate," he concluded, "decreed that the cloak has become an iron cage."[25, 26] Bound to "the technical and economic conditions of machine production" and "the tremendous cosmos of the modern economic order," life in this cage determines "the lives of all the individuals who are born into this mechanism, not only those directly concerned with economic acquisition, with irresistible force." "Perhaps it will so determine them until the last ton of fossilized coal is burnt," Weber adds.[27]

With the spirit of asceticism and its ethic of awe, humility, self-control and restraint gone from capitalism, we may, like pushers and users, have grown dependent upon a destructive way of life we know not how to escape. If so, the answer to Will's question, "Has it been good for our souls?" is Wendell Berry's: "We are not getting something for nothing. We are getting nothing for everything."[28] Here is Chesterton's fear fully realized: The proclamation and pursuit of small things has displaced the proclamation and pursuit of great things. Or worse: The small things are proclaimed and pursued *as* the great things, with little notice of the difference. And the wisdom of every enlightened teacher from time immemorial is lost; namely, that material possessions beyond those needed for survival and simple pleasures should, for the sake of both self and others, be disowned.[29]

Asceticism as soulcraft

What is asceticism's counter to consumerism? What is its kind of discipleship and way of life? How might it be "good for our souls" and the planet's? If we reject the political economy and markets as the chief agents of soulcraft and Earth-keeping, what takes their place? Let one of the masters, immersed in Christian ascetic traditions as well as sacramental and mystical ones, be a guide.

Santa Barbara, California, was the site of a 1997 "Symposium on the Sacredness of the Environment." Bruce Babbitt, Secretary of the Interior in the Clinton administration; Carl Pope, president of the Sierra Club; and His All Holiness Ecumenical Patriarch Bartholomew of Constantinople were all present. If the city rather than the saint is in view, Santa Barbara, like San Francisco, is not a name that leaps to mind for asceticism as a way of life. Yet it is hardly surprising that Bartholomew, leader of 250 million Orthodox

Christians, spoke of it precisely as an "element in our responsibility toward creation." Asceticism, alive since the formative years of the Christian movement and long before in traditions such as Hinduism and Buddhism, has always been about living lightly, gently, and equitably upon the Earth. It "requires . . . a voluntary restraint" and "offers practical examples of conservation." *Enkrateia*, self-control, the Patriarch explained, reduces our consumption and ensures that resources are left for others. *Enkrateia* also frees us from self-directed neediness by centering us in God and in a disciplined life whereby we "work in humble harmony with creation and not in arrogant supremacy against it." It fights the consuming passions of affluence with spiritual richness tethered to material spareness. It "provides an example whereby we may live simply."

Asceticism is "not a flight from society and the world," the black-clad Patriarch told the Santa Barbarans, but "a communal attitude of mind and way of life that leads to the respectful use, and not the abuse of material goods." By contrast, our prevailing "attitude of mind and way of life" abuses. "Many human beings have come to behave as materialistic tyrants." They enshrine abusive behavior in the macroeconomy and "commit crimes against the natural world" that would be considered antisocial and illegal if done to other humans. Labeling these crimes against nature "sins," Bartholomew explained to his audience why they occur. "Excessive consumption may be understood to issue from a worldview of estrangement from self, from land, from life, and from God," he says, in the tradition of the desert fathers and mothers. "Consuming the fruits of the earth unrestrained, we become consumed ourselves, by avarice and greed. Excessive consumption leaves us emptied, out of touch with our deepest self. Asceticism is a corrective practice, a vision of repentance. Such a vision will lead us from repentance to return, the return to a world in which we give, as well as take, from creation."[30]

The same might have been said in secular terms, using the analogy of abuse and the abuser. The abuser is one who does not abide by limits or boundaries. The abuser lacks respect for those boundaries and for the autonomy of his or her victim. Instead, he or she feels somehow entitled to do to the other as he or she desires.

In this case, Bartholomew says, nature is the victim and we are the abusers. His language, however, is steeped in an ascetic religious tradition ("from repentance to return, the return to a world in which we give, as well as take, from creation").

On another occasion, an international symposium on "The Black Sea in Crisis" led by the Ecumenical Patriarch and Jacques Santer, president of the

European Commission, the Patriarch noted further how asceticism is "a corrective practice" and a "vision of repentance." "*It is obvious*," he emphasized, "*that the rapacious exploitation of natural resources, which derives from greed and not from extraordinary circumstances of need, entails a debilitation of nature to the extent that it cannot renew its own productive powers.*" For "the furtherance of natural life" itself, then, "ascetic self-denial" is necessary and "the reduction of many material pleasures" beneficial.[31] In a humanly over-populated world, asceticism is a mandatory pathway to sustainability.

Yet Bartholomew's point is not simply that asceticism and consumerism are contrasting ways of life. The serious charge at the center is that consumerism violates an Earth-honoring ethic and "the true self."

A deeper understanding of asceticism explains why. In ascetic traditions, *encratia/enkrateia* (mastery for moral freedom, or self-restraint and self-control) is achieved by *askesis* (striving, discipline, or training, in the manner of an athlete or a disciple). The word itself is from the Greek verb *askeo*, referring to a working of raw material with training and skill.[32]

This *askesis* is not its own end, however. It is not the latest—or, rather, earliest—diet and self-help program. Nor is its essence the ongoing protest against a life of taking and against the desire for essentially small things. *Askesis* is the soulcraft of a disciplined life centered in God. Both "annunciation" and "renunciation" are consonant with that life. But saying "no" to a distracting way of life is uttered *on the basis* of "yes" to a centered one. A counterworld is thereby nurtured, an alternative to the craving corruptions of a consuming culture in which gratification has displaced gratitude.[33]

It is important to underscore that the "annunciations," and not the protests, are foundational. What is harmful and wrong is harmful and wrong because it contrasts with the better way. Francis doesn't choose voluntary poverty, even vagabondage, in order to protest consumption. His soul is not defined by rebellion or his personality by naysaying. He chooses these because stripping down to such nakedness yields unmediated contact with the beauty of the world in God, and he desires to live in the burdens and wonder of that beauty. He needs, voluntarily, to truly be poor in order to stand with the involuntarily poor and with the self-emptying God of the poor. His faith in God and his humanity set him upon this path of lean, other-directed discipleship.

Like Eastern ascetics, and like Thomas Merton after him, Francis here reflects a theology common to much asceticism. The quest on one level is for our "natural" humanity, our "true" self, the kind of creatures we were created as and, deep down, still are. That quest always entails struggles to overcome the demons. Nonetheless, exorcism as such isn't the goal, anymore than poverty is. The restoration of Adam and Eve, "earth creature" (Adam) and "bearer of life" (Eve), is. Eden is in view, and flashes of its ambit of harmony and innocent desire can be realized in mindful living that heals creation.

Such freedom and innocent desire will not last, however. The "old" (but not aboriginal) self reemerges, ready to do vice-and-virtue battle all over again in a moral struggle that is without end. "Before the mystical experience, the laundry; and after the mystical experience, the laundry" is Buddhist wisdom that pertains equally to the ascetic experience. Since vice and virtue never declare a truce, the ascetic life is a daily contestation and search for the genuine self in God, undertaken with the rigor essential to moral freedom and self-control. It's "confirm thy soul in self-control, thy liberty in law," to recall Bates's prayer for the nation of spacious skies and amber waves of grain.

In sum, a life centered in God frees our natural humanity through sound discipline. That discipline entails specific renunciations, renunciations that, if foregone, lead to practices issuing in a false and abusive self that will act unjustly. Thus fasting counters gluttony, vowed poverty counters possessiveness, abstinence counters "sensuality without heart," frugality counters excess, seclusion and solitude counter excitement and frenzy, prayer counters false allegiance, and a community communism of labor and love counters isolation, tedium, and fixed social status. And while the details of *askesis* vary considerably from time to time, place to place, and tradition to tradition, soulcraft of this sort always includes disciplining the ego and the will as they face ostentation, conspicuous consumption, and loose, exploitative, and violent sex, together with other hedonistic habits of the surrounding world.

Asceticism as a way of life in God includes the "outward" details of any way of life—family and community, clothing and diet, art and architecture, craft and trade, agricultural and healing practices, guiding ritual and rites of passage—as well as the "inward" details—godly qualities of psyche, character, and spirit nurtured by everyday disciplines that shape daily habits. Regulating all the details, inner and outer, is a notion of the Edenic or natural state as a state free of nonessentials and awake with every sense to true, innocent desire. "Can any of you by worrying add a single hour to your span of life?" (Matthew 6:27). It's all "startlingly moral" (Thoreau) and startlingly spiritual (Jesus), together. It is about satisfaction, but satisfaction of the deeper self's need, not greed.

What must not escape us in all this, given a planet in jeopardy at human hands, is that asceticism's sometimes severe "not of this world" dualism does not mean that it is "anti-creation." "Not of this world" is about the world that is "too much with us" (Wordsworth), the world that carries heart, soul, and proper human powers off into alienation from the natural world to which they belong. With due deliberation, practitioners of asceticism seek out the natural world as their spiritual habitat. Frequently that has been desert and mountain wilderness, or other fierce and remote terrain like the "tempestuous winds," "the deep salt sea," and the "old, eternal rocks" of St. Patrick's Celtic asceticism.[34] Or they have created still places, oases of serenity, as patches of Eden amid throbbing centers of (suspect) civilization. In all these, a detailed sense and love of place, attuned to all the signs of local life, marks the ascetic's relationship with the landscape and meticulous attention to garden, field, and craft. "The desert a city," St. Athanasius would write in his famous *Life of St. Anthony*. In his *Festal Epistle* he says about Israel, but true with equal force for the early monks, that they "walked in the wilderness as an inhabited place." For although, "according to the mode of living customary among men, the place was desert; yet, through the gracious gift of the law, and also through their intercourse with angels, it was no longer desolate, but inhabited, yea, more than inhabited."[35]

Thus do ascetics often, and rightly, ascribe holiness to their "inhabited, yea, more than inhabited" wild places. Not by chance, then, desert asceticism issues in desert spirituality, mountain asceticism in mountain spirituality, and coastal asceticism in a spirituality of wind, water, and the land's rocky or sandy boundaries. Images of the divine in art, hymnody, chant, and prayer mirror the land, the sea, and their life. Sacred space is outdoors among the elements, and not indoors only.

High Irish crosses, the art of Celtic monks, are an example. A sun disk rests at the crossing itself, while flora, fauna, biblical figures, and the endless Celtic knot are carved in the stone from top to bottom and left to right. The crosses stand in the open, marking the rough, damp green hills of Ireland and Scotland as places of meditation, holy ground. They gather up and baptize the religious impulses of an earlier nature-religion, that of the Druids.

At the center of the ascetic way is always a life in God. Apart from this, the rest has no point of lasting reference, proper quality, or real power. The choice truly is between God and mammon—mammon as "this world," this corrupting culture.

Our examples to this point have come from Christian asceticism. Yet Christian asceticism is a junior presence in the world of religious asceticism. Hindu and Buddhist asceticisms are older, deeper, and, in some ways, more present in the popular and routine practice of their communities.

They can also be powerful. In chapter 1, we noted the ordination of trees in Thailand, where the elders of the forest are draped with the saffron robes of Buddhist monks as a protest against logging.

Among modern Hindus, few have been as powerful a presence as Mohandas Gandhi. Gandhi turned from his aspiration to be a successful barrister (lawyer) in the best English tradition and, first in South Africa and then at home in India, embraced a life of solidarity with the poor, community self-reliance, simplicity, and inner and outer nonviolence (*ahimsa*) that, in due course, led to Indian independence from the British. ("We have come a long way with the British. We want them to leave, but we want them to leave as friends,"[36] he once said, in the spirit of freedom and reconciliation that would inspire movements elsewhere.)

Not least important to Gandhi's asceticism was an ancient institution, the ashram, a school of discipleship. Simple living, shared labor, a self-reliant community using local materials and craft, daily prayers and instruction, the effort to treat all equally and respectfully as children of God—these markers of ascetic community were the marks of the ashram. And in Gandhi's case, the ashram was an interfaith—and Earth-honoring—community. Hindus, Muslims, Jews, Christians, and Jains all belonged.

Jews rarely think of themselves as religious ascetics, chiefly because much religious asceticism is otherworldly or world-denying in ways wholly out of tune with the Jewish vision of redemption as historical, this-worldly, and Earthbound. Yet the 2008 rabbinical letter from members of the main branches of the American Jewish community was entitled "Wonder and Restraint," two prominent qualities of religious asceticism.

The letter begins with a stirring description:

> *At this very moment, our Earth is hurtling through space at 18.5 miles per second* while the Sun burns with an internal heat of 20 million degrees. Forests and vegetation sweep the planet's atmosphere of carbon dioxide and provide oxygen and food for countless creatures. A 40-ton humpback whale sings a symphonic cycle of songs in the depths of the sea; a tiny hummingbird flaps its wings 4,500 times per minute as it sips nectar from flowers. The million-year-old messages of our DNA repair and reproduce themselves and create a spectacular diversity of human beings on Earth.
>
> These interwoven testaments to the God of Creation, unveiled by our senses and by the probings of science, have stirred millions of people to become mindful guardians of the biosphere.
>
> Now our Jewish tradition must, and can, do likewise.[37]

"We worry," the rabbis say, "that the same factors of abundance and alienation in modern life that have inured people to the pleading voices of nature could inure them, as well, to these voices of Torah." A recital of the voices of Torah follows, together with a call to an awakening.

> ***The awakening we seek begins with wonder: the wonder that turned Moses aside*** to regard the burning bush and realize that he was standing on "holy ground" (Exodus 3:3–5). That vision of light is what we all see every year in the buds of spring, the spawning of new generations, the migrations of birds, mammals and fishes, the cleansing streams of atmosphere and oceans—in all of the miraculous processes by which life awakens from dormancy and recovers from stress, even from disaster, to recreate the world right before our eyes.[38]

A plethora of Jewish expressions of wonder then follows, as does a summons to covenant. "***Two covenantal responsibilities apply most directly to the environmental challenges*** of our time," the letter continues. "The first demands inwardness, the second, outwardness. The first fulfills the traditional Jewish role as a "holy nation," the second, as a "light to the nations."[39]

Inwardness means "*restraint:* to practice restraint in our individual and communal lives." Example after example follows, with interspersed commentary about the need for restraint today: "Human activity is now as consequential to the Earth and its wealth of species as glaciers, volcanoes, winds and tides—so we cannot persist in the illusion that the world is inexhaustible. Human activity has split the seas, brought down manna from heaven, cured pestilence, built vast tabernacles—so we cannot continue to quake and stammer at the prospect of assuming the responsibility given to us along with our power. Instead, we must transform ourselves from nature's children to nature's guardians by learning to say '*dai,*' 'enough,' to ourselves."[40]

Outwardness, the second covenantal obligation, is the obligation to "speak out, and speak truth, to the world's leaders." That obligation is spelled out.

> *We are obliged* to contrast our religious and ethical values with the values of self-indulgence, domination, short-term national security, and money-worship that fuel the ravaging of the Earth.
>
> *We are obliged* to oppose the political empowerment of religious fatalists who view our environmental crisis as a mark of Armageddon and a glad-tiding of redemption.
>
> *We are obliged* to support policies that ease poverty and spare the planet its ravages; that protect underdeveloped countries from serving

as the world's environmental dumping grounds; that tie economic development to environmental stewardship; and that enable poor people to pursue sustainable economic lives.

We are obliged to withdraw support from corporations that act parasitically rather than symbiotically with the natural world, or that tamper with fundamentals of creation without caution, without reverence, but solely for purposes of short-term profit and petty self-interest.

We are obliged to challenge the fever of consumption that drives unsustainable economic growth.

We are obliged to challenge public officials who deify property and wealth, reducing our living planet to a commodity.

We are obliged to seek peace and pursue it—to oppose easy recourse to military violence, outside of legitimate self-defense, not only for its destruction of human life and health, but also for its shattering impact on nature and natural resources.

It is precisely in taking these kinds of prophetic stances, lifting our voices to join protest to prayer, that we renew Judaism's capacity for stirring the *rachamim*, the womb-love, of God and of the human race, thus keeping the gates open to a healthy future for our planet and its inhabitants.[41]

Wonder and restraint, inwardness and outwardness, drawing deeply from the tradition and speaking sharply to the present—here are the telltale marks of a profound, Earth-honoring asceticism.

Ascetic ethics

Finally, what are the elements of asceticism, East and West, that ground the renunciation of consumerism as an Earth-destructive way of life dangerous to the soul, the self, and clear sight? What elements yield an Earth-honoring way of wonder and restraint? Fr. John Chryssavgis's sketch will serve as a summary. He says, "I would define asceticism as":

- traveling light—we can always manage with less than we imagine;
- letting go—we are to learn to relinquish our desire to control;
- opening up—we are called to create bonds, to reunite, to reconcile;
- softening up—how can we make our communities less savage, more inhabitable?
- treading light—we must not hurt, we must stop wounding our environment;

- living simply—not complicating our relationship with each other and with our environment, consuming less;
- simply living—not competing against each other and against nature in order to survive.

Asceticism, Chryssavgis continues, "aims at refinement, not detachment or destruction. Its goal is moderation, not repression. Its content is positive, not negative. It looks to service, not selfishness—to reconciliation, not renunciation or escape. Without asceticism, none of us is authentically human."[42, 43]

This last line—"without asceticism, none of us is authentically human"—may capture all that is needed. It goes to the heart of a humanity crafted by consumerism as the spirit of the age and the global shaper of souls. So the present question may be as simple as, Can we be human now, without asceticism?

Next . . .

The same question, how are we to be human now, is answered somewhat differently in the deep traditions of sacramentalism. We turn to those.

The Sacred and the Commodified

*How can Christianity call itself catholic, if the universe
itself is left out?*

—SIMONE WEIL

*The most important thing to do for the planet is reinvent
the sacred.*

—N. SCOTT MOMADAY

CONSIDER TWO VIGNETTES. On February 15, 2003, more than a hundred cities hosted "apparently the largest coordinated one-day popular protest in the history of the world."[1] The prospective U.S.-led war with Iraq precipitated this ample coalition of the unwilling. Millions marched on every continent, including Antarctica![2]

Digital technologies made the nimble organizing possible. Fluid combinations of social networks and communications dissolved barriers of time and place and mobilized international civil society. Sociologists even spoke of emerging "heterarchies" displacing "hierarchies."

The creative power of such instant community, not to mention its staying power, remains to be seen. Transborder community might set as quickly as it rises. But what *was* seen everywhere in those pulsing ranks was a certain icon: a marbled planet appeared on placard after placard.

Each placard had room for but a few words, arched over bent horizons of sea, land, and sky: No War on Iraq; No War on the World; Not in Our Name. Otherwise the message was the fragile planet itself, still beautiful "beyond the singing of it"[3] but endangered by a species that, without wincing, bethinks itself the planet's trustee. Few if any of the marchers would have known the Russian Orthodox proverb: "Earth is the icon that hangs around God's neck." Yet many sensed just that.

The placarded image was first transmitted by astronauts Frank Borman, William Anders, and James Lovell in 1968. Dostoevsky, picturing Alyosha's rapture in the monastery yard, may have voiced their experience even better than they: "Night, fresh and quiet, almost unstirring, enveloped the earth. . . . The silence of the earth seemed to merge with the silence of the heavens, the mystery of the earth touched the mystery of the stars."[4] The astronauts chose their own words, however, and on Christmas Eve, as the distant jewel disappeared beneath moon's horizon in a silent Earthset, they read from an ancient account: "In the beginning, God created the heavens and the earth." It was simple cosmic poetry.

The second vignette is less dramatic but no less important—a discussion of U.S. energy policy and the fate of the Arctic National Wildlife Refuge. Thomas Friedman, the *New York Times'* foreign affairs columnist, feeling compelled to join a domestic debate about drilling in this wilderness, put aside the economic cost-benefit calculations that usually preoccupy policy wonks in Washington. "I'll let the experts point out the irresponsibility built into the Bush budget," he writes, and moves to another kind of argument altogether. He finds it in Richard Feinberg's concept of wilderness. Wilderness is "immutable," Feinberg writes. "It is like perfection; there are no degrees to it. Oil development in a wilderness, no matter how sensitive, changes the very nature of it. It means it's no longer wilderness. If the drill worshipers prevail in the Arctic Refuge, then there will be no place on this continent where a unique environment will be safe from greed and short-term interests."[5]

Countering Bush's argument that drilling can take place without harming the wilderness, Friedman says: "[That's] like saying you can do online trading in church on your Palm Pilot without disturbing anyone. It violates the very ethic of the place."[6]

"The very ethic of the place." Why is drilling in this "unique environmental cathedral"[7] a moral violation, if indeed it is? Is it truly wrong to text and trade online in church if it bothers no one at prayer and doesn't distract the organist?

Assume for the moment that Friedman, whether finally right or wrong about drilling, has intuited something of moral gravity when he is repulsed by heavy equipment in the cathedral. Moral emotions, not least moral-esthetic ones, ought not to be dismissed as untutored or trivial. They register our initial judgments, if not our final ones, and reveal as much about our nature, values, and sense of holiness as pious emotions do. Add the worries of the global marchers, and the gravity of Friedman's intuition is accentuated. Violate "the very ethic of the place"? Not in our name. Something sacred seems at stake.

The vignettes do not explain moral emotion and gravity, however, any more than they disclose the foundations of a sacramental ethic or determine policy. Numerous stands on warmaking, peacemaking, energy, and security are possible, even after the horror of war and the violation of drilling in the cathedral have been registered with every ounce of being. All who share similar emotions may press their noses to the same pane and gaze at the same scene yet respond in different ways. A shared moral reflex, expressing a shared sense of the sacred, does not dictate a single, unbroken line. We might agree to ban drilling for oil in the Arctic Refuge only to disagree over oil somewhere else or the mix, location, financing, and safety of wind, solar, and nuclear alternatives. In a word, where our loyalties finally thump down isn't clear until the full deliberation of reasoned justification has been made. Nonetheless, those loyalties and the moral emotions attached to them do locate the burden of proof for us. Commonly our first responses are also our strongest ones and become a critical initial element of practical moral reasoning.

Let us proceed, then, on the assumption that Friedman, the astronauts, and the coalitions in the streets have in effect issued an invitation or posed a question. Do tenured religio-moral intuitions, as well as newly written icons, say something compelling about planet-saving issues? If we considered Earth truly home, and if the environment had sacramental status for us—no drilling in the cathedral, please—would it matter for policy and action? More precisely, how does a moral sense of the sacred play out as a way of life? If Earth were a sacrament, how would we treat it?

A sacramental universe

"Saving Souls and Salmon" ran as a feature in the Sunday *New York Times*. What might this conjunction—salmon and souls—mean? Archbishop Alex Brunett led *Times* writer Jim Robbins to the baptismal font of St. James Cathedral in downtown Seattle. "The water isn't just sitting there," he said, pointing to its gentle movement. "We don't baptize people in stagnant water, but flowing water, water that is alive."[8] The waters of life (baptism) and the waters of life (in this case, the Columbia River and salmon) formed the connection. For the archbishop, the connection was sacramental. Saving souls and saving salmon belong to the same universe.

"The Columbia River Watershed: Realities and Possibilities" is a bioregional pastoral letter of Roman Catholic bishops in Montana, Idaho, Washington, Oregon, and British Columbia. A century of unbridled logging, mining, grazing, and dam building had left the great river and its basin in dire straits, if its emblem—the salmon—is any measure. As of 2000, the annual run of an estimated 16 million salmon had dwindled to about 700,000.[9]

No less arresting is the name given the endangered watershed: a "sacramental commons." "We're trying to establish a sacredness in the world around us," the archbishop explained to Robbins. Establishing such sacredness assumes the lead tenet of all, not only Christian, religious sacramentalism: Material reality bears a value humans share and name but do not bestow. Such value is inclusive of all being and the manifestation of "the life-creating, sustaining, and redeeming presence and promise" of the divine throughout creation.[10] Sometimes called the "sacramental principle," the conviction is that life-affirming grace is present to and through creation as God's own abiding presence "for, with, and within the past, present and future of creation in its natural-ecological and socio-historical dimensions."[11] A sacrament is the symbol through which some natural reality, such as water or the work of human hands (bread), is the means by which the divine "is experienced as being presently real."[12] Such symbols both point to and participate in the life and power they symbolize.[13] Paradoxically they reveal the divine in a hidden way—hidden in creation, wrapped in nature, present to the senses.

Don Sampson, a Yakima Indian leader, chuckled in response to the bishops' letter. "Maybe God has spoken to [the bishops]," he said. "I hope the pope gets on board." In a more serious tone he added, "The church is being upfront and dispelling the myth of Manifest Destiny and dominion over the Earth. That's refreshing and welcome."[14]

Great Chain sacramentalism

Sacramentalism hasn't always been set over against dominion. The Great Chain of Being, arguably the most influential of all Christian cosmologies, bundled sacrament and dominion together and sent them sailing the high seas to colonize the New World, Sampson's Yakima nation included. Pope Alexander VI's famous Bull of Donation simply gave—donated—all islands and mainlands "discovered and to be discovered, one hundred leagues to the West and South of the Azores toward India,"[15] and not already occupied or held by any Christian king or prince as of Christmas 1492, to Isabel and Ferdinand of Spain. The pope was utterly clear: European Christian monarchs should rule the world, spread civilization, and save the benighted souls of their non-Christian brothers and sisters. This was "taking" on a grand scale, in the guise of giving.

In keeping with most sacramentalist cosmologies, the Great Chain[16] pictured life as an outflowing of the divine in an endless array of diverse and interdependent lives. For sacramentalism the universe is alive, manifold, and whole. Everything belongs to it and it belongs in the way reflected in the Talmud: "Of all the things in the world, the Holy One did not create a single one that is useless."[17]

The particular ordering of this life as a Great Chain inscribed dominion and hierarchy, however. Humans rank a bit lower than angels, with God above and all else beneath. Within this special species, "crowned with glory and honor" (Psalm 8), men's standing is forever a notch above women's, while (higher) reason, mind, and spirit rule (lesser) emotion and body. Most strikingly, as already noted, empire is sanctioned as conquest and colonization, commerce, and the spread of Christianity. This was the quartet that followed in the wake of Columbus in the Age of Discovery and that we met in Crosby's discussion in chapter 2. In such a scheme, the Great Chain's sacramentalism served a "civilizing mission" in which "inferior" peoples and cultures were the unconsulted beneficiaries of a salvific gospel and way of life.

Superiority of such a racist and cultural cast was brutal. Native peoples, like Sampson's Yakima nation, were killed, moved out, or assimilated, all on European terms. Slaves suffered the Middle Passage, with great loss of life and centuries of ensuing coercion and fear. The underlying morality for all this, cited earlier, was both chilling and theological: "Again and again during the centuries of European imperialism the Christian view that all men are brothers was to lead to persecution of non-Europeans—he who is my brother sins to the extent that he is unlike me."[18]

Religious cosmologies always take an inventory of the universe, bind its elements together, and establish sin, vice, reward, and virtue on the basis of the outcome ("All men are brothers . . . he who is my brother sins to the extent that. . . ."). This particular sacramentalist cosmology did so in ways that ascribed value to life organisms and states of being as "higher" and "lower." Its racism, androcentrism, and hierarchical ordering have persisted a very long time. As recently as 1957, long after Pope Alexander's Bull of Donation, William F. Buckley Jr., guru of conservative Republican thought and editor of the highly influential *National Review*, responded to the U.S. Supreme Court's decision on *Brown v. Board of Education* like this:

> The central question that emerges—and it is not a parliamentary question or a question that is answered by merely consulting a catalogue of rights of American citizens, born equal—is whether the White community in the South is entitled to take such measures as are necessary to prevail, politically and culturally, in areas where it does not predominate numerically? The sobering answer is Yes—the White community

is so entitled because, for the time being, it is the advanced race. . . . *National Review* believes that the South's premises are correct. If the majority wills what is socially atavistic, then to thwart the majority may be, though undemocratic, enlightened. . . . Universal suffrage is not the beginning of wisdom or the beginning of freedom.[19]

Not least the Great Chain conceived the life of the spirit as largely Earth-escaping. While all creatures are alive with the presence of the divine, the chain's hierarchical order placed God as pure Spirit and Mind at the apex and inorganic matter at the base, with union with the divine as the goal of the moral-spiritual life. Because the means of that was ascetic ascent, the closer the human was to God, the farther the human was from the rest of creation "below"; the closer to God, the farther from Earth, that temporary place of pilgrimage.

In short, and in ways that are even more severe in much Protestant thought, God becomes separated from much of nature and relocated in human history; humanity is separated from nature as well, and relocated in history; creation is detached from redemption, which shrinks to a segregated human domain; and pervasive, destructive dualisms are reinforced by dominant instruction and practice (men over women, the rights of humans over nature, Western technology and its ways over subjugated peoples and theirs).[20]

All of which is only to emphasize what was said earlier. A moral plumb line must take the measure of every deep religious tradition and every notion of the sacred, wherever they are grounded. No tradition is pristine and none escapes ethical critique and reconstruction. Noteworthy here is that the bishops of the northwest United States and southwest Canada find an alternative to the oppressions of chain-of-being sacramentalism in a different sacramental sense of the whole. While the alternative informs their Columbia River Watershed pastoral, it comes clearest in another pastoral letter, this one from the U.S. Catholic Conference (the U.S. bishops as a body).

Web-of-life sacramentalism

"Renewing the Earth: An Invitation to Reflection and Action in Light of Catholic Social Teaching" shifts the reigning metaphor from a ranked ladder to "the web of life [as] one."[21] It retains the conviction of both Thomas Aquinas and the Talmud that every creature counts and creation is sacred, but it consciously shifts the common good as the long-standing Catholic ethical norm for human society to a common good inclusive of the planet, a good that includes global "commons" such as the atmosphere and the oceans.

Assuming this living web of planetary good, the bishops "explore the links between concern for the person and for the earth, between natural ecology and social ecology."[22] The environmental crisis is "a moral challenge," they argue. It "calls us to examine how we use and share the goods of the earth, what we pass on to future generations and how we live in harmony with God's creation."[23] Like all sacramentalists, including Great Chain-ers, the bishops view creation as a "commons" with intrinsic linkages "between natural ecology and social ecology." In this tradition of moral theology Earth's goods are a common gift with a common purpose—to meet the fundamental needs of all, including trees, flowers, and animals. So, for example, if capitalist markets and the right to private property aid in the distribution of the goods of the Earth as the commons we belong to and share, they have vital roles to play. If, however, capitalist markets and privatized property effectively close the commons and remove goods from just distribution to those who need them, they fail as legitimate means for achieving and sustaining a just society.

The bishops are acutely aware that privilege and power affect the nexus of "social" and "natural" ecologies. "Renewing the Earth" gives extensive attention to the relationship of richer and poorer nations and the plight of poor people everywhere. "The Option for the Poor embedded in the gospel and the church's teaching," they write, "make us aware that the poor suffer most directly from environmental decline and have the least access to relief from their suffering. Indigenous peoples die with their forests and their grasslands. In Bhopal and Chernobyl it was the urban poor and working people who suffered the most immediate and intense contamination. Nature will truly enjoy its second spring only when humanity has compassion for its weakest members." The choice between "a decent environment and a decent life for workers" is a false one.[24]

The present environmental crisis as moral challenge is sufficiently daunting, the bishops continue, that conversion—turning in another direction—is required. It is a conversion to Earth and God in the same moment and together. "We need a change of heart to preserve and protect the planet for our children and for generations yet unborn."[25]

But where is the power to change hearts? "In the sacramental universe itself," the bishops answer. Nature bears God's presence and power. "Throughout history people have continued to meet the Creator on mountaintops, in vast deserts, and alongside waterfalls and gently flowing springs. In storms and earthquakes, they found expressions of divine power. In the cycle of the seasons and the courses of the stars, they have discerned signs of God's fidelity and wisdom. We still share, though dimly, in that sense of God's presence in nature."[26]

Earth is a sacrament here—a disclosure of God's presence by visible and tangible signs, like the waters of baptism and the waters of the Columbia River and its salmon. Transcendent power is imminent, as close as the grain and the grape of the Eucharist, or the fields, forests, and waterways around us. Those who reverence God's presence in creation and understand themselves as part and parcel of the world as sacrament will be moved to care for creation as "the sacred trust" it is, the bishops contend. In a time when humans are estranged from "the natural scale and rhythms of life on earth" by economic and technological super-development, "a vision of a sacramental universe. . . . can contribute to making the earth a home for the human family once again."[27]

None of this is far from the teachings of Islam. "The Earth is a mosque, and everything in it is sacred. I learned this basic tenet of Islam from my father," writes Ibrahim Abdul-Matin as the first sentences of *Green Deen: What Islam Teaches about Protecting the Planet*.[28]

Nor is it far from Buddhism. Thich Nhat Hanh again: "To me the Kingdom of God or the Pure Land of the Buddha is not a vague idea; it is a reality." He explains: "That pine tree standing on the mountain is so beautiful, solid, and green. To me the pine tree belongs to the Kingdom of God, the Pure Land of the Buddha. Your beautiful child with her fresh smile belongs to the Kingdom of God, and you also belong to the Kingdom of God." The conclusion? "If we're capable of recognizing the flowing river, the blue sky, the blossoming tree, the singing bird, the majestic mountains, the countless animals, the sunlight, the fog, the snow, the innumerable wonders of life as miracles that belong to the Kingdom of God, we'll do our best to preserve them and not allow them to be destroyed."[29]

Judaism shares this sensibility. Wisdom (*hochma*) personifies the pervasive presence of the divine throughout the universe. Recall the rabbinical letter, "Wonder and Restraint": ***The awakening we seek begins with wonder: the wonder that turned Moses aside*** to regard the burning bush and realize that he was standing on "holy ground" (Exodus 3:3–5). That vision of light is what we all see every year in the buds of spring, the spawning of new generations, the migrations of birds, mammals and fishes, the cleansing streams of atmosphere and oceans—in all of the miraculous processes by which life awakens from dormancy and recovers from stress, even from disaster, to recreate the world right before our eyes.[30] Ecumenical Patriarch Bartholomew also drew on sacramentalism at the 1997 Symposium on the Sacredness of the Environment mentioned in the previous chapter. "The Lord suffuses all of creation with His Divine presence in one continuous legato from the substance of atoms to the Mind of God," he said in closing. "Let us renew the harmony between heaven and earth, and transfigure every detail, every particle of life."[31]

Perhaps little more need be said about creation as one continuous legato from the substance of atoms to the Mind of God unless it be to underscore several matters, one of which is creation's exuberance. "Extravagance! Nature will try anything once,"[32] writes Annie Dillard. Or unless it be to mark the Patriarch's conclusion in his *Wall Street Journal* editorial: "For if life is sacred, so is the entire web that sustains it."[33] Or unless it be to underline sacramentalism's most emphatic note: This extravagant and indivisible life is a freely offered *gift of God* and the *medium of grace*, a gift ritually borne into the worshipful presence of God and renewed there in contemplative and liturgical practices. In this tradition the drama of the liturgy is the ritual enactment or reenactment of cosmic community and the drama of creation's redemption.

Web thinking and utility

The moral ethos of leaning into the world in this way is signaled in the word "Eucharist." *Eucharistia* is Greek for "thanksgiving" and is a word implying liturgy and ritual as the form of people's grateful response and as a guide for their living. If the bread of heaven is shared freely and equally with all as God's own provisioning way, and if all are welcome to this welcome table for a sacramental meal together, why do we not do likewise for the other tables of the world?

After all, tables are always microcosms of society. Decisions about who gets to sit at the table, in what places, and in accord with what table manners and social standing are reflective of the order of a community and society. So are choices about who cooks, who serves, who cleans up, who breaks the bread, and who initiates and steers the conversation. Which bodies are present at the table and which are absent matters, as does their health or lack of it. Where does the food come from, who raised it in what way for what purposes? How was it harvested, transported to market, and sold, and at what price? What is the condition of Earth as a consequence of all this? Table fellowship is a reliable map of "eco-nomic" and eco-social well-being, just as it is a reliable map of discrimination, political order and differentiation, social hierarchy and caste. Tables encode how a culture communicates its values, priorities, and organizing systems. How people take, bless, break, and share bread mirrors their way of life. Likewise, the way different religions eat and drink together in their sacred practices reflects their way of life and its table-connection to the world around them. Is it a dominion connection or some alternative to that?

Web-of-life sacramentalism is one alternative. It is almost the antithesis of the working cosmology and theology of the institutions and practices that created the modern world. To them "nature" means natural resources and capital, now extended to human resources and capital, even moral and spiritual resources and capital. These definitions betray the mindset we have described as utilitarian with a vengeance and devoid of sacramental sensibilities. They belong to Weber's "disenchanted" world[34] in which the numinous is bled from the common, the holy is leached from the ordinary, and the mystical is cut away from the everyday. Use, utility, and possession measure all value, just as all are relative to human appropriation and significance. The (human) subject determines the worth of all else, as object, with "object" taking the form of commodities.

We noted earlier that the route to this commodifying practice is part of the industrial paradigm set in motion with the new economy of the rising bourgeoisie. Few have described it with the precision of Marx or understood so well and early (1848) that it portended the destruction of a sense of the sacred and a sense of place.

> Constant revolutionizing of production, uninterrupted disturbance of all social conditions, everlasting uncertainty and agitation distinguish the bourgeois epoch from all earlier ones. All fixed, fast-frozen relations, with their train of ancient and venerable prejudices and opinions, are swept away, all newly-formed ones become antiquated before they can ossify. All that is solid melts into air, all that is holy is profaned, and man is at last compelled to face with sober sense, his real conditions of life, and his relations with his kind.[35]

It is ironic that Marx the atheist is the one to understand the destruction of what religions, whether theistic or nontheistic, have always sought to communicate; namely, that the phenomenon of life merits that highest expression of value humans confer—the sacred. If "all that is holy is profaned," and "all that is solid melts into air," then where are the moral limits to use and abuse?

Even path-finding environmentalists occasionally adopt commodity ethics. Gifford Pinchot, the influential preservationist/conservationist who served as mentor to Teddy Roosevelt in the establishment of the U.S. national parks system, argued that in the end only two realities inhabit the planet— "people" and "resources." The latter are to be preserved and harvested for the sake of the former.

Talk of the "food chain" rather than the "food web" also betrays the mind-set of technological-industrial utility. Human beings regard themselves as at the "top" of the food chain, in keeping with the ranking habits of chain-of-being devotees. What is "lower" on the food chain serves the "higher." Moreover, that which is lower is essentially a resource viewed as a potential commodity, a resource and commodity that can be substituted for or replaced. If we eat too many cows, we can grow more or turn to something else—say, fish. And if we eat most of the wild fish, we can farm fish. If farm fish run short, there are always fruits and vegetables. These are objects abstracted from their habitats, with little attention to consequences other than food on the table for higher-ups. This is industrial chain-of-being thinking devoid of a sense of the webbed and the sacred.

"Food web" by contrast says we belong to a complex system of interconnected links. We eat, say, rabbits and rabbits eat plants. The plants feast on soil nutrients, themselves the work of microorganisms and their ravenous diets. Complex, dynamic relationships are key.

Such webbing means that taking down a key species to put it on the tables of the higher-ups might also take down an ecosystem. Changing relationships have ripple effects when they are woven and webbed. Bluefin tuna, for example, appear to be a key species in their ocean ecosystem. Overfishing them has consequences for other fish and their habitat, together with ocean vegetation.

As it turns out, the system of production and consumption built on "food chain" thinking often rewards eating the harder-to-find animals. In a capitalist system, scarcer tuna command a higher price. Good money can be made in hunting down the remaining tuna for the marketplace. This of course not only renders the dwindling numbers of remaining tuna more vulnerable; it renders the rest of their ocean ecosystem more vulnerable as well.[36]

Food-web thinking, or "foodshed" thinking (on the analogy of "watershed," a foodshed outlines the flow of food within and to an area), asks what food-chain thinking does not. Where does the food on the plate fit in the web? What is the foodshed where we eaters live? How do *we* fit into *it*, not just it into us? What are the ripple effects of diet choices? Are these chain reactions sustainable for the community of life? Thinking "sideways," around curves and corners, and along threads in web fashion is more likely to be truthful than thinking "up and down" with us always "up" and all else "down." As intimated, exactly the same questions and thinking pertain to watersheds. The right question is not, How much water can we extract from the watershed, but how do we fit into it and govern in keeping with it?

This web-of-life thinking is in keeping with web-of-life sacramental ethics. It also speaks to "strong" and "weak" anthropocentrism. Strong human-centeredness in ethics consciously puts human concerns at the center of moral ones while intentionally or arbitrarily placing nonhuman interests outside the circle of those concerns. In both religious and secular traditions such anthropocentrism typically views humans as the crown of creation and the only bearers of intrinsic value and moral standing. Human life is sacred but no other is. The other-than-human world bears instrumental value only. Its raison d'être is to serve the needs and desires of *Homo sapiens*. Master–slave is the long-standing relation here.

By contrast weak anthropocentrism grants intrinsic value to other-than-human nature. Humans, however, are granted moral privilege of place in a ranking scheme that translates as dominion. Humans may also be ranked among themselves by gender, race, or culture that reflects moral ranking and authority. (Colonization ethics, patriarchy, and race-based stratification have consistently done so.)

Great Chain of Being sacramental ethics are those of weak anthropocentrism. So are many notions of stewardship. By way of contrast, web-of-life sacramentalism tries to find its way beyond both strong and weak anthropocentrism to some form of eco-centrism or even cosmo-centrism.[37] It does so while yet acknowledging that value determination and moral decisions are inevitably human endeavors and the product of finite and limited human minds and hearts.[38] Thus some manner of anthropocentrism is unavoidable; our understanding and treatment of nature cannot bypass the filters and effects of human consciousness.

This chapter, "The Sacred and the Commodified," was intended to contrast sacramental ethics and commodity ethics. Yet we were right to first enter the world of sacramental ethics and note two of its varied renditions. A look at Jeffrey Stout's *Blessed Are the Organized* will supplement our discussion and move us from there to commodity ethics.

Sacred disputes

What identifies the sacred, Stout asks, and what is our response to it? "To be sacred is to be worthy of reverence" is his answer; we respond to sacred things "by celebrating their existence and excellences."[39] We also "express horror at the prospect of losing them" and "mourn when they are lost" just as we commemorate sacred things. We are invariably "angered by assaults" on what we deem sacred and we "take offense" when they are profaned. We also do what we can "to protect [sacred things] from violation, destruction, and profanation."[40] Strong moral emotions are at work when value is sacred value.

Stout's chapter is titled "The Contested Sacred." In our society, many visions of the sacred are reverently celebrated, commemorated, and protected. They often clash, sometimes fiercely, and when they do, moral debate and ethical justification turn religious and theological as appeals to divine authority and natural law. ("We hold these truths to be self-evident, that all men are created equal, that they are endowed by their Creator with unalienable rights, that among these are Life, Liberty and the pursuit of Happiness.")[41] Mastery and slavery were said to rest in differences established by nature and/or God. So did patriarchy and dominion theology. As a consequence, they could only be debated by contesting their theological as well as empirical standing. When what is worthy of reverence is in dispute, and sacred value and divine authority are invoked by either side in a debate, even secular communities argue with religious intensity. Marriage as the sacred bond of a man and a woman now extended to same-sex couples presently fuels this dynamic of the disputed sacred, as do arguments over the legitimacy of torture and the conduct of war. To deem something sacred intensifies moral emotions; compromise comes hard, "we"/"they" divisions intensify, and common ground often disappears.

Little wonder, then, that the Enlightenment, in response to the religious wars that wracked Europe following the Reformation, sought an alternative to sacred violence in secular, scientific reason. And little wonder that the new economy of capitalism and industry viewed commerce as civilizing. Promoting economic interests and increasing productivity were ways to do both good and well nonviolently. Religious passions were clearly corrosive; economic and financial interests were not. From a moral point of view a secular utilitarian cost-benefit ethic, even with a bottom-line appeal to calculating self-interest, was preferable to the killing fields of the sacred.[42]

Yet the results of thinking this way, but now with a view to the "urban blight, industrial pollution, robber barons, and hedge fund managers" that have since arrived on the scene, are "first, that the unruly passion of greed for the most part went unnamed and, second, that the continuing relevance of sacred causes to our politics takes us by surprise or even leaves us aghast."[43] Evidently the sacred still has a grip and the idol of worldly economism can go badly awry as the alternative.

Commodity thinking

But there is more—the dangers of commodification and commodity ethics. Stout is our guide here, too.

"To commodify something, in the primary sense," he says, "is to treat it as something to be bought and sold and then perhaps discarded when it no longer has much usefulness."[44] The real-world value of any given thing is quantifiable to me in terms of how much I am willing to spend on it. This "given thing" might be another person. Chattel slavery commodified human beings as property to be bought and sold. "Hired hands," as the phrase implies, are also commodified human labor. Sexual activity might be the given thing. Prostitution and escort services commodify sex for a price. Nature as a standing resource for industry commodifies a forest, prairie, or stream[45] just as mining operations commodify ore and energy companies commodify fossil fuels. No. 2 yellow corn might be commodified in the same way as No. 2 yellow lead pencils. In all these instances and innumerable more, the cost-benefit analysis of instrumental reason serving particular human interests is the working ethic. With the industrialization of food production and eating habits, for example, the aim is not to promote "nutrition, freshness, and quality of taste, but rather transportability, long store and counter shelf life, and uniformity of appearance."[46] Shorn of its ecological and social context, food is treated in much the same way as inanimate things: What counts is its appearance, availability, convenience, and price. Food-like products replace the real thing. And short of some sense of the sacred, with accompanying horror over its violation—"the destruction of a redwood grove . . ., the placement of a sexually provocative billboard next to an elementary school, . . . bribery [as] an instance of the unjust"[47]—there are no limits. Everything has its price and the planet is for sale if utility is the only measure and economic cost-benefit analysis is the only spoken language.

What about the kind of commodification regnant in the consumerist economy that "matured" in and since the 1950s? It has its own framework and setting.

Modern commodification

Modern commodification and modern commodity ethics is the product of an industrial ecology that runs against the grain of nature to mine and undermine it. Commodification also buries or externalizes the costs to nature and perfectly embodies capitalism as a freeloader system of unpaid costs.[48] In both theory and practice Earth's economy is a subset of the human economy. From a scientific point of view, this is exactly backward. Science is clear: The human economy is everywhere and always a subset of the planet's. We have the basic relationship wrong and our commodities embody that error.[49]

While this is the framework, it is not yet the setting. Modern industrial ecology serves urbanized human settlements: Urban peoples of necessity appropriate carrying capacity from elsewhere, through the commodification of market-organized nature. Unfortunately, commercializing nature puts the effects on nature "back home" out of sight for most people, and then out of mind. And with that, peoples' sense of responsibility for the nature they depend upon is quietly put to sleep. At every age and stage of life, the psychological dynamics attending commodification thus cut against the formation and maintenance of moral responsibility for that upon which we depend. We do not truly see and know what we are doing to nature as we consume; and, not seeing and not knowing, we take little thought and do not much care.

If this is so, it is worth a closer look. What do we know about commodities we use daily and what do they "do" in our relationship with them?

We know they are "commodious"—convenient. (The Latin root, *commodus*, traces to "convenience.") Commodities are goods and services placed at our disposal without burdening us. They make life easier, more enjoyable, less troublesome. They do so by handing us the end product only. The good or service in our hands is all foreground, so to speak, with no background in view and no strings attached. It's likely, then, that we know almost nothing of who produced the goods at what cost to themselves and the rest of the ecosphere; all that is hidden from view. Nor does it matter. What matters is the abstracted commodity conveniently available for our use.

Missing here is what sociologists call "manifold engagement." In the case of food, for example, manifold engagement would be joining others to tend the soil, grow and harvest the crops or feed the lambs and calves, take the harvest or the animals to market, and rally the energy needed for safe transport to a store near us. All this and more is lost if we only shop and eat. Our relationship to the persons and the earth, air, fire, water, and light upon whom we literally depend for daily bread is real, to be sure—very real, since without them we would not eat. But we do not engage them. The relationship is narrowly commercial, instrumental, and out of sight.

Such a relationship is a reliable prescription for time-saving convenience, to be certain. It is truly commodious. But it is also a prescription for alienation. A TV dinner is commodious but it is not the bread of life, much less a sacrament, since nothing more is asked of us, or engages us, than a microwave, a fork, and packaging. By contrast, a meal prepared together with others and accompanied by conviviality around a shared table might be bread for both body and soul, even a sacrament. (It might also be just lunch.)

Bottled water for $2.50 from the vending machine is also commodious, just as water from the tap is. But when water is a commodity only, when water is "it" only and never "thou," then water's wonder is lost on us, as is gratitude for the life it births, brings, and sustains. So while a living stream of crystalline waters might strike us as sacred (worthy of reverence) and even a part of us at some profound level, bottled water does not solicit wonder, beckon poetry, or enter the psyche as a primal element that is home to our bodies. Commodities remove the rich world of nature from view, paper it over with glitzy advertisements meant to create product desire, and, with that, diminish both our sense of connection to nature and our sense of personal responsibility for it. When nature, including humans, is packaged for end-use only, we engage it abstractly and reductively, although "engage" hardly seems the right word. Nature becomes a collection of passive objects to be disposed of when their services are ended. This is a prescription for human alienation from nature as alive and a sacred trust. Manifold engagement is reduced to end use.

Real world loss

The biblical story of Rebecca at the well illumines our real-world loss of manifold engagement. When Rebecca went to the well she found not only living water but also companionship, news of the village, and her fiancé. "These strands of her life were woven into a fabric [that] technology has divided and privatized into commodities," writes Albert Borgmann.[50] This is no argument for women as virtual property or the hardship and confinement of village life. But compare Rebecca with, say, a woman standing at the sink on the eleventh floor of a Cleveland studio apartment. What Borgmann calls "the presence of things"—Rebecca's community at the well—is replaced with packaged goods and/or services delivered by anonymous others "without the encumbrance of or the engagement with a context."[51] The engagement is not manifold; it is simplified in the way the industrial paradigm conveniently simplifies all nature for human betterment.

This way of organizing life means that, at the point of something so important as food and other critical goods and services, we lose the common reference points of nature, culture, and social relations. In many ways, it's the loss of community and belonging; it's the pursuit of loneliness[52] and a quiet alienation we hardly notice and never name. So the two forms that "commodity fetishism takes in public philosophy," "utilitarianism and egoism,"[53] turn out to be bad psychology as well as bad ethics. The Buddhist's meditation in the presence of her food never occurs to us: "In this food / I see clearly / the entire universe / supporting my existence."[54]

"Company" would seem the contrasting term to "commodity." It means "breaking bread" (*pan*) "together" (*com*). And like the shared meal around a convivial table, "company" carries a sacramental association. One might even, in such company, "see clearly / the entire universe / supporting my existence."

Yet the first definition of company in the *New Oxford American Dictionary* is "a commercial business." Only thereafter comes an entry for company as "the fact or condition of being with another or others, esp. in a way that provides friendship and enjoyment."[55] Thus do commerce and commodity regularly trump belonging and sacrament. Intentional or not, the order accurately reflects the nonsacramental place of commodified nature in modernity's alienated "engagement" with it.

Another world imagined

The foregoing discussion can be deceptive if we conclude that losing the real-world context of commodities means that they offer or embody no world at all. On the contrary, commodities intend to create their own context and world. They do so through advertising.

Our text is Emilie M. Townes's brilliant treatment of the journey of Aunt Jemima in "Vanishing into Limbo: The Moral Dilemma of Identity as Property and Commodity." Townes begins with a quotation from James Baldwin about the fate of Aunt Jemima and Uncle Tom. Gratefully they are dead, Baldwin writes, only to add: "Before, however, our joy at [their] demise approaches the indecent, we had better ask whence they sprang, how they lived? Into what limbo have they vanished?"[56] Townes and her generation despised Aunt Jemima and were embarrassed by her in the 1960s. They thought she had vanished with the emergence of a black middle class but she had only exited into limbo. Aunt Jemima, Uncle Tom, Topsy, "or any of their kin" would never be banished by black Americans because they were never theirs to control. "They are creations of the White imagination—its fears and its terrors and its stereotypes and its unilateral attempts at justice."[57]

"'I'se in town, Honey': Marketing Aunt Jemima" tracks the history and fate of the famed figure. The backdrop is the cakewalk. Originating with slaves during harvest festivals, it was a minstrel competition in which slaves spoofed the mannerisms of their white masters. First prize was often a cake.

But the cakewalk found another purpose in 1888 when the Pearl Milling Company of St. Joseph, Missouri, produced the first commercial pancake mix under the label "Self-Rising Pancake Flour." While searching for a symbol for their product, the owners happened upon a performance by the blackface minstrel team of Baker and Ferrell. It was a performance that included a cakewalk and the rousing tune of "Old Aunt Jemima," copyrighted a couple years earlier by the white minstrel James Grace. With a white man in blackface dressed as a woman singing away the cares of the plantation South, Pearl Milling had found its symbol.

When Pearl Milling was sold to the R. T. Davis Mill and Manufacturing Company in 1890, Davis designed "the first and one of the most successful campaigns ever launched in U.S. marketing history."[58] Davis found Nancy Green, a former slave who was a nurse in Chicago and a cook already well known for her pancakes. In his hands, she became the Aunt Jemima of Self-Rising Pancake Flour even though Nancy Green never resembled the older, smiling, full-figured housekeeper with the bandana around her head. Instead of Nancy Green of Chicago, Aunt Jemima was a Mammy image whose appeal was that of a smiling black servant in an idealized, bucolic ante- and postbellum South. She soon came to grace the pages of ladies' magazines and became the figure for the hugely successful Aunt Jemima dolls. By 1918 the tally was more than 120 million Aunt Jemima breakfasts served annually, despite black hostility to advertising that consistently presented her as the endearing figure at home in the South she loved. Aunt Jemima nicely "demonstrated the benefits of maintaining the color line and how Black women behaved under proper White control."[59]

Tracing the subsequent history of Aunt Jemima is fascinating. It includes the earliest version of her "life story," *The Life of Aunt Jemima, the Most Famous Colored Woman in the World* by Purd Wright, an advertising executive.[60] That history underscores the point we might make about the treatment of most U.S. commodities. Commodities are about the "interstructuring of class, gender, and race with marketing and profit margins," done in a manner that "accentuates the ways in which history and memory function in U.S. culture and society."[61] Identity itself is commodified and made subject to its marketing handlers. Commodities, then, are not only cut away from their real-world origins and our relationship to them (Borgmann); they carry an alternative identity that appeals to the myths and biases of their target audience. They subtly, or not so subtly, create the fantasy world of those they target. This is another, powerful layer of alienation whereby the fantasies of advertising and packaging displace knowledge of the real world, engagement with it, and responsibility for it. Townes's own conclusion is that "when identity is commodified, we have been beaten by a willfully narrow history that suppresses the richness of who we are. . . . To treat identity as property is one form of the cultural production of evil."[62]

So where have we arrived in the discussion of commodity thinking and commodity ethics? With Marx on "The Fetishism of Commodities and the

Secret Thereof": "A commodity appears, at first sight, a very trivial thing, and easily understood. Its analysis shows that it is, in reality, a very queer thing, abounding in metaphysical subtleties and theological niceties."[63]

Water

But back to "Saving Souls and Salmon." Do we find in a web-of-life sacramental ethic an alternative to the "metaphysical subtleties and theological niceties" (Marx) of commodity ethics? Further attention to water may answer that question. It also offers another opportunity, beyond soil, to think morally about and with a primal element of Earth.

The full name of Santa Fe, New Mexico, is "La Villa Real de la Santa Fe de San Francisco de Asis"—"The Royal City of the Holy Faith of Saint Francis of Assisi." Before the Spanish founded this City of Holy Faith around 1600 and made it the provincial capital of the northern portion of the Spanish Empire ("el Norte") in 1610, it was home to an Indian pueblo known by two names: White Shell Water Place and Dancing Ground of the Sun. Both names reflect the direct relationship to the elements characteristic of Southwest Indian cosmologies and their sacred sense of place. In their high mountain desert home, sun is abundant and intense, water is scarce and essential.

The "Holy Faith" (Santa Fe) of St. Francis fits nicely here as well. His faith, too, is about Earth's sacred, primal elements. Brother Sun, Sister Moon, Brothers Wind and Air, Sister Water, Brother Fire, Mother Earth, and Sister Bodily Death—these are all siblings in Francis's Song of Songs, *The Canticle of the Sun.*[64]

But what do we know about Sister Water?

The deciding element

We know what water does. The source and sustainer of life, the planet's "deciding element,"[65] water births, cleanses, heals, revives, carves, transports, and kills. It wears stone into soil; nourishes flora, fauna, and microorganisms; melts and vaporizes; steams and freezes; and goes liquid. It refreshes and renews bodies and souls. It also drowns some; or, by the awful presence of its absence, dispatches them to their destination as dust. An awesome power, it destroys.

The ultimate shape-shifter, water is a liquid, a solid, and a vapor. It absorbs very large amounts of energy without evaporating and cools and warms slowly enough for life first to be and then to adapt. Your body's water prevents you from simply boiling to death, suddenly looking like an ice sculpture, or dehydrating on the spot like the last stalk of Oklahoma corn.[66] Auden's poem, "First Things First," has it right: "Thousands have lived without love; not one has lived without water."[67] "A little whooping and stomping on the part of sane people"[68] in the presence of water is, then, quite in order.

Yet this only introduces water. The story of water is the reader's story, the story of every cell of every creature that ever was, and the planet's story.

Planet Water

"Earth" is a serious misnomer. "Planet Water" is more accurate. Water, not dry ground, is the planet's basic structure. Its surface is 74.4 percent water and 97.2 percent of that is ocean.[69] From these waters the wonder of life itself likely emerged three billion years ago.

Those three billion years are carried in our blood. The salt in our veins and tears matches the ocean's, just as our body's water mass matches the planet's—70 percent and change. And don't forget that the most dramatic and formative nine months of every human life find us, without exception, growing in salt water, the warm waters of a mother's womb. Dry ground appeared only when your mother had had quite enough and her waters "broke."

It's all quite mystical: We emerged from the ocean and we still carry the ocean within us, rivers of living waters gently coursing through our bodies. The next time you shed tears of joy and sorrow or bleed a bit, remember that. What is blood but glorified water?

We breathe the oceans as well. We live because of green plants. Plants are nature's only "autotrophs," singular creatures who know how to eat the sun so as to create organic matter from inorganic. They do this by combining atmospheric carbon dioxide with water from the soil while converting sunlight into energy through photosynthesis. This autotrophic process not only provides food for all the world's heterotrophs—us and a gazillion other critters on nature's welfare system—it also releases oxygen and water vapor, our life breath, to the only place we can easily get at it, the bottom two to three miles of the atmosphere.

What does this have to do with ocean waters? Plantations of ocean phytoplankton create much of the air we inhale, whether we live near an ocean or not. Usually too small to see with the unaided eye except as a watery green tinge, phytoplankton are the autotrophs that account for half the photosynthetic activity on Planet Water. They also extract lots of CO_2 from the air.

It's a little mystical. What we breathe out—carbon dioxide—the oceans breathe in. What the oceans breathe out—oxygen—we breathe in. We breathe and so does Planet Water. Disable the oceans and we disappear. No blue, no green; no green, no us.

Yet neither we, nor the oceans, nor the planet started here. As we saw in the Prelude, we began long before, in a very different place—in the power-houses of star formation called supernovae. A supernova explosion nursed in a pillar of creation released the elements from which the planet and we even-tually emerged. We, and all else, are starseed. Perhaps that's the truth in Plato's claim that our souls come from the stars. It's a little mystical.

The most popular gas in supernova explosions is hydrogen. The universe by weight is three-quarters hydrogen. Oxygen is the third most popular, and with this odd couple—one large molecule (oxygen) bonding with two small ones (hydrogen) in a wonderful *ménage à trois*—we have the makings of water. Water, then, is both a primal Earth element and a cosmic one. Expen-sive rockets and robots go prospecting for water millions of miles away, not because they couldn't find the treasure closer to home, just down the hall, but because water is the *universal* wonder that, so far as we know to date, is the singular medium of life. "If we ever find aliens, they'll be thirsty."[70]

But Planet Water wasn't always so wet; it wasn't always Planet Water. Somewhere between 4.4 and 4.1 billion years old, the home planet spent a few hundred million years evolving from exploded gases and dust particles into a large, molten mass with a thin rocky crust.[71] How did we get from that molten planet with a sulfuric climate toxic to life to a planet that sings arias?[72] The answer: water. It may have come via a hard rain of meteorites bearing a payload of water and CO_2 in sufficient quantity to kick-start some essential chemical changes.[73] In any event, as massive columns of steam began to con-dense, the first true rains fell . . . and fell . . . and fell. Thrumming rain slammed down day and night for likely some 12,000 years, far more than old Noah could have survived, drunk or sober. Rivers soon formed to carve the hard crust and pool into great seas. With that the molten surface cooled and a rel-atively stable climate eventually emerged. Then, powered by the hydrologic cycle itself, atmospheric processes were created that let *the* miracle happen— cellular life. The same processes have kept the planet and its ecosphere alive ever since.[74]

While I am not certain what counts as sacred for the reader, if water doesn't qualify, little else should. Though we may ordinarily pay it little mind, largely because we confront it as a commodity, something deep within us still senses its mystery and its spell. Many have become everyday mystics in the course of quiet hours beside crystal waters that seem to flow from the throne of God, lost moments as a "pilgrim on Tinker Creek," or dazzling ones while the sun drops into an endless ocean or the moon rises from it. Thundering moments on the Bay of Fundy and terrible tsunamis bespeak the power of forces not our own. Something inside us is pulled into poetry, religion, and fear by water, it seems.

Water rites

Who has met a religion without water rites sitting near its sacramental center, commonly rites of initiation and purification? Consider but a sampling of water rites, all of them reflecting the sacred as "worthy of reverence"[75] and a sacrament as a "participatory symbol through which ... God's gracious promise of life is experienced as being presently real."[76]

The mikveh, Hebrew for a "collection" or "gathering" (of water), is a ritual bath used to ensure or restore ritual purity by, among others, those converting to the Jewish faith, Jewish women before their marriage, and those planning to enter the Temple in Jerusalem. For the convert, the immersion symbolizes release from the past life to enter a new life as a Jew. For married women and those entering the Temple it symbolizes purity of body, mind, and spirit. Ritual cleansing can also take place in other sites of what the Bible names as "living water"—a spring, a river, the sea.

Like the mikveh, Christian baptism symbolizes washing away the past in order to enter or reenter a new life in God. The baptismal life is a daily dying and rising (Paul), a pattern of renewal, with baptism and "being born of water and the Spirit" (John) a portal to the fullness of life.

Muslims are to be ritually pure before approaching God in daily prayer and water is the means. The instructions are given in the Qur'an: "O you who believe! When you prepare for prayer, wash your faces, and your hands (and arms) to the elbows; rub your heads (with water); and (wash) your feet to the ankles" (Qur'an 5:6). The instructions can be exacting. To move in the life of faith toward justice (*adl*) and to be attuned to the Oneness of all creation (*tawhid*) the believer is to wash the hands three times ("for what you have done with those hands"), rinse the mouth three times ("for what you said"), then rinse the nose three times ("to cleanse yourself of any acts of arrogance").[77] Some mosques will have a pool of clear water in the courtyard but most locate the ablutions outside the walls. Ablutions, which play a vital role everywhere in the Islamic world, have different names. *Ghusl* is washing the entire body in pure water and is performed after sexual relations, before Friday prayer, and before the two primary Islamic feasts as well as before touching the Qur'an. Not least, the dead must have the *ghusl* washing before they are buried. *Wudu* is done five times a day before the periods of prayer to remove the impurities of daily life. When at all possible, a mosque will have running water for *wudu* and prayers. But if for some reason no water is available, a third ablution is performed with clean sand. In a nice twist, some Muslims, pursuing a "green Deen" (green way of life), ask, "What's your *wudu* number?" It means how much water you are using for *wudu*, implying that you might use less and then offering ways to do so.[78] Not least, the word *sharia*, the body of Islamic law, has its origin in a desert image. *Sharia* is the path to a place of water, an oasis.

Hindus believe that all water is holy water, whether used for religious ritual or daily needs. Morning cleansing is a basic obligation, a part of Hindu morning prayers. Every temple has a pond near it where devotees often bathe themselves before entering the temple. Rivers are especially sacred waters. Funeral grounds are typically located near them. On the third day after a cremation the ashes are collected and cast onto the holy waters.

In the Theravada Buddhism of Sri Lanka, veneration of the Bodhi tree (a descendent of the tree under which Buddha attained enlightenment) includes bathing the tree with scented water. The twice-monthly Observance Day rituals at the monasteries find monks pouring water to transfer merit to the laity and the laity pouring it to share this with the ancestors. Water is also poured by the monks into a bowl placed before the dead body during a funeral.

In Thai Buddhist weddings, white threads linking the wrists of the couple are first soaked in holy water. Each guest pours a shell of holy water on the hands of the bride and groom and offers sentences of blessing.

For the practitioners of Shintoism, waterfalls are sacred. Shinto rituals include washing before prayer and standing under a waterfall for purification.

Like other religions, Zoroastrianism uses water for purification. But Zoroastrians may be unique in explicitly lifting up water as a *primal* element and concluding that it therefore must not be polluted. People must not urinate, spit, or even wash their hands in a river.[79]

The water rites of the almost countless indigenous religions are too numerous to describe separately. This one, from northern New Mexico, would resonate with many. The Ohkay Owingeh Pueblo begins its annual feast day on June 24 with a procession to the Chama River to bless the waters of the high mountain desert and, with the waters, bless the people, who also go to the river to ritually bathe before the day's dances, some of which are danced prayers. Here is a portion of the early morning blessing down by the riverside:

Blessed are you, Lord God of Mercy, the Creator of heaven and earth, the seas and rivers and all they contain. . . .

We ask you to keep this life-giving source of water always flowing freely and cleanly through our land for our needs of cleaning and re-freshing, for our needs of cooking and baking, for our needs of plant life, for our corn, our squash, our melons, and all our gifts from the breast of Mother Earth. This water is our recreation and a beauty for our eyes to see. May we use it wisely and never take it for granted. May this water always be a grace and never a cause of harm or hurt. May we always respect this gift of water as we ask you to bless it today, and may this life-giving water which continually returns to you and which you continually return to us remind us of the very gift of life itself that comes from you and returns to you. May our lives be an echo back to you of your love for us.[80]

The state of water

How is water faring? From 1950 to 2000, water use more than trebled, going from 1,360 cubic kilometers used in 1950 to 5,190 in 2000 (see the graphs in chapter 2).[81] This is roughly "half the world's readily accessible freshwater run-off."[82] That leaves half for the rest of the biosphere and explains why there is a worldwide crisis of dwindling freshwater supplies—for the rest of nature, for the poor,[83] for future generations. And frankly, we don't know how much water people, now the planet's water hogs, can safely use and still give the rest of life its due. Judging by the precipitous decline in freshwater species—a 35 percent decline in 458 freshwater species in the period from 1970 to 2005[84]—it's likely they're not getting it.

We do know we are overpumping, even for human use alone. More than half the world's population lives in countries where water tables are falling. The World Bank reports that in some of the economically most dynamic countries, the increased use is precipitous. India has drilled 20 million irriga-tion wells, many of which are running dry, while 175 million Indians are being fed with grain produced by overpumping. The World Bank's estimate is that 130 million Chinese are currently fed by overpumping, much of it in the North China Plain, which produces half of China's wheat and one-third of its corn.[85]

Most of our interaction with water is unseen. Each cotton T-shirt, for ex-ample, requires 2,900 liters of water to produce (766 gallons), each pair of jeans 10,855 liters (2867.5 gallons), each couple of pounds of burger beef over 15,000 (3962.55 gallons).[86] But this invisibility doesn't change the fact that every time we interact with water, seen or unseen, "we change it, redirect it or otherwise alter its state."[87] All our activities interact with water and change the Earth system in the process.

Incidentally, bottled water is 2,000 times as energy costly as tap water. Peter Gleick's vivid image for this is to pour each bottle a quarter full of oil. We're drinking carbon emissions.

The key vector of climate change is water. Ocean temperatures drive most atmospheric activity and warming ocean temperatures are now altering the hydrologic cycle itself. The warming at the poles is especially fateful. It is shifting the global temperature gradient and spinning global winds and ocean currents into different patterns. This seems to be speeding up the rate at which water evaporates and falls again as rain or snow; and this higher rate, a change in the hydrologic cycle itself, "seems to make wet regions more sodden, and arid ones drier. It brings longer droughts between more intense periods of rain."[88]

It's important to understand tipping points in light of this warming. Tipping points are critical because in nonlinear systems like the water cycle, even small changes—a degree or two of average mean temperature—can have cascading consequences. Thresholds can be crossed and new or more extreme forces can take over, with effects out of proportion to the initiating cause.[89] Life can fall from its perch.

Here is one list of potential tipping points: permafrost and tundra loss, releasing the powerful greenhouse gas, methane; boreal forest dieback; Arctic sea-ice loss; Greenland ice-sheet melting; Atlantic deep water formation (affecting the great ocean currents like the Gulf Stream); Indian monsoon instability; West African monsoon shift; El Nino southern oscillation; Amazon forest dieback; Sahara desert greening; changes in Antarctic water formation; and the instability of the West Antarctic ice sheet.[90] Every one of these is a game changer, and every one is about water.

What about food and farming? The National Academy of Sciences published a study on major shifts in agriculture that will likely come in the wake of climate change. The conclusion is that present farmers "are the first generation of growers who can't count on historical climate information to help them plan things such as when to plant and what varieties to choose. . . . They can't rely on the calendar to tell them when to plant, they can't rely on the variety of seeds they have always used, and they can't rely on dealing with the same insect pests, because it's all a moving target now."[91] Every dress rehearsal for the future must now start with this: It's all a moving target, uncertain because of what we are doing to water and air. Yet water and air don't people our moral universe (unless you are a serious web-of-life sacramentalist).

Increased pressure from the two chief drivers of planetary change—human population and the global human economy—will only increase pressure on water availability and health. Short of an apocalypse worthy of science fiction, human numbers will continue to grow rapidly, mostly in urban areas where, for the first time in human history, the majority now lives. (In 1900 only 13 percent lived in cities; in 2030 60 percent will.) This historic shift is critical because urbanization is a major intensifier of water use. The other big intensifier is growing wealth and mass consumption.[92] In short, a dramatic turnaround in the factors that produced the steep curves in post-1950s trends is not on the horizon. The world is in greater, not less, need of its chief uncertain resource.

In brief we might modify our basic premise that "planetary health is primary, human well-being is derivative."[93] It could read: planetary *water* health is primary, human health is derivative. To repeat: no blue, no green; no green, no us.

What, then, are we water people to be and do? What ethical issues must be addressed as we live with a freshwater crisis on land, a crisis of the ocean's health, and the rude shocks of a destabilized atmosphere and big changes in the hydrologic cycle?

The subject of any ethic, sacramental or otherwise, is how we live. What makes lives go around well, avoiding harm and contributing to the common good? As we look to water in a world that is small, round, and without an exit ramp, the critical moral matters fall into three categories.

The first is simplest. While morally blue skies are rather rare, sometimes what we ought to do *is* clear as day. The moral issue then is mobilizing sufficient will for effective action. An advertisement placed in the *New York Times* by Water Advocates illustrate this: "Imagine a Water Pump So Remarkable It Quenches Poverty, Fear and Illiteracy."

> To change the world, the best place to start is with clean drinking water. Especially for women and children in developing countries, who can spend up to 60% of each day walking over treacherous paths to find it . . . But with access to clean drinking water, sanitation and hygiene, children have time to attend school. Women have time to earn livelihoods. Fatal bouts of diarrhea are reduced. Dignity is renewed. And, once water and sanitation become accessible, entire

communities are able to achieve sustainable futures. The ripple effect is astonishing.[94]

There is no ethical dilemma here. Clean, accessible water can be made available. It need not compete against other basic needs, the technology is known, and the costs are manageable. Actions readily at hand would reduce the catastrophic toll of unsafe water; only mobilized will and financial resources are missing. Moral complacency on the part of the privileged is the obstacle, not big risks, conflicting claims, or inadequate information.

Many other water matters pose no moral agony, either. Getting better data and sharing it, integrating water policy with food and energy policy, wringing massive inefficiencies out of our present infrastructure—none of these are riddled with moral doubt or conflict. They may require a wakeup call but their achievement draws upon values and commitments already widely held. Matched to good science and technology, they offer "win-win" choices and a shared good.

A second category of ethical issues *does* center on conflicting claims and competing needs, all of which have validity. There is the aforementioned conflict between human needs and those of the rest of nature. And if our moral universe says human water needs should trump those of plants and animals, we don't understand where smug heterotrophs sit on the food chain and in the food web.

Within human society, agricultural and urban needs compete. City peoples demand large amounts of water, often from distant sources where those who live there are not eager to see their water drained away. Moreover, city people cannot grow the acres of food they need. Industrialized agriculture and factory farming demand a huge volume of water, over and over again, to produce that food. (Agriculture claims about three-fourths the world's used water.)

Then there is the matter of diet. When agriculture is for the meaty tastes of Americans and Europeans, 5,000 liters of water per person per day (1,320 gallons) is required. When it's for the vegetarian diets of Asians and Africans, it's 2,000 liters (528 gallons). So diet is a moral issue, too. Of course if, as in an earlier era, the population is small and abundant water can meet all needs, these hard moral choices dissolve. But that is no longer the case, so the lawyers are busy.

What about public health and the economy? There is no longer any uncontaminated place on the planet. And since the hydrologic system is a genuine cycle, toxicity can travel anywhere. Some PCBs (polychlorinated biphenyls) released in Big Spring, Texas, traveled various waterways to end up in seals, polar bears, and the breast milk of Inuktitut mothers on the isolated, far northern island of Broughton.[95] Yet we cannot shut down all industry and agriculture while we do our research, clean up, replace all the offending systems, and reregulate. Public health will compete with ongoing economic needs.

Other examples of conflicting claims and needs that demand hard choices—desalination and its high-carbon-emitting energy requirements and costs, privatization versus public control, the damming of waterways, and cross-border claims to water—could be added. As we confront them, we do well to remember a sentence attributed to Reinhold Niebuhr: "What counts is not the purity of our intentions but the integrity of our compromises."[96] Only now "integrity" has an added meaning: keeping creation's integrity up-permost. The integral functioning of nature's systems must set the basic terms and outer limits for all water policy.

The third area of moral concern is of a different order altogether. It is not about discrete issues and claims, but the larger framework within which water matters are considered. How ought we to regard water in the first place?

Every good ethic includes a description of what is. At present what *is*, in the case of water, is a resource and commodity in the service of the irrational exuberance of the post-1950 global economy. This is the utilitarian view at the heart of the industrial paradigm we have met often and discussed as commodity ethics. In this case it's water as a natural resource at the ready. That use-relationship, so "natural" to us, frames water and its value in our way of life and erodes the mythic, poetic, and esthetic understandings of water. When water is a market commodity in a plastic bottle piled on supermarket shelves, it is no longer sacramental. This loss of sacred meaning in turn affects our moral sense: It's "just water."

The basic ethical reorientation commended here belongs to an eco-spirituality that includes a profoundly sacramental sense. Water is the object of awe and not *only* the object of engineering; it is the medium of the mystical and not *only* a resource for a world of our own making; water is a "thou" and not *only* an "it." It's "Sister Water" (St. Francis) or a pueblo called "White Shell Water Place." It's worthy of reverence.

The ethics of water as a commodity is reflected in IBM's Global Innovation Outlook on water. The Outlook gathers good research and successful water practices from around the world. At that level it is highly commendable. The assumed moral framework is unsettling, however. The introduction says: "[T]here are 2 trillion liters of fresh water for every man, woman and child on Earth. And each of us only needs less than three liters a day. Therefore, what we have is not a shortage of fresh water. What we have is a management problem,"[97] a problem solved with high-quality data, accurate pricing, and the right business models. A reader searches the report in vain—chapters on "Data Drought," "The Business of Water," "The Infrastructure Imperative," "Food, Energy and Water," and "Perception Is Reality"—to see if any life other than human life exists on Planet Water and whether that life has any claims to water. In this light, the last chapter's title, "Perception Is Reality," is telling. In ethics, "perception is reality" means that what people define as real is real in its consequences. And what is defined as real in this report is this: All that matters about water is human need, supply, and use. IBM needs a poster on its corporate headquarters door: "We're all heterotrophs, stupid."

In contrast with command-and-control management such as IBM's, David Groenfeldt proposes the alternative paradigm of "ecological management." The key principle here is maintaining the flow of a river, wetland, or coastal zone needed for their ecosystems. This is akin to South Africa's constitution: Water is a public good with two reserves, the human need reserve and the ecological reserve. Both must be served; one does not trump the other. Human infrastructure and the rest of nature's are both essential.

Ecological management has science on its side, says Groenfeldt, but command-and-control management has politics and business on its side. He then ventures to speak of "sacred water management" and say that "for all practical purposes, a [sacred] approach would be identical to an [ecological] approach, because they share common objectives, the health and sustainability of the whole ecosystem." The difference is in underlying precepts. "A vision of the river as sacred, and its sustainable management as a sacred responsibility to Mother Earth, adds a clarity of purpose which is not found in management models predicated on a secular vision." Groenfeldt's concluding sentence is: "Religion may be just as important as science, in motivating sustainable water management practices and helping all of us weather the emerging challenges of climate change."[98]

The just use of water requires moral systems that attend to the good of the commons as we fashion our shared human good. (As noted, the oceans and atmosphere are classic commons.) A sacramental sense and web-of-life morality are more conducive to that than either chain-of-being sacramentalism or the commodity morality of industrialism. All water engineers need not become Franciscans. But theirs would be sound ecological water management, not command-and-control management, if they adopted Francis's adjectives: "Praised be you my Lord, for Sister Water, so *useful, humble, precious,* and *pure*" (*Canticle of the Sun*). Not least, the way forward requires a renewed sense of sacramental wonder and awe in the presence of the stunning beauty of life. Human beings will always seek out ways to meet their core needs. It is not for us to ravage the sea and the land in the process, however. In the present and foreseeable circumstances, that means, for all practical purposes, whether, under the strains of water needs, water conflict, and climagration, commodity ethics will trump sacrament ethics. If that happens, something essentially human will be lost, not only for water but for the apprehension and value of all life. That "something"—this chapter's effort to let the commodified be addressed by the sacred—is still present in Marilynne Robinson's *Gilead*. The elderly pastor, his ailing heart beating out its mortality, captures his memories in letters to his young son. One goes like this:

> You and Tobias are hopping around in the sprinkler. The sprinkler is a magnificent invention because it exposes raindrops to sunshine. That does occur in nature, but it is rare. When I was in seminary I used to go sometimes to the Baptists down at the river. It was something to see the preacher lifting the one who was being baptized up out of the water and the water pouring off the garments and the hair. It did look like a birth or a resurrection. For us the water just heightens the touch of the pastor's hand on the sweet bones of the head, sort of like making an electrical connection. I've always loved to baptize people, though I have sometimes wished there were more shimmer and splash involved in the way we go about it. Well, but you two are dancing around in your iridescent little downpour, whooping and stomping as sane people ought to do when they encounter a thing so miraculous as water.[99]

Next . . .

The sacramental and the mystical are close cousins. But they are not the same. The mystical addresses alienation in the modern world in profounder ways than the sacramental, despite the latter's profound contrast with the objectified and the commodified. We turn to mystery and the mystical.

10

Mysticism and Alienation

The most beautiful and most profound experience is the sensation of the mystical. It is the sower of all true science. He to whom this emotion is a stranger, who can no longer wonder and stand rapt in awe, is as good as dead.

—ALBERT EINSTEIN

Our life is a faint tracing on the surface of mystery. The surface is not smooth. . . . Nor does it fit together. . . . Mystery is as fringed and intricate as the shape of the air in time.

—ANNIE DILLARD

ON ANOTHER PILGRIM day at Tinker Creek, Annie Dillard suddenly found herself face-to-face with a weasel. "Our eyes locked and someone threw away the key. Our look was as if two lovers, or deadly enemies, met unexpectedly on an overgrown path when each had been thinking of something else,"[1]

Not all mystical experience is so abrupt or so uncertain, whether the locked eyes are those of enemies or lovers. But the mystical *is* always a certain kind of *meeting* and a certain way of *being*. It is subject joined to subject or, in some people's experiences, the dissolution of subjectivity itself in undifferentiated union. In this meeting and union, *direct* experience prevails. Friedrich von Hügel's account, offered by Dorothee Soelle in *The Silent Cry: Mysticism and Resistance*, identifies three enduring elements present in all religion. The historical-institutional addresses itself to mind and memory (in Christianity, the "Petrine" element); the analytical-speculative aligns itself with reason and doctrine (the "Pauline" element); and an intuitive-emotional element directs itself to the will and to love. This is the specifically mystical (identified by Soelle as the "Johannine" in Christianity;[2] like the eagle that symbolizes the Fourth Gospel, the soul has a capacity to look directly into the sun and to soar).[3]

Simone Weil's delightful image for the soul's soaring is one she takes from the Brothers Grimm. A little tailor competes with a giant to see which is the stronger. The giant throws a stone so high and far that it takes a long while to return to earth. The little tailor hurls a small bird that does not come down at all, at least not anywhere in sight. The soul, Weil says, is that bird.

The testimony of religious mystics is that any and all can soar in this manner. All are able to "move beyond the confines of society and history [and] break the bounds of normal human interaction, normal consciousness, and normal physical reality"[4] in order to draw upon a wisdom hidden deep within this world or resident beyond it. For mystics, like ascetics, this is release from the grip of the social ego and socially constructed senses of the body itself. This is direct experience of the divine beyond the stipulations of doctrine and institution. This is truth apprehended apart from the authority of society's keepers of the truth. And this is revelation shorn from common attachments and desires. The way things seem to be is not the way they truly are or might be. For mystics, institutions and their powers are not fates we must accommodate. They are habitual patterns that could be otherwise.

In short, mystics testify to a profound submersion into "the All" (Atman-Brahman in Hinduism), the oceanic experience in which we "touch with our living hearts the Heart of the World and listen to the secret revelations of its unending beat."[5] This is the experience of a reality within or beneath the immediate material reality and the experience of a oneness that includes and encloses everyone and everything in sight. And all this happens in unmediated fashion.

The unmediated mystical experience is beyond formal religion. The mystic knows that in the depths of any and every religion there comes a point at which religion no longer matters at all. Universal truth, beauty, and the good merge, whether formally religious or not.

Sufi master Ibn 'Al-Arabī (1165–1240) underscores the unmediated, direct nature of mystical knowing: "Knowledge of mystical states can only be had by actual experience, nor can the reason of man define it, nor arrive at any cognizance of it by deduction, as is also the case with knowledge of the taste of honey, the bitterness of patience, the bliss of sexual union, love, passion or desire, all of which cannot possibly be known unless one be properly qualified or experience them directly."[6]

Examples of this experience of "an ocean of intimacy"[7] are many. They occur in all traditions and cultures. They may happen without preparation. A person whose only preparation was removing his or her shoes may, upon entering the Al-Aqsa Mosque in Jerusalem, be so captured, as I was, by the soaring spaces and play of light in so vast a quiet that a sense of Allah's overwhelming presence was palpable. Such has also been the experience of God in many a medieval cathedral, in a redwood forest, beside a river, or atop a mesa.

Meditation

Other times the mystical experience is accompanied by disciplined preparation and practice. Contemplation and meditation are religious practices independent of the mystical experience. Yet they often prepare for it and foster it.

Take, for example, the Buddhist *gatha* cited in the previous chapter: "In this food / I see clearly / the entire universe / supporting my existence."[8] It belongs to a large collection of meditations meant to aid the practice of mindfulness, of being intensely present to the images the *gathas* convey. This attentiveness, when part of a regular practice, may issue in the mystical experience.

Here is a practice of what is called "mindful breathing." In this instance, the intent is to look deeply into the roots of fear. (Buddhist practice has contemplative exercises for specific vices and virtues and their moral emotions— love, greed, compassion, anger, etc.) This exercise goes as follows.

> *Breathing in, I know that I am of the nature*
> *to grow old.*
> *Breathing out, I know I cannot escape old age.*
> *Breathing in, I know that I am of the nature*
> *to get sick.*
> *Breathing out, I know that I cannot escape sickness.*
> *Breathing in, I know that I am of the nature*
> *to die.*
> *Breathing out, I know that I cannot escape dying.*
> *Breathing in, I know that one day I will have to*
> *let go of everything and everyone I cherish.*
> *Breathing out, there is no way to bring them*
> *along.*
> *Breathing in, I know that I take nothing with me*
> *except my actions, thoughts, and deeds.*
> *Breathing out, my actions come with me.*

We'll never get out of life alive. But it is one thing to acknowledge that intellectually; it is quite another to come to terms with it deep within my whole being. The former is easy—just look around. The latter may require the repeated practice of meditation.

Contemplative and meditative practices belong to living traditions. So in this case Thich Nhat Hanh, with fears for our present civilization because of its assaults on nature, adds a stanza. He does not wish the death of this civilization and, as an "engaged Buddhist," works for an Earth-honoring transformation of it. Yet he knows that all civilizations are mortal and that sound mental health asks us to face mortality in all forms, including our way of life.

> *Breathing in, I know that this civilization*
> *is going to die.*
> *Breathing out, this civilization cannot escape dying.*[9]

The example should not overwhelm the point: Mystical experience is often accompanied by disciplined practice and not only sudden experience.

Moral agency

One consequence of transcending the hold that the forces have upon us—a part of the oceanic feeling, its ripples and riptides—is strong personal agency. Such moral strength and independence is the spillover of the profound consent to Being and union with the All, a consent and union in which, paradoxically, self falls away, the heresy of "mine" and "thine" falls away as well, and the mystic's quest ends in the cool cosmic fire that some name "God" and others refuse to name at all. Cosmic unity and cosmic community is the mystic's home. It is the very opposite of isolation and self-encapsulated autonomy.

When the mystic returns to intransigent worldly reality, as he or she must, the seemingly autonomous agency does not dissipate. Rather, the mystic is so captured by cosmic beauty and harmony that she or he is permanently dissatisfied with the world around. That world may indeed be fully embraced, with empathy and compassion. But things will not be right until Eden reborn sings with the stars. Mystics cannot deny the wondrous burden of beauty and truth that the moment in God brings.

Soelle reports that this direct experience of transcendence leads to lives of nonviolence, egolessness, and possessionlessness. Those who experience the unity and beauty of all things awaken from the prison in which they have fallen asleep[10] to take up justice as a virtue and way of being. "The flood of fire abated," Dillard writes of her own mystical encounter, "but I'm still spending the power."[11]

Janet Ruffing's collaborative study comes to a similar conclusion. After investigating Jewish, Muslim, and Christian mysticism in various contexts and cultures, Ruffin goes on to say that "beyond these traditions, every tradition of mystical revelation—Buddhist, Hindu, Taoist, and others—points to an alternative *form of culture* and *intends* an alternative way for human beings to dwell together."[12] The mystical experience becomes part of the disciple's way.

In her own idiosyncratic way, Simone Weil (1901–1943) illustrates everything said to this point. *Two Moral Essays* was written as part of her work for the De Gaulle government in exile when Germany occupied France in the early 1940s. The work includes a "Draft for a Statement of Human Obligations" as well as thoughts on "Human Personality." The former begins with as succinct a statement of mysticism as any, albeit offered in the prose of Weil the instructor rather than the poetry of Weil the mystic. That it comes as the lead-in for "a statement of human obligations" only confirms Soelle's and Ruffing's conclusions about mysticism and moral agency.

> There is a reality outside the world, that is to say, outside space and time, outside man's mental universe, outside any sphere whatsoever that is accessible to human faculties.
>
> Corresponding to this reality, at the center of the human heart, is the longing for an absolute good, a longing which is always there and is never appeased by any object in this world. . . .
>
> Just as the reality of this world is the sole foundation of facts, so that other reality is the sole foundation of good.
>
> That reality is the unique source of all the good that can exist in this world: that is to say, all beauty, all truth, all justice, all legitimacy, all order, and all human behaviour that is mindful of obligations. . . .
>
> Although it is beyond the reach of any human faculties, man has the power of turning his attention and love towards it.
>
> Nothing can ever justify the assumption that any man, whoever he may be, has been deprived of this power.
>
> It is a power which is only real in this world in so far as it is exercised. The sole condition for exercising it is consent. . . .
>
> The combination of these two facts—the longing in the depth of the heart for absolute good, and the power, though only latent, of directing attention and love to a reality beyond the world and of receiving good from it—constitutes a link which attaches every man without exception to that other reality.

Whoever recognizes that reality recognizes also that link. Because of it, he holds every human being without any exception as something sacred to which he is bound to show respect.[13]

Weil next argues that every-human-being-as-sacred is not a deduction that can be reasoned from the world as we know it. The world we know is one of "unequal objects unequally solicit[ing] our attention."[14] Some people grab our attention, others remain unidentified and unknown, still others belong only to a collective identity that erases their individuality. Factual world knowledge alone, as the springboard of action, leads, Weil says, to *in*equality of both respect and treatment. From a strictly empirical point of view, "men are unequal in all their relations with the things of this world, without exception."[15]

The point of her essay, however, is "the presence of a link with the reality outside the world" that is identical for all human beings and that has consequences for how all persons are to be understood and treated. All humans have their center "in an unquenchable desire for good" that resides on the other side of that thin place separating the factual world from the world mystical experience imbibes. By attending to that other reality, we arrive at a center that belongs to all.[16] This center funds a dignity and respect that also belongs to all equally. Weil does not hesitate to name it the "sacred" that we all *are*.

This innate desire for the good and the knowledge of our own being as sacred can be beaten from us, die from neglect, or be betrayed. While it is genetic, it is also vulnerable and subject to loss. Weil's response is strong moral obligation to repair the world. "When a man's life is destroyed or damaged by some wound or privation of soul or body, which is due to other men's actions or negligence, it is not only his sensibility that suffers but also his aspiration towards the good. Therefore there has been sacrilege towards that which is sacred in him."[17] To fail through neglect or commission to engage and draw out the sacred that others *are*, is desecration itself. For Weil it is a violation of creation and an offense against God.

Such stark moral-theological reasoning stands behind her argument elsewhere that the only proper love of neighbor is justice, not charity (the charity relationship is subject to object, not subject to subject). Justice is repair of the world that rests in mysticism's knowledge of radical equality and shared subjectivity (all have the same center, all merit the respect due the sacred).[18]

Teeming nature

If moral agency, rooted in profound union with being and consent to it as a communion of sacred subjects, isn't left behind in the mystical experience, neither is nature. On the contrary, teeming nature abounds in much mystical consciousness and holds uncommonly high rank in mystical visions. Consider Hildegard's encounter with the divine: "I, the highest and fiery power, have kindled every living spark . . . I am . . . the fiery life of the divine essence—I am aflame above the beauty of the fields; I shine in the waters; in the sun, the moon and the stars, I burn. And by the means of the airy wind, I stir everything into quickness with a certain invisible life which sustains all."[19]

Or consider Black Elk's vision: "It was when I was five years old that my Grandfather made me a bow and some arrows. The grass was young and I was on horseback. A thunderstorm was coming from where the sun goes down. . . . Then I looked up and at the clouds, and two men were coming there, headfirst like arrows slanting down; as they came they sang a sacred song and the thunder was like drumming. I will sing it for you. The song and the drumming were like this: 'Behold, a sacred voice is calling you; all over the sky a sacred voice is calling.' I sat there gazing at them, and they were coming from the place where the giant marsh lives. . . . When they were gone, the rain came with a big wind and roaring. I did not tell this vision to anyone. I like to think about it, but I was afraid to tell it."[20]

Or consider Weil's complaint, "How can Christianity call itself catholic if the universe itself is left out?"[21] This sentence is in a section, "Love of the Order of the World," itself largely a gloss on the beauty of the world and on love of matter as the proper parallel to love of the human neighbor. "In the beauty of the world," she writes, "brute necessity becomes an object of love. What is more beautiful than the action of gravity on the fugitive folds of the sea waves, or on the almost eternal folds of the mountains?"[22] Nothing less than Christ is present here: "The beauty of the world is the co-operation of divine wisdom in creation. . . . The beauty of the world is Christ's tender smile for us coming through matter."[23]

The association with Jesus Christ robs Weil's mysticism of the romanticism it and other expressions of panentheism sometimes embrace. "God crosses through the thickness of the world to come to us," she says.[24] That crossing includes the cross itself. A world afflicted with suffering, pain, and injustice is the mystic's world. The beauty of the world and of Earth only renders more poignant its distress.

Consider the elder Zosima's instruction in *The Brothers Karamazov*. Like Hildegard's and Weil's, Zosima's spiritual world is equal parts sacramentalism, asceticism, and mysticism. But Dostoevsky's section title gives priority to the mystical: "Of Prayer, of Love and of Contact with Other Worlds." Note in this passage that love of God and love of nature, ourselves included, are the abiding themes. Note also that these are central to Zosima's instruction on sin.

> Brothers, be not afraid of men's sin, love man also in his sin, for this likeness of God's love is the height of love on earth. Love all of God's creation, both the whole of it and every grain of sand. Love every leaf, every ray of God's light. Love animals, love plants, love each thing. If you love each thing, you will perceive the mystery of God in things. Once you have perceived it, you will begin tirelessly to perceive more and more of it every day. And you will at come at last to love the whole world with an entire, universal love. Love the animals: God has given them the rudiments of thought and an untroubled joy. Do not trouble it, do not torment them, do not take their joy from them, do not go against God's purpose. Man, do not exalt yourself above the animals: they are sinless, and you, you with your grandeur, fester the earth by your appearance on it, and you leave your festering traces behind you—alas, almost every one of us does! Love children especially, for they, too, are sinless, like angels, and live to bring us to tenderness and the purification of our hearts and are as a sort of example to us. Woe to him who offends a child.[25]

The wizened Zosima goes on to instruct young monks about the need for *askesis* and forgiveness.

> Brothers, love is a teacher, but one must know how to acquire it, for it is difficult to acquire, it is dearly bought, by long work over a long time, for one ought to love not only for a chance moment but for all time. Anyone, even a wicked man, can love by chance. My young brother asked forgiveness of the birds: it seems senseless, yet it is right, for all is like an ocean, all flows and connects; touch it in one place and it echoes at the other end of the world. Let it be madness to ask forgiveness of the birds, still it would be easier for the birds, and for a child, and for every animal near you, if you yourself were more gracious than you are now, if only by a drop, still it would be easier. All is like an ocean, I say

to you. Tormented by universal love, you, too, would then start praying to the birds, as if in a sort of ecstasy, and entreat them to forgive you your sin. Cherish this ecstasy, however senseless it may seem to people.[26]

Zosima himself laid great store by such ecstasy. He also instructed novices in the morality that accompanies it. His long discourse concludes on this note.

People are always saved after the death of him who saved them. The generation of men does not welcome its prophets and kills them, but men love their martyrs and venerate those they have tortured to death. Your work is for the whole, your deed is for the future. Never seek a reward, for great is your reward on earth without that: your spiritual joy, which only the righteous obtain. Nor should you fear not the noble and powerful, but be wise and ever gracious. Know measure, know the time, learn these things. When you are alone, pray. Love to throw yourself down on the earth and kiss it. Kiss the earth and love it, tirelessly, insatiably, love all men, love all things, seek this rapture and ecstasy. Water the earth with the tears of your joy, and love those tears. Do not be ashamed of this ecstasy, treasure it, for it is a gift from God, a great gift, and it is not given to many, but only to those who are chosen.[27]

Zosima himself dies kissing the earth. He "silently lowered himself from his armchair to the floor and knelt, then bowed down with his face to the ground, stretched out his arms, and, as if in joyful ecstasy, kissing the earth and praying (as he himself taught), quietly and joyfully gave up his soul to God."[28]

Not all mysticism is so consistently life-charged, like the figures in Toni Morrison's and Alice Walker's novels, or so thoroughly drenched with the tears of joy and sorrow that Earth evokes. In some forms of mysticism, nature and earth are left behind as distractions on the path. As was the case with asceticism and sacramentalism, so mysticism must also be plumbed to see whether its morality is truly Earth-honoring.

That said, Zosima's Earth-rich panentheism seems the natural habitat for much mysticism. This means what "panentheism" formally means—the finite bears the infinite; God is present to creation in, through, and as creation; the divine inhabits the ecosocial and geosocial. It means, in different words, that nature is a translucent order with traces of divine habitation everywhere, the medium of God's very presence. Mystical experience might begin, then, like Thomas Merton's, in contemplation of a lone cardinal in a locust tree, or the swirl of humanity at the intersection of 4th and Walnut, Louisville, Kentucky:

> I was suddenly overwhelmed with the realization that I loved all those people, that they were mine and I theirs, that we could not be alien to one another even though we were total strangers. It was like waking from a dream of separateness, of spurious self isolation in a special world, the world of renunciation and supposed holiness. The whole illusion of a separate holy existence is a dream.[29]

Or it might begin with some other encounter—Dillard and the weasel. But it is no surprise that mystics end their moment of transcendent encounter by taking to their gardens, taking to the streets, or taking to their pens. All that is belongs to the living Whole.

Passing the test of whether this ethic is Earth-honoring, and thus fit for the Great Work, can draw from mysticism's strong moral agency rooted in the panentheistic apprehension of God and the universe. Such mysticism is the antithesis of the alienated relationships typical of modernity. In mystical experience, the universe is a communion of subjects rather than a collection of objects.[30] The oceanic feeling, like the ocean itself, encompasses all who dwell therein. The great illusion is the illusion of separateness. The great illusion is that the other is object apart from me, rather than subject in whose presence I am who I am.

Interbeing

No religious tradition is clearer about separateness as illusion than Buddhism. "Interbeing" is constitutive of all that is, not only the human. "When we look deeply into a flower, we see the elements that have come together to allow it to manifest," writes Thich Nhat Hanh. "We can see clouds manifesting as rain. . . . When I touch the flower, I'm touching the cloud and touching the rain. This is not just poetry, it's reality. If we take the clouds and the rain out of the flower, the flower will not be there. . . . The flower cannot be as a separate entity; it has to inter-be with the light, with the clouds, with the rain. The word 'interbeing' is closer to reality than the word 'being.' *Being* really means *interbeing*."[31] Thus can Thich Nhat Hanh see in a forest "our lungs outside our body"[32] and in the sun "the great heart outside our body."[33] "When we see things in this way, we can easily transcend the duality of self and nonself. We see that we must take care of our environment because the environment is us."[34] This is "our large self" and our "true self," joined from the inside to "the forest, the river, and the ozone layer." The "small self" is the one that is self-imprisoned and alienated, when these—forest, river, ozone—are seen, and treated, as though they did not belong to our humanity.[35]

Interbeing as reality means intersubjectivity. In a world of suffering that can only mean empathy and compassion as the heart and soul of the moral life. When Thich Nhat Hanh learned that the Indian Ocean tsunami of 2004 killed thousands of people in Indonesia, Sri Lanka, Thailand, India, and Africa, he responded, "I practiced. I sat down and I practiced looking deeply. And what I saw is that when these people died, we also died with them, because we inter-are with them."[36] Died with them? He explains. When our soul-mate dies, something in us dies as well. Our lives have belonged to one another and are a part of one another. Even after the beloved's death, that presence remains with us, deep in the psyche, lodged as part of who we are. Likewise, if we understand that our lives "inter-are" with other lives, and if we have compassion, "then when we see other people dying, even strangers on the other side of the world, we suffer and die with them." "What we find out," Thich Nhat Hanh continues, "is that they die for us. So we have to live for them. We have to live in such a way that the future will be possible for our children and their children. Whether or not their deaths will have meaning depends on our way of living. That is the insight of interbeing. They are us and we are them."[37]

Descartes's turn

"Interbeing" and a "communion of subjects" is far from modernity's take on the matter. The standard account builds on the famous methodological move of René Descartes (1596–1650). In his quest for certain knowledge Descartes thought it proper "to cast aside the loose earth and sand, that I might reach the rock or the clay."[38] This search for solid ground took him first to his studies, including theology. "I revered our Theology," he writes, "and aspired as much as any one to reach heaven: but being given assuredly to understand that the way is not less open to the most ignorant than to the most learned, and that the revealed truths which lead to heaven are above our comprehension, I did not presume to subject them to the impotency of my Reason."[39] The search sent him traveling as well. "Studying the book of the world, and ... gather[ing] some experience"[40] occupied several years. "[T]he great book of nature" was still another contender for discovering clear and certain knowledge.[41]

Yet neither book, the book of the world nor the book of nature, availed, and Descartes' very next words mark his new path and decisive move: "I at length resolved to make myself an object of study, and to employ all the powers of my mind in choosing the paths I ought to follow."[42] This fabled turn to the human subject for certain knowledge (it became the signature of the Enlightenment) *could* have transpired in numerous ways. He might have asked how certain knowledge belonged to the human subject's embeddedness in its surroundings, or how it emerged as the outcome of communal human ties. Instead, Descartes's—and modernity's—move was to effect disconnection at every point. "During the nine subsequent years, I did nothing but roam from one place to another, desirous of being a spectator rather than an actor in the plays exhibited on the theatre of the world."[43] His life was, he says, "as solitary and retired as in the most remote desert" though not "deprived of any of the conveniences to be had in the most populous cities."[44] This was not, we should note, the ascetic's relocation. Descartes is not searching out "the solace of fierce landscapes"[45] in order to allow them, in solitude and prayer, to work their ways on human selves carefully tuned to their environs for all signs of life and death. His method of radical skepticism was a conscious effort to disconnect mind from body and nature, even society.

The *locus classicus* of Descartes's method, and of the Enlightenment's turn to the autonomous reason of the autonomous subject as essentially a thinking machine, is the following passage, one of the most influential and fateful in human history.

> I observed that, whilst I . . . wished to think that all was false, it was absolutely necessary that I, who thus thought, should be somewhat; and as I observed that this truth, *I think, hence I am*, was so certain and of such evidence, that no ground of doubt, however extravagant, could be alleged by the Skeptics capable of shaking it, I concluded that I might, without scruple, accept it as the first principle of the Philosophy of which I was in search.[46]

What immediately follows, though not oft-noted, is as important as this first principle and belongs to it.

> In the next place, I attentively examined what I was, and as I observed that I could suppose that *I had no body, and that there was no world and*

no place in which I might be, I could not for all that doubt that *I* did not exist.[47]

Dissociated mind and the independent thinking "I" is the foundational reality in this cosmology, the sure ground for knowing the world in pristine detachment from it. It is the human subject as immaterial mind and disembodied rational consciousness and process. And it is described by Descartes as exactly that.

I thence concluded that I was a substance whose whole essence or nature consists only in thinking, and which, that it may exist, has need of no place, nor is dependent on any material thing; so that "I," that is to say, the mind by which I am what I am, is wholly distinct from the body, and is even more easily known than the latter, and is such, that although the latter were not, it would still continue to be all that is.[48]

The easy transit from "I" to the human self and the active human subject implies a human self and subject removed from (the rest of) nature, a self that can imagine itself distinct from body and place and without need of them. The key is that the human mind and its thoughts exist as a different category and on some other plane than the physical world.[49] The world "out there" was cleft from the mind "within." With that cleavage modernity's subjectivism, and its profound alienation from the rest of nature, was born.

This severe Cartesian dualism is, however, not only about knowing. It is about valuing. Descartes's thought experiment was crucial not only for epistemology and science but also for ethics. He could hardly have imagined what a momentous change his experiment to doubt all things possible except the thinking "I" was, and then build up all knowing and ordering from there. But from the seventeenth century onward, a Western culture that had considered meaning and purpose to be written into the order of nature and the cosmos by an awesome and incarnate God now assumed that the meaning and end of all nature has its effective value in the rational will and active agency of autonomous and sovereign humanity. This is the essence of secular modernity. It has reigned in both science and in the day-to-day practices of capitalist political economy. To cite James Miller, the natural world is no longer "an arena of subjectivity to be engaged in a communal relationship." It does not "speak" to humans and becomes only "an object for human purposes rather than a living subject in the planetary ecosystem."[50]

In short, the essence of humanity is consciousness and mind, a consciousness and mind that is lifted from the very biological and evolutionary matrix that made it possible.[51] This essence radically distinguishes us from the rest of nature, which is now "object" to us, rather than "subject." And our relationship to this nature is in the manner of subject-over-object and mind-over-matter in an economic order that assumes nature is slave to humanity as its steward.

The point is not only Descartes's extreme mind/body dualism, however. It is the alienated subject/object relationship they create. The disassociated human mind is ranged over against all else as disconnected objects, including its own body. Immaterial mind over mechanical matter, as reigning subject over against passive object, is the ethic that issued from this worldview as soon as it found real-world affinities in the emerging science, technology, and economy of coming days. Descartes had given the European world the picture of itself that validated its control of nature as the means to imperious human ends. Already in the *Discourse on Method* (1637) comes the triumphalist proclamation of humankind as the "master and possessor of nature,"[52] the same claim we meet three centuries later in Bonhoeffer's analysis of the collective war-and-industry identity and problem-solving ways characteristic of the "thinking, experimenting man" of the Enlightened West.[53] Robert Pogue Harrison's wry comment is that just about the time the divine right of kings was discredited in Europe, Descartes and the Enlightenment transferred its hubris and powers to humanity.[54] Descartes had put in place the profound alienation—that is, nonbelonging—that is born of the ontological separation of the human self from body and world. That separation became the trademark of modernity's master-slave ethic of control.

Gregory Bateson adds the God of Descartes's theological studies and then draws the consequences.

> If you put God outside and set him vis-à-vis his creation and if you have the idea that you are created in his image, you will logically and naturally see yourself outside and against the things around you. And as you arrogate all mind to yourself, you will see the world around you as mindless and therefore not entitled to moral or ethical consideration. The environment will seem yours to exploit. Your survival unit will be you and your folks or conspecifics against the environment of other social units, other races and the brutes and vegetables.[55]

Fairness to Descartes requires that we report the rest of his enterprise. On the basis of clear and distinct ideas working upward as a "chain of truths"[56] from this first principle, he in effect builds up much of the world he has doubted. Thus he acknowledges "that we have a body, and that there exist stars and an earth, and such like."[57] He goes on to prove, to the satisfaction of his own mind, the existence of both God and the soul. The point, however, is that the fundamental relationship we are describing is not thereby altered. This remains the knowledge of a disembodied and "unearthly" mind set over against all that it is not. One cannot live farther from "interbeing" than this.

In any event, Descartes himself, having found bedrock, could not imagine another kind of relationship. For him, alienation of this sort belongs to *being human* in and over against the rest of the (passive) world. Even fellow animals are *automatons*, organic machines cut off not only from reason but from consciousness and feeling. He considered these co-creatures alien to us by nature, in the same manner as Immanuel Kant: "So far as animals are concerned, we have no direct duties. Animals are not self-conscious and are there merely as a means to an end. That end is man."[58] Neither Descartes nor Kant had met Dillard's weasel. Nor could they have, at least not in Dillard's way, given their perspective and cosmology, a perspective and cosmology conducive to industrialized agriculture, feedlots, and animals as meat machines.

Of all this Mab Segrest asks, intriguingly, "What . . . if Descartes had cultivated a community in the years he cultivated isolation? What would experimenting with radical belief in human contexts, rather than experimenting with acute doubt in isolation, have brought . . .? Would mind then have been more than rationality, his body easier then to know, if faith had not been so terroristic, so repressive, and so out of sync with human curiosity?"[59] We can fruitfully pose additional questions: What if Descartes had viewed mind and consciousness as nature's own way of coming to awareness of itself in one of its own species? What if he had entertained mind and consciousness as nature's way of being subject, and not object only, of being Thou to I and not to It alone? What if natural body and natural mind together were nature's own way with us, rather than material body separated from immaterial mind and denatured consciousness, if we were spirited bodies or embodied spirits rather than bodies separated from spirits, if matter were not mindless and mind and consciousness were physical? And what if Descartes and his disciples had not conceived nature, including fellow mammals, as machine, without feeling, sentience, and the capacity to experience suffering, but as kin?

The musings of a philosopher and mathematician, undertaken in isolation as a brilliant twenty- and thirtysomething, would have meant little, however, had they not joined other streams to carve the channels of a new epoch. Descartes's way of knowing—the active, knowing human self as subject/the passive other as object—became the way of modern and eco-modern science, technology, and economy. Descartes is dead; the world he helped create is very much alive.

Marx's insight

Karl Marx can be our guide through the Cartesian world. We have met the following passage before but it bears reading again, this time for our study of modern alienation. Marx, you will recall, was shocked and awed by capitalism, in equal measure.

> The bourgeoisie, during its rule of scarce one hundred years, has cre-
> ated more massive and more colossal productive forces than have all
> preceding generations together. Subjection of Nature's forces to man,
> machinery, application of chemistry to industry and agriculture, steam
> navigation, railways, electric telegraph, clearing of whole continents
> for cultivation, canalization of rivers, whole populations conjured out
> of the ground—what earlier century had even a presentiment that such
> productive forces slumber in the lap of social labor?[60]

That was in 1848 and, indeed, no prior century had entertained such a presentiment. None had so thoroughly subjected nature's forces for so many different ends. Command of the great oceans expanded trade while sharply cutting its costs. Large sailing ships allowed mass emigration to neo-European settler nations as well as the thriving trade in human bodies themselves, regarded simply as "hands." Technological breakthroughs and efficiencies helped create this new world as well. Entrepreneurial capital supplied motive, means, and risk.

The outcome of all this was self-sustaining, world-transforming change. "The need of a constantly expanding market for its products," Marx writes, "chases the bourgeoisie over the whole surface of the globe. It must nestle everywhere, settle everywhere, establish connexions everywhere."[61] These bourgeois adventurers are "revolutionaries," he says.[62]

To his dying day, Marx never shed his own or his epoch's confidence in the possibilities of progress through humanly directed economic transformation. But he was equally impressed by its shocking downside. The assault on settled community, the atomization of society, the generation of poverty accompa-nying the generation of wealth, and the exploitation of those who had naught to sell but their labor, together with the exploitation of the soil—all these were centrifugal spinoffs of capitalist industrialization. He thought it sowed the seeds of its own eventual destruction.

Descartes's disembodied rationality as a way of seeing the world and acting upon it had by then partnered for a hundred years with science, technology, and economics to control and consume the world. Humans under these conditions have little or no sense of belonging to a wider existence. They are strangers in the earthly web of life; the ethos of the cosmos is lost upon them. Alienated from nature and their fellows, they are conscious of them only as external resources and objective conditions. Fixed relations are swept away, new ones are soon obsolete, and what was holy and sacred is profaned or disappears.[63]

What Marx contends, and Descartes did not, is that certain kinds of socioeconomic processes create this alienation. Understanding this demands that we consult Marx on human nature.

Marx, quite taken with Darwin's new theory of nature as dynamic, evolving, and interdependent, conceives human nature dialectically: Human beings and the rest of nature mutually condition one another through ongoing transformations. Marx, drawing on nineteenth-century natural science, discusses these transformations as the humanizing of nature and the naturalizing of man.[64] "Man himself is a product of Nature, which has been developed in and along with its environment," he writes. "[Human] history . . . is a *real* part of *natural history*—of nature developing into man." "The *forming* of the five senses is a labor of the entire history of the world down to the present,"[65] he adds in a line that anticipates conclusions of present-day paleoanthropologists.[66] We *are* our bodies, ourselves, as creatures of ecosocial and geosocial evolution.

This humankind/otherkind dialectic holds for every form of human society. Nature-society is in fact the matrix of the ongoing evolution of human nature as part of the wider world. Industrial society is no exception. It is a certain historical-natural "moment" in the long sweep of nature's—or Earth's—life. "The nature which develops in human history—the genesis of human society—is man's *real* nature; hence nature as it develops through industry, even though in an *estranged* form, is true *anthropological* nature."[67]

But why an "estranged" form in industrialized society, even if a genuinely human one ("anthropological")? Answering that question requires a description of the "objectifying" or "externalizing" that happens as the carefully organized routine of capitalist industrialist orders.

All material production—anywhere, anytime—is "appropriation of nature by the individual within and through a definite form of society."[68] But the "definite form" that is capitalism creates relationships governed by "exchange value" (money). Both human products and human activities are externalized, commodified, and "moneyed" in this kind of society. "The individual carries his social power, as well as his bond with society, in his pocket," Marx quips.[69] The consequence is a vast gathering of resources, division of labor, and chain of consumption that transforms nature so as to create a world seemingly external to us. Marx notes as a prime feature the "autonomization of the world market in which the activity of each individual is included."[70] Yet the individual feels little part of this world except as a seller of labor or as consumer and client. His or her bonds are still genuinely *human* in that they are part and parcel of a humanly constructed way of living. This is our work, not the work of the gods or the fates.

Though thoroughly a human enterprise, this way of living severs our sensuous connections with the rest of nature and one another. Human creations, plus human labor itself, become abstracted commodities, with no lives obviously attached to them. It matters little to us where something is made, by whom, and with what consequences for community, family, and environs. The world of commodities, including our labor, is foreground; all else is background, exterior to us and, for all truly practical purposes, distant and meaningless. Our natural-social bonds are all "in our pockets."[71] The world is plastic, to use a term Marx did not.

Since for Marx we are, by nature, inherently prosocial and ecosocial beings and not self-standing monads, externalizing and objectifying relationships with one another and the rest of nature also means *self*-alienation. It means the loss of the intersubjectivity and interbeing that render us truly human in a normative sense (rather than a purely descriptive one). It means the loss of the belonging that constitutes our genuine "species being" (Marx's term). Treating nature "for the first time" in the history of human societies as "purely an object for humankind, purely a matter of utility,"[72] and reducing our connections with one another to narrow points of labor, goods, and services, all of which end up as abstracted, objective commodities for market exchange, may "conquer" nature and generate the very power and wealth that awed Marx. But this unique subject-object ordering of both society and human nature also renders us alien to the rest of nature, to one another, and to ourselves. By it we create a denaturalized and dehumanized world. Our "species being" is alienated in such externalizing arrangements. Something that on the surface appears only as object to us in fact shapes our consciousness and subjectivity. Thus Marx begins the chapter on "The Fetishism of Commodities and the Secret Thereof" in *Capital* in the way noted earlier: "A commodity appears, at first sight, a very trivial thing. . . . Its analysis shows that it is, in reality, a very queer thing, abounding in metaphysical subtleties and theological niceties."[73]

Marx's own solution was to try and imagine a society that would alter the way people organized their basic relationships with one another so as to overcome this serial alienation. He did not succeed. He did succeed, however, in showing why and how a homeless and alienated self emerges, a self that feels free "to ransack the world storehouse."[74] This disconnected, portable, and alienated self, living in an iron cage of its own making in a world where all is profaned yet somehow seems natural (because it is genuinely our own work), may even come to regard this "complete emptiness"[75] (what Max Weber called "this nullity")[76] as the desired end of history and the epitome of civilization. Such is the bitter accomplishment of modernity. The mystic might ask, with Rumi, "Why, when God's world is so big, did you fall asleep in a prison of all places?"[77]

We should add that Marx, despite the failings of capitalism, opposes those who desire to return to some precapitalist order; he thinks it romantic and impossible. But, like Niebuhr much later, he also opposes those who think that the stage of human evolution brought by industrial-technological capitalism is the final one, the end of history. "It is as ridiculous to yearn [for the former era] as it is to believe that with this complete emptiness history has come to a standstill."[78]

In any event, Friedrich Engels, Marx's partner, sums up with even more precision than Marx the trail whose crumbs lead back to Descartes. This, too, is a passage we have seen before; but it bears repeating here.

> To make earth an object of huckstering—the earth which is our one and all, the first condition of our existence—was the last step toward making oneself an object of huckstering. It was and is to this very day an immorality surpassed only by the immorality of self-alienation. And the original appropriation—the monopolization of the earth by a few, the exclusion of the rest from that which is the condition of their life—yields nothing in immorality to the subsequent huckstering of the earth.[79]

How far such huckstering and its ethic of orderly alienation is, even in eco-modern form, from the "interbeing" of mysticism and its morality of ontological communion is breathtaking. Religious mysticism is wholly counter to alienation's dynamic of rendering external to the self that which inextricably belongs to its existence. Whether the reason for alienation is the manner of knowing (Descartes), the manner of ordering nature-society (Marx), or some other cause of indifference, rejection, dismissal, or discrimination, the other is distanced and objectified, then treated accordingly. The mystic's experience of union, communion, and beauty, from Weil, Dostoevsky, and Berry to Ibn al-Arabi, Thich Nhat Hanh, Black Elk, Merton, and Soelle, refuses to accept the alienated world as the real one—thus the protests and the strong moral impulse of mystics to lead transformed lives of affective communion.

Next . . .

Prophetic-liberative religious traditions share the protests of mystics as well as their impulse of transformation. Their focus and emphasis are quite different, however. To those we turn.

11

Prophetic-Liberative Practices and Oppression

The mountains shall yield peace for the people, and the hills justice.

—Psalm 72:3

We have prayed for impossible things: peace without justice, forgiveness without restitution, love without sacrifice.

—Yom Kippur (Day of Atonement) Concluding Service

THE HEART OF prophetic-liberative religious traditions is justice-centered faith. Its key is shared power. Both express "an unquenchable ontological thirst"[1] for life.

Like the laments of ascetics and mystics, prophetic rage is the result of a vision violated and a dream deferred. Hope and redemption, peace and abundance are the dreams that drive the action, the first words and the last. In Earth-honoring form, hope is hope for the redemption of creation inclusively, the liberation of all life from the cell to the community, a struggle inclusive of the poor, the weak, the marginalized, the diseased, and the disfigured. Not least, it is the liberation of exploited and exhausted nature: "The mountains shall yield peace for the people, and the hills justice" (Psalm 72:3).

The center of the Torah is redemption as freedom for slaves. ("Redemption," a word from economic life referring to manumission, is deliverance from oppression.) The God of mercy and compassion, who creates a people from those who were no people and hews a way where there was none, experiences the suffering of slaves and goes before them on a journey to a teeming land of promise (Exodus 12:19).

Here, in the scriptural account, is also the prophets' picture of Earth redeemed, a picture of abundant life, with all nations streaming to the mountain of the Lord for instruction in the ways of peace (Isaiah 2).

For the Hebrew prophets and the Hebrew Bible as a whole, the life of faith is justice-centered living. Righteousness is the persistent theme—right relations with one another, the land, and God. The fullest possible flourishing of all life is the outcome and the sure sign that justice reigns. Until justice is done, there can be no peace. When justice is done, there is *shalom*. "Peace without justice, forgiveness without restitution," and "love without sacrifice" are "impossible things" (the Yom Kippur liturgy).

James Cone points out what Martin Luther King Jr. kept insisting: Justice is an essential ingredient of Christianity as well as Judaism, yet most Christian theologians have failed to make it their starting point.[2] To the extent this is so, the Hebrew Bible is abandoned, since in it righteousness and justice are at the heart of the covenantal relationship to God and Earth. The very calling of the people of God is to serve as a witness to the *ethnoi* (the "nations" or the "Gentiles") of inclusive righteous community (Isaiah 49:6b).

In the modern era, this ancient prophetic-liberative tradition gained tools it did not previously have. With the great social theorists (Marx, Durkheim, Weber, Sorel) and the development of social scientific analysis, prophetic attention to systems, structures, and policies, and how they might bend in the direction of shared and saving power, attained a certain sophistication.

The subtle and profound ways in which human behavior and character are patterned by the organization of nature-society is the sociologist's insight. *How* life together is ordered makes it easier for people to be and do good and harder for them to be and do evil or, conversely, makes it easier to be and do evil and harder to be and do good. The Social Gospel, Christian Realism, and liberation theologies, together with progressive evangelicalism, have all learned that fashioning and refashioning institutions, with focused attention to the organization and distribution of power, bears directly on righteous living.

The prophets are especially beady-eyed about institutionalized practices—the habits we live by, the routines inculcated as our way of life. The practices of systems and structures are the true judges of how we're doing. Ideological claims, creeds, beliefs, rituals, and the noise of solemn assemblies pale alongside routine practice as the measure of our lives. It is as if the prophets, now with sociological savvy, said: "Tell us your income and your zip code and we will tell you how you live and the world it creates. We'll describe your education, diet, energy use, and transportation. We'll describe the housing you have, the company you keep, the way you spend your leisure time, and how you treat your neighbors and the world. Whether you're Christian, Buddhist, or unaffiliated, gentle of spirit or not, likeable or not, and whatever your race, ethnic identity, and genes, your habitual practices reflect how your living is organized and carried out." "Moreover," the prophet might say, "the word of Jesus is the same as ours: Not all those who can claim Abraham as their father, or who call on God as their Lord, are saved, but only those who *do* the Father's will, whoever and wherever they might be."

Prophetic-liberative traditions not only assume that daily practices are telling, they also assume that no matter how good our intentions, things go awry on a regular basis. Reform is a standing need because of what contemporary prophets, packing sociological tools, name "structural sin."

The words can be blunt, as they are in the papal encyclical, *The Gospel of Life.*

> We are confronted by an even larger reality, which can be described as a veritable *structure of sin.* This reality is characterized by the emergence of a culture which denies solidarity and in many cases takes the form of a veritable "culture of death." This culture is actively fostered by powerful cultural, economic, and political currents which encourage the idea of society excessively concerned with efficiency. . . . In this way a kind of "conspiracy against life" is unleashed.[3]

"Culture of death?" "Conspiracy against life?" "I have set before you life and death, blessings and curses. Choose life so that you and your descendants may live" (Deuteronomy 30:19). Such are the subtleties of prophetic discourse! Rarely capable of nuance, prophets always confront their people with fundamental choices.

These traditions also try to institutionalize reforms, with close attention to ecosocial structures. The Jubilee (Leviticus 25) is an example, though perhaps a failed one. There is little evidence it was ever fully carried out (often the fate of prophetic proposals and demands). In the Jubilee (the fiftieth) year, land and animals rest, debts are canceled, land is returned to its original owners, and Hebrew slaves are freed. The intent is institutional forgiveness and atonement, breaking the cycles of accumulation and impoverishment and putting in place a way to start afresh toward a more just order. Note that in both Jubilee and Sabbath laws (the latter *were* carried out), the regularized practices have in view the recovery and well-being of the land and animals as well as their tillers and keepers.

Power shared

How power is organized is always on the minds of prophets. The proper structuring and restructuring of power, together with accountability to God for its uses, is near the center of the religious ethic of prophetic traditions.

In chapter 7, we addressed environmental racism and the environmental justice movement, launched to address the systematic race, class, age, and gender bias ("structural sin") that underlies our environmental practices. Here is a deep strand of religious ethics focused on systemic reform and the structuring of power for the sake of nature-society, with the knowledge that the fate of society and the fate of the land are inextricably tied to one another.

Later studies, including those of the U.S. Environmental Protection Agency, confirmed what the initial 1987 study of the United Church of Christ showed: while poorer communities fare far worse than affluent ones as sites of commercial toxic waste, poorer peoples of color fare worse than poor whites. Since poor women and children, and especially poor women and children of color, fare worse than men in most communities, negative gender and generational factors correlate as well. In a word, race, class, age, and gender are all intersected by systemically biased environmental practices. Different communities suffer different consequences. The wrong side of the tracks has always been more toxic. Injustice is authorized by privilege and the way privilege organizes power. That most of the privileged are good people is largely beside the point. This is about practice, not individual character and virtue.

This pattern is not a U.S. phenomenon only. Poorer nations and poorer communities within nations, most often nonwhite societies and communities, bear disproportionate burdens in widespread global trashing. This holds for communities functioning both as "resource pools" and as "sinks" (sites for waste and pollution). These communities are not the chief *sources* of Earth's distress, even in their own locales. The chief sources are in the ranks of socioeconomic and racial privilege. But these communities are the most vulnerable, because of the way structural sin works.[4]

All we need add is the prophets' insistence that all this is the proper agenda for Earth-honoring faith's own practice. Addressing structural sin as it affects the whole community of life is a task of discipleship. Justice as creation justice must be authorized and institutionalized.

The environmental justice movement also illustrates the fact that prophetic-liberative traditions are often most effective as movements. While movements are usually remembered by their leaders, identified as prophets, the leaders' power resides in people power, whether latent or organized.

Three exemplars

Three figures we have met before—Dietrich Bonhoeffer, Martin Luther King Jr., and Mohandas Gandhi—will show us how prophetic-liberative traditions were lived out in the twentieth century. Although most attention will be given to King and Bonhoeffer, Gandhi is a prophetic figure for both.

The coincidences startle. Both Bonhoeffer and King died when they were thirty-nine years and four months old. Both died in April, victims of the violence they sought to end. Both were true patriots who died because of, as well as for, their countries. Like other prophets, each loved his country enough to agonize over and confess its wrongs, seek repentance for its crimes, and pursue the dream of a nation and people that lived up to its own best promise. Both reached a fateful personal turning point at age twenty-six, King when the Montgomery bus boycott threw him into the nascent civil rights movement, Bonhoeffer when the appointment of Hitler as Reich Chancellor set the young university professor on the path of costly grace. (Prophets don't choose their own moment.) In graduate school, both vacillated between lectern and pulpit, academy and the parish, as their career calling. Both bore an ecumenical and internationalist vision of a beloved community in which the peoples of the world are one, and both pursued peace and justice as the way of Jesus. Both were inspired to nonviolence by the Sermon on the Mount and both turned to the Hindu Gandhi and his ways for their practical pursuit of Christian nonviolence. Both drew upon Gandhi's Anglican priest friend, Charles Andrews. Bonhoeffer tapped Andrews to help secure an invitation from Gandhi to India; King tapped Andrews for his exposition of Gandhi's ideas. Both earned doctorates in liberal Protestant theology, albeit different brands (Boston Personalism for King; Schleiermacher, Harnack, and Ritschl for Bonhoeffer). Both challenged their liberal theology and instead became theologians of the cross, a theology whose love and justice ethic included a tragic view of life and human nature. With the cross at the very center, both were fierce in their refusal to compromise with evil in high places, including high places backed by standing law and the police powers of the state. Both might have remained in safety yet both returned home to danger out of a sense of responsibility and calling, King from Boston to the Jim Crow South in 1954, Bonhoeffer from New York City to Berlin in 1939. Both did prison time and wrote classics in Christian ethics from their cells. At the end, both identified with Moses standing atop Mount Nebo, peering into the Promised Land he would not enter. This was King's image in the sermon he delivered on the eve of his assassination and Bonhoeffer's in one of his last poems, "The Death of Moses." Both are now Protestant saints remembered in statuary in sacred and public places.

The coincidences startle because these were very different men, of different times on different continents; of different Christian faith traditions and different churches; and of different cultures, nations, education, circumstances, and race. If each has become a universal figure, it was because each was, like "that strange little brown man"[5] they both admired, universal in his own backyard, true to his own people and place.

Now take the coincidences and differences a level or two deeper. What we find is that each is, at heart, a theologian of sociality and solidarity, relationality and mutuality, social ecology and reciprocity. Each is a communitarian for whom the well-being of the other, including the enemy, is placed in the same moral framework as his own. This relationship of self and other is one of equal regard, nicely captured in Josiah Young's phrase as "no difference in the fare."[6] It is also profoundly ecological in a social sense, perfectly captured by King in the words from prison: "We are caught in an inescapable network of mutuality, tied in a single garment of destiny. Whatever affects one directly affects all indirectly."[7]

Bonhoeffer says much the same in *Life Together*. His subject is specifically Christian community, not all society and all humanity. But since for him the reality of the world and the reality of God participate ontologically in one another and both have their center in Jesus Christ, his description of Christian community pertains more broadly. (This expansion is consciously developed in his wartime writing, *Ethics*.)[8]

> In a Christian community, everything depends on whether each individual is an indispensable link in a chain. The chain is unbreakable only when even the smallest link holds tightly with the others. . . . Every Christian community must know that not only do the weak need the strong, but also that the strong cannot exist without the weak. The elimination of the weak is the death of the community.[9]

"The elimination of the weak is the death of the community" is not a general socio-ecological truth only; it is specific and contextual. In Germany, the remaining Jews have been rendered "weak" as Bonhoeffer is writing (1937). They have been deprived of the rights they held under the Weimar constitution, much of their property has been confiscated, their businesses boycotted, and their persons maligned. "The weak" also refers to those who have been labeled *lebensunwertes Leben*—"life unworthy of life." These were persons with genetic and other disabilities who were subjected to race-based medical experiments of all kinds. Many of them were euthanized. For Bonhoeffer, just as the chain would have been *un*breakable had solidarity with them been maintained, so also their deaths and the breaking of the chain mean the fracture and death of the whole community. It is his version of King's "Injustice anywhere is a threat to justice everywhere" and, quoting John Donne, "[a]ny man's death diminishes me."[10]

This communitarian theology of solidarity is also a this-worldly faith that generates motive and energy for transformation. One of the means for this transformation is nonviolent resistance, while the ends are the establishment of rights for the disenfranchised, a different social and political order, and the well-being of future generations—systemic reform to combat structural sin.

Context

All prophetic utterances, however widely they may pertain, are initially addressed to the grave issues of the day. In the cases of King and Bonhoeffer, the contexts differ in some ways but not others.

King's communalism, while in line with one of the cultural languages of the United States, namely, biblical and republican communitarianism, runs counter to the dominant language of American economic and therapeutic individualism. *Habits of the Heart* called the latter "Sheilaism," after Sheila, one of the interviewees who decided that, in the end, her religion was herself and her life.[11] The black churches that nurtured King and the prophetic social gospel ministry were both countercultural and minority traditions in a nation imbued with economic and therapeutic individualism. Their very status as marginal communities, with their own distinctive culture of biblical and republican communitarianism, provided fertile ground for risking resistance when the time ripened.

Bonhoeffer's case is different. He knew at the very outset of Hitler's accession to power that the churches' form and spirituality were not up to the challenge of the new Germany. The church needed to be born anew in a disciplined life through a new monasticism initially strange to German Protestants. It would be a community of formation and dissent. Such a path was utterly alien to a church accustomed to privilege and well settled into its roles as court chaplain, keeper of bourgeois culture, and agent of social cohesion. Bonhoeffer's communalism wasn't counter to a dominant culture of individualism, as was King's; Germans had a strong sense of corporate identity that nurtured personal sacrifice for *das Volk*. Rather, Bonhoeffer's communalism was counter to a cultural Christianity that gave no offense. The following is from 1934: "Christianity stands or falls with its revolutionary protest against violence, arbitrariness and pride of power and with its apologia for the weak.—I feel that Christianity is rather doing too little in showing these points than doing too much. Christianity has adjusted itself much too easily to the worship of power. It should give more offence, more shock to the world, than it is doing. Christianity should [. . .][12] take a much more definite stand for the weak than to consider the potential moral right of the strong."[13]

Those words could have been King's as well, no matter how different their setting.

Rights and resistance

Bonhoeffer's and King's resistance and their struggle for rights issued from their shared ecological sense of society. So accustomed are we to the strides in human rights since World War II that it may be startling to learn that Bonhoeffer was one of the first Protestant theologians to broach the theme, much less put it somewhere near the center of his resistance and his work in *Ethics*. King, of course, personifies the struggle for civil rights. And while that struggle had deep roots in the black churches' centennial struggles for dignity and equality, King, the Southern Christian Leadership Council (SCLC), and other civil rights organizations took this struggle to the streets and the courts on a scale not seen before. Resistance as a mass-based, nonviolent civic initiative of the churches is a post-King phenomenon. Of course there are antecedents—think of labor history and the women's suffrage movement. But a threshold in the history of rights and resistance as an undertaking of civil society was crossed by King and his lieutenants in the wake of the lynching of Emmett Till, Rosa Parks' initiative, and the adoption of Gandhi's methods of nonviolent mass action. It led to the passage of the Civil Rights Act and the Voting Rights Act. Faith communities played an essential role.

Citizen-based mass resistance occurred in other nations as well, thanks to Gandhi and King. Even in his abbreviated lifetime, King belonged to the *world* as the effective champion of an international movement for peace and justice, as his 1964 Nobel Peace Prize acknowledged, yet another case of the prophet more honored outside his own country than at home.

In short, if we now assume religious communitarianism with real backbone is good theology and polity, if we assume that the establishment of civil and human rights is a common good, and if we assume that civil disobedience and other forms of resistance are legitimate means in the pursuit of peace and justice, we do so as plain debtors to those, no doubt numbering in the tens of thousands, who have carried the banners of the prophets, among them Gandhi, King, and Bonhoeffer.

Theology and power

Neither King nor Bonhoeffer, nor others in prophetic-liberative traditions, can be understood if we fail to treat them as keepers of the faith, a faith for which theology matters. Their powerful social ethic is the expression of a powerful theological ethic. King can say that his campaign and place in history are the work of the *Zeitgeist*, the driving spirit of a critical historical moment. But he understands the demands of that *Zeitgeist* theologically. As noted, his theological center is in the African American prophetic social gospel and the cross. It is thoroughly saturated with the scripture that funds it, the Hebrew Bible above all. It is black Baptist in mood and emotional energy and delivery, even though King moves far away from the otherworldliness and biblical literalism of many in his own tradition. (Recasting the faith in a charged and changed moment is another prime mark of prophetic traditions.)

King's God is a personal God who is his living source of support, challenge, and consolation. He sees this God above all in Jesus and his cross, a parallel to the intensely personal relationship with Jesus Christ at the center of Bonhoeffer's life and thought. The animation of King's campaign draws from his theology and that of his colleagues, just as Bonhoeffer's search for a resisting church and his move into the military-political conspiracy draw from his understanding of Christ in and as community. These two were both theologians of relationality and mutuality who thought *as* theologians and whose piety and agency were in accord with their theological ethic.[14]

What about that persistent theme in prophetic-liberative traditions, power? Both men knew that nothing evil happens apart from power. They also knew that nothing good happens apart from power, and for the same reason: Nothing whatsoever *can* happen apart from power. Power is the energy inherent in being itself, the animation of every creature, and the means of construction as well as destruction. Power forms, reforms, and deforms. If we focus on personal and social forms of power, we see both Bonhoeffer and King trying to shape and mobilize a collective spirituality that will help move mountains. In Bonhoeffer's case, power in society must address the propensity of the ego to pursue dominating power. Dominating power, power "over," isolates its wielder from others and fractures mutuality, the only kind of relationality that can achieve the common good. Or, to say it differently, the power of the dominating ego isolates the other from love as the way all are bound together in Christ through the interdependence inherent in creation itself.

The powerful ego's disruption of mutuality is expressed socially in the destructive forces of corporate life. This was brutally evident for Bonhoeffer in antisemitism and racism; in the dehumanizing uses of modern technology; in ruthless forms of capitalism; in the kind of security based upon aggressive collective assertion, including militarism and the power of ideology; and in the way all these came together in goose-stepping Nazism and a romanticized war-and-industry identity.

King might easily have identified with Bonhoeffer's list of socially destructive uses of power. But the parallel realities were American, not German. They were the violence of structural sin as systemic racism; the lack of democratic means of representation and reform extended to black citizens; poverty and the gap between rich and poor in a nation with enough for all; and the criminality and waste of war. "We have committed more war crimes almost than any nation in the world, and I'm going to continue to say it," he preached in a famous sermon on the "Drum Major Instinct." "And we won't stop it because of our pride, and our arrogance as a nation."[15] In the equally famous Riverside Church address, "A Time to Break Silence," he cited his own government, embroiled in a war in Vietnam, as "the greatest purveyor of violence in the world today."[16]

The violence of war and the violence of poverty and race were of apiece, he said at Riverside, mirroring again the prophet's occupation with structural sin. Interlinked violence was the first reason he gave for taking his stand on Vietnam.

> There is at the outset a very obvious and almost facile connection between the war in Vietnam and the struggle I, and others, have been waging in America. A few years ago there was a shining moment in that struggle. It seemed as if there was a real promise of hope for the poor—both black and white—through the poverty program.... Then came the buildup in Vietnam and I watched the program broken and eviscerated as if it were some idle political plaything of a society gone mad on war, and I knew that America would never invest the necessary funds or energies in rehabilitation of its poor so long as adventures like Vietnam continued to draw men and skills and money like some demonic destructive suction tube. So I was increasingly compelled to see the war as an enemy of the poor and to attack it as such.[17]

And while the war was "destroying the soul of our nation" for other reasons as well, King never let up, from this time forward, on poverty as a defining material and moral issue. "A nation that spends $500,000 to kill one enemy ... and only $50 to get one of its own citizens out of poverty is a nation that will be destroyed by its own moral contradictions," he said, adding apocalyptically, "if something doesn't happen soon, I'm convinced that the curtain of doom is coming down on the U.S."[18]

By this time, after the Watts riots and as King was taking the civil rights campaign north to Chicago, he spoke more like Malcolm X and talked, not of the American dream, but the American nightmare. "We've got to begin to ask questions about the whole society," he said at SCLC's tenth anniversary celebration. "We are called upon to help the discouraged beggars in life's market place. But one day we must come to see that an edifice which produces beggars needs restructuring. It means that questions must be raised. 'Who owns the oil?' ... 'Who owns the iron ore?' ... Why is it that people have to pay water bills in a world that is two-thirds water?'"[19]

Thus had King taken the campaign beyond civil rights to economic inequality, foreign policy, oppression abroad, and resource questions. In a historic meeting with Lyndon Johnson, he told the president that the Voting Rights Act had addressed political disenfranchisement and now it was time to address economic disenfranchisement. Yet while King in some ways was at the height of his power and influence, he and the movement were unsuccessful in breaching class in America, that hallowed divide observed by both South and North. As the *New Yorker* put it, "King had begun to perceive that society tends to confine its indignation to injustices that can be attenuated without imperiling fundamental economic relationships."[20] Few even remember that the occasion for the "I Have a Dream" Speech was the March on Washington for Jobs and Freedom. Nonetheless King was determined that now "our struggle is for genuine equality, which means economic equality," as he told the crowd gathered to support the strike of black sanitation workers of Memphis. That struggle was taken up specifically so that "Memphis will see the poor."[21]

It was King's last campaign. A fatal shot rang out April 4, 1968, exactly a year to the day after the Riverside address,[22] as King stood on the balcony of the Lorraine Motel.

These power struggles, achieving great good and suffering great loss, were King's and the movement's burden and accomplishment. But unlike Bonhoeffer, King does not focus on the dominating ego and its abuse of power. At least he does not do so for African Americans and others in the movement. In "The Drum Major Instinct," King compares Gibbons's *Decline and Fall of the Roman Empire* to America and finds the parallels frightening. Yet he immediately says that, while this arrogance and imperial domination is the perversion of the drum major instinct, and while you might have expected Jesus to have said,

"You are out of your place. You are selfish. . . ." Jesus says something quite different. In substance it is this: "Oh, I see, you want to be first. You want to be great. You want to be important. You want to be significant. Well you ought to be. If you're going to be my disciple, you must be." But he reordered priorities. And he said, "Yes, don't give up this instinct. It's a good instinct if you use it right. It's a good instinct if you don't distort it and pervert it. Don't give it up. Keep feeling the need for being important. Keep feeling the need for being first. But I want you to be first in love. I want you to be first in moral excellence. I want you to be first in generosity. That is what I want you to do."[23]

In sum, for both King and Bonhoeffer, power is essential to achieving any peace and any justice. Bonhoeffer, as a privileged German among a talented people gone mad, is wary of the powerful ego and its desire to dominate the many collectivist forms that exhibit what C. Wright Mills once called a "higher order of immorality" (legal, systemic immorality). King knows the way of domination well enough. He is up against powerful egos at work at every turn, but his attention is focused on empowering those who do not yet think sufficiently well of their considerable latent powers to take to the streets, "cast off centuries of paralyzing fear,"[24] and confront the most intractable social ills.

In this connection, note especially the first of three lessons King said he learned from Mohandas Gandhi: "The way of acquiescence leads to moral and spiritual suicide." And note that it accords with the message of a prophet of Islam sharing the same struggles as King, El-Hajj Malik El-Shabazz, Malcolm X.[25] (The other lessons are that while "the way of violence leads to bitterness in the survivors and brutality in the destroyers," "the way of nonviolence leads to redemption and the creation of the beloved community."[26])

King's central theological ideas, that of a personal God and bearing the cross, bolster his discussion of personal power. For him human personality bears an infinite value. He never wavers from this conviction of the dignity and worth of all human beings, including that of his enemies. Like Bonhoeffer, his theology did not allow him to demonize his opponents even when they acted demonically.[27] We cannot hate those for whom we pray, Bonhoeffer told his students.

Differently said, both men are inoculated by their core religious convictions against the very perspectives that issued in virulent racism, disdain for the poor, genocide, and the Holocaust. For them, no people are so loathsome and so alien that they are to be set outside the circle of human compassion and belonging. None are such that we don't have to hear their cries, honor their tears, or respect their dignity, even when those same persons violate the dignity of others together with their own.[28] All belong inside the circle of life.

Why were King and Bonhoeffer both attracted to Gandhi, the Hindu ascetic and prophet? Despite a shared belief in nonviolence, the reasons were quite different for each.

Bonhoeffer and Gandhi

For Bonhoeffer, the crisis of 1933—Hitler's appointment as Reich Chancellor on January 30 and the subsequent one hundred days of legislation that cleared the way for Nazi dictatorship—made starkly clear that German Protestants were not spiritually formed in ways that would effectively resist nationalist appeals draped in Christian rhetoric, state-sponsored fascism, and Aryan racism. Deference to the state and its powers in a time of chaos was ingrained in both church and society. Bonhoeffer writes Erwin Sutz:

> The next generation of pastors, these days, ought to be trained entirely in church-monastic schools, where the pure doctrine, the Sermon on the Mount, and worship are taken seriously—which for all three of these things is simply not the case at the university and under the present circumstances is impossible. It is also time for a final break with our theologically grounded reserve about whatever is being done by the state—which really only comes down to fear. "Speak out for those who cannot speak"[29]—who in the church today still remembers that this is the very least the Bible asks of us in such times as these?[30]

Bonhoeffer recognizes these deficits at once and begins to gather students for a different life together. His motives are twofold: the exhaustion of an adequate German Protestant formation in costly discipleship; and the need for a ministry that will resist the enthusiasm for German rebirth on fascist and racist terms.

Developments in Germany were rapid and dramatic. In only three months, from February through April 1933, most everything legally required for the systemic organization of barbarism and brutality had been put in place by the

Nazi Party. It would not be long before nearly every moral act would be illegal and every legal act immoral.

The immediate circumstance generating both resistance and attention to rights is the treatment of Jews inside and outside the church—that is, secular Jews, observant Jews, and Jewish-Christians. Bonhoeffer is writing "The Church and the Jewish Question" just as the Law for the Reconstitution of the Civil Service is passed (April 7). This legislation banned non-Aryans from the civil service and wrote racial/ethnic discrimination into the law of the land.

The so-called Jewish question is, for Bonhoeffer, the circumstance that demands *status confessionis*—a state of confession in which central truths of faith are at stake.[31] Here, he argues, is the litmus test of the church's very nature *as* church.

What actions are required, if the church is to be a church? His essay outlines three possible responses to state injustice.

In the first the church is a critic that, using the criterion of a just order, publicly asks whether the state's actions are legitimate. The state's proper role, as state, is to keep order and mete out justice.

The second response is to help the victims of any illegitimate, that is, unjust, state action. While again the treatment of the Jews was the precipitating and pressing case, Bonhoeffer's argument pertains to any persons deprived of their rights in a state bearing what he calls either "too much" or "too little" law and order. His argument from rights—specifically their deprivation—found no resonance, however. Despite this, or perhaps because of it, Bonhoeffer carried his attention to rights into his later work in *Ethics* when the subject was still largely absent among German theologians. There he writes of "natural life" and of bodily integrity as "the foundation of all natural rights without exception." And why? "The living human body is always the human person himself or herself."[32] "The most primordial right of natural life," he says, "is the protection of the body from intentional injury, violation, and killing."[33] "Rape, exploitation, torture and the arbitrary deprivation of physical freedom are all serious invasions of the right conferred on human beings at creation."[34] The rights of natural life are "the reflection of the glory of God the Creator in the midst of the fallen world."[35]

The third church responsibility is to bring these crimes to a halt by disabling the state. Here Bonhoeffer made a plea for an international ecumenical council to make a collective decision and take action. Regime change was not a step an individual Christian such as himself could or should take on his or her own. When eventually he did conclude that he must join the military-political conspiracy to overthrow the regime, he did so aware that he was surrendering his reputation in the church.[36]

It is important to recall that these first months of the Nazi juggernaut were a time when the party's attempts to synchronize state and society with the party platform were not everywhere entirely successful, even if a path for dictatorial powers had been legally cleared in a remarkably short time. This is why Bonhoeffer's essay is *not* about the church's response to the Nazi *Party*: his appeal was to the state and its responsibilities, specifically in the matter of the Aryan legislation. In this still-contested space between the end of the Weimar Republic and the full implementation of the Nazi state, and in the hope that a legitimate constitutional state might yet be rescued, Bonhoeffer made his appeal to the church and its responsibilities: Let the state be a proper state; and if it is not, restore it to its rightful roles of order and justice.

Putting an end to the fateful theological deference to the state and speaking up for those who cannot speak, the Jews above all, requires, then, both a disciplined Christian resistance in the churches and beyond. These needs direct his interest to Gandhi's ashram. Gandhi, too, is an ardent disciple of Jesus and the Sermon on the Mount, and Bonhoeffer wonders aloud whether the Gospel itself may not now be found in other words and other deeds in the East. So he seeks an invitation to live in the ashram and learn the arts of nonviolent discipleship and close community.

Bonhoeffer received the invitation from Gandhi that he sought. But he never got to the ashram, feeling compelled instead to accept the call to Finkenwalde Seminary, to train students in a new school of Christian discipleship.

King and Gandhi

King did get to India, although only after Indian independence and Gandhi's death. The visit was "one of the most concentrated and eye-opening experiences of our [his and Coretta's] lives."[37] His interest in Gandhi is theological: King's theology of the beloved community finds in Gandhi its practitioner. But the source of this theology of love is not Gandhi. When King told the story of the Montgomery bus boycott, he spoke of "a basic philosophy" that "guided the movement" and said it had been referred to variously as "nonviolent resistance, noncooperation, and passive resistance." But, he goes on, "in the first days of the protest, none of these expressions was mentioned. The phrase most often heard was Christian love. It was the Sermon on the Mount, rather than a doctrine of passive resistance, that initially inspired the Negroes of Montgomery to dignified social action. It was Jesus of Nazareth that stirred the Negroes to protest with the creative weapon of love." When he did speak of method, King put it this way: "Nonviolent resistance had emerged as the technique of the movement, while love stood as the regulating idea. Christ furnished the spirit and motivation, while Gandhi furnished the method." Yet King also saw in the Gandhian campaigns the same love he saw in Jesus and the Sermon on the Mount. (We should not overlook the fact that all three of these men were strongly drawn to Jesus and the Sermon on the Mount,[38] and that the Sermon is a body of prophetic teaching that belongs to the wisdom tradition as well.)

King articulated this kind of love in many places, one of them his account of the Montgomery bus boycott. Singling out *agape* love for extended comment, King says:

> *Agape* is love seeking to preserve and create community. It is insistence on community even when one seeks to break it. *Agape* is a willingness to go to any length to restore community. It doesn't stop at the first mile, but goes the second mile to restore community. It is a willingness to forgive, not seven times, but seventy times seven to restore community. The resurrection is a symbol of God's triumph over all the forces that seek to block community. The Holy Spirit is the continuing community-creating reality that moves through history.
>
> In the final analysis, *agape* means a recognition of the fact that all life is interrelated. . . . Whether we call it an unconscious process, an impersonal Brahman, or a Personal Being of matchless power and infinite love, there is a creative force in the universe that works to bring the disconnected aspects of reality into a harmonious whole.[39]

Theologically framed with this kind of creative love present throughout creation,[40] and understanding that following Jesus would mean hardship and suffering, King is interested above all in nonviolence as a way of life that develops effective means for the oppressed to wage their own struggles on their own terms. "I left India more convinced than ever before that nonviolent resistance is the most potent weapon available to oppressed people in their struggle for freedom."[41]

King, like others standing in prophetic traditions, is aware that practical nonviolence requires the purging of violence within. It requires new habits of heart, soul, and mind. "Our goal," he said in an *Ebony* interview, "is to create a beloved community and this will require a qualitative change in our souls as well as a quantitative change in our lives."[42] Here is the prophetic call to be a changed people; nonviolence as a means of society's transformation will not work apart from the moral imagination and the virtues of nonviolent spirituality. Both inwardness and outwardness are engaged, together. King fully subscribed to Gandhi's conviction that "[n]onviolence is not a garment to be put on and off at will. Its seat is in the heart, and it must be an inseparable part of our very being."[43] Yet King already had, in the black churches, a couple of centuries of spiritual formation for this struggle. He had a community, and a movement, that could tap the redemptive energy of nonviolent power, and it was his genius to mobilize it for this-worldly reform via mass nonviolent action. King thus achieved with Gandhian means what Bonhoeffer, without that kind of community or movement, could not. Furthermore, that movement and community could not, and cannot, be created in the midst of the crisis itself. Soulcraft, individual and collective, is a long, slow process. It takes generations but it is as indispensable to achieving peace and justice as is statecraft.

The communitarian ethic of both King and Bonhoeffer is inherently a prophetic love ethic. All—self and other—belong in the same framework of moral reference and concern, and bear the same dignity as children of God. Sharing vulnerability and sharing power for life keeps the circle of love intact. Double standards and using power to privilege "us" over "them," and to sacrifice "them" for our sins as well as theirs, break the circle of love and destroy community. Resistance for the sake of community restoration and structural justice is thus a requirement of peace itself. Peace without justice, forgiveness without restitution, and love without sacrifice are all "impossible things" (the Yom Kippur liturgy).

Or, to say it differently: Both King and Bonhoeffer understand goodness as a healing power. The power of organized goodness is expressed through moral agency that is based in empathy and equal regard for the other. It often takes the form of resistance.[44]

This resistance is a means, not an end. For Bonhoeffer, resistance is a means to bring an end to war and Germany's crimes against humanity through nothing less than regime change and the establishment of "the other Germany."[45] For King, it is also means, not end. It is the means to enact and enforce laws that end discrimination and realize the constitutional promise of a genuine democracy organized around the common good. It is the means as well to challenge economic inequity and generate jobs and wealth sufficient to realize the dream of a decent life for all. Here King and the movement came up against the full force of American socioeconomic and cultural values that the movement was not prepared to counter. It was not prepared for the degree to which, in the United States, individual success, ownership, the market, and economic power override human solidarity, mutuality, and the well-being of society's most vulnerable members. Privatizing property, maximally deregulating markets, and individualizing freedom and choice converged to override the classic democratic task of balancing freedom, equality, and community. The theology of ownership and voluntary philanthropy subverted the theology of sociality and solidarity. The common good was subordinated to the good of individuals and their choices.

Whatever else King and Bonhoeffer bequeathed to religious ethics after their deaths, they, together with Gandhi, handed us, in word and deed, ecological theologies of sociality and solidarity focused so laser-sharp on peace and justice that resistance and the defense of rights in the interest of a comprehensive common good now belong to religious ethics at its core. As with others in prophetic traditions, justice and power both issue from and test the faith.

Yet how to muster a viable social ecology now, as members of what King called "the world house,"[46] when we must add that other threatened ecology, the physical ecology of earth (soil), air, fire (energy), and water, is the prophetic-liberative task they have left us.

Gandhi beyond King and Bonhoeffer

Whatever Gandhi's attraction to Jesus, his Hinduism put him beyond King and Bonhoeffer in ways that are important to "the world house" (King) and to religious ethics in a new key. The Vedantic Hindu cosmology that Gandhi embraced conceived all reality as unified and interconnected in such a way that no sharp ontological boundaries separate animate and inanimate. Rocks and rivers as well as trees are powerful beings that bear the intrinsic value accorded being itself.[47] Gandhi, from his youth onward, internalized this and gave it expression in a life committed to nonviolence and "respectful justice toward all beings."[48] He would speak of the goal as "self-realization," but it was self-realization of a sort foreign to that of Western cultures (with the exception of some mystics). Self-realization is identification with the totality of life. "My doctrine means that I must identify myself with life, with everything that lives, that I must share the majority of life in the presence of God. The sumtotal of this life is God."[49] "I believe in the essential unity of man and for that matter of all that lives."[50] His ethics, he went on to say, "not only permits me to claim, but requires me to own kinship with not merely the ape, but the horse and the sheep, the lion and the leopard, the snake and the scorpion . . . I want to realize brotherhood or identity not merely with the beings called human, but . . . with all life, even with such things as crawl upon the earth . . . We claim descent from the same God."[51] (Gandhi was well known for not allowing trees to be cut or snakes to be killed in his ashram.)

Self-realization in Gandhi's religious ethic thus understood the realized person to see the cosmic Self in all beings and all beings in the Self. From there the realized person regards all beings, not with the arrogant eye, but with the equal eye. (The Bhagavad-Gītā, 6:29, reads: "A true yogi observes Me in all beings and also sees every being in Me. Indeed, the self-realized person sees Me, the same Supreme Lord, everywhere.")[52]

In Gandhi's case, such comprehensive ecospheric consciousness led him to address issues of social justice above all—the caste system and the oppressions of the colonial system—and to do so in ways committed to nonviolence as an encompassing way of life and not only as a shrewd strategy on the part of those who did not have arms to bear or privilege to exercise. While King and Bonhoeffer have a version of *advaita*, the nondualism Gandhi calls the "rock-bottom foundation" of his thinking,[53] Gandhi's nondualism has none of the anthropocentrism that is ingrained in modern Western cultures. For Gandhi, humans are not ontologically superior to other life forms.[54]

Legacies extended

"Where do we go from here, chaos or community?" King asks in the lead essay of a book by that title. The concluding essay of that book, published the year he was assassinated, is entitled "The World House." This is how it begins:

> Some years ago a famous novelist died. Among his papers was found a list of suggested plots for future stories, the most prominently under-scored being this one: "A widely separated family inherits a house in which they have to live together." This is the great new problem of man-kind. We have inherited a large house, a great "world house" in which we have to live together—black and white, Easterner and Westerner, Gentile and Jew, Catholic and Protestant, Moslem and Hindu—a family unduly separated in ideas, culture and interest, who, because we can never again live apart, must learn somehow to live with each other in peace.[55]

The following pages are, for an account written almost fifty years ago, a remarkable description of globalization processes that render us all neigh-bors. His conclusions, however, underscore dimensions of globalization that are *not* strictly material. Again sounding the prophet's theme, "our problem" in this "world house"

> is that we have allowed the internal to become lost in the external. We have allowed the means by which we live to outdistance the ends for which we live. So much of modern life can be summarized in that sugges-tive phrase of Thoreau: "Improved means to an unimproved end." This is . . . the deep and haunting problem confronting modern man. Enlarged material powers spell enlarged peril if there is not proportionate growth of the soul. . . . Our hope for creative living in this world house . . . lies in our ability to re-establish the moral ends of our lives in personal charac-ter and social justice. Without this spiritual and moral reawakening we shall destroy ourselves in the misuse of our own instruments.[56]

That is almost the book's end, but not quite. Its penultimate page includes a passage that was also a part of the Riverside Church address: "A genuine revolution of values means in the final analysis that our loyalties must become ecumenical rather than sectional. Every nation must now develop an over-riding loyalty to mankind as a whole in order to preserve the best in their individual societies." The very last lines are these: "We still have a choice today: nonviolent coexistence or violent coannihilation. This may well be mankind's last chance to choose between chaos or community."[57]

As exemplars of prophetic-liberative courage, King and the movement pose a question to us: How might the legacy of their twentieth-century struggle be extended?

Any reply must include what King and Bonhoeffer did not, yet given their moral sensibilities, likely would have: the coalescence of "the social question" and "the ecological," the reality of planetary suffering across the community of human and beyond-human life together. "Earth and its distress," by an-other name.

The prophetic-liberative tradition tries to ferret out causes of distress and uses the tools of detailed observation to do so. Just as the social sciences gave this tradition important tools for understanding and reforming society, so the ecological sciences combined with social and historical studies offer assis-tance. Consider some examples.

Canadians William Rees and Mathis Wackernagel pioneered a scientific means for measuring the local, regional, national, continental, and global impact of human economies on nature's. These impacts, called "ecological footprints," tally ecological assets and ecological deficits for designated areas.

What is measured is "the size of the human enterprise compared to the biosphere, and to what extent humanity is in ecological overshoot. Overshoot is possible in the short-term because humanity can liquidate its ecological capital rather than living off annual yields."[58] In short, scientific specificity can be given the meaning of sustainability and nonsustainability for any section of the globe by comparing actual demand to the "biocapacity" of the region.[59] In this way footprint analysis includes what economists and the world of business conveniently omit—economic externalities. And because ecological footprints internalize the economic externalities, they secure a more accurate picture of human economies than, say, the *Wall Street Journal*'s. While I will not go to the changing details of selected regions, cities, or nations, I report a "macro" datum: Midway between 1981 and 1991 total world demand crossed the threshold from sustainability to unsustainability. In 1961 world demand was half of the world's biocapacity. Around 1985 they were a match. But in 2002 we were living at 1.2 times the biocapacity of the Earth, and that number has steadily risen. In 2010 humanity used nature's services 50 percent faster than Earth could renew them.[60] In short, we're using up indispensable capital rather than living off its yield, and King's "world house" is in serious ecological deficit. The restructuring King said was necessary for U.S. society, in order to address poverty, must simultaneously address the impoverished health of the biosphere and atmosphere upon which all other health depends.

Enter Jared Diamond. Diamond's first book, *Guns, Germs, and Steel*, was provoked by a Papuan New Guinea friend who asked, "Why does the white man have so much cargo, and we do not?" Diamond knew the answer was not in native intelligence or genes. So he set off to explain the inequity of our world. The role of geography (or environment) and history is key, he concluded, as these play out in the domestication of plants and animals. Together with "guns, germs, and steel," these are the great modes of conquest of territories and peoples. They explain the advantages some societies and civilizations have had and why they rose and ruled at the expense of others.[61]

But what explains why so many fell? More poignantly, why did so many fall near the height of their power and numbers, and often rather quickly? That query led to Diamond's second book, *Collapse*. Unlike most works in economics and business, it always has the complex and dynamic interrelationship of economy, equity, *and* environment in view, together.

Diamond's quest is fundamentally a moral one. He wants to know what lessons of history might help us to sustain Earth's economy in the very course of overcoming the insecurity and destructiveness of a world cleaved by haves and have-nots. "How Societies Choose to Fail or Succeed" is Diamond's phrase for this moral endeavor.[62] It is about choice and living together, about a way or ways of life.

By "collapse" Diamond means "a drastic decrease in human population size and/or political/economy/social complexity, over a considerable area, for an extended time."[63] "Collapse" is an extreme form of decline.

In all cases of collapse, degraded environments, usually "unintended eco-logical suicide,"[64] is *a* factor though not always *the* factor, whether we cite an ancient civilization such as the Mayan, or recent collapses, such as the Soviet Union. (In our discussion of the Fertile Crescent, assisted soil suicide was a very heavy factor though not the only one.)[65] There are eight processes by which people have undermined the biological capacity on which they depend: "deforestation and habitat destruction, soil problems (erosion, salinization, and soil fertility losses), water management problems, overhunting, overfish-ing, effects of introduced species on native species, human population growth, and increased per capita impact of people."[66]

To these eight, all present in some combination in past collapses, Dia-mond adds four that are new because they are products of modernity: human-caused climate change, the buildup of toxic chemicals in the environment, energy shortages, and full human utilization of the Earth's photosynthetic capacity.[67] (Photosynthetic capacity is the maximum rate at which leaves can fix carbon during photosynthesis, thus affecting the amount of carbon in the atmosphere.) Diamond's conclusion is that most all twelve of these will be "globally critical within the next few decades: either we solve the problems by then, or the problems will undermine [both Two-Thirds World and] First World societies."[68] He doesn't foresee the apocalyptic collapse of civilization, or the extinction of the human species. More likely is "a future of significantly lower living standards, chronically higher risks, and the undermining of what we now consider some of our key values. Such a collapse could assume various forms, such as the worldwide spread of diseases or else of wars, triggered ulti-mately by scarcity of environmental resources."[69]

Diamond is not a determinist; his whole purpose is to learn how to over-come the inequities and degradation that lead to collapse. Based on his study, he proposes a framework for assessing societies' responses: What they do about five factors sets their course.

Noted already is the one he finds present in every case: self-generated envi-ronmental damage. The others are: climate change, hostile neighbors, friendly trade partners, and the manner and effectiveness of societies' responses to their environmental problems. *Collapse* uses these factors as a grid to investigate present-day Montana and Southern California, Norse Greenland, Easter Island, the ancient Pueblo peoples of the Southwest United States, Rwanda, the Dominican Republic and Haiti, China, Australia, and the Netherlands. The sober bottom line is that no present society has sufficiently addressed the total complex of factors. This aligns Diamond's conclusion with that of the Global Footprint Network: "Our world society is presently on a non-sustainable course."[70]

The factors that produce this nonsustainable course will get "resolved" one way or another, Diamond says. "The only question is whether they will become resolved in pleasant ways of our own choice, or in unpleasant ways not of our choice, such as warfare, genocide, starvation, disease epidemics, and collapses of societies. While all of those grim phenomena have been endemic to humanity throughout our history, their frequency increases with environmental degradation, population pressure, and the resulting poverty and political instability."[71]

Finally, if anyone gets Diamond's nod of approval, it's the Dutch. They realize better than most that the whole world is now a *polder*. Polders are the below-sea-level lands the Dutch have been reclaiming for a millennium. Dutch wisdom says that "[y]ou have to be able to get along with your enemy, because he may be the person operating the neighboring pump in your polder." The person who passed that along to Diamond went on to say: "And we're all down in the polders together. It's not the case that rich people live safely up on the tops of the dikes while poor people live down in the polder bottoms below sea level. If the dikes and pumps fail, we'll all drown together." He continues, "If global warming causes polar ice melting and a world rise in sea level, the consequences will be more severe for the Netherlands than for any other country in the world, because so much of our land is already under sea level. That's why we Dutch are so aware of our environment. We've learned through our history that we're all living in the same polder, and that our survival depends on each other's survival."[72] The moral ecology that King and Bonhoeffer said belongs to theological ethics seems to have an empirical real-world counterpart. The "world house" as the entire ecosphere is a polder.

Power analysis

Whatever the journey chosen, wisdom won in Earth-honoring struggles should inform our fateful choices. There are important lessons about power in prophetic-liberative traditions. These and the power analysis that prophets insist upon bring this chapter to a close.

* Before power is "power over," "power with," or "power on behalf of," it is "power to," the energy and agency of all existence, the power of creation itself. This means that nothing happens apart from power, nothing evil, nothing good, nothing at all.

> Beginning with this assumption, good power analysis specifies the kind or kinds of power(s) at hand: Is it power to as power on behalf of? Power over? Power with and among? Power within or from within? What kind of human/more-than-human/extra-human power mix moves through these? Is it reputational power, coalitional power, communicational power, structural power, charismatic power, or some other form such as the power of song? Is it overt or covert, actual or latent? In short, what kind of power is operating by what dynamics and constitutive of what manner of relationships? Good work in religious ethics mandates specificity about power.

*Just as in prophetic-liberative traditions the experience of divinity is always a dimension of other relations, so also personal, communal, moral-spiritual power is a dimension of political, economic, and other material and structural power dynamics. The material world as the terrain of the Spirit means that power analysis belongs to a theological-ethical method from the outset. It does not first appear when the discourse broaches some classic topic in public ethics, such as the role of government and the powers of the state. Nor does it first appear after some ecosocial or other problem has been described by science. Power analysis is not an auxiliary tool for religious ethics, waiting to be taken from the shelf; it is a systemic element of method.

* Binary thinking usually vitiates good power analysis. It does so by positing vital subjects in ethics, such as love and power or freedom and power, as contrasting end points on a moral spectrum that sunders private from public (itself a binary). Good analysis teases out the togetherness of public and private, deeply personal and broadly social, inner and outer, habitual and random, close in and distant, and, not least, human and beyond-human. Our experience of power begins at home in our tender years; there are connections between the patterns of power in intimate circles and the patterns of power in broader ones. Binary thinking obscures these.

* We should be self-conscious about our ecosocial location and its power matrix. We should be sufficiently self-critical to ask what our power location means for our perception of power itself and the privileges and liabilities it

bears. We should welcome the perspectives of others. In Saul Alinsky's words about all exercise of power, "Solo is dodo."

* For power analysis informed by prophetic-liberative traditions, we do not begin with stated theological claims or moral principles but concrete practices. Thinking itself emerges from practices and each human practice (career work, parenting, keeping house, civic engagement, and making music, poetry, war, or love) engenders its own perception and behavior, its own virtues, values, and obligations. Our experience of power, including divine power, is embedded in these practices. They are the initial and primary subject of power analysis, rather than credos, principles, moral ideas, or intellectual traditions.

* In analyzing practices, the "capillaries"[73] are vital but often neglected. This means going to the farthest points in the flow of power, the region of the extremities, to analyze concrete practices and outcomes there. We have it on good authority that "by their fruits you will know them" (Matthew 7:16). From the outcomes at the extremities, including the extremities of the planet's soil, air, water, and energy, we can trace power back through the circulatory system to learn how it works, rather than going first to the centers of power to examine the reigning views there. Good prophetic-liberative religious ethics destabilizes the established, taken-for-granted thinking about power, who wields it and how. Analyzing power from the view of those most completely invested in its present accumulation and justification is a mistake. The focus should be on how things are constructed, structured, patterned, and finally work out. What most counts is what people and other creatures do and what they experience.

* Only a multilayered analysis of ecosocial and geosocial practices is valid. What is the history of these practices? From whence do they arise? Why are they the shape they are? Who has benefited and who has suffered from them? What are the currencies of power in these practices—who has credibility and voice for what reasons? High verbal skills? Economic clout? Extraordinary spirit? Commanding presence? The ability to compromise? What is the role of race? Gender? Class? Sexual preference? Physical ability? Culture and religious faith? Technology and its impact? Other-than-human nature's capacities and conditions? Negatively stated: While single-factor power analysis may be common fare, it is rarely sufficient.

* Prophetic-liberative ethics has priorities. Special attention is given those whose ecosocial and geosocial location deprives them of their full share of reigning power or makes them vulnerable to the consequences of power's abuse. They know something about power that others in other strata do not.

From what Du Bois called the "veiled corner"[74] that is hidden to the majority, those suffering a deficit of reigning power see what the worldview of the privileged does not. A second priority is hearing from those most affected by the decisions made. What is the concrete experience of those deciding or responding to others' decisions? We should question the traditions in religious ethics that, in the name of supposed disinterestedness and fairness, assign those outside the circle of first effect to "represent" the well-being of other affected parties. Representation of this kind is sometimes necessary, even indispensable (speaking for those already rendered mute, to remember Bonhoeffer, or speaking for degraded soils, to recall one of our examples). But it is almost always less desirable than articulation by the parties themselves. They need spokespersons in high places less than they need to be heard as they speak for themselves in their own places. Prophetic-liberative ethics asks if that is happening and if not, why not. I only add that the power seen in figures like Gandhi is less that of "representation," with its notion of power as power-on-behalf-of, and more that of "articulation." Such figures evoke a power the subjects recognize as their own claim upon the God-shared power that courses through all things great and small. This was nicely captured by Filipino farmers: "We are the people we've been waiting for!"

* No one's moral vision is 20/20. Yet together we might figure out whether the beast we touch is an elephant, camel, aardvark, or one another. Working together from difference enlarges and enhances the experiences and interpretations of power that inform the analysis. None of us is as smart as all of us; and all of us are smarter when we are not homogenized.

* Language analysis is a key to power analysis. To revisit an earlier example, recall that the biggest human-caused environmental disaster in U.S. history to date, the BP oil rig explosion in the Gulf of Mexico, was and still is referred to as a "spill." While "spill"—a mild word about a regrettable mess—is on one side, on the other is aggressive technological problem-solving. Here, the language is not mild, but violent. The language is of top kill, bottom kill, static kill, junk shot, choke line, kill line. The escaping oil is itself the aggressor, moreover, not those doing the killing. It is the "ogre that keeps coming at us."[75] Here, in the vocabulary of power, is the war-and-industry identity we met earlier. Close attention to words and images illustrates language as a key to understanding the perception of power.

* Earth's deep distress means to be attentive to evil and surprised by nothing. It is useful to keep in mind Richard Rorty's comment about Heidegger: Heidegger was a Nazi, "a coward, a liar, and the greatest philosopher of the twentieth century."[76] Nor ought we to forget the tragic character of

existence we will meet in Fritz Haber.[77] Power is not only given to corruption. Sometimes it just goes awry, wreaking havoc when motives are laudatory rather than venal. And it is invariably ambiguous. Its many forms—power over, on behalf of, with and within—can all serve justice and injustice. That does not translate as moral equivalence of all forms. It means daunting moral complexity at times and some Monday morning surprises.

 * Not least, prophetic-liberative power analysis understands power as the only possible vehicle of good itself. Analysis attuned only to suspicion and conspiracy will not uncover the routine goodness of ordinary human and other-than-human achievements (like the power of love and renewal, or the power of a seed). It will not reveal all those wondrous workings of common grace, like arriving alive in Victoria Station when alive was what you wanted to be and Victoria Station was exactly where you wanted to be that way.[78] The aim of power analysis is not to bolster the ranks of the cynics or generate moral relativism. It is to aid the justice of creation's flourishing.

Next . . .

Creation's flourishing on a tough, new planet during a time of transitions will require both ongoing crisis management and prophetic-liberative savvy and imagination. It will also require wisdom, a word that has surfaced now and again in this and other chapters. Beyond its meaning in common parlance, however, "Wisdom" is a set of pan-human moral traditions and, not least, a prominent figure in religious traditions. To Wisdom we turn.

12

Wisdom and Folly

Where is the life we have lost in living? Where is the wis-
dom we have lost in knowledge? Where is the knowledge we
have lost in information?

—T. S. ELIOT

Truth is One, the wise call It by many names.

—HINDU ADAGE

WISDOM MAY BE *the* biblical eco-theology and ethic. Creation is a teacher of wisdom; measured human responsibility follows.[1]

Here is Wisdom's autobiography, according to one ancient account.

(1) Does not wisdom call,
and does not understanding raise her voice?
(2) On the heights, beside the way,
at the crossroads she takes her stand;
(3) beside the gates in front of the town,
at the entrance of the portals she cries out;
(4) "To you, O people, I call,
and my cry is to all that live. . . .
(22) YHWH had me (as) the beginning of his way,
the earliest of his works of yore.
(23) Of old I was woven, from the very beginning,
even before the earth itself.
(24) When the deeps were not existent, I was birthed.
When the wellsprings were not yet laden with water,
(25) when the mountains were not yet anchored,
before the hills themselves, I was brought forth.
(26) Before [YHWH][2] made the earth abroad,
and the first clods of soil,

(27) when he established the heavens, I was there.
When he circumscribed the surface of the deep,
(28) when he secured the skies,
and stabilized the springs of the deep,
(29) when he assigned the sea its limit
(lest the waters transgress his decree),
when he inscribed the foundations of the earth,
(30) I was beside him growing up,
I was his delight day by day,
playing before him every moment,
(31) playing with his inhabited world,
delighting in the offspring of *'ādām*.

Proverbs 8:1–4; 22–31.[3]

The book of Proverbs, from which this autobiography is taken, belongs to the deep tradition of Wisdom, at home with God and whimsically at play in the cosmos even before the creation of Earth. So do Job, Ecclesiastes, the Song of Songs, and portions of the Psalms, together with numerous strands in other writings reflecting oral traditions in circulation long before their literary collection.

Wisdom traditions offer yet another distinctive approach to religious ethics and Earth's healing. Her speech is not the prophet's shrill warning that the violating ways of the people, unless we turn around, will bring sure ruin. Nor, for that matter, does Wisdom indulge in soaring prophetic visions of harmonies never known to history; Wisdom never advises children to play over the den of asps or newborn lambs to find a lion to rest against.[4] While Wisdom does find extraordinary beauty and harmony in creation, and delights in them, she does not witness all nations streaming to Zion's mountain in global peace.[5] Instead, Sophia (the commonly used Greek word for wisdom and its personification) assumes that conflict and difference will continue and poses the question, How, then, since we cannot live apart, shall we live together?

Wisdom does not sound the apocalyptic song of the end times, either. Her assumption is that creation and Earth endure within limits established by their Creator: "He secured the skies, and stabilized the springs of the deep . . . he assigned the sea its limit . . . [and] inscribed the foundations of the earth" (Proverbs 8:28–29). "Gaining wisdom" does not depend on decoding bizarre dreams of cataclysmic events or unraveling cosmic mysteries. Instead, "gaining wisdom" requires careful, patient observation of nature, then learning from its patterns how to craft human responsibility aright. The assumption is that the functioning of creation can be known by all who are attentive and that instructed human power can be exercised freely, soberly, and well.

While only God is Truth in its fullness, and only God creates and fully comprehends the Logos of the cosmos (its principle of intelligibility), no truth anywhere is alien to God or forbidden to those who walk in Wisdom's way. "While Truth is One," it has "many names" by which the wise know it.[6] Those heeding Wisdom's call "at the crossroads" (Proverbs 8:2) are thus wholly capable of acquiring knowledge, acting prudently, and exercising their vocation as tillers and keepers.

In short, no rancid odor of apocalypse and no battlefield ethic typify Wisdom's way. Instead, confidence in sound knowledge attained by young and old abounds. Careful discernment of nature will reveal what is needful for life together. "We" eliminating "them," destroying the village in order to save it, is neither necessary nor prudent.[7]

The sages of old were the village elders and the court scientists and philosophers who, as edifying teachers, taught skills of discernment and practical arts of application—in commerce, governance, family life, and all the domains of daily living.[8] Wise parents and grandparents, aunts and uncles, any who oversaw the raising up of children in the way they should go, were also Wisdom's couriers. Town tradesmen and tradeswomen, artists, musicians, and potters, might be mentors as well. Wisdom's messenger might be anyone. Even the village idiot, the naïve child, the holy fool, or an animal at play might unwittingly offer wisdom. And in homely folk tales, a genre of Wisdom literature, they do. (*The Animal's Lawsuit against Humanity*, discussed earlier, belongs to Wisdom's trove.) In some manner or another, all these study human nature with an eye to detail and the tutelage of experience. Insight follows and daily responsibility is instructed.

Norman Habel, a scholar of biblical Wisdom, asks: "Have you ever wondered why a frog always jumps like a frog and never runs like an ant? Have you ever been fascinated by the way a baby bird learns to fly as a bird rather than swim like an eel?"[9] It's the sort of question Wisdom's sages ask: What is the nature of each creature, why is it so, and what might we learn in its presence? Is there some essential and instinctual structure, some internal impulse, that mediates insight for our own ways? Does creation's unbounded and mysterious work betray helpful instruction for human life?

The ways of Wisdom, then, are the ways of nature understood, human nature included. A hefty burden falls on human knowing, human skill, and human agency. Wisdom's ways can be fathomed; to transgress them leads to grave human loss.

Not that gaining wisdom is ever finished. Wisdom, a steadfast "tree of life to those who take hold of her" (Proverbs 3:18), is ever-renewing and ever-branching. Even the wise elder will die an unfinished open book. Wisdom's boundlessness is little reason to cease the quest for it, however.

> (1:2) To know wisdom and instruction,
>   to understand words of insight,
> (1:3) to gain effective instruction,
>   as well as righteousness, justice, and equity,
> (1:4) to teach prudence to the inexperienced,
>   knowledge and discretion to the young,
> (1:5) Let the wise also hear and gain erudition,
>   and the discerning to acquire skill,
> (1:6) to understand a proverb and a figure,
>   the words of the wise and their enigmas.
> (1:7) The fear of YHWH is the beginning of knowledge,
>   fools despise wisdom and instruction.[10]

Universal wisdom

Wisdom traditions are pan-human, open to all and found in all cultures and religions. She is anything but sectarian and secretive; she is universal, with common themes. One is enlightenment, a theme of the seven verses above. Discernment, insight, clear eyes, acquiring skills, and learning prudence are parts of this; so is acquiring a sense of the worth and dignity of all life, far beyond my tribe's. Another theme, also common to every religious tradition, is suffering and sacrifice as part of the process of transformation and of learning responsibility. While Wisdom is confident that human beings can live cooperatively with one another, she is also clear those relationships can be corrupted and in need of repentance that exacts a cost. For Wisdom, too, "peace without justice, forgiveness without restitution, and love without sacrifice" are "impossible things" (the Yom Kippur liturgy). Not least, God (YHWH in the passage above) in the Wisdom traditions is never a deus ex machina, the rescuer God who bails out human beings when they are complacent about righteous living. Rather, the presence of the divine is available to all who stand in awe—the "fear" of verse 7—and empowers them as they strive for the fullest possible flourishing of all that is. Humans participate with the rest of nature in the down-to-earth presence of the sacred and the powers of the divine. They, together with all else, tap creation's genius and thirst for life.

But humans are thinking creatures that carry responsibility for their actions. Their brains and hearts are Wisdom's pathways. Social learning and cumulative cultural adaptation set humans off from other creatures. Yes, the agency behind all creation is God, with Wisdom the child and companion of God who instructs receptive humans in ways that bring out creation's goodness, beauty, and wonder. But divine agency, for humans, is joined to their own power and judgments. They can go terribly wrong in their choices, just as they can will the good and do it. Human responsibility is both possible and mandatory, given the kind of creature we are, with Wisdom as a guide but never a proxy. Human responsibility is a bright line across all wisdom traditions.

Wisdom's genre

The forms of Sophia's instruction vary widely. The form may be, and often is, a collection of didactic sayings and stories or questions that teach life lessons. They are practical, accessible, easily remembered, pithy, and to the point.

> When you were born, you cried and the world rejoiced.
> Live your life so that when you die, the world cries and you rejoice.
>
> White Elk

> If you want others to be happy, practice compassion.
> If you want to be happy, practice compassion.
>
> The Dalai Lama

> There is no fire like greed,
> No crime like hatred,
> No sorrow like separation,
> No sickness like hunger of heart,
> And no joy like the joy of freedom.
> Look within. Be still.
> Free from fear and attachment.
> Know the sweet joy of living in the way.
>
> The Buddha

And which of you, by worrying, can add a single hour to your span
of life?

Jesus

It is not yours to finish the task, but neither are you free to take no
part in it.

Jewish Wisdom of the Fathers

How shall we love you, Holy hidden Being, if we love not the world
that you have made?

(Hymn, "Maker Eternal, Ruler of Creation," text by
Laurence Housman)

Stories are favored ways to teach. They, too, are easily remembered.

The disciples were absorbed in a discussion of Lao-tzu's dictum:

"Those who know, do not say;
Those who say, do not know."

When the master entered, they asked him what the words meant.
   Said the master, "Which of you knows the fragrance of a rose?"
   All of them indicated that they knew.
   Then he said, "Put it into words." All of them were silent.

Crowfoot, a Blackfoot warrior, teaches by posing a big question and offering common, memorable images but saying no more.

What is life?
It is the flash of a firefly in the night.
It is the breath of a buffalo in the wintertime.
It is the little shadow which runs across the grass and loses itself in the
   sunset.

Often wisdom is straightforward advice remembered because the images are borrowed from familiar surroundings, as in this Pueblo Indian
prayer:

Hold on to what is good, even if it's a handful of dirt,
Hold on to what you believe, even if it's a tree that stands by itself.

Hold on to what you must do, even if it's a long way from here.
Hold on to your life, even if it's easier to let go.
Hold on to my hand, even if someday I'll be gone away from you.[11]

Other passages take a different form and serve a different purpose. Treatises meant to grapple with life's most difficult or perplexing circumstances—disease, calamity, boom and bust, the drama of good and evil—these pose irresolvable questions. Why do bad things happen to good people? Why do the wicked prosper? Is all toil and vanity? Is there nothing new under the sun? Here wisdom comes as hard-won, if transient, insight gleaned from unending exchange with harsh reality. The Book of Job is the ancient classic of this genre but hardly the only one. Qoheleth, the consummate empiricist who wrote Ecclesiastes, undertakes the heroic quest only to return empty-handed.[12] "Life sucks, though it has its moments" might be an accurate, if crude, translation of his finding. There is wisdom for every season and circumstance, even the dire and fruitless ones.

Falling between popular adages and treatises that wrestle with unanswerable questions are prayers, meditations, parables, and passages that invite a return visit over and again, each time giving rise to edifying reflection. Gandhi once spelled out wisdom as the Seven Deadly Social Sins:

politics without principle;
wealth without work;
commerce without morality;
pleasure without conscience;
education without character,
science without humanity,
[and] worship without sacrifice.[13]

Or the wisdom of Reinhold Niebuhr cited in an earlier chapter:

Nothing that is worth doing can be achieved in our lifetime; therefore we must be saved by hope. Nothing which is true or beautiful or good makes complete sense in any immediate context of history; therefore we must be saved by faith. Nothing we do, however virtuous, can be accomplished alone; therefore we are saved by love. No virtuous act is quite as virtuous from the standpoint of our friend or foe as it is from our standpoint. Therefore we must be saved by the final form of love which is forgiveness.[14]

Beyond passages for meditation, there are easily remembered stories, with instruction implicit or attached. Fairy tales and folk tales, all manner of children's stories, and stories about the doings of gods and goddesses are vehicles for "gaining effective instruction" (Proverbs 1:3). Since there is no "app" for moral judgment, most of them in one way or another aim at character instruction and moral formation. Frequently, as in this Cherokee Nation tale, wisdom passes from an elder to a child, in this case from grandfather to grandson:

> "A fight is going on inside me," the grandfather said to the boy. "It is a terrible fight between two wolves."
>
> The grandson listened intently.
>
> "One wolf is evil, unhappy, and ugly: He is anger, envy, war, greed, selfishness, sorrow, guilt, resentment, inferiority/superiority, false pride, coarseness, and arrogance. He spreads lies, deceit, fear, hatred, blame, scarcity, poverty, and divisiveness."
>
> "The other wolf is beautiful and good: He is friendly, joyful, loving, worthy, serene, humble, kind, benevolent, just, fair, empathetic, generous, honest, compassionate, grateful, brave, and inspiring, resting wholeheartedly in deep vision beyond ordinary wisdom."
>
> The grandson paused in deep reflection on what his grandfather had just said. Then he exclaimed: "Oyee!" (in recognition).
>
> Grandfather continued. "This same fight in going on inside you, and inside all human beings as well."
>
> The grandson paused in deep recognition of what his grandfather had just said. Then he finally cried out deeply: "Oyee! Grandfather, which wolf will win this horrific war?"
>
> Grandfather replied, "The wolf that you feed. That wolf will surely win!"[15]

The means of gaining wisdom might as easily have been the petitions of prayer. Like so much wisdom, this sample also finds nature the teacher.

> Earth teach me quiet—
> as the grasses are still with new light.
> Earth teach me suffering—
> as old stones suffer with memory.
> Earth teach me humility—
> as blossoms are humble with beginning.

Earth teach me caring—
as mothers nurture their young.
Earth teach me courage—
as the tree that stands alone.
Earth teach me limitation—
as the ant that crawls on the ground.
Earth teach me freedom—
as the eagle that soars in the sky.
Earth teach me acceptance—
as the leaves that die each fall.
Earth teach me renewal—
as the seed that rises in the spring.
Earth teach me to forget myself—
as the melted snow forgets its life.
Earth teach me to remember kindness—
as dry fields weep with rain.

—Ute prayer[16]

Practices

Nor is the form of instruction only oral or written. Wisdom's most effective media are repeated practices that tap something essential about human experience and creation's ways in order to give direction and meaning.

The practice of Sabbath-keeping illustrates this. Any number of other religious practices, associated with weekly, seasonal or annual festivals and the liturgical marking of time and meaning, might have been chosen. The point of all of them is the same: repeated practices are centering points, or maybe cairns, for marking a life well-lived. They instruct by offering new or renewed meanings and direction at different times and stages of life, or for life in altered circumstances. Those fortunate enough to have a long look back as their dying day approaches often remember such practices with gratitude and deep satisfaction.

"Ancient Wisdom," an article by Nan Chase in *Hemispheres* magazine,[17] relayed her discovery of the sanity of the Sabbath in a society that boasts, rather than repents, of offering everyone everything all the time. Sabbath on such frenzied terrain, she writes, is a "mental health tool" that can "work for anyone, no matter what religion you practice (or don't practice)." It's "a way to stop the onslaught of obligations, improve your social life, keep the house clean, revive your tired marriage, elevate spiritual awareness, and improve productivity at work, all overnight and without cost!" Given results like these, Chase's conclusion that Sabbath is the greatest gift the Hebrews gave humanity comes as no surprise.

Her Sabbath began in a marriage counselor's office. During their second session (it turned out to be the last), Nan and Saul Chase hit on a day off together once a week to improve their marriage. A disarmingly simple solution, it worked—for the marriage, for the family, for their harried lives. Furthermore, it didn't entail new commitments: no elaborate rituals, no hours in prayer or study at synagogue. It did get them reading the theology of Sabbath together, however, and they became fascinated with ancient wisdom and its relevance for modern lives.

Chase's discovery of Sabbath as an effective mental-health tool is undoubtedly significant. Her life, including her career, was the better for this ancient practice. A saving rhythm insinuated itself into her otherwise zany week, relaxation coupled itself with recreation and good eats, and—perhaps most important—quality time with her spouse and children reappeared just when it and the marriage seemed to be slipping away. Little wonder that her happy testimonial ends with the comment, "I look forward to my weekly holiday. As the sun goes down each Friday evening, I take off my wristwatch, and for a night and a day, time stands still."

Scolding Nan Chase for a utilitarian, secular use of Sabbath would be in poor taste. Her search for a sanity-inducing "weekly holiday" only mirrors the narcissism and solipsism of millions of her compatriots and may even be the right remedy for the most anti-Sabbath society in history. After all, what could be healthier than a good, strong, weekly countercultural moratorium on the madness of the "good life" that mandates getting and having and spending 24 hours a day/7 days a week/365 days a year?

But is a healthy day off truly Sabbath, even when it is considered "ancient wisdom" reborn? Maybe it is, if in due course it leads the Chases from the good of bodily rest and enjoyment of one another into wonder and praise of God and the gift of life, that endpoint for religious wisdom.

Yet there are deeper meanings to be discovered, meanings intended to instruct life beyond the good the Chases have already found. After all, one of the two remembrances in "Remember the Sabbath Day, to keep it holy" is *cher le'ma'aseh b'ereyshit* (in remembrance of the events of creation). All interference in the natural order is disallowed and all the "tilling and hammering and carrying and burning"[18] that tallies as the relentless human transformation of the material world is forbidden. Don't even think about commerce;

"Lay off all work" is the command. And walk, don't drive. Worlds inside worlds reveal themselves to those who take notice at very low speeds. Wisdom's lesson is that the grandeur of the universe is to be appreciated on its own terms, apart from any human use and as a steady reminder of our total dependence upon a core belonging not of our own doing. All things bright and beautiful, great and small, wise and wonderful, flow from their source in *Eloheynu*, the Creator and Sustainer of all that ever was, is, and will be. So lose yourself in wonder at the giftedness of life, its pleasures and its God. Pray, read the Torah, and enjoy. Rabbi Abraham Heschel's response is Wisdom's: "Just to be is a blessing; just to live is holy."[19]

Perhaps, then, the Chases have it right after all, if their discovery of true wealth eventually leads them to the Source and to quiet praise of God.

Yet Nan Chase's gratitude for Sabbath doesn't include the second remembrance: *zeycher le' tziyat mitzrayim* (in remembrance of going out from Egypt). Sabbath is post-Exodus legislation. It is remembrance of liberation from slavery and the passionate God who struggles against the anti-life forces loose in the world, just as it is remembrance that the People of God are chosen as joint participants in the sublime cause of forging just community. Their righteousness is their part in a redemption that joins history to nature.

Chase's Sabbath falls short of Wisdom's full instruction here. It divorces spirituality from politics and economics. In the biblical Sabbath and Wisdom there is no such divorce, no sundering of worship and prayer from the Monday work of justice, no sundering of liturgy from daily chores and demands. Whenever such sundering does occur, it invokes God's wrath. The God of Sabbath rejects "the noise of solemn assemblies" (Amos) and raises up a prophet to remind the people yet one more time that ritual and morality are two manifestations of the same life. Awe and wonder before the God of life ("in remembrance for the events of creation") is coupled with fiery discontent over life's violations ("in remembrance of going out from Egypt"). The God who spins out galaxies without end and assigns the cells of all creatures their tasks is the God of divine pathos who commands human transformation of the world in accord with righteousness. The Creator redeems, and the Redeemer creates, in a reach that spans inner spiritual, social, and cosmic realms. Creation's God and liberation's God are one.

Nan Chase is right in her unfolding discovery and celebration of Sabbath; we would all sing our lives better with the practice of Sabbath than without. And she is right that Sabbath is a great Hebrew gift available to all.

Still, no one can be whole in a broken world. Sabbath, then, is not only, or chiefly, about personal adjustment, relief, mental health, or haven. It doesn't let the world be what it is the rest of the week, with no thought of its betterment beyond my own.

Or, to give it a different twist, the remembrances that keep the Sabbath Day holy are not a creation and projection of ourselves, even for our own good.[20] The Sabbath command is not hearing our own voice, only louder, as God's. And Sabbath is certainly not meant as a weekly private enclave in a world of public pain. Sabbath is Wisdom's word of life that comes by opening ourselves to God. Sabbath and its remembrances are a projection, not of ourselves, but of creation and creation's God. Keeping the Sabbath holy is a weekly, Earth-honoring practice that joins a mystery surpassing us and a purpose outstripping us. Like all of Wisdom's ways, it includes the burning mysteries of our own unique lives. Its practice is Wisdom's insinuation into otherwise small worlds. It helps answer Mary Oliver's question: "Tell me, what is it you plan to do with your one wild and precious life?"[21]

Speaking of Mary Oliver, poetry is a common genre for wisdom. "The Summer Day," from which the line above is taken, is classic wisdom: the themes outlined earlier, with their questions large and small and their careful attention to nature, are Oliver's.

> Who made the world?
> Who made the swan, and the black bear?
> Who made the grasshopper?
> This grasshopper, I mean—
> the one who has flung herself out of the grass,
> the one who is eating sugar out of my hand,
> who is moving her jaws back and forth instead of up and down—
> who is gazing around with her enormous and complicated eyes.
> Now she lifts her pale forearms and thoroughly washes her face.
> Now she snaps her wings open, and floats away.
> I don't know exactly what a prayer is.
> I do know how to pay attention, how to fall down
> into the grass, how to kneel down in the grass,
> how to be idle and blessed, how to stroll through the fields,
> which is what I have been doing all day.
> Tell me, what else should I have done?
> Doesn't everything die at last, and too soon?
> Tell me, what is it you plan to do
> with your one wild and precious life?[22]

The Earth Charter

Wisdom doesn't end, nor are its forms limited to those cited—adages, poetry, didactic instruction, stories, parables, meditations, and practices. While most of Wisdom's treasures are indeed gifts of the past, every present must also discover its own wisdom and work out its own salvation as fitted to its own circumstances. The forms might be the same, with different authors and maybe different sites—a new play, a new song, even posters, T-shirts, and notes on the refrigerator door.

But the form might also be more ambitious and far-reaching, like that of the Earth Charter, a cross-cultural dialogue aimed at an international agreement with standing in international law.[23] The Charter bears many strong marks of Wisdom. It is an important example of wisdom-in-the-making as the practical wisdom for ecological rather than industrial civilization.

Wisdom's dream of a common earth ethic and the unity of humankind is at least as old as the Hebrew prophets, Confucius, the Buddha, and Plato. That should surprise no one since religions, together with ancient philosophies and the primordial visions of First Peoples, have consistently staked out the audacious claim that "community" not only includes Earth as a whole but the cosmos. Creation as a community has been the enduring dream and a basic religious, moral, and metaphysical claim.

The Earth Charter belongs to the dream of Earth as a comprehensive community guided by a shared ethic. There are new twists, however. The most remarkable one, at least for the children of modernity, is the one this book promotes; namely, to derive the ethics of *Homo sapiens* from Earth's requirements and to consider the whole community of life the bearer of compelling moral claims. "Respect Earth and life in all its diversity,"[24] itself a wisdom formulation, is the fundamental principle of the Charter. It parallels human dignity, or respect for every human life, as the baseline of the Universal Declaration of Human Rights.

But the parallel hides a moral revolution that is in keeping with an understanding of creation in the Wisdom tradition. The Charter rejects the Enlightenment's turn to the human subject for modern Western ethics—a turn underlying modern psychology, philosophy, economics, politics, and the science and technology of the industrial paradigm itself. Although its language is careful and consensual, and never truly confrontational, the Earth Charter is an assault on the institutionalized anthropocentrism of reigning practices, especially patterns of production and consumption. To say "humanity is part of a vast evolving universe"[25] and to view Earth as a remarkable niche in that universe, alive because it is the bearer and sustainer of a unique community of life, is already to dislodge the autonomous, transcendent human subject and invert the orientation of prevailing ethics. Like so much ancient wisdom, the Charter locates the ecology of human action within the economy of Earth itself and tempers the sovereign swagger of idolatrous human power parading mastery on a grand scale. At the same time, the Charter affirms the dignity of all human beings, their freedom, equality, and right to respect. Here is Wisdom's assumption that human economies can be attuned to Earth's and to mutual benefit, if humans assume their proper place in the "vast evolving universe."

Another theme puts the Earth ethic of the Charter closer to Wisdom's moral reach but far from the reigning moral universe of present institutions and habits. Cosmologies now emerging in science, in which the web of life spreads to embrace distant galaxies and all 13 to 15 billion years of cosmic and planetary evolution, have little place in most modern moral conventions. They still regard us as an ecologically segregated species, morally speaking, even in eco-modern mode. The Earth Charter does not.

Like Wisdom itself, the Earth Charter tries to flesh out what Earth as community means for human life and human moral agency. It does so by decentering the sovereign human self and calling for common efforts that mean, in the words of a penultimate draft, no less than "reinvent[ing] industrial-technological civilization." This primacy of Earth community for ethics is the new twist, at least for the modern era. It is Wisdom's communitarian understanding of nature and society together, with creation's economy basic to all and instructive for all.

This means the Charter is an Earth ethic and not an environmental ethic. Ecological integrity is certainly its theme but the Charter recognizes that the goals of ecological protection, the eradication of poverty, equitable economic development, respect for human rights, democracy, and peace, are interdependent and indivisible. The whole of Earthly life is the domain, not "the environment."

Still another remarkable quality of the Earth Charter is the drafting process itself. The Charter was to be the product of international negotiations, set to climax the 1992 Earth Summit in Rio de Janeiro. But governments could not agree and that did not happen. The Earth Charter Commission, created in 1996, then decided to launch the effort as a global civil-society initiative. The most inclusive process ever associated with an international declaration, with grassroots participation by communities and associations of all kinds across all sectors of society, achieved "a people's treaty." It is not a true treaty, however, since it was not negotiated by heads of government and ratified by their national bodies. But substantively it is a genuine charter that, through the United Nations, seeks universal recognition and international backing as a "soft-law" document, morally binding upon those who subscribe to it. The Charter is also an inspirational document and an educational tool for developing global consciousness and offering guidance and instruction for action by all manner of organizations, from local to global, and all social sectors, including youth.

What stands out about the Charter's genesis is its difference from previous efforts to device a pan-human Earth ethic. Few have been generated from the bottom up; or more precisely, from high levels of participation cutting across all sectors of society, with a determined effort to include historically underrepresented voices. Past efforts were far less representative, and none were carried out by way of a cross-cultural, democratic consultative process open to so much revision over a decade-long drafting and redrafting of common goals and shared values. The Charter, made possible by electronic globalization as well as face-to-face meetings everywhere, is a remarkable instance of what in fact may be an emerging global society tuned to local communities and bioregions as well as to expertise from every quarter—government, business, academe, and the varied expressions of civil society. Not least, the world's religions are sources of the Charter's accumulated wisdom.

These two qualities, then, command the attention of religious ethics: the Charter's high levels of representation and agency in the effort to realize the ancient dream of an Earth ethic; and its moral universe, with respect for the full community of life and its diversity as foundational. Steven Rockefeller's own lean summary of the Charter echoes this: "Interconnectedness and responsibility are the two main themes of the Earth Charter."[26] (Rockefeller was the first chairman of the Charter Commission.)

If the Earth Charter is a response to what is happening to the planet and the inadequacy of modern ways to address it, where are the rubs? What does the Earth Charter assume, cherish, and pursue that will be difficult to achieve because of present forces? What does Wisdom in this form face as obstacles to living well? Where is it subversive? (Remember that new wisdom is initially subversive—think of the teachings of Lao-Tzu, Buddha, and Jesus.) Only one obstacle is discussed here, albeit a far-reaching one: the conflict between the Charter's kind of democracy and global capitalism's.

The vernacular for the ways of global capitalism is the language of "globalization," the porous movement of information, money, goods, images, ideas, and people across countries and cultures, driven by the progressive integration of these elements into a single geopolitical economy. Players are many but most prominent are those Thomas Friedman tags "corporations on steroids."[27]

Most discussions of sustainable development assume the globalizing economy of corporate capitalism and seek to green that. Sustainable development is the effort to wrap the global environment around the global economy in such a way that both the economy and the environment can continue indefinitely.

The Earth Charter, too, uses the language of sustainable development. Yet its spirit and direction better accord with sustainable community. Sustainable community works on the principle of subsidiarity. Subsidiarity asks how economy and environment are wrapped around local communities and bioregions. As a principle, subsidiarity is always in search of the most appropriate "whole" to address challenges and problems. But it begins in decentralized fashion with local communities and their assets. If they can address basic needs with those assets, no further course need be pursued. If they cannot, or, rather, when and where they cannot, then the effort is made to draw upon or create a more encompassing "whole." In a contracting world, that whole may easily require international cooperation. But subsidarity's principle is always the same: begin with the local and solve problems at the so-called lowest appropriate level with the resources available there. This is to "consult the genius of the place," to recall Wes Jackson's phrase.

In contrast to sustainable development as global corporate capitalism, Big Economics and Big Politics greened, sustainable community is the effort to preserve or create all together or in part: greater economic self-sufficiency locally and regionally, with a view to the bioregions themselves as basic to human organization; agriculture appropriate to a region and in the hands of local owners and workers using local knowledge and crop varieties, with the ability to save their own seeds and treat their own plants and soils with their own products; the preservation of local and regional traditions, language, and cultures and a resistance to global homogenization of culture and values; a revival of religious life and a sense of the sacred, in place of a way of life that leaches the sacred from the everyday and reduces life to the utilitarian; the repair of the moral fiber of society on some terms other than sovereign consumerism; resistance to the full-scale commodification of things, including knowledge; the internalization of costs to the local, regional, and global environment in the price of goods; and the protection of ecosystems and the cultivation of Earth, in the language of the Charter, as "a sacred trust held in common."

All this is global democratic community, not nativist localism. It is not asking *whether* to "globalize," but *how*. And the Charter's answer—democratic community democratically arrived at—is *global* community by virtue of both its planetary consciousness and the impressive networking of citizens around the world made possible by electronic globalization. Adherents of sustainable community have this, rather than "development" in mind, because they are not trying to wrap the global environment around the integrating global economy of corporations. They are asking, "What makes for healthy community on successive levels—local, regional, sometimes national, and global—and how do we achieve a healthy economy and environment together, aware that Earth's requirements are fundamental?" They are attentive to questions that global capitalism, even as sustainable development, rarely asks: What are the essential bonds of human community and culture, as well as the bonds with the more-than-human world? What is the meaning of such primal bonds for a healthy, concrete way of life? What are cultural wealth and biological wealth and what wisdom do we need to sustain them in the places people live with the rest of life's community?

In sum, the Earth Charter is both an example of present wisdom-in-the-making and a call for that wisdom in the face of forces that diminish planetary life. Wisdom has found a home here.[28]

Moral tragedy

The good work of the Earth Charter and innumerable other efforts at sustainable community will not escape moral tragedy and life's contradictions and ironies. Wisdom that is not roomy enough for these is not genuine wisdom, it is only cheery self-help. All of human experience, including deep lamentation and the cry that "all things are wearisome, more than one can express" (Ecclesiastes 1:8), has a home in Wisdom. "What do people gain from all the toil at which they toil under the sun? A generation goes, and a generation comes, but the earth remains forever" (Ecclesiastes 1:3–4). All is in vain.

Moral tragedy belongs to human experience even when it is not the daily fare of every life. Even when it is, it rarely reaches that tragic depth of Fritz Haber.

Fritz Haber belonged to that extraordinary cadre of German Jews who won fourteen of the thirty-eight Nobel prizes between 1905 and 1936. The circle included Haber's close friend, Albert Einstein. Haber himself won in 1920, for "improving the standards of agriculture and the well-being of mankind." Together with Carl Bosch, he is credited for what some have claimed was the most important invention of the twentieth century, a synthetic way to fix nitrogen. The Haber-Bosch process uses heat and pressure in chemical "crackers" to synthesize nitrogen from the air, turning it into ammonia which is then used to produce fertilizers.[29] Vaclav Smil says that from two to every five humans on Earth today would not be alive apart from this invention, since it became the means to mass monocrop production of basic food crops—corn, soybeans, wheat, rice.[30] It meant significantly increased food surpluses that, in some lands, including China, staved off famine and starvation. (China's first order after its opening to the West in 1972 was for thirteen massive fertilizer factories from the United States.) It also made possible the growth in meat-based diets. Michael Pollan goes so far as to say that the discovery of synthetic nitrogen "changed everything—not just for the corn plant and the farm, not just for the food system, but also for the way life on earth is conducted."[31]

The reason is this: All life depends on nitrogen as nature's building block for assembling amino acids, proteins, and nucleic acid. "The genetic information that orders and perpetuates life is written in nitrogen ink." Thus do "scientists speak of nitrogen as supplying life's quality, while carbon provides the quantity."[32]

Yet while Earth's atmosphere is 80 percent nitrogen, it is essentially useless in that form to plants and animals. Nitrogen becomes usable via the work of bacteria in the roots of leguminous plants and the shock of lightning, which breaks the nitrogen bonds in the air and delivers it via rain as fertility to the soil. But this is a limited and uncertain process. European scientists had already decided by 1900 that unless a way were found to augment the naturally occurring nitrogen, "the growth of the human population would soon grind to a very painful halt."[33] What the Haber-Bosch process did was to "fix" nitrogen by splitting nitrogen atoms and joining them to atoms of hydrogen. The heat and pressure of the process are supplied by large amounts of electricity, and the hydrogen is supplied by oil, coal, and, most commonly now, natural gas.[34] This made possible both mass industrialized agricultural production and an unprecedented human population.

Haber himself never saw the outcome that we experience now; namely, the abandonment of most traditional agriculture in favor of fossil-fueled, industrialized agriculture, and factory farming, with its deleterious consequences for humans and the rest of nature, including dead zones in the oceans due to nitrogen runoff and nitrogen in the water supply of many cities and in rural wells. The shift from full reliance on the energy of the sun to reliance on

fossil fuels put fertility in a bag or tank and allowed farmers a certain liberation from some age-old biological restraints. The farm no longer needs "to
generate and conserve its own fertility by maintaining a diversity of species";[35]
it can, via synthetic fertilizer, turn to monocultures instead. Industrial principles take over, with their economies of scale and mechanical efficiency. All of
this permits the food chain "to turn from the logic of biology and embrace
the logic of industry. . . . Instead of eating exclusively from the sun, humanity
now began to sip petroleum," Michael Pollan concludes.[36] One result is depleted soils, since petroleum fertilizers prefer direct injections for plant
growth to upbuilding the soil's fertility.

Haber's context was World War I and he, the devoted patriot scientist,
threw himself into his nation's war effort. When Britain choked off Germany's
supply of nitrates from abroad, Haber created a synthetic nitrate that allowed
das Vaterland to continue making bombs. When the German war machine
became mired in the trenches of France, Haber turned his genius to developing poison gases—ammonia and chlorine. He personally directed their use
on the battlefield and returned home a hero, a rare feat in an utterly humili-
ated, defeated nation. His wife, a fellow chemist sickened by her husband's
contribution to the war, picked up his army pistol and shot herself. Though
Haber himself later converted to Christianity, Aryan racism brooked no exceptions and Haber fled Germany for Switzerland. He died, utterly broken, in
a Basel hotel room.

Karl-Friedrich Bonhoeffer, older brother of Dietrich, was mentored by
Haber and, like Haber, had volunteered for service in World War I. After the
"Great War" Bonhoeffer attained international renown as a physical chemist,
working closely with Nobel laureates Otto Hahn and Fritz Haber. At twenty-
four Bonhoeffer became Haber's assistant at the prestigious Kaiser Wilhelm
Institute in Berlin and soon established his reputation with groundbreaking
work on the hydrogen molecule. Bonhoeffer stopped his work on "heavy
water," however, when he suspected it could be used to develop a weapon of
mass destruction, some kind of nuclear fission device, a subject of much interest and work among his good friends. Near the onset of World War II,
Bonhoeffer switched from physical chemistry to electrochemistry. Mean-
while his friend and colleague, Otto Hahn, joined Fritz Strassmann at the
Kaiser Wilhelm Institute in successfully splitting the uranium nucleus, the
first recorded instance of planned atomic fission. (This was the event that
Niels Bohr reported in his four-month stay at Princeton in early 1939 and that
eventuated in the Manhattan Project after Enrico Fermi and I. I. Rabi brought
news of it to the physics department of Columbia University.)

When Karl-Friedrich (who, in the manner of a righteous Gentile, harbored Jews at his institute until the end of the war in 1945) heard of Haber's death, he organized a memorial for him and wrote a speech for it. The Nazi Ministry of Education and Culture reacted fiercely and forbade Karl-Friedrich's address. He gave it anyway, but at a private funeral ceremony. For the public event, Karl-Friedrich asked his colleague, Otto Hahn, to stand in for him. Hahn gave the address. But it was Karl-Friedrich's, word for word.

Here is Karl-Friedrich's letter to the Haber children: "I have just learned from the newspaper of the death of your respected father. I am so dismayed by it that I can hardly find words. [I am so sorry] that he had to die at this moment! Everything good and beautiful which I owe to him comes back to me, and I cannot suppress the feeling of bitterness at our powerlessness to support him in these last difficult years. I shall always remember his wisdom and goodness, and as long as I live I shall do everything in my power to nurture and keep his memory alive in our field. I am grateful to the fate which for many years brought me close to such an extraordinary man as your father, and I hope that I will have an opportunity to express publicly how much Germany owes to him and also what I feel for him. Since I do not know where his grave is, I intend to have a wreath laid at the Haber-Linde as a sign of my gratitude. . . . With deep sympathy, always your Karl-Friedrich Bonhoeffer."[37]

The clouds of tragedy hang heavy here. Karl-Friedrich says he regrets that Haber died at this moment [1934], that he will keep Haber's memory alive, and that he desires to publicly express all that Germany owes Haber, the brilliant patriot scientist. But at this moment Karl-Friedrich Bonhoeffer did not know, and Fritz Haber could not know, what the state would do with another of Haber's inventions. Fritz Haber not only gave the world food for billions, via synthetic nitrogen as fertilizer and industrialized agriculture; he invented Zyklon B, hydrogen cyanide, the death-camp gas used against his own people in the Holocaust. Haber had developed Zyklon B to exterminate vermin. The Nazis said that was exactly what they were doing.

This is raw moral tragedy. Haber, the well-meaning patriot, the same brilliant scientist doing the same brilliant science, invents the death-camp gas of the Holocaust and helps cut the now-dubious path to unsustainable agriculture and unsustainable human population.

For such moral tragedy as this, there is no redemption. There is only infinite sorrow and compassion. If and where religious wisdom is present, it is not present as the motif of redemption prominent in much so-called Western religion, that a redeeming good will somehow make its way and new life will somehow emerge from the depths of tragedy. Often it does not. Instead,

Wisdom bears a motif usually associated with Eastern religion, the motif of a pervasive sorrow that is enveloped, though not forgotten, in ongoing compassionate living, a sorrow painfully embraced as the burden it is. The broken heart remains broken but life goes on.

Differently said, Wisdom knows there is no full rational explanation for suffering, death, meaning, and purpose. Neither science nor theology is up to the task of final and satisfactory explanations. Any "yes" to life comes instead with the existential choice of a life pathway, and living it as well as uncertain life permits.[38]

Folly

Wisdom counters folly: feeding the wrong wolf, for example, or ignoring what Norman Habel names "the Joseph principle"—times of prosperity are precisely the times to prepare for scarcity and a diminished world.

Pharaoh had a dream about seven fat cows and seven lean ones. The lean ones consume the fat ones but they remain as thin as they were. Joseph, an outsider now in Pharaoh's court, interprets the dream as portending famine, and he convinces Pharaoh to store up grain in the years of plenty so as to survive the years of scarcity. That is done and Egypt, together with its needy neighbors, is saved from disaster.[39]

Habel's comment is that we, like Egypt's neighbors, choose folly if the years when climate change is not yet doing its worst (except perhaps of late in Habel's native Australia!) are not used to prepare present and future generations for oncoming disasters.

Another folly, on the grandest of scales, is the one shadowing every page of this book: our collective insistence about undertaking a huge, uncontrolled planetary experiment to see if there are limits to infinite economic growth and where calamitous tipping points may occur. "Burn, then learn" is foolish advice. So is oil for soil, and a few annual crop varieties rather than many perennial ones.

John Adams discusses another foolish course in his article "Heading Off Next Big Bailout—of Nature." Bailouts, he points out, inevitably cost far more than preventive measures. "Building water purification systems is far more costly than conserving natural watersheds" and "rebuilding cities is enormously expensive compared to the cost of conserving forests and coral reefs that protect against floods and storms."[40] When watersheds no longer provide freshwater, forests no longer prevent droughts and floods, and oceans no longer support and supply healthy fish stocks, then governments must scramble to find other ways to supply these basic goods and services. The alternative paths are usually far more expensive and more difficult, fraught with potential conflict as competition intensifies. Nonetheless, in 2010 "expenditures on extracting natural resources globally [dwarfed] spending on conserving nature by over 100 to 1."[41] This is folly, if not madness. Wisdom says that it's long since time "to start accounting for nature."[42]

Wisdom sits in places

Wisdom accounting for nature is wisdom that "sits in places," Dudley Patterson (Western Apache) tells Keith Basso. "It's like water that never dries up. You need to drink water to stay alive, don't you? Well, you also need to drink from places."[43] "Place-worlds" we know well,[44] the ones that truly "bind and fasten us" (*religare*—religion), become inner landscapes as well as outer. The configurations of earth, air, fire, water, and light in locales that are home to us become cultural symbols and metaphors. They belong to a whole way of living and take on sacramental and mystical power as we consciously and unconsciously commune with them. Far more than a zip code and address, place-worlds are the means by which we appropriate the Earth where we live, move, and have our bodily being.

The appropriation is reciprocal: As we invest our lives in the physical landscapes to which we belong, they become part of our fundamental experience and perception. We shape them and they shape us. N. Scott Momaday (Kiowa) says that, from the human side, this interaction is "primarily a matter of imagination which is moral in kind."[45] That is, we become who we are in keeping with the way creatures of symbolic consciousness construe their living relationship with their physical worlds. A physical landscape is fashioned into a meaningful human universe, replete with virtue, value, and duty.[46] Our sense of place is a close companion of heart and mind.[47]

Certainly Dudley Patterson thinks it is so. His discourse continues: "You ... need to drink from places. You must remember everything about them. You must learn their names. You must remember what happened at them long ago. You must think about it and keep on thinking about it. Then your mind will become smoother and smoother. Then you will see danger before it happens. You will walk a long way and live a long time. You will be wise. People will respect you."[48] Patterson, having tapped "the genius of the place" (Jackson), cherishes the remains of Earth and draws wisdom and instruction from them.

Genuine place-worlds yield the ethos of *oikos* (home and household, dwelling place) and the "stable" society discussed in previous pages,[49] an ethos formative and expressive of human character and conduct. The place-world might be a New Yorker's Central Park, a farmer's fields, or Patterson's White Mountains of present-day Arizona. But its yield is knowing who we are because we know where we belong and how to "be" there.

What happens as place-worlds are degraded or destroyed? What happens to human meaning and the human moral world when, in an unsettled age, "large portions of the earth's surface are being ravaged by industrialism . . . when on several continents indigenous peoples are being forcibly uprooted by wanton encroachments upon their homelands . . . when American Indian tribes are mounting major legal efforts to secure permanent protection for sacred sites now controlled by federal agencies . . . when philosophers and poets are asserting that attachments to geographical localities contribute fundamentally to the formation of personal and social identities . . . [and] when new forms of 'environmental awareness' are being more radically charted and urgently advocated than ever in the past"?[50] What happens when climate change alters landscapes and seasons so dramatically that the place we call home no longer looks or feels the same? The consequence, writes William deBuys, is a "*demoralized* landscape," demoralized because, for those who have lived there as part of it and it as part of them, massive changes in the composition of their world empties it of meaning.[51] Sacred places are ruined or gone and the land seems strange and alien.

Then paradoxically, and precisely because wisdom *always* sits in places, it becomes all the more imperative consciously to tap the genius of a changing and altered place and to discover anew the integrity of creation there. The unsettled world of hard transitions on a tough, new planet, rather than the settled world that formed the character and conduct of the ancestors, becomes the new arena for learning what we are to value and how we are to live. A "*re-moralization* of the landscape" (deBuys)[52] becomes the collective religious and cultural task as people struggle to find a new identity while caught in the throes of death and renewal. Singing the Lord's song in a strange land, treating each locale as a sacred trust worthy of well-being, and "doing first works over" (Baldwin) are done well only if they include a profound and ongoing sense of place, a sense of place that, like wisdom itself, continually listens to and learns from nature.

Next and nearly last . . .

In some ways Wisdom brings us full circle. The concluding pages of William Brown's masterful chapter on "Wisdom's World: Cosmos as Playhouse in Proverbs 8:22–31," in his *The Seven Pillars of Creation*, gather in themes that tie us back to our chapter 1, "The Creature We Are."

Wisdom traditions are more poetry than science, certainly more than modern science. Most would not pass muster as credible Earth science. This includes ancient Wisdom's assumptions of Earth's stability and unchanging repetition—the anchored mountains, the circumscribed seas, the trustworthy seedtimes and harvests with the same flora and fauna ages on end. When the wisdom we know was gathered, human experience knew nothing of Earth's wildly different "ages" or the planet's billion-year dynamism. The conventional wisdom of much ancient Wisdom was, on this count, foolish rather than wise.

Yet Wisdom does share with science the conviction that creation is "wonderfully intelligible" and that the universe "exhibits a rational order," with "lawful regularities" and stunning uniformity across space-time.[53] At the same time—here Wisdom and the sciences of Earth and cosmos also align— humanity's place in the universe merits little attention. Yes, the very purpose of wisdom is for human instruction, that we might live long and well on the land. But, as Brown notes, there is *no strong anthropic principle* here. The universe is not finely tuned or designed to yield hominids and the line of *Homo sapiens*. If anything, creation's principle is "sophic." The cosmos is "finely and firmly constructed for Wisdom's sake, for her growth, delight, and play, far beyond humanity's. The cosmos exists in delightful intelligibility"[54] whether or not *Homo sapiens* is present. "Wisdom has two partners: God and creation."[55] You and I and our kind appear within that frame, a single, lovely detail in a distant corner, a twig on a great tree, a dot that requires a big arrow with the words, "You are here."

This delightful intelligibility of the creation to which we belong, rather than the one that belongs to us in either a possessive or teleological sense, returns us to the "binding together" of Wisdom in her cosmic play.[56] All is born to belonging as complex interconnectedness. Einstein found the connections ascertained by quantum physics across space-time "spooky" but scientifically correct. Objects can be very far apart in space, yet behave as a single entity. They are entangled rather than separate. A primordial bonding and belonging is the common finding of the ancient poet and the modern scientist. (Dante called it the love that moves the sun and the other stars.[57]) The cosmos is ordered and alive.

Finally, Wisdom accords with science on adaptive challenges. Can we make the long, hard transitions we ought and must? "We are capable" is the only reply Wisdom and science offer. It must suffice, since we cannot know the future. We are capable because "gaining wisdom," or "growing in wisdom," takes place, in evolutionary perspective, as a process of adaptation. It takes place as fitting in and achieving the "functional efficacy"[58] we associated with Darwin's finding that "[it]t is not the strongest of the species that survives, not the most intelligent that survives, but the one that is most adaptable to change."[59] It also takes place in the knowledge that the altruistic and the selfish in human nature are always present, and that what enchants also tempts and deceives.

Gaining wisdom, then, is more than genes for humans; more than brains, too. It's learning, including the collective social learning and cooperation of cultural innovation and adaptation.

Learning, gaining wisdom, requires varied angles of vision, some sufficiently askew of the going paradigms so as to supply the breakthrough insight of another way, whether in science or daily living. Thinking outside the paradigm, too, belongs to cultural innovation and adaptation.

There is more, at least for Wisdom, if not for science. Gaining wisdom and fitting in, good judgment and appropriate action ("functional efficacy"), include moral and religious valuation. Maturity and good judgment as the earthlings we are entails multidimensional intelligence that includes tutored moral emotions and cultivated religious sensibilities. These are more than puzzling things out with cognitive intelligence. "To gain effective instruction, as well as righteousness, justice, and equity"[60]—to cultivate true wisdom, in other words—is to merge sound cognition, morality, and faith—not for their own sake, but for a life well lived that belongs to a creation deemed good.[61] Brown summarizes Proverbs in a way that pertains nicely: "Wisdom seeks both the common good and the common God; it fosters reverence of the creator of all and cultivates 'justice, righteousness, and equity' (1:3). The myriad proverbs in the book present various, even conflicting views about life and the world, all to develop the reader's critical, meta-cognitive intelligence, that is, to cultivate wisdom."[62] Fidelity to God lived as fidelity to Earth. May it be so.

13

Closing

These words are not a list to be read. They are not even a sermon to be preached. They are a score to be played and a program to be enacted.

—JOHN DOMINIC CROSSAN

Give us the courage to enter the song.

—MARTY HAUGEN, "Gather Us In"

IN 2006, FORMER U.S. Secretary of State Madeline Albright told the American Academy of Religion that she expected the big issues of the twenty-first century to be religion, ecology, and the Asian economy.[1]

Of those, the Asian economy—China, India, Japan, Korea, Indonesia, Malaysia, Thailand, and Singapore—might have been named by most people in, say, 1990, as belonging to the triumvirate of leading factors. A few would have named ecology as well. None would have given religion any such standing.[2]

Startlingly moral

These pages have been woven around three assumptions.

First, "our whole life is startlingly moral."[3] In one sense it has been ever thus. Moral is the kind of creature *Homo sapiens* is, by nature. We cannot be nonmoral. Choice, habits, perspectives, dispositions, institutions, decisions, duties, aims, and actions play decisive roles in the score we play and the program we enact (Crossan). Morality can go terribly wrong, and does, but it is always present and always consequential.

Yet now our lives are startlingly moral for a second reason: The fateful presence of cumulative human power on the planet. We affect all things, including the weather and the course of evolution. Even proverbial "acts of God" are no longer cleanly differentiated from the mounting consequences of human activities. Intensified storms, landslides and avalanches, rising sea levels, droughts and deluge, shifting seasons, and migrating pests and disease—these fall inside rather than outside the circle of human-induced impact and responsibility, just as mounting human numbers and needs do. Daily decisions and half-conscious habits have global reach. We are geosocial creatures as well as biosocial and ecosocial.

There is a third reason our lives are startlingly moral. It rests in the constructive work to be undertaken when one way of life must of needs give way to another. The subject of ethics is how we and others are to survive and flourish. So when a turning point arrives and a time of transition from one way of life to another intrudes, moral inertia no longer suffices and all that belongs to the present moral life must of needs be engaged anew—cosmology; community reformation of human character and conduct; the understanding of what is morally normative; and the shape, behavior, and outcome of systems, structures, and practices. All these belong to the work of human responsibility as the way is forged from the industrial-technological era to an ecospheric one. The Great Work is moral to the core, across a wide range.

John Paul Lederach says it well: Turning points ask for a horizon of awareness that exceeds the normal. At such times, the fate of the human journey does not turn only "on which specific forms of governing political, economic, or social structures we devise." Nor does it rotate "primarily around finding answers to ever-present and pressing issues of population growth, environmental degradation, use of natural resources, or poverty." It doesn't even find its essence "in the search to understand the roots of violence, war, or terrorism, or solutions to the same." Much less will "learning a few good communication skills, new facilitation methodologies, or teachable techniques for resolving conflicts" do the trick. While "each of these is important, and represent the core challenges we face," they do not constitute the capacity to create a turning point "that orients us toward a new and more humane horizon." That which does is "our moral imagination."[4] Moral imagination, addressing the question of what manner of living befits life in and for an ecozoic era, is uppermost. The full range of human being and doing, including imagination, is startlingly moral.

The unit of survival

The second assumption of this work is that the unit of survival of human society is the ecosphere and nature comprehensively. Our origin, ongoing life, and destiny reside in membership here and nowhere else. Our belonging is ecospheric and cosmic. Religions and moralities that do not account for this near their pulsing centers are quaint, false, and now dangerous.

Dangerous religions and moralities perpetuate what Norman Wirzba names a "reconciliation deficit disorder," a disorder that stems from two misguided beliefs: (1) "that God cares only for human beings, and (2) that people can flourish while the memberships of creation languish."[5]

In contrast to the first, Wirzba presses the fundamental conviction that creation as a whole is the subject of God's presence and love. God seeks, not to be free from creation and part of "the fellowship of a few disembodied, placeless minds," but at home in the universe as sacred abode, dwelling "among a reconciled creation."[6] In contrast to the second belief, Wirzba rallies an evolutionary and ecological account in keeping with which we began. We, together with all else, belong. "To live is to be in a body in a place joined to all the bodies of creation."[7]

Earth-honoring Faith has used varied rubrics for addressing this reconciliation deficit: Centering the primal elements of all life in our moral universe; measuring all our moral and religious impulses by the stringent criterion of whether or not they are Earth-honoring; attending to more reality than is immediately visible and at hand, perhaps best expressed in the manner of Buddhist mindfulness and awakening; promoting change that has a quality of transcendence and creativity such that it nurtures possibilities not imagined in current practices; focusing on transitions that reconcile economics and ecology as "eco-nomics"; fostering discipleship communities that anticipate a different future by meeting present adaptive challenges in sustainable ways, utilizing resources from the millennial traditions of religious communities; and living the present in the awareness that the eyes of future generations look back at us.

All of these assume a fundamental "consent to being" as the basic human stance. Consent to being is a trust in the triumph of life, its continuation and renewal. From there, and with the good of the whole in view, "we are," in James Gustafson's words, "to conduct life so as to relate to all things in a manner appropriate to their relations to God."[8] Nicholas Lash's version of this is "learning to see all things in the way God sees them: as worth infinite expenditure of understanding, interest, and care."[9] Given our eons-deep Earthly and cosmic belonging, we could also say that we are to relate to all things in a manner appropriate to their relations to ourselves. Which is to say that if some manner of anthropocentrism is inevitable—and it is, because we relate to all things only through human consciousness—let it be framed by consent to being and rooted in that even bigger-than-life arena apart from which we could and would not be: nature and nature's God.

Reconciliation of this scope is a multigenerational task. It is the task of moving from a resolutely consumerist global civilization, largely secular in its practices and with little sense of mystery and the sacred, to a world of bioregional clusters populated with ecologically viable communities.

Contributions

The third assumption is this: The interacting threesome of religion, ecology, and economy (Asian and otherwise) merits more attention and better analysis than it gets, not only for the place this triumvirate does play in our lives but also for what, when coupled to human imagination and responsibility, it might contribute. Part II of this volume is one attempt to do so.

In 1944, Karl Polanyi looked down the remaining decades of his century and into ours:

> To allow the market mechanism to be sole director of the fate of human beings and their natural environment, indeed, even of the amount and use of purchasing power, would result in the demolition of society. For the alleged commodity "labor power" cannot be shoved about, used indiscriminately, or even left unused, without affecting the human individual who happens to be the bearer of this commodity. In disposing of a man's labor power the system would, incidentally, dispose of the physical, psychological, and moral entity of "man" attached to the tag. Robbed of the protective covering of cultural institutions, human beings would die as the victims of acute social dislocation through vice, perversion, crime, and starvation. Nature would be reduced to its elements, neighborhoods and landscapes defiled, rivers polluted, military safety jeopardized, the power to produce food and raw materials destroyed.[10]

Polanyi saw this before, not after, the post-1950 transformations that bring to an end the Great Transformation of the industrial-technological era. He saw it at the very time a conscious choice was being made in Washington, D.C., and Bretton Woods, New Hampshire, to shift the war-based economy to an economy of accelerated mass consumption in which economic time fatefully learned to outrun biological time.[11]

Now another Great Transformation awaits, if not a new Axial Age, aided and sometimes led, we have said, by anticipatory communities attending to the full range of the "startlingly moral" life humans live as they seek to create ecological civilization. We have said as well that religious communities have gifts and talents for the common work of a common good. Indeed, the most creative moments for religions have been those times of death and renewal when they have given birth to their own anticipatory communities, some of them Earth-honoring. They, to adapt what Robert Pogue Harrison says about garden sanctuaries, "become places of rehumanization in the midst of, or in spite of, the forces of darkness."[12]

But what are the contributions?

To believe in God is to disbelieve in the world as it is. It is not to disbelieve in the world, but only the world "as it is." Ours is a good Earth and a good world gone wrong, not a wrong Earth and world—that Manichean mistake that keeps on giving. And to believe in God's presence in all life is to offer more, a "more" already borne by the ecosphere's tenacious insistence that life *will be* and it will flourish. Here, in believing in God's presence and disbelieving in the necessity of the world as it is, is the proximate source and energy for Earth-honoring religious ethics. (The ultimate source is God and grace.) Here, in the disciplined ways of sacramentalism, mysticism, asceticism, prophetic-liberative practices, and wisdom, are the spirited lifeways that renew and recast human responsibility. They renew and recast responsibility in ways that offer alternatives to the ethic of unqualified utilitarian expediency that marks global consumerism and corporate capitalism.

To be certain, no one who sings these songs has perfect pitch. Or, to shift the metaphor, none of these traditions is unsullied. Many prophetic-liberative strands, for example, have yet to overcome the anthropocentrism of their social justice traditions. Theirs is not yet truly creation justice.

Too, numerous streams of all these traditions still leave out much of the universe in their cosmologies, to recall Simone Weil's complaint about a Christianity not genuinely catholic. They are stuck with people still inured to the indispensability and sheer wonder of life beyond the human. A few even "scoff at the stars" (Heschel) or see in a redwood only lumber.

Some also know the temptation of which Thomas Merton writes—"to diddle around in the contemplative life, making itsy-bitsy statues"[13] rather than fall under the activists' beatitude, "blessed are the organized."[14]

Still, ascetic gymnasts of the soul, those athletes of God who choose the simple life, powerfully expose consumerism as the deceitful sire of a diminished self who lives a life of real tinsel[15] rather than false. People of sacramental imagination and piety cultivate critical virtues of humility, care, awe, respect, and reverence in a world that is itself an extraordinary stanza in the "hymn of the universe,"[16] a world worthy of so much more than the ransacked storehouse modernity has made of it. The mystic's union with all that is peels back layer upon layer of Earth-destructive, other-destructive, and self-destructive alienation and lives out another possibility quietly, resolutely, gently; a life of surpassing beauty, serenity, and solidarity. Prophets, with less patience and little quiet, expose how carefully constructed power either fractures or promotes justice for the community of life. Theirs is an "applied reverence."[17] Wisdom gathers in the tried and tested ways of creation itself, as mediated by cultural and religious experience, then passes the treasures along for the edification of any and all, whatever their age, state, or credo.

As with any typology, these idealized types are sifted and sorted to display their driving logic, infrastructure, and traffic. Types tend first to simplify, then exaggerate. By contrast lived life finds them merged and nuanced. Around the world, innumerable practices of diverse indigenous peoples simply reject the sharp dualism of nature and culture as they pass along the wisdom of a sacred universe and the mystery of belonging to it. Ecumenical Patriarch Bartholomew couldn't instruct in the ways of Orthodox Christian discipleship without braiding asceticism, mysticism, and sacramentalism together. Mohandas Gandhi, drawing from Indian village culture, placed a powerful popular Hindu asceticism in the service of liberative ends. Dorothy Day took her uncompromisingly prophetic stance against war-making and poverty-making into the field, but nurtured it with the sacramental piety of daily mass at the Catholic Worker. Thich Nhat Hanh's engaged Buddhist discipleship joins his ascetic regime and mystical meditation to wisdom and liberative example. From the New York City Mayor's Office, and working with youth, Ibrahim Abdul-Matin views "the Earth [as] a Mosque" and marshals Muslim discipleship to embody Islam as a "Green Deen" (path or way of life).[18] In Connecticut Adamah Farm trains college youth in organic farming and a ranging Jewish spirituality. Hazon, the largest Jewish environmental organization in the United States, has the largest single network of Community Supported Agriculture farms.[19]

Orchestrating deep traditions in varied ways as the symphony of discipleship is itself wise. The very strengths of a dominant tradition can, when left to their own devices, become its weakness. The ascetic, mystical, and sacramental, for example, are all skilled schools of virtue. Each focuses its powers on qualities of character that move hearts and minds to empathy, compassion, and just deeds. Yet this indispensable attention to fundamental moral-spiritual formation tends to neglect that careful institution-building and hard politics by which direct attention to "behavioral changes [that] *precede* attitudinal ones" makes the singular difference. Virtue then fails to realize the power of its own transforming potential. By contrast, prophetic-liberative traditions generally "do" institutional justice better than virtue traditions. Through systemic practices they organize the life of the polis and *oikos* without assuming that virtue will always find its way. Prophetic traditions are, however, oftentimes impatient with the long, slow schooling of the very character and conscience they cannot do without. They organize union members and college students but not preschoolers. Here wisdom is wiser. While not self-sufficient as a tradition, it draws from nature and the deep traditions in ways attentive to both ongoing moral formation *and* the institutional scaffolding of a just way of life.

Differently said, an Earth-honoring consequences ethic and a duty ethic are not sustainable apart from a virtue ethic. Neither will an Earth-honoring virtue ethic bear fruit if it neglects to give structural and strategic attention to desired ends or moral bottom-lines. Creation justice requires the moral powers each and all of these traditions provide. Earth-honoring ways of life fitted for the long, hard transitions to an "Ecozoic" from a "Technozoic" Age will draw upon the full range of these traditions. In brief, all are required for a comprehensive ethic of responsibility fitted to the demands of a new era, the Anthropocene.

Such traditions, even when tarnished, are places to stand. They carry the kind of tenacity and devotion that religion, and little else, provides. They offer cross-cultural and interfaith resources that nurture the moral-esthetic emotions needed to guide and fuel our lives. Not least, they are treasures shared by most religions across millennia and, as such, bridge world faiths in order, together, to counter consumerism, utilitarianism, alienation, oppression, and folly. Alliances of this sort embody what religious traditions bring to the communities needed for the Great Work, whether their Earth-honoring emphasis is ecojustice, with its attention to just institutions that grant the ecosphere its due; or stewardship as adaptive management, backing away from modernity's efforts to conquer nature but not backing away from human interventions that fit in; or eco-spirituality as virtue's efforts to become human again, this time as citizens of a belonging marked by biophilia and cosmophilia. Whether one, another, or some blend of these strategies of engagement, the deep traditions of Part II offer substance and moral-spiritual energy for the birth and rebirth work of sustainable communities.

Not least, the deep traditions offer the kind of thinking and the kind of language that characterizes the empathetic, or sympathetic, mind, in contrast to the reductionist economic, utilitarian mind. While vivid with imagination and possibility, empathetic understanding, like the religious traditions that nurture it, is aware of humanity's presumption and ignorance. It counsels caution and the arts of humble living. It learns from the millennial experience of peoples who have dreamed, worked, succeeded, and failed. It conceives reality as interdependent wholes rather than isolated parts and knows that landscape and culture belong together. It accepts that we are creatures "living in a world of creatures, all of which are mortal, fallible, and related in complex ways."[20] It knows we are accountable to those who have gone before and the generations of those who follow, both human and other-than-human. Most important, it asks the question that is rarely, if ever, asked by economic and utilitarian thinking: How do we "become worthy to use what must be used"?[21]

Leaders

In 1932 Howard Becker made a study of personality types in societies undergoing transition. Since it was provoked by "secularization," the study contrasted older understandings of the holy in societies, which were rather closed to change, and more recent patterns of freedom and openness in post-Enlightenment secularizing societies.

The results surprised many. Not surprising was Becker's finding that some people abandoned ties to older traditions as they embraced the new. For them, the new displaced the old. They wanted modernity's freedom and nothing else. Not surprising, either, was the fact that others held fast to the old and, for them, the sacred, only to discover themselves without influence in the new order and alienated from it.

The surprise was that the most creative leadership in transition times came from "sacred strangers in secular society" (Becker's term). The sacred stranger embraced the new possibilities, even sought to create some, but in so doing did not abandon the values, meanings, and insights of older sacred orders. Such "strangers" recast older understandings in new patterns in the process of meeting the adaptive challenges of the day. Indeed, the traditions the stranger knew provided some of the makings of the vision of the emerging order. The sacred stranger participated fully in, but was not captured by, the emerging secular culture.[22]

The deep, shared traditions we have outlined equip religious communities to be the sacred strangers needed for leading new communities of moral-spiritual formation. Drawing from their own wells, these religious communities aid the anticipatory communities required for a more viable and durable way of life. Amid the shaking of the foundations of industrial-technological civilization, these communities of the long obedience of discipleship offer a sturdy place to stand, anchored to the good work of countless generations of both the famous and the forgotten. They equip their members for sustainable adaptability. Paradoxically, when such sacred strangers in secular society live Earth-honoring faith, they are the people most at home, most in tune with Planet Home. Its elements are their own.

Final note

We began with song. We end with it as well.

The last note of "Ode to Joy" in Beethoven's Ninth Symphony is not the purpose or goal of either the Ode or the symphony. The meaning of that note, or any before it, is not teleological. The meaning is in the music as a whole and the making of it. The meaning of life, too, is in the living of it, just as the meaning of the dance is in the dancing.[23] This book has only tried to say that the meaning of life is living it, together, inside Earth-honoring faith as a song of many songs, the hymn of the universe in a million variations. So we end with an invitation and a petition: "Give us the courage to enter the song" (Marty Haugen).

Postlude

We must remember the worlds our ancestors traveled.
Always wear the songs they gave us.
Remember that we are made of prayers.
Now we leave wrapped in blankets of love and wisdom.
—Diné (Navajo)

My life flows on in endless song
    above earth's lamentations;
I hear the real though far off hymn
    that hails a new creation.

Adoration Point is the name fiber artist Nicole Dunn gave the quilt that is this book's cover.[1] It befits a work in religious ethics, not least because the center of this desert landscape is a tree of life, arguably the most popular religious symbol across all cultures. The only viable contenders are other natural manifestations, the sacred mountains and rivers of crystalline waters. All are points of adoration.

While the tree is at the center, as is this book's effort to draw upon shared religious traditions—mysticism, prophetic-liberative practices, asceticism, sacramentalism, wisdom—the careful observer will also find a cross in the background, off to the side. The reason is not only that the author is working from the tradition he knows best. The more important reason is the conscious intent of this work to exemplify how religious ethics might be done—as a medley of melodies, a Song of Songs. The Song itself is Earth-honoring faith, but its expression is via innumerable *songs*. How might we work in the traditions we know best while at the same time drawing from others so that our voices are a collaborative religious effort, a symphony? The cross on the cover, then, is not a subtle way to render Christianity normative. It is to mark the author's tradition and to invite others of other faiths to mark theirs in parallel fashion. Another song, drawing upon different sources, might still have a tree of life at the center, but with a crescent, menorah, flame, feather, or chalice off to the side and in the background. This book will succeed when others draw out their own renderings of Earth-honoring faith.

An encounter with Elie Wiesel nicely makes the point. Wiesel was invited to speak to Protestant pastors in Detroit. As he prepared to speak, he opened his Hebrew Bible, paused, looked up, and said, "Let me be clear about something. I'm not going to try and convert anyone here to Judaism, and I would appreciate it very much if you didn't try to convert me to Christianity. What I am trying to do is to be the best Jew that I can be, so that you can be the best Christian that you can be. Let's study together."[2]

"Let's study together" is not only the immediate aim of this book; it is the ultimate aim, each reader drawing from his or her own path while respecting the paths of others, all in order to rally living traditions for Earth-honoring faith.

Notes

PRELUDE

1. Carl Sagan, "A Pale Blue Dot," excerpt from the public lecture given at Cornell University, October 13, 1994, available from The Big Sky Astronomy Club, http://bigskyastroclub.org/pale_blue_dot.html.
2. Ibid.
3. Bill McKibben, *Eaarth: Making a Life on a Tough New Planet* (New York: Times Books, 2010), 1.
4. From the subtitle of McKibben, *Eaarth*.
5. The title of Thomas Friedman's *Hot, Flat, and Crowded* (New York: Farrar, Straus & Giroux, 2008).
6. Alex Doherty and Robert Jensen, "A World in Collapse?," The New Left Project, an interview online at: http://www.newleftproject.org/index.php/site/article_comments/a_world_in_collapse/
7. "Unveiling," rather than "end," is the meaning of the Greek word for "apocalypse."
8. Phrases from "The Holden Prayer," commonly prayed at Holden Village, an ecumenical retreat and renewal center in the Lutheran tradition, Chelan, Washington. The prayer is part of Morning Prayer (Matins) in *The Lutheran Book of Worship* (Minneapolis: Augsburg, 1978), 137.
9. From "The Greening of the World's Religions," Mary Evelyn Tucker and John Grim, in *Religious Studies News* (May 2007): 15.
10. See Steven Mithen, *The Singing Neanderthals: The Origins of Music, Language, Mind and Body* (Boston: Harvard University Press, 2008).
11. A reference to the hymn by Robert Lowry, "How Can I Keep From Singing?" in *Bright Jewels for the Sunday School* (New York: Biglow and Main), 1869.
12. A reference to Thomas Berry's discussion of "the Great Work." See the discussion in chapter 3 below, "The Faith We Seek."
13. Denise Levertov, "Beginners," *Candles in Babylon* (New York: New Directions, 1982), 82–83.

CHAPTER 1

1. The title of the book by Mab Segrest: *Born to Belonging: Writings on Spirit and Justice* (New Brunswick, NJ: Rutgers University Press, 2002).

2. "Hymn of the universe" is the title of a book by the priest and paleontologist Pierre Teilhard de Chardin. See Teilhard de Chardin, *Hymn of the Universe* (New York: Perennial Library, 1972).

3. From Charles Darwin, *On the Origin of Species*, first published in London in 1869. This citation of Darwin's closing lines is that of Stephen Jay Gould in "This View of Life," *Natural History* 12 (1992): 19.

4. This is the close of the first edition of *On the Origin of Species*. After the enormous religious controversy elicited by the book, Darwin inserted "by the Creator" in the sixth edition: "There is grandeur in this view of life, with its several powers, having been originally breathed by the Creator into a few forms or into one; and that, whilst this planet has gone cycling on according to the fixed law of gravity, from so simple a beginning endless forms most beautiful and most wonderful have been, and are being, evolved." The 6th edition is available from GRIN Verlag, Norderstedt, Germany.

5. Michael Sanderson and his colleagues at the University of Arizona have used super-computers to crunch the DNA data from thousands of species of plants in order to see how all the estimated five hundred thousand plant species are related to one another. They hope eventually to present the entire evolutionary tree of plants. But, Sanderson says, "We have no way to visualize such a tree at the moment." Plants by themselves, even without the rest of life, would end up a blurry, inscrutable thicket. "Crunching the Data for the Tree of Life," *New York Times*, February 10, 2009, D1.

6. Ursula Goodenough and Terrence W. Deacon, "From Biology to Consciousness to Morality," *Zygon* 38, no. 4 (December 2003): 805.

7. Ibid.

8. Cited from Carl Zimmer, "You Are Here," a review of Richard Dawkins, *The Ancestor's Tale: A Pilgrimage to the Dawn of Evolution*, in *New York Times Book Review*, Sunday, October 17, 2004, 30.

9. Psalm 139:13–16.

10. The materials to this point, on "born to belonging," are also published in revised form as part of the my chapter, "Creating the Commons," in *Justice in a Global Economy*, ed. Pamela K. Brubaker, Rebecca Todd Peters, and Laura A. Stivers (Louisville, KY: Westminster John Knox Press, 2006), 101–12. Used with permission.

11. Walt Whitman, *Leaves of Grass*, Stanza 31, cited from www.Bartleby.com. Great Books Online. The stanza begins: "I believe a leaf of grass is no less than the journey work of the stars, And the pismire is equally perfect, and a grain of sand, and the egg of the wren."

12. William Bryant Logan, "Stardust," in his *Dirt: The Ecstatic Skin of the Earth* (New York: W. W. Norton, 1995), 7, 125.

13. Cited from "Letters," a feature found at www.joannamacy.net.

14. Maya Angelou, *On the Pulse of Morning: An Inaugural Poem* (New York: Random House, 1993), n.p.

15. Annie Dillard, *Pilgrim at Tinker Creek* (New York: HarperCollins, 1974), 178.

16. Annie Dillard, *Pilgrim at Tinker Creek* (New York: HarperCollins Perennial Classics, 1998), 146. The remainder of the passage is this: "If creation had been left up to me, I'm sure I wouldn't have had the imagination or courage to do more than shape a single, reasonably sized atom, smooth as a snowball, and let it go at that. No claims of any and all revelations could be so far-fetched as a giraffe."

17. From Charles Darwin, *On the Origin of Species*, first published in London in 1869. This citation of Darwin's closing lines is that of Stephen Jay Gould in "This View of Life," 19.

18. Brian Swimme and Thomas Berry, *The Universe Story: From the Primordial Flaring Forth to the Ecozoic Era* (San Francisco: HarperSanFrancisco, 1992), 74.

19. Dillard, *Pilgrim at Tinker Creek*, 11.

20. Logan, *Dirt*, 124–25.

21. Peter G. Brown, Mark Goldberg, Nicolas Kolsoy, and Robert Nadeau, from a working syllabus, "Civilization and Environment," 6. Made available to the author at the Yale Conference on The Journey of the Universe, March 24–26, 2011.

22. Thich Nhat Hanh, *The World We Have: A Buddhist Approach to Peace* (Berkeley, CA: Parallax Press, 2008), 99.

23. Swimme and Berry, *Universe Story*, 70–78.

24. Ibid., 72 and 79 for the respective quotations.

25. See the argument in Martin A. Nowak with Roger Highfield, *Supercooperators: Altruism, Evolution, and Why We Need Each Other to Succeed* (New York: Free Press, 2011).

26. Beverly Wildung Harrison has elaborated this best for religious ethics and ethics generally. See *Making the Connections* (Boston: Beacon Press, 1985) and *Justice in the Making* (Louisville, KY: WJK Press, 2004).

27. David Suzuki, Foreword, in Tim Flannery, *Now or Never: Why We Must Act Now to End Climate Change and Create a Sustainable Future* (New York: Atlantic Monthly Press, 2009), vii.

28. A title in the Science Times section of the *New York Times'* feature on evolution, June 26, 2007, D1–D10. The article by this title includes an accessible explanation about what genes are and how they work. "Genes are stretches of DNA that can be switched on so that they produce molecules know as proteins. Proteins can then do a number of jobs in the cell or outside it, working to make parts of organisms, switching other genes on and so on" (D4).

29. Neil Shubin, *Your Inner Fish: A Journey into the 3.5 Billion-Year History of the Human Body* (New York: Random House, First Vintage Books, 2009), 184–85.

30. Ibid., 152–53.

31. Ibid., 152–54.

32. Ibid., passim.

33. The title of Shubin's chapter subsection, ibid., 173–78.

34. Ibid., 149.

35. Ibid., 123.

36. "Early life forms set the platform for an increasing flexibility and freedom within the phenomenon of life." William Hurlbut, "From Biology to Biography," *The New Atlantis: A Journal of Technology and Society* 3 (Fall 2003): 50.

37. See the account of Margulis's work in Rob Dunn, *Every Living Thing: Man's Obsessive Quest to Catalog Life, from Nanobacteria to New Monkeys* (New York: Collins Books, 2009), 138–43.

38. Shubin, *Your Inner Fish*, 123.

39. Carl Zimmer, "Our Microbiomes, Ourselves," *New York Times*, Sunday Review, December 4, 2011, 12.

40. There may be as many as 150 million species of microbes on the planet, while there are only about 5,400 species of mammals. They can exist under conditions that would kill most higher forms of life, such as humans, and are clearly the vast majority of organisms on Earth. "Scientists Start a Genomic Catalog of Earth's Abundant Microbes," *New York Times*, December 29, 2009, D3.

41. Logan, *Dirt*, 55.

42. A million billion billion, or 10 with 24 zeros.

43. Paul Hawken does not provide the bibliographic data for the sentence from Darwin. These citations from Hawken, as well as the data in the prior paragraph, are from his "Commencement Address to the Class of 2009," University of Portland, May 3, 2009, n.p. The address is available online at http://www.paulhawken.com/paulhawken_frameset.html.

44. Gregory of Nazianzus, Gregory of Nyssa, Basil, and Macrina. Yet another theologian of the human person as microcosm of the macrocosm is Nemesius of Emesa. While there is much bad science in the science of his day, his *On the Nature of Man* argues in ways largely congruent with the story of evolution. Namely, that higher orders of creation are rooted in lower orders and that there are no ontological leaps in nature from one order to the next. See Nemesius, "On the Nature of Man," in *The Library of Christian Classics*, vol. 4, *Cyril of Jerusalem and Nemesius of Emesa*, ed. Wm. Telfer (Philadelphia: Westminster Press, 1955). It is also worthy of note that Gregory of Nyssa understands the human microcosm of the macrocosm as a unitary being. "The root cause of our constitution is neither soul without the body, nor the body without the soul, but that, from ensouled and living bodies, our nature is generated at the first as a living and ensouled being." From Gregory of Nyssa, *The Making of Man*, as quoted in Francis M. Young, "Adam and Anthropos," *Vigiliae Christianae* 37, no. 2 (1983): 118.

45. It may be coincidental but it is hardly unfitting that the cosmologist who first proposed the Big Bang as the theory of creation, Georges Lemaitre, was a priest; the paleontologist who placed us amid the epic drama of evolution, Pierre Teilhard de Chardin, was also a priest; and the father of genetics, Gregor Mendel, was a monk.

Their religious sense of a sacred cosmos as a community merged with the minutiae of the science that awed them. By such reckoning as theirs, and countless persons of religious conviction over centuries, the primary and primordial revelation of God is the universe itself, and creation as community is the hymn of the universe.

46. St. Augustine, *City of God*, trans. by Henry Bettenson (New York: Modern Library Classics, 2000), 1 10:12.

47. Abraham Heschel, in *I Asked for Wonder: A Spiritual Anthology*, ed. Samuel Dresner (New York: Crossroad, 1983), 20.

48. Craig Childs, *The Secret Knowledge of Water* (New York: Little, Brown, 2000), 61.

49. Ibid., 64–65.

50. "Deep under the Sea, Boiling Founts of Life Itself," Science Times, *New York Times*, September 9, 2003, F1, F4.

51. Diane Ackerman, "Worlds within Worlds," *New York Times*, December 4, 1995, sec. 4.

52. Hurlbut, "From Biology to Biography," 49.

53. Wes Jackson, *Consulting the Genius of the Place* (Berkeley, CA: Counterpoint Press, 2010), x.

54. Ibid.

55. Cited by Jackson, ibid., 64.

56. Ibid., 65.

57. Cited from Thich Nhat Hanh, *World We Have*, 43.

58. "Key Human Traits Tied to Shellfish Remains," *New York Times*, October 18, 2007, A6.

59. From the review, "A Little Help From Your Friends," by Oren Harman of Martin A. Nowak with Roger Highfield, *Supercooperators: Altruism, Evolution, and Why We Need Each Other to Succeed* (New York: Free Press, 2011) in *New York Times Book Review*, April 20, 2011, 18. Harman does not give a page number and simply says "near the end of the book" for the story about Mahler and Walter.

60. From the discussion on myth in Robin R. Meyers, *Saving Jesus from the Church* (San Francisco: HarperOne, 2009), 102.

61. This section on what symbols do is indebted to William Hurlbut, "From Biology to Biography," 50–53.

62. Robert Pogue Harrison, *Gardens: An Essay on the Human Condition* (Chicago: University of Chicago Press, 2008), 115–16.

63. Meyers, *Saving Jesus from the Church*, 105.

64. Harrison, *Gardens*, 115–16.

65. James Miller, "Connecting Religion and Ecology," 1–2. Unpublished paper, used with the author's permission.

66. The phrase is the title of Michael Oleksa's fine volume, *Orthodox Alaska: A Theology of Mission* (Crestwood, NJ: St. Vladimir's Seminary Press, 1992).

67. See, for example, Swimme and Berry, *Universe Story*.

68. Thomas Berry, *The Great Work: Our Way into the Future* (New York: Bell Tower, 1999), 3.

69. For a full account, see Larry Rasmussen, "Bishop Moses and the Trees," in *Frontiers of African Christianity: Essays in Honour of Inus Daneel*, ed. Greg Cuthbertson, Hennie Pretorius and Dana Robert (Pretoria: University of South Africa Press, 2003), 69–74.

70. See the work of Charles Taylor as reported in "Canadian Is Awarded Spirituality Prize," *New York Times*, March 15, 2007, A20.

71. David Sloan Wilson, as reported in "The Origin of Religions, From a Distinctly Darwinian View," *New York Times*, December 24, 2002, F2.

72. "We Will Not Forget You," *Gates of Repentance: The New Union Prayerbook for the Days of Awe* (New York: Central Conference of American Rabbis, 1978), 21–22.

73. James Miller, "Connecting Religion and Ecology," 4. Unpublished paper, used with author's permission.

74 *Gates of Repentance*, 102.

75. Jeffrey Kluger, "What Makes Us Moral," Science section of *Time*, December 3, 2007, 55.

76. Ibid.

77. One of three meditations offered for Memorial Day weekend in the bulletin of the United Church of Santa Fe, the original source not given.

78. Kluger, "What Makes Us Moral," 55.

79. Wolfgang W. E. Samuel, *German Boy: A Child in War* (New York: Random House, 2001), 253.

80. These distinctions draw upon my article, "Moral Community and Moral Formation," in *Ecclesiology and Ethics: Costly Commitment*, ed. Thomas F. Best and Martin Robra (Geneva: World Council of Churches, 1995), 54–55.

81. As reported by Kluger, "What Makes Us Moral," 57.

82. From Frans de Waal as reported by Kluger, ibid.

83. Both the elephant and fox examples are from Marc Bekoff, "Animal Passions and Beastly Virtues: Cognitive Ethology as the Unifying Science for Understanding the Subjective, Emotional, Empathic, and Moral Life of Animals," *Zygon* 41, no. 1 (March 2006): 73 (inclusive page nos. 71–104).

84. From the citation above at the outset of the subsection "Born to Meaning."

85. Bekoff, "Animal Passions and Beastly Virtues," 74–75.

86. These studies are all reported by Bekoff, "Animal Passions and Beastly Virtues," 83.

87. Bekoff, "Animal Passions and Beastly Virtues," 76.

88. Charles Darwin, *The Descent of Man and Selection in Relation to Sex* (New York: Random House, 1936), 163. The original publication date is 1871.

89. Bekoff, "Animal Passions and Beastly Virtues," 80.

90. These questions are suggested by "An Evolutionary Theory of Right and Wrong," *New York Times*, Science Times, October 31, 2006, D1–2.

91. "Is 'Do Unto Others' Written into Our Genes?," *New York Times*, Science Times, September 18, 2007, D1.

92. The title of Christian Smith's *Moral, Believing Animals: Human Personhood and Culture* (New York: Oxford University Press, 2003).

CHAPTER 2

1. Matthew Fox interviewed by Jeffrey Mishlove on "Creation Spirituality" for the program, *Thinking Allowed, Conversations on the Leading Edge of Knowledge and Discovery*. The interview text is available at http://www.intuition.org/txt/fox.htm.

2. Herman Melville, *Moby-Dick or, The Whale* (New York: Modern Library, 1992), 90.

3. Carl Safina cited by Browning, *New York Times Book Review*, January 16, 2011, 11.

4. H. Richard Niebuhr, *The Purpose of the Church and Its Ministry: Reflections on the Aims of Theological Education* (New York: Harper & Row, 1956), 38. Italics are mine.

5. I draw here from Larry L. Rasmussen, *Earth Community, Earth Ethics* (Maryknoll, NY: Orbis Books, 1996), 127.

6. James Baldwin, *The Price of the Ticket: Collected Nonfiction, 1948–1985* (New York: St. Martin's Press, 1985), xix. Baldwin was not sanguine about white Americans' ability to do their first works over. In a dialogue with Reinhold Niebuhr at the time of the civil rights movement, he had this to say: "The only people in this country at the moment who believe either in Christianity or in the country are the most despised minority in it.... It is ironical... the people who were slaves here, the most beaten and despised people here... should be at this moment... the only hope this country has.... None of the descendants of Europe seem to be able to do, or have taken it on themselves to do, what Negroes are now trying to do. And this is not a chauvinistic or racial outlook. It probably has something to do with the nature of life itself. It forces you, in any extremity, any extreme, to discover what you really live by, whereas most Americans have been for so long, so safe and so sleepy, that they don't any longer have any real sense of what they live by. I think they really think it may be Coca-Cola." From the audiotape of the dialogue, n.d., as reported by James H. Cone in *The Cross and the Lynching Tree* (Maryknoll, NY: Orbis Books, 2011), 54.

7. I take the phrase from Cornel West and his discussion in Cornel West, *Prophesy Deliverance! An Afro-American Revolutionary Christianity* (Philadelphia: Westminster Press, 1982), 53ff.

8. This is the term of W. E. B. Du Bois in *The Souls of Black Folks* (New York: New American Library, 1960; original publication, 1903). "Two-ness" means, in Du Bois's exposition, that African Americans must of necessity know two worlds, their own and that of white folks, for the sake of their survival as an out-of-favor minority. It also refers to the consequences for their souls and psyche of living on this ledge. "One ever feels his two-ness—An American, and a Negro; two souls, two thoughts, two unreconciled strivings; two warring ideals in one dark body" (ibid., 5).

9. Cited from *Autobiography of Mark Twain*, edited by Harriet Elinor Smith and other editors of the Mark Twain Project, vol. 1 (Berkeley: University of California Press, 2010), 16.

10. James Baldwin, "White Man's Guilt," reprinted in *Black on White: Black Writers on What It Means to be White*, ed. David R. Roediger (New York: Schocken Books, 1998), 321.

11. See the Prelude.

12. Walter Rauschenbusch, *Christianity and the Social Crisis* (New York: Macmillan, 1907), 211.

13. Ibid.

14. Ibid.

15. Ibid.

16. Ernst Troeltsch, *The Social Teaching of the Christian Churches* (Chicago: University of Chicago Press, 1981), 2:1010.

17. Karl Marx, *The Communist Manifesto* (Chicago: Henry Regnery, 1954), 23.

18. As an aside, 2008 was the first year on record when the proportion of the world's population without sufficient food ratcheted upward. The 250-million-person increase in a single year was the largest in human history. In a global capitalist economy food security has joined sufficient secure energy and sufficient safe water as great twenty-first-century issues. Frederick Kaufman, "The Food Bubble: How Wall Street Starved Millions and Got Away with It," *Harper's* 321, no. 1022 (July 2010): 28.

19. As I write, the BP oil catastrophe in the Gulf of Mexico has become the largest spill thus far. This from the corporate giant that for some years advertised itself as "Beyond Petroleum" and the champion of alternatives to it.

20. This section on the social and ecological question was originally published as follows: Larry Rasmussen, "Give Us Word of the Humankind We Left to Thee: Globalization and its Wake," *EDS Occasional Papers* 4 (August 1999): 1–3.

21. The test site for the A-bomb was named by Oppenheimer. It refers to the Christian God. Oppenheimer had been reading the sonnets of John Donne during sleepless nights in the summer as the countdown to the test proceeded apace. One sonnet, the one that inspired the name, goes as follows:

    Batter my heart, three-personed God: for you
    As yet but knock, breathe, shine, and seek to mend;
    That I may rise and stand, o'erthrow me, and bend
    Your force, to break, blow, burn, and make me new.

    Cited by Jennet Conant in *109 East Palace* (New York: Simon & Schuster, 2005), 237.

22. Ibid., 308.

23. Jornada del Muerto is a stretch of New Mexico desert dangerous for those who try and cross it. "Jornada" is a reference to how far a person can normally walk in a day. The little town that is the destination on the far edge of the desert is Socoro— "succor," "consolation."

24. Items about the Neolithic Revolution are from Rasmussen, *Earth Community, Earth Ethics*, 55.

25. Jackson, *Consulting the Genius of the Place*, 75.

26. Ibid., 68.

27. Edward B. Barbier, *Scarcity and Frontiers: How Economies Have Developed through Natural Resource Exploitation* (Cambridge: Cambridge University Press, 2011), 665.

28. Berry's questions are cited by Jackson, *Consulting the Genius of the Place*, 69.

29. David Suzuki, Foreword, in Tim Flannery, *Now or Never: Why We Must Act Now to End Climate Change and Create a Sustainable Future* (New York: Atlantic Monthly Press, 2009), vii.

30. I am using Karl Polanyi's phrase and drawing on his work. See Karl Polanyi, *The Great Transformation: The Political and Economic Origins of Our Time* (Boston: Beacon Press, 1944), passim.

31. What we call "the Plague" was, at the time, called "the Great Mortality." Muslim nations, who lost a portion of the population similar to Europe's, referred to it as "The Year of Annihilation."

32. A paraphrase of Michael Crofeet as cited by Sam Bingham, *The Last Ranch: A Colorado Community and the Coming Desert* (New York: Pantheon Books, 1996), 345. Bingham does not give the source for Crofeet.

33. Randy Udall, "The Big Bonfire," *High Country News*, December 21, 2009, 21.

34. From Wes Jackson, "Where We Are Going," *The Land Institute*, 2, n.d. Available at www.LandInstitute.org.

35. Alan T. Durning, *How Much Is Enough?* (London: Earthscan, 1992), 38.

36. "Remove far from me falsehood and lying; give me neither poverty nor riches; feed me with the food that I need, or I shall be full, and deny you, and say, 'Who is the Lord?' or I shall be poor, and steal, and profane the name of my God."

37. Berry, *The Great Work*, 1–4.

38. Friedman, *Hot, Flat, and Crowded*, 26–27.

39. E.C.E. is Energy Climate Era. See *Hot, Flat, and Crowded*, 26.

40. With kind permission from Springer Science+Business Media: W. L. Steffen et al., *Global Change and the Earth System* (Berlin and New York: Springer, 2004), v. Figure 2.1 was originally Figure 3.66 and Figure 2.2 was originally Figure 3.67.

41. Steffen et al., *Global Change and the Earth System*, 81.

42. J. R. McNeill, *Something New under the Sun: An Environmental History of the Twentieth-Century World* (New York: W. W. Norton, 2000), 4.

43. Ibid., 16.

44. Durning, *How Much Is Enough?*, 38.

45 *Pocket World in Figures: 2011 Edition*, 103. *Pocket World* is a publication of *The Economist*.

46. Bill McKibben, *Eaarth: Making a Life on a Tough New Planet*. New York: Times Books, 2010, 144.

47. John Maynard Keynes, *Essays in Persuasion* (New York: W. W. Norton), 358.

48. Cited from Fareed Zakaria, "Fueling the Future," a review of Daniel Yergin, *The Quest: Energy, Security, and the Remaking of the Modern World* (New York: Penguin Press, 2011), in *New York Times Book Review*, September 25, 2011, 15.

49. "Thinking Big," *New Mexican*, November 13, 2007, C1. At the time West was the director of the Santa Fe Institute, a science think tank on chaos and complexity theory.

50. James Gustave Speth, *The Bridge at the Edge of the World: Capitalism, the Environment, and Crossing from Crisis to Sustainability* (New Haven: Yale University Press, 2008), 4.

51. Heather Eaton, "Reflections on Water," unpublished paper, n.p., made available by the author.

52. McNeill, *Something New under the Sun*, 4.

53. McKibben, *Eaarth*, title page.

54. Ibid., 47.

55. Jackson, *Consulting the Genius of the Place*, 81–82.

56. This discussion of the big, orienting ideas and the reversal Friedman sees as necessary is from *Hot, Flat, and Crowded*, 18–19.

57. John Rawls, *A Theory of Justice* (Boston: Belknap Press of Harvard University Press, 1971), passim.

58. "The Address: All This We Will Do," *New York Times*, January 21, 2009, P2.

59. Ibid.

60. This is a slight modification of the list of William McDonough and Michael Braungart in "The Next Industrial Revolution," *Atlantic Monthly*, October 1998, 85.

61. Alfred W. Crosby, *Ecological Imperialism: The Biological Expansion of Europe, 900–1900* (Cambridge: Cambridge University Press, 1986), 131.

62. Adam Smith, *An Inquiry into the Nature and Causes of the Wealth of Nations* (New York: Modern Library, 1994), 675.

63. Ibid., 675–76.

64. Ibid., 605.

65. While I have cited Darwin from Crosby, the original is in Chap. XIX, "Australia," Darwin's diary account in *The Voyage of the Beetle*, first published in 1839.

66. Marx, *Communist Manifesto*, 15–16.

67. Karl Marx, *Capital: A Critique of Political Economy*, vol. 1, trans. Samuel Moore and Edward Aveling, ed. Frederick Engels (New York: International Publishers, 1967), 507.

68. Frederick Engels, "Outlines of a Critique of Political Economy," in Karl Marx, *The Economic and Philosophic Manuscripts of 1844*, 210, as cited in *Marx and Engels on Ecology*, ed. Howard Parsons (Westport, CT: Greenwood Press, 1977), 173.

69. While I have cited from Crosby, the original can be found in Charles Lyell, *Principles of Geology* (New York: Penguin Books, 1997), 276. *Principles of Geology* was first published in 1830.

70. Theodore Roosevelt, *The Winning of the West: From the Alleghenies to the Mississippi, 1769–1776* (Middlesex, UK: Echo Library, 2007), 59. First published in 1894.

71. From Charles Marsh, *The Earth as Modified by Human Action* (New York: Charles Scribner, Armstrong, 1874), as cited in William Ashworth, *The Economy of Nature: Rethinking the Connections between Ecology and Economics* (New York: Houghton Mifflin, 1995), 11. Ashworth doesn't cite the page number from *The Earth as Modified by Human Action*.

72. See the discussion in Sallie McFague, *Super, Natural Christians: How We Should Love Nature* (Minneapolis: Fortress Press, 1997), 67–69.

73. John Milton, in *Paradise Lost*, puts in verse form the arrogance he traces to Adam's fall. In this section of the epic poem he writes of the consequences for Earth: by [Adam] first,

> *Men also, and by his suggestion taught,*
> *Ransacked the center, and with impious hands*
> *Rifled the bowels of their mother earth*
> *For treasures better hid. Soon had his crew*
> *Opened into the hill a spacious wound*
> *And digged out ribs of gold. Let none admire*
> *That riches grow in hell; that soil may best*
> *Deserve the precious bane.*

John Milton, *Paradise Lost*, 2nd ed. (New York: W. W. Norton, 1993), 29. The original was published in 1674.

74. Alfred Crosby, *The Columbian Exchange* (Westport, CT: Greenwood Press, 1974), 12.

75. Bonhoeffer, "The Right to Self-Assertion," *DBWE* 11: 250–51.

76. Ibid., 251–52.

77. Ibid., 252.

78. Dietrich Bonhoeffer, *Letters and Papers from Prison*, *DBWE* 8:500.

79. There are numerous references in the letters. Here see the aforementioned "Outline for a Book," in *Letters and Papers from Prison*, *DBWE* 8:499–504.

80. Bonhoeffer, "The Right to Self-Assertion," *DBWE* 11: 252.

81. This section on Bonhoeffer is a modified excerpt of a chapter I authored for a book edited by Peter Frick, to be published in 2012 by Peter Lang Publishers, Frankfurt, in the series, International Bonhoeffer Interpretations, ed. Ralf Wuestenberg et al.

82. Daniel C. Maguire, *Whose Church? A Concise Guide to Progressive Catholicism* (New York: New Press, 2008), 38. Emphasis Maguire's.

83. Only a portion of the list in Wendell Berry, "Does Community Have a Value?" in *Home Economics* (San Francisco: North Point Press, 1987), 179.

84. While Ludovico Ariosto's *Orlando Furioso* is, argues Robert Pogue Harrison, one of the few epic poems of the modern era, it is full of insights into "the behavioral disorder of our times" (Robert Pogue Harrison, *Gardens: An Essay on the Human Condition* [Chicago: University of Chicago Press, 2008,] 151). Cast as a look back to a bygone era, it centers on the formidable knight Orlando who, like the other knights, is a picture of action that feeds upon itself and a need for ever-new challenges and exploits. With little attention to consequences, this is an identity of self-affirmation "through contest, conflict, and conquest" (Harrison, *Gardens*, 155). The problem per se is not, however, the unquiet heart or the Western spiritual restlessness seen in Orlando

and the knights, but the fact that Earth itself suffers the destruction of this identity and action, albeit undertaken by noble and well-meaning knights.

85. Harrison, *Gardens*, 158–59.

86. McKibben, *Eaarth*, 27.

87. Ibid., 28.

88. McKibben, *Eaarth*, xii, citing Richard Ingham, "Act Now on Floods, Drought, Says Forum," *Age* (Australia), March 18, 2009.

89. Ibid., xii.

90. Cited by Nicholas D. Kristof, "Our Beaker Is Starting to Boil," *New York Times*, Week in Review, July 18, 2010, 10.

91. McKibben, *Eaarth*, 26–27.

92. Ibid., 5.

93. "U.S. Clings to Climate Disbelief," *New Mexican*, September 26, 2011, A-5.

94. McKibben, *Eaarth*, xiv.

95. Ibid., xiv.

96. "U.S. Clings to Climate Disbelief."

97. Ibid.

98. Ibid.

99. Cited from Friedman, *Hot, Flat and Crowded*, 44.

100. Ibid., 37–38.

101. Ibid., 44.

102. Albert Einstein as first cited in "Atomic Education Urged by Einstein," *New York Times*, May 25, 1946 and quoted a month later by Michael Amrine in "The Real Problem Is in the Heart of Man," *New York Times Magazine*, June 23, 1946.

103. The term is Aiden Davison's in Aiden Davison, *Technology and the Contested Meanings of Sustainability* (Albany: State University of New York Press, 2001), passim.

104. A reference to the earlier discussion.

105. The phrases are from the Anglican hymn, "All Things Bright and Beautiful."

106. See chapter 1, "The Creature We Are."

107. Norman Wirzba, who does not categorically oppose genetic modification and patenting of food needs, offers this comment: "Far from signaling an end to genetic research, appropriate research will respect the integrity of creatureliness and honor the divine logos (the principles of life and intelligibility) in things. Research that serves the narrow purposes of profitability and power (the glorification of a corporation) rather than the nurture and health of the world, is a desecration." Norman Wirzba, *Food and Faith: A Theology of Eating* (Cambridge: Cambridge University Press, 2011), 204n49.

108. Reported in "Starting Over," *New York Times Book Review*, September 2, 2007, 12. It was not only Monsanto, however, but the chemical industry as a whole that berated

and attacked Carson's work, *Silent Spring* (New York: Houghton Mifflin, 1962). For more details, see Paul Hawken, *Blessed Unrest: How the Largest Movement in the World Came into Being and Why No One Saw It Coming* (New York: Viking Press, 2007).

109. Berry, "Does Community Have a Value?" in *Home Economics*, 179.

110. This is an adaptation from the list Bruce C. Birch and I used in *The Predicament of the Prosperous* (Philadelphia: Westminster Press, 1978), 44–45. I also used it in the volume with Daniel C. Maguire, *Ethics for a Small Planet* (Albany: State University of New York Press, 1998), 88–89.

111. Frederic Morton, *Crosstown Sabbath: A Street Journey through History* (New York: Grove Press, 1987), 31.

112. The cover and feature story of *The Economist*, May 26–June 3, 2011, "Welcome to the Anthropocene: Geology's New Age," illustrates this stance as well. The feature describes an unprecedented era of Earth under human eco-stress and says it "means thinking afresh about the relationship between people and their world and acting accordingly." But the story is new wine in old wineskins, as perfectly captured by the cover. Except for a few empty, unfinished patches, the surface of the entire planet is all steel plates, riveted together. The remaining holes await the completion of this human project by the master species. This is the Anthropocene as industrial eco-modern.

113. James Gustave Speth, "Towards a New Economy and a New Politics," *Solutions* 5, available online at http://thesolutionsjournal.com, n.p.

114. All these bullet-pointed paragraphs except the first combine the discussion of Speth with my own. Even when not quoted directly, they draw from James Gustave Speth, "Towards a New Economy and a New Politics," *Solutions* 5, available online at http://thesolutionsjournal.com, passim.

115. Thomas Berry, "Conditions for Entering the Ecozoic Era," *Ecozoic Reader* 2, no. 2 (Winter 2002): 10.

116. Thomas Friedman, "Connecting Nature's Dots," *New York Times*, Week in Review, August 23, 2009, 8.

CHAPTER 3

1. Thomas Berry, *The Great Work: Our Way into the Future* (New York: Bell Tower, 1999), 7–8.

2. See the previous chapter's discussion of the parable of Jesus in Luke 5:36–39.

3. Titled the Song of Solomon in some Bibles and Canticle of Canticles in a few.

4. Eight short chapters.

5. Bonhoeffer, "Basic Questions of a Christian Ethic," *DBWE* 10: 377–78.

6. He never was released. He was hanged in April 1945 for his part in the conspiracy to overthrow the Nazi regime.

7. Dietrich Bonhoeffer and Maria von Wedemeyer, *Love Letters from Cell 92*, ed. Ruth-Alice Bismarck and Ulrich Kabitz, trans. John Brownjohn (Nashville: Abingdon Press, 1995), 162.

8. Ibid., 64.

9. Bonhoeffer, *Letters and Papers from Prison*, DBWE 8:492.

10. 7:6 is "How fair and pleasant you are, O loved one, delectable maiden!"

11. Bonhoeffer, *Letters and Papers from Prison*, DBWE 8:394. The emphasis is Bonhoeffer's.

12. Ibid., *DBWE* 8:410.

13. Ibid., *DBWE* 8:394.

14. Ibid., *DBWE* 8:394. The emphasis is Bonhoeffer's.

15. From Virginia Cover, "Dietrich Bonhoeffer: A Wealth of Themes," unpublished paper, 18.

16. I am grateful to Jacquelyn Helin and Karen Marrolli of the United Church of Christ, Santa Fe, for their help in researching cantus firmus as a musical style. Especially important was the pointer to cantus firmus in *The New Grove Dictionary of Music and Musicians*, vol. 3, ed. Stanley Sadie (New York: Macmillan, 1980), 738–41.

17. Bonhoeffer, *Letters and Papers from Prison*, DBWE 8:394.

18. Bonhoeffer, "Thy Kingdom Come! The Prayer of the Church-Community for God's Kingdom on Earth," *DBWE* 12:286.

19. Ibid., *DBWE* 12:286.

20. Bonhoeffer, *Letters and Papers from Prison*, DBWE 8:485–86.

21. In *Creation and Fall* and elsewhere.

22. Bonhoeffer, "Thy Kingdom Come!," *DBWE* 12:292.

23. This is the exegesis in Phyllis Trible's landmark volume, *God and the Rhetoric of Sexuality* (Philadelphia: Fortress Press, 1978).

24. Sometimes the cruciform is literal. In the course of two-and-one-half centuries of slavery, 5,500 African Americans were lynched in the United States and an untold number of Native peoples killed or moved off their lands. See James H. Cone, *The Cross and the Lynching Tree* (Maryknoll, NY: Orbis Books, 2011).

25. Bonhoeffer, *Letters and Papers from Prison*, DBWE 8:447–48.

26. Ibid., *DBWE* 8:213.

27. Annie Dillard, *Pilgrim at Tinker Creek* (New York: HarperCollins Perennial Classics, 1998), 278.

28. See the previous chapter.

29. E. O. Wilson, *The Future of Life* (New York: Knopf), 94.

30. *De Nabuthe Jezraelita* 3, 11, cited from Rosemary Radford Ruether, "Sisters of Earth: Religious Women and Ecological Spirituality," *The Witness* (May 2000): 14–15.

31. This is the phrase of Brock and Parker describing Augustine's commentary on Genesis. From Rita Nakashima Brock and Rebecca Ann Parker, *Saving Paradise: How Christianity Traded Love of This World for Crucifixion and Empire* (Boston: Beacon Press, 2008), 104. This account of Ambrose and Augustine draws from *Saving Paradise*, 99–100.

32. Augustine's Sermon 169.4, as cited by Johannes Van Oort in *Saving Paradise*, 104. Van Oort's text is available at http://home.um.edu.mt/philosophy/activities. html.

33. This is a succinct anticipation of Max Weber on the modern nation-state. The nation-state's distinguishing mark is not the renunciation of violence but sanctioned legal control of it.

34. Augustine cites as the source of this exchange Cicero's *De Reb.*, 3, 14, 24. The full passage is from Augustine's *The City of God*, Book IV, chap. 5, sec. 4, 139 of the Penguin Classics Edition, 1984.

35. Brock and Parker, *Saving Paradise*, 102–5.

36. Slightly adapted from Daniel Maguire, *A Moral Creed for All Christians* (Minneapolis: Fortress Press, 2005), 5.

37. "A Hen's Space to Roost," *New York Times*, The Week in Review, August 15, 2010, 3.

38. The largest volcanic explosion in modern times, which took place in Indonesia (1883).

39. Dillard, *Pilgrim at Tinker Creek*, 146.

40. Michael Crofoot as cited by Sam Bingham, *The Last Ranch*, 345, emphasis in the original. Bingham does not give the source.

41. James Martin-Schramm and Robert Stivers, *Christian Environmental Ethics: A Case Method Approach* (Maryknoll, NY: Orbis, 2003).

42. The term is Aiden Davison's in *Technology and the Contested Meanings of Sustainability*.

43. This is Niebuhr's recurring theme; but see especially vol. 2 of Reinhold Niebuhr, *The Nature and Destiny of Man* (New York: Charles Scribner's Sons, 1943), the chapter entitled "The Kingdom of God and the Struggle for Justice."

44. Jeremiah 17:9.

45. Reinhold Niebuhr, *Moral Man and Immoral Society* (New York: Charles Scribner's Sons, 1932), 164.

46. Frederick Douglass, "West India Emancipation," August 3, 1857 address in Canandaigua, New York, available at http://www.blackpast.org.

47. Niebuhr, *Moral Man and Immoral Society*, xxiii.

48. I am using Jeffrey Stout's formulation, in *Blessed Are the Organized: Grassroots Democracy in America* (Princeton: Princeton University Press, 2010), 63, but it is precise for Niebuhr as well.

49. Niebuhr, *Moral Man and Immoral Society*, 117.

50. The phrase is Jeffrey Stout's in *Blessed Are the Organized*, xv.

51. Reinhold Niebuhr, *The Children of Light and the Children of Darkness* (New York: Charles Scribner's Sons, 1944), xiii.

52. Niebuhr, *Moral Man and Immoral Society*, 64.

53. Niebuhr, *The Nature and Destiny of Man*, vol. 1 (New York: Scribner's, 1964 [1941]), 190–91.

54. Ibid., 191.

55. Cited by Crosby, *Ecological Imperialism*, 131.

56. Joseph Sittler, "An Open Letter," in response to the Statement on Peace and Politics of the Lutheran Church in America, March 7, 1984, available in the Joseph A. Sittler Archives, Lutheran School of Theology at Chicago, and online at http://www.josephsittler.org/.

57. By no means is slavery gone entirely. Sex trafficking happens the world over and in many societies women's status is still tied to male property and privilege. On another front, see Douglas A. Blackmon, *Slavery by Another Name: The Re-Enslavement of Black Americans from the Civil War to World War II* (New York: Anchor Books, 2008).

58. A reference to the title of Thomas Friedman's book.

59. Simon Singh, "Even Einstein Had His Off Days," *New York Times*, Week in Review, January 2, 2005, 9.

60. At the Church of the Pilgrims, Washington, D.C.

61. The subtitle and title of Rosen's book, *The Most Powerful Idea in the World: A Story of Steam, Industry, and Invention* (New York: Random House, 2010).

62. The Rigveda as cited from Hinduism, the Open Source Faith, available at hinduismtheopensourcefaith.blogspot.com.

63. Joseph Sittler, "A Theology of Earth," reprinted in Richard C. Foltz, ed., *Worldviews, Religion, and the Environment: A Global Anthology* (Belmont, CA: Wadsworth/Thomson, 2003), 17.

64. Pierre Teilhard de Chardin, "The Mass on the World," in his *Hymn of the Universe* (London: William Collins Sons; New York, Harper & Row, 1965), 25.

65. From the Lutheran Eucharist liturgy, *Lutheran Book of Worship* (Minneapolis: Augsburg, 1979), 88.

66. Denise Levertov, from the poem, "Annunciation," in *The Door in the Hive* (New York: New Directions, 1984), 85.

67. Douglas John Hall, "Against Religion: The Case for Faith," *Christian Century* 128, no. 1 (January 11, 2011): 32.

68. Ibid., 31.

69. Meditation 12, *The Gates of Repentance*, 5.

70. The phrase is taken from "Time and Possibilities," Judith Shulevitz's review of James L. Kugel, *In the Valley of the Shadow: On the Foundation of Religious Belief* (New York: Free Press, 2010), *New York Times Book Review*, February 12, 2011, 22.

71. Harrison, *Gardens*, 33.

72. Montaigne, as cited by Anthony Robinson, "Articles of Faith," a guest column in *The Seattle PI*, January 9, 2009, available online at http://www.seattlepi.com/local/395457_faith10.html.

73. "The Hills Are Bare at Bethlehem," *Lutheran Book of Worship*, 61.

74. Martin Luther King Jr., "The Current Crisis in Race Relations," in James M. Washington, *A Testament of Hope: The Essential Writings of Martin Luther King, Jr.* (San Francisco: Harper & Row, 1986), 88, as part of King's comments to "Faith."

75. Willis Jenkins, *Ecologies of Grace: Environmental Ethics and Christian Theology* (New York: Oxford University Press, 2008), 240.

76. Ibid., 229.

77. Ibid.

78. Fyodor Dostoyevsky, *The Brothers Karamazov*, trans. Richard Pevear and Larissa Volokhonsky (New York: Alfred A. Knopf, Everyman Library, 1927), 245.

79. For this discussion see Irving Greenberg, "Cloud of Smoke, Pillar of Fire: Judaism, Christianity, and Modernity after the Holocaust," in *Auschwitz: Beginning of a New Era?*, ed. Eva Fleishner (New York: KTAV, 1974).

80. Hayim Bialik, "After My Death," *Songs from Bialik: Selected Poems of Hayim Nahman Bialik*, trans. and adapted from the Hebrew by Atar Hadari (Syracuse: Syracuse University Press, 2000), 59.

81. My thanks to Richard Crouter, *Reinhold Niebuhr: On Politics, Religion, and Christian Faith* (New York: Oxford University Press, 2010) for this note on the fugue. Crouter is writing of Niebuhr, however, not Bonhoeffer.

82. Bonhoeffer, *Letters and Papers from Prison*, *DBWE* 8:306. The chorale, "Vor Deinem Thron tret'ich allhier," was often handed down together with *The Art of the Fugue*.

83. Reinhold Niebuhr, *The Irony of American History* (New York: Charles Scribner's Sons, 1952), 63.

84. Dillard, *Pilgrim at Tinker Creek*, 178.

85. Bonhoeffer, *Love Letters from Cell 92*, 229.

86. Jenkins, *Ecologies of Grace*, 234.

87. This appropriates the discussion of Judith Lewis Herman, *Trauma and Recovery* (New York: Basic Books, 1992), 319. She is not speaking specifically to human response to environmental suffering.

88. From "Letter to the Churches," appendix 1 of Wesley Granberg-Michaelson, *Redeeming the Creation, the Rio Earth Summit: Challenge to the Churches* (Geneva: WCC Publications, 1992), 73.

89. Brock and Parker, *Saving Paradise*, 29.

90. The title of the last chapter of Jenkins, *Ecologies of Grace*.

91. Robin Meyers, drawing on Marcus Borg's *Heart of Christianity*, summarizes "faith" as follows. Faith is *fiducia* as radical trust in God, *fidelitas* as loyalty in one's relationship to God, and *visio* as a way of seeing creation as gracious. See the discussion in Meyers, *Saving Jesus from the Church*, 36–38.

CHAPTER 4

1. Holmes Ralston III, "Saving Creation: Faith Shaping Environmental Policy," *Harvard Law and Policy Review* 4 (2010): 121. This essay is posted on the website of Dieter Hessel, www.EcoJusticeNow.org.

2. James Miller, "Connecting Religion and Ecology," 9. Unpublished paper, used with permission.

3. Vaclav Havel, "Address of the President of the Czech Republic, His Excellency Vaclav Havel, on the Occasion of the Liberty Medal Ceremony," Philadelphia, July 4, 1994, 2; photocopied manuscript made available by the Czech Republic Mission, New York City.

4. Ibid., 3.

5. Ibid., 3.

6. Ibid., 5–6.

7. Ibid., 6.

8. Ibid., 7.

9. Ibid.

10. Ibid., 7–8.

11. Ibid., 8–9.

12. Ibid., from the passage cited above.

13. Ibid., 9.

14. Ibid., 10.

15. This exposition of Havel's address is a modified version of my essay, "The Integrity of Creation," published in the *Annual of the Society of Christian Ethics* (1995): 167–71.

16. Bonhoeffer, Letter of April 30, 1944, *Letters and Papers from Prison*, DBWE, 8:367.

17. From the essay by Henry David Thoreau, "An Address to All Intelligent Men," published in many places.

18. See chapter 2, "The World We Have."

19. Cited from David Owen, "The Efficiency Dilemma: If Our Machines Use Less Energy, Will We Just Use Them More?," *New Yorker*, December 20 and 27, 2010, 79.

20. Roger L. Shinn, *Forced Options: Social Decisions for the Twenty-First Century*, 3rd ed. (Cleveland: Pilgrim Press, 1991), 3.

21. From the Fourth of July address cited earlier.

22. Thomas Berry, "Conditions for Entering the Ecozoic Era," *Ecozoic Reader* 2, no. 2 (Winter 2002): 11.

23. Berry, "Conditions for Entering the Ecozoic Era," 10.

24. The Earth Charter is available online at www.earthcharter.org.

25. Derrick Jensen, "Forget Shorter Showers: Why Personal Change Does Not Equal Political Change," *Orion* (July/August 2009): 18–19.

26. Bill McKibben, "Multiplication Saves the Day: How Just a Few of Us Can Rescue the Planet," *Orion* (November/December 2008): 19 (inclusive pages 18–19).

27. Bill McKibben, "Duty Dodgers," *Orion* (July/August 2010): 11.

28. "A Buddhist-Christian Common Word on Structural Greed: A Joint Statement," 4, available on the World Council of Churches website: www.oikoumene.org/resources/documents/wcc-programmes/interreligious-dialogue-and-cooperation/interreligious-trust-and-respect/buddhist-christian-common-word-on-structural-greed.html. The document is dated September 9, 2010, and was issued from a conference in Chiang Mai, Thailand.

29. From "The Age of Anxiety" as cited by Wes Jackson, *Consulting the Genius of the Place* (Berkeley, CA: Counterpoint Press, 2010), 96.

30. See the discussion of Galileo and a major tenet of science, that *"perception is not always reality,"* in Jackson, *Consulting the Genius of the Place,* 94–96.

31. See "Diminished Expectations," a review of Gideon Rachman's *Zero-Sum Future* in *New York Times Book Review,* January 30, 2011, 19.

32. Cited from http://en.wikiquote.org.

33. "The Year of Big Questions at SFI," *The New Mexican,* December 26, 2011, A-1, A-5.

34. William deBuys, *A Great Aridness: Climate Change and the Future of the American Southwest* (Oxford and New York: Oxford University Press, 2011), 59–60.

35. I use the subtitle of Sherry Turkle's book. She extends this habit of industrial-technological civilization to the world of digital technologies and social networking. See Sherry Turkle, *Alone Together: Why We Expect More from Technology and Less from Each Other* (New York: Basic Books, 2011).

36. Henry David Thoreau, *Walden* (New York: W. W. Norton, 1992), 146.

CHAPTER 5

1. The epigraph is from Langdon Gilkey, *Shantung Compound* (New York: Harper & Row, 1966), 113.

2. This note on language is from Paul Lehmann, *Ethics in a Christian Context* (New York: Harper & Row, 1963), 23–25.

3. This point is Aldo Leopold's in his classic essay, "The Land Ethic": "I have purposely presented the land ethic as a product of social evolution because nothing so important as an ethic is ever 'written.' Only the most superficial student of history supposes that Moses 'wrote' the Decalogue; it evolved in the minds of a thinking community, and Moses wrote a tentative summary of it for a 'seminar.' I say tentative because evolution never stops." Aldo Leopold, "The Land Ethic," in Leopold, *A Sand County Almanac* (New York: Ballantine Books, 1966), 263.

4. See the reference at the beginning of the previous chapter.

5. Gilkey, *Shantung Compound.*

6. Ibid., 109.

7. Ibid.

8. Ibid.

9. Ibid., 110.

10. David Brooks, "The Responsibility Deficit," *New York Times,* September 24, 2010, A25.

11. While I have drawn directly from Gilkey in *Shantung Compound,* the account here also paraphrases the one I and Bruce Birch provided in Bruce C. Birch and Larry L. Rasmussen, *Bible and Ethics in the Christian Life,* rev. and expanded ed. (Minneapolis: Augsburg Fortress, 1989), 48–50. The paraphrase is from the second edition. A third edition is underway with additional coauthors Jacqueline Lapsley and

Cynthia Moe-Lobeda. The Grant/Gilkey exchange may or may not be part of that edition.

12. Borgmann is quoting from Churchill's collected speeches, in Robert Rhodes James, ed., *Winston S. Churchill: His Complete Speeches 1897–1963*, vol. 7 (New York: Chelsea House, 1974), 68–69.

13. Alfred Borgmann, *Real American Ethics: Taking Responsibility for Our Country* (Chicago: University of Chicago Press, 2006), 160–88.

14. Aristotle, *Nicomachean Ethics*, II.i.4–5, trans. H. Rackam, Loeb Classical Library, vol. 19 (Cambridge: Harvard University Press, 1926; Reprint, 1982), 73.

15. Mary Evelyn Tucker, "The Alliance of World Religions and Ecology," *SGI Quarterly: A Buddhist Forum for Peace, Culture and Education* 61 (July 2010): 4.

16. Langdon Gilkey, *Maker of Heaven and Earth: The Christian Doctrine of Creation in the Light of Modern Knowledge* (Garden City, NY: Doubleday, 1959); *Nature, Reality, and the Sacred: The Nexus of Science and Religion* (Minneapolis: Augsburg Fortress, 1993). While these volumes prepare for ecological theology, Gilkey's attention is not to the ecosphere and what is happening to it. Their focus is the impact of modern science on the claims of theology and religion.

17. Gilkey, *Shantung Compound*, 110.

18. Ibid., 113.

19. Havel, "Address by the President of the Czech Republic," 8–9.

20. Tom L. Beauchamp and James F. Childress, *Principles of Biomedical Ethics* (New York: Oxford University Press, 1979), 29. As with the Shantung Compound case study, the discussion here includes some paraphrase of the discussion in Birch and Rasmussen, *Bible and Ethics in the Christian Life*, 52–58.

21. John Rawls, *A Theory of Justice* (Boston: Belknap Press of Harvard University Press, 1971), passim.

22. The Earth Charter is available at www.earthcharter.org.

23. From an unpublished paper by Roy Branson, "Apocalyptic and the Moral Imagination," proceedings from a conference on "Bioethics: Old Models and New," held at Loma Linda University, November 1986, 1–2. Made available to the authors and cited with permission in Birch and Rasmussen, *Bible and Ethics in the Christian Life*, rev. and expanded ed., 1989, 58.

24. Cited from Edward Ball, "Gone with the Myths," *New York Times*, Week in Review, December 19, 2010, 8.

25. Thomas Jefferson, "Commerce between Master and Slave," 1782, in Paul Leicaster Ford, *Works of Thomas Jefferson*, Federal Edition, 4:83.

26. Arundhati Roy, *Outlook India*, "The Trickledown Revolution," available online at http://www.outlookindia.com/article.aspx?267040. The citation is the last two paragraphs of the article. The preceding paragraphs are these: "Judging from what is happening in Russia and China and even Vietnam, eventually communist and capitalist societies have one thing in common—the dna of their dreams. After their revolutions, after building socialist societies that millions of workers and peasants paid

for with their lives, both countries now have unbridled capitalist economies. For them too, the ability to consume has become the yardstick by which progress is measured. For this kind of 'progress' you need industry. To feed the industry you need a steady supply of raw material. For that you need mines, dams, domination, colonies, war. Old powers are waning, new ones rising. Same story, different characters—rich countries plundering poor ones. Yesterday, it was Europe and America, today it's India and China. Maybe tomorrow it'll be Africa. Will there be a tomorrow? Perhaps it's too late to ask, but hope has little to do with reason. . . . Can we expect that an alternative to what looks like certain death for the planet will come from the imagination that has brought about this crisis in the first place? It seems unlikely. The alternative, if there is one, will emerge from the places and the people who have resisted the hegemonic impulse of capitalism and imperialism instead of being coopted by it."

27. Ibid.

28. "World house" is Martin Luther King's phrase for an ecumenical and interfaith notion of the world. See Martin Luther King Jr., "The World House," *Where Do We Go from Here: Chaos or Community?* (Boston: Beacon Press, 1968), 167. "This is the great new problem of mankind," King writes. "We have inherited a large house, a great 'world house' in which we have to live together—black and white, Easterner and Westerner, Gentile and Jew, Catholic and Protestant, Moslem and Hindu—a family unduly separated in ideas, culture and interest, who, because we can never again live apart, must learn somehow to live with each other in peace."

29. The notion of the economy of God is a continuing motif in the Eastern Orthodox tradition of Christianity. See, e.g., Fr. John Chryssavgis, ed., *Cosmic Grace, Humble Prayer: The Ecological Vision of the Green Patriarch Bartholomew I* (Grand Rapids, MI: Eerdmans, 2003); note especially "Divine Economy and Human Ecology," 141–42. Protestant liberal and evangelical traditions also utilize the theme. See M. Douglas Meeks, *God the Economist: The Doctrine of God and the Political Economy* (Augsburg: Fortress, 1989); and Jonathan Wilson-Hargrove, *God's Economy: Redefining the Health and Wealth Gospel* (Grand Rapids, MI: Zondervan Press, 2009).

30. See Daniel Bell, *The Cultural Contradictions of Capitalism* (New York: Basic Books, 1976), the last chapter.

31. The dedication of Thomas Berry, *The Great Work: Our Way into the Future* (New York: Bell Tower, 1999). Italics mine.

32. Plato, *The Republic*, 2nd rev. ed. (Baltimore: Penguin Books, 1974), 107.

33. Ibid., 108.

34. The Glaucon example draws from Birch and Rasmussen, *Bible and Ethics in the Christian Life*, 43.

35. Michael Sandel, *Justice: What's the Right Thing to Do?* (New York: Farrar, Straus & Giroux, 2009), 19.

36. Ibid., 34.

37. Michael Sandel, in "Competing American Traditions of Public Philosophy," *Ethics and International Affairs*, no. 20 (Fall 1997), (New York: Carnegie Council on Ethics and International Affairs Newsletter), 7.

38. Douglas Sturm, "Faith, Ecology, and the Demands of Social Justice: On Shattering the Boundaries of Moral Community," in *Religious Experience and Ecological Responsibility*, ed. Donald A. Crosby and Charley D. Hardwick, vol. 3 of *American Liberal Religious Thought* (New York: Peter Lang, 1996), 306.

39. Ibid., 307.

40. *The Animals' Lawsuit against Humanity: A Modern Adaptation of an Ancient Animal Rights Tale*, trans. and adapt. Rabbi Anson Laytner and Rabbi Dan Bridge, edited by Matthew Kaufmann, introduced by Seyyed Hossein Nasr, illustrated by Kulsum Begum (Louisville, KY: Fons Vitae Press, 2005), vii–viii.

41. Ibid., 7.

42. Ibid., 11.

43. Ibid., 10.

44. Ibid., 16–17.

45. Ibid., 16.

46. Ibid., 78.

47. "Hochmah" is Hebrew for "wisdom."

48. *The Animals' Lawsuit*, 78–81.

49. Ibid., xiii.

50. Ibid., xiii–xiv.

CHAPTER 6

1. Francis Fukuyama, "The Great Disruption: Human Nature and the Reconstitution of Social Order," *Atlantic Monthly* 283, no. 5 (May 1999): 59.

2. Diana Eck, *Encountering God: From Bozeman to Banaras* (Boston: Beacon Press, 1993), 203.

3. Howard Thurman, *The Search for Common Ground: An Inquiry into the Basis of Man's Experience of Community* (Richmond, IN: Friends United Press, 1986), 104.

4. Tibor Scitovsky, *The Joyless Economy: The Psychology of Human Satisfaction*, rev. ed. (New York: Oxford University Press, 1992).

5. Robert E. Lane, *The Loss of Happiness in Market Democracies* (New Haven and London: Yale University Press, 2000), selected from 319–24 and cited by James Gustave Speth. *The Bridge at the Edge of the World: Capitalism, the Environment, and Crossing from Crisis to Sustainability* (New Haven: Yale University Press, 2008), 135–36.

6. Readers can find detailed analyses of the "happiness literature" published since the 1970s, with references to the wisdom of the ages as well, in two volumes: Sissela Bok, *Exploring Happiness: From Aristotle to Brain Science* (New Haven: Yale University Press, 2011); and Derek Bok, *The Politics of Happiness: What Government*

Can Learn from the New Research on Well-Being (Princeton: Princeton University Press, 2011). Both are reviewed by Timothy Renick, "Pursuing Happiness," *Christian Century* 128, no. 1 (January 11, 2011): 22–26.

7. Ed Diener and Martin E. P. Seligman, "Beyond Money: Toward an Economy of Well-Being," *Psychological Science in the Public Interest* 5, no. 1 (2004): 18–19, as cited by Speth, *Bridge at the Edge of the World*, 135.

8. Michael Walzer, *Spheres of Justice* (New York: Basic Books, 1983), 31.

9. Martin Buber, *Paths in Utopia* (Boston: Beacon Press, 1958), 133.

10. Douglas Sturm, "Faith, Ecology, and the Demands of Social Justice: On Shattering the Boundaries of Moral Community," in Donald A. Crosby and Charley D. Hardwick, eds., *Religious Experience and Ecological Responsibility*, vol. 3 of *American Liberal Religious Thought*, 305.

11. Richard Rohr, "Why Does Psychology Always Win?" *Sojourners* 20 (November 1991): 14.

12. Michael Walzer, "The Idea of Civil Society," *Dissent* (Spring 1991): 293.

13. Adam Smith, *The Theory of Moral Sentiments*, ed. D. D. Raphael and A. L. Macfie (Oxford: Clarendon Press, 1976), 9.

14. Smith as cited in Alan Wolfe, *Whose Keeper? Social Science and Moral Obligation* (Berkeley, Los Angeles, and London: University of California Press, 1989), 29.

15. Adam Smith, *The Wealth of Nations* (New York: Modern Library, 1937), 14. The original was published in 1776.

16. Smith here is cited by Christopher Lasch, *The True and Only Heaven: Progress and Its Critics* (New York: W. W. Norton, 1991), 55. Lasch is citing *The Theory of Moral Sentiments* but he does not say where this phrase is found.

17. Smith as cited in Wolfe, *Whose Keeper?*, 29.

18. These pages draw heavily on my work in Larry Rasmussen, *Moral Fragments and Moral Community: A Proposal for Church in Society* (Minneapolis: Fortress Press, 1993), 41–45.

19. Mark Lilla, "The President and the Passions," in "The Way We Live Now," *New York Times Magazine*, December 19, 2010, 14.

20. Wolfe, *Whose Keeper?*, 30.

21. Ibid.,

22. Edward Ross, *Social Control: A Survey of the Foundations of Order*, 432, as cited by Thomas Bender, *Community and Social Change in America* (New Brunswick, NJ: Rutgers University Press, 1978), 35.

23. Maria Erling and Mark Granquist, *The Augustana Story* (Minneapolis: Fortress Press), 7.

24. Paraphrased from my *Moral Fragments and Moral Community*, 35.

25. Gary Becker, *The Economic Approach to Human Behavior* (Chicago: University of Chicago Press, 1976), passim.

26. Ibid. Again, I have drawn from my own discussion in *Moral Fragments and Moral Community*, 49–50.

27. See Michael J. Sandel, "What Isn't for Sale?," *Atlantic Monthly* 309, no. 3 (April 2012): 62–66.

28. All citations are from George W. Bush, "Second Inaugural Address," January 20, 2005, available from Inaugural Address of the Presidents, at Bartleby.com.

29. "The Rich and the Rest: A Special Report on the Global Elite," *Economist*, January 22–28, 2011, 7.

30. Joseph E. Stiglitz, "Of the 1%, by the 1%, for the 1%," *Vanity Fair*, April 14, 2011, 1–2 of the online version, available at http://www.vanityfair.com/society/features/2011/05/top-one-percent-201105.

31. Ibid.

32. "Rich and the Rest," 7.

33. Richard Wilkinson and Kate Pickett, *The Spirit Level: Why Greater Equality Makes Society Stronger* (New York: Bloomsbury Press, 2009), passim.

34. While I am using my discussion in *Moral Fragments and Moral Community*, 61–76, I draw from the argument of Herman E. Daly and John B. Cobb Jr. in their volume, *For the Common Good: Redirecting the Economy toward Community, the Environment, and a Sustainable Future* (Boston: Beacon Press, 1989).

35. F. A. Hayek, *The Road to Serfdom: Texts and Documents*, ed. Bruce Caldwell (Chicago: University of Chicago Press, 2007 [original 1944]), 48.

36. Ibid.

37. Octavio Paz, "Poetry and the Free Market," *New York Times Book Review*, December 8, 1991, sec. 7, 56.

38. Michael Sandel, "Competing American Traditions of Public Philosophy," *Ethics and International Affairs* 20 (Fall 1997): 7.

39. Ibid., 10.

40. Ibid., 8.

41. Ibid.

42. Alan Wolfe, *Whose Keeper?*, 189. I have drawn from Wolfe but also freely added to his list of what we learn in microcosm in close community.

43. This section on market and state draws heavily on my volume, *Moral Fragment and Moral Community*, 61–76.

44. Ronald Heifetz, *Leadership without Easy Answers* (Cambridge, MA: Belknap Press, 1994), 183. "Creative deviance on the front line" is the title of chap. 8.

45. I am drawing from my own summary of Ronald Heifetz, *Leadership without Easy Answers*, in Rasmussen, "Shaping Communities," *Practicing Our Faith: A Way of Life for a Searching People*, ed. Dorothy Bass (1st ed., San Francisco: Jossey-Bass, 1997; 2nd ed., 2009), 119–32.

46. See the Havel discussion at the beginning of chapter 4, "The Ethic We Need: Change and Imagination."

47. Again I draw from my own writing on Heifetz, *Leadership without Easy Answers* in Rasmussen, "Shaping Communities," *Practicing Our Faith*, 119–32.

48. This information has been gathered from the website of the Focolare Movement: http://www.focolare.us; and from Lorna Gold, "The Roots of the Focolare

Movement's Economic Ethic," *Journal of Markets and Morality* 6, no. 1 (Spring 2003): 1–14.

49. Michael Pollan, *The Omnivore's Dilemma: A Natural History of Four Meals* (New York: Penguin, 2008), 203.

50. Ibid., 138.

51. Ibid., 134.

52. Ibid., 140.

53. Ibid., 229.

54. I have drawn from and altered the text found in Rasmussen, *Moral Fragments and Moral Community*, 30.

CHAPTER 7

1. A chapter in René Dubos, *A God Within: A Positive Philosophy for a More Complete Fulfillment of Human Potentials* (New York: Charles Scribner's Sons, 1972), 153–74.

2. From Ian Morris, *Why the West Rules—For Now: The Patterns of History, and What They Reveal about the Future* (New York: Straus & Giroux, 2010), as cited by Orville Schell in his review of Morris, "The Final Conflict," *New York Times Book Review*, December 12, 2010, 19.

3. Dubos, *A God Within*, 153–54.

4. From "Little Gidding," in T. S. Eliot, *Four Quartets* (New York: Houghton Mifflin Harcourt, 1943), 63.

5. Daniel Maguire, *A Moral Creed for All Christians* (Minneapolis: Fortress Press, 2005), 4. Maguire is borrowing in part from biblical scholar Gerd Theissen,

6. Cited from Wes Jackson, *Consulting the Genius of the Place*, 103. Jackson notes that "The Epic of Gilgamesh" can be found in several places and cites as one example *World Mythology: An Anthology of the Great Myths and Epics*. He does not cite a page number.

7. Plato, *The Timaeus and Critias of Plato*, trans. Thomas Taylor (New York: Kessinger, 2003), 235–36. For a discussion of this passage as related to trees, see Larry Rasmussen, "Or Bare Ruined Choirs," in *Earth Community, Earth Ethics*, 212–17.

8. Cited from Jackson, *Consulting the Genius of the Place*, 104.

9. Ibid., 106–7.

10. Reported by Jackson, ibid., 105.

11. Ibid., 130.

12. Aldo Leopold, *A Sand County Almanac* (New York: Ballantine, 1966), 258.

13. This section uses an address I gave at the Festival of Faiths, Louisville, Kentucky, in November 2010. The theme for this ten-day event was "Sacred Soil." Its Honorary Co-Chairs were Wes Jackson and Wendell Berry.

14. Cited by Robert Pogue Harrison. *Gardens: An Essay on the Human Condition* (Chicago: University of Chicago Press, 2008), 63. Harrison is citing from Plato, *Phaedrus and Letters VII and VIII*, trans. Walter Hamilton (New York: Penguin, 1986), 99.

15. Paraphrased from Harrison, *Gardens*, 63–64.

16. I am grateful to Christopher Chapple for his discussion in his paper, "Jainism, Life, and Environmental Ethics," presented at the Yale "Journey of the Universe" Conference, March 2011. Chapple's citations from the *Acaranga Sutras* that I have used are taken from Herman Jacobi, trans. *Jaina Sutras, Part One* (Oxford: Clarendon Press, 1884), 8, 19.

17. Sutra 13:5 in the chapter, "Thunder," *The Koran* (New York: Penguin Classics, 1990), 171.

18. As cited from *The Meaning of the Noble Koran*, available online at www.pdf-Koran.com.

19. Martin Luther, "That These Words of Christ, 'This Is My Body,' etc. Still Stand Firm against the Fanatics," *Luther's Works*, vol. 37 (Minneapolis: Augsburg Fortress, 1986), 57.

20. Martin Luther, "Confession Concerning Christ's Supper," in Martin Luther, "The Sacrament of the Body and Blood of Christ—Against the Fanatics," in *Martin Luther's Basic Theological Writings*, ed. Timothy Lull (Minneapolis: Augsburg Fortress, 2005), 323.

21. Martin Luther, *Lectures on Genesis*, ed. Jaroslav Pelikan (St. Louis: Concordia, 1958), 1:52.

22. Luther, "Sacrament of the Body and Blood of Christ," 323.

23. Theodore Hiebert, *The Yahwist's Landscape: Nature and Religion in Early Israel* (New York: Oxford University Press, 1996), 158.

24. Wendell Berry, *Home Economics*, as cited by Theodore Hiebert, *The Yahwist's Landscape: Nature and Religion in Early Israel* (New York: Oxford University Press, 1996), 62.

25. The discussion of Luther is from Larry Rasmussen, "Luther and a Gospel of Earth," *Union Seminary Quarterly Review* 51, nos. 1–2 (1997): 1–28.

26. William Bryant Logan's subtitle for his book, *Dirt: The Ecstatic Skin of the Earth* (New York: W. W. Norton, 1995).

27. Dillard, *Pilgrim at Tinker Creek*, 96.

28. Logan, *Dirt*, 123.

29. Ibid., 125.

30. Rainer Maria Rilke, Sonnet 12, *The Sonnets to Orpheus: First Series*, trans. A. Poulin Jr., in *Duino Elegies and the Sonnets to Orpheus* (New York: Mariner, 2007), emphasis in the original.

31. Chief Luther Standing Bear, cited from Native American Wisdom, www.sapphyr.net.

32. This is taken from the permanent exhibit of the Museum of Northern Arizona, Flagstaff, Arizona.

33. J. M. Ledgard's "Revolution from Within," *New York Times Book Review*, Feb. 13, 2011, 16, a review of Nelson Mandela, *Conversations with Myself*, David James Smith, *Young Mandela*, and Richard Stengel, *Mandela's Way*.

34. Logan, *Dirt*, 125. Logan doesn't supply the source in Hartman.

35. Harrison, *Gardens*, 33.

36. Ibid., 33–34.

37. As cited by Wes Jackson, *Consulting the Genius of the Place*, 59.

38. Ibid., 59.

39. Maya Angelou, *A Brave and Startling Truth* (New York: Random House, 1995), n.p.

40. Bill McKibben, *Eaarth*, 25.

41. An allusion to Genesis 2:9.

42. See the chapter, "Fratricide and Ecocide: Rereading Genesis 2–4," by Brigitte Kahl, in *Earth Habitat: Eco-Injustice and the Church's Response*, ed. Dieter Hessel and Larry Rasmussen (Minneapolis: Fortress Press, 2001), 53–68.

43. Jackson, *Consulting the Genius of the Place*, 75.

44. Sutra 11:23, the *Qu'ran*.

45. Harrison, *Gardens*, 37.

46. Commission for Racial Justice, *Toxic Wastes and Race in the United States* (New York: United Church of Christ, 1987).

47. "Principles of Environmental Justice," adopted at the First National People of Color Environmental Leadership Summit on October 27, 1991, Washington, D.C.

48. This account of the EJ movement draws heavily from my chapter, "Resisting Eco-Injustice, Watering the Garden," in *Resist! Christian Dissent for the 21st Century*, ed. Michael G. Long (Maryknoll, NY: Orbis Books, 2008), 127–30.

49. Margaret Mead, in her Earth Day address to the United Nations, March 22, 1977, as cited by Louise Jones in *Environmentally Responsible Design: Green and Sustained Design* (Hoboken, NJ: John Wiley, 2008), 65. Also available online at http://www.earthsite.org/mead77.htm.

50. Alexei Torres-Fleming, Presentation in the Series on Environmental Racism, Union Theological Seminary, September 17, 2002.

51. The phrase and example are taken from Berry, *The Great Work*, 2.

52. Words used freely from Psalm 80:5.

53. For an account in the literature of environmental justice that does make the proper connections, see Cone, "Whose Earth Is It, Anyway?," in *Earth Habitat: Eco-Injustice and the Church's Response*, ed. Dieter Hessel and Larry Rasmussen (Minneapolis: Fortress Press, 2001), 23–32.

54. This citation, as much of the discussion here about omitted themes, is from "Ecopsychology and the Deconstruction of Whiteness: An Interview with Carl Anthony," in *Ecopsychology: Restoring the Earth, Healing the Mind*, ed. Theodore Roszak, Mary E. Gomes, and Allen D. Kanner (San Francisco: Sierra Club Books, 1995), 263–78. The citation is from 266.

55. Ibid., 266.

56. Ibid., 263–78.

57. Mary Midgeley, "Duties Concerning Islands," in *Environmental Ethics*, ed. Robert Elliot (New York: Oxford University Press, 1995), 97.

58. Ibid.

59. All three quotations are from the Preamble of *The Earth Charter*. The full text is available in many places. For the text as well as numerous activities related to the Charter, see www.earthcharter.org.

60. These phrases are taken from the seventeen Principles of Environmental Justice.

61. See Andrew Dobson's contrast of "environmentalism" and "ecologism" in his *Green Political Thought*, 3rd ed. (New York: Routledge, 2000), 2.

62. This phrase is the subtitle of an impressive case made by Thad Williamson, David Imbroscio, and Gar Alperowitz in *Making a Place for Community: Local Democracy in a Global Era* (New York: Routledge, 2002).

63. See the case made by Jeffrey Stout, *Blessed Are the Organized: Grassroots Democracy in America* (Princeton: Princeton University Press, 2010). See also Alastair McIntosh, *Soil and Soul: People versus Corporate Power* (London: Aurum Press, 2001).

64. Karl Marx, *The Economic and Philosophic Manuscripts of 1844*, trans. Martin Milligan and ed. Dirk J. Struik (New York: International Publishers, 1964), 112.

65. J. R. McNeill, *Something New under the Sun: An Environmental History of the Twentieth-Century World* (New York: W. W. Norton, 2000).

66. This discussion is indebted to the article by Peter Singer, "Navigating the Ethics of Globalization," in *The Chronicle of Higher Education*, October 11, 2002, n.p.: http://chronicle.com/article/Navigating-the-Ethics-of/28293.

67. Karl Marx, *Capital: A Critique of Political Economy*, in *Karl Marx: A Reader*, ed. Jon Elster (Cambridge: Cambridge University Press, 1986), 1:507.

68. Engels, "Outlines of a Critique of Political Economy," in Marx, *The Economic and Philosophic Manuscripts of 1844*, 210.

69. All citations are from Richard Lewontin, "Genes in the Food!," *New York Review of Books* 48, no. 10, 84.

70. E. O. Wilson, *Consilience: The Unity of Knowledge* (New York: Knopf, 1998), 297–98.

71. This coupling is taken from Cynthia Moe-Lobeda, "Christian Ethics toward Earth-honoring Faiths," in *The Union Seminary Quarterly Review: Festschrift for Larry L. Rasmussen*, ed. Daniel Spencer and James Martin-Schramm, vol. 58, nos. 1–2 (2004): 135.

72. As reported by Andrew Dobson, *Justice and the Environment: Conceptions of Environmental Sustainability and the Dimensions of Social Justice* (London and New York: Oxford University Press, 1998), 24.

73. Robert D. Bullard, "Decision Making," in Laura Westra and Bill E. Lawson, *Faces of Environmental Racism: Confronting Issues of Global Justice*, 2nd ed. (New York: Rowman & Littlefield, 2001), 4–9.

74. Ibid., 23.

75. See Dobson's *Justice and the Environment*. While the entire volume is concerned with these questions, Part II is the guide for the discussion: "Three Conceptions of Environmental Sustainability" and "The Dimensions of Social Justice, " 33–86.

76. Willis Jenkins, *Ecologies of Grace: Environmental Ethics and Christian Theology* (Oxford and New York: Oxford University Press, 2008), 63. This discussion and the pointer to Jenkins are courtesy of Richard R. Bohannon II and Kevin J. O'Brien, chap. 9, "Saving the World (and the People in It, Too)," in *Inherited Land: The Changing Grounds of Religion and Ecology*, ed. Whitney A. Bauman, Richard R. Bohannon II, and Kevin J. O'Brien (Eugene, OR: Pickwick, 2011), 181–84.

77. See this chapter, above.

78. H. Richard Niebuhr, *The Purpose of the Church and Its Ministry: Reflections on the Aims of Theological Education* (New York: Harper & Row, 1956), 38.

79. Reported in Shridath Ramphal, *Our Country, the Planet: Forging a Partnership for Survival* (Washington, DC: Island Press, 1992), 211.

80. The reference is to the discussion in chapter 1.

81. Barbara Brown Taylor, *Leaving Church: A Memoir of Faith* (New York: HarperSan-Francisco, 2006), 22, as cited by William P. Brown, *The Seven Pillars of Creation: The Bible, Science, and the Ecology of Wonder* (New York: Oxford University Press, 2010), 79.

82. For the questions raised in these paragraphs I have drawn on the work of Nancie Erhard, "To Love the Earth Fiercely," in *The Union Seminary Quarterly Review: Festschrift for Larry L. Rasmussen*, ed. Daniel Spencer and James Martin-Schramm, vol. 58, nos. 1–2 (2004): 120–31; and that of Cynthia Moe-Lobeda, "Christian Ethics toward Earth-honoring Faiths," in the same volume, 132–50.

83. Aldo Leopold was keenly aware that the "land ethic" he proposed in 1949 entailed new habits of heart and mind: "No important change in ethics was ever accomplished without an internal change in our intellectual emphasis, loyalties, affections, and convictions." From Leopold, "The Land Ethic," in *A Sand County Almanac* (New York: Ballantine, 1966), 246. *A Sand County Almanac* was initially published by Oxford University Press in 1949.

INTERLUDE

1. The epigraph is from a traditional bluegrass gospel song, "As I Went Down to the River to Pray."

2. This paragraph and the next draw from materials in Rasmussen, *Earth Community, Earth Ethics*, 177–79.

3. Harrison, *Gardens*, 81–82.

4. Harrison, *Gardens*, 162, citing 165 of Calvino's *Invisible Cities*.

5. "From the Editors," *Orion: Nature/Culture/Place*, January/February 2011, 1.

6. Ibid.

7. An aside: Earth-honoring faith shouldn't even *try* for one religion for all people. The plains of history are littered with the corpses of only-one-way religion; one, and only one, true faith. Ironically, this faith is unfaithful. The gracious and all-merciful God is a spacious God while one-way faith is neither gracious and spacious nor merciful.

8. Meyers, *Saving Jesus from the Church*, 15.

9. Ibid., 11.

10. John Howard Yoder, *Body Politics: Five Practices of the Christian Community before the Watching World* (Harrisonburg, VA: Herald Press, 2001), ix, 2.

11. I have used these in my chapter, "Shaping Communities," in Bass, ed., *Practicing our Faith*, 128. Most in this list reflect the influence of John Howard Yoder.

12. Dag Hammarskjold, *Markings* (New York: Alfred Knopf, 1964), 205.

13. I use a familiar citation of Dietrich Bonhoeffer's sentence. The new translation in Bonhoeffer's *Discipleship*, DBWE 4:87, is "Whenever Christ calls us, his call leads us to death."

14. *United Church of Santa Fe Whole Earth Covenant*, United Church of Santa Fe, n.p.

15. Many of these, including "singing our lives," "saying Yes and saying No," "testimony," "honoring the body," and "forgiveness," are taken from Bass, *Practicing Our Faith*.

CHAPTER 8

1. The poet of the quote in the epigraph is Katharine Lee Bates, 1850–1929. The daughter of a Congregational minister and a professor of English at Wellesley College, she penned the four stanzas of *America the Beautiful* atop Pike's Peak at the end of a hike up the 14,000-foot-high mountain. The preceding phrase, "God mend thine every flaw," is also in the ascetic tradition.

2. Cited from Paul Briens, Mary Gallway, Douglas Hughes, Azfar Hussain, Richard Law, Michael Myers, Michael Neville, Roger Schlesinger, Alice Spitzer, and Susan Swan, eds., *Reading about the World*, 3rd ed. (Fort Worth, TX: Harcourt College, 1999), 2:127.

3. Ibid.

4. Derrick Jensen, "The Tyranny of Entitlement," *Orion* (January/February 2011): 10.

5. An example of reborn asceticism in the United States is "The New Monasticism Project." Its twelve marks are: (1) Relocation to the abandoned places of Empire; (2) Sharing economic resources with fellow community members and the needy; (3) Hospitality to the stranger; (4) Lament for racial divisions within the church and our communities combined with the active pursuit of a just reconciliation; (5) Humble submission to Christ's body, the church; (6) Intentional formation in the way of Christ and the rule of the community (along the lines of the old novitiate); (7) Nurturing common life among members of intentional community; (8) Support for celibate singles alongside monogamous married couples

and their children; (9) Geographical proximity to community members who share a common rule of life; (10) Care for the plot of God's earth given to us along with support of our local economies; (11) Peacemaking in the midst of violence and conflict resolution within communities along the lines of Matthew 18; (12) Commitment to a disciplined contemplative life. Information is available at http://www.newmonasticism.org. One instance of the new monasticism is an intentional community in Camden, New Jersey, that combines elements of Benedictine and Mennonite asceticism in ways appropriate to the conditions and needs of Camden.

6. Cited from Walter Goodman, "God and Politics: Nothing New under the American Sun," *New York Times*, Week in Review, September 10, 2000, 4.

7. Kevin Phillips, in *American Theocracy: The Perils and Politics of Radical Religion, Oil, and Borrowed Money in the 21st Century* (New York: Viking Penguin, 2006), argues that the pursuit of oil after World War II has been one of the defining elements of U.S. policy in the world. He calls it a kind of "petro-imperialism, the key aspect of which is the U.S. military's transformation into a global oil-protection force," which "puts up a democratic façade, emphasizes freedom of the seas (or pipeline routes) and seeks to secure, protect, drill and ship oil, not administer everyday affairs." As cited by Alan Brinkley in his review of Phillips, *New York Times Magazine*, March 19, 2006, 10. My response is somewhat different and broader, although it includes oil together with other energy sources. It is that the keys to U.S. policy since the boom following World War II are the exacting requirements of U.S. affluence, now regarded as the American way of life itself.

8. Cited from George F. Will's review of Brink Lindsey, *The Age of Abundance: How Prosperity Transformed America's Politics and Culture* (New York: Collins/HarperCollins, 2007), in *New York Times Book Review*, June 10, 2007, 16.

9. Morgenthau's address is cited from U.S. Department of State, *Proceedings and Documents of the United Nations Monetary and Financial Conference, Bretton Woods, New Hampshire, July 1–22, 1944*, 1:790. I am indebted to Daniel Maguire in his "Whom the Gods Would Destroy, They First Make Myopic," *Union Seminary Quarterly Review* 63, nos. 1–2 (2006): 73–74, for pointing to Morgenthau's address.

10. Bill McKibben, *Eaarth*, 211.

11. These are Rostow's phrases in chap. 2, where he introduces all five in summary fashion: Walter Rostow, *The Stages of Economic Growth: A Non-Community Manifesto* (Cambridge: Cambridge University Press, 1960).

12. J. R. McNeill, *Something New under the Sun*, xv–xvi.

13. See the section "Earth Movers," in ibid., 30–49.

14. Allen T. Durning, *How Much Is Enough?* (London: Earthscan, 1992), 38.

15. The *Life* essay and Twentieth Century Fund study are cited by Lizabeth Cohen in "A Consumers' Republic: The Politics of Mass Consumption in Postwar America,"

Miller Center Report, a Publication of the Miller Center of Public Affairs, University of Virginia 19, no. 1 (Winter 2003): 6.

16 *Handbook for Newlyweds* is cited by Cohen, "A Consumer's Republic," 7, as are the titles by Nathan and Bowles mentioned above.

17. "China, New Land of Shoppers, Builds Malls on Gigantic Scale," *New York Times*, May 25, 2005, A1, C7.

18. Ibid., A1.

19. Ibid., A1, C7.

20. Cited from George W. Will's review of Brink Lindsey's *The Age of Abundance* in *New York Times Book Review*, June 10, 2007,16.

21. Cited from William Leach, *Land of Desire* (New York: Vintage, 1993), 348.

22. Robert Pogue Harrison, *Gardens*, 82.

23. Max Weber, *The Protestant Ethic and the Spirit of Capitalism* (New York: Charles Scribner's Sons, 1958), 182. The original was published in German in 1904. "Specialists without spirit, sensualists without heart; this nullity imagines that it has attained a level of civilization never before achieved" is itself a quotation in Weber's text. He does not cite its source.

24. Ibid., 181–82. The emphasis is mine, made in order to connect Weber's description ("mechanical foundations") to the earlier discussion of the economy's systemic requirement of materialist consumption.

25. Ibid., 181. "Like a light cloak, which can be thrown aside at any moment" is a quotation Weber takes from *Saints' Everlasting Rest*, chap. xii, by the prominent seventeenth-century Puritan divine, Richard Baxter.

26. Explanations for the rise of what becomes mass affluence are many and Weber's thesis of a certain mix of Protestant inner-worldly asceticism and early capitalism has been vigorously challenged and debated. Of recent note among economic historians is the work of Gregory Clark of the University of California at Davis. While he does not concur with Weber, and takes issue with both those who argue the lead role of institutions-channeling-behavior as well as those who, like Jared Diamond in *Guns, Germs, and Steel*, argue the advantage of those who gained immunity to crucial pandemic diseases at the same time that they domesticated productive animals and wild grains, Clark's own tentative conclusions are akin to Weber's in a key respect. A Malthusian trap was in place from 1200 to 1800, he contends, along with many others. That is, "each time new technology increased the efficiency of production a little, the population grew, the extra mouths ate up the surplus, and average income fell back to its former level." Breaking out of this cycle came about in no small part because of an increase in people's preference for saving over consumption. His explanation for this is a certain ethic and way of life that came to prevail; or, if not prevail, at least gain sufficient mass that many escaped the Malthusian trap. Clark's summary is this: "Thrift, prudence, negotiation and hard work were becoming values for communities that previously had

been spendthrift, impulsive, violent and leisure loving." What is intriguing is Clark's findings about these particular communities as he reads wills, tracks interest rates and literacy rates, and so on. The key communities are those of the relatively well-off. Because wealthier people then had large families, with more children than poor families, downward mobility came about as the children of the well-off sought to make their own way in a world that had relatively few slots in the ranks of the rich. Clark contends that this population generated the ethic decisive to the rise of capitalism and the Industrial Revolution. While in contrast to Weber (he does not direct his attention to the religious-moral impulses of ascetic Protestants) his conclusions about the critical place of a change in human behavior in accord with a guiding ethic of hard work, thrift, prudence, deferred gratification, nonviolence, and restraint are strikingly similar. Moreover, what is still needed for the Clark thesis is attention to populations Weber cited but Clark does not, at least to date: namely, those who embraced this ethic but who were not the downwardly mobile from the ranks of the well-off. Weber, for example, cites the early Methodists, who were typically poor workers in mining regions, just as he cites the carriers of the Radical Reformation, who were rural and small-town people long accustomed to poverty. See the report on Clark's work in the Science Times section of the *New York Times*, August 7, 2007, D1, D4.

27. Weber, *Protestant Ethic*, 181.
28. Wendell Berry, *Life Is a Miracle* (Washington, DC: Counterpoint Press, 2000), Dedication Page.
29. Robin R. Meyers, *Saving Jesus from the Church*, 200.
30. Address of Ecumenical Patriarch Bartholomew, Symposium on the Sacredness of the Environment, Santa Barbara, California, Final Delivery Text, 4–6.
31. "Ascesis and Consumption," in Fr. John Chryssavgis, ed., *Cosmic Grace, Humble Prayer*, 197.
32. Another text of the Ecumenical Patriarch also treats the meaning of asceticism. See His All Holiness Ecumenical Patriarch Bartholomew, *Encountering the Mystery* (New York: Doubleday, 2008), 100–103.
33. From Harrison, *Gardens*, 82.
34. The phrases are from the hymn attributed to St. Patrick, "I Bind unto Myself Today," stanza 2, as cited from #188 in *The Lutheran Book of Worship*.
35. Cited by Philip Rousseau in *Pachomius: The Making of a Community in Fourth-Century Egypt* (Berkeley: University of California Press, 1975), 11–12.
36. From the script of Richard Attenborough's *Gandhi*, the movie. See www.scribd.com/doc/45864526/Gandhi.
37. "Wonder and Restraint: A Rabbinic Call to Environmental Action." The editor is Lawrence Bush, editor of *Jewish Currents*, as well as editor of *Reconstructionist Today* (Accord, New York). The text is available online at: http://www.coejl.org/

about/rabbinicletter_revfin.pdf. The citations above are from p. 1. All the bolded, italicized text cited in my discussion is in the original.

38. Ibid., 2.

39. Ibid., 3.

40. Ibid., 4.

41. Ibid., 4–5.

42. From the Introduction in Chryssavgis, *Cosmic Grace and Humble Prayer*, 31.

43. Portions of this essay, especially the sections on Ecumenical Patriarch Bartholomew and the ascetic ethic, are a reworking and amendation of an article done for *DIALOG: A Journal of Theology*. That article addresses other traditions as well as asceticism: sacramentalism, mysticism, and prophetic-liberative practices. See Larry Rasmussen, "Drilling in the Cathedral," *DIALOG: A Journal of Theology* 42, no. 3 (Fall 2003): 202–25. An earlier version of this essay as a whole was published in *Crosscurrents* 57, no. 4. The issue, dedicated to "Asceticism Today," includes my essay, "Earth-Honoring Asceticism and Consumerism," 498–513. Used with permission.

CHAPTER 9

1. The epigraph is from Simone Weil, *Waiting for God* (New York: G. P. Putnam's Sons, 1951), 101. The Momaday citation is taken from Hendrik Hertzberg, "The Talk of the Town," *New Yorker*, March 17, 2003, 68.

2. The Antarctica contingent consisted of fifty scientists at the McMurdo Station on the Ross Sea.

3. The phrase is Alan Paton's, about South Africa under apartheid, in *Cry the Beloved Country*. Shridath Ramphal makes the connection between country and planet explicit in his book, *Our Country, The Planet: Forging a Partnership for Survival* (Washington, DC: 1992). The book is dedicated to the memory of Barbara Ward and Rene Dubos and "to all who continue their mission for Our Country, The Planet."

4. Fyodor Dostoyevsky, *The Brothers Karamazov*, trans. Richard Pevear and Larissa Volokhonsky (New York: Alfred A. Knopf, The Everyman Library, 1927), 362.

5. Fineberg as cited by Thomas Friedman, "Drilling in the Cathedral," *New York Times*, March 2, 2003, A23.

6. Ibid.

7. Ibid.

8. "Saving Souls and Salmon," *New York Times Week in Review*, October 22, 2000, 5.

9. Ibid.

10. Therese DeLisio, *Stretching the Sacramental Imagination in Sacramental Theology, Liturgy, and Life: A Trinitarian Proposal for a Cosmologically Conscious Age*, Ph.D. thesis, Union Theological Seminary, New York, 2007, 13. DeLisio's focus is the Triune God of Christianity. I have taken the liberty of extending her statement to all notions of divine presence.

11. Ibid., 226.

12. Ibid., 230.

13. Ibid., 233. DeLisio is drawing on the discussion of symbols in the work of Karl Rahner and Paul Tillich.

14. "Saving Souls and Salmon," *New York Times Week in Review*, October 22, 2000, 5.

15. Cited from Vandana Shiva, *Biopiracy: The Plunder of Nature and Knowledge* (Toronto: Between the Lines Press, 1997), 1. Shiva is citing the bull's text from Walter Ullmann's *Medieval Papalism: The Political Theories of the Medieval Papalists*, published in 1949.

16. The phrase was made popular by Arthur Lovejoy, *The Great Chain of Being* (New Brunswick: Transaction Press, 2009; original publication by Harvard University Press, 1936).

17. Tractate Shabbat 77b. Available at http://halakhah.com/pdf/moed/Shabbath.pdf.

18. Alfred W. Crosby, *The Columbian Exchange* (Westport, CT: Greenwood Press, 1974), 12.

19. Cited by Bob Herbert, "Looking Back at an Ugly Time," *New York Times*, February 24, 2003, A17. The influence of Buckley's "Great Chain" Catholicism is found in much of his writing. See, for example, his *God and Man at Yale: The Superstitions of "Academic Freedom"* (Chicago: Regnarey/Gateway, 1977).

20. This summary, taken from Ian Barbour, is discussed extensively by Dieter Hessel in "The Church Ecologically Reformed," in *Earth Habitat: Eco-Injustice and the Church's Response*, ed. Dieter Hessel and Larry L. Rasmussen (Minneapolis: Fortress Press, 2001), 185–206.

21. While the web-of-life image is a recent one for much Christianity, such as the Catholicism discussed here, in some quarters it is an ancient tradition. Celtic Christianity of the fourth through sixth centuries c.e. developed beyond the boundaries of neo-Platonic Roman Christianity and practiced a web-of-life rather than a chain-of-being faith.

22. U.S. Catholic Bishops, *Renewing the Earth—An Invitation to Reflection and Action in Light of Catholic Social Teaching* (Washington, DC: U.S. Catholic Conference, November 14, 1991), I. A. Aims of This Statement, 2. John Hart's *What Are They Saying about Environmental Theology?* (Costa Mesa, CA: Paulist Press, 2004) is a detailed guide to Roman Catholic social teaching on the environment. I have drawn upon Hart's work here.

23. U.S. Catholic Bishops, *Renewing the Earth*, Signs of the Times, 1.

24. U.S. Catholic Bishops, *Renewing the Earth* III. D. Available online at http://www.usccb.org/sdwp/ejp/bishopsstatements.html.

25. Ibid., I. D.

26. Ibid., III. D.

27. Ibid. My thanks to Drew Christiansen, S.J., for pointing me to these passages in *Renewing the Earth*.

28. Ibrahim Abdul-Matin, *Green Deen: What Islam Teaches about Protecting the Planet* (San Francisco: Berrett-Koehler Publications, 2010), 1.

29. Reprinted from *The World We Have: A Buddhist Approach to Peace and Ecology* (2008) by Thich Nhat Hanh, with permission of Parallax Press, Berkeley, California, www.parallax.org., 97–98.

30. "Wonder and Restraint: A Rabbinic Call to Environmental Action." The editor is Lawrence Bush, editor of *Jewish Currents*, as well as editor of *Reconstructionist Today* (Accord, New York). The text is available online at: http://www.coejl.org/about/rabbinicletter_revfin.pdf. The citations above are from p. 1. All the bolded, italicized text cited in my discussion is in the original.

31. The address of His All Holiness Ecumenical Patriarch Bartholomew at the Environmental Symposium is available in Fr. John Chryssavgis, ed., *Cosmic Grace, Humble Prayer*. This citation is from 166 of the prepublication manuscript, courtesy of John Chryssavgis.

32. Annie Dillard, *Pilgrim at Tinker Creek: A Mystical Excursion into the Natural World* (New York: Bantam Books, 1975), 67. Another passage reads: "This, then, is the extravagant landscape of the world, given, given with pizzazz, given in good measure, pressed down, shaken together, and running over" (149).

33. Ecumenical Patriarch Bartholomew, "Our Indivisible Environment," *Wall Street Journal*, October 25, 2009, at http://online.wsj.com/article/SB10001424052748704500604574485341504345488.html.

34. This is a reference to the famous description by Max Weber at the conclusion of *The Protestant Ethic and the Spirit of Capitalism* and to which we will refer in the discussion below. We discussed it in part in chapter 8 "Asceticism and Consumerism."

35. Karl Marx and Friedrich Engels, *The Communist Manifesto* (New York: Norton Critical Edition, 2003; from the English edition edited by Friedrich Engels, 1888), 4.

36. "Forget the Food Chain—Think Food Web," *New Mexican*, February 28, 2011, A-1, A-4.

37. The work of two Roman Catholic priests, Pierre Teilhard de Chardin and Thomas Berry, is an effort to shift sacramental ethics from anthropocentrism to eco- and cosmo-centrism.

38. This discussion is indebted to DeLisio, *Stretching the Sacramental Imagination*, 5–8.

39. Jeffrey Stout, *Blessed Are the Organized*, 211.

40. Ibid., 211–12.

41. From what is commonly called simply *The Declaration of Independence*. The full title is: *In Congress, July 4, 1776, the Unanimous Declaration of the Thirteen United States of America*.

42. Stout, *Blessed Are the Organized*, 216–17.

43. Ibid., 217.

44. Ibid., 219.

45. Ibid.

46. Norman Wirzba, *Food and Faith: A Theology of Eating* (Cambridge: Cambridge University Press, 2011), 23.

47. Stout, *Blessed Are the Organized*, 220.

48. See the discussion in "The Ethic We Need: Community Matrix."

49. See the fine discussion of Peter G. Brown and Goeffrey Garver, working from Quaker perspectives, in *Right Relationship: Building a Whole Earth Economy* (San Francisco: Berrett-Koehler Publishers, 2009).

50. Albert Borgmann, *Technology and the Character of Contemporary Life* (Chicago and London: University of Chicago Press, 1984), 119. Borgmann has borrowed the Rebecca example from Daniel Boorstin.

51. Borgmann, *Technology and the Character of Contemporary Life*, 47.

52. The title of the book by Philip Slater, *The Pursuit of Loneliness: American Culture at the Breaking Point* (Boston: Beacon Press, 1970). Slater says that U.S. households find it perfectly normal to seek a private means of transportation, a private laundry, and self-service stores; moreover, when economically feasible, a private room for each of the kids, with a separate phone, stereo, and maybe TV. Then when there is a restless spirit or low-level depression, the answer is another gadget, fad, or diverting experience.

53. Stout, *Blessed are the Organized*, 225.

54. Cited from Thich Nhat Hanh, *World We Have*, 110.

55. Entries from *The New Oxford American Dictionary*, 2nd ed. (New York: USA Oxford University Press, 2005).

56. Emilie M. Townes, *Womanist Ethics and the Cultural Production of Evil* (New York: Palgrave Macmillan, 2006), 29, citing James Baldwin, "Too Many Thousands Gone," in *Notes of a Native Son* (Boston, MA: Beacon Press, 1955), 27.

57. Ibid., 36.

58. Ibid., 37.

59. Ibid., 39.

60. Ibid.

61. Ibid.

62. Ibid., 55.

63. Karl Marx, *Capital*, in *Karl Marx: A Reader*, ed. Jon Elster (Cambridge: Cambridge University Press, 1986), 63.

64. From St. Francis's *Canticle of the Sun*.

65. E. O. Wilson in *The Future of Life* (New York: Knopf, 2002), p. 1 of chap. 1, "To the Ends of Earth": "Water is the deciding element on planet earth. It may be no more than a transient film on grains of sand, it may never see sunlight, it may be boiling hot or super cooled, but there will be some kind of organism living in or upon it."

66. Heather Eaton, "Reflections on Water: Ecological, Political, Economic, and Theological," n.p., available at http://www.nccecojustice.org/downloads/water/Reflections_on_Water.pdf.

67. W. H. Auden, in the poem, "First Things First," from *Selected Poems*, W. H. Auden, author, and Edward Mendelsohn, ed., expanded 2nd ed. (New York: Random House, 2007), 245.

68. Marilynne Robinson, *Gilead* (New York: Farrar Straus Giroux, 2004), 63.

69 http://ep.yimg.com/ca/I/skyimage_2065_43429339.

70. An interview with Seth Shostak in "Take Us to Your Water," *Good* (Summer 2009): 83.

71. Eaton, "Reflections on Water: Ecological," n.p

72. Brian Swimme, interview in *The Awakening Universe*, a film by Neal Rogin, available at www.AwakeningUniverse.com.

73. John Johnson, "Spatial Delivery," in *The New Mexican*, June 6, 2009, D1–2.

74. Eaton, "Reflections on Water," n.p.

75. Stout, cited earlier, from *Blessed Are the Organized*, 211.

76. DeLisio, *Stretching the Sacramental Imagination*, 230.

77. The quotations as well as the words in parens in the Qur'an text are those of Ibrahim Abdul-Matin in *Green Deen*, 134–35.

78. Ibrahim Abdul-Matin in *Green Deen*, 136–39.

79. Information from Water in Religion, available at http://www.africanwater.org and from "Teaching Religion in Schools," available at http://www.brighthub.com/education/k-12.

80. Text made available to the author and other participants in the Blessing of the Waters at Ohkay Owingeh, 2009.

81. McNeill, *Something New Under the Sun*, 120.

82. Elizabeth Kolbert, "The Sixth Extinction?", *New Yorker*, May 25, 2009, 58.

83. Oxfam reports that 97 percent of all resource-related deaths take place in developing countries.

84 *The Living Planet Report 2008*, p. 10.

85. World Bank data cited by Lester R. Brown, "The New Geopolitics of Food," *Foreign Policy* (May–June 2011): 58.

86. "Water Footprint," *The Living Planet Report 2008*, 20–21. The water footprint is the total volume of water used by inhabitants to produce goods and services.

87. From "Water: A Global Innovation Outlook Report," n.p. This IBM-sponsored project is available on-line at: www.ibm.com/ibm/gio/water.html.

88. "Sine agua non," *The Economist*, April 11, 2009, 60.

89. William duBuys, *A Great Aridness: Climate Change and the Future of the American Southwest* (Oxford and New York: Oxford University Press, 2011), 60.

90. Taken from "Figure 1: Potential Tipping Points in Climate Systems," in Anthony Costello et al., "Managing the Health Effects of Climate Change," *Lancet* 373 (May 16, 2009), 1696.

91. "Study: Climate Change Threatens Key Crops," *New Mexican*, September 7, 2009, A-4. The citations are from David Walter Wolfe of Cornell University, commenting to the study by North Carolina University.

92. Some of this is because wealth commonly brings with it a shift from vegetarian to meaty diets, the latter much more water-intensive.

93. Thomas Berry, in many of his writings, one of which is *Evening Thoughts: Reflecting on Earth as Sacred Community* (San Francisco: Sierra Club Books, 2006), 19.

94. "Imagine a Water Pump so Remarkable It Quenches Poverty, Fear and Illiteracy," advertisement in the *New York Times*, July 23, 2007, n.p.

95. Eaton, "Reflections on Water," n.p.

96. I have been unable to find this in Niebuhr's writings.

97. *Global Innovation Outlook*, cover page, available at http://www.ibm.com/ibm/fio/water.html.

98. David Groenfeldt, "Reinventing Water Management," unpublished paper presented at the Third International Conference of the International Society for the Study of Religion, Nature, and Culture (ISSRNC), Amsterdam, July 23–26, 2009, 9. Used with permission.

99. Robinson, *Gilead*, 63.

CHAPTER 10

1. The first epigraph is from Albert Einstein, as quoted in Phillipp Frank, *Einstein: His Life and Times*, chap. 12, sec. 5 (1947), from Einstein's address, "The Merger of Spirit and Science." The second epigraph is from Dillard, *Pilgrim at Tinker Creek*, 145. The frontispiece of *Pilgrim at Tinker Creek*, "The Tree With Lights," is another mystical account of Dillard's that arrived abruptly. She excerpted it from a later passage in the book. "One day I was walking along Tinker Creek thinking of nothing at all and I saw the tree with the lights in it. I saw the backyard cedar where the mourning doves roost charged and transfigured, each cell buzzing with flame. I stood on the grass with the lights in it, grass that was wholly fire, utterly focused and utterly dreamed. It was less like seeing than like being for the first time seen, knocked breathless by a powerful glance. The flood of fire abated, but I'm still spending the power . . . I had been my whole life a bell, and never knew it until at that moment I was lifted and struck" (n.p.).

2. Dorothee Soelle, *The Silent Cry: Mysticism and Resistance* (Minneapolis: Fortress Press, 2001), 1.

3. From Simone Weil, *Waiting for God*, trans. Emma Craufurd (New York: G. P. Putnam's Sons, 1951), 127.

4. Roger Gottlieb, "The Transcendence of Justice and the Justice of Transcendence: Mysticism, Deep Ecology, and Political Life," *Journal of the American Academy of Religion* 67, no. 1 (March 1999): 150.

5. Ibid., 149.

6. Ibn 'Al-Arabī, *Futūbāt, I*, 31, cited in Ibn 'Al-Arabī, *The Bezels of Wisdom* (Mahwah, NJ: Paulist Press, 1980), 25.

7. Brian Thomas Swimme and Mary Evelyn Tucker, *Journey of the Universe* (New Haven: Yale University Press, 2011), 115.

8. Reprinted from *The World We Have: A Buddhist Approach to Peace and Ecology* (2008) by Thich Nhat Hanh, with permission of Parallax Press, Berkeley, California, www.parallax.org, 110.

9. The *gathas* are cited from Thich Nhat Hanh, *World We Have*, 106 and 111; the breathing exercise is from 53–55.

10. The image is from the Afghan poet Rumi, cited by Soelle in her Introduction: "Why, when God's world is so big, did you fall asleep in a prison of all places?" (*Silent Cry*, 1).

11. Dillard, *Pilgrim at Tinker Creek*, 35.

12. Janet Ruffing, R. S. M., ed., *Mysticism and Social Transformation* (Syracuse, NY: Syracuse University Press, 2001), xi. Emphasis in the original.

13. Simone Weil, *Two Moral Essays* (Wallingford, PA: Pendle Hill Publications, 1981), 5–6.

14. Ibid., 6.

15. Ibid.

16. Ibid., 7.

17. Ibid.

18. See her discussion in the essay, "Forms of the Implicit Love of God," the section on "The Love of Our Neighbor," in *Waiting for God*, 84–99.

19. Hildegard of Bingen, *The Book of Divine Works*, excerpts from the section, "The Source of All Being," in *Hildegard of Bingen: Mystical Writings*, ed. Fiona Bowie and Oliver Davies (New York: Crossroad, 1990), 91.

20. Black Elk, *Black Elk Speaks* (New York: Pocket Books, 1972), 15–16.

21. Weil, *Waiting for God*, 101.

22. Ibid., xxxiii of the Introduction, as cited by Leslie Fiedler.

23. Ibid., 104.

24. Weil, *Gravity and Grace*, trans. Arthur Wills with an introduction by Gustave Thibon (Lincoln: University of Nebraska Press, 1952), 142.

25. Fyodor Dostoyevsky, *The Brothers Karamazov*, trans. Richard Pevear and Larissa Volokhonsky (New York: Alfred A. Knopf, The Everyman Library, 1927), 318–19.

26. Ibid., 319–20.

27. Ibid., 322.

28. Ibid., 324.

29. Thomas Merton, *Conjectures of a Guilty Bystander*, (London: Sheldon Press, 1965), 153–154. 4th and Walnut is the intersection in Louisville, Kentucky, where Merton, a Trappist monk at nearby Gethsemene monastery, had this mystical vision.

30. The language is again that of Thomas Berry in *The Great Work: Our Way into the Future* (New York: Bell Tower, 1999).

31. Thich Nhat Hanh, *World We Have*, 99.

32. Ibid., 82.

33. Ibid., 81.
34. Ibid.
35. Ibid., 82.
36. Ibid., 41.
37. Ibid., 41–42.
38. René Descartes, *Discourse on the Method of Rightly Conducting the Reason, and Seeking Truth in the Sciences* (Chicago: Open Court Publishing Company, 1927), 33.
39. Ibid., 7–8.
40. Ibid., 10.
41. Ibid., 8.
42. Ibid., 10.
43. Ibid., 30.
44. Ibid., 33.
45. The reference is to Belden C. Lane's *The Solace of Fierce Landscapes: Exploring Desert and Mountain Spirituality* (New York: Oxford University Press, 1998).
46. Descartes, *Discourse on Method*, 35.
47. Ibid. Emphasis added.
48. Ibid., 35–36.
49. This is a strong theme in Russell Shorto, *Descartes' Bones: A Skeletal History of the Conflict between Faith and Reason* (New York: Doubleday, 2008).
50. James Miller, "Connecting Religion and Ecology," p. 8 of an unpublished paper. Cited with the author's permission.
51. James Miller, "Ecology, Aesthetics and Daoist Body Cultivation," p. 2 of an unpublished paper. Cited with the author's permission.
52. Cited from Robert Pogue Harrison, *Gardens: An Essay on the Human Condition* (Chicago: University of Chicago Press, 2008), 113. Harrison does not provide the page number in Descartes.
53. Bonhoeffer, *Ethics*, in *Dietrich Bonhoeffer Works, English Edition*, vol. 6 (Minneapolis: Fortress Press, 2005), *DBWE* 6:373. Bonhoeffer's criticism of the Enlightenment conception of ethics includes the following: "These assertions [Bonhoeffer's own conception of ethics] stand in stark contrast to the understanding of the ethical as a generally valid rational principle that entails the negation of everything concrete and specific to time and place. . . . Wherever the ethical is construed as apart from any determination by time and place, apart from the question of authorization, and apart from anything concrete, there life disintegrates into an infinite number of unrelated atoms of time, just as human community disintegrates into discrete atoms of reason" (373).
54. Harrison, *Gardens*, 113.
55. Gregory Bateson, *Steps to an Ecology of Mind* (New York: Random House, 1972), 472.
56. Descartes, *Discourse on Method*, 44.

57. Ibid., 41.

58. Immanuel Kant, "Duties to Animals and Spirits," in *Lectures on Ethics*, trans. Louis Infield (New York: Harper Torchbooks, 1963), 239.

59. Mab Segrest, *Born to Belonging: Writings on Spirit and Justice* (New Brunswick, NJ: Rutgers University Press, 2002), 12.

60. Karl Marx, *The Communist Manifesto*, intro. Stefan T. Possony (Chicago: Henry Regnery, 1954), 23.

61. Ibid., 227.

62. Ibid., 226.

63. A reference to the passage from *The Communist Manifesto* cited and commented upon in chapter 9, "The Sacred and the Commodified."

64. See Karl Marx, *The Economic and Philosophical Manuscripts of 1844*, in *Marx and Engels on Ecology*, ed. Howard L. Parsons (Westport, CT: Greenwood Press, 1977), 101–14.

65. Both this quotation and the one immediately preceding it are from *The Economic and Philosophical Manuscripts of 1844* as a selection in Howard L. Parsons, *Marx and Engels on Ecology* (Westport, CT: Greenwood Press, 1977). Parsons only gives the inclusive pages of the *Manuscripts*, however, and not the individual pagination of the original. In Parsons's compilation the latter sentence is on p. 215, the former on p. 217. The inclusive pages from the *Manuscripts* that Parsons has selected are 132–46.

66. See the fascinating paleoanthropological account of the human/other nature dialectic as creative of human being in Rick Potts, *Humanity's Descent: The Consequences of Ecological Instability* (New York: William Morrow, 1996).

67. Marx, *Economic and Philosophical Manuscripts*, as cited by Parsons, *Marx and Engels on Ecology*, 217.

68. Marx, in the Introduction to the *Grundrisse*, in Elster, *Karl Marx: A Reader*, 7.

69. Ibid., 48.

70. Ibid., 52.

71. This bare sketch of social bonds and what happens to them in capitalist society is described at great length by Marx in different volumes. See, among other places, the monumental work, *Capital*.

72. Marx, *Grundrisse*, in Parsons, *Marx and Engels on Ecology*, 410.

73. Karl Marx, *Capital*, as selected by Elster, *Karl Marx: A Reader*, 63.

74. Daniel Bell, *The Cultural Contradictions of Capitalism* (New York: Basic Books, 1976), 13.

75. From Marx, *Grundrisse*, in Elster, *Karl Marx: A Reader*, 53.

76. Max Weber, *The Protestant Ethic and the Spirit of Capitalism*, trans. Talcott Parsons (New York: Charles Scribner's Sons, 1958; original published in German 1904), 182.

77. From the above-noted introduction in Soelle's *The Silent Cry*, 1.

78. Marx, *Grundrisse* as selected by Elster, *Karl Marx: A Reader*, 53. The parallels between Marx's discussion in these pages and Weber's conclusions, cited in our

chapter 9, "The Sacred and the Commodified," about "specialists without spirit" and "sensualists without heart" who imagine "this nullity" the high point of "civilization" are fascinating, even though Weber is writing in conscious opposition to Marx.

79. Friedrich Engels, *Outlines of a Critique of Political Economy*, in Karl Marx, *Economic and Philosophic Manuscripts of 1844*, 210.

CHAPTER II

1. The Yom Kippur epigraph is taken from the Yom Kippur Concluding Service, *The Gates of Repentance*, 498. The phrase "an unquenchable ontological thirst" is cited from Mircea Eliade, *The Sacred and the Profane: The Nature of Religion* (New York: Harper Torchbooks, 1959), 4, by James Cone in *The Cross and the Lynching Tree* (Maryknoll, NY: Orbis Books, 2011), 3. Cone's full sentence is: "Both the cross and the lynching tree represented the worst in human beings and at the same time 'an unquenchable ontological thirst' for life that refuses to let the worst determine our final meaning." This thirst for life that refuses to let the worst determine the final meaning holds for the prophets.

2. See James Cone, *Risks of Faith: The Emergence of a Black Theology of Liberation* (Boston: Beacon Press, 1999), xvi–vii. "It is one thing to think of Martin King as a civil rights activist who transformed America's race relations and quite another to regard the struggle for racial justice as having theological significance. . . . While he never regarded himself as an academic theologian, he transformed our understanding of the Christian faith by making the practice of justice an essential ingredient of its identity. . . . It could be argued that Martin King's contribution to the identity of Christianity in America and the world was as far-reaching as Augustine's in the fifth century and Luther's in the fourteenth. Before King, no Christian theologian showed so conclusively in his actions and words the great contradiction between racial segregation and the gospel of Jesus."

3. John Paul II, *Evangelium vitae (The Gospel of Life)* (Washington, DC: United States Catholic Conference Office of Publishing and Promotion Services, 1995), 141, available from the United States Catholic Conference Office of Publishing and Promotion Services, Washington, D.C. *Evangelium vitae* was promulgated in 1995.

4. A more extended discussion is found in the chapter on "Environmental Apartheid" in Rasmussen, *Earth Community, Earth Ethics* (Maryknoll, NY: Orbis, 1996), 75–89. The discussion above draws, sometimes directly, on this chapter.

5. "The little brown saint of India" was King's affectionate term for Gandhi, likely taken from the title of F. B. Fisher's, *That Strange Little Brown Man, Gandhi* (New York: R. Long & R. R. Smith, 1932).

6. The title of Young's book on Bonhoeffer: Josiah Ulysses Young III, *No Difference in the Fare: Dietrich Bonhoeffer and the Problem of Racism* (Grand Rapids, Mich.: Eerdmans, 1998).

7. "Letter from Birmingham Jail," in James M. Washington, *A Testament of Hope: The Essential Writings of Martin Luther King, Jr.* (San Francisco: Harper & Row, 1986), 290.

8. Bonhoeffer's *Ethics* is vol. 6 of the *Dietrich Bonhoeffer Works, English Edition.*

9. Dietrich Bonhoeffer, *Life Together, DBWE* 5:95–96.

10. "Remaining Awake through a Great Revolution," a Passion Sunday sermon at the National Cathedral (Episcopal) in Washington, D.C., cited in Washington, *A Testament of Hope*, 269–70.

11. See Robert Bellah, Richard Madsen, William M. Sullivan, and Ann Swidler, *Habits of the Heart: Individualism and Commitment in American Life* (Berkeley: University of California Press, 1985).

12. Illegible insert.

13. Sermon for Evening Worship Service on 2 Corinthians 12:9, *DBWE* 13 (3/19): 402–3.

14. See the chapter, "Bearing the Cross and Staring Down the Lynching Tree: Martin Luther King Jr.'s Struggle to Redeem the Soul of America," in Cone, *Cross and the Lynching Tree*, 65–92.

15. Cited from Washington, *A Testament of Hope*, 265.

16. Ibid., 232.

17. Martin Luther King Jr., "A Time to Break Silence," from Washington, *A Testament of Hope*, 232–33.

18. As cited by James Cone, *Martin & Malcolm & America: A Dream or a Nightmare* (Maryknoll, NY: Orbis Books, 1991), 240.

19. "Presidential Address," SCLC Tenth Anniversary Celebration, August 16, 1967, Atlanta, Georgia, as cited by Cone, *Martin & Malcolm & America*, 224.

20. Ibid.

21. From the excerpted portion of Taylor Branch, "At Canaan's Edge," *Time*, January 9, 2006, 51.

22. "A Time to Break Silence."

23. Cited from Washington, *Testament of Hope*, 265.

24. Cone, *Cross and the Lynching Tree*, 66.

25. I add that the meaning of "prophet" here is not the same as its meaning in Islam. There the title is reserved for the last, or "Seal," of the prophets, the Prophet Muhammad, and for the prophets (messengers of God) named in the Qur'an. My use of "prophet" in this chapter is more general, a way to highlight motifs and work shared by strong faith-based reformers of nature-society. Specific religious traditions may or may not designate these articulate critics as "prophets," though many do.

26. Cited from "My Trip to the Land of Gandhi," in Washington, *Testament of Hope*, 25.

27. Beyond my use of original sources, I draw upon James H. Cone, *Cross and the Lynching Tree*; Cone, *Malcolm & Martin & America*; and the discussion of King in Gary Dorrien, *The Making of American Liberal Theology: Crisis, Irony, & Modernity, 1950–2005* (Louisville, KY: Westminster John Knox Press, 2006), 143–61.

28. This paragraph uses, for its commentary on King and Bonhoeffer, a paraphrase of portions of Leonard Pitts Jr., "Bad Treatment of Gays Isn't the Holocaust; however . . ." in *Houston Chronicle*, Opinion, May 2, 2005.

29. Proverbs 31:8.

30. *DBWE* 13:217.

31. See also *DBWE* 12 (Berlin, 1932–33), Part 2, Document 14, Memorandum "The Jewish-Christian Question as Status Confessionis." It should be noted that even if Bonhoeffer acknowledges in this essay that the church is to help all victims, *status confessionis* for him concerns only whether or not the church will institute an Aryan paragraph and exclude "non-Aryan" members. Nowhere does he explicitly say that *status confessionis* arises in the state's treatment of non-Christian Jews.

32. *DBWE* 6:214.

33. Ibid., 185–86.

34. Ibid., 214.

35. Ibid., 180.

36. Eberhard Bethge, *Dietrich Bonhoeffer: A Biography*, rev. ed., rev. and ed. Victoria J. Barnett (Minneapolis: Fortress Press, 2000), 275.

37. King, "My Trip to the Land of Gandhi," in Washington, *Testament of Hope*, 24.

38. Matthew 5–7.

39. All the direct quotations in this account of the bus boycott, Gandhi, and love are from King, *Stride toward Freedom: The Montgomery Story*, as excerpted in "An Experiment in Love," in Washington, *Testament of Hope*, 20.

40. Reinhold Niebuhr, too, was a theologian of the cross who made the norms of justice and *agape* love his core ethic. But see the important discussion of the differences of King and Niebuhr on agape in Cone, *Cross and the Lynching Tree*, 70–72. "Although Martin Luther King Jr. was strongly influenced by Reinhold Niebuhr, he had a different take on love and justice because he spoke to and for powerless people whose faith, focused on the cross of Jesus, mysteriously empowered them to fight against impossible odds. In contrast to Niebuhr, King never spoke about *proximate* justice or about what was *practically* possible to achieve. That would have killed the revolutionary spirit in the African American community. Instead, King focused on and often achieved what Niebuhr said was impossible" (72).

41. Ibid., 25.

42. King, "Nonviolence: The Only Road to Freedom, " *Ebony*, October 1966, as cited in *Catholic Worker* 75, no. 2 (March–April 2008): 1.

43. From Gandhi's 1948 writings as cited here from John Dear, "The Consistent Ethic of Life," July 15, 2008, available at www.persistentpeace.com.

44. The power of goodness is available not only for resistance. Such power, inherent in creation itself, is available for all sectors of life. For a touching account of this in his family and culture, see Bonhoeffer's poem, "Powers of Good," in *Letters and Papers from Prison*, *DBWE* 8:400–401.

45. A phrase used to describe the Germany sought by the military-political conspiracy.

46. See the essay with this title in King's *Where Do We Go From Here, Chaos or Community?* (Boston: Beacon Press, 1967).

47. David L. Haberman, "Hinduism, Deep Ecology and the Universe Story," a paper given at the Yale Conference on the Journey of the Universe, March 23–26, 2011, 3. Used with permission.

48. Ibid., 3.

49. Ibid., 3–4. Haberman here is citing Gandhi as quoted in *The Deep Ecology Movement: An Introductory Anthology*, ed. Alan Drengson and Yuichi Inoue (Berkeley, CA: North Atlantic Books, 1995), 146.

50. Ibid., 4, quoting from M. Gandhi, *All Men Are Brothers* (Lausanne: United Nations Educational, Scientific and Cultural Organization, 1958), 118.

51. Gandhi, *All Men Are Brothers*, 119.

52. *Bhagavad-gītā as It Is*, Complete Edition (Los Angeles, CA: International Society for Krishna Consciousness, 1983), 337.

53. Gandhi, *All Men Are Brothers*, 118.

54. Haberman, "Hinduism, Deep Ecology and the Universe Story," 5.

55. Martin Luther King Jr., "The World House," *Where Do We Go from Here: Chaos or Community?"* 167.

56. Ibid., 172–73.

57. Ibid., 190–91.

58. P. 1 of "Humanity's Footprint 1961–2002," available at www.footprintnetwork.org/gfn_ sub.p[hp?content=global_footprint.

59. This resource, "Global Footprint Network," is available at www.footprintnetwork.org.

60. See the *2010 Living Planet Report* of the World Wildlife Federation, available at www.footprintnetwork.org.

61. Jared Diamond, *Guns, Germs, and Steel: The Fates of Human Societies* (New York: W. W. Norton, 1997), passim.

62. The subtitle of *Collapse*.

63. Jared Diamond, *Collapse: How Societies Choose to Fail or Succeed* (New York: Viking, 2005), 3.

64. Ibid., 6.

65. See above.

66. Ibid., 6.

67. Ibid., 7.

68. Ibid.

69. Ibid.

70. Ibid., 498.

71. Ibid.

72. Ibid., 519–20.

73. The term is Michel Foucault's in *Power/Knowledge: Selected Interviews and Other Writings 1972–1977*, ed. Colin Gordon (New York: Pantheon Books, 1980).

74. W. E. B. Du Bois, *Darkwater: Voices from within the Veil* (Mineola, NY: Dover Publications, 1999).

75. *New Mexican*, August 5, 2010, A1, A8.

76. Quoted in L. S. Klepp, "Every Man a Philosopher-King," *The New York Times Magazine*, December 2, 1990, Section 6:57.

77. See above.

78. An image from G. K. Chesterton, *The Man Who Was Thursday* (New York: G. P. Putnam's Sons, 1960), 10.

CHAPTER 12

1. T. S. Eliot, from "The Rock" (1934), *Collected Poems, 1909–1962* (New York: Houghton Mifflin Harcourt, 1963), 147.

2. YHWH is one of the Hebrew words for God, often translated as "the Lord."

3. Proverbs 8:1–4; 22–31 in William P. Brown's translation in his *The Seven Pillars of Creation: The Bible, Science, and the Ecology of Wonder* (New York and London: Oxford University Press, 2010), 164. I use his translation because I also draw on his discussion, a discussion that stays close to the phrases as he has translated them.

4. Allusions to Isaiah 11:6.

5. Isaiah 2:2.

6. The Hindu adage cited at the outset of the chapter.

7. An allusion to a statement by a U.S. commander in Vietnam after a fierce battle: "It's a shame, but we had to destroy the village to save it."

8. This approach is that of Norman Habel, "Earth-Mission: The Third Mission of the Church," in *Currents in Theology and Mission* 37, no. 2 (April 2010): 120–22. This issue of *Currents* is on "Faith and Earthkeeping: A Tribute to the Environmental Ministry of David Rhoads."

9. Habel, "Earth-Mission: The Third Mission of the Church," 120.

10. I again use the arrangement and translation of Proverbs 1 by William Brown, *Seven Pillars of Creation*, 162.

11. With the exception of the Matthew text, all the texts cited are from the collections of wisdom found on the website www.sapphyr.net.

12. See William Brown's discussion, "The Dying Cosmos," in *Seven Pillars of Creation*, 177–96.

13. From Mohandas Gandhi, "Young India," May 7, 1925.

14. Reinhold Niebuhr, *The Irony of American History* (New York: Charles Scribner's Sons, 1952), 63.

15. Slightly adapted text, available at Native Wisdom, http://www.rainbowbody.net.

16. Cited from Native American Wisdom, www.sapphyr.net.

17. *Hemispheres*, United Airlines In-Flight Magazine, July 1997 issue.

18. Dorothy C. Bass, "Keeping Sabbath," in *Practicing Our Faith: A Way of Life for a Searching People*, ed. Dorothy C. Bass (San Francisco: Jossey-Bass, 1997), 80.

19. Abraham Heschel, *I Asked for Wonder: A Spiritual Anthology*, ed. Samuel H. Dresner (New York: Crossroad, 1983), 65.

20. I draw here upon my article, "Chase's Sabbath," in *The Living Pulpit* (April–June 1998): 20–21.

21. "The Summer Day." *House of Light* by Mary Oliver, Published by Beacon Press Boston. Copyright © 1990 by Mary Oliver. Reprinted by permission of The Charlotte Sheedy Literary Agency Inc.

22. Ibid.

23. As a so-called soft law document, meaning that it is morally, rather than legally, binding on those who subscribe to it.

24. Principle 1 from Section I of the charter, 2.

25. From the Preamble, the section "Earth, Our Home," 1.

26. Rockefeller as quoted in "Earth Charter Launched at The Hague," *Boston Research Center for the 21st Century Newsletter* 16 (Winter 2001): 12. Rockefeller, who had worked with Maurice Strong and Mikhail Gorbachev on the Earth Charter project since 1994, served as chair of the International Drafting Committee from 1997 to 2000, when the drafting was completed. (Communication to the author, September 8, 2011.)

27. Thomas L. Friedman, "Corporations on Steroids," *New York Times*, February 4, 2000, A29.

28. The text of the Earth Charter and its many ongoing activities are available at: www.EarthCharter.org.

29. Michael S. Northcott, *A Moral Climate: The Ethics of Climate Change* (Maryknoll, NY: Orbis, 2007), 244–45.

30. Cited from Michael Pollan, *The Omnivore's Dilemma: A National History of Four Meals* (New York: Penguin, 2008), 42. The full account is available in Vaclav Smil, *Enriching the Earth: Fritz Haber, Carl Bosch, and the Transformation of World Food* (Cambridge, MA: MIT Press, 2000).

31. Pollan, *Omnivore's Dilemma*, 42.

32. Ibid.

33. Ibid., 43.

34. Ibid.

35. Ibid., 45.

36. Ibid.

37. Cited from Eberhard Bethge, "The Non-Religious Scientist and the Confessing Theologian," in *Bonhoeffer for a New Day: Theology in a Time of Transition*, ed. John de Gruchy (Grand Rapids, MI: Eerdmans, 1997), 43–44.

38. While these are my words, they were stimulated by the remarks of Steven Rockefeller at the Yale Conference on the Journey of the Universe, Yale University, March 23–26, 2011.

39. Genesis 41.

40. John S. Adams, "Heading Off Next Big Bailout—of Nature," *New Mexican*, March 21, 2010, B2.

41. Ibid.

42. Ibid.

43. Cited in Keith Basso, *Wisdom Sits in Places: Landscape and Language among the Western Apache* (Albuquerque: University of New Mexico Press, 1996), 127.

44. The term is Basso's, used throughout *Wisdom Sits in Places*.

45. Basso's citation, 64, in N. Scott Momaday, "Native American Attitudes to the Environment," in *Seeing with a Native Eye: Essays on Native American Religion*, ed. W. Capps (New York: Harper & Row, 1974), 80.

46. Basso, *Wisdom Sits in Places*, 40.

47. Ibid., 106.

48. Ibid., 127.

49. The dimensions of *oikos* are discussed in chapter 5; ethos as a reference to "stable" and "stability" is found in the same chapter.

50. The words are Basso's, drawing from the journal *Cultural Survival Quarterly*, in his *Wisdom Sits in Places*, 105.

51. William deBuys, *A Great Aridness: Climate Change and the American Southwest* (New York: Oxford University Press, 2011), 267. DeBuys is drawing on the work of Keith Basso; I am grateful to deBuys for pointing me to that work.

52. Ibid.

53. Brown, *Seven Pillars of Creation*, 168.

54. Ibid., 169.

55. Ibid., 176.

56. Ibid., 169, uses the Greek translation from the Septuagint (LXX) for Prov. 8:30: "I was beside him [God] binding together."

57. The closing of Dante's *Paradiso*.

58. Brown, *Seven Pillars of Creation*, 173. Brown takes the phrase from Jeffrey P. Schloss, "Wisdom Traditions as Mechanisms for Organismal Integration: Evolutionary Perspectives on Homeostatic Laws of Life," in *Understanding Wisdom: Sources, Science, and Society*, ed. Warren S. Brown (Philadelphia: Templeton Foundation Press, 2000), 153–91.

59. See "The Ethic We Need," above.

60. Proverbs 1:3, Brown's rendition.

61. Genesis 1:31.

62. Brown, *Seven Pillars of Creation*, 173–74.

CHAPTER 13

1. The first epigraph is from John Dominic Crossan, *The Historical Jesus: The Life of a Mediterranean Peasant* (New York: HarperCollins, 1992), xiii. Crossan's reference is the Sermon on the Mount of Jesus. The second epigraph is from the song, "Gather Us In," in the musical collection of the same title: Marty Haugen, *Gather Us In* (Chicago: GIA Publications). The Albright reference is from my notes of Susan

Thistlethwaite's interview with Madeline Albright at the 2006 meeting of the American Academy of Religion.

2. For an insightful account of the adventure of Asia and modernity, see Patrick Smith, *Somebody Else's Century: East and West in a Post-Western World* (New York: Random House, 2011).

3. Henry David Thoreau, *Walden* (New York: W. W. Norton, 1992), 146.

4. John Paul Lederach, *The Moral Imagination: The Art and Soul of Building Peace* (New York: Oxford University Press, 2005), 23.

5. Norman Wirzba, *Food and Faith: A Theology of Eating* (Cambridge: Cambridge University Press, 2011), 174.

6. Ibid.

7. Ibid., 175.

8. James M. Gustafson, *Ethics from a Theocentric Perspective*, vol. 1, *Theology and Ethics* (Chicago: University of Chicago Press, 1981), 113.

9. Nicholas Lash, *Believing Three Ways in the One God: A Reading of the Apostle's Creed* (Notre Dame, IN: University of Notre Dame, 1992), 22.

10. Karl Polanyi, *The Great Transformation: The Political and Economic Origins of Our Time* (Boston: Beacon Press, 2001; original ed., 1944), 76.

11. See the discussion in the chapter "Asceticism and Consumerism."

12. Robert Pogue Harrison, *Gardens: An Essay on the Human Condition* (Chicago: University of Chicago Press, 2008), 71.

13. Cited, without bibliographic data, by Annie Dillard in *Pilgrim at Tinker Creek*, 276.

14. The title of Jeffrey Stout's book, cited earlier.

15. With apologies to H. L. Mencken, who is supposed to have said this about Hollywood.

16. The reference is to the book by the French priest and paleontologist, Pierre de Chardin, himself both a Roman Catholic sacramentalist and a Catholic Earth mystic. See Pierre Teilhard de Chardin, *Hymn of the Universe* (London: William Collins Sons; New York, Harper & Row, 1965).

17. The term of Kathleen Dean Moore as influenced by Rachel Carson. See Lisa H. Sideris and Kathleen Dean Moore, *Rachel Carson: Legacy and Challenge* (Albany: SUNY Press, 2008).

18. See Ibrahim Abdul-Matin, *Green Deen: What Islam Teaches about Protecting the Planet* (San Francisco: Berrett-Koehler, 2010).

19. For a discussion of Adamah Farm and Hazon, see Fred Bahnson, *Soil and Sacrament: Four Seasons among the Keepers of the Earth* (forthcoming from Free Press).

20. Wirzba, *Food and Faith*, 197.

21. Wendell Berry, "Two Minds," in *Citizenship Papers* (Washington, DC: Shoemaker and Hoard, 2003), 91, as cited by Wirzba, *Food and Faith*, 197. I have adapted both Wirzba's and Berry's discussions to echo the themes of this book.

22. This is a summation of Howard Becker, "Processes of Secularization: An Ideal-Typical Analysis with Special Reference to Personality Change as Affected by Population Movement," *Sociological Review* 24 (1932): 138–54, 266–86.

23. The comments to "Ode to Joy" were part of a conversation at the Yale conference accompanying the premiere of the film, "Journey of the Universe," March 24–26, 2011.

POSTLUDE

1. The second epigraph is from a hymn attributed to Robert Lowry, "How Can I Keep from Singing?" in *Bright Jewels for the Sunday School* (New York: Biglow and Main), 1869. The stanza continues: "No storm can shake my inmost calm, while to that rock I'm clinging; while love is Lord o'er heaven and earth, how can I keep from singing?"

2. Reported by Robin Meyers in *Saving Jesus from the Church* (San Francisco: HarperOne, 2009), 181.

Bibliography

ARTICLES

2010 Living Planet Report. The World Wildlife Federation. At www.footprintnetwork.org.

"A Buddhist-Christian Common Word on Structural Greed: A Joint Statement," 4, available on the World Council of Churches website: www.oikoumene.org/resources/documents/wcc-programmes/interreligious-dialogue-and-cooperation/interreligious-trust-and-respect/buddhist-christian-common-word-on-structural-greed.html.

"A Hen's Space to Roost." *New York Times*, Week in Review, August 15, 2010, 3.

"The Rich and the Rest: A Special Report on the Global Elite." *Economist*, January 22–28, 2011.

"An Evolutionary Theory of Right and Wrong." *New York Times*, Science Times, October 31, 2006, D1–2.

"China, New Land of Shoppers, Builds Malls on Gigantic Scale." *New York Times*, May 25, 2005, A1, C7.

"Deep under the Sea, Boiling Founts of Life Itself." *New York Times*, Science Times, September 9, 2003, F1, F4.

"Diminished Expectations." Review of Gideon Rachman's *Zero-Sum Future* in *New York Times Book Review*, January 30, 2011, 19.

"Ecopsychology and the Deconstruction of Whiteness: An Interview with Carl Anthony." In *Ecopsychology: Restoring the Earth, Healing the Mind*, ed. Theodore Roszak, Mary E. Gomes, and Allen D. Kanner. San Francisco: Sierra Club Books, 1995, 263–78.

"Environmental Apartheid." In Larry Rasmussen, *Earth Community, Earth Ethics*. Maryknoll, NY: Orbis Books, 1996, 75–89.

"Forget the Food Chain—Think Food Web." *New Mexican*, February 28, 2011, A-1, A-4.

"From the Editors." *Orion: Nature/Culture/Place*, January/February 2011, 1.

"Global Footprint Network." At www.footprintnetwork.org.

"The Holden Prayer." Morning Prayer (Matins). *The Lutheran Book of Worship*. Minneapolis: Augsburg Publishing House, 1978.

"How Can I Keep from Singing." A hymn attributed to Robert Lowry. In *Bright Jewels for the Sunday School*. New York: Biglow and Main, 1869.

"Humanity's Footprint 1961–2002." At www.footprintnetwork.org.

"Is 'Do Unto Others' Written into Our Genes?" *New York Times*, Science Times, September 18, 2007, D1.

"Key Human Traits Tied to Shellfish Remains." *New York Times*, October 18, 2007, A6.

"Letter to the Churches." Appendix 1 of Wesley Granberg-Michaelson, *Redeeming the Creation, the Rio Earth Summit: Challenge to the Churches*. Geneva: WCC Publications, 1992.

"The New Monasticism Project." http://www.newmonasticism.org.

"Principles of Environmental Justice." The First National People of Color Environmental Leadership Summit on October 27, 1991, Washington, D.C. At www.ejnet.org/ej/principles.html.

"Promoting Tolerance & Compassion Through Religion in Schools." http://www.brighthub.com/education/k-12/articles/69391.aspx.

"Saving Souls and Salmon." *New York Times Week in Review*. October 22, 2000, 5.

"Sine agua non." *Economist*, April 11, 2009.

"Study: Climate Change Threatens Key Crops." *New Mexican*, September 7, 2009, A-4.

"U.S. Clings to Climate Disbelief." *New Mexican*, September 26, 2011, A-5.

"Water Footprint." *The Living Planet Report 2008*. Gland, Switzerland: World Wildlife Fund, 2008.

"Water: A Global Innovation Outlook Report." IBM project online: www.ibm.com/ibm/gio/water.html.

"Welcome to the Anthropocene: Geology's New Age." *Economist*, May 28–June 3, 2011.

"Wonder and Restraint: A Rabbinic Call to Environmental Action." Lawrence Bush, ed., *Jewish Currents and Reconstructionist Today*. Accord, NY. At http://www.coejl.org/about/rabbinicletter_revfin.pdf.

BOOKS

Abdul-Matin, Ibrahim. *Green Deen: What Islam Teaches about Protecting the Planet*. San Francisco: Berrett-Koehler Publications, 2010.

Ackerman, Diane. "Worlds within Worlds." *New York Times*, December 4, 1995, sec. 4.

Adams, John S. "Heading Off Next Big Bailout—of Nature." *New Mexican*, March 21, 2010, B2.

Angelou, Maya. *A Brave and Startling Truth*. New York: Random House, 1995.

———. *On the Pulse of Morning: An Inaugural Poem*. New York: Random House, 1993.

The Animals' Lawsuit against Humanity: A Modern Adaptation of an Ancient Animal Rights Tale. Trans. and adapted by Rabbi Anson Laytner and Rabbi Dan Bridge, ed.

Matthew Kaufmann, intro. Seyyed Hossein Nasr, illus. Kulsum Begum. Louisville, KY: Fons Vitae Press, 2005.

Aristotle. *Nicomachean Ethics*. Trans. H. Rackam. Loeb Classical Library, vol. 19. Cambridge: Harvard University Press, 1926; reprint ed., 1982.

Attenborough, Richard. *Gandhi*. The film script. At www.scribd.com/doc/45864526/Gandhi.

Auden, W. H. "First Things First." *Selected Poems*. Ed. Edward Mendelsohn. Expanded 2nd ed. New York: Random House, 2007.

Bahnson, Fred. *Soil and Sacrament: Four Seasons among the Keepers of the Earth*. Forthcoming from Free Press.

Baldwin, James. *Black on White: Black Writers on What It Means to be White*. Ed. David R. Roediger. New York: Schocken Books, 1998.

———. *Notes of a Native Son*. Boston, MA: Beacon Press, 1955.

———. *The Price of the Ticket: Collected Nonfiction, 1948–1985*. New York: St. Martin's Press, 1985.

Barbier, Edward B. *Scarcity and Frontiers: How Economies Have Developed through Natural Resource Exploitation*. Cambridge: Cambridge University Press, 2011.

Bass, Dorothy C. "Keeping Sabbath." In *Practicing Our Faith: A Way of Life for a Searching People*, ed. Dorothy C. Bass. San Francisco: Jossey-Bass, 1997.

Basso, Keith. *Wisdom Sits in Places: Landscape and Language among the Western Apache*. Albuquerque: University of New Mexico Press, 1996.

Bateson, Gregory. *Steps to an Ecology of Mind*. New York: Random House, 1972.

Bauman, Whitney A., Richard R. Bohannon II, and Kevin J. O'Brien, eds. *Inherited Land: The Changing Grounds of Religion and Ecology*. Eugene, OR: Pickwick Publications, 2011.

Beauchamp, Tom L., and James F. Childress. *Principles of Biomedical Ethics*. New York: Oxford University Press, 1979.

Becker, Gary. *The Economic Approach to Human Behavior*. Chicago: University of Chicago Press, 1976.

Becker, Howard. "Processes of Secularization: An Ideal-Typical Analysis with Special Reference to Personality Change as Affected by Population Movement." *Sociological Review* 24 (1932): 138–54, 266–86.

Bekoff, Marc. "Animal Passions and Beastly Virtues: Cognitive Ethology as the Unifying Science for Understanding the Subjective, Emotional, Empathic, and Moral Life of Animals." *Zygon* 41, no. 1 (2006): 71–104.

Bell, Daniel. *The Cultural Contradictions of Capitalism*. New York: Basic Books, 1976.

Bellah, Robert, Richard Madsen, William M. Sullivan, and Ann Swidler. *Habits of the Heart: Individualism and Commitment in American Life*. Berkeley: University of California Press, 1985.

Bender, Thomas. *Community and Social Change in America*. New Brunswick, NJ: Rutgers University Press, 1978.

Berry, Thomas. "Conditions for Entering the Ecozoic Era." *Ecozoic Reader, The Center for Ecozoic Studies* 2, no. 2 (Winter 2002).

———. *Evening Thoughts: Reflecting on Earth as Sacred Community*. San Francisco: Sierra Club Books, 2006.

———. *The Great Work: Our Way into the Future*. New York: Bell Tower, 1999.

Berry, Wendell. *Home Economics*. San Francisco: North Point Press, 1987.

———. *Life Is a Miracle*. Washington, DC: Counterpoint Press, 2000.

———. "Two Minds." *Citizenship Papers*. Washington, DC: Shoemaker and Hoard, 2003.

Bethge, Eberhard. *Dietrich Bonhoeffer: A Biography*. Revised ed. Rev. and ed. Victoria J. Barnett. Minneapolis: Fortress Press, 2000.

———. "The Non-Religious Scientist and the Confessing Theologian." In *Bonhoeffer for a New Day: Theology in a Time of Transition*, ed. John de Gruchy. Grand Rapids, MI: Eerdmans, 1997.

Bialik, Hayim. *Songs from Bialik: Selected Poems of Hayim Nahman Bialik*. Trans. and adapted from the Hebrew by Atar Hadari. Syracuse, NY: Syracuse University Press, 2000.

Bingen, Hildegard of. *The Book of Divine Works*. In *Hildegard of Bingen: Mystical Writings*, ed. Fiona Bowie and Oliver Davies. New York: Crossroad, 1990.

Bingham, Sam. *The Last Ranch: A Colorado Community and the Coming Desert*. New York: Pantheon Books, 1996.

Birch, Bruce C., and Larry L. Rasmussen. *Bible and Ethics in the Christian Life*. Rev. and expanded ed. Minneapolis: Augsburg Fortress, 1989.

———. *The Predicament of the Prosperous*. Philadelphia: Westminster Press, 1978.

Black Elk. *Black Elk Speaks*. New York: Pocket Books, 1972.

Blackmon, Douglas A. *Slavery by Another Name: The Re-Enslavement of Black Americans from the Civil War to World War II*. New York: Anchor Books, 2008.

The Blessing of the Waters at Ohkay Owingeh, 2009. Text made available to the author.

Bok, Derek. *The Politics of Happiness: What Government Can Learn from the New Research on Well-Being*. Princeton: Princeton University Press, 2011.

Bok, Sissela. *Exploring Happiness: From Aristotle to Brain Science*. New Haven: Yale University Press, 2011.

Bonhoeffer, Dietrich. "Basis Questions of a Christian Ethic." In *Dietrich Bonhoeffer Works, English Edition*. Vol. 10. Minneapolis: Fortress Press, 2008.

———. *Ethics. Dietrich Bonhoeffer Works, English Edition*. Vol. 6. Minneapolis: Fortress Press, 2005.

———. *Letters and Papers from Prison. Dietrich Bonhoeffer Works, English Edition*. Vol. 8. Minneapolis: Fortress Press, 2010.

———. *Life Together. Dietrich Bonhoeffer Works, English Edition*. Vol. 5. Minneapolis: Fortress Press, 1996.

———. "The Right to Self-Assertion." *Dietrich Bonhoeffer Works, English Edition*. Vol. 11. Minneapolis: Fortress Press, 2012.

———. "Sermon for Evening Worship Service on 2 Corinthians 12:9." *Dietrich Bonhoeffer Works, English Edition*. Vol. 13. Minneapolis: Fortress Press, 2007.

———. "Thy Kingdom Come! The Prayer of the Church-Community for God's King-dom on Earth." *Dietrich Bonhoeffer Works, English Edition*. Vol. 12. Minneapolis: Fortress Press, 2009.

Bonhoeffer, Dietrich, and Maria von Wedemeyer. *Love Letters from Cell 92*. Ed. Ruth-Alice Bismarck and Ulrich Kabitz. Trans. John Brownjohn. Nashville: Abingdon Press, 1995.

Borgmann, Albert. *Real American Ethics: Taking Responsibility for Our Country*. Chicago: University of Chicago Press, 2006.

———. *Technology and the Character of Contemporary Life*. Chicago and London: University of Chicago Press, 1984.

Branch, Taylor. "At Canaan's Edge." *Time*, January 9, 2006, 51.

Branson, Roy. "Apocalyptic and the Moral Imagination." Proceedings from "Bioethics: Old Models and New," Loma Linda University, November 1986.

Briens, Paul, Mary Gallway, Douglas Hughes, Azfar Hussain, Richard Law, Michael Myers, Michael Neville, Roger Schlesinger, Alice Spitzer, and Susan Swan, eds. *Reading About the World*. 3rd ed. Vol. 2. Fort Worth, TX: Harcourt College Publishers, 1999.

Brooks, David. "The Responsibility Deficit." *New York Times*, September 24, 2010, A25.

Brown, Lester R. "The New Geopolitics of Food." *Foreign Policy* (May–June 2011): 55–62.

Brown, Peter G., and Goeffrey Garver. *Right Relationship: Building a Whole Earth Economy*. San Francisco: Berrett-Koehler Publishers, 2009.

Brown, William P. *The Seven Pillars of Creation: The Bible, Science, and the Ecology of Wonder*. New York and London: Oxford University Press, 2010.

Brubaker, Pamela K., Rebecca Todd Peters, and Laura A. Stivers, eds. *Justice in a Global Economy*. Louisville, KY: Westminster John Knox Press, 2006.

Buber, Martin. *Paths in Utopia*. Boston: Beacon Press, 1958.

Buckley, William, Jr. *God and Man at Yale: the Superstitions of "Academic Freedom."* Chicago: Regnarey/Gateway, 1977.

Bullard, Robert D. "Decision Making." In *Faces of Environmental Racism: Confronting Issues of Global Justice*, ed. Laura Westra and Bill E. Lawson. 2nd ed. New York: Rowman & Littlefield, 2001, 4–9.

Bush, George W. "Second Inaugural Address," January 20, 2005. At: Inaugural Address of the Presidents, at Bartleby.com.

Chapple, Christopher. "Jainism, Life, and Environmental Ethics." Paper presented at the Yale Journey of the Universe Conference, March 2011. Used with permission.

Chesterton, G. K. *The Man Who Was Thursday*. New York: G. P. Putnam's Sons, 1960.

Childs, Craig. *The Secret Knowledge of Water*. New York: Little, Brown, 2000.

Chryssavgis, Fr. John, ed. *Cosmic Grace, Humble Prayer: The Ecological Vision of the Green Patriarch Bartholomew I*. Grand Rapids, MI: Eerdmans, 2003.

Commission for Racial Justice. *Toxic Wastes and Race in the United States*. New York: United Church of Christ, 1987.

Conant, Jennet. *109 East Palace*. New York: Simon & Schuster, 2005.

Cone, James H. *The Cross and the Lynching Tree*. Maryknoll, NY: Orbis Books, 2011.

——. *Risks of Faith: The Emergence of a Black Theology of Liberation*. Boston: Beacon Press, 1999.

——. "Whose Earth Is It, Anyway?" In *Earth Habitat: Eco-Injustice and the Church's Response*, ed. Dieter Hessel and Larry Rasmussen. Minneapolis: Fortress Press, 2001, 23–32.

Costello, Anthony, et al. "Managing the health effects of climate change," *Lancet* 373 (May 16, 2009): 1693–1733.

Cover, Virginia. "Dietrich Bonhoeffer: A Wealth of Themes." Unpublished paper, 18.

Crosby, Alfred W. *The Columbian Exchange*. Westport, CT: Greenwood Press, 1974.

——. *Ecological Imperialism: The Biological Expansion of Europe, 900–1900*. Cambridge: Cambridge University Press, 1986.

Crossan, John Dominic. *The Historical Jesus: The Life of a Mediterranean Peasant*. New York: HarperCollins, 1992.

Crouter, Richard. *Reinhold Niebuhr: On Politics, Religion, and Christian Faith*. New York: Oxford University Press, 2010.

Daly, Herman E., and John B. Cobb Jr. *For the Common Good: Redirecting the Economy toward Community, the Environment, and a Sustainable Future*. Boston: Beacon Press, 1989.

Dante, Alighieri. *Paradiso*. Trans. Robert Hollander and Jean Hollander. New York: Anchor Books, 2007.

Darwin, Charles. *The Descent of Man and Selection in Relation to Sex*. New York: Random House, 1936; original publication 1871.

——. *On the Origin of Species*. New York: D. Appleton, 1869.

Davison, Aiden. *Technology and the Contested Meanings of Sustainability*. Albany: State University of New York Press, 2001.

deBuys, William. *A Great Aridness: Climate Change and the Future of the American Southwest*. Oxford and New York: Oxford University Press, 2011.

de Chardin, Pierre Teilhard. *Hymn of the Universe*. London: William Collins Sons; New York, Harper & Row, 1965.

DeLisio, Therese. *Stretching the Sacramental Imagination in Sacramental Theology, Liturgy, and Life: A Trinitarian Proposal for a Cosmologically Conscious Age*. Ph.D. thesis, Union Theological Seminary, New York, 2007.

Descartes, René. *Discourse on the Method of Rightly Conducting the Reason, and Seeking Truth in the Sciences*. Chicago: Open Court Publishing Company, 1927.

Diamond, Jared. *Collapse: How Societies Choose to Fail or Succeed*. New York: Viking, 2005.

——. *Guns, Germs, and Steel: The Fates of Human Societies*. New York: W. W. Norton, 1997.

Diener, Ed, and Martin E. P. Seligman. "Beyond Money: Toward an Economy of Well-Being." *Psychological Science in the Public Interest* 5, no. 1 (2004): 18–19.

Dillard, Annie. *Pilgrim at Tinker Creek: A Mystical Excursion into the Natural World.* New York: Bantam Books, 1975.

———. *Pilgrim at Tinker Creek: A Mystical Excursion into the Natural World.* New York: HarperCollins Perennial Classics, 1998.

Dobson, Andrew. *Green Political Thought.* 3rd ed. New York: Routledge, 2000.

———. *Justice and the Environment: Conceptions of Environmental Sustainability and the Dimensions of Social Justice.* London and New York: Oxford University Press, 1998.

Doherty, Alex, and Robert Jensen. "A World in Collapse?" The New Left Project, at: http://www.newleftproject.org/index.php/site/article comments/a_world_in_collapse/.

Dorrien, Gary. *The Making of American Liberal Theology: Crisis, Irony, and Modernity, 1950–2005.* Louisville, KY: Westminster John Knox Press, 2006.

Dostoyevsky, Fyodor. *The Brothers Karamazov.* Trans. Richard Pevear and Larissa Volokhonsky. New York: Alfred A. Knopf, The Everyman Library, 1927.

Douglass, Frederick. "West India Emancipation." August 3, 1857 address in Canandaigua, New York. At http://www.blackpast.org.

Douthwaite, Richard. *The Growth Illusion.* Totnes, UK: Green Books, 1999.

Drengson, Alan, and Yuichi Inoue, eds. *The Deep Ecology Movement: An Introductory Anthology.* Berkeley, CA: North Atlantic Books, 1995.

Du Bois, W. E. B. *Darkwater: Voices from within the Veil.* Minneola, NY: Dover Publications. 1999.

———. *The Souls of Black Folks.* New York: New American Library, 1960; original publication, 1903.

Dubos, René. *A God Within: A Positive Philosophy for a More Complete Fulfillment of Human Potentials.* New York: Charles Scribner's Sons, 1972.

Dunn, Rob. *Every Living Thing: Man's Obsessive Quest to Catalog Life, from Nanobacteria to New Monkeys.* New York: Collins Books, 2009.

Durning, Allen T. *How Much Is Enough?* London: Earthscan, 1992.

The Earth Charter. At www.earthcharter.org.

Eaton, Heather. "Reflections on Water: Ecological, Political, Economic, and Theological." Available at http://www.nccecojustice.org/downloads/water/Reflections_on_Water.pdf.

Eck, Diana. *Encountering God: From Bozeman to Banaras.* Boston: Beacon Press, 1993.

Einstein, Albert. As first cited in "Atomic Education Urged by Einstein," *New York Times*, May 25, 1946 and quoted a month later by Michael Amrine in "The Real Problem Is in the Heart of Man," *New York Times Magazine*, June 23, 1946.

Eliade, Mircea. *The Sacred and the Profane: The Nature of Religion.* New York: Harper Torchbooks, 1959.

Eliot, T. S. *Four Quartets.* "Little Gidding." New York: Ballantine Books, 1966.

———. "The Rock." *Collected Poems, 1909–1962.* New York: Houghton Mifflin Harcourt, 1963.

Engels, Frederick. "Outlines of a Critique of Political Economy." In Karl Marx, *The Economic and Philosophic Manuscripts of 1844*, as cited in *Marx and Engels on Ecology*, ed. Howard Parsons. Westport, CT: Greenwood Press, 1977.

The Epic of Gilgamesh. In *World Mythology: An Anthology of the Great Myths and Epics*. Lincolnwood, IL: Donna Rosenberg National Textbook, 1986.

Erhard, Nancie. "To Love the Earth Fiercely." *Union Seminary Quarterly Review: Festschrift for Larry L. Rasmussen* 58, nos. 1–2 (2004): 120–31.

Erling, Maria, and Mark Granquist. *The Augustana Story*. Minneapolis: Fortress Press.

Fisher, F. B. *That Strange Little Brown Man, Gandhi*. New York: R. Long & R. R. Smith, 1932.

Flannery, Tim. *Now or Never: Why We Must Act Now to End Climate Change and Create a Sustainable Future*. New York: Atlantic Monthly Press, 2009.

Focolare Movement. Information from http://www.focolare.us/

Foucault, Michel. *Power/Knowledge: Selected Interviews and Other Writings 1972–1977*. Ed. Colin Gordon. New York: Pantheon Books, 1980.

Fox, Matthew. Interviewed by Jeffrey Mishlove on "Creation Spirituality" for the program, *Thinking Allowed, Conversations on the Leading Edge of Knowledge and Discovery*. At http://www.intuition.org/txt/fox.htm.

Frank, Phillipp. *Einstein: His Life and Times*. New York: Alfred A. Knopf, 1947.

Friedman, Thomas L. "Connecting Nature's Dots." *New York Times Week in Review*, August 23, 2009, 8.

———. "Corporations on Steroids." *New York Times*, February 4, 2000, A29.

———. "Drilling in the Cathedral." *New York Times*, March 2, 2003: A23.

———. *Hot, Flat, and Crowded*. New York: Farrar, Straus & Giroux, 2008.

Fukuyama, Francis. "The Great Disruption: Human Nature and the Reconstitution of Social Order." *Atlantic Monthly* 283, no. 5 (May 1999): 55–80.

Gandhi, Mohandas. *All Men Are Brothers*. Lausanne: United Nations Educational, Scientific and Cultural Organization, 1958.

———. "Young India." May 7, 1925.

———. 1948 writings as cited from John Dear, "The Consistent Ethic of Life." July 15, 2008. At www.persistentpeace.com.

Gates of Repentance: The New Union Prayerbook for the Days of Awe. New York: Central Conference of American Rabbis, 1978.

Gilkey, Langdon. *Maker of Heaven and Earth: The Christian Doctrine of Creation in the Light of Modern Knowledge*. Garden City, NY: Doubleday, 1959.

———. *Nature, Reality, and the Sacred: The Nexus of Science and Religion*. Minneapolis: Augsburg Fortress, 1993.

———. *Shantung Compound*. New York: Harper & Row, 1966.

Global Innovation Outlook, cover page, at http://www.ibm.com/ibm/fio/water.html.

Gold, Lorna. "The Roots of the Focolare Movement's Economic Ethic." *Journal of Markets and Morality* 6, no. 1 (Spring 2003): 1–14.

Goodenough, Ursula, and Terrence W. Deacon. "From Biology to Consciousness to Morality." *Zygon* 38, no. 4 (December 2003): 805.

Goodman, Walter. "God and Politics: Nothing New under the American Sun." *New York Times Week in Review*, September 10, 2000, 4.

Gottlieb, Roger. "The Transcendence of Justice and the Justice of Transcendence: Mysticism, Deep Ecology, and Political Life." *Journal of the American Academy of Religion* 67, no. 1 (1999): 149–66.

Gould, Stephen Jay. "This View of Life." *Natural History* 12 (1992): 19.

Greenberg, Irving. "Cloud of Smoke, Pillar of Fire: Judaism, Christianity, and Modernity after the Holocaust." In *Auschwitz: Beginning of a New Era?*, ed. Eva Fleishner. New York: KTAV, 1974.

Gregory of Nyssa. *The Making of Man*. Cited in Francis M. Young, "Adam and Anthropos." *Vigiliae Christianae* 37, no. 2 (1983): 118.

Groenfeldt, David. "Reinventing Water Management." Unpublished paper presented at the Third International Conference of the International Society for the Study of Religion, Nature, and Culture (ISSRNC), Amsterdam, July 23–26, 2009. Used with permission.

Gustafson, James M. *Ethics from a Theocentric Perspective*. Vol. 1: Theology and Ethics. Chicago: University of Chicago Press, 1981.

Habel, Norman. "Earth-Mission: The Third Mission of the Church." *Currents in Theology and Mission* 37, no. 2 (2010): 120–22.

Haberman, David L. "Hinduism, Deep Ecology and the Universe Story." A paper given at the Yale Conference on the Journey of the Universe, March 23–26, 2011. Used with permission.

Hall, Douglas John. "Against Religion: The case for Faith." *Christian Century* 128, no. 1 (January 11, 2011): 32.

Hammarskjold, Dag. *Markings*. Trans. Leif Sjöberg and W. H. Auden. New York: Alfred Knopf, 1964.

Harris, Sam. *The Moral Landscape: How Science Can Determine Human Values*. New York: Free Press, 2010.

Harrison, Beverly Wildung. *Justice in the Making*. Louisville, KY: WJK Press, 2004.

———. *Making the Connections*. Boston: Beacon Press, 1985.

Harrison, Robert Pogue. *Gardens: An Essay on the Human Condition*. Chicago: University of Chicago Press, 2008.

Hart, John. *What Are They Saying about Environmental Theology?* Mahwah, NJ: Paulist Press, 2004.

Haugen, Marty. "Gather Us In." In the musical collection of the same title, *Gather Us In*. Chicago: GIA Publications, n.d.

Havel, Vaclav. "Address of the President of the Czech Republic, His Excellency Vaclav Havel, on the Occasion of the Liberty Medal Ceremony." Philadelphia, July 4, 1994. Made available by the Czech Republic Mission, New York City.

Hawken, Paul. *Blessed Unrest: How the Largest Movement in the World Came into Being and Why No One Saw It Coming*. New York: Viking Press, 2007.

———. "Commencement Address to the Class of 2009." University of Portland, May 3, 2009. At http://www.paulhawken.com/paulhawken_frameset.html.

Hayek, F. A. *The Road to Serfdom: Texts and Documents*. Ed. Bruce Caldwell. Chicago: University of Chicago Press, 2007, original 1944.

Heifetz, Ronald. *Leadership without Easy Answers*. Cambridge, MA: Belknap Press, 1994.

Hemispheres. United Airlines In-Flight Magazine, July 1997.

Herbert, Bob. "Looking Back at an Ugly Time." *New York Times*, February 24, 2003, A17.

Herman, Judith Lewis. *Trauma and Recovery*. New York: Basic Books, 1992.

Hertzberg, Hendrik. "The Talk of the Town." *New Yorker*, March 17, 2003.

Heschel, Abraham. *I Asked for Wonder: A Spiritual Anthology*. Ed. Samuel Dresner. New York: Crossroad, 1983.

Hessel, Dieter. "The Church Ecologically Reformed." In *Earth Habitat: Eco-Injustice and the Church's Response*, ed. Dieter Hessel and Larry L Rasmussen. Minneapolis: Fortress Press, 2001, 185–206.

Hiebert, Theodore. *The Yahwist's Landscape: Nature and Religion in Early Israel*. New York: Oxford University Press, 1996.

His All Holiness Ecumenical Patriarch Bartholomew. "Ascesis and Consumption." In *Cosmic Grace and Humble Prayer*, ed. Fr. John Chryssavgis. Grand Rapids, MI: Eerdmans, 2003.

———. *Encountering the Mystery*. New York: Doubleday, 2008.

———. "Our Indivisible Environment." *Wall Street Journal*, October 25, 2009. At http://online.wsj.com/article/SB100014240527487045006045744853415043454 88.html

Hurlbut, William. "From Biology to Biography." *New Atlantis: A Journal of Technology and Society* 3 (2003): 50.

Ibn 'Al-Arabī. *The Bezels of Wisdom*. Mahwah, NJ: Paulist Press, 1980.

In Congress, July 4, 1776, the Unanimous Declaration of the Thirteen United States of America.

Ingham, Richard. "Act Now on Floods, Drought, Says Forum." *Age (Australia)*, March 18, 2009.

Jackson, Wes. *Consulting the Genius of the Place*. Berkeley, CA: Counterpoint Press, 2010.

———. "Where We Are Going." *The Land Institute*. N.d. At www.LandInstitute.org.

James, Robert Rhodes, ed. *Winston S. Churchill: His Complete Speeches 1897–1963*. Vol. 7. New York: Chelsea House, 1974.

Jefferson, Thomas. "Commerce between Master and Slave." In Paul Leicaster Ford, *Works of Thomas Jefferson. Federal Edition*. Vol. 4. 1782.

Jenkins, Willis. *Ecologies of Grace: Environmental Ethics and Christian Theology*. New York: Oxford University Press, 2008.

Jensen, Derrick. "Forget Shorter Showers: Why Personal Change Does not Equal Political Change." *Orion* (July/August 2009): 18–19.

———. "The Tyranny of Entitlement." *Orion* (January/February 2011): 10.

John Paul II. *Evangelium vitae (The Gospel of Life)*. Washington, DC: United States Catholic Conference Office of Publishing and Promotion Services, 1995.

Johnson, John. "Spatial Delivery." *New Mexican*, June 6, 2009, D1–2.

Kahl, Brigitte. "Fratricide and Ecocide: Rereading Genesis 2–4." In *Earth Habitat: Eco-Injustice and the Church's Response*, ed. Dieter Hessel and Larry L. Rasmussen. Minneapolis: Fortress Press, 2001.

Kant, Immanuel. *Lectures on Ethics*. Trans. Louis Infield. New York: Harper Torchbooks, 1963.

Kaufman, Frederick. "The Food Bubble: How Wall Street Starved Millions and Got Away with It." *Harper's* 321, no. 1022 (2010): 28.

Keynes, John Maynard. *Essays in Persuasion*. New York: W. W. Norton, 1963.

King, Martin Luther, Jr. "The Current Crisis in Race Relations." In Washington, *A Testament of Hope: The Essential Writings of Martin Luther King, Jr*. San Francisco: Harper & Row, 1986.

———. "An Experiment in Love." In *Stride toward Freedom: The Montgomery Story*. In James M. Washington, *A Testament of Hope*.

———. "Letter from Birmingham Jail." In Washington, *A Testament of Hope*.

———. "My Trip to the Land of Gandhi." In Washington, *A Testament of Hope*.

———. "Nonviolence: The Only Road to Freedom." *Ebony*, October 1966.

———. "Presidential Address." SCLC Tenth Anniversary Celebration. Cited by James Cone, *Martin & Malcolm & America*. Maryknoll, NY: Orbis Books, 1991.

———. "Remaining Awake through a Great Revolution." In Washington, *A Testament of Hope*.

———. "A Time to Break Silence." Cited by James Cone, *Malcolm & Martin & America*. Maryknoll, NY: Orbis Books, 1991.

———. *Where Do We Go from Here, Chaos or Community?* Boston: Beacon Press, 1968.

Klepp, L. S. "Every Man a Philosopher-King." *New York Times Magazine*, December 2, 1990, sec. 6.

Kluger, Jeffrey. "What Makes Us Moral." Science section of *Time*, December 3, 2007, 55.

Kolbert, Elizabeth. "The Sixth Extinction?" *New Yorker*, May 25, 2009.

Kristof, Nicholas D. "Our Beaker Is Starting to Boil." *New York Times Week in Review*, July 18, 2010, 10.

Lane. Belden C. *The Solace of Fierce Landscapes: Exploring Desert and Mountain Spirituality*. New York: Oxford University Press, 1998.

Lane, Robert E. *The Loss of Happiness in Market Democracies*. New Haven and London: Yale University Press, 2000.

Lasch, Christopher. *The True and Only Heaven: Progress and Its Critics*. New York: W. W. Norton, 1991.

Lash, Nicholas. *Believing Three Ways in the One God: A Reading of the Apostle's Creed*. Notre Dame, IN: University of Notre Dame, 1992.

Leach, William. *Land of Desire*. New York: Vintage Books, 1993.

Lederach, John Paul. *The Moral Imagination: The Art and Soul of Building Peace*. New York: Oxford University Press, 2005.

Ledgard, J. M. "Revolution From Within." *New York Times Book Review*, Feb. 13, 2011, 16, a review of Nelson Mandela, *Conversations with Myself*, David James Smith, *Young Mandela*, and Richard Stengel, *Mandela's Way*.

Lehmann, Paul. *Ethics in a Christian Context*. New York: Harper & Row, 1963.

Leopold, Aldo. *A Sand County Almanac*. New York: Ballantine Books, 1966.

Levertov, Denise. "Annunciation." *The Door in the Hive*. New York: New Directions, 1984.

———. "Beginners." *Candles in Babylon*. New York: New Directions, 1982.

Lewontin, Richard. "Genes in the Food!" *New York Review of Books* 48, no. 10.

Lilla, Mark. "The President and the Passions." The Way We Live Now, *New York Times Magazine*, December 19, 2010.

Lindsey, Brink. *The Age of Abundance: How Prosperity Transformed America's Politics and Culture*. New York: Collins/HarperCollins, 2007.

Logan, William Bryant. *Dirt: The Ecstatic Skin of the Earth*. New York: W. W. Norton, 1995.

Lovejoy, Arthur. *The Great Chain of Being*. New Brunswick, NJ: Transaction Press, 2009; original publication 1936.

Luther, Martin. "Confession Concerning Christ's Supper." In Martin Luther, "The Sacrament of the Body and Blood of Christ—Against the Fanatics." In *Martin Luther's Basic Theological Writings*, ed. Timothy Lull. Minneapolis: Augsburg Fortress, 2005.

———. *Lectures on Genesis. Luther's Works 1*. Ed. Jaroslav Pelikan. St. Louis: Concordia, 1958.

———. "That These Words of Christ, 'This Is My Body,' etc. Still Stand Firm against the Fanatics." *Luther's Works* 37. Minneapolis: Augsburg Fortress.

Lutheran Book of Worship. Minneapolis: Augsburg, 1979.

Lyell, Charles. *Principles of Geology*. New York: Penguin Books, 1997; original publication 1830.

Macy, Joanna. "Letters." At www.joannamacy.net.

Maguire, Daniel C. *A Moral Creed for All Christians*. Minneapolis: Fortress Press, 2005.

———. "Whom the Gods Would Destroy, They First Make Myopic." *Union Seminary Quarterly Review* 63, nos. 1–2 (2006): 67–83.

———. *Whose Church? A Concise Guide to Progressive Catholicism*. New York: New Press, 2008.

Maguire, Daniel C., and Larry L. Rasmussen. *Ethics for a Small Planet*. Albany: State University of New York Press, 1998.

Marsh, Charles. *The Earth as Modified by Human Action*. New York: Charles Scribner, Armstrong, 1874. Cited in William Ashworth, *The Economy of Nature: Rethinking the Connections between Ecology and Economics*. New York: Houghton Mifflin, 1995.

Martin-Schramm, James, and Robert Stivers. *Christian Environmental Ethics: A Case Method Approach*. Maryknoll, NY: Orbis, 2003.

Marx, Karl. *Capital: A Critique of Political Economy*. Vol. 1. Trans. Samuel Moore and Edward Aveling and ed. Frederick Engels. New York: International Publishers, 1967.

———. *Capital*. In *Karl Marx: A Reader*, ed. Jon Elster. Cambridge: Cambridge University Press, 1986.

———. *The Communist Manifesto*. Intro. Stefan T. Possony. Chicago: Henry Regnery, 1954.

———. *The Economic and Philosophical Manuscripts of 1844*. In *Marx and Engels on Ecology*, ed. Howard L. Parsons. Westport, CT: Greenwood Press, 1977.

———. *Grundrisse*. In *Karl Marx: A Reader*, ed. Jon Elster. Cambridge: Cambridge University Press, 1986.

Marx, Karl, and Friedrich Engels. *The Communist Manifesto*. New York: Norton Critical Edition, 2003; from the English edition edited by Friedrich Engels, 1888.

McDonough, William, and Michael Braungart. "The Next Industrial Revolution." *Atlantic Monthly*, October 1998.

McFague, Sallie. *Super, Natural Christians: How We Should Love Nature*. Minneapolis: Fortress Press, 1997.

McIntosh, Alastair. *Soil and Soul: People versus Corporate Power*. London: Aurum Press, 2001.

McKibben, Bill. "Duty Dodgers." *Orion*, July/August 2010, 11.

———. *Eaarth: Making a Life on a Tough New Planet*. New York: Times Books, 2010.

———. "Multiplication Saves the Day: How Just a Few of Us Can Rescue the Planet." *Orion* (November/December 2008): 18–19.

McNeill, J. R. *Something New under the Sun: An Environmental History of the Twentieth-Century World*. New York: W. W. Norton, 2000.

Mead, Margaret. Earth Day address to the United Nations, March 22, 1977. Cited by Louise Jones, *Environmentally Responsible Design: Green and Sustained Design*. Hoboken, NJ: John Wiley, 2008. At http://www.earthsite.org/mead77.htm.

The Meaning of the Noble Koran. At www.pdf-Koran.com.

Meeks, M. Douglas. *God the Economist: The Doctrine of God and the Political Economy*. Minneapolis: Augsburg Fortress, 1989.

Melville, Herman. *Moby-Dick or, The Whale*. New York: Modern Library, 1992; original published in 1851.

Merton, Thomas. *Conjectures of a Guilty Bystander*. London: Sheldon Press, 1965.

Meyers, Robin R. *Saving Jesus from the Church*. San Francisco: HarperOne, 2009.

Midgeley, Mary. "Duties Concerning Islands." In *Environmental Ethics*, ed. Robert Elliot. New York: Oxford University Press, 1995.

Miller, James. "Connecting Religion and Ecology." Unpublished paper, used with permission.

———. "Ecology, Aesthetics and Daoist Body Cultivation." Unpublished paper, used with permission.

Milton, John. *Paradise Lost*. 2nd ed. New York: W. W. Norton, 1993; original published in 1674.

Mithen, Steven. *The Singing Neanderthals: The Origins of Music, Language, Mind and Body*. Boston: Harvard University Press, 2008.

Moe-Lobeda, Cynthia. "Christian Ethics toward Earth-honoring Faiths." *Union Seminary Quarterly Review: Festschrift for Larry L. Rasmussen*, ed. Daniel Spencer and James Martin-Schramm 58, nos. 1–2 (2004).

Momaday, N. Scott. "Native American Attitudes to the Environment." In *Seeing with a Native Eye: Essays on Native American Religion*, ed. W. Capp. New York: Harper & Row, 1974, 79–85.

Montaigne. Cited by Anthony Robinson, "Articles of Faith." *The Seattle PI*, January 9, 2009. At http://www.seattlepi.com/local/395457_faith10.html.

Morgenthau, Robert. Address cited from U.S. Department of State, Proceedings and Documents of the United Nations Monetary and Financial Conference, Bretton Woods, New Hampshire, July 1–22, 1944. Vol. 1.

Morris, Ian. *Why the West Rules—For Now: The Patterns of History, and What They Reveal about the Future*. New York: Straus & Giroux, 2010.

Morton, Frederic. *Crosstown Sabbath: A Street Journey through History*. New York: Grove Press, 1987.

Nakashima Brock, Rita, and Rebecca Ann Parker. *Saving Paradise: How Christianity Traded Love of This World for Crucifixion and Empire*. Boston: Beacon Press, 2008.

Native American Wisdom. At www.sapphyr.net.

Native Wisdom. At http://www.rainbowbody.net.

Nemesius of Emesa. "On the Nature of Man." In *The Library of Christian Classics*. Vol. 4, *Cyril of Jerusalem and Nemesius of Emesa*. Ed. Wm. Telfer. Philadelphia: Westminster Press, 1955.

The New Grove Dictionary of Music and Musicians. Vol. 3. Ed. Stanley Sadie. New York: Macmillan, 1980.

The New Oxford American Dictionary. 2nd ed. New York: USA Oxford University Press, 2005.

Niebuhr, H. Richard. *The Purpose of the Church and Its Ministry: Reflections on the Aims of Theological Education*. New York: Harper & Row, 1956.

Niebuhr, Reinhold. *The Children of Light and the Children of Darkness*. New York: Charles Scribner's Sons, 1944.

———. *The Irony of American History*. New York: Charles Scribner's Sons, 1952.

———. *Moral Man and Immoral Society*. New York: Charles Scribner's Sons, 1932.

———. *The Nature and Destiny of Man*. New York: Charles Scribner's Sons, 1943.

Northcott, Michael S. *A Moral Climate: The Ethics of Climate Change*. Maryknoll, NY: Orbis, 2007.

Nowak, Martin A., with Roger Highfield. *Supercooperators: Altruism, Evolution, and Why We Need Each Other to Succeed*. New York: Free Press, 2011.

Obama, Barack. "All This We Will Do." *New York Times*, January 21, 2009, P2.

Oleksa, Michael. *Orthodox Alaska: A Theology of Mission*. Crestwood, NJ: St. Vladimir's Seminary Press, 1992.

Oliver, Mary. "The Summer Day." *House of Light*. Boston: Beacon Press, 1990.

Owen, David. "The Efficiency Dilemma: If Our Machines Use Less Energy, Will We Just Use Them More?" *New Yorker*, December 20 and 27, 2010, 79.

Paz, Octavio. "Poetry and the Free Market." *New York Times Book Review*, December 8, 1991, sec. 7.

Phillips, Kevin. *American Theocracy: The Perils and Politics of Radical Religion, Oil, and Borrowed Money in the 21st Century*. New York: Viking Penguin, 2006.

Pitts, Leonard, Jr. "Bad Treatment of Gays Isn't the Holocaust; however . . ." *Houston Chronicle*, Opinion, May 2, 2005.

Plato. *Phaedrus and Letters VII and VIII*. Trans. Walter Hamilton. New York: Penguin, 1986.

———. *The Republic*. Trans. G. M. A. Grube. 2nd rev. ed. Baltimore: Penguin Books, 1974.

———. *The Timaeus and Critias of Plato*. Trans. Thomas Taylor. New York: Kessinger, 2003.

Pocket World in Figures: 2011 Edition. London: Economist, 2011.

Polanyi, Karl. *The Great Transformation: The Political and Economic Origins of Our Time*. Boston: Beacon Press, 2001; originally published, 1944.

Pollan, Michael. *The Omnivore's Dilemma: A Natural History of Four Meals*. New York: Penguin, 2008.

Potts, Rick. *Humanity's Descent: The Consequences of Ecological Instability*. New York: William Morrow, 1996.

Queenborough, Simon A., and Liza S. Comita. "Should Ecological Science Be Ethical?" *Union Seminary Quarterly Review* 53, nos. 1–2: 18–25.

Ralston, Holmes, III. "Saving Creation: Faith Shaping Environmental Policy." *Harvard Law and Policy Review* 4 (2010): 121. At www.EcoJusticeNow.org.

Ramphal, Shridath. *Our Country, the Planet: Forging a Partnership for Survival*. Washington, DC: Island Press, 1992.

Rasmussen, Larry. "Bishop Moses and the Trees." In *Frontiers of African Christianity: Essays in Honour of Inus Daneel*, ed. Greg Cuthbertson, Hennie Pretorius, and Dana Roberts. Pretoria: University of South Africa Press, 2003.

———. "Chase's Sabbath." *Living Pulpit* (April–June 1998): 20–21.

———. "Drilling in the Cathedral." *DIALOG: A Journal of Theology* 42, no. 3 (2003): 202–25.

———. *Earth Community, Earth Ethics*. Maryknoll, NY: Orbis, 1996.

———. "Earth-honoring Asceticism and Consumerism." *Crosscurrents* 57, no. 4 (2009): 498–513.

———. "Give Us Word of the Humankind We Left to Thee: Globalization and Its Wake." *EDS Occasional Papers*, no. 4, August 1999.

———. "The Integrity of Creation." *Annual of the Society of Christian Ethics* 15, no. 1 (1995): 167–71.

———. "Luther and a Gospel of Earth." *Union Seminary Quarterly Review* 51, nos. 1–2 (1997): 1–28.

———. "Moral Community and Moral Formation." In *Ecclesiology and Ethics: Costly Commitment*, ed. Thomas F. Best and Martin Robra. Geneva: World Council of Churches, 1995, 105–11.

———. "Resisting Eco-Injustice, Watering the Garden." In *Resist! Christian Dissent for the 21st Century*, ed. Michael G. Long. Maryknoll, NY: Orbis, 2008, 127–30.

———. "Shaping Communities." In *Practicing Our Faith: A Way of Life for a Searching People*, ed. Dorothy Bass. 1st ed. San Francisco: Jossey-Bass, 1997. 2nd ed., 2009.

Rauschenbusch, Walter. *Christianity and the Social Crisis*. New York: Macmillan, 1907.

Rawls, John. *A Theory of Justice*. Boston: Belknap Press of Harvard University Press, 1971.

Renick, Timothy. "Pursuing Happiness," *Christian Century* 128, no. 1 (January 11, 2011): 22–26.

Rilke, Rainer Maria. Sonnet 12, *The Sonnets to Orpheus: First Series*. Trans. A. Poulin Jr. In *Duino Elegies and the Sonnets to Orpheus*. New York: Mariner, 2007.

Robinson, Marilynne. *Gilead*. New York: Farrar Straus & Giroux, 2004.

Rockefeller, Steven. "Earth Charter Launched at The Hague." *Boston Research Center for the 21st Century Newsletter* 16 (Winter 2001).

Rohr, Richard. "Why Does Psychology Always Win?" *Sojourners* 20 (November 1991): 14.

Roosevelt, Theodore. *The Winning of the West: From the Alleghenies to the Mississippi, 1769–1776*. Middlesex, UK: Echo Library, 2007; original publication 1894.

Rosen, William. *The Most Powerful Idea in the World: A Story of Steam, Industry, and Invention*. New York: Random House, 2010.

Ross, Edward Alsworth. *Social Control: A Survey of the Foundations of Order*. New York: Macmillan, 1901.

Rostow, Walter. *The Stages of Economic Growth: A Non-Community Manifesto*. Cambridge: Cambridge University Press, 1960.

Rousseau, Philip. *Pachomius: The Making of a Community in Fourth-Century Egypt*. Berkeley: University of California Press, 1975.

Roy, Arundhati. *Outlook India*, "The Trickledown Revolution." At http://www.outlookindia.com/article.aspx?267040.

Ruether, Rosemary Radford. "Sisters of Earth: Religious Women and Ecological Spirituality." *The Witness*, May 2000.

Ruffing, Janet R. S. M., ed. *Mysticism and Social Transformation*. Syracuse, NY: Syracuse University Press, 2001.

Safina, Carl. "The View from Lazy Point." Cited by Dominique Browning, "Delicate Planet," *New York Times Book Review*, January 16, 2011.

Sagan, Carl. *A Pale Blue Dot*. Public lecture, Cornell University, October 13, 1994. At http://bigskyastroclub.org/pale_blue_dot.html.

Samuel, Wolfgang W. E. *German Boy: A Child in War*. New York: Random House, 2001.

Sandel, Michael. "Competing American Traditions of Public Philosophy." *Ethics and International Affairs* 20 (Fall 1997). New York: Carnegie Council on Ethics & International Affairs Newsletter.

————. *Justice: What's the Right Thing to Do?* New York: Farrar, Straus & Giroux, 2009.

Sanderson, Michael. "Crunching the Data for the Tree of Life." *New York Times*, February 10, 2009, D1.

Schell, Orville. "The Final Conflict." *New York Times Book Review*, December 12, 2010.

Schloss, Jeffrey P. "Wisdom Traditions as Mechanisms for Organismal Integration: Evolutionary Perspectives on Homeostatic Laws of Life." In *Understanding Wisdom: Sources, Science, and Society*, ed. Warren S. Brown. Philadelphia: Templeton Foundation Press, 2000. 153–91.

Scitovsky, Tibor. *The Joyless Economy: The Psychology of Human Satisfaction.* Rev. ed. New York: Oxford University Press, 1992.

Segrest, Mab. *Born to Belonging: Writings on Spirit and Justice.* New Brunswick, NJ: Rutgers University Press, 2002.

Shinn, Roger L. *Forced Options: Social Decisions for the Twenty-First Century.* 3rd ed. Cleveland: Pilgrim Press, 1991.

Shiva, Vandana. *Biopiracy: The Plunder of Nature and Knowledge.* Toronto: Between the Lines Press, 1997.

Shorto, Russell. *Descartes' Bones: A Skeletal History of the Conflict between Faith and Reason.* New York: Doubleday, 2008.

Shostak, Seth. "Take Us to Your Water." *Good* (Summer 2009).

Shubin, Neil. *Your Inner Fish: A Journey into the 3.5 Billion-Year History of the Human Body.* New York: Random House, First Vintage Books, 2009.

Shulevitz, Judith. "Time and Possibilities," a review of James L. Kugel, *In the Valley of the Shadow: On the Foundation of Religious Belief. New York Times Book Review,* February 12, 2011, 22.

Sideris, Lisa H., and Kathleen Dean Moore. *Rachel Carson: Legacy and Challenge.* Albany, NY: SUNY Press, 2008.

Singer, Peter. "Navigating the Ethics of Globalization." *Chronicle of Higher Education,* October 11, 2002. Cited from http://chronicle.com/article/Navigating-the-Ethics-of/28293.

Singh, Simon. "Even Einstein Had His Off Days." *New York Times Week in Review,* January 2, 2005, 9.

Sittler, Joseph. "An Open Letter," March 7, 1984. The Joseph A. Sittler Archives, Lutheran School of Theology at Chicago. http://www.josephsittler.org/.

————. "A Theology of Earth." In *Worldviews, Religion, and the Environment: A Global Anthology,* ed. Richard C. Foltz. Belmont, CA: Wadsworth/Thomson, 2003.

Slater, Philip. *The Pursuit of Loneliness: American Culture at the Breaking Point.* Boston: Beacon Press, 1970.

Smil, Vaclav. *Enriching the Earth: Fritz Haber, Carl Bosch, and the Transformation of World Food.* Cambridge, MA: MIT Press, 2000.

Smith, Adam. *An Inquiry into the Nature and Causes of the Wealth of Nations.* New York: Modern Library, 1994; original published 1776.

——. *The Theory of Moral Sentiments*. Ed. D. D. Raphael and A. L. Macfie. Oxford: Clarendon Press, 1976.

Smith, Christian. *Moral, Believing Animals: Human Personhood and Culture*. New York: Oxford University Press, 2003.

Smith, Patrick. *Somebody Else's Century: East and West in a Post-Western World*. New York: Random House, 2011.

Soelle, Dorothee. *The Silent Cry: Mysticism and Resistance*. Minneapolis: Fortress Press, 2001.

Speth, James Gustave. *The Bridge at the Edge of the World: Capitalism, the Environment, and Crossing from Crisis to Sustainability*. New Haven: Yale University Press, 2008.

——. "Towards a New Economy and a New Politics." *Solutions*, Issue no. 5. At http://thesolutionsjournal.com.

St. Augustine. *City of God*. Trans. Henry Bettenson. New York: Modern Library Classics, 2000.

——. *The City of God*. Trans. Henry Bettenson. New York: Penguin Classics Edition, 1984.

——. Sermon 169.4. Cited by Johannes Van Oort. At http://home.um.edu.mt/philosophy/activities.html.

St. Francis. *Canticle of the Sun*. Ed. Betty Buchanan. Middleton, WI: A-R Editions, 2006.

St. Patrick. "I Bind unto Myself Today." *The Lutheran Book of Worship*. Minneapolis: Augsburg, 1979.

Standing Bear, Chief Luther. Cited from Native American Wisdom. At www.sapphyr.net.

Steffen, W. L., et al. *Global Change and the Earth System*. Berlin and New York: Springer, 2004.

Stern, Fritz. *Einstein's German World*. Princeton: Princeton University Press, 1999.

Stiglitz, Joseph E. "Of the 1%, by the 1%, for the 1%." *Vanity Fair*, April 14, 2011. At http://www.vanityfair.com/society/features/2011/05/top-one-percent-201105.

Stout, Jeffrey. *Blessed Are the Organized: Grassroots Democracy in America*. Princeton: Princeton University Press, 2010.

Sturm, Douglas. "Faith, Ecology, and the Demands of Social Justice: On Shattering the Boundaries of Moral Community." In *Religious Experience and Ecological Responsibility*, ed. Donald A. Crosby and Charley D. Hardwick. Vol. 3, *American Liberal Religious Thought*. New York: Peter Lang, 1996.

Swimme, Brian. *The Awakening Universe*. A film by Neal Rogin. At www.Awakening Universe.com.

Swimme, Brian, and Thomas Berry. *The Universe Story: From the Primordial Flaring Forth to the Ecozoic Era*. San Francisco: HarperSanFrancisco, 1992.

Swimme, Brian Thomas, and Mary Evelyn Tucker. *Journey of the Universe*. New Haven: Yale University Press, 2011.

Taylor, Barbara Brown. *Leaving Church: A Memoir of Faith*. New York: HarperSanFrancisco, 2006.

Taylor, Charles. "Canadian Is Awarded Spirituality Prize." *New York Times*, March 15, 2007, A20.

Thich Nhat Hanh. *The World We Have: A Buddhist Approach to Peace and Ecology.* Berkeley, CA: Parallax, 2008.

Thistlethwaite, Susan. Interview with Madeline Albright at the 2006 meeting of the American Academy of Religion, Washington, D.C.

Thoreau, Henry David. "An Address to All Intelligent Men." Part of a review by Thoreau, "Paradise (To Be) Regained," of J. A. Etzler, *The Paradise within the Reach of All Men, Without Labor, by Powers of Nature and Machinery; An Address to All Intelligent Men.* In *The Writings of Henry David Thoreau.* Vol. 4, *Cape Cod and Miscellanies.* Boston: Houghton Mifflin, 1906, 280–305.

———. *Walden.* New York: W. W. Norton, 1992.

Thurman, Howard. *The Search for Common Ground: An Inquiry into the Basis of Man's Experience of Community.* Richmond: Friends United Press, 1986.

Tödt, Heinz Eduard. *Authentic Faith: Bonhoeffer's Theological Ethics in Context.* Trans. David Stassen. Grand Rapids, MI: Eerdmans, 2007.

Torres-Fleming, Alexei. Presentation in the Series on Environmental Racism. Unpublished paper, Union Theological Seminary, September 17, 2002.

Townes, Emilie M. *Womanist Ethics and the Cultural Production of Evil.* New York: Palgrave Macmillan, 2006.

Trible, Phyllis. *God and the Rhetoric of Sexuality.* Philadelphia: Fortress Press, 1978.

Troeltsch, Ernst. *The Social Teaching of the Christian Churches.* Vol. 2. Trans. Olive Wyon. Chicago: University of Chicago Press, 1981.

Tucker, Mary Evelyn. "The Alliance of World Religions and Ecology." *SGI Quarterly: A Buddhist Forum for Peace, Culture and Education* no. 61 (July 2010).

Tucker, Mary Evelyn, and John Grim. "The Greening of the World's Religions." *Religious Studies News* (May 2007).

Turkle, Sherry. *Alone Together: Why We Expect More from Technology and Less from Each Other.* New York: Basic Books, 2011.

Twain, Mark. *Autobiography of Mark Twain.* Vol. 1. Ed. Harriet Elinor Smith and other editors of the Mark Twain Project. Berkeley: University of California Press, 2010.

Twentieth Century Fund Study. Cited by Lizabeth Cohen in "A Consumers' Republic: The Politics of Mass Consumption in Postwar America," *Miller Center Report* 19, no. 1 (Winter 2003).

Udall, Randy. "The Big Bonfire." *High Country News*, December 21, 2009, 21.

Ullmann, Walter. *Medieval Papalism: The Political Theories of the Medieval Papalists.* Political Science no. 36. London: Routledge Library Editions, 2009.

United Church of Santa Fe Whole Earth Covenant. United Church of Santa Fe.

U.S. Catholic Bishops. *Renewing the Earth—An Invitation to Reflection and Action in Light of Catholic Social Teaching.* Washington, DC: U.S. Catholic Conference, November 14, 1991.

Walzer, Michael. "The Idea of Civil Society." *Dissent* (Spring 1991).

——. *Spheres of Justice*. New York: Basic Books, 1983.

Water in Religion. At http://www.africanwater.org.

Weber, Max. *The Protestant Ethic and the Spirit of Capitalism*. Trans. Talcott Parsons. New York: Charles Scribner's Sons, 1958; original published in German 1904.

Weil, Simone. *Gravity and Grace*. Trans. Arthur Wills. Lincoln: University of Nebraska Press, 1952.

——. *Two Moral Essays*. Wallingford, PA: Pendle Hill, 1981.

——. *Waiting for God*. Trans. Emma Craufurd. New York: G. P. Putnam's Sons, 1951.

West, Cornel. *Prophesy Deliverance! An Afro-American Revolutionary Christianity*. Philadelphia: Westminster Press, 1982.

West, Goeffrey. "Thinking Big." *New Mexican*, November 13, 2007, C1.

Whitman, Walt. *Leaves of Grass*. At www.Bartleby.com.

Wilkinson, Richard, and Kate Pickett. *The Spirit Level: Why Greater Equality Makes Society Stronger*. New York: Bloomsbury Press, 2009.

Will, George F. Review of Brink Lindsey, *The Age of Abundance: How Prosperity Transformed America's Politics and Culture*. *New York Times Book Review*, June 10, 2007, 16.

Williamson, Thad, David Imbroscio, and Gar Alperowitz. *Making a Place for Community: Local Democracy in a Global Era*. New York: Routledge, 2002.

Wilson, David Sloan. "The Origin of Religions, From a Distinctly Darwinian View." *New York Times*, December 24, 2002, F2.

Wilson, E. O. *Consilience: The Unity of Knowledge*. New York: Knopf, 1998.

——. *The Future of Life*. New York: Random House, 2003.

Wilson-Hargrove, Jonathan. *God's Economy: Redefining the Health and Wealth Gospel*. Grand Rapids, MI: Zondervan Press, 2009.

Wirzba, Norman. *Food and Faith: A Theology of Eating*. Cambridge: Cambridge University Press, 2011.

Wisdom collection. At www.sapphyr.net.

Wolfe, Alan. *Whose Keeper? Social Science and Moral Obligation*. Berkeley, Los Angeles, London: University of California Press, 1989.

Yoder, John Howard. *Body Politics: Five Practices of the Christian Community before the Watching World*. Harrisonburg, VA: Herald Press, 2001.

Young, Josiah Ulysses, III. *No Difference in the Fare: Dietrich Bonhoeffer and the Problem of Racism*. Grand Rapids, MI: Eerdmans, 1998.

Zakaria, Fareed. "Fueling the Future." Review of Daniel Yergin, *The Quest: Energy, Security, and the Remaking of the Modern World*. *New York Times Book Review*, September 25, 2011, 15.

Zimmer, Carl. "Our Microbiomes, Ourselves." *New York Times*, Sunday Review, December 4, 2011, 12.

——. "You Are Here." Review of Richard Dawkins, *The Ancestor's Tale: A Pilgrimage to the Dawn of Evolution*. *New York Times Book Review*, October 17, 2004, 30.

Index

Index of Scripture Passages